Magnetism, EMI & AC

for JEE Main & Advanced

(Study Package for Physics)

- Head Office : B-32, Shivalik Main Road, Malviya Nagar, New Delhi-110017

- Sales Office : B-48, Shivalik Main Road, Malviya Nagar, New Delhi-110017
  Tel. : 011-26691021 / 26691713

Page Layout : Prakash Chandra Sahoo

Typeset by Disha DTP Team

Printed at: **Repro Knowledgecast Limited, Thane**

For further information about the books from DISHA,
Log on to www.dishapublication.com or email to info@dishapublication.com

STUDY PACKAGE IN PHYSICS FOR JEE MAIN & ADVANCED

Booklet No.	Title	Chapter Nos.	Page Nos.
1	Units, Measurements & Motion	Ch 0. Mathematics Used in Physics Ch 1. Units and Measurements Ch 2. Vectors Ch 3. Motion in a Straight Line Ch 4. Motion in a Plane	1-202
2	Laws of Motion and Circular Motion	Ch 5. Laws of Motion and Equilibrium Ch 6. Circular Motion	203-318
3	Work Energy, Power & Gravitation	Ch 7. Work, Energy and Power Ch 8. Collisions and Centre of Mass Ch 9. Gravitation	319-480
4	Rotational Motion	Ch 1. Rotational Mechanics	1-120
5	Properties of Matter & SHM	Ch 2. Properties of Matter Ch 3. Fluid Mechanics Ch 4. Simple Harmonic Motion	121-364
6	Heat & Thermodynamics	Ch 5. Thermometry, Expansion & Calorimetry Ch 6. Kinetic Theory of Gases Ch 7. Laws of Thermodynamics Ch 8. Heat Transfer	365-570
7	Waves	Ch 9. Wave – I Ch 10. Wave –II	571-698
8	Electrostatics	Ch 0. Mathematics Used in Physics Ch 1. Electrostatics Ch 2. Capacitance & Capacitors	1-216
9	Current Electricity	Ch 3. DC and DC circuits Ch 4. Thermal and Chemical effects of Current"	217-338
10	Magnetism, EMI & AC	Ch 5. Magnetic Force on Moving Charges & Conductor Ch 6. Magnetic Effects of Current Ch 7. Permanent Magnet & Magnetic Properties of Substance Ch 8. Electromagnetic Induction Ch 9. AC and EM Waves	339-618
11	Ray & Wave Optics	Ch 1. Reflection of Light Ch 2. Refraction and Dispersion Ch 3. Refraction at Spherical Surface, Lenses and Photometry Ch 4. Wave optics	1-244
12	Modern Physics	Ch 5. Electron, Photon, Atoms, Photoelectric Effect and X-rays Ch 6. Nuclear Physics Ch 7. Electronics & Communication	245-384

Contents

Magnetic Force on Moving Charges & Conductor (339-394)

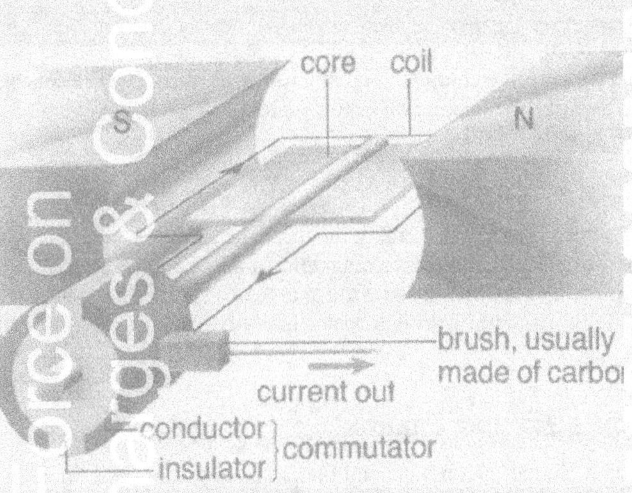

5.1 MAGNETISM : AN INTRODUCTION

The first magnetic phenomenon observed were those associated with naturally occurring magnets; pieces of iron found near Magnesia (hence the term "magnet"). The study of magnetic phenomenon remained confined for thousand of years to magnets made in this way. In 1820 Danish scientist Hans Christian Oersted observed that a compass was deflected when it placed near a current carrying wire. This made the connection between electrical and magnetic phenomenon. On this basis Oersted thus demostrated that magnetic effect could be produced by moving charge. It is now known that all magnetic phenomena result from forces between electric charges in motion. That is, charges in motion relative to an observer produces a magnetic field as well as an electric field.

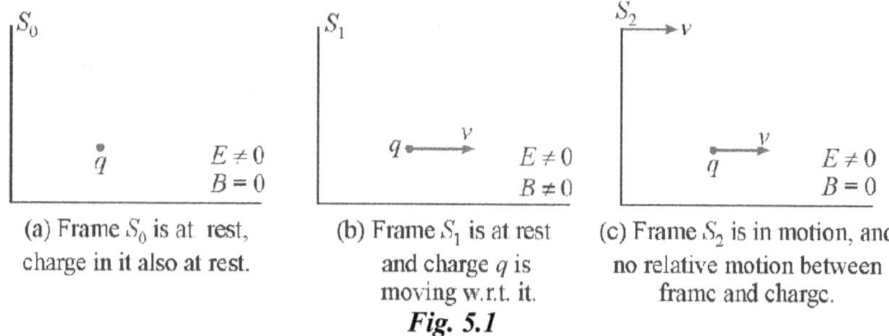

(a) Frame S_0 is at rest, charge in it also at rest.

(b) Frame S_1 is at rest and charge q is moving w.r.t. it.

(c) Frame S_2 is in motion, and no relative motion between frame and charge.

Fig. 5.1

5.2 THE MAGNETIC FIELD

In finding the force between the charges, it is very useful to introduce the concept of electric field and to describe the interaction in two stages :

(i) Charge creates an electric field $\vec{E}$ in the space surrounding it;

(ii) The electric field $\vec{E}$ exerts a force $\vec{F} = q\vec{E}$ on a charge placed in the field.

We shall follow the same pattern in describing the forces on a moving charge.

(i) A moving charge or a current creates a magnetic field in the space surrounding it;

(ii) The magnetic field exerts force on a moving charge or a current in the field.

Like electric field, magnetic field is a vector quantity. We shall use the symbol $\vec{B}$ for magnetic field.

5.3 FORCE ON A MOVING CHARGE

The electric force on a charge does not depend on its velocity; it is same whether the charge is moving or not. The magnetic force, conversely, is found to have a magnitude that increases with speed. Further more, the direction of the force depends on the direction of the field $\vec{B}$ and the velocity $\vec{v}$. The force $\vec{F}$ always perpendicular to both $\vec{B}$ and $\vec{v}$.

The magnitude of force $\vec{F}$ is found proportional to the component of $\vec{v}$ perpendicular to the field. The force is zero when $\vec{v}$ and $\vec{B}$ are parallel or antiparallel. Therefore the magnetic force

$$F \;=\; qv_\perp B = qvB_\perp = qvB \sin\theta$$

Direction of force

The direction of magnetic force can be obtained by either of the two rules.

1. **Right hand rule :** If we wrap the fingers of the right hand around the line perpendicular to the plane of $\vec{v}$ and $\vec{B}$ so that they curl around with the sense of rotation, then thumb points in the direction of force $\vec{F}$.

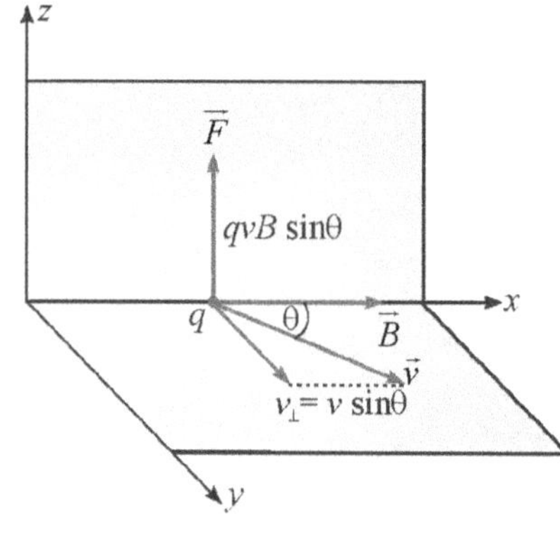

Fig. 5.2

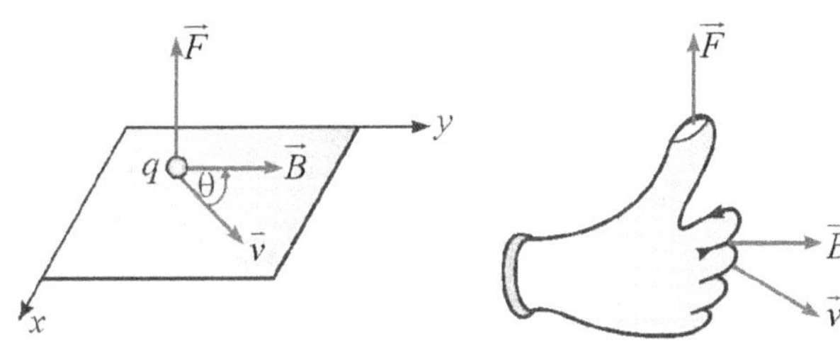

Fig. 5.3

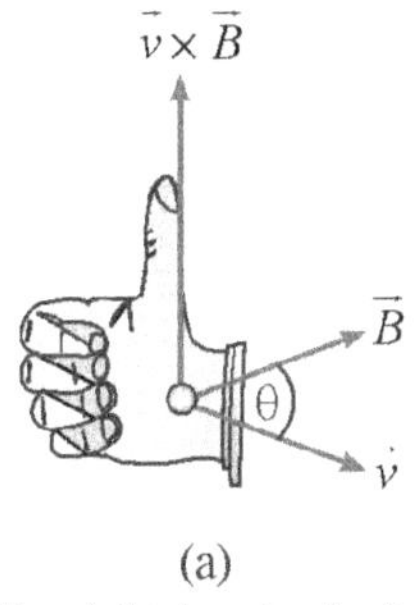

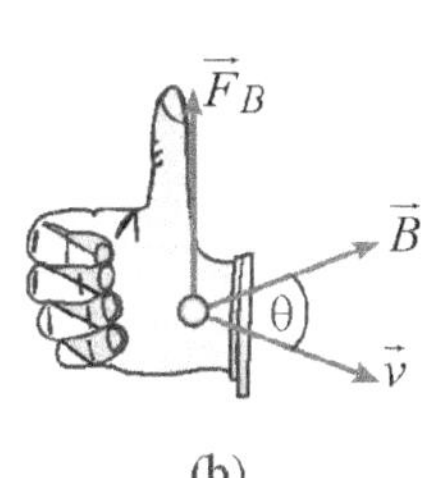

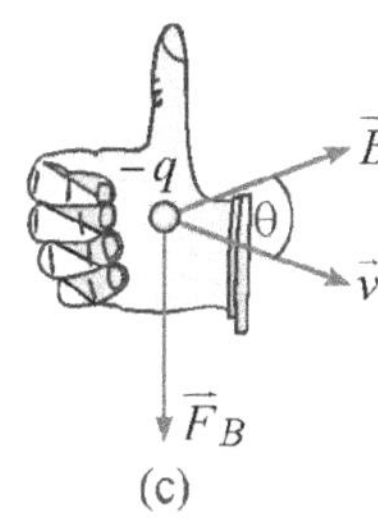

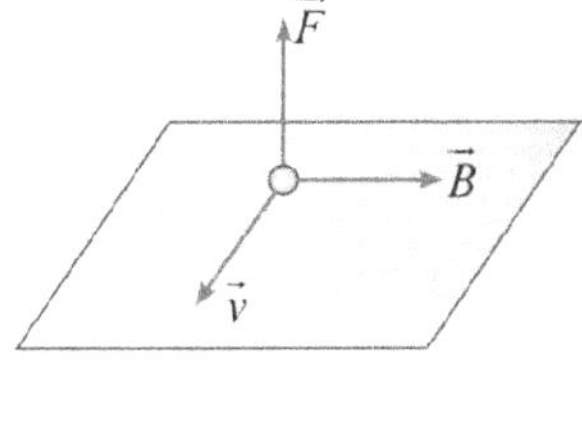

(a)

The right-hand rule (in which $\vec{v}$ is swept into $\vec{B}$ through the smaller angle θ between them) gives the direction of $\vec{v} \times \vec{B}$ as the direction of the thumb.

(b)

If q positive, then the direction of $\vec{F}_B = q\vec{v} \times \vec{B}$ is in the direction of $\vec{v} \times \vec{B}$.

(c)

If q negative, then the direction of $\vec{F}_B$ is opposite to that of $\vec{v} \times \vec{B}$.

(a)

(b)

Fig. 5.5

Fig. 5.4

In the diagram shown the force on the charge

$$\vec{F} \quad = \quad qvB\sin\theta\hat{k}.$$

In vector notation, we can write

$$\vec{F} \quad = \quad q\left(\vec{v} \times \vec{B}\right)$$

2. **Fleming's left hand rule (FLHR) :** If we hold fore finger, middle finger and thumb of the left hand mutually perpendicular to each other; the fore finger shows the direction of $\vec{B}$, the middle finger shows the direction of the velocity of positive charge, then thumb indicates the direction of force.

More about magnetic field

1. Other name used for magnetic field are :
   (i) Magnetic induction (old name).
   (ii) Magnetic flux density.
2. Magnetic field can be represented by lines, called lines of field, just as the electric field. $\vec{B}$ is related to its line of induction in the following ways :
   (i) The tangent drawn at any point to a line of field gives the direction of $\vec{B}$ at that point.
   (ii) The number of lines per unit area gives an idea about the magnitude of the magnetic field vector $\vec{B}$. This field is large if lines are closer and small if they are apart.

The direction of $\vec{B}$ is represented as follows :

(a) Equally spaced dots represent the field pointing out of the page and perpendicular to it.

(b) Equally spaced crosses represent the field into the page and perpendicular to it.

Fig. 5.6

3. **The unit of $\vec{B}$:** The unit of $\vec{B}$ can be obtained from $\dfrac{F}{qv}$.

Thus SI unit of $\vec{B}$ is N/A-m.

$$1 \text{ N/A-m} = 1 \text{ tesla.}$$

Also
$$1T = 10^4 \text{ gauss,}$$
$$= 1 \text{ Wb/m}^2.$$

Lorentz force

When a charged particle moves through a region of space where both electric and magnetic fields are acting, the net force on the charged particle is equal to the vector sum of the forces exert by both the fields. Thus net force

$$\vec{F} = \vec{E}q + q\left(\vec{v} \times \vec{B}\right)$$

This net force is called Lorentz force.

More about magnetic force

1. The magnetic force on a charged particle is zero, if either $v = 0$ or $\theta = 0°$ or $180°$.

2. The magnetic force will be maximum, for $\theta = 90°$, which is $F = qvB \sin 90° = qvB$.

3. The magnetic force is always perpendicular to the direction of motion of charged particle, and therefore magnetic force does no work on it. Hence the kinetic energy of moving charged particle in magnetic field remains constant.

4. In using the formula $F = qvB \sin\theta$, put the value of the charge q without sign.

5. In using the formula $\vec{F} = q(\vec{v} \times \vec{B})$, put the value of the charge with the proper sign.

Ex. 1 An electron is moving with a velocity $\left(2\hat{i} + 3\hat{j}\right)$ m/s in an electric field of intensity $\left(3i + 6\hat{j} + 2\hat{k}\right)$ V/m and a magnetic field of $\left(2\hat{j} + 3\hat{k}\right)$ tesla. Find the magnitude and direction of the Lorentz force acting on the electron.

Sol. Lorentz force is given by

$$\vec{F} = q\left(\vec{E} + \vec{v} \times \vec{B}\right)$$

$$= -1.6 \times 10^{-19}\left[\left(3\hat{i} + 6\hat{j} + 2\hat{k}\right) + \left(2\hat{i} + 3\hat{j}\right) \times \left(2\hat{j} + 3\hat{k}\right)\right]$$

$$= -1.6 \times 10^{-19}\left[3\hat{i} + 6\hat{j} + 2\hat{k} + 9\hat{i} - 6\hat{j} + 4\hat{k}\right]$$

$$= -1.6 \times 10^{-19}\left[12\hat{i} + 6\hat{k}\right] = 9.6 \times 10^{-19}\left(2\hat{i} + \hat{k}\right)$$

$$\therefore \quad F = 9.6 \times 10^{-19}\sqrt{2^2 + 1^2} = 2.15 \times 10^{-18} \text{ N}$$

It is in xz-plane, making an angle θ with the x-axis, where

$$\theta = \cos^{-1}\frac{2}{\sqrt{5}}. \qquad \textit{Ans.}$$

Ex. 2 A proton beam moves through a region of space where there is a uniform magnetic field of magnitude 2.0 T, with direction along the positive z-axis as shown in *fig.5.7*. The protons have velocity of magnitude 3×10^5 m/s in the xz plane, at an angle $30°$ to the positive z-axis. Find force on proton. $\left(q = 1.6 \times 10^{-19} C\right)$

Sol.

The magnitude of force

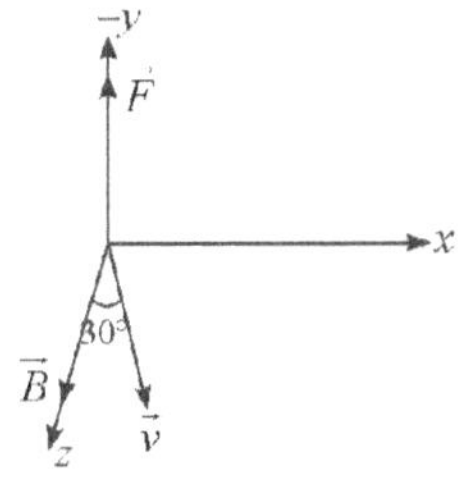

$$F \quad = \quad qv_\perp B$$

$$= \quad q \times v \sin 30° \times B$$

$$= \quad \left(1.6 \times 10^{-19}\right) \times \left(3 \times 10^5\right) \times \left(\frac{1}{2}\right) \times (2) \quad \textit{Fig. 5.7}$$

$$= \quad 4.8 \times 10^{-14} \, N$$

The direction of force is along negative y-axis, thus

$$\vec{F} \quad = \quad 4.8 \times 10^{-14} \left(-\hat{j}\right) N \qquad \textit{Ans.}$$

Ex. 3 An experimenter's diary reads as follows : "a charged particle is projected in a magnetic field of $\left(7.0\hat{i} - 3.0\hat{j}\right) \times 10^{-3}$ T. The acceleration of a particle is found to be $\left(\Box\,\hat{i} + 7.0\hat{j}\right) \times 10^{-6}$ m/s^2". The number to be left of $\hat{i}$ in the last expression was not readable. What can this number be ?

Sol.

As magnetic force is perpendicular to the magnetic field, so

$$\vec{B} \cdot \vec{F} \quad = \quad 0$$

or $$\vec{B} \cdot \vec{a} \quad = \quad 0.$$

Let value in box provided is k.

$$\therefore \quad 7k - 3 \times 7 \quad = \quad 0 \Rightarrow k = 3 \qquad \textit{Ans.}$$

5.4 MOTION OF CHARGED PARTICLE IN UNIFORM MAGNETIC FIELD

The path of charged particle in magnetic field depends on the angle θ between $\vec{v}$ and $\vec{B}$. Depending on different values of θ, the possible cases are :

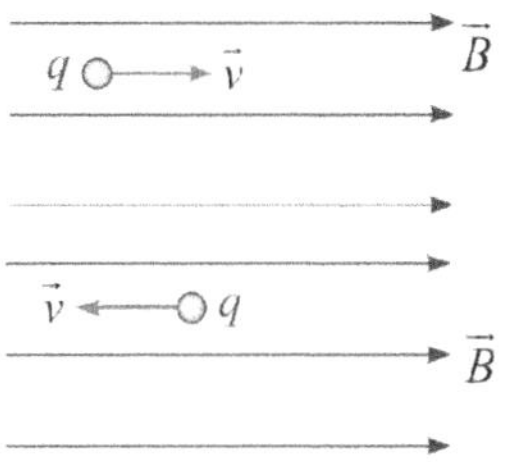

Case 1 : When θ is $0°$ or $180°$:

For $\theta = 0°$ or $180°$, the force on the moving charge $F = qvB \sin\left(0° \text{ or } 180°\right) = 0$,

and therefore particle goes undeviated along a straight path.

Case 2 : When $\theta = 90°$:

(i) **When particle is projected from inside the field,** it experiences a force which always perpendicular to the velocity and so its path will be circular. The necessary centripetal force is provided by the magnetic force. If r be the radius of the path, then

$$\frac{mv^2}{r} \quad = \quad qvB \sin 90°$$

or $$r \quad = \quad \frac{mv}{qB}$$

or we can write

$$r \quad = \quad \frac{mv_\perp}{qB} \qquad \qquad ...(1)$$

or $$r \quad = \quad \frac{v}{\left(\dfrac{q}{m}\right) B}$$

Let $\dfrac{q}{m} = \alpha$, is called specific charge,

$\therefore$ The equation (1) can be written in the form :

$$r \quad = \quad \frac{v}{\alpha B}$$

The K.E. of the particle $\quad K \quad = \quad \dfrac{P^2}{2m}$

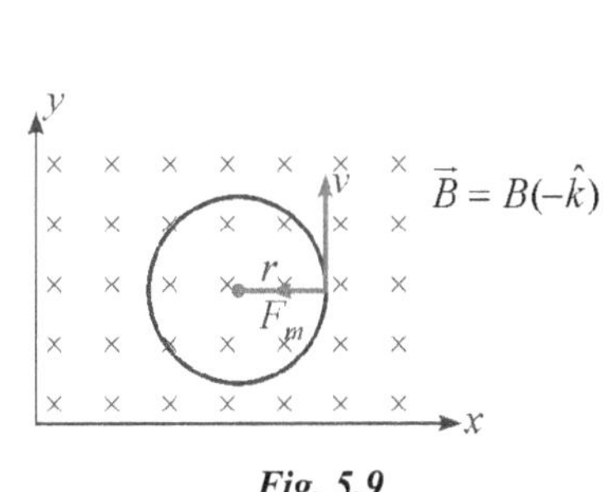

Fig. 5.8

Fig. 5.9

or
$$P = \sqrt{2mK}$$

If charged particle is accelerated by potential V, then
$$K = qV$$

$\therefore$
$$r = \frac{P}{qB} = \frac{\sqrt{2mK}}{qB} = \frac{\sqrt{2mqV}}{qB} \qquad \text{...(2)}$$

Time period :

$$T = \frac{\text{Length of path}}{\text{speed}}$$

$$= \frac{2\pi r}{v} = \frac{2\pi \times \dfrac{mv}{qB}}{v}$$

or
$$T = \frac{2\pi m}{qB}$$

Also linear frequency of rotation

$$f = \frac{1}{T} = \frac{qB}{2\pi m},$$

and angular frequency
$$\omega = 2\pi f = \frac{Bq}{m}.$$

Note: 1. Time period T, f and ω are independent of v.

2. The velocity at any instant can be written as

$$\vec{v} = v_x \hat{i} + v_y \hat{j}$$

(ii) **When particle is projected out side the field:** If the length of the magnetic field is enough, then the angle with which the charged particle emerges out will equal to the angle with which it enters into the field. Thus we have two cases:

(a) Time spend in magnetic field

$$t = \frac{T}{2} = \frac{\pi m}{qB}$$

$$PQ = 2r$$

(b) The time spend in magnetic field

$$t = \frac{2\theta}{2\pi}[T] = \frac{\theta}{\pi}[T], \quad \text{where} \quad T = \frac{2\pi m}{qB}$$

$$PQ = 2r\sin\theta$$

Case 3 : **When particle is projected at an angle θ, which is not equal to 0°, 90° or 180°:**

The velocity of the particle can be resolved into two components; one along $\vec{B}$, that is $v\cos\theta$ and other perpendicular to $\vec{B}$ that is $v\sin\theta$. The velocity $v\sin\theta$ will provide circular path and the velocity $v\cos\theta$ will provide a straight line. The resulting path is a helical path.

(i)
$$r = \frac{mv_\perp}{qB} = \frac{mv\sin\theta}{qB}$$

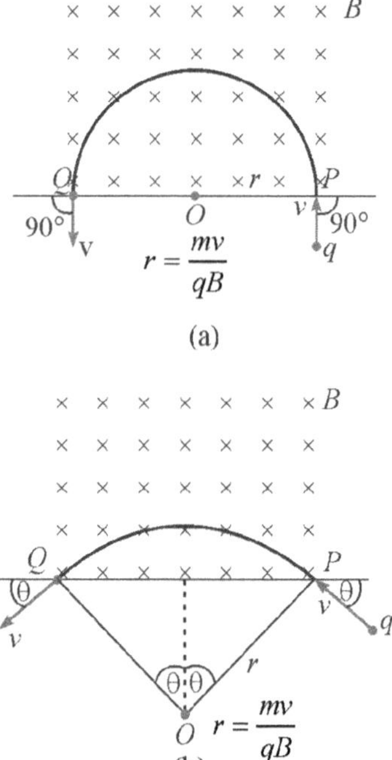

Fig. 5.10

(ii) Since time period of rotation does not depend on velocity, therefore

$$T = \frac{2\pi m}{qB}$$

(iii) Pitch (p) : The centre to centre distance between two consecutive circular paths is called pitch. Thus

$$p = v\cos\theta \times T$$

$$= v\cos\theta \times \frac{2\pi m}{qB} = \frac{2\pi m v\cos\theta}{qB}$$

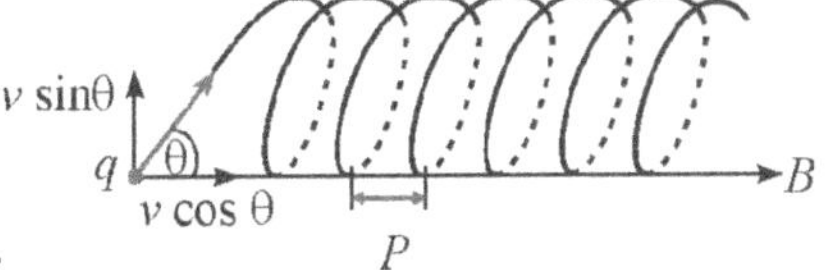

Fig. 5.11

Comparison of paths in $\vec{E}$ - field and $\vec{B}$ - field

1.	$\theta = 0°$ $q \quad \vec{v}$ $\longrightarrow E$ Straight line path	1.	$\theta = 0°$ $q \quad \vec{v}$ $\longrightarrow B$ Straight line path
2.	$\theta = 90°$ $\vec{v}$ $q \longrightarrow \vec{E}$ Parabolic path	2.	$\theta = 90°$ $\vec{v}$ $q \longrightarrow \vec{B}$ Circular path
3.	$0° < \theta < 90°$ $\vec{v}$ $q \,\theta \longrightarrow \vec{E}$ Parabolic path	3.	$0° < \theta < 90°$ $\vec{v}$ $q \,\theta \longrightarrow \vec{B}$ Helical path

Deviation of charged particle in magnetic field

Suppose a charged particle q enters normally in a uniform magnetic field $\vec{B}$. The magnetic field extends to a distance x, which is less than or equal to radius of the path, that is $x \le r$.

(i) The radius of path

$$r = \frac{mv}{qB}$$

and

$$\sin\theta = \frac{x}{r}$$

Above relation can be used when $x \le r$

(ii) For $x > r$

$$r = \frac{mv}{qB}$$

and deviation, $\theta = 180°$ as clear from the diagram.

(iii) If particle moves for time t inside the field, then

$$\theta = \omega t$$

$$= \left(\frac{Bq}{m}\right) t$$

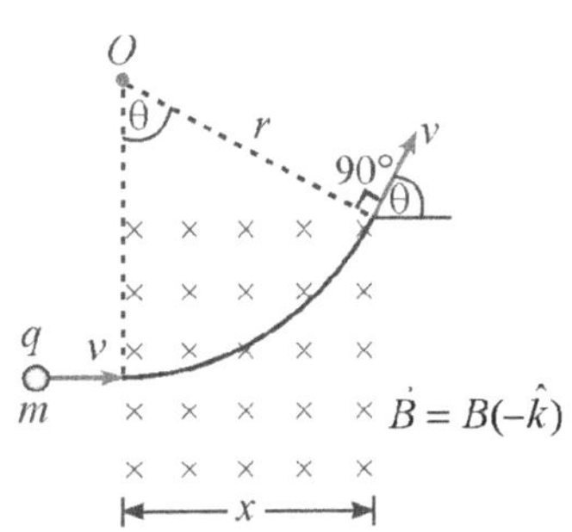

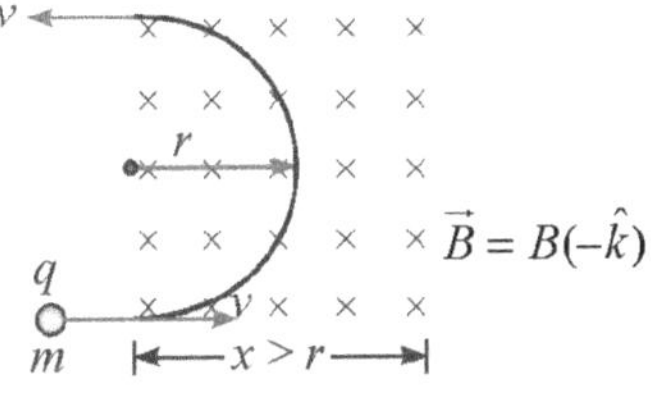

Fig. 5.12

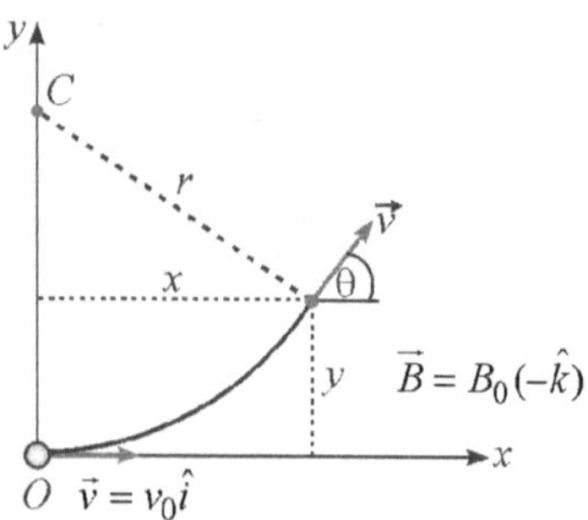

Fig. 5.13

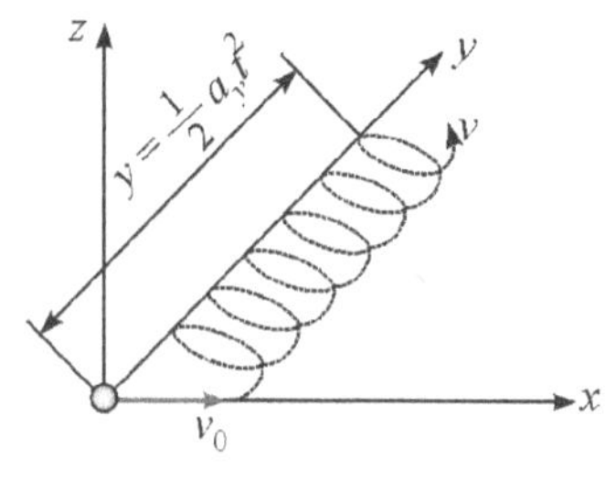

Fig. 5.17

As $\qquad \alpha = q/m$

$\therefore \qquad \theta = B\alpha t$

(iv) Velocity of particle :

We have, $\theta = B_0\alpha t$, $\qquad r = \dfrac{v_0}{\alpha B_0}$

Velocity of particle at any time t, $\vec{v} = v_x\hat{i} + v_y\hat{j}$

$$= v_0\cos\theta\,\hat{i} + v_0\sin\theta\,\hat{j}$$

On substituting the value of θ, we have

or $\qquad \vec{v} = v_0\cos\left(B_0\alpha t\right)\hat{i} + v_0\sin\left(B_0\alpha t\right)\hat{j}$

(v) Position of particle :

$$\vec{r} = x\hat{i} + y\hat{j}$$

$$= r\sin\theta\,\hat{i} + \left(r - r\cos\theta\right)\hat{j}$$

$$= r\left[\sin\theta\,\hat{i} + \left(1 - \cos\theta\right)\hat{j}\right]$$

$$= \dfrac{v_0}{B_0\,\alpha}\left[\sin\left(B_0\,\alpha t\right)\hat{i} + \left\{1 - \cos\left(B_0\,\alpha t\right)\right\}\hat{j}\right]$$

Motion of charged particle in both electric and magnetic field

Case 1 :   When $\vec{E}\parallel\vec{B}$ and particle velocity is perpendicular to both the fields

Consider a particle of charge q and mass m projected from the origin with velocity $\vec{v} = v_0\hat{i}$ into a region having electric and magnetic field i.e., $\vec{E} = E_0\hat{j}$ and $\vec{B} = B_0\hat{j}$. The electric field exerts force only along y-direction and therefore particle accelerates in this direction with the acceleration $a_y = \dfrac{F_y}{m} = \dfrac{qE_0}{m}$. The velocity component in y-direction goes on increasing with time. The magnetic field rotates the particle in a circle in xz-plane. The resultant path of the particle is a helical path with increasing pitch. The velocity of a particle at any time t would be

$$\vec{v} = v_x\hat{i} + v_y\hat{j} + v_z\hat{k}$$

Here $\qquad v_y = a_yt = \dfrac{qE_0t}{m}$

and $\qquad v_x^2 + v_z^2 = v_0^2 = \text{constant}$

where $\qquad v_x = v_0\cos\theta = v_0\cos\left(\dfrac{Bqt}{m}\right)$

and $\qquad v_z = v_0\sin\theta = v_0\sin\left(\dfrac{Bqt}{m}\right)$

$$\theta = \omega t = \dfrac{Bq}{m}t$$

$\therefore \qquad \vec{v} = v_0\cos\left(\dfrac{Bqt}{m}\right)\hat{i} + \left(\dfrac{qE_0t}{m}\right)\hat{j} + v_0\sin\left(\dfrac{Bqt}{m}\right)\hat{k}$

Similarly position vector of the particle

$$\vec{r} = x\,\hat{i} + y\,\hat{j} + z\,\hat{k}$$

$$= \left(r\sin\theta\right)\hat{i} + \left(\frac{1}{2}a_y t^2\right)\hat{j} + \left(r - r\cos\theta\right)\hat{k}$$

or

$$\vec{r} = \left(\frac{mv_0}{Bq}\right)\sin\left(\frac{Bqt}{m}\right)\hat{i} + \left(\frac{1}{2}\frac{qE}{m}t^2\right)\hat{j}$$
$$+ \left(\frac{mv_0}{Bq}\right)\left\{1 - \cos\left(\frac{Bqt}{m}\right)\right\}\hat{k}$$

Note :

While moving on a helical path the particle touches the y-axis after every T second,

where $T = \dfrac{2\pi m}{qB}$.

Case 2:   When $\vec{E} \perp \vec{B}$ and the particle is released at rest : Consider a particle of charge q and mass m, is placed at the origin with zero initial velocity into a region of uniform electric and magnetic field. Let field $\vec{E}$ is acting along x-axis and field $\vec{B}$ is along y-axis, that is $\vec{E} = E_0\hat{i}$ and $\vec{B} = B_0\,\hat{j}$.

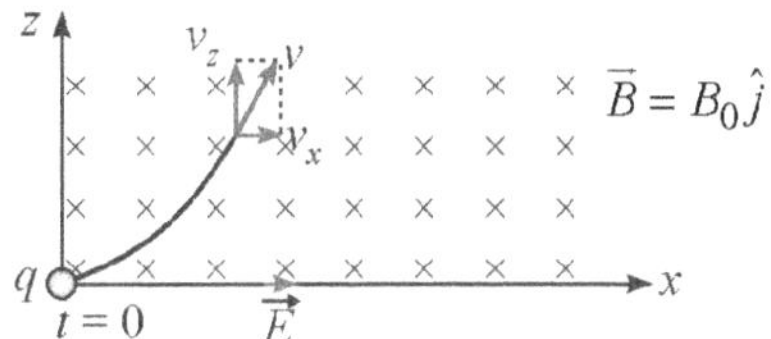

Fig. 5.18

The electric force accelerates the particle along x-axis and so, the particle starts gaining velocity along x-axis. As soon as particle starts moving, the magnetic force starts acting and bends the particle. The resulting motion of particle is in xz- plane.

At any instant its velocity

$$\vec{v} = v_x\,\hat{i} + v_z\,\hat{k}$$

The resultant force is thus given by

$$\vec{F} = q\left(\vec{E} + \vec{v} \times \vec{B}\right)$$

$$= q\left[E_0\hat{i} + \left(v_x\,\hat{i} + v_z\,\hat{k}\right) \times \vec{B}_0\,\hat{j}\right]$$

$$= qE_0\hat{i} + qv_x B_0\hat{k} + qv_z B_0\left(-\hat{i}\right)$$

or

$$\vec{F} = q\left(E_0 - v_z B_0\right)\hat{i} + qv_x B_0\hat{k} \qquad \text{...(i)}$$

and acceleration

$$\vec{a} = \frac{\vec{F}}{m} = \frac{q}{m}\left(E_0 - v_z B_0\right)\hat{i} + \frac{q}{m}v_x B_0\,\hat{k} \qquad \text{...(ii)}$$

This acceleration has two components

$$a_x = \frac{dv_x}{dt} = \frac{q}{m}\left(E_0 - v_z B_0\right) \qquad \text{...(iii)}$$

and

$$a_z = \frac{dv_z}{dt} = \frac{q}{m}v_x B_0 \qquad \text{...(iv)}$$

Differentiating equation (iii) w.r.t. time, we get

$$\frac{d^2 v_x}{dt^2} = -\frac{q}{m}B_0\left(\frac{dv_z}{dt}\right)$$

Now substituting $\dfrac{dv_z}{dt}$ from equation (iv), we have

$$\frac{d^2 v_x}{dt^2} = -\left(\frac{qB_0}{m}\right) \times \left(\frac{q}{m} v_x B_0\right)$$

or

$$\frac{d^2 v_x}{dt^2} = -\left(\frac{qB_0}{m}\right)^2 v_x \qquad \text{...(v)}$$

This is the equation similar to equation of SHM i.e.,

$$\frac{d^2 x}{dt^2} = -\omega^2 x$$

where

$$\omega = \left(\frac{qB_0}{m}\right)$$

and its solution for v_x is

$$v_x = A \sin(\omega t + \phi) \qquad \text{...(vi)}$$

At $t = 0$, $v_x = 0$, hence $\phi = 0$

Again,

$$\frac{dv_x}{dt} = \omega A \cos \omega t \qquad \text{...(vii)}$$

From equation (iii), at $t = 0$, $v_z = 0$

and

$$\frac{dv_x}{dt} = \frac{qE_0}{m}$$

Now we have

$$\omega A \cos(\omega \times 0) = \frac{qE_0}{m}$$

or

$$A = \frac{qE_0}{m\omega}$$

where

$$\omega = \left(\frac{qB_0}{m}\right)$$

$\therefore$

$$A = \frac{qE_0}{m \dfrac{qB_0}{m}} = \frac{E_0}{B_0}$$

Therefore equation (vi) becomes

$$v_x = \frac{E_0}{B_0} \sin \omega t \qquad \text{...(viii)}$$

Now from equation (iv), we have

$$\frac{dv_z}{dt} = \frac{q}{m} v_x B_0$$

$$= \frac{qB_0}{m} \times \frac{E_0}{B_0} \sin \omega t$$

or

$$\frac{dv_z}{dt} = \frac{qE_0}{m} \sin \omega t$$

or

$$dv_z = \frac{qE_0}{m} \sin \omega t \, dt$$

or

$$v_z = \frac{qE_0}{m} \int_0^t \sin \omega t \, dt$$

$$= \frac{qE_0}{m\omega}\left(1 - \cos\omega t\right)$$

$$= \frac{qE_0}{m \times \left(\frac{qB_0}{m}\right)}\left(1 - \cos\omega t\right)$$

or $\qquad v_z = \dfrac{E_0}{B_0}\left(1 - \cos\omega t\right)$ $\qquad$ ...(ix)

From equation (viii), we have

$$\frac{dx}{dt} = \frac{E_0}{B_0}\sin\omega t$$

or $\qquad x = \dfrac{E_0}{B_0}\displaystyle\int_0^t \sin\omega t\, dt$

$$= \frac{E_0}{B_0\omega}\left|-\cos\omega t\right|_0^t$$

or $\qquad x = \dfrac{E_0}{B_0\omega}\left(1 - \cos\omega t\right)$ $\qquad$ ...(1)

Also from equation (ix), we have

$$\frac{dz}{dt} = \frac{E_0}{B_0}\left(1 - \cos\omega t\right)$$

or $\qquad z = \dfrac{E_0}{B_0}\displaystyle\int_0^t \left(1 - \cos\omega t\right) dt$

or $\qquad z = \dfrac{E_0}{B_0\omega}\left(\omega t - \sin\omega t\right)$ $\qquad$ ...(2)

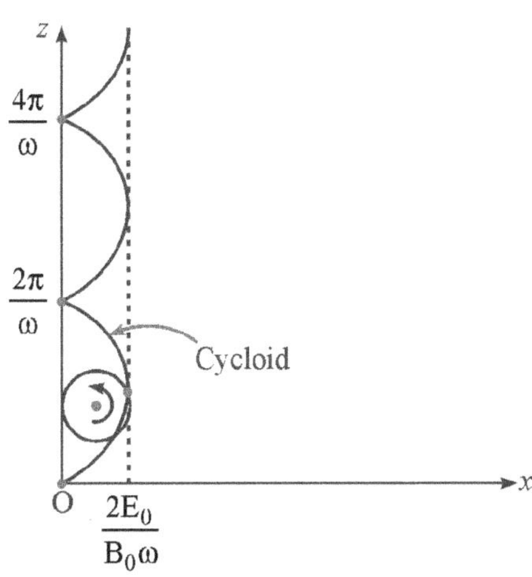

Fig. 5.19

Equations (1) and (2), together represents a **cycloid** which is defined as the path generated by the point on the circumference of a wheel rolling on the ground.

Ex. 4 When a proton is released from rest in a room, it starts with an initial acceleration a_0 towards west. When it is projected towards north with a speed of v_0, it moves with an initial acceleration $3a_0$ towards west. Find the electric field and the minimum possible magnetic field in the room.

Sol.

When proton released, it experiences only electric force, so

$$F_e = ma_0 = Eq$$

$$\therefore \quad E = \frac{ma_0}{q} = \frac{ma_0}{e}, \text{ towards west}$$

$$\textit{Ans.}$$

When proton is projected, it experiences force due to both the fields, and so

$$F_e + F_m = m\,(3a_0)$$

As $\qquad F_e = ma_0,$

$$\therefore \qquad F_m = 2ma_0.$$

The magnetic force on the proton will be ev_0B, therefore

$$ev_0B = 2ma_0,$$

$$\therefore \qquad B = \frac{2ma_0}{ev_0} \text{ downward} \qquad \textit{Ans.}$$

Ex. 5 A particle of mass m and charge q is projected into a region having a perpendicular magnetic field B. Find the angle of deviation (*fig. 5.14*) of the particle as it comes out of the magnetic field if the width d of the region is very slightly smaller than

(a) $\dfrac{mv}{qB}$ $\qquad$ (b) $\dfrac{mv}{2qB}$ $\qquad$ (c) $\dfrac{2mv}{qB}$

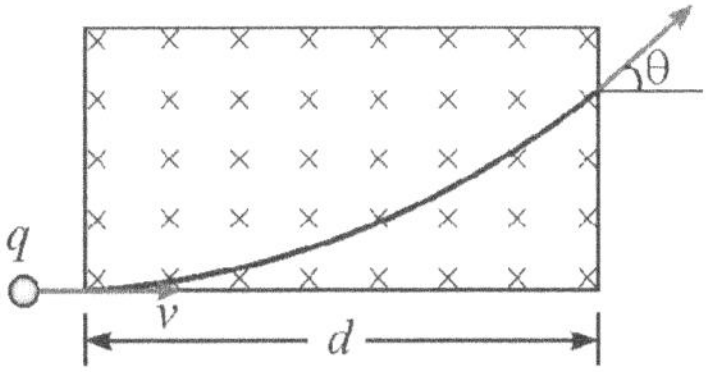

Fig. 5.14

Sol. The radius of path $r \;=\; \dfrac{mv}{qB}$

For $d \le r$, we have $\sin\theta \;=\; \dfrac{d}{r}$

(a) $d = \left(\dfrac{mv}{qB}\right) = r,\ \therefore \sin\theta \;=\; \dfrac{\left(\dfrac{mv}{qB}\right)}{\left(\dfrac{mv}{qB}\right)} = 1$

    or $\theta \;=\; \dfrac{\pi}{2}$ radian   *Ans.*

(b) $d = \left(\dfrac{mv}{2qB}\right) < r,\ \ \sin\theta \;=\; \dfrac{d}{r}$

$$= \dfrac{\dfrac{mv}{2qB}}{\dfrac{mv}{qB}} = \dfrac{1}{2}$$

    or $\theta \;=\; \dfrac{\pi}{6}$ radian   *Ans.*

(c) $d = \left(\dfrac{2mv}{qB}\right) > r$, the deviation of particle is therefore $\theta = \pi$ radian.

                                             Ans.

Ex. 6   **Electrons emitted with negligible speed from an electron gun are accelerated through a potential difference V along the x-axis. These electrons emerge from a narrow hole into a uniform magnetic field B directed along this axis. However, some of the electrons emerging from the hole make slightly divergent angles as shown in *fig. 5.15*.**

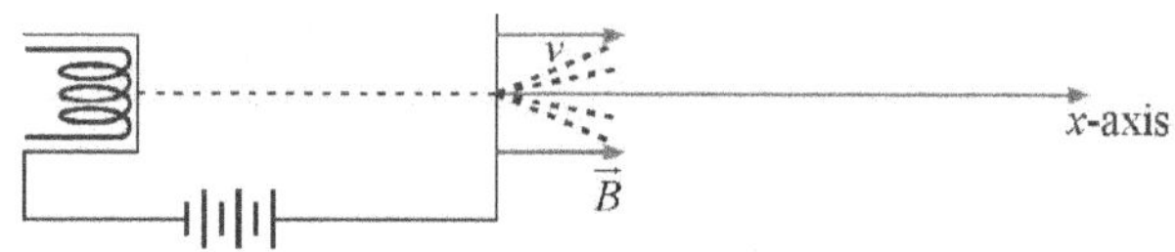

Fig. 5.15

Show that these paraxial electrons are refocused on the x-axis at a distance $x = \sqrt{\dfrac{8\pi^2 mV}{eB^2}}$.

Sol.   The velocity of electrons as they emerge out,

$$\tfrac{1}{2}mv^2 \;=\; eV$$

    or $v \;=\; \sqrt{\dfrac{2eV}{m}}$

The velocity can be resolved into two perpendicular components, $v\cos\theta$ along x-axis and $v\sin\theta \perp$ to it. The time taken to complete a circle

$$T \;=\; \dfrac{2\pi m}{eB}$$

In this time the distance travelled by electrons along x-axis

$$x \;=\; v\cos\theta \times T$$

$$= \left(\sqrt{\dfrac{2eV}{m}} \times \dfrac{2\pi m}{eB}\right)\cos\theta$$

for small θ, $\cos\theta = 1$

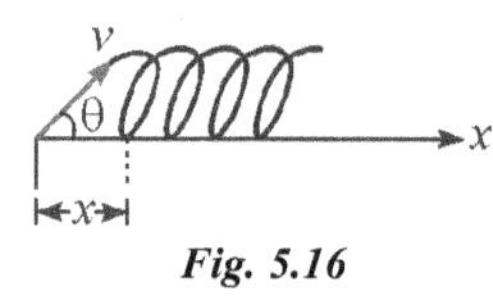

Fig. 5.16

$\therefore$ $x \;=\; \sqrt{\dfrac{8\pi^2 mV}{eB^2}}$ *Proved*

5.5   HALL EFFECT : 1879

According to Hall, if a current carrying conductor is placed in a transverse magnetic field, an emf is setup across the conductor perpendicular to both current and magnetic field. This was first observed by Hall, and therefore is called Hall effect.

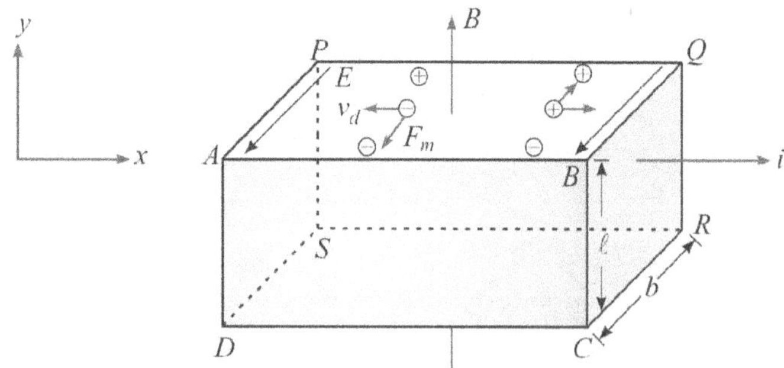

Fig. 5.20

Suppose we have a steady current i flowing in a uniform conducting strip along x-axis. If the strip is placed in a uniform magnetic field B, acting along the y-axis, the field $\vec{B}$, will exert a deflecting force on electrons along z-axis and on positive ions along negative z-axis. Because of this force, the electrons displace towards front face, $ABCD$ and positive ions on back face $PQRS$. The displacement of charge carriers gives rise to a transverse field, known as Hall electric field which acts along positive z-axis, and opposes the side ways drift of the carriers. When equilibrium is reached in which the magnetic deflecting force on the charge carriers is just balanced by the electric force caused by Hall electric field. Thus

$$ev_d B = E_H e$$

or $$E_H = v_d B \qquad ...(1)$$

The Hall potential

$$V_H = E_H \times b$$
$$= v_d B\, b$$

Also $$v_d = \frac{i}{neA}$$

As $$A = b\ell,$$

$\therefore$ $$V_H = \frac{i}{neb\ell} Bb$$

or $$V_H = \frac{iB}{ne\ell}. \qquad ...(2)$$

5.6 MASS SPECTROGRAPH

It is used to find mass number, to determine the relative abundance of isotopes or to produce separated isotopes.

An instrument in which we use a photographic plate and obtain a series of lines on it are known as mass spectrographs. Another instrument in which an electric or magnetic field is adjusted to make each part of the spectrum in turn to fall on a fixed detecting slit and measured electrically are called **mass spectrometers**.

All mass spectroscopes start with an ion source where the ions are produced by electron bombardment of gases. The ions are first set in motion with the help of an accelerating potential.

In the spectrograph designed by **Bainbridge**, a velocity selector is used to obtain ions of particular velocity v. The velocity selector allows a beam of a positive ions having the same velocity v to pass undeviated through crossed electric and magnetic fields $\vec{E}$ and $\vec{B}$.

In this case forces due to these fields are equal and opposite. i.e.,

$$F_e = F_m$$

or $$qE = qvB$$

$\therefore$ $$v = \frac{E}{B} \qquad ...(i)$$

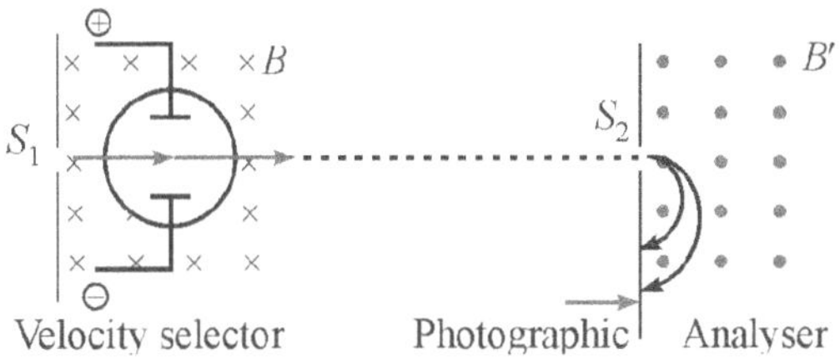

Fig. 5.21 Mass Spectrograph.

All the ions having the same velocity, $v = E/B$ enter the analysing chamber through slit. In this chamber another magnetic field B is applied perpendicular to the plane of paper and in outward direction. Due to this field, ions of different masses move in circles of different radii such that

$$\frac{mv^2}{r} = qvB'$$

or $$m = \frac{qrB'}{v} \qquad \text{...(ii)}$$

Assuming equal charges on each ion, the mass of each ion is proportional to the radius of its path. Ions of different isotopes converse at different points on the photographic plate. The relative abundance of the isotopes is measured from the densities of the photographic images they produce. For two isotopes of masses m_1 and m_2, we have

$$\frac{m_1}{m_2} = \frac{r_1}{r_2}.$$

5.7 CYCLOTRON

Cyclotron is a device which is used to accelerate positive particles like α-particle, deuteron etc.

It is based on the fact that the electric field accelerates a charged particle and the magnetic field keeps it revolving in circular orbits of increasing radius.

It consists of two hollow D-shaped metallic chambers D_1 and D_2 called dees. The dees are connected to the source of high frequency electric field. The whole apparatus is placed between the two poles of a strong electromagnet N–S as shown in *Fig. 5.22*. The magnetic field acts perpendicular to the plane of the dees.

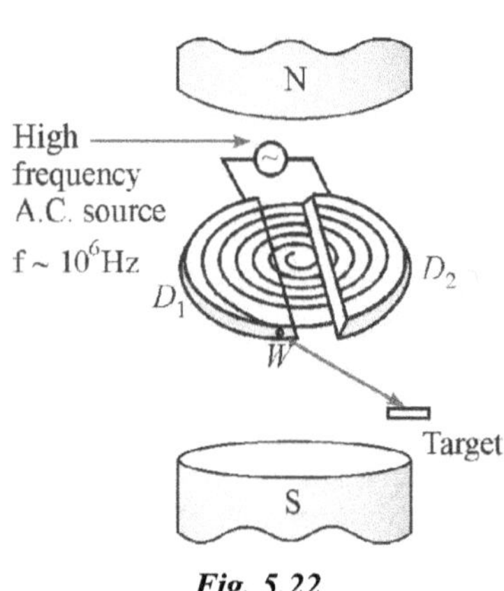

Fig. 5.22

(i) **Cyclotron frequency :** Time taken by charged particle to describe a semicircular path,

$$t = \frac{\pi r}{v} = \frac{\pi m}{qB}$$

The period of oscillating electric field

$$T = 2t = \frac{2\pi m}{qB}$$

and cyclotron frequency $f = \dfrac{1}{T} = \dfrac{Bq}{2\pi m}.$

(ii) **Maximum kinetic energy of the particle :**

(a) We have $$r = \frac{mv}{qB}$$

for $$r_0 = \frac{mv_0}{qB} \Rightarrow v_0 = \frac{r_0 qB}{m}$$

(r_0, maximum radius of circular path)

$$\therefore \quad \text{K.E.} = \frac{1}{2}mv_0^2 = \frac{1}{2}m\left(\frac{r_0 qB}{m}\right)^2 = \left(\frac{q^2 B^2}{2m}\right)r_0^2$$

(b) Also, K.E. = work done by electric source

$$\therefore \quad \text{K.E.} = f \times \left[qV \times 2\right]$$
$$= 2fqV.$$

Ex. 7 Two positive ions having the same charge q but different masses, m_1 and m_2 are accelerated horizontally from rest through a potential difference V. They then enter a region where there is uniform field $\vec{B}$ normal to the plane of the trajectory.

(a) Show that, if the beam entered the magnetic field along x-axis, the value of the y-coordinate for each ion at any time t is approximately

$$y = Bx^2 \left(\frac{q}{8mV}\right)^{\frac{1}{2}}$$

provided x remain much smaller than y.

(b) Can this arrangement be used for isotope separation ?

Sol.

(a) The path of ion is shown in *fig. 5.23*. The magnetic force provides an acceleration which is towards the centre of path C. At any instant the acceleration

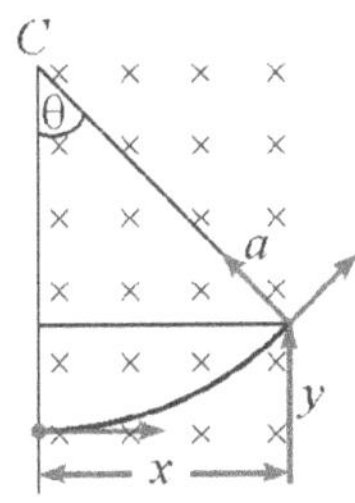

Fig. 5.23

$$a_c = \frac{F}{m} = \frac{qvB}{m}$$

and $\qquad a_y = a_c \cos\theta$

for small x, $\theta \to 0$, $\cos\theta \to 1$

$$\therefore \qquad a_y \simeq a_c = \frac{qvB}{m}$$

For $\qquad x = vt,$ ...(i)

$$y = \frac{1}{2} a_y t^2 \qquad \text{...(ii)}$$

From above equations, we get

$$y = \frac{1}{2} a_y \left(\frac{x}{v}\right)^2 = \frac{1}{2}\left(\frac{qvB}{m}\right)\frac{x^2}{v^2}$$

$$= \frac{1}{2}\frac{qBx^2}{mv} \qquad \text{...(iii)}$$

Since ions are accelerated through potential V,

$$\therefore \qquad \frac{1}{2}mv^2 = qV$$

Which gives $\qquad v = \sqrt{\frac{2qV}{m}}$.

Now $\qquad y = \frac{1}{2}\frac{qBx^2}{m\sqrt{\frac{2qB}{m}}} = Bx^2\left(\frac{q}{8mV}\right)^{\frac{1}{2}}$

(b) From equation (iii) $m \propto \dfrac{1}{y}$

$$\therefore \qquad \frac{m_1}{m_2} = \frac{y_2}{y_1}.$$

Ex. 8 A particle of charge $+q$ and mass m moving under the influence of a uniform field $E\hat{i}$ and a uniform magnetic field $B\hat{k}$ follows a trajectory from P to Q. The velocities at P and Q are $v\,i$ and $-2v\hat{j}$. Find the rate of doing work by the fields.

Sol. Magnetic field does no work on the moving charged particle. It bends the path of the particle. Electric field does work on the particle. Due to which its speed changes.

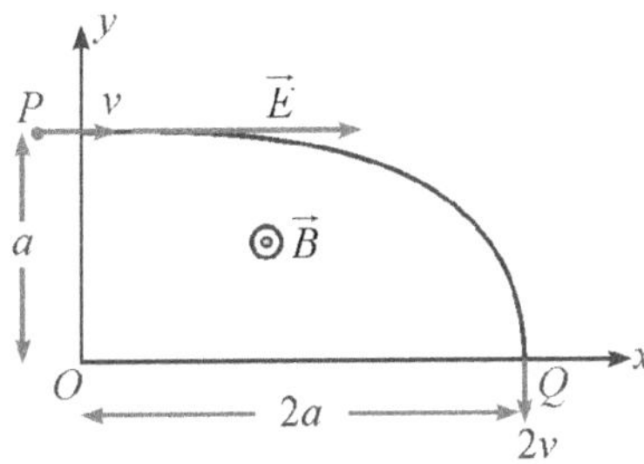

Fig. 5.24

$\therefore$ Workdone by electric field $= \Delta$K.E

or $\qquad \vec{F_e} \cdot \vec{s} = \Delta$K.E.

or $\qquad (Eq) \times 2a = \frac{1}{2}m\left[(2v)^2 - v^2\right]$

or $\qquad (Eq) = \frac{3mv^2}{4a}$

Now rate of doing work at P

$$= \vec{F_e} \cdot \vec{v} = (Eq) \times v \times \cos 0°$$

$$= \frac{3mv^2}{4a} \times v$$

$$= \frac{3}{4}\frac{mv^3}{a}. \qquad \textit{Ans.}$$

Ex. 9 A circular wire loop of radius r can with stand a radial force T before breaking. A particle of mass m and charge q ($q > 0$) is sliding over the wire. A magnetic field B is applied normal to the plane of the wire. What maximum speed v_{max} the particle can have before the loop breaks ?

Sol.

The centripetal force available is

$$= (T + qvB)$$

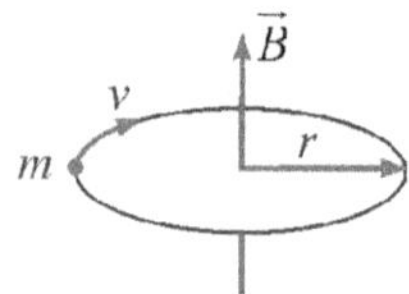

Fig. 5.25

From Newton's second law

$$(T + qvB) = \frac{mv^2}{r}$$

or

$$\frac{mv^2}{r} - qvB - T = 0$$

Solving above equation for v, we get

$$v_{max} = \frac{r}{2m}\left[qB + \sqrt{q^2B^2 + \frac{4Tm}{r}} \right] \qquad .Ans.$$

Ex. 6

A particle carries a charge of 4×10^{-9} C. When it moves with a velocity v_1 of 3×10^4 m/s at 45° above the x-axis in the xy-plane, a uniform field exerts a force F_1 along negative z-axis. When the particle moves with a velocity v_2 of 2×10^4 m/s along the z-axis, there is a force of 4×10^{-5} N exerted on it along the x-axis. What are the magnitude and direction of the magnetic field ?

Sol.

Given,

$$\vec{v}_1 = \left(3\times10^4\right)\left(\cos45^\circ \hat{i} + \sin45^\circ \hat{j}\right)$$

$$= 3\times10^4\left(\frac{\hat{i}}{\sqrt{2}} + \frac{\hat{j}}{\sqrt{2}}\right)$$

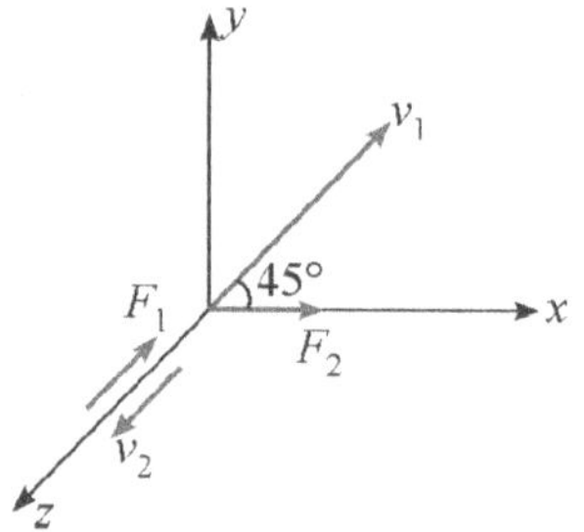

Fig. 5.26

In first case;

The force acts along z-axis, so field may be

$$\vec{B} = B_x\hat{i} + B_y\hat{j}.$$

In the second case,

$$\vec{F}_2 = q\left(\vec{v} \times \vec{B}\right)$$

or

$$4\times10^{-5}\hat{i} = \left(4\times10^{-9}\right)\left[2\times10^4\hat{k}\times\left(B_x\hat{i} + B_y\hat{j}\right)\right]$$

or

$$4\times10^{-5}\hat{i} = \left(4\times10^{-9}\right)\left(2\times10^4\right)\left[B_x\left(-\hat{j}\right) + B_y\left(-\hat{i}\right)\right]$$

or

$$4\times10^{-5}\hat{i} = 8\times10^{-5}\left[-B_x\hat{j} - B_y\hat{i}\right]$$

On comparing both sides of above expression, we get

$$B_x = 0 \text{ and } B_y = -0.5$$

Thus

$$\vec{B} = 0 + \left(-0.5\hat{j}\right)T$$

$$= -0.5\hat{j}\ T \qquad \textbf{\textit{Ans.}}$$

Ex. 11

A proton accelerated by a potential difference $V = 500$ kV flies through a uniform transverse magnetic field with induction $B = 0.51$ T. The field occupies a region of space $d = 10$ cm thickness (see *fig. 5.27*). Find the angle through which the proton deviates from the initial direction of motion.

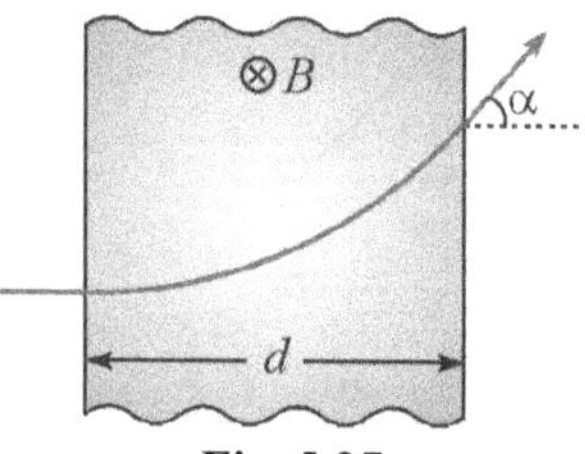

Fig. 5.27

Sol. If v is the speed of the proton, then

$$\frac{1}{2}mv^2 = qV$$

or

$$v = \sqrt{\frac{2qV}{m}}.$$

Here q and m are the charge and mass of the proton respectively. The proton traverses circular path of radius R in the magnetic field, where

$$R = \frac{mv}{qB}$$

From the figure

$$\sin\alpha = \frac{d}{R}$$

$$= \frac{d}{\dfrac{m\left(\sqrt{\dfrac{2qV}{m}}\right)}{qB}}$$

$$= Bd\sqrt{\frac{q}{2mV}} \qquad \textbf{Fig. 5.28}$$

On substituting the values, we get $\alpha = 30^\circ$ \qquad **Ans.**

Ex. 12

A particle with specific charge q/m moves rectilinearly due to an electric field $E = E_0 - ax$, where a is a positive constant, x is the distance from the point where the particle was initially at rest. Find

(a) the distance covered by the particle till the moment it come to a stand still;

(b) the acceleration of the particle at that moment.

Sol. The force exerted by the electric field on the particle
$$F = Eq = q\,(E_0 - ax).$$
Acceleration of the particle
$$v\frac{dv}{dx} = \frac{q}{m}\left(E_0 - ax\right) \qquad \text{...(i)}$$
Upon integrating, we have
$$\frac{1}{2}v^2 = \frac{q}{m}\left(E_0 x - \frac{1}{2}ax^2\right) + C$$
Given at $x = 0$, $v = 0$; $\therefore$ $C = 0$.

Thus
$$v^2 = \frac{2q}{m}\left(E_0 x - \frac{1}{2}ax^2\right) \qquad \text{...(ii)}$$

(a) The velocity of the particle again will be zero.
$$0 = \frac{2q}{m}\left(E_0 x - \frac{1}{2}ax^2\right)$$

or
$$x = x_m = \frac{2E_0}{a}. \qquad \textbf{\textit{Ans.}}$$

(b) The corresponding acceleration, from equation (i)
$$= \frac{q}{m}\left(E_0 - a \times \frac{2E_0}{a}\right)$$
$$= -\frac{qE_0}{m}. \qquad \textbf{\textit{Ans.}}$$

Ex. 13 A slightly divergent beam of non-relativistic charged particles accelerated by a potential difference V propagates from a point A along the axis of a straight solenoid. The beam is brought into focus at a distance ℓ from the point A at two successive values of magnetic induction B_1 and B_2. Find the specific charge q/m of the particles.

Sol.

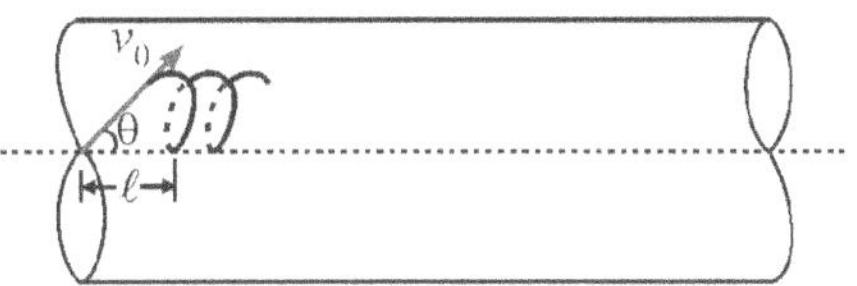

Fig. 5.29

Suppose v_0 is the velocity of the particle, then
$$\frac{1}{2}mv_0^2 = qV$$

or
$$v_0 = \sqrt{\frac{2qV}{m}} \qquad \text{...(i)}$$

For slightly divergent particle, $\theta \to 0$
$$\therefore \qquad v_0\cos\theta \simeq v_0.$$

If t is the time to travel a distance ℓ, then $t = \dfrac{\ell}{v_0}$. In this duration, let particle completes n circles for B_1 and $(n + 1)$ for B_2, then
$$\frac{\ell}{v_0} = n\frac{2\pi m}{qB_1}$$
$$= (n+1)\frac{2\pi m}{qB_2} \qquad \text{...(ii)}$$

On solving
$$n = \frac{B_1}{B_2 - B_1}$$

Substituting this values of v_0 and n in equation (ii) and solving, we get
$$\frac{\ell}{\sqrt{\dfrac{2qV}{m}}} = \left(\frac{B_1}{B_2 - B_1}\right)\frac{2\pi m}{qB_1}$$

or
$$\frac{q}{m} = \frac{8\pi^2 V}{\ell^2\left(B_2 - B_1\right)^2}. \qquad \textbf{\textit{Ans.}}$$

5.8 MAGNETIC FORCE ON CURRENT CARRYING CONDUCTOR

When a current carrying conductor is placed in a magnetic field, magnetic force is acted upon the moving charges (electrons) within the conductor. This force is transmitted to the material of the conductor, and the conductor as a whole experiences a force distributed along its length.

Suppose a conducting wire of length ℓ carrying current i, lies in a magnetic field $\vec{B}$ (see *fig. 5.30*).

Consider a small element of length $d\vec{\ell}$ of the wire. The free electrons drift with a speed v_d opposite to the direction of the current. We know that $i = jA = neAv_d$. Here A is the area of cross section of the wire and n is the number of free electrons per unit volume. Each electron experiences an average magnetic force
$$\vec{f}_m = -e\left(\vec{v}_d \times \vec{B}\right)$$

The number of free electrons in the element is $nAd\ell$. Thus the magnetic force on the wire is
$$d\vec{F}_m = \left(nAd\ell\right)\vec{f}_m$$

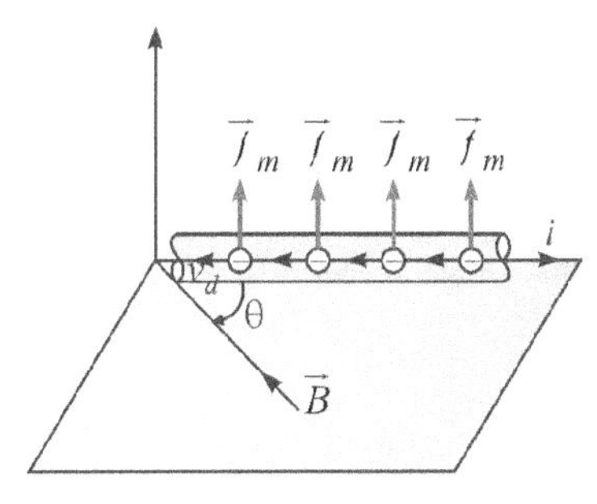

Fig. 5.30

$$= \left(nAd\ell\right)\left[-e\left(\vec{v}_d \times \vec{B}\right)\right]$$

If we take $d\vec{\ell}$ along the direction of the current, then $-\vec{v}_d\left(d\ell\right) = v_d\left(d\vec{\ell}\right)$ and the above expression becomes

$$d\vec{F}_m = nAev_d\left(d\vec{\ell} \times \vec{B}\right)$$

or

$$d\vec{F}_m = i\left(d\vec{\ell} \times \vec{B}\right)$$

$$= id\vec{\ell} \times \vec{B}$$

Quantity $id\vec{\ell}$ is called current element.

The force on the wire of length ℓ

$$\vec{F}_m = i\vec{\ell} \times \vec{B}.$$

The above equation can be used in two stages

To find the magnitude of force by $F = Bi\ell \sin\theta$ and the direction of force can be obtained by Fleming left hand rule or by right hand palm rule.

Force on curved conductor

Let us consider a conducting wire of arbitrary shape and is placed in uniform magnitude field $\vec{B}$.

The force on $d\vec{\ell}$ length of the conductor $d\vec{F}_m = id\vec{\ell} \times \vec{B}$. To get force on the whole wire, integrate above equation over the length of the wire. Thus

$$\vec{F}_m = \int_P^Q id\vec{\ell} \times \vec{B}$$

$$= i\left[\int_P^Q d\vec{\ell}\right] \times \vec{B}$$

$$= i\,\overrightarrow{PQ} \times \vec{B}.$$

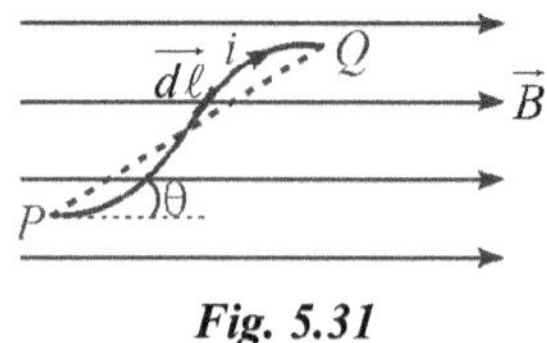
Fig. 5.31

The other simpler way to get the force on current carrying wire is : draw straight line joining the ends of the conductor (here PQ), and then find its component perpendicular to $\vec{B}$, here it is $PQ \sin\theta$. Therefore

$$F = Bi(PQ \sin\theta).$$

Ex. 14 Find the force on the conductors placed in uniform magnetic field as shown in the figure.

Sol.

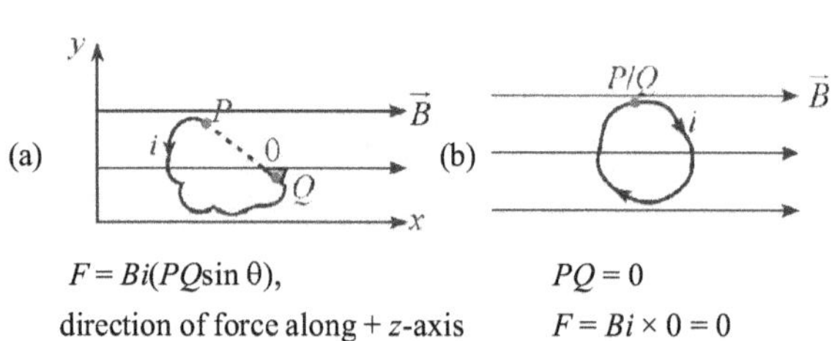

(a) $F = Bi(PQ\sin\theta),$
direction of force along $+z$-axis

(b) $PQ = 0$
$F = Bi \times 0 = 0$

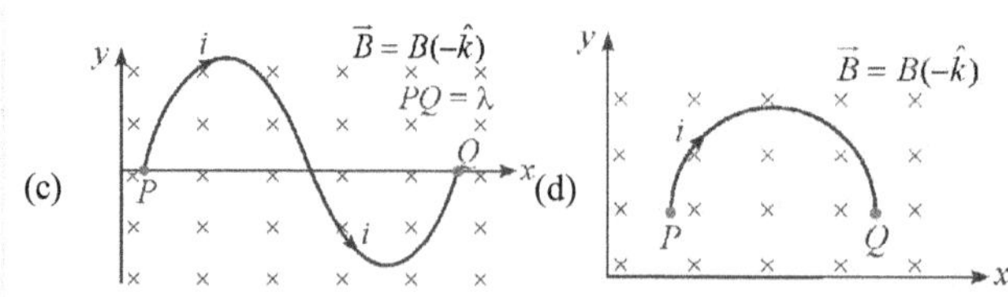

(c) $F = Bi \times PQ = Bi\,\lambda,$
direction of force along $+y$-axis

(d) $F = Bi\,(PQ),$
direction of force along $+y$-axis
(perpendicular to line PQ)

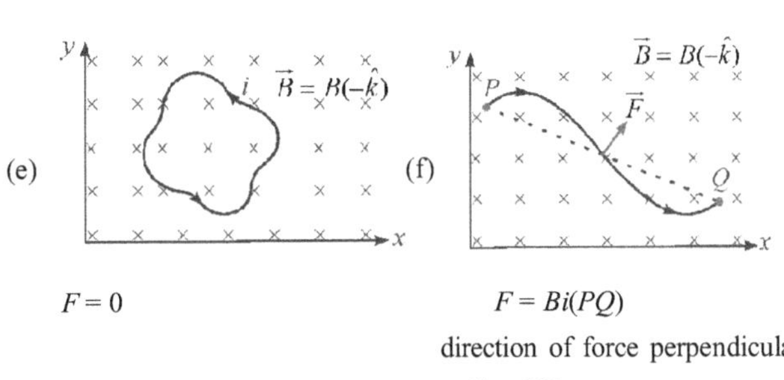

(e) $F = 0$

(f) $F = Bi(PQ)$

direction of force perpendicular to line PQ.

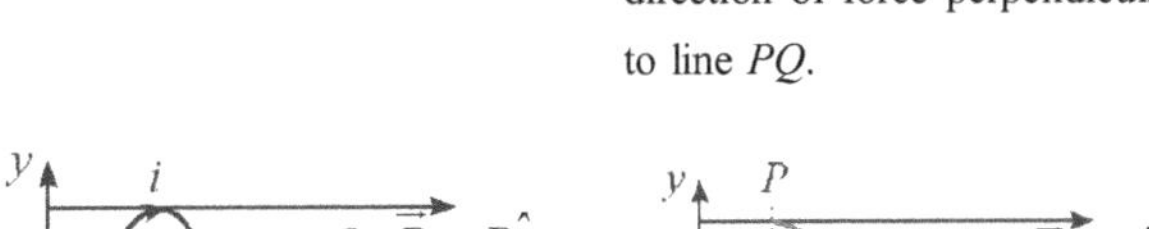

(g) $\vec{F} = 0$

(h) $\vec{F} = Bi\lambda\hat{k}$

Note: Magnetic force on any close loop in a uniform field acting perpendicular to plane of loop always be zero.

Ex. 15

In the *fig. 5.32* shown a semi-circular wire loop of radius R is placed in a uniform magnetic field B. The plane of the loop is perpendicular to the magnetic field. Find magnetic force on the loop.

Sol.

Consider an element of length $d\,1 = Rd\theta$ in segment PS. The force on it $dF = Bid\,1 = Bi(Rdq)$ the direction of force is normal to $d\vec{\ell}$. Similar element is taken in segment QS, and will have the same force.

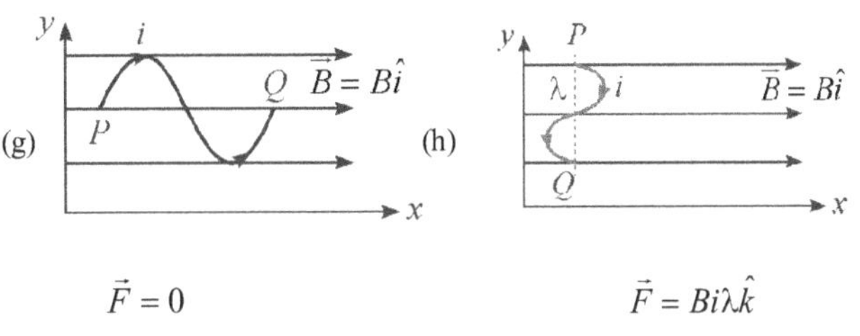

Fig. 5.32

The resultant force on these elements

$$= 2dF\sin q$$
$$= 2\,Bi(Rdq)\sin q$$

The resultant force on the entire loop

$$F = \int_0^{\frac{\pi}{2}} dF$$

$$= 2BiR\int_0^{\frac{\pi}{2}} \sin\theta\, d\theta$$

$$= 2BiR\left|-\cos\theta\right|_0^{\pi/2}$$

$$= 2BiR\left[-\cos\frac{\pi}{2} - \left(-\cos 0\right)\right]$$

$$= Bi \times \left(2R\right)$$

or $\qquad F = Bi\,(PQ) \qquad\qquad$ **Ans.**

The direction of force is perpendicular to line PQ. i.e., along y-axis.

Ex. 16

Find in brief the force on the conductor shown in *fig. 5.33*.

Sol.

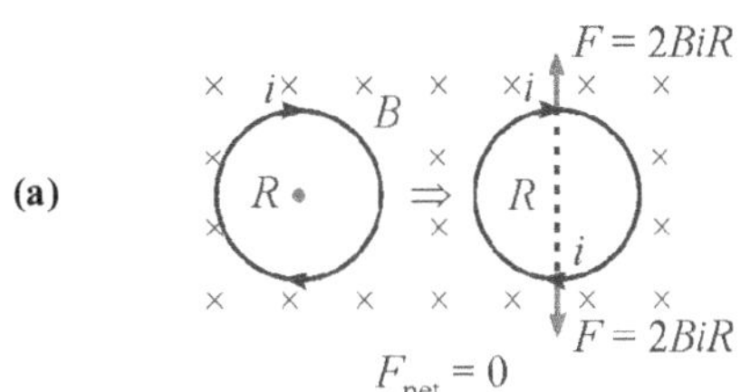

(a)

$$F_{net} = 0$$

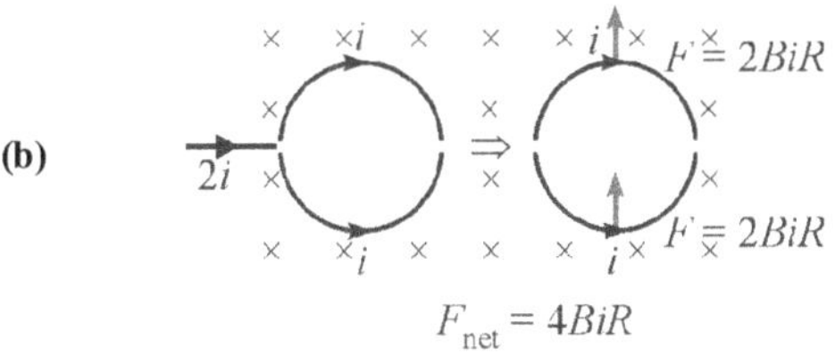

(b)

$$F_{net} = 4BiR$$

Fig. 5.33

Ex. 17

A circular loop of radius a, carrying a current i, is placed in a two dimensional magnetic field. The centre of the loop concides with the centre of the field as shown in *Fig. 5.34*. The strength of the magnetic field at the periphery of the loop is B. Find the magnetic force on the wire.

Sol.

Consider an element of length $d\ell$, the force on it $dF = Bi(d\ell)$ $\sin 90^0 = Bi(d\ell)$ and perpendicular to $d\vec{\ell}$ and $\vec{B}$, that is along z-axis. For any of the element of the loop, the direction is along z-axis. Therefore force on entire loop

$$\vec{F} = \int_0^{2\pi a} Bi(d\ell)\hat{k}$$

$$= Bi\int_0^{2\pi a} d\ell\,\hat{k}$$

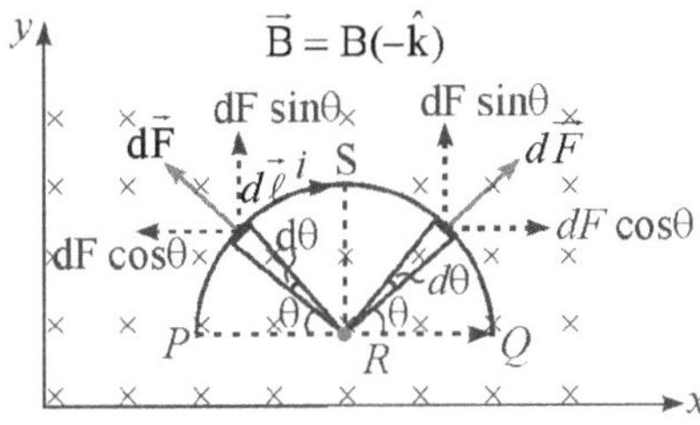

or $\qquad \vec{F} = Bi\left(2\pi a\right)\hat{k} \qquad$ **Fig. 5.34** **Ans.**

Ex. 18

A hypothetical magnetic field existing in a region is given by $\vec{B} = B_0\vec{e}_r$, where $\vec{e}_r$ denotes the unit vector along the radial direction. A circular loop of radius a, carrying a current i, is placed with its plane parallel to the xy- plane and the centre at $(0, 0, d)$. Find the magnitude of the magnetic force acting on the loop.

Sol. The situation is shown in the *fig. 5.35*.

$$\sin\theta = \frac{a}{\sqrt{a^2 + d^2}}$$

The given field can be resolved into two components: $B_0\sin\theta$, which acts all round the periphery of loop and lie in the plane of the loop and other component $B_0\cos\theta$ acts all round the periphery and perpendicular to the plane of the loop.

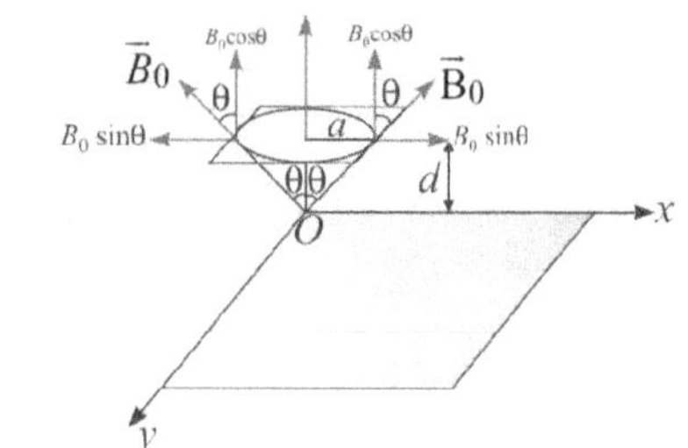

Fig. 5.35

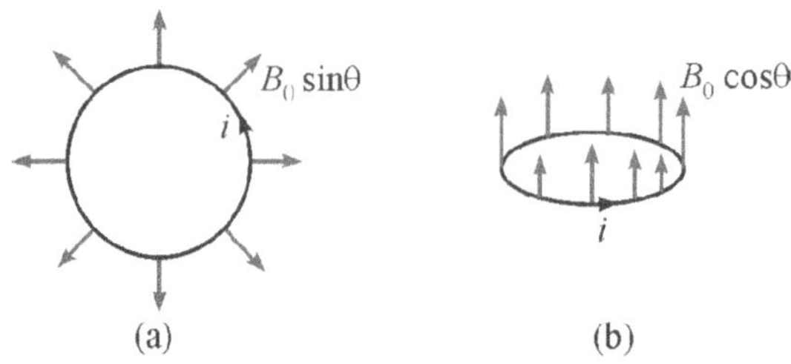

(a)   (b)

Fig. 5.36

Force on the loop due to $B_0\cos\theta$ is zero. The force is only due to $B_0\sin\theta$, which is

$$F = \left(B_0\sin\theta\right)i \times 2\pi a$$

$$= 2Bi\pi a \times \frac{a}{\sqrt{a^2 + d^2}}$$

or $\qquad F = \dfrac{2Bi\pi a^2}{\sqrt{a^2 + d^2}}.$ *Ans.*

Ex. 19 *Fig. 5.37* shows a circular wire-loop of radius a, carrying a current i, placed in a perpendicular magnetic field B.
(a) Take a small part *dl* of the wire. Find force on this part of the wire exerted by the magnetic field.
(b) Find the force of compression in the wire.

Sol.

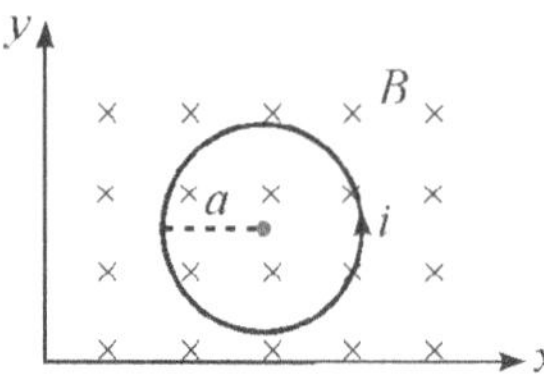

Fig. 5.37

(a) The force on the element by magnetic field $dF = Bi(dl)$, towards the centre of loop (By FLHR).
(b) Let us now consider an element, cutout from the loop. The force exerted by rest part of loop on the element is shown in *fig. 5.38*. Let this force is T.

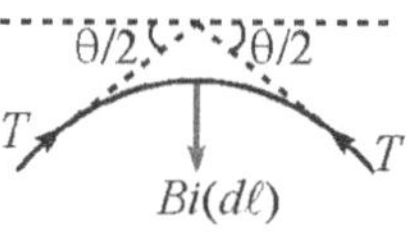

Fig. 5.38

Since net force on the entire loop is zero, so the net force on its element also be zero. Therefore the equilibrium of element gives

$$2T\sin\frac{\theta}{2} = Bi(dl)$$

for small θ, $\sin\dfrac{\theta}{2} \simeq \dfrac{\theta}{2}$

$$\therefore \qquad 2T \times \frac{\theta}{2} = Bi(a\theta) \qquad [dl = a\theta]$$

which gives $\qquad T = Bia$ *Ans.*

Ex. 20 The magnetic field existing in a region is given by

$$\vec{B} = B_0\left[1 + \frac{x}{\ell}\right]\hat{k}.$$

A square loop of edge ℓ and carrying a current i, is placed with its edges parallel to x-y axis. Find the magnitude of the net magnetic force experienced by the loop.

Sol.

Magnetic field at $x = 0$,

$$\vec{B}_1 = B_0\hat{k}$$

and at $x = \ell$,

$$\vec{B}_2 = 2B_0\,\hat{k}$$

The situation is shown in the *fig. 5.39*.
The forces on the sides BC and DA are equal and opposite and get cancelled.
The force on side AB,

$$\vec{F}_1 = B_0 i\ell\,\hat{j}$$

And the force on side CD,

$$\vec{F}_2 = -2B_0 i\ell\,\hat{j}$$

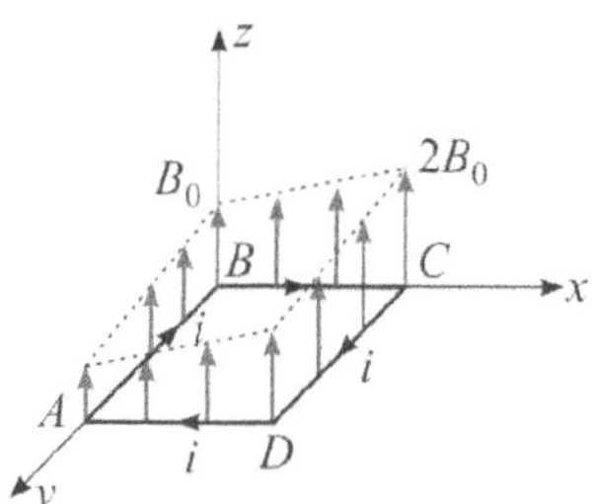

Fig. 5.39

Therefore net force on the loop

$$\vec{F} = \vec{F}_1 + \vec{F}_2$$

$$= -B_0 i\ell\,\hat{j}$$

or $\qquad F = B_0 i\ell.$ *Ans.*

5.9 TORQUE ON A CURRENT LOOP IN MAGNETIC FIELD

Let us consider a rectangular loop $(a \times b)$ is placed in a magnetic field $\vec{B}$. The normal of loop makes an angle θ with the direction of $\vec{B}$.

The force exerted by the magnetic field on four sides of the loop is shown in *fig. 5.41*. On sides AB and CD, the force $Bia\cos\theta$ is equal and opposite and their line of action is same. While on sides BC and AD, the force on each is Bib and opposite in directions. Their line of actions are at a separation of $a\sin\theta$. Therefore the net force on entire loop, $F_{net} = 0$. But there is a net torque which is

$$\tau = Bib \times a\sin\theta$$

$$= Bi(a \times b)\sin\theta$$

$$= BiA\sin\theta$$

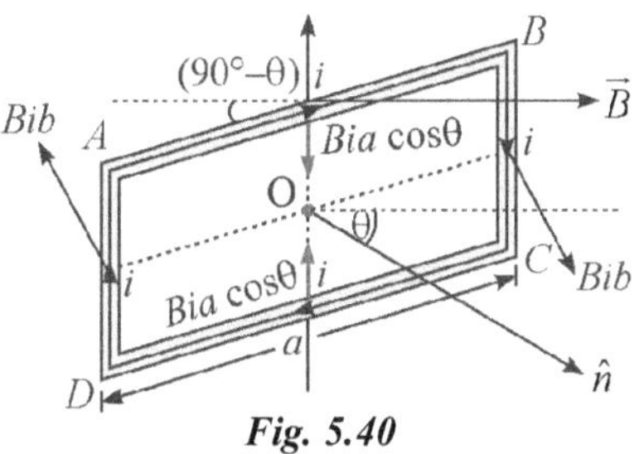

Fig. 5.40

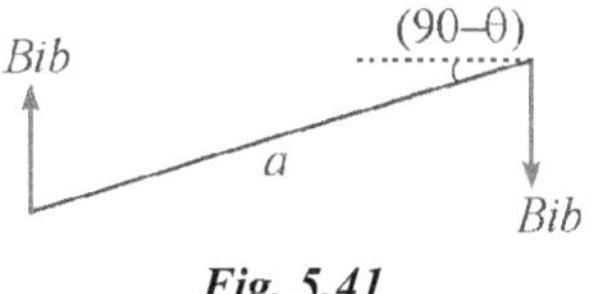

Fig. 5.41

If coil consists of N turns, the torque on entire coil is

$$\tau = (NiA)\,B\sin\theta$$

$$\text{or}\qquad \tau = MB\sin\theta \qquad \text{...(1)}$$

where $M = NiA$, is known as magnetic moment of the loop of N-turns.

In vector notation, it can be written as

$$\vec{\tau} = \vec{M} \times \vec{B} \qquad \text{...(2)}$$

5.10 POTENTIAL ENERGY OF MAGNETIC DIPOLE

When the current loop or a magnetic dipole is placed in magnetic field $\vec{B}$, work must be done by an external agent to change the orientation of the dipole. This work done by agent becomes the potential energy of the magnetic dipole. Magnetic energy is assumed to be zero when $\vec{M}$ is $\perp$ to $\vec{B}$. If the dipole is rotated through an angle θ from zero energy position, then

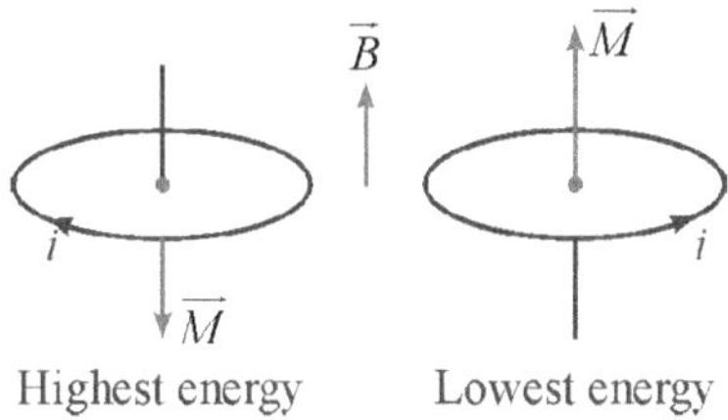

Fig. 5.42

$$U = W_{agent} = \int_{90°}^{\theta} \tau\, d\theta$$

$$= MB \int_{90°}^{\theta} \sin\theta\, d\theta$$

$$\text{or}\qquad U = -MB\cos\theta$$

$$\text{or}\qquad U = -\vec{M} \cdot \vec{B}$$

Note :   Above results are derived for rectangular loop. But they can be used for a plane loop of any shape.

1. For circular loop :
$$M = iA = i\pi R^2$$
and
$$\tau = MB\sin\theta = (i\pi R^2)\,B\sin\theta$$
$$F_{net} = 0$$

2. For solenoid : If windings are closely spaced, the solenoid can be approximated by a number of circular loops.
$$\tau = NiAB\sin\theta.$$

Analogy between electric dipole and magnetic dipole

	Electric dipole		Magnetic dipole
1.	$\vec{P} = q\vec{\ell}$ direction from $-q$ to $+q$	1.	$\vec{M} = i\vec{A}$ direction from S to N
2.	$\vec{F}_{net} = 0$	2.	$\vec{F}_{net} = 0$
3.	$\vec{\tau} = \vec{P} \times \vec{E}$	3.	$\vec{\tau} = \vec{M} \times \vec{B}$
4.	$U = -PE\cos\theta$	4.	$U = -MB\cos\theta$

More about magnetic moment $\vec{M}$

(a) The direction of $\vec{M}$ is the direction of thumb of the right hand if the fingers of this curl around the loop are in the direction of the current.

(b) Direction of $\vec{M}$ can also be determined as in the case of electric dipole, the dipole moment $\vec{P}$ has a direction from negative to positive charge. In the similar way direction of $\vec{M}$ is from south magnetic pole to north magnetic pole. The south and north poles can be determined by the sence of flow of current. The side from where the current seems to be clockwise becomes south pole [S] and the opposite side from it seems anticlockwise becomes north pole [N].

(c) $\vec{M}$ of a rectangular square loop can also the determined by this method

$$\vec{M} = i\vec{A}$$
$$= i\left(A\vec{B} \times B\vec{C}\right)$$
$$= i\left(B\vec{C} \times C\vec{D}\right)$$
$$= i\left(C\vec{D} \times D\vec{A}\right)$$
$$= i\left(D\vec{A} \times A\vec{B}\right)$$

Gyro-magnetic Ratio $\dfrac{M}{C}$: The ratio of angular momentum to magnetic moment is called Gyro-magnetic ratio.

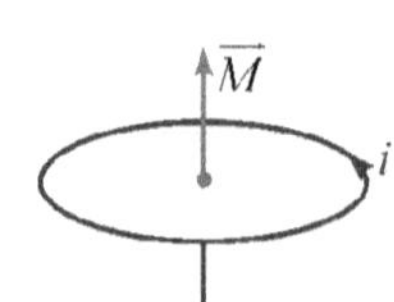

Fig. 5.44(a)

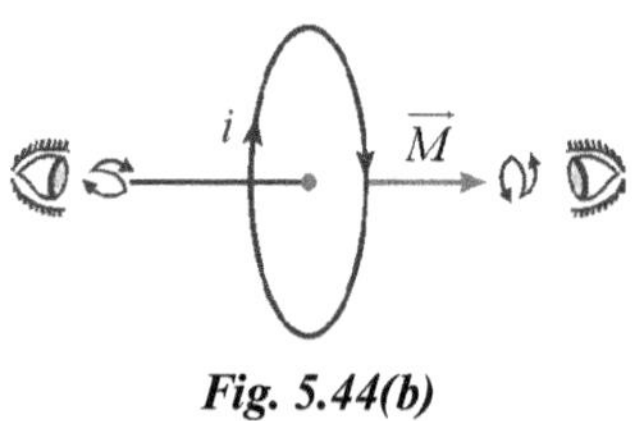

Fig. 5.44(b)

Fig. 5.45

Ex. 21 The *fig. 5.43* shows four orientations, at an angle θ, of a magnetic dipole moment $\vec{M}$ in a magnetic field. Find :

(a) the magnitude of the torque on the dipole and

(b) the potential energy of the dipole.

Sol.

For the dipole

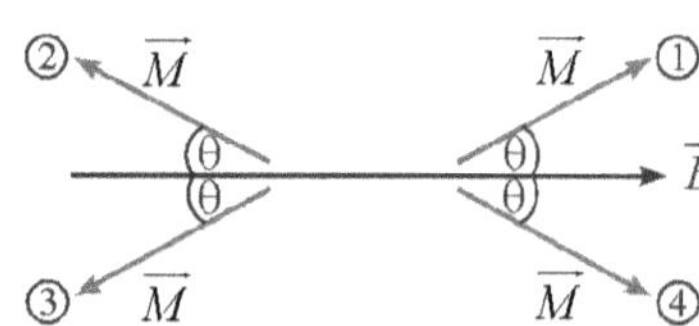

Fig. 5.43

1,	$\theta_1 = \theta$
2,	$\theta_2 = (180° - \theta)$
3,	$\theta_3 = (180° + \theta)$
4,	$\theta_4 = (360° - \theta)$

(a) Torque on the dipole is given by $\tau = MB\sin\theta$.

$$\tau_1 = MB\sin\theta$$
$$\tau_2 = MB\sin(180° - \theta) = MB\sin\theta$$
$$\tau_3 = MB\sin(180° + \theta) = -MB\sin\theta$$
$$\tau_4 = MB\sin(360° - \theta) = -MB\sin\theta$$

(b) Potential energy of a dipole in magnetic field is given by $U = -MB\cos\theta$.

$$U_1 = -MB\cos\theta$$
$$U_2 = -MB\cos(180° - \theta) = MB\cos\theta$$
$$U_3 = -MB\cos(180° + \theta) = MB\cos\theta$$
$$U_4 = -MB\cos(360° - \theta) = -MB\cos\theta$$

Ex. 22 A square loop of side ℓ carries a current i. It is placed as shown in *Fig. 5.46*. Find the magnetic moment of the loop.

Sol. Method I :

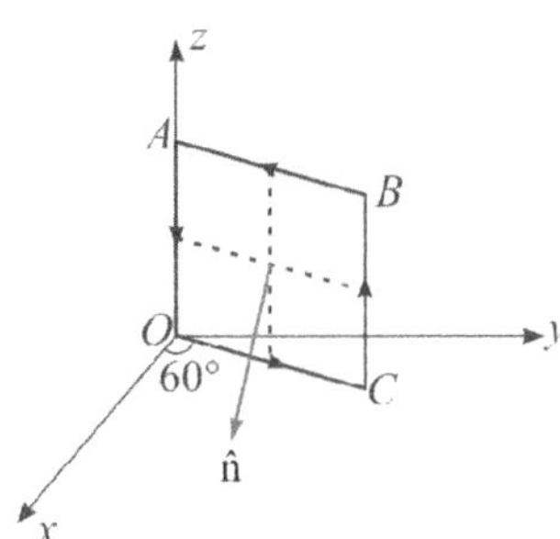

Fig. 5.46

$$\vec{M} = iA\hat{n}$$

where $$M = i\ell^2$$

and $$\hat{n} = \sin 30°\hat{i} + \cos 30°\hat{j}$$

$$= \frac{\hat{i}}{2} - \frac{\sqrt{3}\,\hat{j}}{2}$$

$\therefore$ $$\vec{M} = \frac{i\ell^2}{2}\left(\sqrt{3}\hat{i} - \hat{j}\right)$$

Method II : $$\vec{M} = i\left(\vec{OC} \times \vec{CB}\right)$$

Here $$\vec{OC} = \ell\cos 60°\hat{i} + \ell\sin 60°\hat{j}$$

$$= \frac{\ell\hat{i}}{2} + \frac{\sqrt{3}\ell\hat{j}}{2} = \ell\left[\frac{i}{2} + \frac{\sqrt{3}}{2}\hat{j}\right]$$

and $$\vec{CB} = \ell\,\hat{k}$$

$\therefore$ $$\vec{M} = i\,\ell^2\left[\left(\frac{i}{2} + \frac{\sqrt{3}}{2}\hat{j}\right) \times \hat{k}\right]$$

$$= i\,\ell^2\left[\frac{-\hat{j}}{2} + \frac{\sqrt{3}}{2}\hat{i}\right]$$

$$= \frac{i\,\ell^2}{2}\left[\sqrt{3}\,\hat{i} - \hat{j}\right].$$ *Ans.*

Ex. 23 Find the magnitude of magnetic moment of the current carrying loop *ABCDEFA*. Each side of the loop is ℓ and current in the loop is *i*.

Sol. The given loop can break into two loops to get magnetic moment that is in *ABEFA* and *BCDEB*.

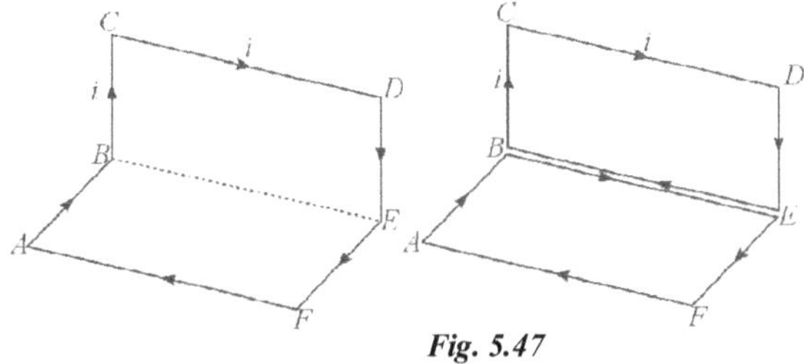

Fig. 5.47

The magnetic moment of each loop

$$M = i\,A$$
$$= i\,\ell^2$$

Their magnetic moments are perpendicular to each other. Hence

$$M_{net} = \sqrt{2}\,M = \sqrt{2}\,i\,\ell^2.$$ *Ans.*

Ex. 24 A thin uniform ring of radius *R* carrying uniform charge *q* and mass *m* rotates about its axis with angular velocity ⍵. Find the ratio of its magnetic moment and angular momentum.

Sol. The equivalent current in the ring

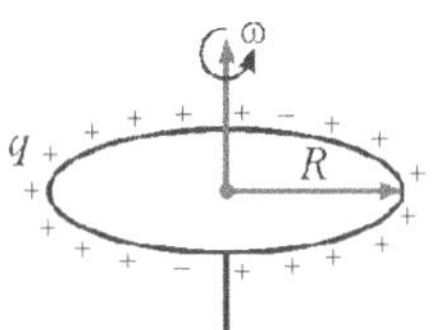

Fig. 5.48

$$i = \frac{q}{T} = \frac{q}{\dfrac{2\pi}{\omega}} = \frac{q\omega}{2\pi}$$

Magnetic moment $$M = i\,A$$

$$= \frac{q\omega}{2\pi} \times \pi R^2$$

$$= \frac{q\omega R^2}{2}$$

Angular momentum $$L = I\,\omega$$
$$= (mR^2)\omega$$

$\therefore$ $$\frac{M}{L} = \frac{q}{2m}.$$ *Ans.*

Ex. 25 A positive charge *q* is distributed over a circular ring of radius *a*. It is placed in a horizontal plane and is rotated about its axis at a uniform angular speed ⍵. A horizontal magnetic field *B* exists in the space. Find the torque acting on the ring due to the magnetic force.

Sol.

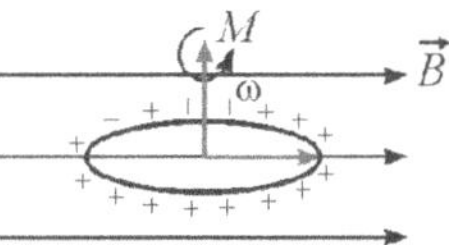

Fig. 5.49

We know that $$\tau = MB\sin\theta$$
Here $$\theta = 90°$$
$\therefore$ $$\tau = MB = i\,AB$$

$$= \left(\frac{q}{\dfrac{2\pi}{\omega}}\right) \times \pi a^2 B$$

$$= \frac{1}{2}q\omega a^2 B.$$ *Ans.*

Ex. 26   A thin insulated wire forms a plane spiral of N light turns carrying a current i. The radii of inside and outside turns are equal to a and b. Find the magnetic moment of the spiral with a given current.

Sol. Consider dr width of the spiral, at a distance r from the centre. Number of turns in this

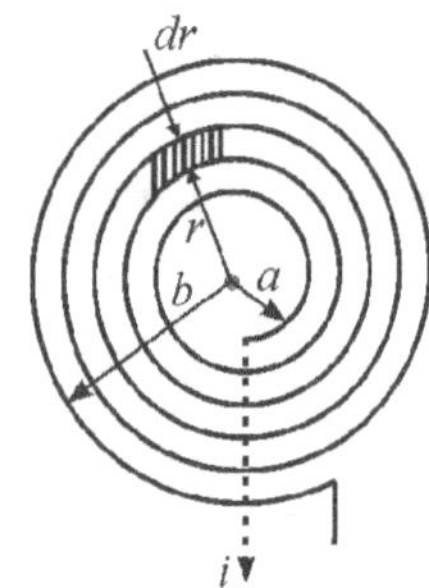

Fig. 5.50

$$dN = \frac{N}{(b-a)}dr$$

The magnetic moment of current loop, having dN turns is,
$$dM = (dN)\,i\,A$$
Total magnetic moment

$$M = \int dM$$

$$= \int_a^b dN\,iA$$

$$= \left(\frac{N}{b-a}\right)\int_a^b dr\,i \times \pi r^2$$

$$= \frac{\pi\,N\,i}{(b-a)}\int_a^b r^2\,dr$$

$$= \frac{\pi\,N\,i}{3(b-a)}\left(b^3 - a^3\right). \qquad \textbf{\textit{Ans.}}$$

Ex. 27 *Fig. 5.51 shows a circular coil with 250 turns, an area A*

of $2.52 \times 10^{-4}\,\text{m}^2$*, and a current of 100 μ A. The coil is at rest in a uniform magnetic field of magnitude $B = 0.85$ T with its magnetic dipole moment $\vec{M}$ initially aligned with B.*

(a)   **What is the direction of the current in the coil ?**

(b)   **How much work would the torque applied by an external agent to do on the coil to rotate it 90° from its initial orientation, so that $\vec{M}$ is perpendicular to $\vec{B}$ and the coil is again at rest ?**

Sol.

(a)   According to the right-hand rule, the direction of the current through the wires from the right side of the coil is from top to bottom (see figure).

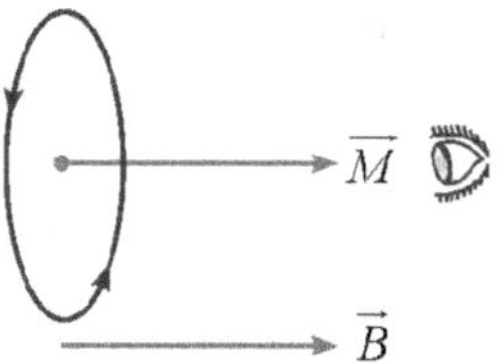

Fig. 5.51

(b)   Work done by the agent is given by

$$W = \int_{\theta_1}^{\theta_2} \tau\,d\theta = \int_{\theta_1}^{\theta_2} MB\,\sin\theta\,d\theta$$

$$= MB\big[\cos\theta_1 - \cos\theta_2\big]$$

Given $\theta_1 = 0°$, $\theta_2 = 90°$

$$\therefore \qquad W = MB\,[\cos0° - \cos90°]$$
$$= MB$$
$$= N\,i\,AB$$

$$= (250)\left(100 \times 10^{-6}\right)\left(2.52 \times 10^{-4}\right)(0.85)$$

$$= 5.4 \times 10^{-6}\,J = 5.4\,\mu\,J \qquad \textit{Ans.}$$

Ex. 28 **The flat insulating disc of radius a carries an excess charge on its surface is of σ C/m^2. Consider disc to rotate around the axis passing through its centre and perpendicular to its plane with angular speed ω rad/s. If a magnetic field $\vec{B}$ is directed perpendicular to the rotation axis, then find the torque acts on the disc.**

Sol.

Suppose the disc is placed in xy-plane and is rotated about the z-axis. Consider an annular ring of radius r and of thickness dr, the charge on this ring

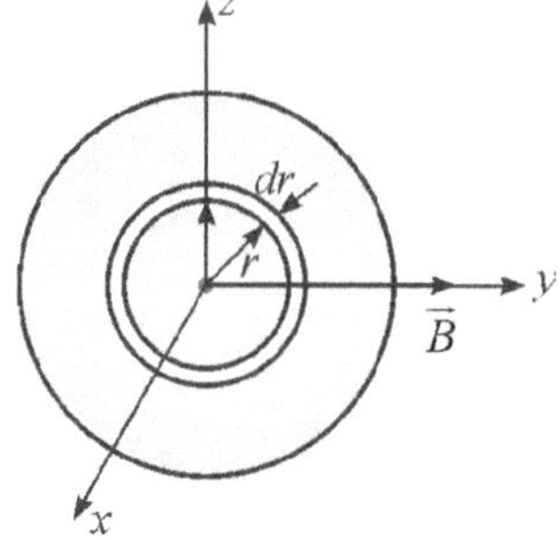

Fig. 5.52

$$dq = \sigma(2\pi r\,dr)$$

As the ring rotates with angular velocity ω, so the current

$$i = \frac{dq}{dt} = \frac{\sigma\left(2\pi r dr\right)}{\dfrac{2\pi}{\omega}}$$

$$= \sigma\omega r\,dr$$

The torque on the current loop

$$\tau = i\,\vec{A} \times \vec{B}.$$

Hence the torque on this annular ring

$$d\tau = i\left(d\vec{A} \times \vec{B}\right)$$

$$= \sigma\omega r\,dr\left(\pi r^2 B \sin 90°\right)$$

$$= \pi\sigma\omega r^3\,Bdr$$

and

$$\tau = \pi\sigma\omega\,B\int_0^a r^3\,dr$$

$$= \frac{\pi\sigma\omega Ba^4}{4}. \qquad \textit{Ans.}$$

Ex. 29

Consider a non conducting plate of radius a and mass m which has a charge q distributed uniformly over it. The plate is rotated about its axis with an angular speed ω. Show that the magnetic moment M and the angular momentum L of the plate are related as $\dfrac{M}{L} = \dfrac{q}{2m}$.

Sol. If σ is the surface charge density, then

$$q = \sigma\pi a^2.$$

Current $\qquad i = \sigma\omega r dr$ (calculated in previous example)

The magnetic moment of the element ring

$$dM = i\,(dA)$$

$$= \sigma\omega r dr\,(\pi r^2)$$

$$= \pi\sigma\omega r^3\,dr$$

and

$$M = \pi\sigma\omega\int_0^a r^3\,dr$$

$$= \frac{\pi\sigma\omega a^4}{4}$$

$$= \left(\pi a^2\sigma\right)\frac{\omega a^2}{4} = \frac{q\omega a^2}{4}$$

The angular momentum of the disc about its axis

$$L = \frac{ma^2}{2}\omega.$$

The ratio

$$\frac{M}{L} = \frac{\dfrac{q\omega a^2}{4}}{\dfrac{\omega ma^2}{2}} = \frac{q}{2m}. \qquad \textit{Ans.}$$

Ex. 30

Two metal strips, each of length ℓ, are clamped parallel to each other on a horizontal floor with a separation b between them. A wire of mass m lies on them perpendicular as shown in *Fig. 5.53*. A vertically upward magnetic field of strength B exists in the space. The metal strips are smooth but the coefficient of friction between wire and the floor is μ. A current i is established when the switch S is closed at the instant t = 0. Discuss the motion of the wire after the switch is closed. How far away from the strips will the wire reach ?

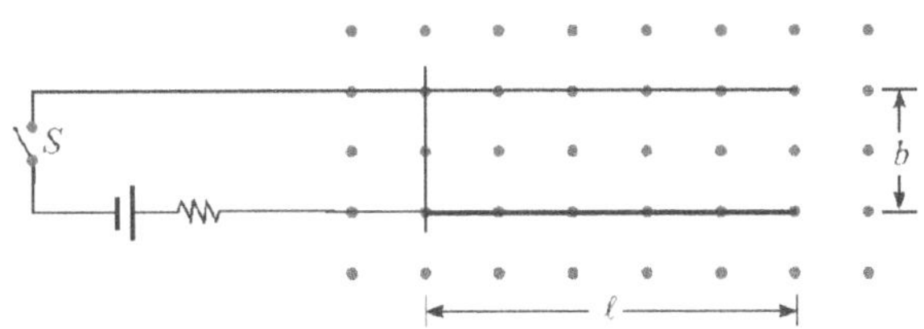

Fig. 5.53

Sol.

When current starts flowing in the wire, it experiences a force, F = Bib of constant magnitude. Due to which it accelerates on the metal strips. Thereafter when wire falls on to the floor, it retards due to friction and finally stops. Thus

$$a = \frac{F}{m} = \frac{Bib}{m}.$$

The velocity gained by the wire on the strips

$$v^2 = 0 + 2a\ell$$

$$= 2\frac{Bib\ell}{m}$$

Let x be the distance moved by the wire on the floor, its final velocity becomes zero, and so

$$0 = 2v^2 - a'x$$

or

$$x = \frac{v^2}{2a'}$$

Here

$$a' = \frac{\mu mg}{m} = \mu g$$

$$\therefore \qquad x = \frac{\left[\dfrac{2Bib\ell}{m}\right]}{2\mu g} = \frac{Bib\ell}{\mu mg}. \qquad \textit{Ans.}$$

Review of formulae & Important Points

1. **Force on a moving charge :** The force on a charge q moving with velocity $\vec{v}$ in a magnetic field is given by

$$F = qvB\sin\theta,$$

and the direction of force is given by Fleming left hand rule. In vector notation, we can write

$$\vec{F} = q\left(\vec{v} \times \vec{B}\right)$$

2. **Lorentz force :** When a charged particle moves through a region of space having both $\vec{E}$ and $\vec{B}$ field, the net force on the particle called Lorentz force and is given by

$$\vec{F} = q\left(\vec{E} + \vec{v} \times \vec{B}\right).$$

3. In magnetic field speed and hence kinetic energy of the charged particle remain constant.

4. When charged particle is projected perpendicular to the magnetic field, its path will be circular.
The radius of path

$$r = \frac{mv}{qB}$$

The time to complete the circle

$$T = \frac{2\pi m}{qB}.$$

5. When charged particle is projected at an angle θ with the magnetic field, its path will be helical. The radius of path

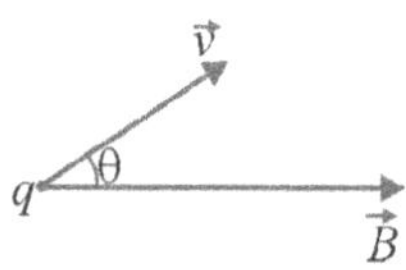

$$r = \frac{mv\sin\theta}{qB},$$

and pitch ,

$$p = \frac{2\pi mv\cos\theta}{qB}$$

6. A charged particle q enters normally in a uniform magnetic field $\vec{B}$. The magnetic field extends to a distance x, which is less than or equal to the radius of the path, then deviation angle θ is given by

$$\sin\theta = \frac{x}{r}.$$

7. **Hall effect :** Hall potential is given by

$$V_H = \frac{iB}{ne\ell}.$$

8. **Mass spectrograph :** For two isotopes of mass numbers m_1 and m_2,

$$\frac{m_1}{m_2} = \frac{r_1}{r_2}.$$

9. **Cylotron :** If V is the potential and f is the frequency of the AC source used in cylotron, then K.E. of the particle q will be

$$K = 2fqV.$$

10. **Magnetic force on current carrying conductor :**

$$F = Bi\ell \sin\theta,$$

and the direction of force can be obtained by Flemings left hand rule. In vector notation $\vec{F} = i\vec{\ell} \times \vec{B}$.

11. **Force on curved conductor :**

$$\vec{F} = \int_{P}^{Q} id\vec{\ell} \times \vec{B}$$

12. **Torque on a current loop :**

$$\vec{\tau} = \vec{M} \times \vec{B},$$

where $\vec{M} = Ni\vec{A}$, is called magnetic moment of the loop.

13. Magnetic moment of an electron moving in a circle of radius r with speed v

$$M = \frac{evr}{2}.$$

★ ★ ★

LEVEL - 1

Only one option correct

1. The figure shows four directions for the velocity vector $\vec{v}$ of a positively charged particle moving through a uniform electric field $\vec{E}$ (directed out of the page and represented with an encircled dot) and a uniform magnetic field $\vec{B}$. Of all four directions, which might result in a net force of zero ?

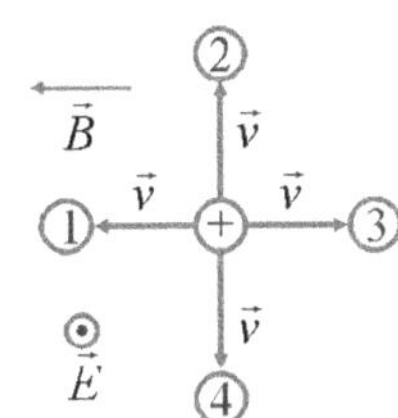

   (a) 1   (b) 2
   (c) 3   (d) 4

2. The figure shows a metallic, rectangular solid that is to move at a certain speed v through the uniform magnetic field $\vec{B}$. You have three choices for the direction of the velocity of the solid : v_x, v_y and v_z parallel to x, y and z directions respectively. For which choice is the front face at lower potential ?

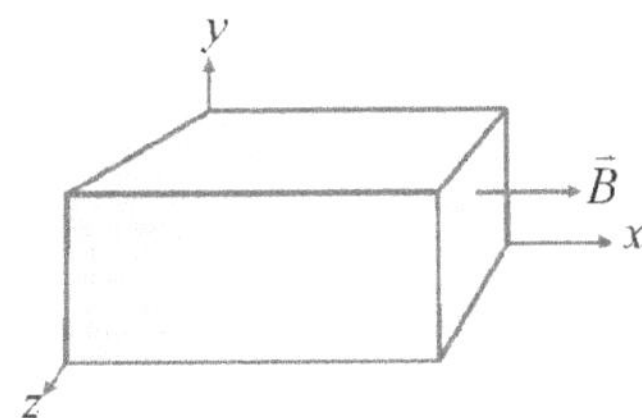

   (a) v_x (b) v_y
   (c) v_z (d) none

3. Figure shows three situations in which a positive particle of velocity $\vec{v}$ moves through a uniform magnetic field $\vec{B}$ and experiences a magnetic force $\vec{F}_B$. In which situation(s) the orientations of the vectors are physically reasonable

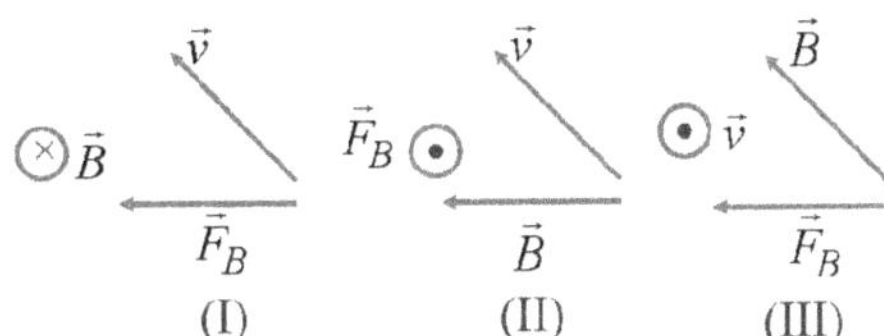

   (a) I   (b) II, III
   (c) III   (d) I, II, III

4. A particle is projected in a plane perpendicular to a uniform magnetic field. The area bounded by the path described by the particle is proportional to
   (a) the velocity   (b) the momentum
   (c) the kinetic energy   (d) none of these

5. A positively charged particle projected towards east is deflected towards north by a magnetic field. The field may be
   (a) downward   (b) upward
   (c) towards west   (d) towards south

6. Given, B = magnetic induction and R = radius of the path, the energy of a charged particle coming out of a cyclotron is given by

   (a) $\dfrac{qB^2R^2}{2m}$ (b) $\dfrac{q^2BR^2}{2m}$

   (c) $\dfrac{q^2BR}{2m}$ (d) $\dfrac{q^2B^2R^2}{2m}$

7. A uniform electric field and a uniform magnetic field are produced, pointed in the same direction. An electron is projected with its velocity pointing in the same direction
   (a) the electron will turn to its right
   (b) the electron will turn to its left
   (c) the electron velocity will increase in magnitude
   (d) the electron velocity will decrease in magnitude

8. Two particles X and Y having equal charges, after being accelerated through the same potential difference, enter a region of uniform magnetic field and describes circular path of radius R_1 and R_2 respectively. The ratio of mass of X to that of Y is

   (a) $\left(\dfrac{R_1}{R_2}\right)^{1/2}$ (b) $\dfrac{R_2}{R_1}$

   (c) $\left(\dfrac{R_1}{R_2}\right)^{2}$ (d) $\dfrac{R_1}{R_2}$

9. The radius of curvature of the path of the charged particle in a uniform magnetic field is directly proportional to
   (a) the charge on the particle
   (b) the momentum of the particle
   (c) the energy of the particle
   (d) the intensity of the field

Answer Key	1	(d)	2	(b)	3	(d)	4	(c)	5	(a)
Sol. from page 383	6	(d)	7	(d)	8	(c)	9	(b)		

10. If a particle of charge 10^{-12} coulomb moving along the $\hat{x}$ – direction with a velocity 10^5 m/s experiences a force of 10^{-10} newton in $\hat{y}$ – direction due to magnetic field, then the minimum magnetic field is

(a) 6.25×10^3 tesla in $\hat{z}$ – direction

(b) 10^{-15} tesla in $\hat{z}$ – direction

(c) 6.25×10^{-3} tesla in $\hat{z}$ – direction

(d) 10^{-3} tesla in $\hat{z}$ – direction

11. An electron and a proton enter region of uniform magnetic field in a direction at right angles to the field with the same kinetic energy. They describe circular paths of radius r_e and r_p respectively. Then

(a) $r_e = r_p$

(b) $r_e < r_p$

(c) $r_e > r_p$

(d) r_e may be less than or greater than r_P depending on the direction of the magnetic field.

12. A charge moves in a circle perpendicular to a magnetic field. The time period of revolution is independent of

(a) magnetic field   (b) charge

(c) mass of the particle   (d) velocity of the particle

13. An electron and a proton with equal momentum enter perpendicularly into a uniform magnetic field, then

(a) the path of proton shall be more curved than that of electron

(b) the path of proton shall be less curved than that of electron

(c) both are equally curved

(d) path of both will be straight line

14. Two particles A and B of masses m_A and m_B respectively and having the same charge are moving in a plane. A uniform magnetic field exists perpendicular to this plane. The speeds of the particles are v_A and v_B respectively, and the trajectories are as shown in the figure. Then

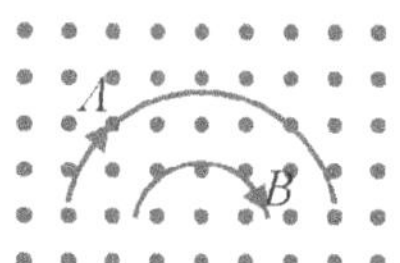

(a) $m_A v_A < m_B v_B$

(b) $m_A v_A > m_B v_B$

(c) $m_A < m_B$ and $v_A < v_B$

(d) $m_A = m_B$ and $v_A = v_B$

15. A charged particle is released from rest in a region of steady uniform electric and magnetic fields which are parallel to each other the particle will move in a

(a) straight line   (b) circle

(c) helix   (d) cycloid

16. A particle of mass M and charge Q moving with velocity $\vec{v}$ describes a circular path of radius R when subjected to a uniform transverse magnetic field of induction B. The work done by the field when the particle completes one full circle is

(a) $BQv2\pi R$ (b) $\left(\dfrac{Mv^2}{R}\right)2\pi R$

(c) zero   (d) $BQ2\pi R$

17. A particle of charge -16×10^{-18} coulomb moving with velocity 10 ms^{-1} along the x-axis enters a region where a magnetic field of induction B is along the y-axis, and an electric field of magnitude 10^4 V/m is along the negative z-axis. If the charged particle continues moving along the x-axis, the magnitude of B is

(a) 10^{-3} Wb/m^2 (b) 10^3 Wb/m^2

(c) 10^5 Wb/m^2 (d) 10^{16} Wb/m^2

18. A very long straight wire carries a current I. At the instant when a charge $+Q$ at point P has velocity $\vec{v}$, as shown, the force on the charge is

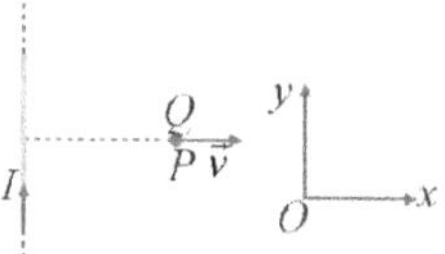

(a) opposite to OX (b) along OX

(c) opposite to OY (d) along OY

19. A rectangular loop carrying a current i is situated near a long straight wire such that the wire is parallel to one of the sides of the loop and is in the plane of the loop. If a steady current I is established in wire as shown in figure, the loop will

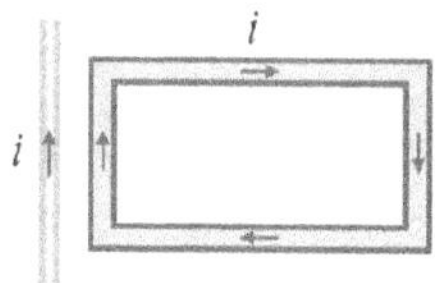

(a) rotate about an axis parallel to the wire

(b) move away from the wire or towards right

(c) move towards the wire

(d) remain stationary

20. A conducting circular loop of radius r carries a constant current i. It is placed in a uniform magnetic field $\vec{B}$, such that $\vec{B}$ is perpendicular to the plane of the loop. The magnetic force acting on the loop is

(a) $ir\vec{B}$ (b) $2\pi ri\vec{B}$

(c) Zero   (d) $\pi ri\vec{B}$

21. If a current is passed in a spring, it

(a) gets compressed   (b) gets expanded

(c) oscillates   (d) remains unchanged

Answer Key	10	(d)	11	(b)	12	(d)	13	(c)	14	(b)	15	(a)
Sol. from page 383	16	(c)	17	(b)	18	(d)	19	(c)	20	(c)	21	(a)

22. A stream of electrons is projected horizontally to the right. A straight conductor carrying a current is supported parallel to electron stream and above it. If the current in the conductor is from left to right then what will be the effect on electron stream?
(a) The electron stream will be pulled upward
(b) The electron stream will be pulled downwards
(c) The electron stream will be retarted
(d) The electron beam will be speeded up towards the right

23. Two long conductors, separated by a distance d carry current I_1 and I_2 in the same direction. They exert a force F on each other. Now the current in one of them is increased to two times and its directions is reversed. The distance is also increased to 3d. The new value of the force between them is
(a) $-2F$ (b) $F/3$
(c) $2F/3$ (d) $-F/3$

24. Two thin, long, parallel wires, separated by a distance d carry a current i A in the same direction. They will

(a) attract each other with a force of $\mu_0 i^2 / \left(2\pi d^2\right)$

(b) repel each other with a force of $\mu_0 i^2 / \left(2\pi d^2\right)$

(c) attract each other with a force of $\mu_0 i^2 / \left(2\pi d\right)$

(d) repel each other with a force of $\mu_0 i^2 / \left(2\pi d\right)$

25. A particle of charge q and mass m moves in a circular orbit of radius r with angular speed ω. The ratio of the magnitude of its magnetic moment to that of its angular momentum depends on
(a) ω and q (b) ω, q and m
(c) q and m (d) ω and m

26. A conducting loop carrying a current I is placed in a uniform magnetic field pointing into the plane of the paper as shown. The loop will have a tendency to

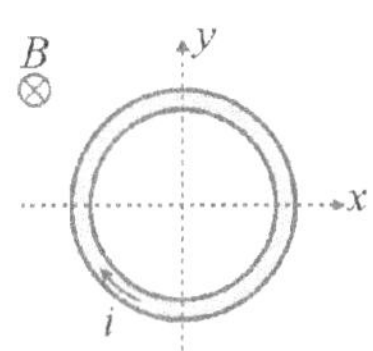

(a) contract (b) expand
(c) move towards + ve x-axis (d) move towards –ve x-axis

27. A current carrying loop is placed in a uniform magnetic field in four different orientations, I, II, III and IV arrange them in the decreasing order of potential energy.

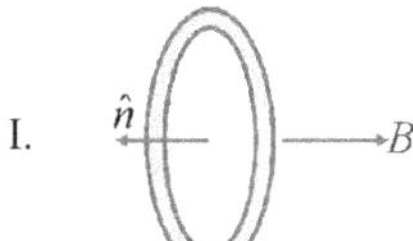 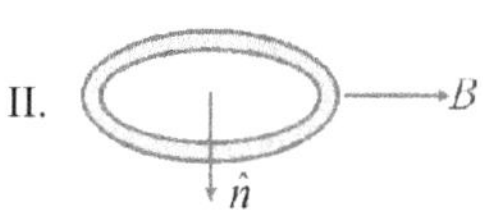

 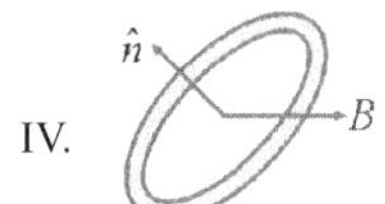

(a) I > III > II > IV (b) I > II > III > IV
(c) I > IV > II > III (c) III > IV > I > II

28. Two very long, straight and parallel wires carry steady currents I and I respectively. The distance between the wires is d. At a certain instant of time, a point charge q is at a point equidistant from the two wires in the plane of the wires. Its instantaneous velocity v is perpendicular to this plane. The magnitude of the force due to the magnetic field acting on the charge at this instant is

(a) $\dfrac{\mu_0 Iqv}{2\pi d}$ (b) $\dfrac{\mu_0 Iqv}{\pi d}$

(c) $\dfrac{2\mu_0 Iqv}{\pi d}$ (d) 0

29. An electron moving with a speed u along the positive x-axis at $y = 0$ enters a region of uniform magnetic field $\vec{B} = -Bo\hat{k}$ which exists to the right of y-axis. The electron exists from the region after some time with the speed v at co-ordinate y, then

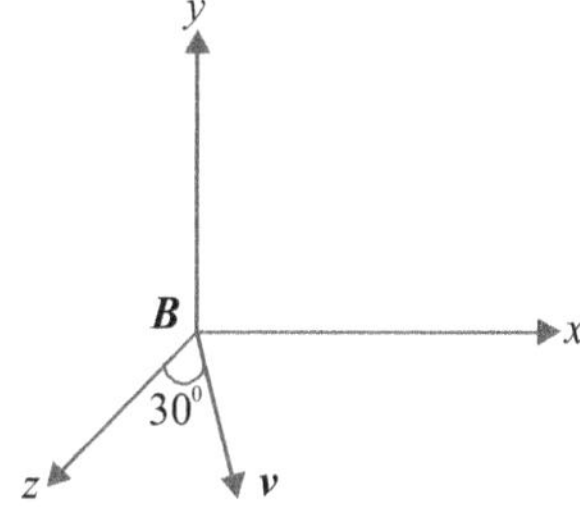

(a) $v > u, y < 0$ (b) $v = u, y > 0$
(c) $v > u, y > 0$ (d) $v = u, y < 0$

30. A proton beam moves through a region of space where there exists a uniform magnetic field of magnitude 4.0 T along z-axis. The protons have a velocity of 4×10^5 m/s in the x-z plane at an angle of 30° to the positive z-axis. The force on the proton is :

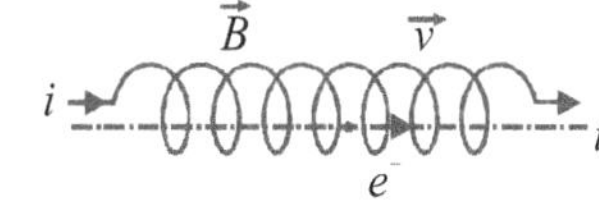

(a) 25.6×10^{-14} j N (b) -25.6×10^{-14} j N
(c) -12.8×10^{-14} j N (d) 12.8×10^{-14} j N

31.

Work done on an electron moving in a solenoid along its axis is equal to
(a) zero (b) $-evB$
(c) $1/B$ (d) None of the above

Answer Key	22	(b)	23	(c)	24	(c)	25	(c)	26	(b)
Sol. from page 383	27	(c)	28	(d)	29	(d)	30	(c)	31	(a)

32. The figure shows three situations when an electron moves with velocity $\vec{v}$ travels through a uniform magnetic field $\vec{B}$. In each case, what is the direction of magnetic force on the electron.

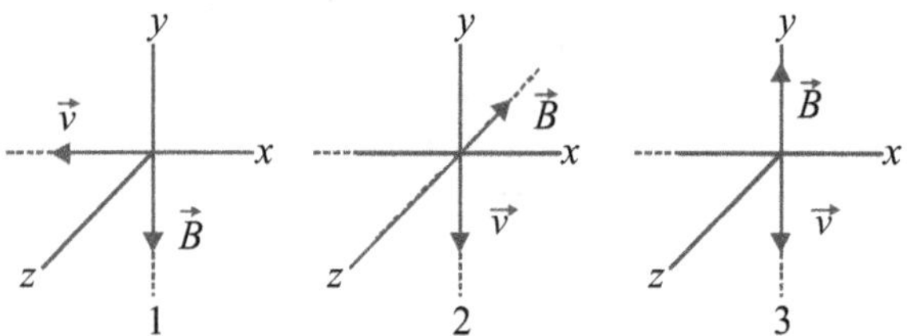

1 2 3

 (a) +ve z-axis, −ve x-axis, + ve y-axis
 (b) −ve z-axis, −ve x-axis and zero
 (c) +ve z-axis, +ve y-axis and zero
 (d) −ve z-axis, +ve x–axis and zero

33. A closed loop $PQRS$ carrying a current is placed in a uniform magnetic field. If the magnetic forces on segment PS, SR and RQ are F_1, F_2 and F_3 respectively and are in the plane of the paper and along the directions shown, the force on the segment QP is

 (a) $\sqrt{\left(F_3 - F_1\right)^2 - F_2^2}$

 (b) $F_3 + F_1 - F_2$

 (c) $F_3 - F_1 + F_2$

 (d) $\sqrt{\left(F_3 - F_1\right)^2 + F_2^2}$

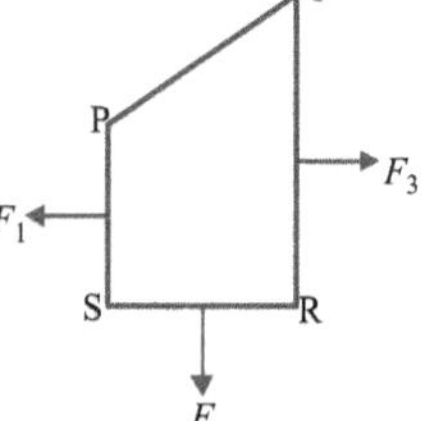

34. A charged particle moves along a circle under the action of constant electric field and magnetic field. Which of the following are possible

 (a) $E = 0, B \neq 0$ (b) $E = 0, B = 0$

 (c) $E \neq 0, B = 0$ (d) $\vec{E} \neq 0, B \neq 0$.

35. A proton of mass 1.67×10^{-27} kg and charge $1.6 \times 10^{-19}\, C$ is projected with a speed of $2 \times 10^6\, m/s$ at an angle of $60°$ to the x-axis. If a uniform magnetic field of 0.104 tesla is applied along y-axis, the path of proton is

 (a) a circle of radius = 0.2 m and time period $\pi \times 10^{-7} s$

 (b) a circle of radius = 0.1 m and time period $2\pi \times 10^{-7} s$

 (c) a helix of radius = 0.1 m and time period $2\pi \times 10^{-7} s$

 (d) a helix of radius = 0.2 m and time period $4\pi \times 10^{-7} s$

36. A proton (or charged particle) moving with velocity v is acted upon by electric field E and magnetic field B. The proton will move undeflected if
 (a) E is perpendicular to B
 (b) E is parallel to v and perpendicular to B

 (c) E, B and v are mutually perpendicular and $v = \dfrac{E}{B}$

 (d) E and B both are parallel to v

37. A homogeneous electric field E and a uniform magnetic field $\vec{B}$ are pointing in the same direction. A proton is projected with its velocity parallel to $\vec{E}$. It will

 (a) go on moving in the same direction with increasing velocity
 (b) go on moving in the same direction with constant velocity.
 (c) turn to its right
 (d) turn to its left

38. An ionized gas contains both positive and negative ions. If it is subjected simultaneously to an electric field along the $+ x$ direction and a magnetic field along the $+ z$ direction, then
 (a) positive ions deflect towards $+ y$ direction and negative ions towards $- y$ direction
 (b) all ions deflect towards $+ y$ direction
 (c) all ions deflect towards $- y$ direction
 (d) positive ions deflect towards $- y$ direction and negative ions towards $+ y$ direction

39. A particle of mass m and charge q moves with a constant velocity v along the positive x direction. It enters a region containing a uniform magnetic field B directed along the negative z direction, extending from $x = a$ to $x = b$. The minimum value of v required so that the particle can just enter the region $x > b$ is
 (a) $qb\, B / m$ (b) $q(b - a)\, B / m$
 (c) $qa\, B/m$ (d) $q(b + a)\, B / 2m$

40. A and B are two conductors carrying a current i in the same direction. x and y are two electron beams moving in the same direction

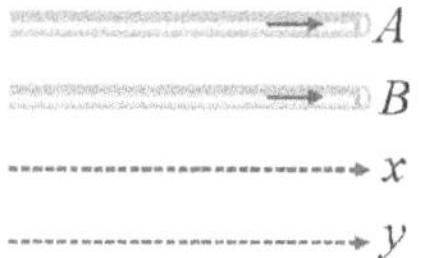

 (a) There will be repulsion between A and B attraction between x and y
 (b) There will be attraction between A and B, repulsion between x and y
 (c) There will be repulsion between A and B and also x and y
 (d) There will be attraction between A and B and also x and y

41. A metallic block carrying current I is subjected to a uniform magnetic induction $\vec{B}$ as shown in the figure. The moving charges experience a force $\vec{F}$ given by ......which results in the lowering of the potential of the face.........Assume the speed of the carriers to be v

 (a) $evB\hat{k}$, $ABCD$

 (b) $evB\hat{k}$, $EFGH$

 (c) $-evB\hat{k}$, $ABCD$

 (d) $-evB\hat{k}$, $EFGH$

42. Two insulated rings, one of slightly smaller diameter than the other are suspended along their common diameter as shown. Initially the planes of the rings are mutually perpendicular. When a steady current is set up in each of them

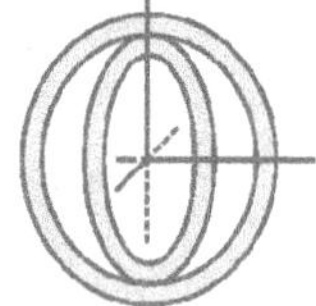

 (a) the two rings rotate into a common plane
 (b) the inner ring oscillates about its initial position
 (c) the inner ring stays stationary while the outer one moves into the plane of the inner ring
 (d) the outer ring stays stationary while the inner one moves into the plane of the outer ring

Answer Key	32	(b)	33	(d)	34	(a)	35	(c)	36	(c)	37	(a)
Sol. from page 383	38	(c)	39	(b)	40	(b)	41	(a)	42	(a)		

Only one option correct

1. For four situations, here is the velocity $\vec{v}$ of a proton at a certain instant as it moves through a uniform magnetic field $\vec{B}$:

   (i) $\vec{v} = 2\hat{i} - 3\hat{j}$ and $\vec{B} = 4\hat{k}$ (ii) $\vec{v} = 3\hat{i} + 2\hat{j}$ and $\vec{B} = -4\hat{k}$

   (iii) $\vec{v} = 3\hat{j} - 2\hat{k}$ and $\vec{B} = 4\hat{i}$ (iv) $\vec{v} = 20\hat{i}$ and $\vec{B} = -4\hat{i}$

   If F_1, F_2, F_3 and F_4 are the magnitude of forces in the four situations respectively, then

   (a) $F_1 = F_2 = F_3 = F_4$ (b) $F_1 = F_2 ; F_3 = F_4$

   (c) $F_1 = F_2 = F_3 , F_4 = 0$ (d) $F_1 = F_2 = F_3 = 0, F_4 \neq 0$

2. A magnetic field $\vec{B} = B_0 \hat{j}$ exists in the region $a < x < 2a$ and $\vec{B} = -B_0 \hat{j}$ in the region $2a < x < 3a$, where B_0 is a positive constant. A positive point charge moving with a velocity $\vec{v} = v_0 \hat{i}$ where v_0 is a positive constant, enters the magnetic field at $x = a$. The trajectory of the charge in this region can be like :

   (a) 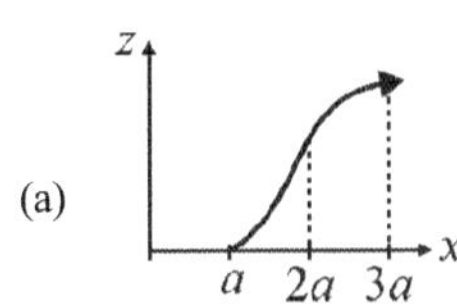

   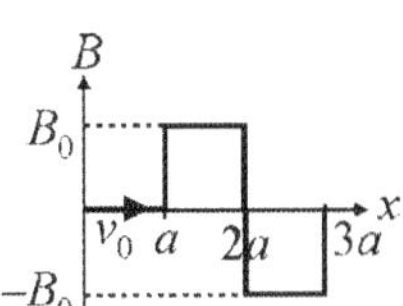

   (b) 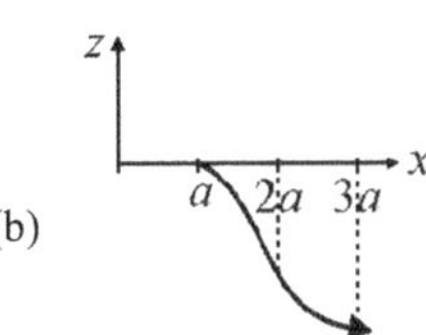

   (c) 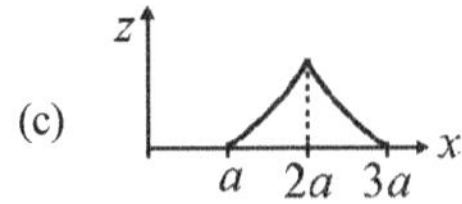

   (d) 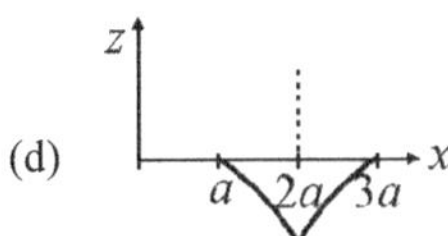

3. A proton, a deuteron and an α–particle having the same kinetic energy are moving in circular trajectories in a constant magnetic field. If r_p, r_d and r_α denote respectively the radii of the trajectories of these particles, then

   (a) $r_\alpha = r_p < r_d$ (b) $r_\alpha > r_d > r_p$

   (c) $r_\alpha = r_d > r_p$ (d) $r_p = r_d = r_\alpha$

4. Four wires each of length 2.0 metres are bent into four loops P, Q, R and S and then suspended into uniform magnetic field. Same current is passed in each loop. Which statement is correct?

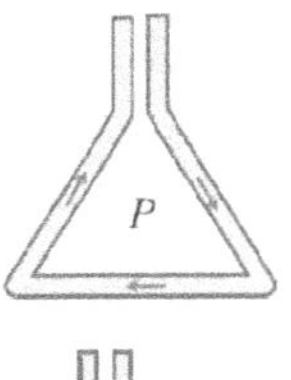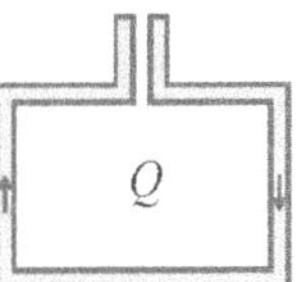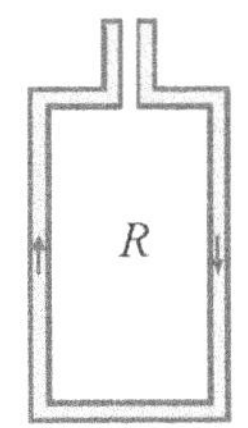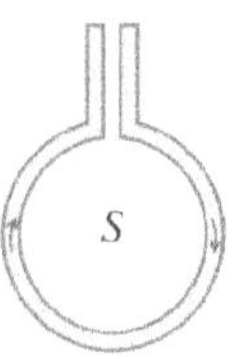

   (a) couple on loop P will be the highest
   (b) couple on loop Q will be the highest
   (c) couple on loop R will be the highest
   (d) couple on loop S will be the highest

5. For a positively charged particle moving in a x-y plane initially along the x-axis, there is a sudden change in its path due to the presence of electric and/or magnetic fields beyond P. The curved path is shown in the x-y plane and is found to be non-circular. Which one of the following combinations is possible.

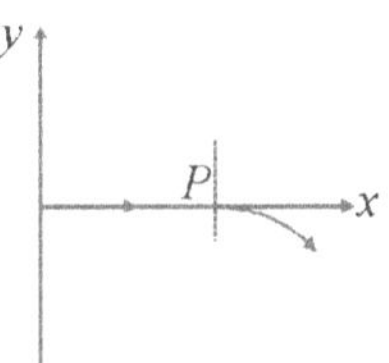

   (a) $\vec{E} = 0; \vec{B} = b\hat{i} + c\hat{k}$ (b) $\vec{E} = a\hat{i}; \vec{B} = c\hat{k} + a\hat{i}$

   (c) $\vec{E} = 0; \vec{B} = c\hat{j} + b\hat{k}$ (d) $\vec{E} = a\hat{i}; \vec{B} = c\hat{k} + b\hat{j}$

6. A wire $ABCD$ is bent in the form shown here in the figure. Segments AB and CD are of length 1 m each while the semicircular loop is of radius 1 m. A current of 5 A flows from A towards the end D and the whole wire is placed in a magnetic field of 0.5 T directed out of the page. The force acting on the wire is :

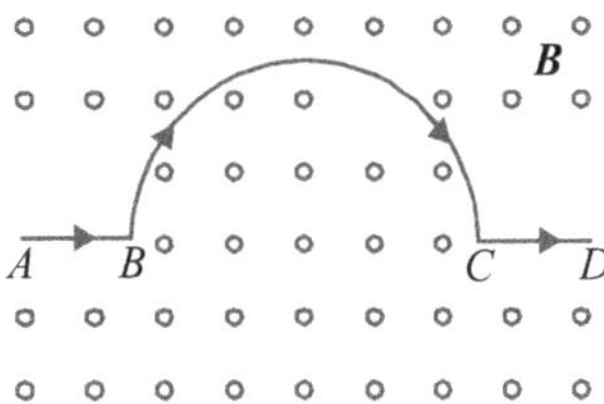

   (a) 40 N (b) 5 N
   (c) 10 N (d) 20 N

Answer Key	1	(c)	2	(a)	3	(a)	4	(d)
Sol. from page 384	5	(b)	6	(c)				

7. A charged particle moves along the x-axis in crossed magnetic and electric fields given as $\vec{B} = B\hat{z}$ and $\vec{E} = E\hat{y}$. The motion of the particle as observed in the laboratory frame will look like :

(a)
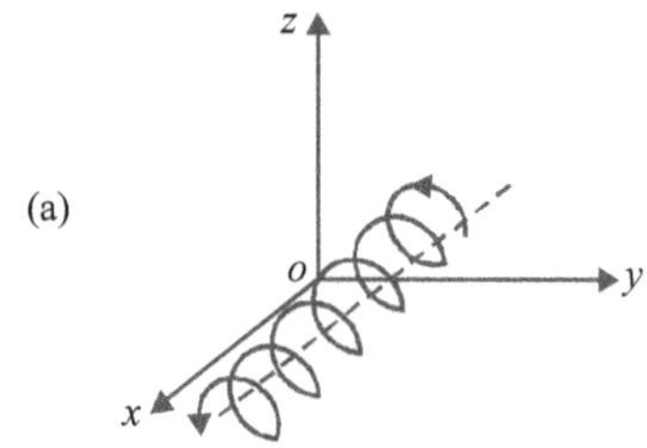

(b)
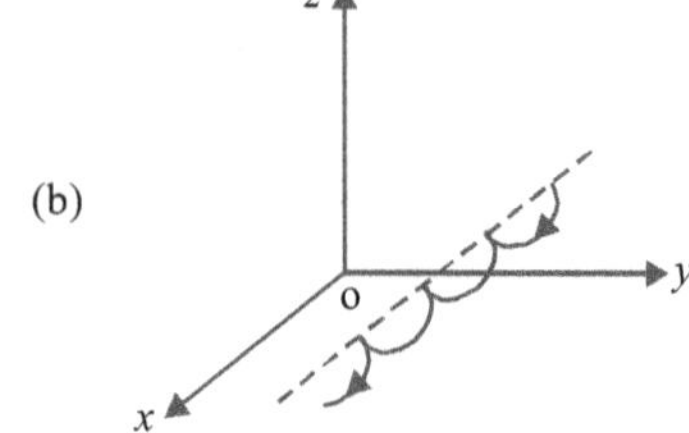

(c)
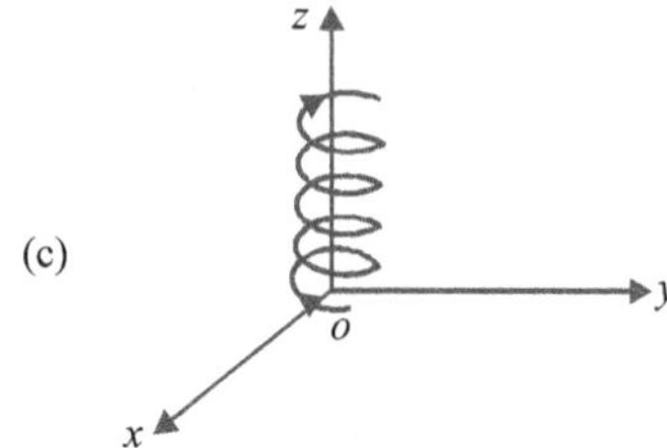

(d)
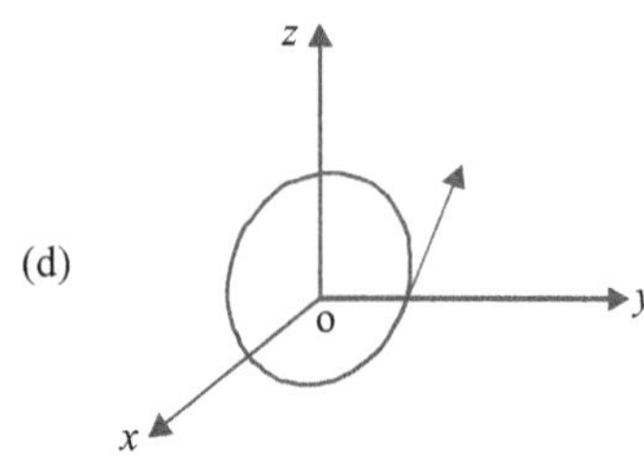

8. An electron moving with a velocity $\vec{v}_1 = 1\hat{i}$ m/s at a point in a magnetic field experiences a force $\vec{F}_1 = -e\hat{j}$ where e is the charge of the electron. If the electron is moving with a velocity $\vec{v}_2 = (1\hat{i} + 1\hat{j})$ m/s at the same point. It experiences a force $\vec{F}_2 = e(\hat{i} - \hat{j})$. The force the electron would experience if it were moving with a velocity $\vec{v}_3 = \vec{v}_1 \times \vec{v}_2$, at the same point is :

(a) $-e(\hat{i} + \hat{j})$

(b) $e(\hat{i} + \hat{j})$

(c) zero

(d) $e\hat{j}$

9. A mass spectrograph is a device for separating charged particles having different masses. Consider two particles of the same charge q but different masses m_1 and m_2 injected into the region of a uniform magnetic field B with a known velocity v normal to the magnetic field as shown in the figure. The particles are separated by a distance d, given by :

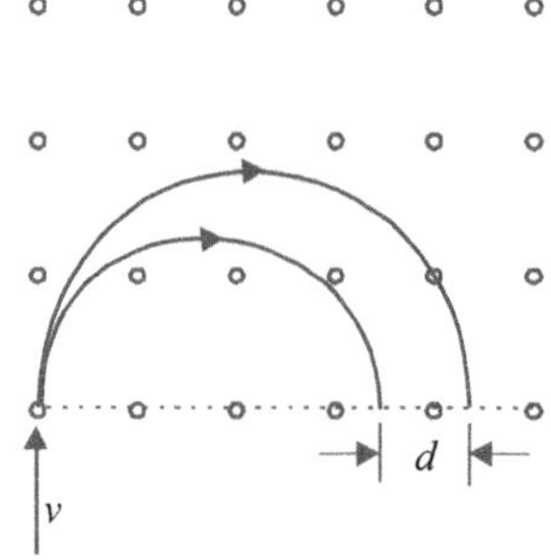

(a) $d = \dfrac{|(m_2 - m_1)v|}{|qB|}$

(b) $d = \dfrac{|2(m_2 - m_1)v|}{|qB|}$

(c) $d = \dfrac{|(m_2 - m_1)v|}{|2qB|}$

(d) $d = \dfrac{|(m_2 - m_1)v|}{|4qB|}$

10. The electric field and the magnetic field in a region are given by $\vec{E} = \hat{i}\vec{E}_0$ and $\vec{B} = \hat{j}B_0$. Consider a frame of reference moving with a velocity $v_0 \hat{k}$. The electric field in this frame will be zero if v_0 is equal to :

(a) $\dfrac{E_0}{B_0}$

(b) $\dfrac{2E_0}{B_0}$

(c) $\dfrac{E_0}{2B_0}$

(d) none of these

11. A positive electric charge q is distributed over a circular ring of radius a. It is placed in a horizontal plane and is rotated about its axis at a uniform angular speed ω. A horizontal magnetic field B exists in the space. The torque acting on the ring due to the magnetic force is :

(a) $q\omega a^2 B$

(b) $\dfrac{1}{2} q\omega a^2 B$

(c) $\dfrac{1}{\pi} q\omega a^2 B$

(d) $\dfrac{1}{2\pi} q\omega a^2 B$

12. An insulating rod of length l carries a charge q distributed uniformly on it. The rod is pivoted at an end and is rotated at a frequency f about a fixed perpendicular axis. The magnetic moment of the system is :

(a) zero

(b) $\pi q f l^2$

(c) $\dfrac{1}{2} \pi q f l^2$

(d) $\dfrac{1}{3} \pi q f l^2$

Answer Key	**7**	(b)	**8**	(c)	**9**	(b)	**10**	(a)
Sol. from page 384	**11**	(b)	**12**	(d)				

13. A particle of charge q and mass m starts moving from the origin under the action of an electric field $\vec{E} = E_0\,\hat{i}$ and $\vec{B} = B_0\,\hat{i}$ with velocity $\vec{v} = v_0\hat{j}$. The speed of the particle will become $2v_0$ after a time

(a) $t = \dfrac{2mv_0}{qE}$

(b) $t = \dfrac{2Bq}{mv_0}$

(c) $t = \dfrac{\sqrt{3}Bq}{mv_0}$

(d) $t = \dfrac{\sqrt{3}mv_0}{qE}$

14. A mass spectrometer is a device which select particle of equal mass. An in with electric charge $q > 0$ starts at rest from a source S and is accelerated through potential difference V. It passes through a hole into a region of constant magnetic field $\vec{B}$ perpendicular to the plane of the paper as shown in the figure. The particle is deflected by the magnetic field and emerges through the bottom hole at a distance d from the top hole. The mass of the particle is

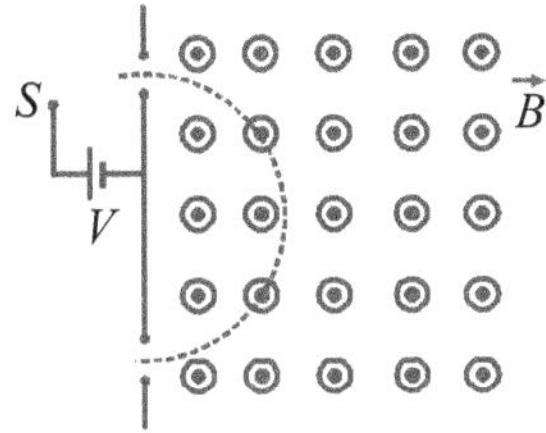

(a) $\dfrac{qBd}{V}$

(b) $\dfrac{qB^2d^2}{4V}$

(c) $\dfrac{qB^2d^2}{8V}$

(d) $\dfrac{qBd}{2V}$

15. $OABC$ is current carrying square loop an electron is projected from the centre of loop along its diagonal AC as shown. Unit vector in the direction of initial acceleration will be

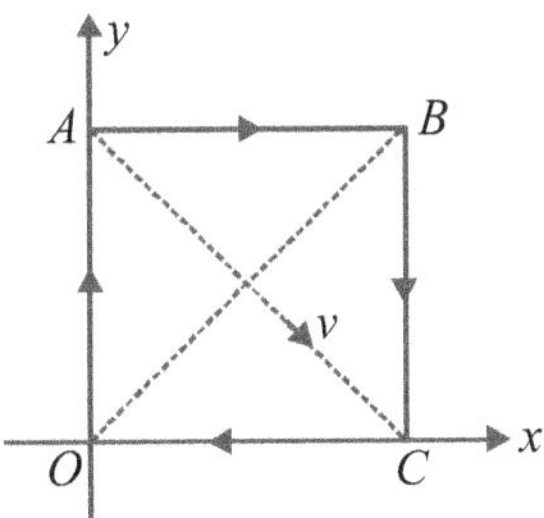

(a) $\hat{k}$

(b) $-\left(\dfrac{\hat{i} + \hat{j}}{\sqrt{2}}\right)$

(c) $-\hat{k}$

(d) $\dfrac{\hat{i} + \hat{j}}{\sqrt{2}}$

16. A conducting wire bent in the form of a parabola $y^2 = 2x$ carries a current $i = 2\,A$ as shown in figure. This wire is placed in a uniform magnetic field $\vec{B} = -4\hat{k}$ tesla. The magnetic force on the wire (in newton)

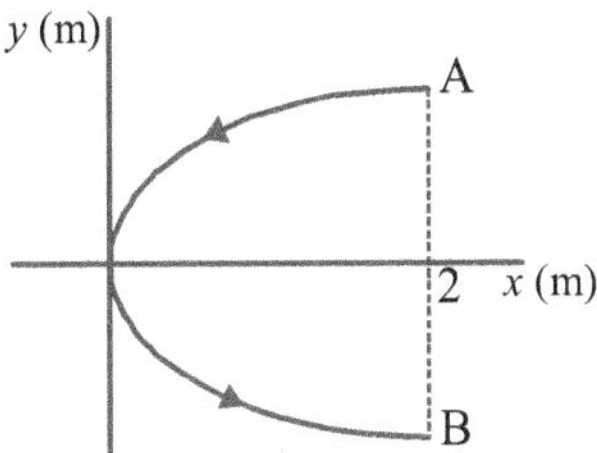

(a) $-16\hat{i}$

(b) $32\hat{i}$

(c) $-32\hat{i}$

(d) $16\hat{i}$

17. A circular current loop of radius a is placed in a radial field B as shown. Then net force acting on the loop is

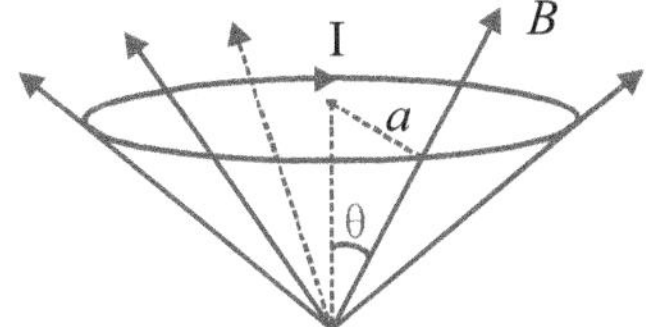

(a) zero

(b) $2\pi BaI\cos\theta$

(c) $2\pi aIB\sin\theta$

(d) none

18. Figure shows a square current carrying loop $ABCD$ of side 10 cm and current $i = 10A$. The magnetic moment $\vec{M}$ of the loop is

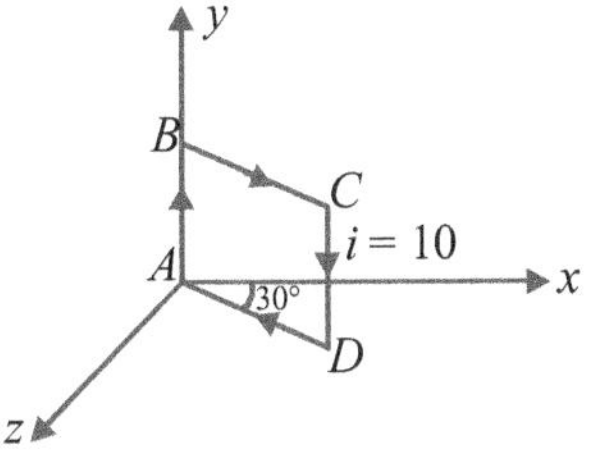

(a) $(0.05)\left(\hat{i} - \sqrt{3}\hat{k}\right)$ A-m^2

(b) $(0.05)\left(\hat{j} + \hat{k}\right)$ A-m^2

(c) $(0.05)\left(\sqrt{3}\hat{i} + \hat{k}\right)$ A-m^2

(d) $\left(\hat{i} + \hat{k}\right)$ A-m^2

19. A charged particle with charge q enters a region of constant uniform and mutually orthogonal fields $\vec{E}$ and $\vec{B}$ with a velocity $\vec{v}$ perpendicular to both $\vec{E}$ and $\vec{B}$, and comes out without any change in magnitude or direction of $\vec{v}$. Then

(a) $\vec{v} = \vec{E} \times \vec{B} / B^2$

(b) $\vec{v} = \vec{B} \times \vec{E} / B^2$

(c) $\vec{v} = \vec{E} \times \vec{B} / E^2$

(d) $\vec{v} = \vec{B} \times \vec{E} / E^2$

Answer Key	**13**	(d)	**14**	(c)	**15**	(b)	**16**	(b)
Sol. from page 384	**17**	(c)	**18**	(a)	**19**	(a)		

20. A current carrying loop is placed in a uniform magnetic field pointing in negative z direction. Branch $PQRS$ is a three quarter circle, while branch PS is straight. If force on branch PS is F, force on branch PQR is

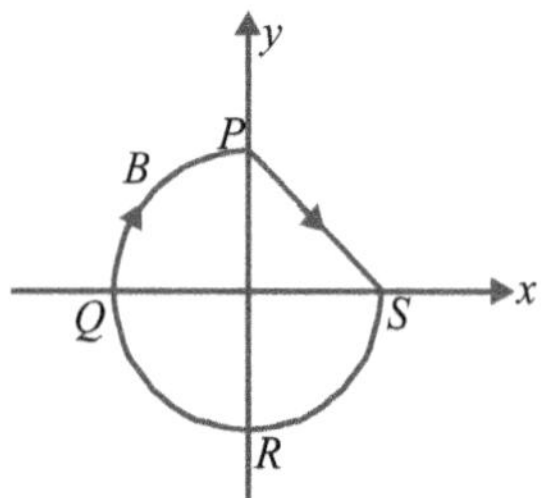

(a) $\sqrt{2}F$

(b) $\dfrac{F}{\sqrt{2}}$

(c) $\dfrac{\pi F}{\sqrt{2}}$

(d) $\sqrt{2}\pi F$

21. A vertical wire of length ℓ has its both ends fixed. Space around the wire has a horizontal magnetic field of strength B. If current i is passed through the wire such that its mid-point is deflected by amount x, tension in the wire is

(a) $\dfrac{Bi\ell^2}{x}$

(b) $\dfrac{Bi\ell^2}{4x}$

(c) $\dfrac{Bix^2}{\ell}$

(d) $\dfrac{Bix^2}{4\ell}$

22. Two particles A and B of same mass and having charges of same magnitude but of opposite nature are thrown into a region of magnetic field (as shown) with speed v_1 and v_2 ($v_1 > v_2$). At the time particle A escapes out of the magnetic field, angular momentum of particle B w.r.t. particle A is proportional to (Assume both the particles escape the region after traversing half circle)

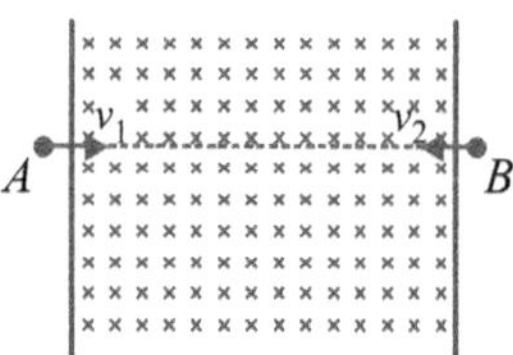

(a) $v_1 + v_2$

(b) $v_1 - v_2$

(c) $v_1^2 - v_2^2$

(d) $v_1^2 + v_2^2$

23. A particle of mass m and charge q enters a region of magnetic field (as shown) with speed v. There is a region in which the magnetic field is absent, as shown. The particle after entering the region collides elastically with a rigid wall. Time after which the velocity of particle becomes antiparallel to its initial velocity is

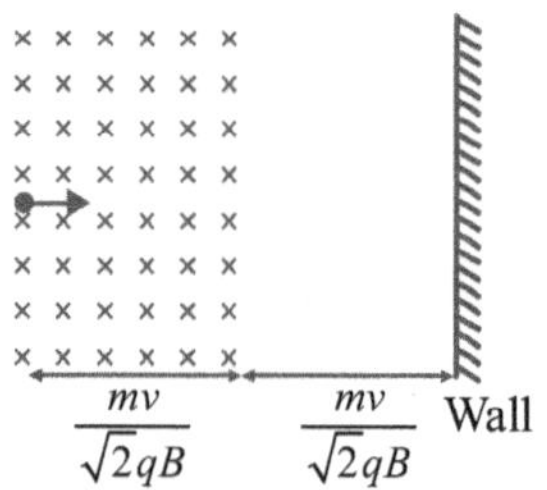

(a) $\dfrac{m}{2qB}(\pi + 4)$

(b) $\dfrac{m}{qB}(\pi + 2)$

(c) $\dfrac{m}{4qB}(\pi + 2)$

(d) $\dfrac{m}{4qB}(2\pi + 3)$

24. A jumper of mass m and length ℓ is placed on two parabolic rails in x-y plane. Shape of the rails can be described by
Rail 1 : $y = x^2$ (and $z = 0$)
Rail 2 : $y = x^2$ (and $z = \ell$)
If x is horizontal and y is vertical direction and magnetic field in the space is $B_0\hat{j}$, the jumper can remain in equilibrium when y coordinate of its ends is (i = current in jumper)

(a) $\dfrac{iB_0\ell}{2mg}$

(b) $\dfrac{iB_0\ell}{mg}$

(c) $\left(\dfrac{iB_0\ell}{mg}\right)^2$

(d) $\left(\dfrac{iB_0\ell}{2mg}\right)^2$

25. A conducting loop is placed in a magnetic field of strength B perpendicular to its plane. Radius of the loop is r, current in the loop is i and linear mass density of the wire of loop is m. Speed of any transverse wave in the loop will be

(a) $\sqrt{\dfrac{Bir}{m}}$

(b) $\sqrt{\dfrac{Bir}{2m}}$

(c) $\sqrt{\dfrac{2Bir}{m}}$

(d) $2\sqrt{\dfrac{Bir}{m}}$

26. A charged sphere of mass m and charge $-q$ starts sliding along the surface of a smooth hemispherical bowl, at position P. The region has a transverse uniform magnetic field B. Normal force by the surface of bowl on the sphere at position Q is

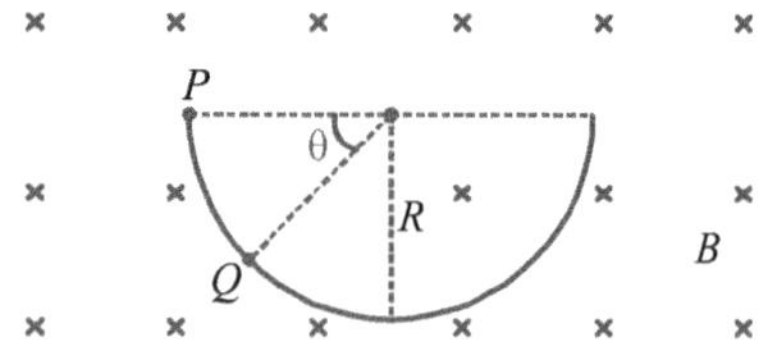

(a) $mg\sin\theta + qB\sqrt{2gR\sin\theta}$

(b) $3mg\sin\theta + qB\sqrt{2gR\sin\theta}$

(c) $mg\sin\theta - qB\sqrt{2gR\sin\theta}$

(d) $3mg\sin\theta - qB\sqrt{2gR\sin\theta}$

Answer Key		**20**	(a)	**21**	(b)	**22**	(c)	**23**	(d)
Sol. from page 384		**24**	(d)	**25**	(a)	**26**	(b)		

27. The figure shows two infinite semi-cylindrical shells: shell-1 and shell-2. Shell-1 carries current i_1, in inward direction normal to the plane of paper, while shell-2 carries same current i_1, in opposite direction. A long straight conductor lying along the common axis of the shells is carrying current i_2 in direction same as that of current in shell-1. Force per unit length on the wire is

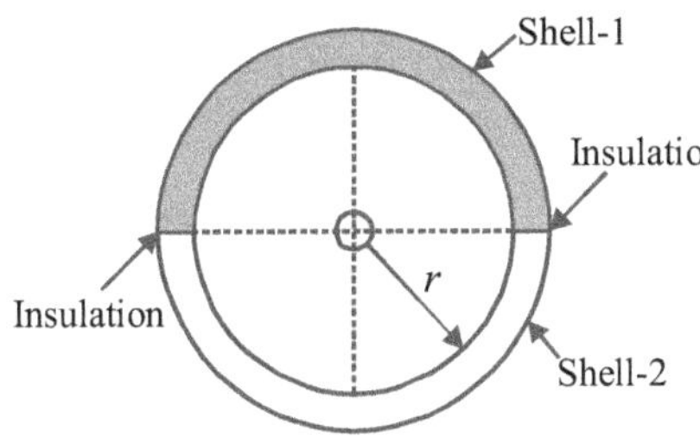

(a) zero

(b) $\dfrac{\mu_0 i_1 i_2}{2\pi r}$

(c) $\dfrac{2\mu_0 i_1 i_2}{\pi r}$

(d) $\dfrac{2\mu_0 i_1 i_2}{\pi^2 r}$

28. A square loop of side ℓ carrying current i is part of the shown arrangement. Minimum current i to just move the block up the inclined plane is

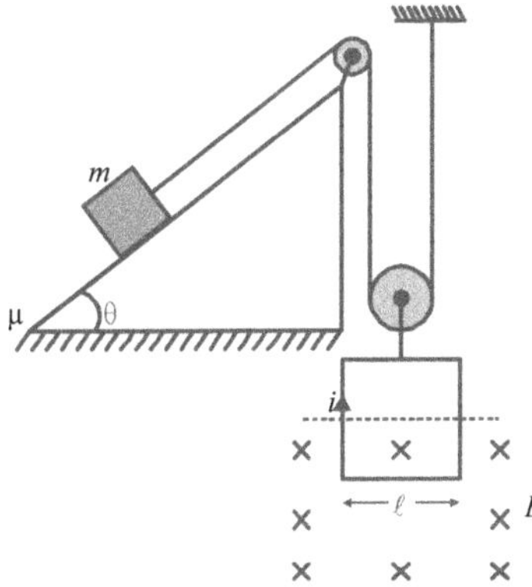

(a) $\dfrac{mg\sin\theta + \mu mg\cos\theta}{B\ell}$

(b) $\dfrac{mg\sin\theta + \mu mg\cos\theta}{2B\ell}$

(c) $\dfrac{2mg\sin\theta + 2\mu mg\cos\theta}{B\ell}$

(d) $\dfrac{mg\sin\theta - \mu mg\cos\theta}{B\ell}$

29. An electron and a positron are projected in a transverse magnetic field (of strength B) with speed v each. If width of magnetic field region is kr (where k is a constant, r is radius of revolution of each of the particle). Time spent by each of the particles in magnetic field is one-fourth of the time period of revolution of particles for k equal to (Assume elastic collision, if particles collide)

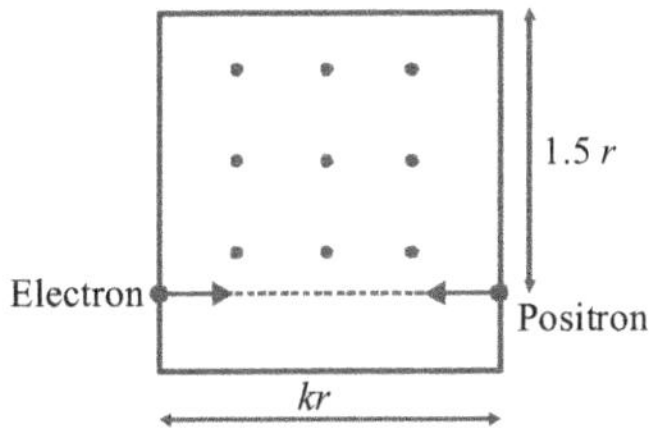

(a) 1

(b) $\sqrt{2}$

(c) $\dfrac{1}{\sqrt{2}}$

(d) 2

30. A particle of mass m and charge q is thrown from origin at $t = 0$ with velocity $2\hat{i} + 3\hat{j} + 4\hat{k}$ units in a region with uniform magnetic field $2\hat{i}$ units. After time $t = \dfrac{\pi m}{qB}$, an electric field $\vec{E}$ is switched on, such that particle moves on a straight line with constant speed. $\vec{E}$ may be

(a) $5\hat{i} - 10\hat{j}$ units

(b) $-6\hat{i} - 9\hat{k}$ units

(c) $-6\hat{k} + 8\hat{j}$ units

(d) $6\hat{i} + 8\hat{k}$ units

31. Shown in the figure are two horizontal parallel conducting rails separated by distance ℓ. A uniform magnetic field B exists in vertical upward direction. A wire of mass m can slide on the rails. The rails are connected to a source, which drives current i in the circuit given by $i = at - bt^2$ between $t = 0$ and $t = \dfrac{a}{b}$, where a and b are positive constants. Coefficient of friction between the rails and the wire is μ. Minimum μ so that wire does not slide is

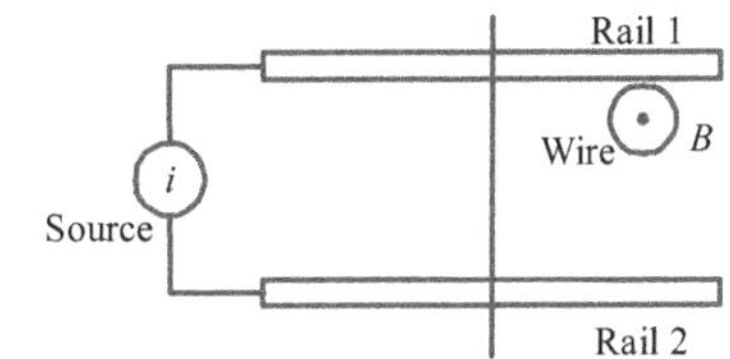

(a) $\dfrac{Ba^2\ell}{b\,mg}$

(b) $\dfrac{Ba^2\ell}{2b\,mg}$

(c) $\dfrac{Ba^2\ell}{4b\,mg}$

(d) $\dfrac{Ba^2\ell}{8b\,mg}$

32. Consider the figure shown. A proton enters a uniform magnetic field region with velocity $\vec{v} = 6\hat{i}$ m/s. Thickness of magnetic field region is $\dfrac{r}{2}$, where r is radius of rotation of the proton in the magnetic field. A large plane mirror in x-z plane is moving with constant velocity $3\hat{i} - 2\hat{j}$ m/s. Velocity of the image of proton in mirror when the proton comes out of the field is

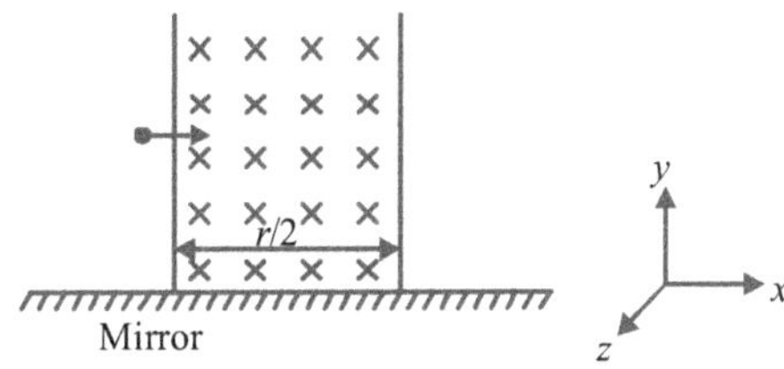

(a) $3\sqrt{3}\,\hat{i} - 5\hat{j}$ m/s

(b) $3\sqrt{3}\,\hat{i} - 7\hat{j}$ m/s

(c) $\left(3 + 3\sqrt{3}\,\hat{i}\right) - 5\hat{j}$ m/s

(d) $\left(3 + 3\sqrt{3}\,\hat{i}\right) - 7\hat{j}$ m/s

Answer Key	27	(d)	28	(c)	29	(b)	30	(c)
Sol. from page 384	31	(c)	32	(b)				

33. A particle (mass m and charge q) is at rest at origin. An electric field $\vec{E} = 10\hat{k}$ units and magnetic field $\vec{B} = -8\hat{i} + 6\hat{j}$ units is switched on in the region. Speed of the particle as function of its z-coordinate is

(a) $\sqrt{\dfrac{10qz}{m}}$ (b) $\sqrt{\dfrac{20qz}{m}}$

(c) $\sqrt{\dfrac{30qz}{m}}$ (d) $\sqrt{\dfrac{40qz}{m}}$

34. A charged particle (of charge q and mass m) is projected with velocity $v_1\hat{k}$ at a point R as shown. Electric and magnetic fields in the region are $E_0\hat{k}$ and $B_0\hat{j}$ respectively. Velocity at another point S in the region is $-v_2\hat{i}$ (as shown). Choose the correct alternate

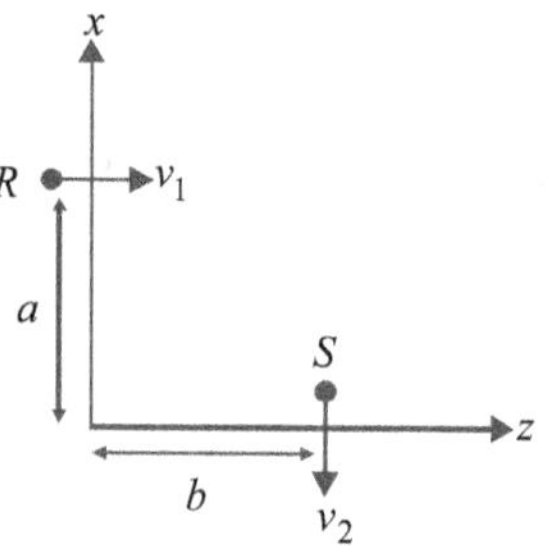

(a) $2qE_0b = m\left(v_1^2 - v_2^2\right)$ (b) $2E_0a = m\left(v_2^2 - v_1^2\right)$

(c) $2qE_0b = m\left(v_2^2 - v_1^2\right)$ (d) $2qE_0a = m\left(v_1^2 - v_2^2\right)$

Answer Key	33	(b)	34	(c)				
Sol. from page 384								

Magnetism   # MCQ Type 2   *Exercise 5.2*

Multiple correct options

1. The radius of curvature of the path of a charged particle moving in a static uniform magnetic field is :
   (a) directly proportional to the magnitude of the charge or the particle
   (b) directly proportional to the magnitude of the linear momentum of the particle
   (c) directly proportional to the kinetic energy of the particle
   (d) inversely proportional to the magnitude of the magnetic field

2. If a charged particle kept at rest experiences an electromagnetic force,
   (a) the electric field must be there
   (b) the magnetic field must be there
   (c) the magnetic field may or may not be there
   (d) the electric field may or may not be there.

3. A charged particle moves in a gravity free space without change in velocity. Which of the following is/are possible ?
   (a) $E \neq 0, B = 0$ (b) $E = 0, B = 0$
   (c) $E = 0, B \neq 0$ (d) $E \neq 0, B \neq 0$.

4. If a charged particle goes without any acceleration in a region containing electric and magnetic fields,
   (a) $\vec{E}$ must be perpendicular to $\vec{B}$
   (b) $\vec{v}$ must be perpendicular to $\vec{E}$
   (c) $\vec{v}$ must be perpendicular to $\vec{B}$
   (d) E must be equal to vB.

5. A particle of mass m and charge q, moving with velocity v enters region II normal to the boundary as shown in the figure. Region II has a uniform magnetic field B perpendicular to the plane of the paper. The length of the region II is ℓ. Choose the correct choice(s)

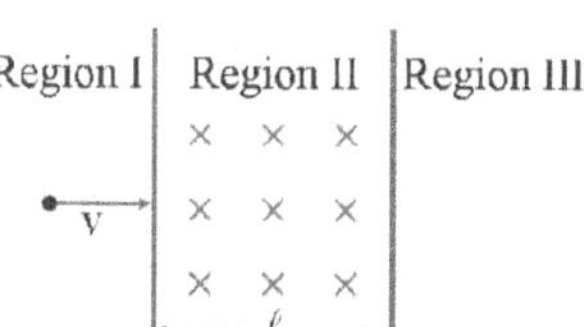

(a) the particle enters region III only if its velocity $v > \dfrac{q\ell B}{m}$

(b) the particle enters the region III only if its velocity $v < \dfrac{q\ell B}{m}$

(c) path length of the particle in region II is maximum when velocity $v < \dfrac{q\ell B}{m}$

(d) time spent in region II is same for any velocity v as long as the particle returns to region I.

6. A particle of charge $+q$ and mass m moving under the influence of a uniform electric field $E\hat{i}$ and a uniform magnetic field $B\hat{k}$ follows trajectory from P to Q as shown in figure. The velocities at P and Q are $v\hat{i}$ and $-2v\hat{j}$ respectively. Which of the following statement(s) is/are correct?

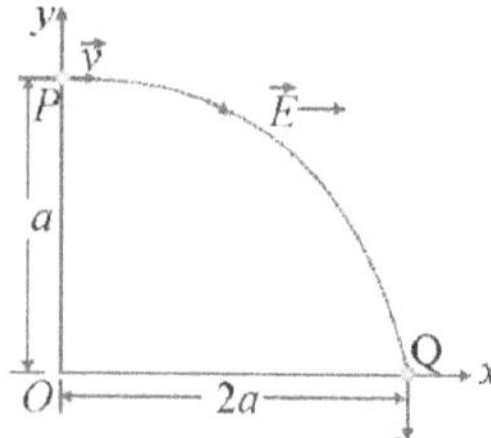

(a) $E = \dfrac{3}{4}\dfrac{mv^2}{qa}$

(b) Rate of work done by electric field at P is $\dfrac{3}{4}\dfrac{mv^3}{a}$

(c) Rate of work done by electric field at P is zero

(d) Rate of work done by both the fields at Q is zero

Answer Key	1	(b, d)	2	(a, c)	3	(b, c, d)	4	(a, b)
Sol. from page 388	5	(a, c)	6	(a, b, d)				

<table>
<tr><td>**Magnetism**</td><td># Statement Questions</td><td>*Exercise 5.3*</td></tr>
</table>

Read the two statements carefully to mark the correct option out of the options given below:
(a) If both the statements are true and the *statement - 2* is the correct explanation of *statement - 1*.
(b) If both the statements are true but *statement - 2* is not the correct explanation of the *statement - 1*.
(c) If *statement - 1* true but *statement - 2* is false.
(d) If *statement - 1* is false but *statement - 2* is true.

1. *Statement -1*

Magnetic field can not accelerate the charged particle.

Statement - 2

Magnetic field can not change the speed of the charged particle.

2. *Statement - 1*

The free electrons in a conducting wire are in continuous thermal motion. If such a wire, without current is placed in a magnetic field, the force on the wire is zero.

Statement - 2

The each free electron in the wire experiences magnetic force.

3. *Statement - 1*

The net magnetic force on a current carrying loop in magnetic field is always zero.

Statement - 2

The resultant force on the loop is the vector sum of the forces on its elements.

4. *Statement - 1*

The kinetic energy of a charged particle in a perpendicular magnetic field B is K. When the magnetic field becomes $3B$, the kinetic energy of the particle becomes $3K$.

Statement - 2

The magnetic force always acts perpendicular to the velocity vector of the particle.

5. *Statement - 1*

Cyclotron does not accelerate electron.

Statement - 2

Mass of the electron is very small.

6. *Statement - 1*

Cyclotron is a device which is used to accelerate the positive charged particles.

Statement - 2

Cyclotron frequency depends upon the velocity of the charged particle.

7. *Statement - 1*

A current carrying loop placed in a magnetic field must experience a torque.

Statement - 2

Torque on the loop is given by τ=MBsinθ.

8. *Statement - 1*

The net charge in a current carrying wire is zero and so magnetic force on the wire in magnetic field is zero.

Statement - 2

The force on a current carrying wire is given by $F=Bi\ell$ sinθ.

9. *Statement - 1*

A charged particle in a region passes undeviated. The region must not have electric field

Statement - 2

The region may have electric field only or both electric and magnetic field.

10. *Statement - 1*

A charged particle moves in a uniform magnetic field. The velocity of the particle at same instant makes an acute angle with the magnetic field. The path of the particle is a helix with constant pitch.

Statement - 2

The force on the particle is given by $\vec{F} = q\left(\vec{v} \times \vec{B}\right)$.

11. *Statement - 1*

The figure shows the circular paths of two particles : electron and proton that travel at the same speed in a uniform magnetic field $\vec{B}$, which is directed into the page. The electron follows the path of smaller radius.

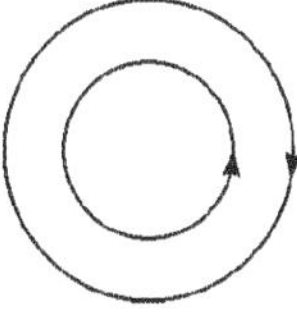

Statement - 2

The radius of path in the perpendicular magnetic field is given by

$$r = \frac{mv}{qB}.$$

Answer Key	1	(d)	2	(a)	3	(d)	4	(d)	5	(a)	6	(c)
Sol. from page 389	7	(d)	8	(d)	9	(d)	10	(b)	11	(a)		

12. *Statement - 1*

The figure shows a current i through a wire in a uniform magnetic field $\vec{B}$, as well as the magnetic force $\vec{F}_B$ acting on the wire. The direction of field must be along negative *y*-axis.

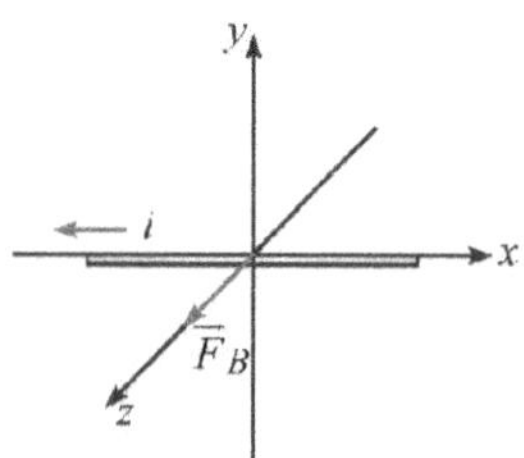

Statement - 2

The force $\vec{F}_B = \left(i\vec{\ell} \times \vec{B} \right)$.

13. A charged particle moving through crossed fields with the forces $\vec{F}_e$ and $\vec{F}_B$ in opposition. If $v = \dfrac{E}{B}$, then particle moves undeviated.

Statement - 2

If $v < \dfrac{E}{B}$, the charged particle bends towards electric field.

14. *Statement - 1*

A proton of charge +e and of mass m enters a uniform magnetic field $\vec{B} = B\hat{i}$ with an initial velocity $\vec{v} = \vec{v}_{ox}\hat{i} + \vec{v}_{oy}\hat{j}$. The x-component of proton velocity v_{ox} remains constant.

Statement - 2

The *x* and *y* components of proton velocity : v_{ox} and v_{oy} change but speed of the proton remains constant.

Answer Key	**12**	(a)	**13**	(b)	**14**	(d)		
Sol. from page 389								

Magnetism	Passage & Matrix	*Exercise 5.4*

PASSAGES

Passage for Q. 1 to Q.3.

In a television tube, each of the electrons in the beam has a kinetic energy of 12.0 *keV*. The tube is oriented so that the electrons move horizontally from geomagnetic south to geomagnetic north. The vertical component of earth's magnetic field points down and has a magnitude of 55.0 μ*T*.

1. The direction in which beam deflects :

    (a) east   (b) west

    (c) north-east   (d) south-west

2. The acceleration of any electron due to the magnetic field is:

    (a) $3.14 \times 10^{14} \, \text{m/s}^2$ (b) $4.28 \times 10^{14} \, \text{m/s}^2$

    (c) $5.56 \times 10^{12} \, \text{m/s}^2$ (d) $6.28 \times 10^{14} \, \text{m/s}^2$

3. The transverse deflection of the beam after travelling 20.0 cm through the television tube :

    (a) 1.96 mm   (b) 2.98 mm

    (c) 4.24 mm   (d) none of these

Passage for Q. 4 to Q.6.

A certain commercial mass spectrometer is used to separate uranium ions of mass $3.92 \times 10^{-25} \, kg$ and charge $3.20 \times 10^{-19} \, C$ from related species. The ions are accelerated through a potential difference of 100 kV and then pass into a uniform magnetic field, where they are bent in a path of radius 1.0 m. After traveling through 180° and passing through a slit of width 1.00 mm and height 1.00 cm, they are collected in a cup.

4. The magnitude of the perpendicular magnetic field in the separation:

    (a) 495 *mT*   (b) 585 *mT*

    (c) 625 *mT*   (d) 835 *mT*

5. If the machine is used to separate out 100 mg of material per hour, then the current of the desired ions in the machine is :

    (a) 22.7 *mA*   (b) 33.51 *mA*

    (c) 45.2 *mA*   (d) 66.7 *mA*

6. The thermal energy produced in the cup in 1.00 h is :

    (a) 4.07 MJ   (b) 5.30 MJ

    (c) 8.17 MJ   (d) 10.00 MJ

Answer Key	**1**	(a)	**2**	(d)	**3**	(b)	**4**	(a)	**5**	(a)
Sol. from page 389	**6**	(c)								

Passage for Q. 7 to Q.9.

A particle of mass m and charge q is moving in a region where uniform, constant electric and magnetic fields E and B are present. E and B are parallel to each other. At time $t = 0$, the velocity v_0 of the particle is perpendicular to $\vec{E}$. Assume that its speed is always $< c$, (the speed of light in vacuum). Express all the required answers in terms of t, q, m, the vectors $\vec{E}$ and $\vec{B}$ and their magnitudes v_0, E and B.

7. Suppose electric field is acting along positive direction of x and v_x is the x-component of the velocity of the particle at any time t, then v_x is

(a) $\dfrac{qE}{m}t$

(b) $\dfrac{E}{B}$

(c) $\dfrac{2qE}{m}t$

(d) none of these

8. If v_y is the y-component of the velocity of the particle, then

(a) $v_y = 2\dfrac{Eq}{m}t$

(b) $v_y = v_0 \sin\left(\dfrac{Bt}{2m}\right)$

(c) $v_y = \dfrac{v_0}{2}\cos\left(\dfrac{Bt}{m}\right)$

(d) $v_y = v_0 \cos\left(\dfrac{Bqt}{m}\right)$

9. The resultant velocity, v of the particle at any time t is given by

(a) $v = v_0 \cos\left(\dfrac{Bt}{m}\right)$

(b) $\vec{v} = \left(\dfrac{qE}{m}\right)t\,\hat{i} + v_0 \cos\left(\dfrac{Bqt}{m}\right)\hat{j} + v_0 \sin\left(\dfrac{Bqt}{m}\right)\hat{k}$

(c) $\vec{v} = \left(\dfrac{qE}{m}\right)t\,\hat{i} + v_0 \cos\left(\dfrac{Bqt}{m}\right)\hat{j}$

(d) none of these.

Paragraph for questions no. 10 and 11

A current loop $ABCD$ is held fixed on the plane of the paper a as shown in the figure. The arcs BC (radius $= b$) and DA (radius $= a$) of the loop are joined by two straight wires AB and CD. A steady current I is flowing in the loop. Angle made by AB and CD at the origin O is 30°. Another straight thin wire with steady current I_1 flowing out of the plane of the paper is kept at the origin.

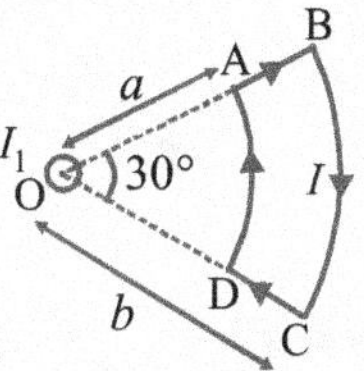

10. The magnitude of the magnetic field (B) due to the loop $ABCD$ at the origin (O) is

(a) zero

(b) $\dfrac{\mu_0 I (b-a)}{2\pi ab}$

(c) $\dfrac{\mu_0 I (b-a)}{4\pi ab}$

(d) $\dfrac{\mu_0 I}{4\pi}\left[2(b-a) + \pi/3(a+b)\right]$

11. Due to presence of the current I_1 at the origin
(a) The force on AB and DC are zero
(b) The forces on AD and BC are zero
(c) The magnitude of the net force on the loop is given by

$$\dfrac{I_1 I}{4\pi}\mu_0\left[2(b-a) + \pi/3(a+b)\right]$$

(d) The magnitude of the net force on the loop is given by

$$\dfrac{\mu_0 I I_1}{2\pi ab}(b-a)$$

Answer Key	7	(a)	8	(d)	9	(b)	10	(b)	11	(b)
Sol. from page 389										

12. A square loop of side a and carrying current i as shown in the figure is placed in gravity free space having magnetic field $B = B_0 \hat{k}$. Now match following :

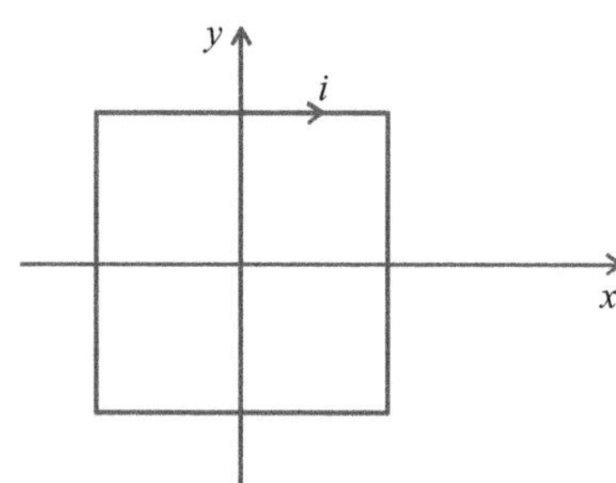

	Column-I		Column -II
A.	Torque on loop	(p)	is zero
B.	Net force on loop	(q)	is in direction $(-\hat{k})$
C.	Potential energy of loop	(r)	has minimum magnitudes
D.	Magnetic moment of loop	(s)	has maximum magnitudes

13. A charged particle having charge q and mass m is to be subjected to a combination of constant uniform magnetic field $(\vec{B})$ and a constant uniform gravitational field $(\vec{G})$. Apart from these field forces there exists no other force. Now match the column.

	Column-I		Column -II
(A)	The charged particle moves without change in its direction.	(p)	It is possible that both $\vec{B}$ and $\vec{G}$ are zero.
(B)	The charged particle moves without change in its velocity.	(q)	It is possible that both $\vec{B}$ and $\vec{G}$ are non zero.
(C)	The charged particle takes a circular path	(r)	It is possible that $\vec{B}$ is zero and $\vec{G}$ is not zero.
(D)	The charged particle takes a parabolic path	(s)	It is possible that $\vec{B}$ is non zero and $\vec{G}$ is zero.

Answer Key	**12**	A-p, s ; B-p ; C- s ; D-q	**13**	A-p,q,r s ; B-p, q, s ; C- s ; D-r
Sol. from page 389				

14. Find correct match for the figure in column I as shown with the items given in column II :

Column I   **Column II**

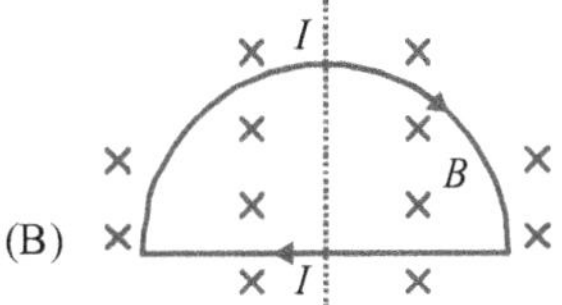

(A)   (p) $F \neq 0$

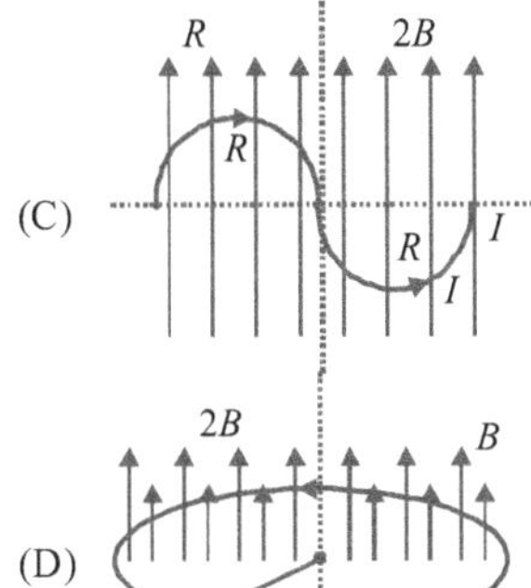

(B)   (q) $F = 0, \bar{\tau} \neq 0$

(C)   (r) $F = 0, \bar{\tau} = 0$

(D)   (s) $F \neq 0, \bar{\tau} = 0$

Answer Key	14	A-q ; B-r ; C- s ; D-r

Sol. from page 389

Magnetism   # Subjective Integer Type   *Exercise 5.5*

Solution from page 391

1. An alpha particle is accelerated by a potential difference of 10^4 V. Find the change in its direction of motion, if it enters normally in a region of thickness 0.1 m having transverse magnetic induction 0.1 T. (Given mass of α - particle $6.4 \times 10^{-27} kg$). ***Ans.*** 30°.

2. Figure shows a convex lens of focal length 12 cm lying in a uniform magnetic field B of magnitude 1.2 T parallel to its principal axis. A particle having a charge 2.0×10^{-3} C and mass 2.0×10^{-5} kg is projected perpendicular to the plane of the diagram with a speed of 4.8 m/s. The particle moves along a circle with its centre on the principal axis at a distance of 18 cm from the lens. Show that the image of the particle goes along a circle and find the radius of that circle.

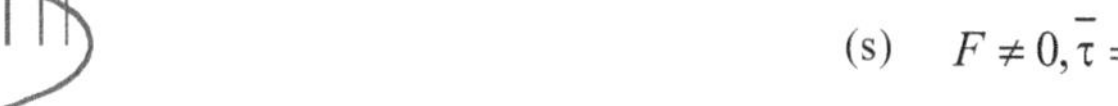

Ans. 8 cm.

3. At the moment $t = 0$ an electron leaves one plate of a parallel plate capacitor with a negligible velocity. An accelerating voltage, varying as $V = at$, where $a = 100$ V/s, is applied between the plates. The separation between the plates is $\ell = 5.0$ cm. What is the velocity of the electron at the moment it reaches the opposite plate ? ***Ans.*** 16 km/s

4. An electron accelerated by a potential difference $V = 1.0$ kV moves in a uniform magnetic field at an angle $\alpha = 30°$ to the vector $\vec{B}$ whose modulus is $B = 29$ mT. Find the pitch of the helical trajectory of the electron.

Ans. $p = 2\pi\sqrt{2mV/eB^2} \cos\alpha = 2.0$ *cm.*

5. An electron moves through a uniform magnetic field given by $\vec{B} = B_x\vec{i} + (3B_x)\hat{j}$. At a particular instant, the electron has the velocity $\vec{v} = (2.0\hat{i} + 4.0\hat{j}) m/s$ and the magnetic force acting on it is $(6.4 \times 10^{-19}\hat{k})N$. Find B_x. ***Ans.*** –2.0 T.

6. A wire of 62.0 cm length and 13.0 g mass is suspended by a pair of flexible leads in a uniform magnetic field of magnitude 0.44 T (figure). What are the magnitude and direction of the current required to remove the tension in the supporting leads ?

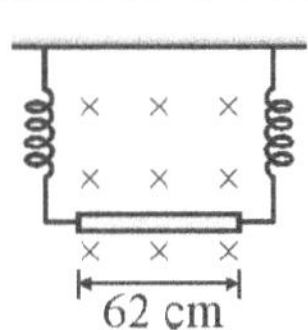

Ans. 467 m A towards right.

Solution from page 391

1. A charge of 1.0 μC moves with a speed of 2.0×10^6 m/s along the positive x-axis. A magnetic field $\vec{B}$ of strength $\left(0.20\hat{j} + 0.40\hat{k}\right)T$ exists in space. Find the magnetic force acting on the charge.

Ans. $\left(-0.8\hat{j} + 0.4\hat{k}\right)N$

2. A proton, a deutron and an alpha particle moving with equal kinetic energies enter perpendicularly into a magnetic field. If r_p, r_d and r_α are the respective radii of the circular paths, find the ratio $\dfrac{r_p}{r_d}$ and $\dfrac{r_p}{r_\alpha}$.

Ans. $\dfrac{1}{\sqrt{2}}, 1$

3. A particle having a charge of 20 μC and mass 20 μg moves along a circle of radius 5.0 cm under the action of a magnetic field $B = 1.0$ T. When the particle is at a point P, a uniform electric field is switched on and it is found that the particle continues on the tangent through P with a uniform velocity. Find the electric field.

Ans. 0.5 V/m, the direction of field is radially outward at P.

4. A narrow beam of singly-charged carbon ions, moving at a constant velocity of 6.0×10^4 m/s, is sent perpendicularly in a rectangular region having uniform magnetic field $B = 0.5$ T (see figure). It is found that two beams emerge from the field in the backward direction, the separations from the incident beam being 3.0 cm and 3.5 cm. Identify the isotopes present in the ion beam. Take the mass of an ion $= A\left(1.6 \times 10^{-27}\right)$ kg, where A is the mass number.

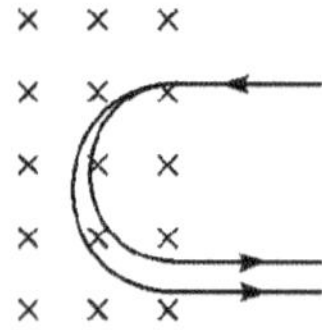

Ans. ^{12}C and ^{14}C.

5. A particle of mass $m = 1.6 \times 10^{-27}$ kg and charge $q = 1.6 \times 10^{-19}$C moves at a speed of 1.0×10^7 m/s. It enters a region of uniform magnetic field at a point E, as shown in figure. The field has a strength of 1.0 T. (a) The magnetic field directed into the plane of the paper. The particle leave the region of the field at the point F. Find the distance EF and the angle θ. (b) If the field is coming out of the paper, find the time spent by the particle in the region of the magnetic field after entering it at E.

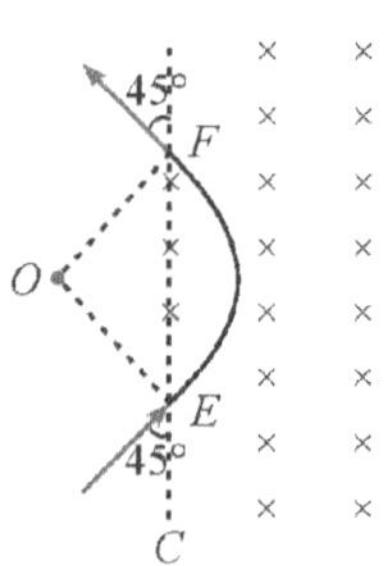

Ans. (a) 14 cm (b) 4.7×10^{-8} s.

6. An electron is released from the origin at a place where a uniform electric field E and a uniform magnetic field B exist along the negative y-axis and the negative z-axis respectively. Find the displacement of the electron along the y-axis when its velocity becomes perpendicular to the electric field for the first time.

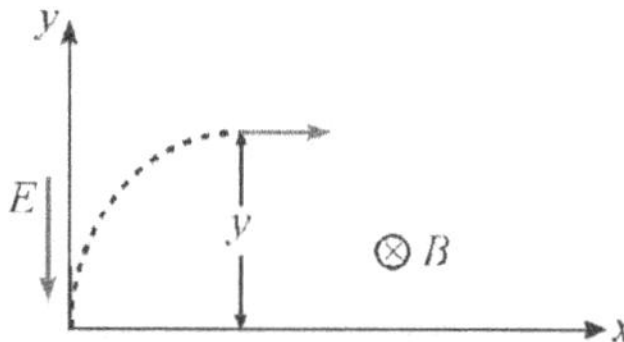

Ans. $y = \dfrac{2Em}{eB^2}$.

7. A current loop of arbitrary shape lies in a uniform magnetic field B. Show that the net magnetic force acting on the loop is zero.

8. A wire of length ℓ carries a current i along the x-axis. A magnetic field exists which is given as $\vec{B} = B_0\left(\hat{i} + \hat{j} + \hat{k}\right)T$. Find the magnitude of the magnetic force acting on the wire.

Ans. $\sqrt{2}\,B_0 i\ell$

9. A rectangular wire-loop of width a is suspended from the insulated pan of a spring balance as shown in figure. A current i exists in the anticlockwise direction in the loop. A magnetic field B exists in the lower region. Find the change in the tension of the spring if the current in the loop is reversed.

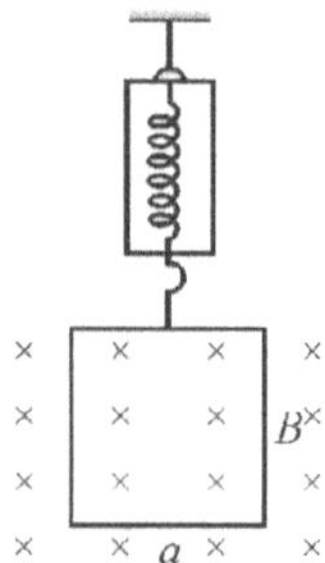

Ans. $2Bia$

10. (a) A wire loop carrying a current I is placed in xy-plane as shown in figure. If a particle of charge $+Q$ and mass m is placed at the centre P and given a velocity $\vec{v}$ along NP. Find its instantaneous acceleration.

(b) If an external uniform magnetic field $\vec{B} = B\hat{i}$ is applied, find the force and the torque acting on the loop due to this field.

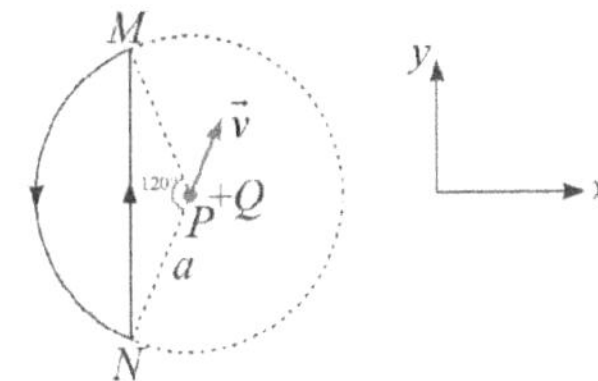

Ans. (a) $a = \dfrac{0.109\mu_0 IQV}{ma}$, at $30°$ with negative x-axis.

(b) $\tau = 0.6136\, a^2 IB$ along y-axis.

11. A coil in the shape of an equilateral triangle of side 0.02 m is suspended from a vertex such that it is hanging in a vertical plane between the pole pieces of a permanent magnet producing a horizontal magnetic field of 5×10^{-2} T. Find the couple acting on the coil when a current of 0.1 A is passed through it and the magnetic field is parallel to its plane. **Ans.** $5\sqrt{3}\times10^{-7}\,N-m.$

12. A circular loop carrying a current i has wire of total length L. A uniform magnetic field B exists parallel to the plane of the loop. (a) Find the torque on the loop.
(b) If the same length of the wire is used to form a square loop, what would be the torque ? Which is larger ?

Ans. (a) $\dfrac{BiL^2}{4\pi}$ (b) $\dfrac{BiL^2}{16}$

13. Consider a solid sphere of mass m which has a charge q distributed uniformly over its volume. The sphere is rotated about a diameter with an angular speed ω. Show that the magnetic moment M and the angular momentum L of the sphere are related as $\vec{M} = \dfrac{q}{2m}\vec{L}.$

14. A proton moves at a constant velocity of $+50$ m/s along an x-axis through crossed electric and magnetic fields. The magnetic field is $\vec{B} = \left(2.0\hat{j}\right)mT.$ What is the electric field? **Ans.** $-0.10\,\hat{k}\,\dfrac{V}{m}.$

15. Two concentric, circular wire loops, of radii 20.0 and 30.0 cm, are located in the xy-plane; each carries a clockwise current of 7.00 A (see figure).

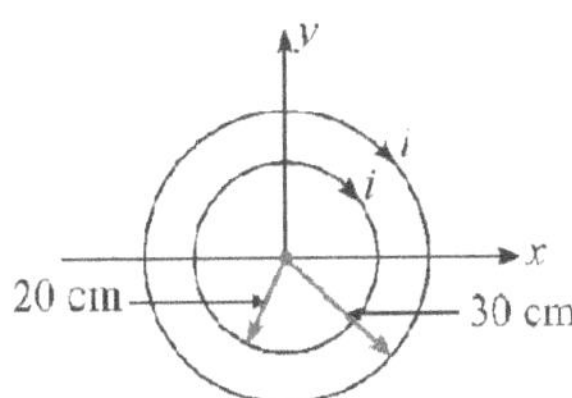

(a) Find the net magnetic dipole moment of this system.
(b) Repeat for reversed current in the inner loop.
Ans. (a) 2.86 A–m², (b) 1.10 A–m².

16. A beam of electrons whose kinetic energy is K emerges from a thin-foil "window" at the end of an accelerator tube. There is a metal plate a distance d from this window and perpendicular to the direction of the emerging beam (figure). Show that we can prevent the beam from hitting the plate if we apply a uniform magnetic field $\vec{B}$ such that $B \geq \sqrt{\dfrac{2mK}{e^2 d^2}}$, in which m and e are the electron mass and charge. How should $\vec{B}$ be oriented ?

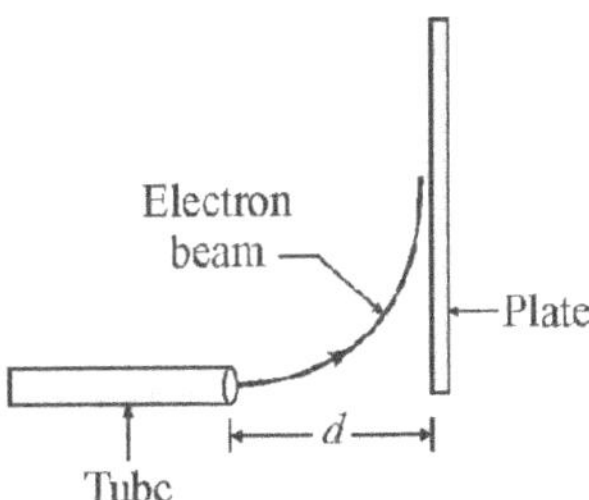

17. Figure shows a wire ring of radius a that is perpendicular to the general direction of a radially symmetric, diverging magnetic field. The magnetic field at the ring is everywhere of the same magnitude B, and its direction at the ring everywhere makes an angle θ with a normal to the plane of the ring. Find the magnitude and direction of the force the field exerts on the ring if the ring carries a current i.

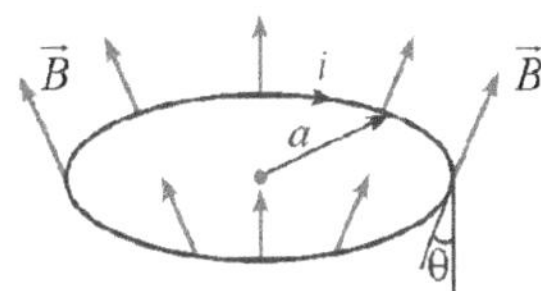

Ans. $2\pi\, a\, i\, B\,\sin\theta$ (up).

18. Figure shows a rectangular 20-turn coil of wire, of dimensions 10 cm by 5.0 cm. It carries a current of 0.10 A and is hinged along one long side. It is mounted in the xy-plane, at $30°$ to the direction of a uniform magnetic field of magnitude 0.50 T. Find the magnitude and direction of the torque acting on the coil about the hinge line.

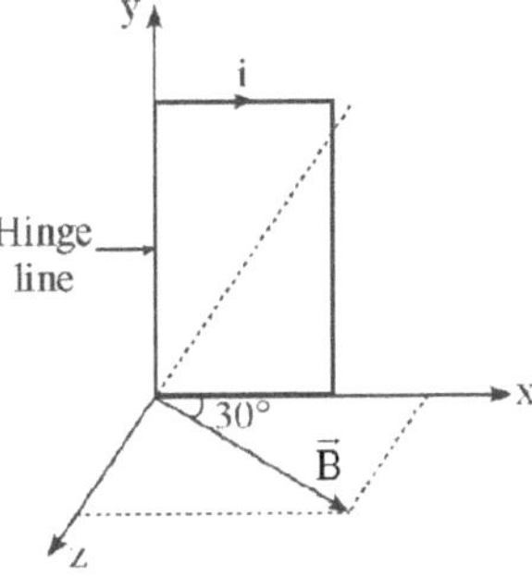

Ans. 4.3×10^{-3} N-m; negative y.

19. Two protons move parallel to each other with an equal velocity $v = 300$ km/s. Find the ratio of forces of magnetic and electrical interaction of the protons.

Ans. $\dfrac{v^2}{c^2} = 1\times10^{-6}$

20. In figure, the long straight wire carries a current of 30 A and the rectangular loop carries a current of 20 A. Calculate the resultant force acting on the loop. Assume that $a = 1.0$ cm, $b = 8.0$ cm, and $L = 30$ cm.

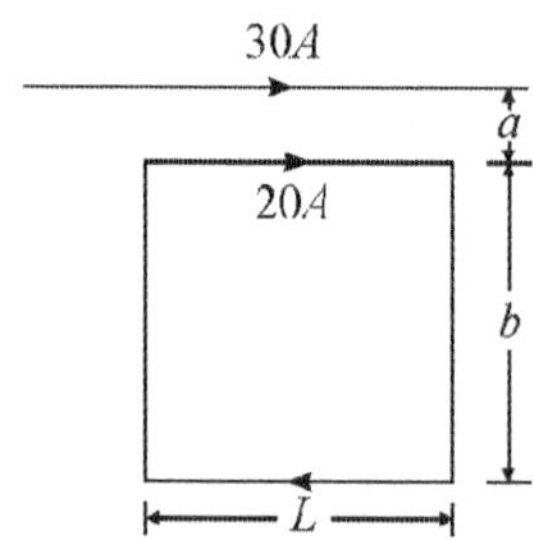

Ans. 3.2 mN, towards the wire.

21. Figure shows a wood cylinder of mass $m = 0.250$ kg and length $L = 0.100$ m, with $N = 10.0$ turns of wire wrapped around it longitudinally, so that the plane of the wire coil contains the axis of the cylinder. What is the least current i through the coil that will prevent the cylinder from rolling down a plane inclined at an angle θ to the horizontal, in the presence of a vertical, uniform magnetic field of magnitude 0.500 T, if the plane of the coil is parallel to the inclined plane ?

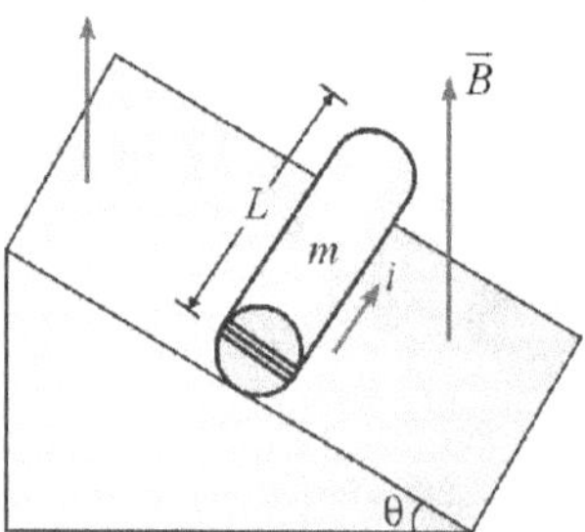

Ans. 2.45 A.

22. Figure shows a current loop $ABCDEFA$ carrying a current 2 A. The sides of the loop are parallel to the coordinate axes, with $AB = 10.0$ cm, $BC = 20.0$ cm, and $FA = 5.0$ cm. Calculate the magnitude and direction of the magnetic dipole moment of this loop.

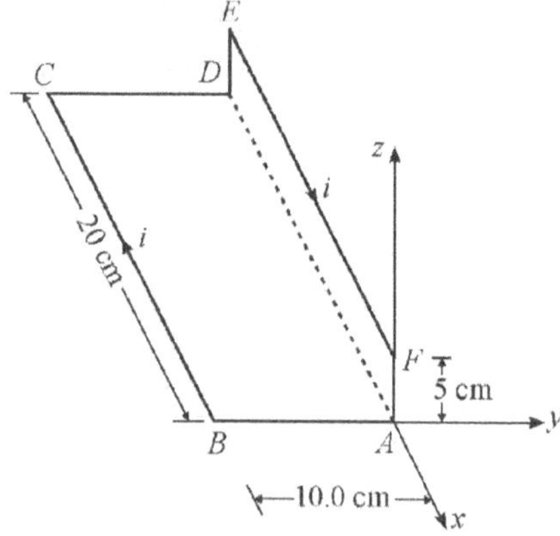

Ans. $\vec{M} = \left(0.02\,\hat{j} - 0.04\,\hat{k}\right) A - m^2$

★ ★ ★

Hints & Solutions

1. (d) The electric force on the positive charge particle is upward and so magnetic force must be downwards. For this magnetic field it is best represented in (4).

2. (b) If velocity of the solid along y-axis, the electrons will accumulate at the front face. So, this face will be at lower potential.

3. (d) Use Fleming's left hand rule to get the answer.

4. (c) As $r = \dfrac{mv}{qB} = \dfrac{P}{qB}$

   $\therefore$ Area, $A = \pi r^2 = \pi\left(\dfrac{P}{qB}\right)^2$

   $= \dfrac{\pi P^2}{qB} = \dfrac{2\,m\pi}{qB}K$

5. (a)

6. (d) We have, $R = \dfrac{mv}{qB}$, or $mv = RqB$.

   Thus kinetic energy, $K = \dfrac{1}{2}mv^2 = \dfrac{P^2}{2m} = \dfrac{(RqB)^2}{2m}$

7. (d) Electric field exerts force on electron in opposite direction of projection.

8. (c) For equal charges, $\dfrac{1}{2}m_1 v_1^2 = qV$ and $\dfrac{1}{2}m_2 v_2^2 = qV$

   $\therefore$ $m_1 v_1^2 = m_2 v_2^2$

   Now, $\dfrac{R_1}{R_2} = \dfrac{m_1 v_1/qB}{m_2 v_2/qB} = \left(\dfrac{m_1}{m_2}\right)^{1/2}$

   or $\dfrac{m_1}{m_2} = \dfrac{R_1^2}{R_2^2}$

9. (b) $r \propto (mv)$

10. (d) $F = qvB \sin\theta$

   or $B_{min} = \dfrac{F}{qv}$ $\qquad (\sin\theta = 1)$

   $= \dfrac{10^{-10}}{10^{-12}\times 10^5} = 10^{-3}\,T$, in z-direction.

11. (b) $\dfrac{r_e}{r_p} = \dfrac{P_e/eB}{P_p/eB} = \dfrac{\sqrt{2m_e K}}{\sqrt{2m_p K}} = \sqrt{\dfrac{m_e}{m_p}}$

   As, $m_p > m_e$, so, $r_p > r_e$

12. (d) Time period, $T = \dfrac{2\pi m}{qB}$, and so T does not depend on the velocity of the particle.

13. (c) $\dfrac{r_e}{r_p} = \dfrac{P/eB}{P/eB} = 1$

14. (b) For equal charge of the particles, radius

   $r \propto (mv)$ and so

   $m_A v_A > m_B v_B$

15. (a) When charge particle is released at rest in electric and magnetic field, the electric force moves it along the direction of electric field.

16. (c) The work done by magnetic field for any displacement will be zero, because it always acts perpendicular to the velocity vector.

17. (b) $B = \dfrac{E}{v} = \dfrac{10^4}{10} = 10^3\,Wb/m^2$.

18. (d) By Fleming's left hand rule, the force on the particle is along OY.

19. (c) The forces on the loop are as shown. It shows that the loop will move towards the wire $(F_1 > F_2)$.

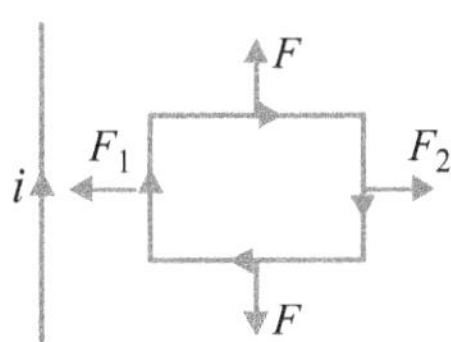

20. (c) The net force on current carrying loop in uniform magnetic field will be zero.

21. (a) The force between two neighbouring turns will be of attractive nature, and so spring will get compressed

22. (b) By Fleming's left hand rule, the force on the electron stream is downwards.

23. (c) $F \propto \dfrac{i_1 i_2}{r}$, and so $F' = \dfrac{2F}{3}$.

24. (c) Force, $F = \dfrac{\mu_0}{2\pi}\cdot\dfrac{i_1 i_2}{r}\ell = \dfrac{\mu_0}{2\pi}\cdot\dfrac{i^2}{d}\ell$.

25. (c) $\dfrac{M}{L} = \dfrac{q}{2m}$

26. (b) By Fleming's left hand rule, each element of the loop experiences radially outward force.

27. (c) Potential energy, $U = -MB\cos\theta$, and so, it greatest when $\theta = 180°$ or $U = -MB\cos 180° = MB$.

28. (d) The angle between magnetic field produced by the wires and velocity of the charge particle will be zero, and so

   $F = qvB \sin 0° = 0$.

29. (d) The electron will experiences a downward force and so electron will move along negative y-axis, speed of the electron remains constant in magnetic field

30. (c) $\vec{F} = q\,(\vec{v} \times \vec{B})$

$$= 1.6 \times 10^{-19}[4 \times 10^5 (\sin 30° \hat{i} + \cos 30° \hat{k}) \times 4\hat{k}]$$

$$= -12.8 \times 10^{-14}\,\hat{j}\,N$$

31. (a) The angle between $\vec{v}$ and $\vec{B}$ is zero and so,

$$F = qvB \sin 0° = 0$$

32. (b) Use Fleming's left hand rule.

33. (d) If F_4 is the force on segment QP, then

$$\vec{F_1} + \vec{F_2} + \vec{F_3} + \vec{F_4} = 0$$

and

$$\vec{F_4} = -(\vec{F_1} + \vec{F_2} + \vec{F_3})$$

or

$$F_4 = \sqrt{(F_3 - F_1)^2 + F_2^2}.$$

34. (a) Charge particle moves along a circular path under magnetic field only.

35. (c) $r = \dfrac{mv \sin 30°}{qB} = \dfrac{(1.67 \times 10^{-27}) \times (2 \times 10^6)\sin 30°}{1.6 \times 10^{-19} \times 0.104} = 0.1\ \text{m}$

$$T = \dfrac{2\pi m}{qB} = \dfrac{2\pi \times 1.67 \times 10^{-27}}{1.6 \times 10^{-19} \times 0.104} = 2\pi \times 10^{-7}\ \text{s}.$$

36. (c) For undeflected charged particle,

$$\vec{F_m} + \vec{F_e} = 0$$

or $q\,(\vec{v} \times \vec{B}) + \vec{E}q = 0$

or $\qquad v = \dfrac{E}{B}.$

37. (a) Magnetic force on the proton is zero. The electric force will accelerate the proton.

38. (c) Both types of ions experience force along $-y$, direction.

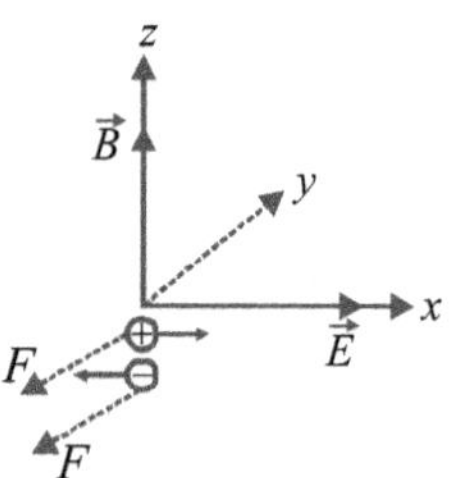

39. (b) The radius of path, $r = (b - a)$. If v is the required velocity, then

$$r = (b - a) = \dfrac{mv}{qB}$$

or $\qquad v = \left[\dfrac{qB(b - a)}{m}\right]$

40. (b) There is only magnetic force of attraction between A and B. While in x and y there is more electric repulsion.

41. (a) Use Fleming's left hand rule.

42. (a) When current is set up in the rings, they produce magnetic field along the axis. So one ring exerts torque on the other, $\tau = mB \sin 90°$.

1. (c) $\vec{F_1} = q\,(\vec{v} \times \vec{B}) = q[(2\hat{i} - 3\hat{j}) \times 4\hat{k}] = q(-8\hat{j} - 12\hat{i})$

$\vec{F_2} = q\,(\vec{v} \times \vec{B}) = q[(3\hat{i} + 2\hat{j}) \times (-4\hat{k})] = q(8\hat{j} - 12\hat{i})$

$\vec{F_3} = q\,(\vec{v} \times \vec{B}) = q[(3\hat{j} - 2\hat{k}) \times (4\hat{i})] = q(-12\hat{k} - 8\hat{j})$

$\vec{F_4} = q\,(\vec{v} \times \vec{B}) = q[(20\hat{i}) \times (-4\hat{i})] = 0$

It shows $F_1 = F_2 = F_3$ and $F_4 = 0$

2. (a) For $x = a$ to $2a$;

$$\vec{F} = q\,(\hat{v} \times \vec{B}) = q\,(v_0\hat{i} \times B_0\hat{j}) = qv_0B_0\hat{k}$$

For $x = 2a$ to $3a$;

$$\vec{F} = q[v_0\hat{i} \times (-B_0\hat{j})] = -qv_0B_0\hat{k}$$

It represents graph as in (a) is correct.

3. (a) Radius, $\qquad r = \dfrac{P}{qB} = \dfrac{\sqrt{2mk}}{qB}$

$$r_P = \dfrac{\sqrt{2mk}}{qB},$$

$$r_\alpha = \dfrac{\sqrt{2 \times (2m)k}}{qB},$$

and $\qquad r_\alpha = \dfrac{\sqrt{2 \times (4m)k}}{(2q)B} = r_P$

4. (d) $\tau = mB \sin\theta = iAB \sin\theta$. Area of circular loop is maximum for given perimeter, and so τ will be maximum in case (d).

5. (b) For non-circular path, there must be presence of $\vec{E}$-field and $\vec{B}$-field. For the given path the magnetic force is initially along $-y$- axis, and so magnetic field must have a component along z-axis and may have a component along x-axis.

6. (c) $\qquad \vec{F} = \vec{F}_{AB} + \vec{F}_{BC} + \vec{F}_{CA}$

or $\qquad F = Bi \times 1 + Bi \times 2 + Bi \times 1$

$$= 4\,Bi = 4 \times 0.5 \times 5 = 10\ \text{N}$$

7. (b) The path of the charged particle in this case will be cycloid. See theory of the chapter.

8. (c) $\qquad \vec{F_1} = -e\hat{j} = -e[\hat{i} \times (B_x\hat{i} + B_y\hat{j} + B_z\hat{k})]$

$\Rightarrow \qquad B_z = -1$

and
$$\vec{F}_2 = e(\hat{i}+\hat{j})$$
$$= -e[(\hat{i}+\hat{j})\times(B_x\hat{i}+B_y\hat{j}+B_z\hat{k})]$$
$$v_3 = \vec{v}_1\times\vec{v}_2 = \hat{i}\times(\hat{i}+\hat{j}) = \hat{k}$$

Now
$$\vec{F} = -e(\vec{v}_3\times\vec{B}_1) = -e[\hat{k}\times(-\hat{k})] = 0$$

9. (b) If R_1 and R_2 are the radii of paths of charged particles, then

$2R_1 + d = 2R_2$. Also $R_1 = \dfrac{m_1 v}{qB}$ and $R_2 = \dfrac{m_2 v}{qB}$,

$$\therefore \quad d = \frac{|2(m_2 - m_1)v|}{|qB|}$$

10. (a) For zero electric field,
$$\vec{F}_e + \vec{F}_m = 0$$
or $q\vec{E} + q(\vec{v}_0\times\vec{B}) = 0$
or
$$v_0 = \frac{E_0}{B_0}$$

11. (b)
$$i = \frac{q}{T} = \frac{q\omega}{2\pi}$$
Now,
$$\tau = MB\sin\theta$$
$$= iAB\sin 90°$$
$$= \frac{q\omega}{2\pi}\times\pi a^2 B = \frac{q\omega a^2 B}{2}$$

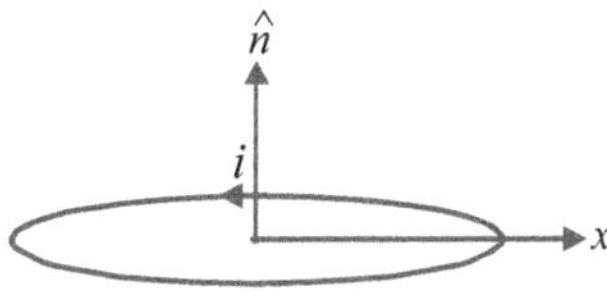

12. (d) The charge on the element, $dq = \dfrac{q}{\ell}dx$.

Current,
$$i = \frac{dq}{T} = \frac{q(dx)}{\ell}f$$

Now,
$$M = \int iA = \int_0^\ell \frac{q(dx)f}{\ell}\times\pi x^2$$
$$= \frac{\pi q f \ell^2}{3}$$

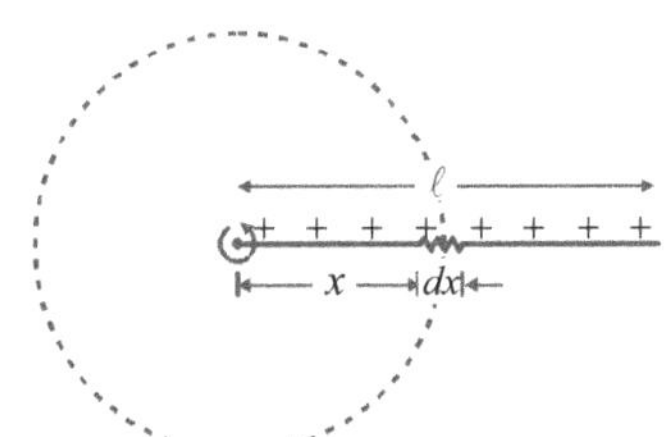

13. (d) Electric force on the particle, $F = Eq$, and

displacement $\quad s = \dfrac{1}{2}at^2 = \dfrac{1}{2}\left(\dfrac{Eq}{m}\right)t^2.$

Now, $\quad W = \Delta K,$

or $\quad Fs = \dfrac{1}{2}m\left(v_f^2 - v_i^2\right)$

or $Eq\times\dfrac{1}{2}\left(\dfrac{Eq}{m}\right)t^2 = \dfrac{1}{2}m[(2v_0)^2 - v_0^2]$

$$\therefore \quad t = \frac{\sqrt{3}\,mv_0}{qE}.$$

14. (c) Radius $\quad r = \dfrac{d}{2}$

$$= \frac{mv}{qB}$$

Also $\quad qV = \dfrac{1}{2}mv^2$ or $v = \sqrt{\dfrac{2qV}{m}}$

$$\therefore \quad \frac{d}{2} = \frac{m\left(\sqrt{\dfrac{2qV}{m}}\right)}{qB}$$

or $\quad m = \dfrac{qB^2 d^2}{8V}.$

15. (b) $\vec{B} = -c\hat{k}$, and $\vec{v} = v\cos 45°\hat{i} - v\sin 45°\hat{j} = \dfrac{v}{\sqrt{2}}\hat{i} - \dfrac{v}{\sqrt{2}}\hat{j}.$

Thus, $\quad \vec{F} = q(\vec{v}\times\vec{B})$

$$= q\left[\left(\frac{v}{\sqrt{2}}\hat{i} - \frac{v}{\sqrt{2}}\hat{j}\right)\times(-c\hat{k})\right]$$
$$= qcv\left[\frac{\hat{i}+\hat{j}}{\sqrt{2}}\right]$$

$$\therefore \quad \vec{a} = \left[\frac{\hat{i}+\hat{j}}{\sqrt{2}}\right].$$

16. (b) At $x = 2$, $y^2 = 2x = 2\times 2$ or $y = 2$.
Thus separation, $AB = 4$ cm
The force, $F = Bi\,(AB) = 4\times 2\times 4 = 32$ N.

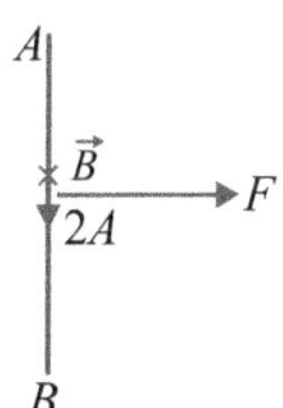

17. (c) Loop experiences the magnetic force due to radial component of magnetic field. Thus
$$F = (B\sin\theta)\times I\times \text{perimeter}$$
$$= B\sin\theta\times I\times 2\pi a.$$

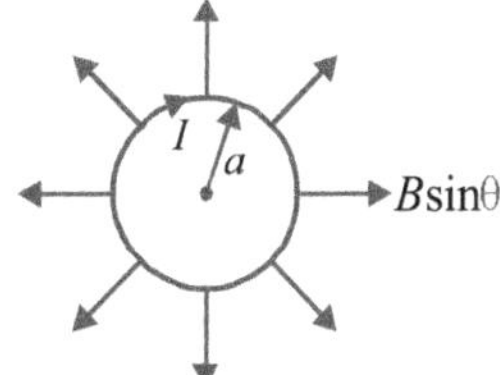

18. (a)
$$\vec{M} = iA(\cos 60^\circ \hat{i} - \sin 60^\circ \hat{j})$$
$$= 10 \times (10 \times 10 \times 10^{-4})\left(\frac{\hat{i}}{2} - \frac{\sqrt{3}\hat{j}}{2}\right)$$
$$= 0.05(\hat{i} - \sqrt{3}\hat{j}) \text{ A-m}^2$$

19. (a)
$$\vec{F}_m = \vec{F}_e$$
or $\quad q(\vec{v} \times \vec{B}) = q\vec{E}$
or $\quad \vec{v} \times \vec{B} = \vec{E}$
or $\quad \vec{v} = \dfrac{\vec{E} \times \vec{B}}{B^2}$.

20. (a) Forces of the different parts of the loop are shown in figure. The force on part RS is also F. The net force on the close loop is zero and so
$$F' = \sqrt{F^2 + F^2}$$
$$= \sqrt{2}F.$$

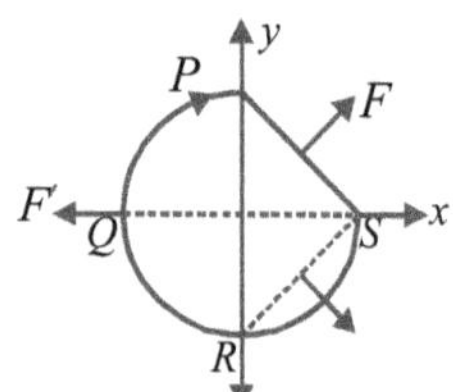

21. (b) Magnetic force on the wire
$$F = Bi\frac{\ell}{2}\sin\theta \approx Bi\frac{\ell}{2}\tan\theta$$
$$= Bi\frac{\ell}{2} \times \frac{\ell/2}{x}$$
$$= \frac{Bi\ell^2}{4x}$$

22. (c)
$$L = mvr = mv\left(\frac{mv}{qB}\right) = \frac{m^2v^2}{qB}$$
so
$$L_1 - L_2 = \frac{m^2}{qB}\left(v_1^2 - v_2^2\right)$$

23. (a)
$$r = \frac{mv}{qB}$$
$$\sin\theta = \frac{x}{r}$$
$$= \frac{\dfrac{mv}{\sqrt{2}qB}}{\dfrac{mv}{qB}} = \frac{1}{\sqrt{2}}$$
or $\quad \theta = \dfrac{\pi}{4}$

Time to complete the circle (2π), $T = \dfrac{2\pi m}{qB}$

$\therefore$ time taken to traverses $\dfrac{\pi}{4}$, $t = \dfrac{\pi m}{4qB}$

Time taken to travel horizontal distance
$$t_1 = \frac{\dfrac{mv}{\sqrt{2}qB}}{\dfrac{v}{\sqrt{2}}} = \frac{m}{qB}$$

Total time taken $= 2t + 2t_1$
$$= \frac{m}{2qB}(\pi + 4)$$

24. (d) $\quad F = B_0 i\,\ell, \ y = x^2$

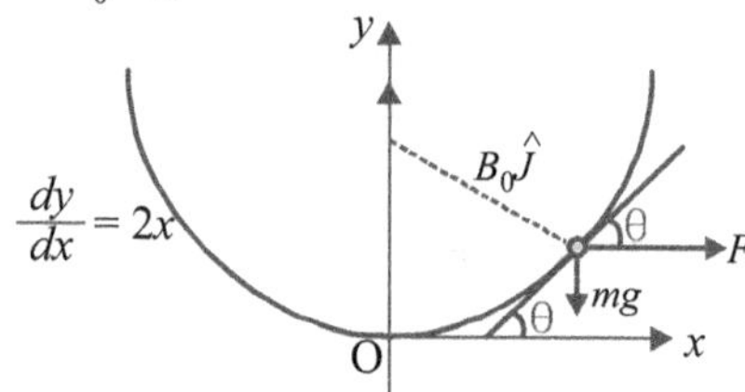

$$\frac{dy}{dx} = 2x$$

For equilibrium,
$$F\cos\theta = mg\sin\theta$$
or $\quad \tan\theta = \dfrac{F}{mg} = \dfrac{B_0 i\ell}{mg}$
or $\quad \dfrac{dy}{dx} = \dfrac{B_0 i\ell}{mg}$
or $\quad 2x = \dfrac{B_0 i\ell}{mg}$
or $\quad x = \dfrac{B_0 i\ell}{2mg}$
or $\quad \sqrt{y} = \dfrac{B_0 i\ell}{2mg}$
or $\quad y = \left(\dfrac{B_0 i\ell}{2mg}\right)^2$

25. (a)
$$F = Bi\ell$$
$$2T\sin\frac{\theta}{2} = F$$
or $\quad 2T\left(\dfrac{\theta}{2}\right) = Bi(r\theta)$
$\therefore \qquad T = Bir$

Now speed, $v = \sqrt{\dfrac{T}{m}}$
$$= \sqrt{\dfrac{Bir}{m}}$$

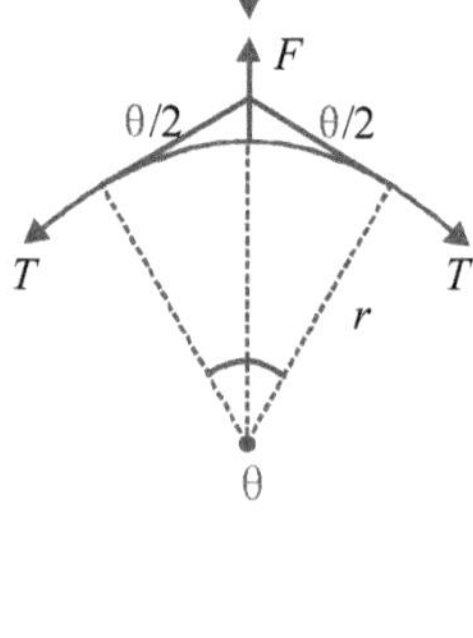

26. (b)

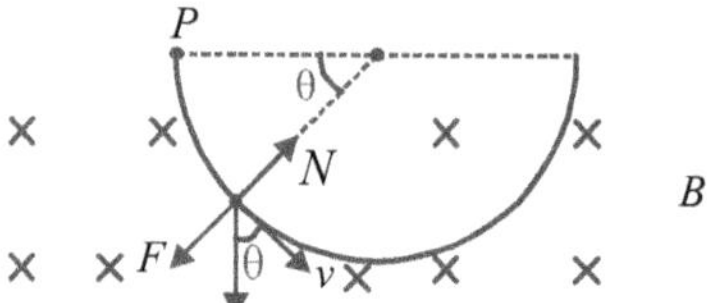

$$v = \sqrt{2gR\sin\theta}$$

and $\qquad F = qvB$

Now

$$N-(F+mg\sin\theta) = \frac{mv^2}{R}$$

$\therefore \qquad N = F + mg\sin\theta + \dfrac{mv^2}{R}$

$$= qB\sqrt{2gR\sin\theta} + mg\sin\theta + 2mg\sin\theta$$

$\therefore \qquad N = 3mg\sin\theta + qB\sqrt{2gR\sin\theta}$

27. (d)

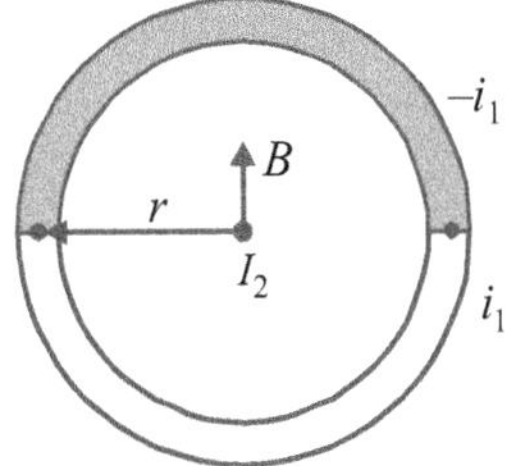

Magnetic field at the centre of the shell $= 2\dfrac{\mu_0 i_1}{\pi^2 r}$

Force per unit length of the wire

$$F = Bi_2 \times 1$$

$$= \left[2\frac{\mu_0 i_1 i_2}{\pi^2 r}\right]$$

28. (c)

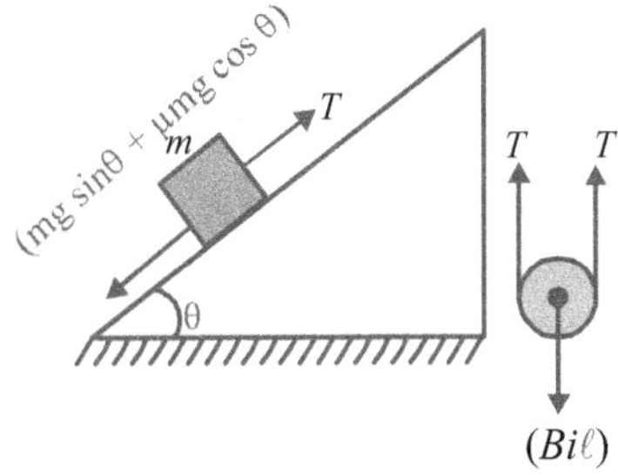

To just move the block up,

$$T = mg\sin\theta + \mu mg\cos\theta$$

and $\qquad 2T = Bi\ell$

$\therefore \qquad i = \left[\dfrac{2mg\sin\theta + 2\mu mg\cos\theta}{B\ell}\right]$

29. (b)

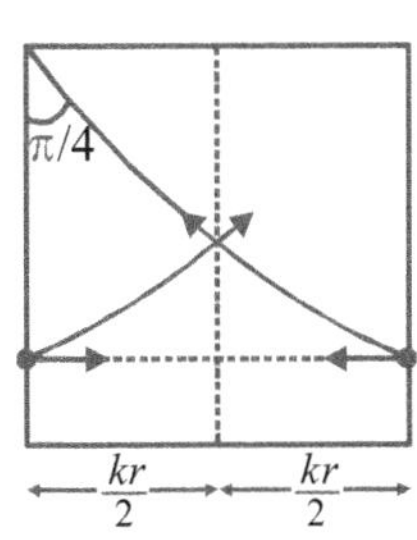

$$\sin\theta = \frac{x}{r}$$

or $\qquad \sin\dfrac{\pi}{4} = \dfrac{\frac{kr}{2}}{r}$

$\therefore \qquad k = \sqrt{2}$

30. (c) $\qquad \vec{F}_m = q\left(\vec{v}\times\vec{B}\right)$

$$= q\left(2\hat{i}+3\hat{j}+4\hat{k}\right)\times 2\hat{i}$$

$$= q\left(-6\hat{k}+8\hat{j}\right)$$

$$\vec{F}_m + \vec{F}_e = 0$$

$\therefore \qquad \vec{F}_e = \vec{F}_m$

$$= -q\left(-6\hat{k}+8\hat{j}\right)$$

After $\dfrac{\pi m}{qB} = \dfrac{T}{2}$, the direction of motion becomes opposite to initial and so applied field may be

$$\vec{E} = \left(-6\hat{i}+8\hat{j}\right) \text{ units}$$

31. (c) For wire not to slide on the rails,

$$f = F_{magnetic}$$

or $\qquad \mu mg = Bil$

$\therefore \qquad \mu = \dfrac{Bil}{mg}$

$$= \frac{B\left(at-bt^2\right)\ell}{mg}$$

For minimum value of μ, $\dfrac{d\mu}{dt} = 0$

or $\qquad a - 2bt = 0$

or $\qquad t = \dfrac{a}{2b}$

or $\qquad \mu_{min} = \dfrac{Ba^2\ell}{4bmg}$

32. (b)

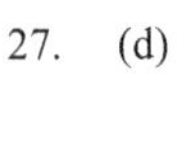

$$\sin\theta = \frac{\frac{r}{2}}{r} = \frac{1}{2}$$

or $\qquad \theta = \dfrac{\pi}{6}$ rad

So velocity of image of proton

$$\vec{v} = 6\cos\dfrac{\pi}{6}\hat{i} + 6\sin\dfrac{\pi}{6}\hat{j}$$

$$= 3\sqrt{3}\hat{i} + 3\hat{j} \text{ m/s}$$

Velocity of object w.r.t. minor (perpendicular to minor)

$$\vec{v}_{0\,\text{mirror}} = \left(3\sqrt{3}\,\hat{i} + 3\hat{j}\right) + \left(2\hat{j}\right)$$

$$= \left(3\sqrt{3}\hat{i} + 5\hat{j}\right) \text{ m/s}$$

Velocity of image w.r.t. mirror

$$= \left(3\sqrt{3}\hat{i} - 5\hat{j}\right) \text{ m/s}$$

Velocity of image w.r.t. ground observer

$$= \left(3\sqrt{3}\,\hat{i} - 5\hat{j}\right) - \left(2\hat{j}\right)$$

$$= \left(3\sqrt{3}\,\hat{i} - 7\hat{j}\right) \text{ m/s}$$

33. (b)
$$a_z = \dfrac{F_z}{m} = \dfrac{\vec{E}q}{m} = \dfrac{10q}{m}$$

Now $\qquad v^2 = 0 + 2az$

or $\qquad v = \sqrt{2az} = \sqrt{\dfrac{20qz}{m}}$

34. (c)
$$W = \Delta K$$

or $\qquad E_0 q \times b = \dfrac{1}{2}m\left(v_2^2 - v_1^2\right)$

or $\qquad 2E_0 qb = m\left(v_2^2 - v_1^2\right)$

Solutions EXERCISE-5.2

1. (b, d) Radius of charged particle in magnetic field,

$$r = \dfrac{mv}{qB}, \text{ and so}$$

$$r \propto (mv) \text{ and } r \propto \dfrac{1}{B}$$

2. (a, c) The charged particle at rest, experiences force due to electric field.

3. (b, c, d) For without change in velocity, either $\vec{E} = 0$, or $\vec{E} \neq 0$ and $\vec{B} \neq 0$, so that $F_e = F_m$.

4. (a, b) For without acceleration, velocity of the particle must be constant. For this $F_e = F_m$. The possible case may be shown in figure.

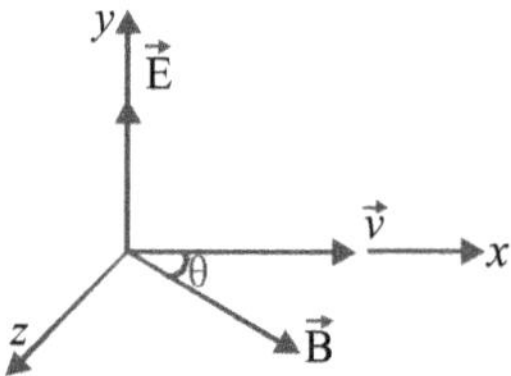

5. (a, c) If r is the radius of path, the

$$r = \ell = \dfrac{mv}{qB}$$

or $\qquad v = \dfrac{q\ell B}{m}$

For $v > \dfrac{q\ell B}{m}$, the particle will enter into region III.

For $v < \dfrac{q\ell B}{m}$, the particle follows the path as shown.

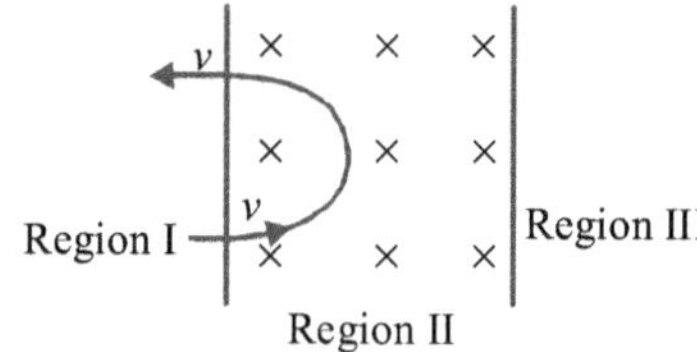

6. (a, b, d) The work is only done by electric field, and so

$$Eq \times 2a = \dfrac{1}{2}m\left[(2v)^2 - v^2\right]$$

or $\qquad E = \dfrac{3}{4}\dfrac{mv^2}{qa}.$

Rate of work done at P,

$$= Fv \cos 0°$$
$$= Eqv$$
$$= \dfrac{3}{4}\dfrac{mv^2}{qa} \times qv = \dfrac{3}{4}\dfrac{mv^3}{a}$$

Rate of work done at Q,

$$= F \times 2v \times \cos 90° = 0$$

Solutions EXERCISE-5.3

1. (d) Magnetic field can not change the speed, but can change the velocity, and so can cause acceleration.

2. (a) Because of random motion of the free electrons, the force on the electron is also randomly oriented and so net force on the conductor becomes zero.

3. (d) The magnetic force on the loop is only zero when it placed in uniform field.

4. (d) Magnetic field can not change the kinetic energy of the particle, because magnetic force is always perpendicular to its velocity vector.

5. (a) The mass of electron has relativity effect.

6. (c)

7. (d) The value of torque depends on θ. For $\theta = 0$, $\tau = MBx$ $\sin 0° = 0$.

8. (d) The magnetic force acts only on moving electrons, and so net force on the conductor is non-zero.

9. (d) If charged particle projected in the line of electric field, it goes undeviated. Or particle is projected in both the field such that $qE = qvB$, then it also goes undeviated.

10. (b) Self explanatory.

11. (a) The radius of path, $r = \dfrac{mv}{qB}$. As mass of electron is smaller than mass of proton, so radius of electron is smaller.

12. (a) Use Fleming's left hand rule.

13. (b) For $v = \dfrac{E}{B}$, $F_m = F_e$ or $qvB = Eq$. For $v < \dfrac{E}{B}$, magnetic force F_m becomes smaller than electric force.

14. (d) In magnetic field, the speed of charged particles remains constant.

Solutions EXERCISE-5.4

Passage for Q. 1 to Q. 3

1. (a) By Fleming's left hand rule, the force on electrons will be along east.

2. (d)
$$\frac{1}{2}mv^2 = K$$

or
$$v = \sqrt{\frac{2K}{m}} = \sqrt{\frac{2 \times 12 \times 10^3 \times 1.6 \times 10^{-19}}{9.1 \times 15^{31}}}$$
$$= 6.48 \times 10^{+7} \text{ m/s.}$$

Radius of path, $r = \dfrac{mv}{qB} = \dfrac{9.1 \times 10^{-31} \times 6.48 \times 10^7}{1.6 \times 10^{-19} \times 55 \times 10^{-6}}$
$$= 6.7 \text{ m}$$

Acceleration of the electron
$$a = \frac{v^2}{r} = \frac{(6.48 \times 10^7)^2}{6.7}$$
$$= 6.23 \times 10^{14} \text{ m/s}^2$$

3. (b) If y is the required deflection, then
$$(r - y)^2 + x^2 = r^2$$
Here, $x = 20$ cm, and $r = 6.7$ m.
After substituting the values and simplifying, we get
$$y = 2.98 \text{ mm}$$

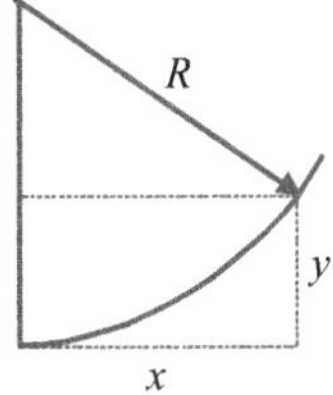

Passage for Q. 4 to Q. 6

4. (a)
$$v = \sqrt{\frac{2K}{m}}$$
$$= \sqrt{\frac{2 \times 3.2 \times 10^{-19} \times 100 \times 10^3}{3.92 \times 10^{-25}}}$$
$$= 4.04 \times 10^5 \text{ m/s}$$

Now $r = \dfrac{mv}{qB}$

$\therefore$ $B = \dfrac{mv}{qr} = \dfrac{3.92 \times 10^{-25} \times 4.04 \times 10^5}{3.20 \times 10^{-19} \times 1}$
$$= 495 \times 10^{-3} \text{ T.}$$

5. (a) The number of ions in the machine
$$= \frac{100 \times 10^{-6}}{3.92 \times 10^{-25}} = 25.51 \times 10^{19}$$

Current, $i = \dfrac{q}{t} = \dfrac{25.51 \times 10^{19} \times 3.20 \times 10^{-19}}{3600}$
$$= 22.7 \times 10^{-3} \text{ A.}$$

6. (c) Charge flows in one hour,
$$q = 25.51 \times 10^{19} \times 3.20 \times 10^{-19}$$
$$= 81.6 \text{ C.}$$
Now work done, $W = Vq$
$$= (100 \times 10^3) \times 81.6$$
$$= 8.17 \times 10^6 \text{ J.}$$

Passage for Q. 7 to Q. 9 :

7.

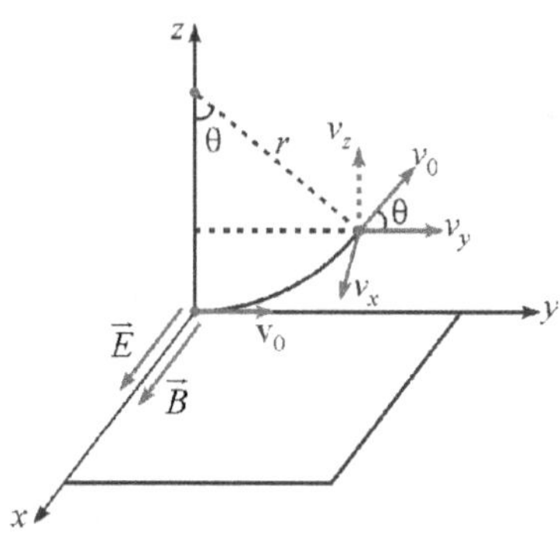

$$\theta = \omega t = \frac{Bqt}{m}$$

$$v_x = a_x\, t = \frac{Eq}{m}t\ .$$

$$v_y = v_0 \cos\theta = v_0 \cos\left(\frac{Bqt}{m}\right)$$

and $\quad v_z = v_0 \sin\theta = v_0 \sin\left(\frac{Bqt}{m}\right).$

Also $\vec{v} = v_x\,\hat{i} + v_y\,\hat{j} + v_z\hat{k}$.]

8. (b)

9. (b)

Passage for Q. 10 to Q. 12 :

See examples.

13. **A-p, q, r, s; B-p, q, s; C-s; D-r**

14. **A-q; B-r; C-p; D-s**

$$\int dF = \int I\vec{d\ell} \times \vec{B};\ \ \vec{\tau} = \vec{\mu} \times \vec{B}$$

Solutions EXERCISE-5.5

1. The situation is shown in figure.

Given, $\qquad \dfrac{1}{2}mv^2 = qV$

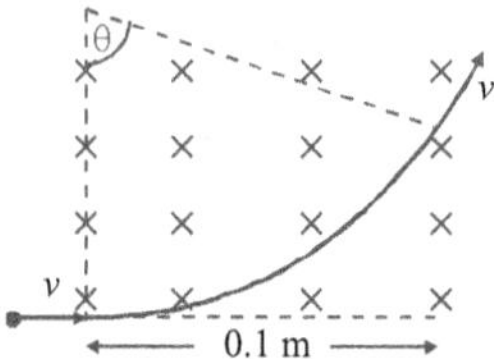

∴ $\qquad v = \sqrt{\dfrac{2qV}{m}}$

$$= \sqrt{\frac{2\times(2\times1.6\times10^{-19})\times10^4}{6.4\times10^{-27}}}$$

$$= 10^6 \text{ m/s}$$

Radius of path, $\qquad r = \dfrac{mv}{qB}$

$$= \frac{6.4\times10^{-27}\times10^6}{2\times(1.6\times10^{-19})\times0.1}$$

$$= 0.2 \text{ m}$$

∴ $\qquad \sin\theta = \dfrac{x}{r} = \dfrac{0.1}{0.2} = \dfrac{1}{2}$

or $\qquad \theta = 30°.$ **Ans.**

2. Radius of the circle, $\qquad r = \dfrac{mv}{qB}$

$$= \frac{(2\times10^{-5})\times(4.8)}{2\times10^{-3}\times1.2}$$

$$= 4\times10^{-2} \text{ m}$$

By lens formula, $\qquad \dfrac{1}{v} - \dfrac{1}{-18} = \dfrac{1}{+12}$

or $\qquad v = 36 \text{ cm}$

Now $\qquad \dfrac{I}{O} = \dfrac{v}{u}$

∴ $\qquad I = \dfrac{v}{u}O = \dfrac{36}{18}\times4 = 8 \text{ cm}$ **Ans.**

3. Electric field, $\qquad E = \dfrac{V}{\ell} = \dfrac{100t}{\ell}$

The acceleration of electron,

$$a = \frac{Ee}{m} = \frac{(100t/\ell)e}{m}$$

or $\qquad \dfrac{dv}{dt} = \dfrac{100t\,e}{m\ell}$

or $\qquad \displaystyle\int_0^v dv = \int_0^t \dfrac{100te}{m\ell}dt$

∴ $\qquad v = \dfrac{50e}{m\ell}t^2$ $\qquad$ ...(i)

Again $\qquad \dfrac{dx}{dt} = \dfrac{50e}{m\ell}t^2$

∴ $\qquad \displaystyle\int_0^x dx = \int_0^t \dfrac{50e}{m\ell}t^2 dt$

or $\qquad x = \dfrac{50et^3}{3m\ell}$ $\qquad$ ...(ii)

For $\qquad x = \ell$, we have

$$\ell = \frac{50et^3}{3m\ell}$$

∴ $\qquad t = \left[\dfrac{3m\ell^2}{50e}\right]^{1/3}$

Substituting this value in equation (i), we get

$$v = \frac{50e}{m\ell}\left[\frac{3m\ell^2}{50e}\right]^{2/3} = 16 \text{ km/s} \quad \textbf{Ans.}$$

4. If v is the velocity of the electron, then

$$\frac{1}{2}mv^2 = eV$$

$$\therefore \qquad v = \sqrt{\frac{2eV}{m}}$$

$$\text{Pitch} = v\cos\alpha \times T = v\cos\alpha \times \frac{2\pi m}{eB}$$

$$= \frac{2\pi m}{eB}\sqrt{\frac{2eV}{m}}\cos\alpha$$

$$= 2\pi\sqrt{\frac{2mV}{eB^2}}\cos\alpha \qquad \textbf{\textit{Ans.}}$$

5. Magnetic force,
$$\vec{F} = q(\vec{v}\times\vec{B})$$

or
$$6.4\times10^{-19}\hat{k} = -e\left[(2.0\hat{i}+4.0\hat{j})\times(B_x\hat{j}+3B_y\hat{j})\right]$$

$$\therefore \qquad B_x = -2.0 \text{ T} \qquad \textit{Ans.}$$

6. The tension in the leads will be zero, if

weight of wire = magnetic force in upwards direction

or
$$mg = Bi\ell$$

or
$$i = \frac{mg}{B\ell} = 467\text{mA} \text{ towards right.}$$

Solutions EXERCISE-5.6

1.
$$\vec{F} = q=(\vec{v}\times\vec{B})$$

$$= 1\times10^{-6}[2\times10^6\hat{i}\times(0.20\hat{j}+0.40\hat{k})]$$

$$= -0.8\hat{j}+0.4\hat{k} \ N$$

2. We know that,
$$P = \sqrt{2mK}$$

We have,
$$r = \frac{mv}{qB} = \frac{P}{qB} = \frac{\sqrt{2mK}}{qB}$$

$$\therefore \qquad \frac{r_p}{r_d} = \frac{\sqrt{2mK}/qB}{\sqrt{2(2m)K}/qB} = \frac{1}{\sqrt{2}}$$

and
$$\frac{r_p}{r_\alpha} = \frac{\sqrt{2mK}/qB}{\sqrt{2(4m)K}/(2q)B} = 1 \qquad \textbf{\textit{Ans.}}$$

3. For the given condition electric force on the particle is equal to magnetic force. Thus

$$qvB = qE$$

$$\therefore \qquad E = vB$$

$$= \left[\frac{rqB}{m}\right]B$$

$$= \frac{0.05\times20\times10^{-6}\times1^2}{20\times10^{-9}}$$

$$= 0.5 \text{ V/m.} \qquad \textbf{\textit{Ans.}}$$

4. We have
$$r = \frac{mv}{qB}$$

$$\therefore \qquad m = \frac{rqB}{v}$$

or
$$m = \frac{0.015\times1.6\times10^{-19}\times0.5}{6.0\times10^4}$$

$$= 2\times10^{-26} \text{ kg}$$

$$\therefore \qquad A = \frac{m}{1.6\times10^{-27}} = 12.5$$

It will be 12. So the isotopes are of mass number 12 and 14. These are ^{12}C and ^{14}C.

5. (a) The radius of the path

$$r = \frac{mv}{qB} = \frac{(1.6\times10^{-27})\times(1\times10^7)}{(1.6\times10^{-19})\times1} = 0.1 \text{ m}$$

$$EF = 2r\sin45° = 2\times0.1\times\frac{1}{\sqrt{2}}$$

$$= 0.14 \text{ m} \qquad \textbf{\textit{Ans.}}$$

(b) Time period, $T = \dfrac{2\pi m}{qB} = \dfrac{2\pi\times1.6\times10^{-27}}{1.6\times10^{-19}\times1} = 6.28\times10^{-18}\text{s}$

When magnetic field is reverse in direction, the particle covers angle 270° inside magnetic field.

$$\therefore \qquad t = \frac{3T}{4} = 4.7\times10^{-8} \text{ s} \qquad \textbf{\textit{Ans.}}$$

6. Given, $\vec{E} = -E\hat{j}$ and $\vec{B} = -B\hat{k}$.

The net force of the electron

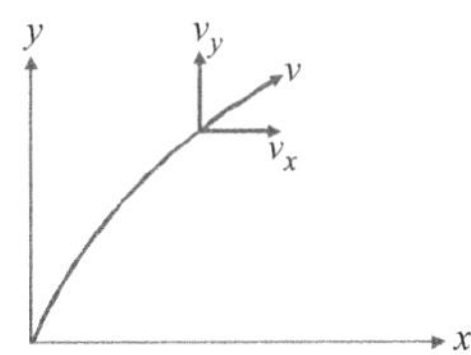

$$\vec{F} = q\vec{E}+q(\vec{v}\times\vec{B})$$

$$= (-e)(-E\hat{j})+(-e)[(v_x\hat{i}+v_y\hat{j})\times(-B\hat{k})]$$

$$= eE\hat{j}-ev_xB\hat{j}+ev_yB\hat{i}$$

$$= ev_yB\hat{i}+e(E-v_xB)\hat{j}$$

The acceleration
$$\vec{a} = \frac{\vec{F}}{m} = \frac{ev_yB}{m}\hat{i}-\frac{e}{m}(E-v_xB)\hat{j}$$

$$\therefore \qquad \vec{a}_x = \frac{dv_x}{dt} = \frac{ev_yB}{m} \qquad \text{... (i)}$$

and
$$a_y = \frac{dV_y}{dt} = \frac{e}{m}(E-v_xB) \qquad \text{... (ii)}$$

Differentiating equation (ii) w.r.t , we get

$$\frac{d^2 v_y}{dt^2} = \frac{e}{m}\left(\frac{dv_x}{dt}\right)B \qquad \dots\text{(iii)}$$

Now from equations (i) and (iii), we have

$$\frac{d^2 v_y}{dt^2} = -\frac{e}{m}\left(\frac{ev_y}{m}\right)B = -\left(\frac{eB}{m}\right)^2 v_y \ \dots\text{(iv)}$$

This equation is similar to

$$\frac{d^2 x}{dt^2} = -\omega^2 x$$

$$\therefore \qquad \omega = \left(\frac{eB}{m}\right)$$

and $\qquad v_y = A\sin(\omega t + \theta)$

At $t = 0$, $\qquad v_y = 0$

$\therefore \qquad 0 = A\sin(0 + \theta)$

or $\qquad \theta = 0$

Also $\qquad \dfrac{dv_y}{dt} = \omega A\cos(\omega t + 0) \qquad \dots\text{(v)}$

In eq (ii) at t = 0, $v_x = 0$,

$$\therefore \qquad \frac{dv_y}{dt} = \frac{eE}{m}$$

From equation (v), At t = 0,

$$\frac{dv_y}{dt} = \omega A \qquad \dots\text{(vi)}$$

$$\therefore \qquad \omega A = \frac{eE}{m}$$

or $\qquad A = \dfrac{eE}{\omega m} = \dfrac{eE}{\left(\dfrac{eB}{m}\right)m} = \dfrac{E}{B}$

Thus, $\qquad v_y = \dfrac{E}{B}\sin\omega t \qquad \dots\text{(vii)}$

For $v_y = 0$,

or $\qquad 0 = \dfrac{E}{B}\sin\omega t$

$\therefore \quad \omega t = 0$, or $\omega t = 0, \pi, 2\pi$

For first time, $\quad t = \dfrac{\pi}{\omega}$

Now from equation (vii), we have

$$\frac{dy}{dt} = \frac{E}{B}\sin\omega t$$

or $\qquad \displaystyle\int_0^t dy = \frac{E}{B}\int_0^{\pi/\omega}\sin\omega t\,dt$

or $\qquad y = \dfrac{E}{B}\left|\dfrac{-\cos\omega t}{\omega}\right|_0^{\pi/\omega}$

$$= \frac{E}{B\omega}[-\cos\pi + \cos 0]$$

$$= \frac{2E}{B\omega} = \frac{2E}{B(eB)/m} = \frac{2Em}{eB^2}. \qquad \textbf{\textit{Ans.}}$$

7.   The force on each element of loop in uniform magnetic field is zero. So there net is found equal to zero.

8.
$$\vec{F} = i\vec{\ell} \times \vec{B}$$

$$= i[\ell\hat{i} \times B_0(\hat{i} + \hat{j} + \hat{k})] = B_0 i\ell(\hat{k} - \hat{j})$$

or $\qquad F = \sqrt{2}\,B_0 i\ell. \qquad \textbf{\textit{Ans.}}$

9.   The force on vertical sides of the loop is cancelled out. The force on lower horizontal direction change by $= -Bi\ell - Bi\ell = -2Bi\ell$.**Ans.**

10. (a)   The magnetic field due to wire loop

$$\vec{B} = \frac{\mu_0 (1/3)I}{2a}\hat{k} - \frac{\mu_0}{4\pi}\cdot\frac{I}{a\cos 60°}[\sin 60° \times 2]\hat{k}$$

$$= \frac{\mu_0 I}{2a}\left[\frac{1}{3} - \frac{\sqrt{3}}{\pi}\right]\hat{k} = -\frac{\mu_0 I}{2a}(0.222)\hat{k}$$

$$= -\frac{\mu_0 I}{a}(0.11\hat{k})$$

Given, $\qquad \vec{v} = v\cos 60°\hat{i} + v\sin 60°\hat{j}$

$$= \left(\frac{v}{2}\hat{i} + \frac{v\sqrt{3}}{2}\hat{j}\right)$$

Force $\qquad \vec{F} = Q(\vec{v} \times \vec{B})$

$$= Q\left[\left(\frac{v}{2}\hat{i} + \frac{v\sqrt{3}}{2}\hat{j}\right) \times \left(\frac{-\mu_0 I}{a}(0.11\hat{k})\right)\right]$$

$$= \frac{Qv\mu_0 I}{a}\left[\left(\frac{\hat{i}}{2} + \frac{\sqrt{3}}{2}\hat{j}\right) \times (-0.11\hat{k})\right]$$

$$= Q\frac{v\mu_0 I}{a}\left[\frac{+0.11}{2}\hat{j} - \frac{\sqrt{3}}{2} \times 0.11\hat{i}\right]$$

or $\qquad F = \dfrac{0.109\,\mu_0 IQv}{a}$

$\therefore \qquad a = \left[\dfrac{0.109\,\mu_0 IQv}{ma}\right] \qquad \textbf{\textit{Ans.}}$

(b) $\qquad \vec{\tau} = i\vec{A} \times \vec{B}$

$$= i(\text{Area of loop }\hat{k} \times \vec{B})$$

$$= 0.6136\ a^2 IB \text{ along y-axis} \quad \textbf{Ans.}$$

11.   The area of the coil, $A = \dfrac{1}{2} \times a \times a\sin 60°$

$$= \frac{1}{2} \times 0.02 \times 0.02 \times \frac{\sqrt{3}}{2}$$

$$= 1.7\sqrt{3} \times 10^{-4} \ \text{m}^2$$

Torque, $\quad \tau \ = \ iAB\sin\theta$

$$= 0.1 \times \sqrt{3} \times 10^{-4} \times 5 \times 10^{-2} \sin 90^\circ$$

$$= 5\sqrt{3} \times 10^{-7} \ \text{N-m} \qquad \textbf{\textit{Ans.}}$$

12. **(a)** Given, $\quad 2\pi R \ = \ L$

$$\therefore \quad R \ = \ \frac{L}{2\pi}$$

The area of the loop, $\quad A \ = \quad \pi R^2 = \pi \left[\frac{L}{2\pi}\right]^2 = \frac{L^2}{4\pi}$

Torque, $\quad \tau \ = \ iAB$

$$= \ i \times \frac{L^2}{4\pi} B = \frac{BiL^2}{4\pi} \ \text{N-m} \qquad \textbf{\textit{Ans.}}$$

(b) For square of side $a, a \ = \ L/4$

Area, $\quad A \ = \ a^2 = \frac{L}{4} \times \frac{L}{4} = \frac{L^2}{16}$

Torque $\quad \tau \ = \ iAB$

$$= \ i \frac{L^2}{16} \times B$$

$$= \ \frac{BiL^2}{16} \ \text{N - m} \qquad \textbf{\textit{Ans.}}$$

13. $\frac{M}{L}$ for a uniformly charged disc is found equal to $\frac{q}{2m}$. From the sphere, take a disc of volume dV, so we can write

$$\frac{M}{L} \ = \ \frac{\left[\dfrac{q}{(4/3)\pi R^3}\right] dV}{2\left[\dfrac{m}{(4/3)\pi R^3}\right] dV} = \frac{q}{2m}.$$

Clearly for the sphere of total charge q and mass m

$$\vec{M} \ = \ \frac{q}{2m} \vec{L}.$$

14. For constant speed, net force on the particle is zero. So

$$\vec{F} \ = \ 0 = q(\vec{E} + \vec{v} \times \vec{B})$$

or $\quad 0 \ = \ +e[\vec{E} + 50\hat{i} \times 2 \times 10^{-3}\hat{j}]$

or $\quad 0 \ = \ [\vec{E} + 0.10\hat{k}]$

$$\therefore \quad \vec{E} \ = \ -0.10\hat{k} \ V/m \qquad \textbf{\textit{Ans.}}$$

15. **(a)** $\quad M \ = \ i(A_1 + A_2)$

$$= \ 2.86 \ A \ \text{m}^2$$

(b) $\quad M \ = \ i(A_2 - A_1)$

$$= \ 1.10 \ \text{A- m}^2$$

16. If $\boldsymbol{v}$ is the speed of the electron, then

$$\frac{1}{2}mv^2 \ = \ K$$

$$\therefore \quad v \ = \ \sqrt{\frac{2K}{m}}$$

We have $\quad r \ = \ d = \frac{mv}{eB}$

$$\therefore \quad B \ = \ \frac{mv}{ed} = \frac{m\sqrt{\dfrac{2K}{m}}}{ed}$$

$$= \ \sqrt{\frac{2mK}{e^2 d^2}}$$

Thus to prevent the beam from hitting, we have

$$B \ \geq \ \sqrt{\frac{2mK}{e^2 d^2}}.$$

17. The magnetic field can be resolved into two components; B_x and B_y, These are

$$B_x \ = \ b\sin\theta \ \text{and} \ B_y = B\cos\theta$$

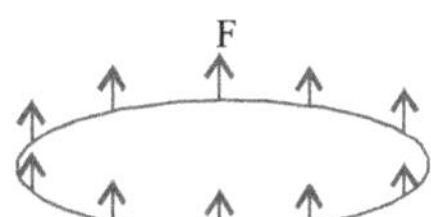

The force due to Bx is

$$F \ = \ \int_0^{2\pi a} B_x i dl$$

$$= \ B_x \times 2\pi a i$$

$$= \ 2\pi a i B \sin\theta$$

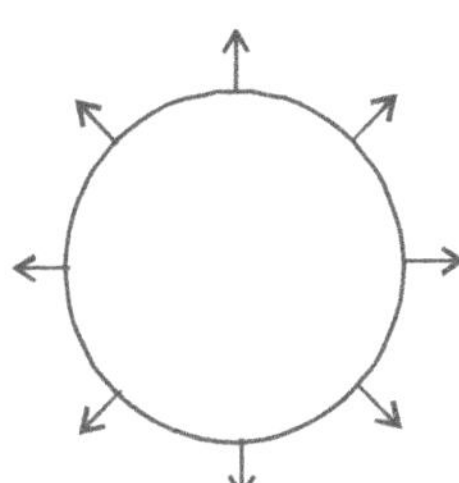

The force due to B_y is zero.

18. The area of loop, $A = 0.1 \times 0.05 = 5 \times 10^{-3} m^2$

The torque, $\quad \tau \ = \ NiAB\sin\theta$

$$= \ 20 \times 0.10 \times (5 \times 10^{-3}) \times 0.5 \sin 60^\circ$$

$$= \ 4.3 \times 10^{-3} \ \text{N-m} \qquad \textbf{\textit{Ans.}}$$

19. We know that

$$\frac{F_m}{F_e} = \frac{v^2}{e^2}$$

$$= \frac{(300\times10^3)^2}{(3\times10^8)^2} = 1\times10^{-6} \qquad \textbf{Ans.}$$

20. The force between wire and loop

$$F = F_1 - F_2$$

$$= \frac{\mu_0}{2\pi}\left[\frac{(30\times20)\times L}{a} - \frac{(30\times20)\times L}{(a+b)}\right]$$

$$= 3.2 \text{ mN} \qquad \textbf{Ans.}$$

21. For the equilibrium of the cylinder, we have

$$\tau_{\text{magnetic}} = \tau_{\text{weight}}$$

$$NiAB\sin\theta = mg\sin\theta\times R$$

$$\therefore \quad i = \frac{mgR}{NAB}$$

$$= \frac{0.25\times9.8\times R}{10\times(L\times2R)\times0.5}$$

$$= 2.45 \text{ A} \qquad \textbf{Ans.}$$

22. The given loop can be spitited into two loops of area,

$$A_1 = 0.20 \times 0.1 = 0.02 \text{ m}^2$$

and

$$A_2 = 0.20 \times 0.05 = 0.01 \text{ m}^2$$

The net magnetic moment

$$\vec{M} = i[A_1(-\hat{k}) + A_2\hat{j}]$$

$$= 2[0.02(-\hat{k}) + 0.01\hat{j}]$$

$$= [0.02\hat{j} - 0.04\hat{k}] \text{ A-m}^2 \qquad \textbf{Ans.}$$

✯ ✯ ✯

Magnetic Effect of Current (395-448)

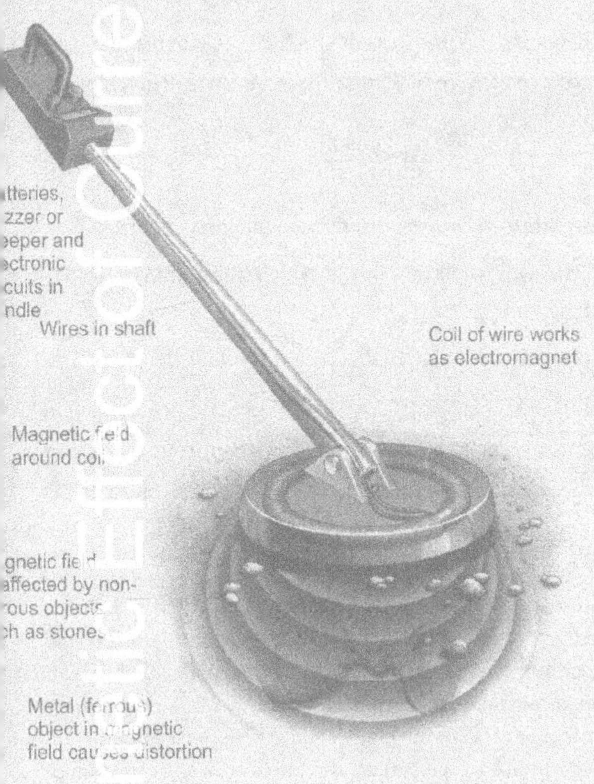

6.1 MAGNETIC FIELD OF MOVING CHARGE

We know that a point charge q, at rest in the observer's inertial frame, produces an electric field along the radius vector and is given by

$$\vec{E} = \left(\frac{1}{4\pi\,\epsilon_0}\right)\frac{q}{r^3}\,\vec{r}.$$

If the charge is moving relative to the observer's inertial frame, it produces a magnetic field in addition to electric field. The magnitude of which is proportional to the speed of the charge relative to the observer provided ($v < c$). The magnetic field vector $\vec{B}$ at the point P, a distant $\vec{r}$ from the charge q moving with a velocity $\vec{v}$ is found to be

$$\vec{B} = \left(\frac{\mu_0}{4\pi}\right)\frac{q}{r^3}(\vec{v}\times\vec{r}). \quad \dots(1)$$

The direction of $\vec{B}$ is thus perpendicular to the plane of $\vec{v}$ and $\vec{r}$. It is in the direction of advance of a right handed screw rotated from $\vec{v}$ to $\vec{r}$. Its magnitude is given by

$$B = \left(\frac{\mu_0}{4\pi}\right)\frac{qv\sin\theta}{r^2} \quad \dots(2)$$

The following points should be remembered regarding with the magnetic field :

1. The magnetic field $\vec{B}$ is zero at all points on a line on which charge moves. That is when $\theta = 0$ or $\theta = 180°$, $\vec{B} = 0$.

2. It is maximum in the plane perpendicular to the $\vec{v}$ and through the charge, as $\sin\theta = 1$, at all points in this plane :

3. $\vec{B}$ remains unaltered in magnitude at all points on the circumference of circle passing through P and lying in a plane perpendicular to $\vec{v}$ with its centre on the velocity direction.

4. The direction of $\vec{B}$ is given by either :
   (a) **Maxwell's right hand screw rule :** If the direction of current through the conductor or the direction of velocity of positive charge is represented by the linear motion of the screw motion, then the direction of the magnetic field can be represented by the direction of rotation of the screw.
   (b) **Right hand claps rule :** If a current carrying conductor is clapsed in the right hand so that the thumb indicates the current direction, then the direction of the magnetic field is represented by the finger tips round the wire.

Electromagnetic field

So far, we have considered electric and magnetic fields separately, without establishing any clear relation between them. This could be done only because the two fields were static. In other cases, however, it is impossible. It will be shown that electric and magnetic fields must always be considered together as a single total electromagnetic field. In other words, it turns out that electric and magnetic fields are in certain sense the components of a single physical object which we call the **electromagnetic field**. The division of the electromagnetic field into electric and magnetic fields is to relative nature since it depends to a very large extent to the reference system in which the phenomenon are considered.

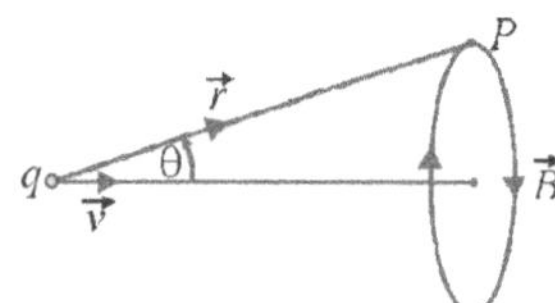

Fig. 6.1

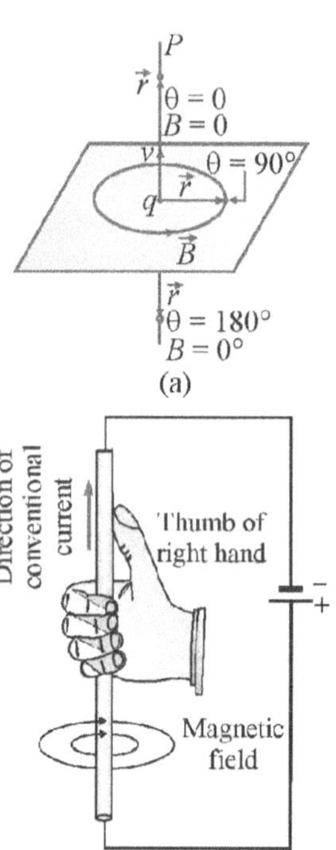

Fig. 6.2

Force between moving charges

The force acting on a charge q_2, moving with velocity v_2 in a magnetic field produced by charge q_1 moving with a velocity v_1 is

$$\vec{F}_{21} = q_2(\vec{v}_2 \times \vec{B}_1)$$

$$= q_2\left[\vec{v}_2 \times \frac{\mu_0 q_1}{4\pi r^3}(\vec{v}_1 \times \vec{r})\right]$$

$$= \frac{\mu_0}{4\pi}\frac{q_1 q_2}{r^3}[\vec{v}_2 \times (\vec{v}_1 \times \vec{r})].$$

The magnitude of force which they exert on each other

$$F_m = \frac{\mu_0}{4\pi}\frac{q_1 q_2 v_1 v_2}{r^2}$$

For

$$v_1 = v_2 = v$$

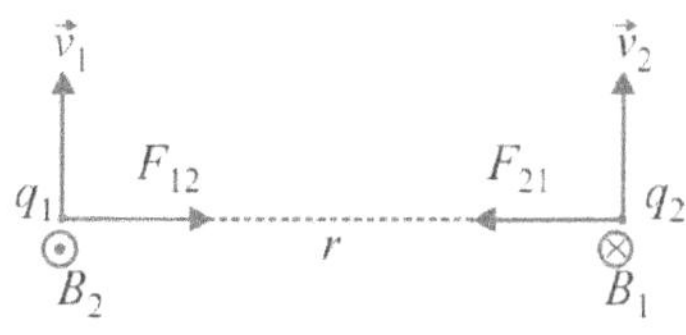

Fig. 6.3

$$F_m = \frac{\mu_0}{4\pi}\frac{q_1 q_2}{r^2}v^2 \qquad .....(i)$$

In addition to the magnitude force, there is an electric force between them, whose magnitude is given by

$$F_e = \frac{1}{4\pi \in_0}\frac{q_1 q_2}{r^2}. \qquad ......(ii)$$

This force is of repulsive nature. On dividing equation (i) by (ii), we have

$$\frac{F_m}{F_e} = v^2 \mu_0 \in_0$$

As

$$c = \sqrt{\frac{1}{\mu_0 \in_0}}.$$

$$\therefore \qquad \frac{F_m}{F_e} = \frac{v^2}{c^2}. \qquad .....(3)$$

Since $v < c$, and so $F_m < F_e$. As $F_m < F_e$, so the net force between the charges is of repulsive nature.

6.2 THE BIOT SAVARTS LAW

Biot-Savarts law is the fundamental law of the magnetics. It gives the magnetic field by a small current element and is based on the experimental facts. Let us consider a small element $d\vec{\ell}$ of a wire of cross-sectional area A carrying current i. If n is the number of charge carries per unit volume, each of charge q and moving with a drift velocity $\vec{v}_d$, then

$$i = neAv_d$$

The quantity of charge flowing in time dt,

$$dq = idt = neAv_d(dt)$$

Since $v_d(dt) = d\ell$, $\therefore$

$$dq = neAd\ell.$$

The magnetic field due to the current element $d\vec{\ell}$ at any point P at a distance $\vec{r}$

$$d\vec{B} = \frac{\mu_0}{4\pi}\frac{dq(\vec{v}_d \times \vec{r})}{r^3}$$

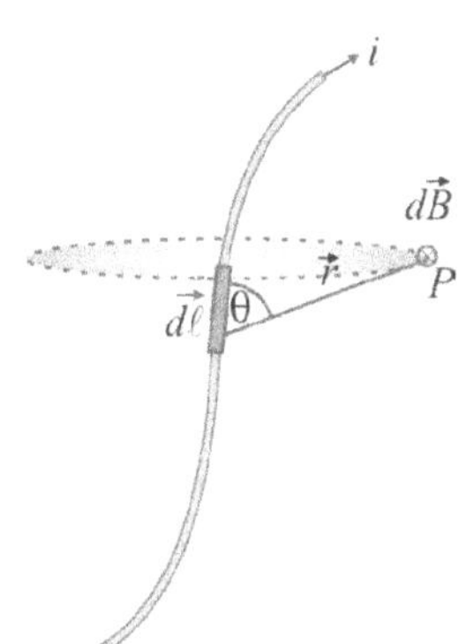

Fig. 6.4

$$= \frac{\mu_0}{4\pi} \frac{(neAd\ell)(\vec{v}_d \times \vec{r})}{r^3}$$

$$= \frac{\mu_0}{4\pi}(neAv_d)\frac{(d\vec{\ell} \times \vec{r})}{r^3}$$

or $$d\vec{B} = \frac{\mu_0}{4\pi}\frac{id\vec{\ell} \times \vec{r}}{r^3} \qquad \ldots(1)$$

This is called Biot-Savarts law.

The field due to the whole current carrying conductor is given by

$$\vec{B} = \int d\vec{B}$$

or $$\vec{B} = \frac{\mu_0}{4\pi}\int\frac{i(d\vec{\ell} \times \vec{r})}{r^3} = \frac{\mu_0}{4\pi}\frac{i\vec{\ell} \times \vec{r}}{r^3} \qquad \ldots(2)$$

Magnetic field due to a straight current carrying conductor

Consider a straight wire carrying current i. Its ends subtend angles θ_1 and θ_2 at point P at which field is to be determined.

Take a small element $d\vec{\ell}$ of the wire at a distance ℓ from O. The magnetic field due to element is

$$dB = \frac{\mu_0}{4\pi}\frac{id\ell\sin(90° + \theta)}{x^2} \qquad \ldots(i)$$

The direction of field at P is perpendicular to the plane of the diagram and going into it. The direction of the field is the same for all elements of the wire and hence net field due to the wire is obtained by integrating equation (i).

From the diagram, $$\frac{\ell}{r} = \tan\theta$$

or $$\ell = r\tan\theta$$

and $$d\ell = r\sec^2\theta d\theta.$$

Putting in equation (i),

$$dB = \frac{\mu_0}{4\pi}\frac{i(r\sec^2\theta d\theta)}{x^2}\cos\theta$$

Also $$\frac{x}{r} = \sec\theta \text{ or } x = r\sec\theta$$

$$\therefore \quad dB = \frac{\mu_0}{4\pi}\frac{i}{r}\cos\theta d\theta$$

Total field $$B = \frac{\mu_0}{4\pi}\frac{i}{r}\int_{-\theta_2}^{\theta_1}\cos\theta d\theta$$

or $$B = \frac{\mu_0}{4\pi}\frac{i}{r}(\sin\theta_1 + \sin\theta_2)$$

We can draw magnetic field lines in the same way that of electric field lines. A tangent to a magnetic field line gives the direction of the magnetic field existing at that point. For a long straight wire, the field lines are circles with their centres on the wire.

Fig. 6.5

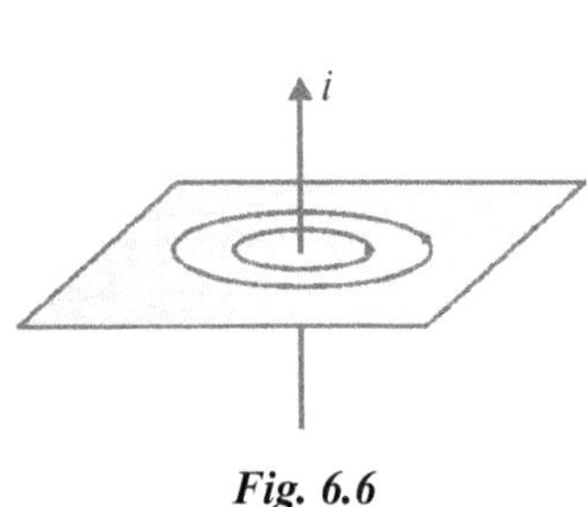

Fig. 6.6

Special cases :

(a) Field due to a long straight wire

$$\theta_1 = \frac{\pi}{2} \text{ and } \theta_2 = \frac{\pi}{2}$$

$$\therefore \quad B = \frac{\mu_0}{2\pi} \cdot \frac{i}{r}$$

(b) Field along the end of the wire

$$\theta_1 = 0 \text{ and } \theta_2 = \pi/2$$

$$\therefore \quad B = \frac{\mu_0}{4\pi} \cdot \frac{i}{r}$$

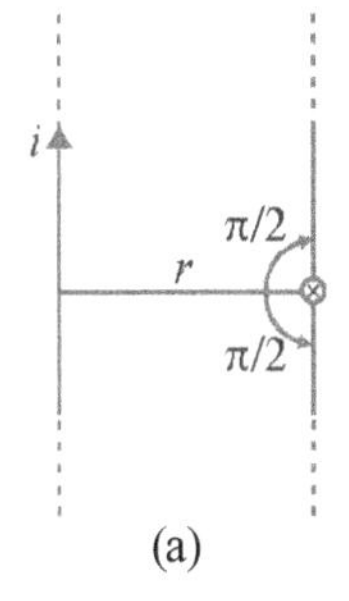

(a)

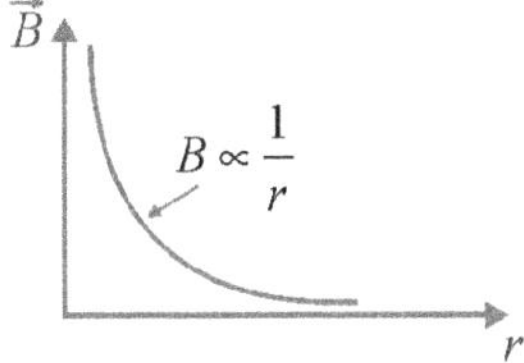

(b) Variation of $\vec{B}$ with r.

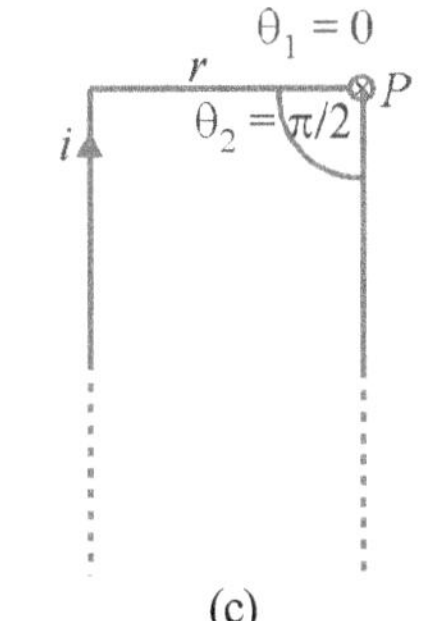

(c)

Fig. 6.7

Force between two parallel current carrying wires

Consider two long straight wires kept parallel to each other at a distance r and carrying currents i_1 and i_2 respectively in the same direction.

Magnetic force on the small element $d\vec{\ell}$ of the wire 2 due to the magnetic field of 1 is

$$d\vec{F} = i_2 (d\vec{\ell} \times \vec{B}_1)$$

The magnitude of the force

$$dF = i_2 (d\ell) B_1 \sin 90°$$

where

$$B_1 = \frac{\mu_0}{2\pi} \frac{i_1}{r}$$

$$\therefore \quad dF = \frac{\mu_0}{2\pi} \frac{i_1 i_2 (d\ell)}{r}$$

or

$$\frac{dF}{d\ell} = \frac{\mu_0}{2\pi} \frac{i_1 i_2}{r}$$

Thus force per unit length of wire 2 due to 1 is $\dfrac{\mu_0}{2\pi} \dfrac{i_1 i_2}{r}$. The same amount of force 1 exerts on 2.

The direction of force on wires are towards each other that is attraction (By FLHR).

If direction of currents in wires are opposite, the force between them will be repulsive.

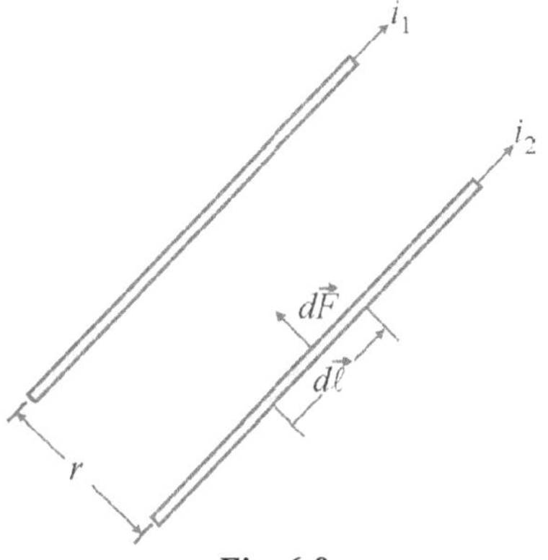

Fig. 6.8

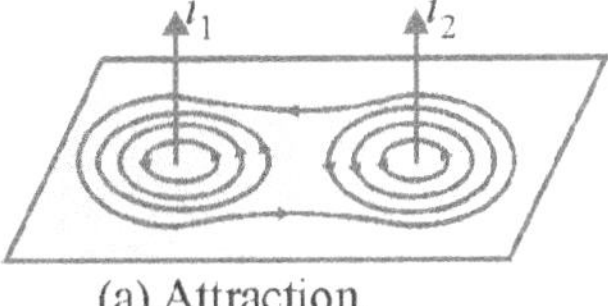

(a) Attraction.

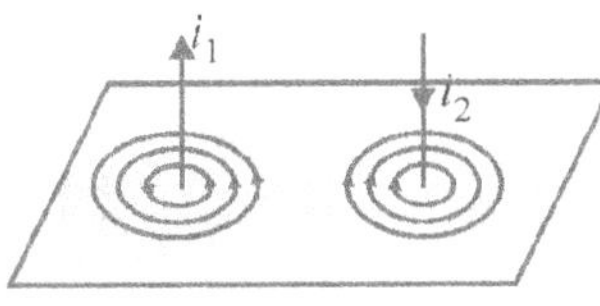

(b) Repulsion.

Fig. 6.9

 There is no electrical interaction between the wires, because they have no net charges.

Field due to a circular current carrying coil

Consider a circular loop of radius a carrying current i. We have to find the magnetic field at a point P on the axis of the loop at a distance x from the centre of the loop. Consider a current element $i\,d\vec{\ell}$ of the wire. The magnetic field at P due to this element is

$$d\vec{B} = \frac{\mu_0}{4\pi} i \frac{d\vec{\ell} \times \hat{r}}{r^2}$$

As $d\vec{\ell}$ is perpendicular to the plane of the paper, and so $d\vec{\ell} \times \hat{r}$ must lie in the plane of paper, as shown in figure.

The magnitude of the field

$$dB = \frac{\mu_0}{4\pi}\frac{id\ell}{r^2}$$

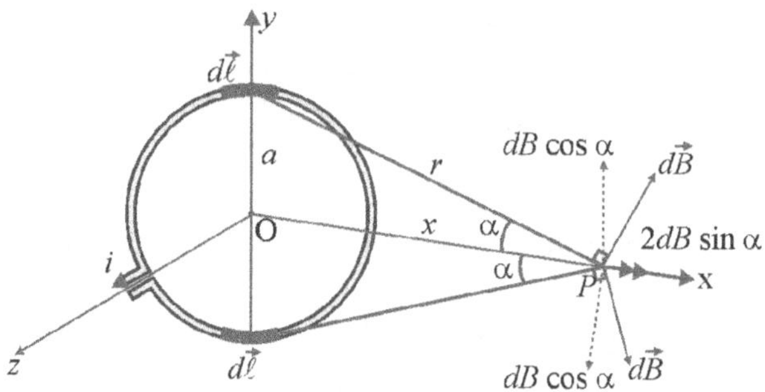

Fig. 6.10

Another element on the diametrically opposite point produces the same amount of field on the point P. The resultant field due to these elements $= 2dB\sin\alpha$.

The effective field of one element at P, $= dB\sin\alpha$

Field due to complete loop

$$B = \int dB\sin\alpha$$

$$= \frac{\mu_0}{4\pi}\int_0^{2\pi a}\frac{id\ell}{r^2}\sin\alpha$$

$$= \frac{\mu_0}{4\pi}\frac{i\times 2\pi a}{r^2}\times\frac{a}{r}$$

or $$B = \frac{\mu_0}{4\pi}\frac{2i\pi a^2}{r^3}$$

Since $$r = \sqrt{a^2+x^2}$$

$\therefore$ $$B = \frac{\mu_0 ia^2}{2(a^2+x^2)^{3/2}} \qquad \ldots(1)$$

As $$i(\pi a^2) = iA = M, \text{ where } A \text{ is the area of the loop}$$
$$= \text{ magnetic moment of the loop,}$$

$\therefore$ $$B = \frac{\mu_0}{4\pi}\cdot\frac{2M}{(a^2+x^2)^{3/2}} \qquad \ldots(2)$$

Field at a point far away from the centre $x >> a$,

$$B = \frac{\mu_0}{4\pi}\frac{2M}{x^3} \qquad \ldots(3)$$

From equation (1), we can get field at the centre of loop, $x = 0$

$$B = \frac{\mu_0 i}{2a}.$$

If there are N turns in the loop

$$B = \frac{\mu_0 Ni}{2a} \qquad \ldots(4)$$

1. Equations (3) and (4) are derived for circular loop, but they can be used for other shape of the loop also which has symmetry about the axis of the loop.
2. In equation (4), N may be a whole number or fraction or decimal number.
3. For the figure shown

$$N = \left(\frac{\theta}{2\pi}\right)$$

$$\therefore \qquad B = \frac{\mu_0\left(\dfrac{\theta}{2\pi}\right)i}{2a}.$$

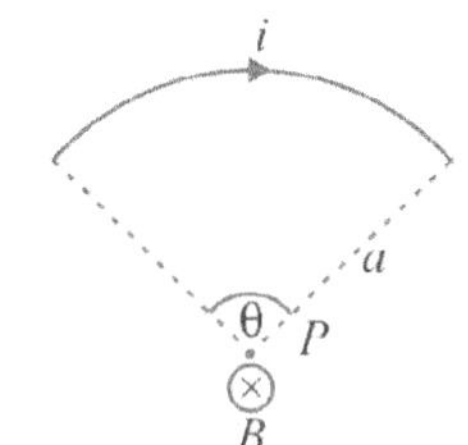

Fig. 6.11

4. The magnetic field at a point not on the axis of the loop is mathematically difficult to calculate. The field lines for the circular loop are not circles, but they are closed curves that link the conductor.

Field between two similar coaxial circular loops

Let us consider two loops, each having N turns and carrying current i are placed at a distance $2d$ apart.

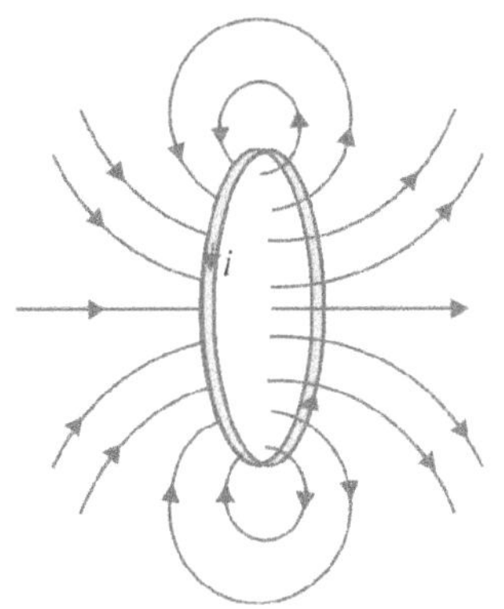

Magnetic field due to a circular loop

Fig. 6.12

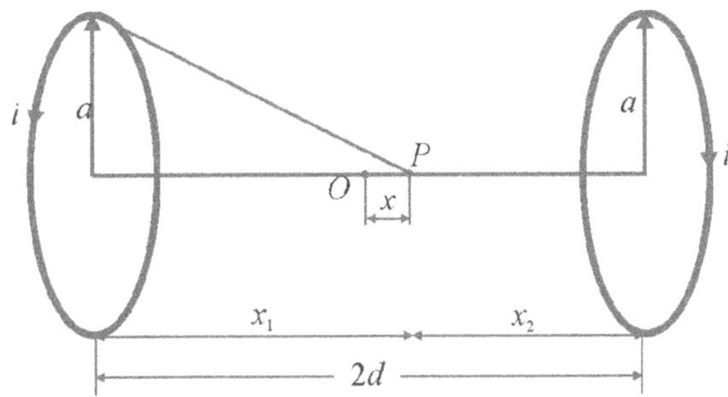

Fig. 6.14

Assuming the current is flowing in the same direction in each coil, the magnetic field at a short distance x from midway point O

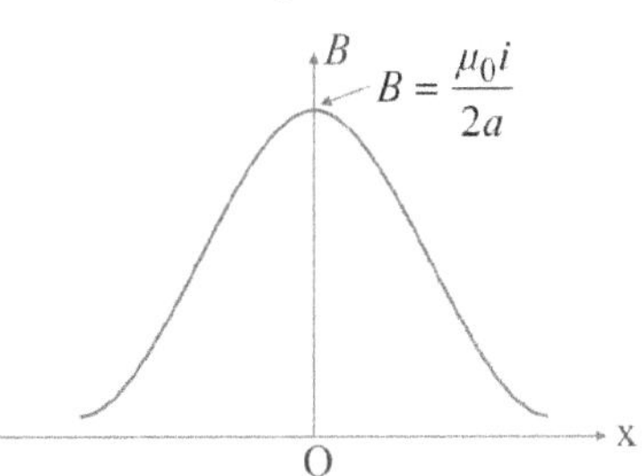

Fig. 6.13

$$B = \frac{\mu_0 N i a^2}{2}\left[\frac{1}{(a^2 + x_1^2)^{3/2}} + \frac{1}{(a^2 + x_2^2)^{3/2}}\right]$$

$$= \frac{\mu_0 N i a^2}{2}\left[\frac{1}{[a^2 + (d+x)^2]^{3/2}} + \frac{1}{[a^2 + (d-x)^2]^{3/2}}\right]$$

The field will be uniform between the loops, if $\dfrac{dB}{dx} = 0$ i.e.,

$$\frac{\mu_0 N i a^2}{2}\left[(-3)\frac{(d+x)}{[a^2 + (d+x)^2]^{5/2}} + 3\frac{(d-x)}{[a^2 + (d-x)^2]^{5/2}}\right] = 0$$

or $\qquad (d+x)\,[a^2 + (d-x)^2]^{5/2} = (d-x)\,[a^2 + (d+x)^2]^{5/2}$ ......(i)

Now $\qquad [a^2 + (d+x)^2]^{5/2} = [a^2 + d^2 + x^2 + 2xd]^{5/2}$

Since x is small, so neglecting x^2, we have

$$= [a^2 + d^2 + 2xd]^{5/2}$$

$$= (a^2 + d^2)^{5/2}\left[1 + \frac{2xd}{(a^2 + d^2)}\right]^{5/2}$$

$$\simeq (a^2 + d^2)^{5/2}\left[1 + \frac{5xd}{a^2 + d^2}\right]$$

$$\because \qquad \frac{2xd}{a^2 + d^2} \ll 1$$

Similarly $\qquad [a^2 + (d - x)^2]^{5/2} = (a^2 + d^2)^{5/2}\left[1 - \frac{5xd}{a^2 + d^2}\right]$

Substituting these values in equation (i), we get

$$(d + x)\left[1 - \frac{5xd}{a^2 + d^2}\right] = (d - x)\left[1 + \frac{5xd}{a^2 + d^2}\right]$$

or $\qquad \dfrac{5d^2}{(a^2 + d^2)} = 1, \qquad \because d = a/2, \ \text{ or } \ a = 2d$

and $\qquad B = 2\left[\dfrac{\mu_0 Nia^2}{2}\dfrac{1}{\left[a^2 + \left(\dfrac{a}{2}\right)^2\right]^{3/2}}\right]$

or $\qquad B = \dfrac{8\mu_0 Ni}{5\sqrt{5}a}.$ $\qquad\qquad …(2)$

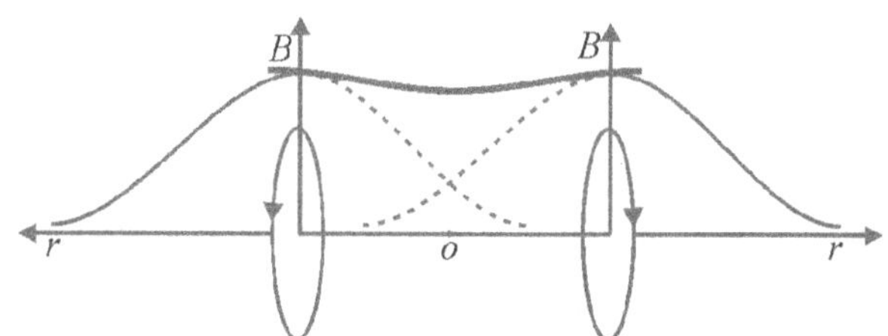

Fig. 6.15 *Variation of magnetic field between the loops.*

Ex. 1 A wire carrying current i has the configuration shown in *fig. 6.16*. Two semi-infinite straight sections, both tangent to the same circle, are connected by a circular arc, of central angle θ, along the circumference of the circle, with all sections lying in the same plane. What must θ be in order for B to be zero at the centre of the circle?

Sol. The field due to the straight parts of the wire

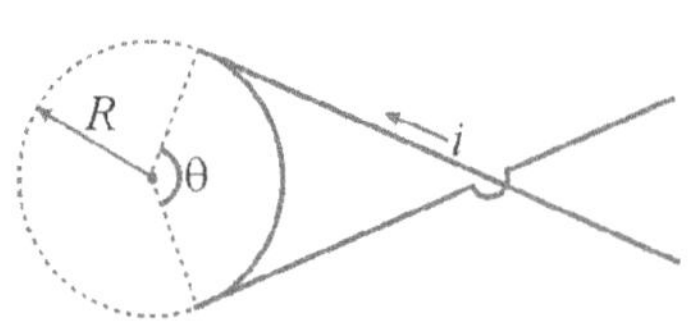

Fig. 6.16

$$B_1 = 2\left[\frac{\mu_0}{4\pi}\frac{i}{R}\right],$$

out of the plane

and field due to curved part of the wire

$$B_2 = \frac{\mu_0\left(\dfrac{\theta}{2\pi}\right)i}{2R}, \text{ into the plane of the wire.}$$

The resultant field at the centre to be zero

$$B_1 = B_2$$

or $\qquad 2\left[\dfrac{\mu_0}{4\pi}\dfrac{i}{R}\right] = \dfrac{\mu_0\left(\dfrac{\theta}{2\pi}\right)i}{2R} \Rightarrow \theta = 2 \text{ rad} \qquad ***Ans.***$

6.3 SOLENOID

A solenoid is a wire wound in a closely spaced spiral over a hollow cylindrical non-conducting core. The wire is coated with an insulating material so that the adjacent turns physically touch each other, but they are electrically insulated.

$$dN = ndx$$

If n is the number of turns per unit length, each carrying a current i, uniformly wound round a cylinder of radius a, then the number of turns in length dx is ndx. Thus the magnetic field at the axial point P due to the element

$$dB = \frac{\mu_0(ndx)i}{2(a^2+x^2)^{3/2}}$$

The direction of magnetic field is along the axis of the solenoid and in the sense of advance of a right handed screw. From geometry, we have

$$x = a\cot(180° - \theta) = -a\cot\theta$$

and

$$dx = a\,\mathrm{cosec}^2\theta\, d\theta \text{ and hence}$$

$$dB = \frac{\mu_0 ni\sin\theta\, d\theta}{2}$$

Total field

$$B = \frac{\mu_0 ni}{2}\int_{\theta_1}^{\theta_2}\sin\theta\, d\theta$$

$$= \frac{\mu_0 ni}{2}\left|-\cos\theta\right|_{\theta_1}^{\theta_2}$$

or

$$B = \frac{\mu_0 ni}{2}[\cos\theta_1 - \cos\theta_2]. \qquad …(1)$$

Special cases :

Case 1 : Solenoid is of infinite length and the point chosen is at the middle

$$\theta_1 = 0, \theta_2 = \pi$$

$$\therefore \qquad B = \mu_0 ni$$

Case 2 : Solenoid is of infinite length and the point is at the end of the solenoid

$$\theta_1 = \pi/2,\ \theta_2 = \pi$$

$$\therefore \qquad B = \frac{\mu_0 ni}{2}$$

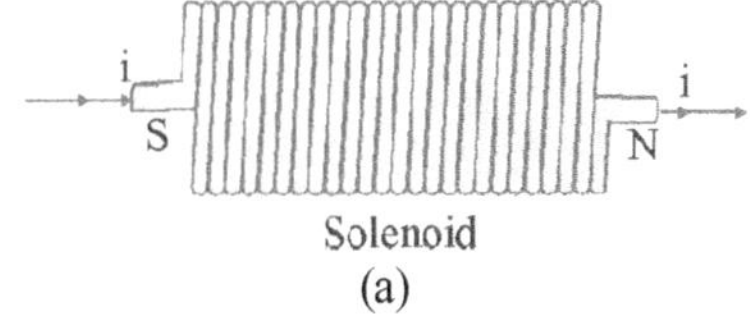

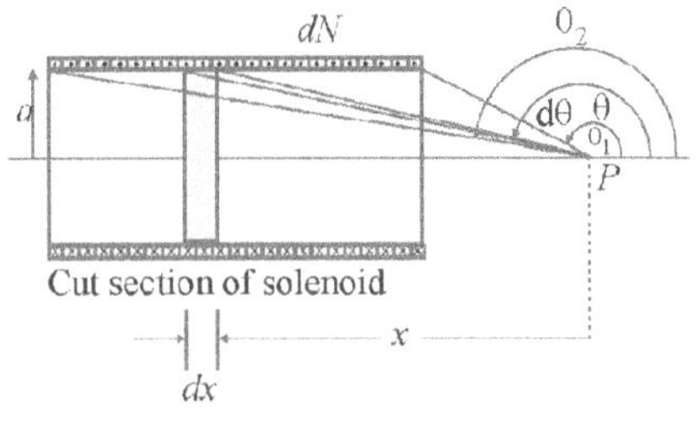

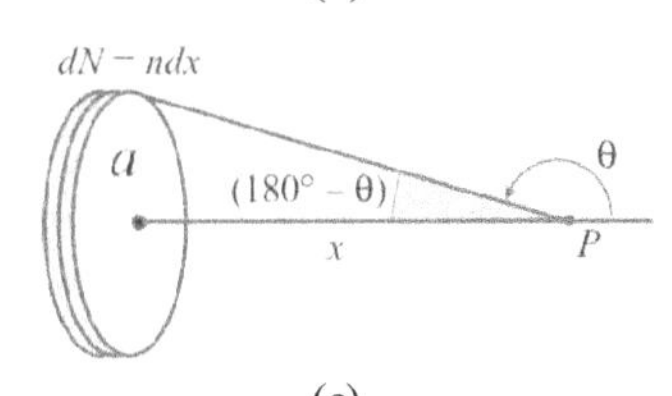

Fig. 6.17

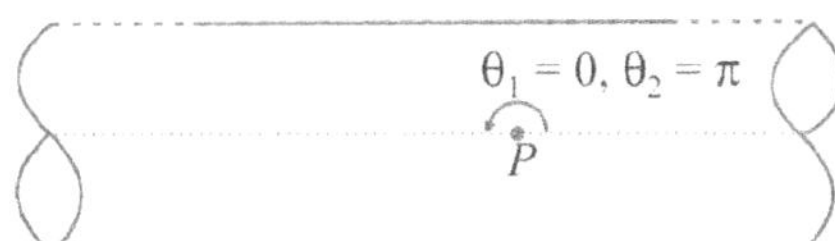

Fig. 6.18

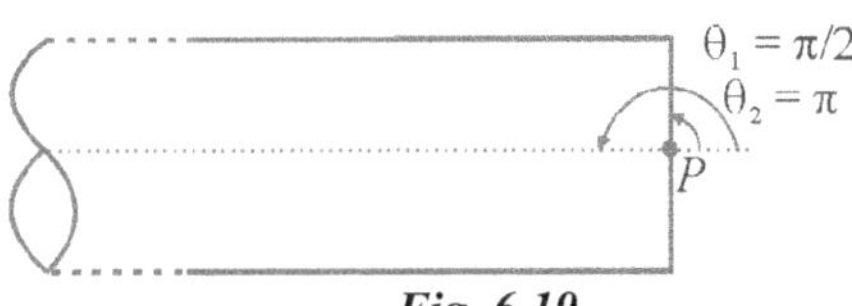

Fig. 6.19

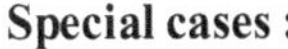

Note :

1. If the length of the solenoid is large compared with its radius, the internal field near its centre is very nearly uniform and parallel to axis, and the external field near the centre is very small. In practice we take the magnetic field inside very tightly wound long solenoid is uniform everywhere and zero outside it.

2. If some material medium is present inside solenoid, the magnetic field inside it is $B = \mu_r\mu_0 ni$; where μ_r is the relative permeability of the medium.

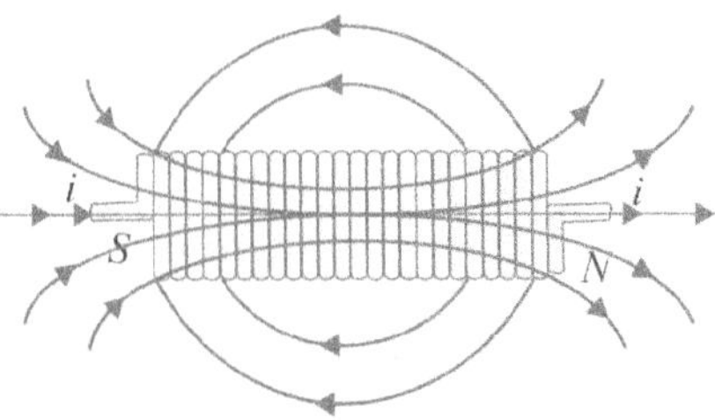

Fig. 6.20

6.4 TOROID OR ANCHOR RING

It is a solenoid of small radius bent round to form a toroid. In an ideal toroid, the field is confined entirely within the core and is uniform. The value of magnetic field at any point on the mean circumferential line is given by

$$B = \mu_0 n i$$

If N is the total turns in the toroid, then

$$n = \frac{N}{2\pi R},$$

$$= \mu_0 \left(\frac{N}{2\pi R}\right) i$$

$$\therefore \qquad B = \mu_0 \left(\frac{N}{2\pi R}\right) i$$

or $\qquad B = \dfrac{\mu_0 N i}{2\pi R}.$

where R is the mean radius of the ring.

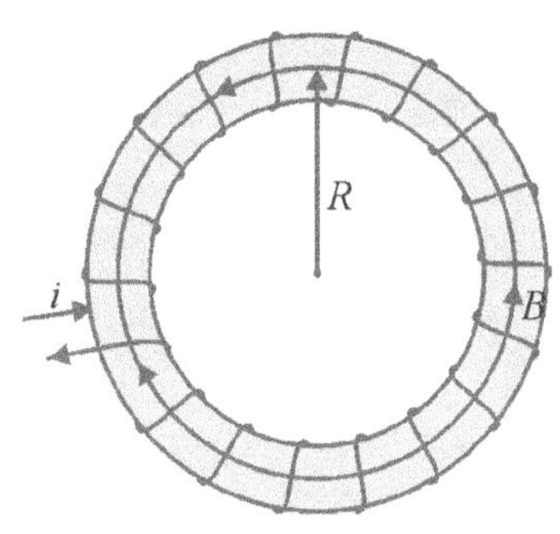

Fig. 6.20

Ex. 2   A steady current is set up in a cubical network of resistive wires, connected as in *fig. 6.22*. Find magnetic field at the centre of the cube.

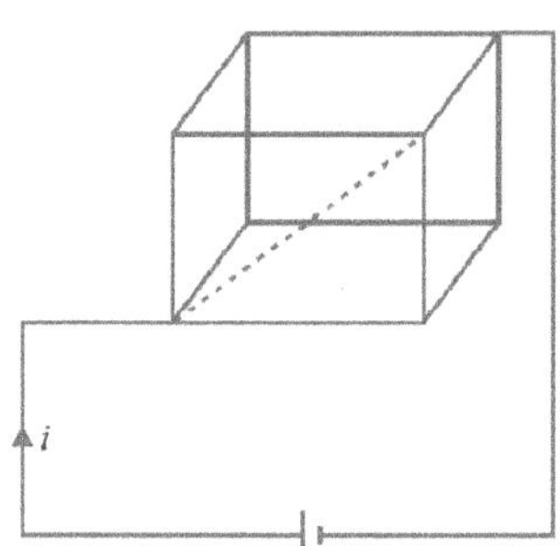

Fig. 6.22

Sol. The currents in the wires distribute symmetrically about the dotted diagonal. And so currents of resistances of one face cancel the magnetic field of its front face. Thus

$$B_{net} = 0. \qquad \textit{Ans.}$$

Ex. 3   A current I flows along a thin wire shaped as a regular polygon with n sides which can be inscribed into a circle of radius R. Find the magnetic induction at the centre of the polygon. Analyse the obtained expression at $n \to \infty$.

Sol. In a regular polygon of n-sides, each of its side subtends an angle $\dfrac{2\pi}{n}$ at the centre of the polygon. The angle $\theta = \dfrac{\pi}{n}$. If B_1 is the field produced by each side of the polygon, then total magnetic induction

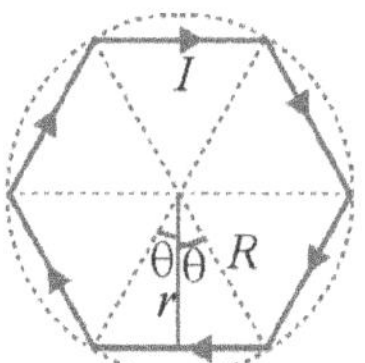

Fig. 6.23

$$B = n B_1$$

$$= n \frac{\mu_0 I}{4\pi} \frac{\left[\sin\dfrac{\pi}{n} + \sin\dfrac{\pi}{n}\right]}{r}$$

where $\qquad r = R \cos\dfrac{\pi}{n}.$

Thus $\qquad B = n \dfrac{\mu_0}{4\pi} I \times \dfrac{2\sin\pi/n}{R\cos\pi/n}$

$$= \frac{\mu_0 n I}{2\pi R} \tan\frac{\pi}{n} \qquad \textit{Ans.}$$

For $n \to \infty$, we can write

$$B = \frac{\mu_0 I}{2R} \lim_{n\to\infty}\left[\frac{\tan\pi/n}{\pi/n}\right]$$

$$= \frac{\mu_0 I}{2R} \qquad \textit{Ans.}$$

Polygon of infinite sides is a circle, and so its magnetic induction at the centre is equal to that due to a circular loop.

Ex. 4   A current $I = 5.0$ A flows along a thin wire shaped as shown in *fig. 6.24*. The radius of a curved part of the wire is equal to $R = 120$ mm, the angle $2\phi = 90°$. Find the magnetic induction of the field at the point O.

Sol.   The curved part of the wire is equal to $\dfrac{3}{4}$ turn. If B_1 and B_2 are the magnetic inductions due to the curved and straight parts of the wire, then

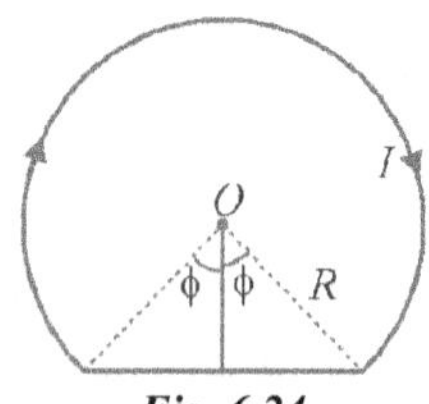

Fig. 6.24

$$B_1 = \frac{\mu_0 (3/4) I}{2R} = \frac{3\mu_0 I}{8R},$$

and

$$B_2 = \frac{\mu_0}{4\pi} I \frac{(\sin 45° + \sin 45°)}{r},$$

where

$$r = R \sin 45°$$

$$\therefore \qquad B_2 = \frac{\mu_0 I}{4\pi} \frac{2\sin 45°}{R \sin 45°}$$

$$= \frac{\mu_0 I}{2\pi R}.$$

Thus total magnetic induction,

$$B = B_1 + B_2$$

$$= \frac{\mu_0 I}{R}\left[\frac{3}{8} + \frac{1}{2\pi}\right]$$

On substituting the values, we get

$$B = 28 \ \mu T. \qquad \textit{Ans.}$$

Ex. 5 Find the magnetic induction of the field at the point O in a current carrying wire has the shape shown in *fig. 6.25 a, b, c.* The radius of the curved part of the wire is R, the linear parts are assumed to be very long.

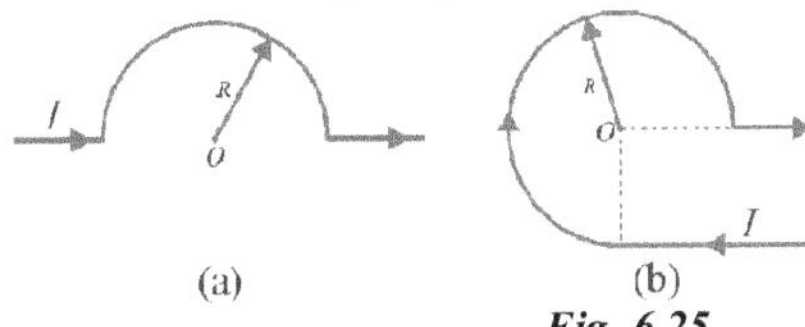
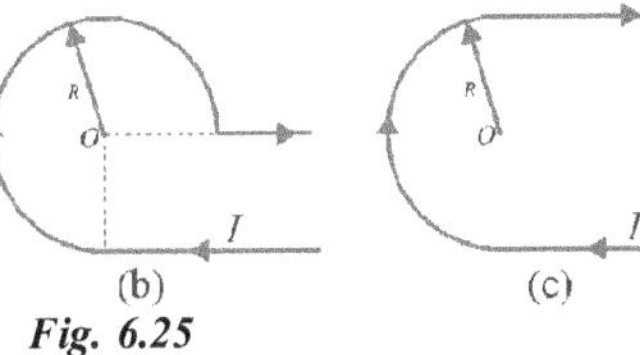

(a)   (b)   (c)

Fig. 6.25

Sol. (a)   Straight part of the wire produces no magnetic induction at O. So magnetic induction is only due to the curved part.

$$B = \frac{\mu_0 \left(\frac{1}{2}\right) I}{2R} = \frac{\mu_0 I}{4R} \qquad \textit{Ans.}$$

(b)   The magnetic induction due to upper straight wire at O will be zero and due to lower straight part is $\frac{\mu_0 I}{4\pi R}$. The magnetic induction due to curved part is $\frac{\mu_0 \left(\frac{3}{4}\right) I}{2R}$. Thus total induction

$$B = B_{\text{straight}} + B_{\text{curved}}$$

$$= \frac{\mu_0 I}{4\pi R}\left[1 + \frac{3\pi}{2}\right] \qquad \textit{Ans.}$$

(c)   In this case all parts of the wire produce non zero magnetic induction at O.

The total induction $= 2B_{\text{straight}} + B_{\text{curved}}$

$$= 2\frac{\mu_0 I}{4\pi R} + \frac{\mu_0 \left(\frac{1}{2}\right) I}{2R}$$

$$= \frac{\mu_0 I}{4\pi R}[2 + \pi] \qquad \textit{Ans.}$$

Ex. 6 Find the magnetic induction of the field at the point O if the wire carrying a current I has the shape shown in *fig. 6.26 a, b, c.* The radius of the curved part of wire is R, the linear parts of the wire are very long.

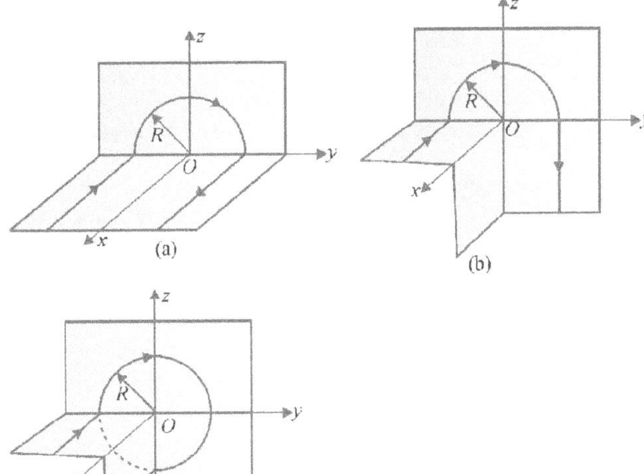

Fig. 6.26

Sol.

(a)   The magnetic induction due to straight part is

$$\vec{B}_{\text{straight}} = 2\left[\frac{\mu_0 I}{4\pi R}\right](-\hat{k}), \text{ and due to curved part is}$$

$$\vec{B}_{\text{curved}} = \left[\frac{\mu_0 \left(\frac{1}{2}\right) I}{2R}\right](-\hat{i})$$

Thus total magnetic induction

$$\vec{B} = \vec{B}_{\text{straight}} + \vec{B}_{\text{curved}}$$

$$= 2\left[\frac{\mu_0 I}{4\pi R}\right](-\hat{k}) + \left[\frac{\mu_0 I}{4R}\right](-\hat{i})$$

$$= -\frac{\mu_0 I}{4\pi R}\left[\pi \hat{i} + 2\hat{k}\right] \qquad \textit{Ans.}$$

(b)

$$\vec{B} = \vec{B}_{\text{straight}} + \vec{B}_{\text{curved}}$$

$$= \left[\frac{\mu_0 I}{4\pi R}(-\hat{k}) + \frac{\mu_0 I}{4\pi R}(-\hat{i})\right] + \left[\frac{\mu_0 \left(\frac{1}{2}\right) I}{2R}\right](-\hat{i})$$

$$= -\frac{\mu_0 I}{4\pi R}[(\pi + 1)\hat{i} + \hat{k}]. \qquad \textit{Ans.}$$

(c)   In this case current in the curved conductor is divided into two parts. The length of upper curved part is thrice that of hidden lower part and so currents in them are $\frac{I}{4}$ and $\frac{3I}{4}$ respectively.

Thus

$$\vec{B} = \vec{B}_{\text{straight}} + \vec{B}_{\text{curved}}$$

$$= \left[\frac{\mu_0 I}{4\pi R}(-\hat{k}) + \frac{\mu_0 I}{4\pi R}(-\hat{j})\right] + \left[\frac{\mu_0\left(\frac{3}{4}\right)\left(\frac{I}{4}\right)}{2R}(-\hat{i}) + \frac{\mu_0\left(\frac{1}{4}\right)\left(\frac{3I}{4}\right)}{2R}\hat{i}\right]$$

$$= -\frac{\mu_0 I}{4\pi R}(\hat{j} + \hat{k}) \qquad\qquad Ans.$$

Ex. 7   A non-conducting sphere of radius R charged uniformly with surface density σ rotates with an angular velocity ω about the axis passing through its centre. Find the magnetic induction at the centre of the sphere.

Sol.   Take an element in the form of ring of angular width $d\theta$ at a position θ. The charge on ring

$$dq = \sigma(dA) = \sigma(2\pi R\sin\theta)R d\theta$$

Due to its rotation, the equivalent current

$$i = \frac{dq}{dt} = \frac{\sigma(2\pi R\sin\theta)R d\theta}{(2\pi/\omega)}$$

$$= \omega\sigma R^2\sin\theta d\theta$$

The magnetic induction at the centre of the sphere

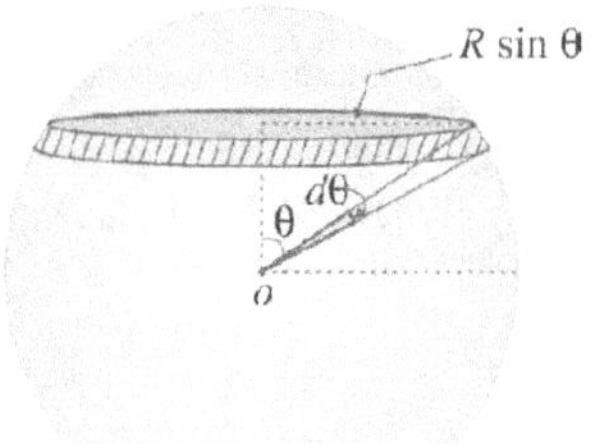

Fig. 6.27

$$dB = \frac{\mu_0}{4\pi}\cdot\frac{2M}{x^3}$$

$$= \frac{\mu_0}{4\pi}\cdot\frac{2idA}{R^3}$$

$$= \frac{\mu_0}{4\pi}\cdot\frac{2(\omega\sigma R^2\sin\theta d\theta)}{R^3}\{(R\sin\theta)^2\}$$

$$= \frac{\mu_0}{2}\omega\sigma R\sin^3\theta d\theta$$

$$\therefore \qquad B = \frac{\mu_0}{2}\omega\sigma R\int_0^{\pi/2}\sin^3\theta d\theta$$

$$= \frac{\mu_0}{2}\omega\sigma R\int_0^{\pi/2}(1-\cos^2\theta)\sin\theta d\theta$$

$$= \frac{\mu_0}{2}\omega\sigma R\int_0^{\pi/2}(1-\cos^2\theta)d\cos\theta$$

$$= \frac{\mu_0}{2}\omega\sigma R\left|\cos\theta - \frac{\cos^3\theta}{3}\right|_0^{\pi/2}$$

$$= \frac{1}{3}\mu_0\omega\sigma R \qquad\qquad Ans.$$

Ex. 8   A straight segment OC (of length L meter) of a circuit carrying a current i A is placed along the x-axis (see *fig. 6.28*). Two infinity long straight wire A and B, each extending from $z=-\infty$ to $+\infty$, are fixed at $y=-a$ metre and $y=+a$ metre respectively as shown in *fig. 6.28*. If the wire A and B each carry a current i A into the plane of the paper, obtain the expression for the force acting on the segment OC. What will be the force on OC if the current in the wire B is reversed.

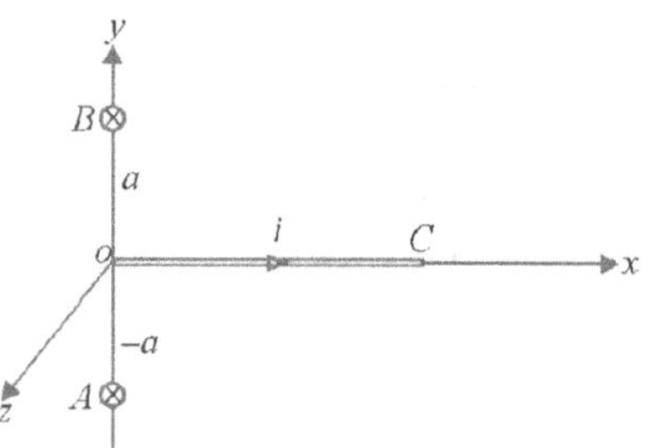

Fig. 6.28

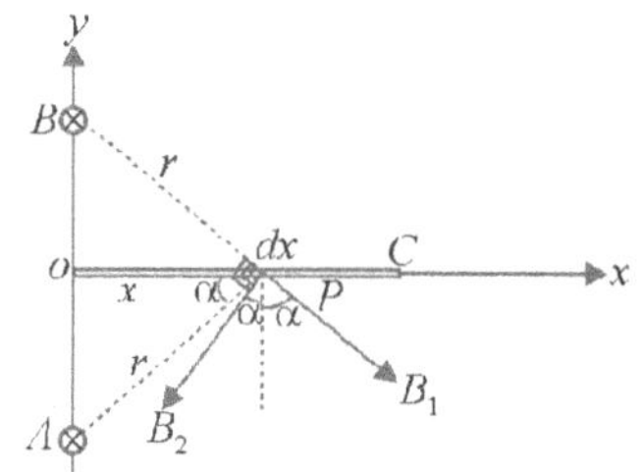

Fig. 6.29

Sol.

The magnetic field due to the wire at a distance x from O can be obtained as follows:

If B_1 and B_2 are the magnetic fields of wire A and B respectively then resultant field at P

$$B = 2B_1\cos\alpha \qquad \text{As }(B_1 = B_2)$$

$$= 2\frac{\mu_0 i}{2\pi r}\cos\alpha$$

$$= 2\frac{\mu_0}{2\pi}\frac{i}{r}\times\frac{x}{r} = \frac{\mu_0}{\pi}\cdot\frac{ix}{r^2}$$

$$= \frac{\mu_0}{\pi}\frac{ix}{(x^2+a^2)} \qquad \text{along } y\text{-axis.}$$

The force on the small length dx of the conductor OC

$$d\vec{F} = i(d\vec{\ell}\times\vec{B})$$

$$= id\vec{x}\times B(-\hat{j})$$

$$= \frac{\mu_0 i^2}{\pi}\frac{xdx}{x^2+a^2}(-\hat{k})$$

The force on the whole conductor

$$\vec{F} = \frac{\mu_0 i^2}{\pi}(-\hat{k})\int_0^L \frac{x\,dx}{x^2 + a^2}$$

$$= \frac{\mu_0 i^2}{\pi}(-\hat{k})\left|ln(x^2 + a^2)\right|_0^L$$

$$= \frac{\mu_0 i^2}{2\pi}(-\hat{k})\left[ln(L^2 + a^2) - lna^2\right]$$

$$= \frac{\mu_0 i^2}{2\pi}(-\hat{k})ln\left(\frac{L^2 + a^2}{a^2}\right). \qquad \textbf{\textit{Ans.}}$$

6.5 AMPERE'S LAW

We know that the lines of magnetic field are continuous and do not arise from any source in the way as lines of electric field originate from charges. These thus form loops without any beginning or end. This property may be used to go through the nature of magnetic field and for calculating the field in certain situation of high symmetry.

The field of a long round current carrying wire $B = \dfrac{\mu_0}{2\pi}\dfrac{i}{r}$. The field lines are concentric around the wire in the plane of the paper if the wire is perpendicular to this plane. The line integral around the path of radius r, starting at any point and returning to the same point is ;

$$\oint \vec{B}.d\vec{\ell} = B\oint d\ell \cos 0°$$

$$= B\oint d\vec{\ell} = \frac{\mu_0}{2\pi}.\frac{i}{r} \times 2\pi r$$

$$= \mu_0 i.$$

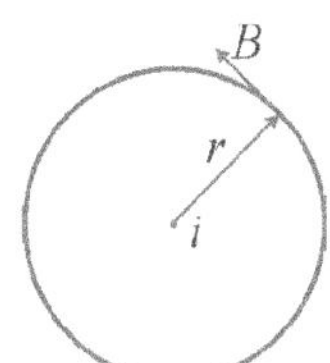

Fig. 6.30

Although the above result is derived for the special case of the field of a long straight conductor, the law is true for conductors and path of any shape. Thus the line integral of the magnetic field $\vec{B}$ around any closed path is equal to μ_0 times the net current across the area bounded by the path. Hence

$$\oint \vec{B}.d\vec{\ell} = \mu_0 i_{\text{in}}.$$

It is called **Ampere's law**. It plays the same role in magnetics as Gauss's law plays in electrostatics.

Note:

1. The magnetic field $\vec{B}$ on the left hand side in Ampere's law is the resultant field due to all the currents existing anywhere while on the right hand side the current i_{in} is due to the conductors inside the close loop.

2. Let us consider a closed plane curve as shown in figure. If direction of integration is taken along the path as shown then i_1 and i_3 will be positive and i_2 will be negative.
   Thus the total current crossing the loop is $(i_1 - i_2 + i_3)$. Any current outside the area is not included in writing the right hand side of the equation. Thus

$$\oint \vec{B}.d\vec{\ell} = \mu_0(i_1 - i_2 + i_3)$$

3. Consider two current carrying conductors, carrying currents i_1 and i_2 in the same direction and a close path as shown in *fig. 6.32*. For the close path

$$\oint \vec{B}.d\vec{\ell} = \mu_0(i_1 - i_2)$$

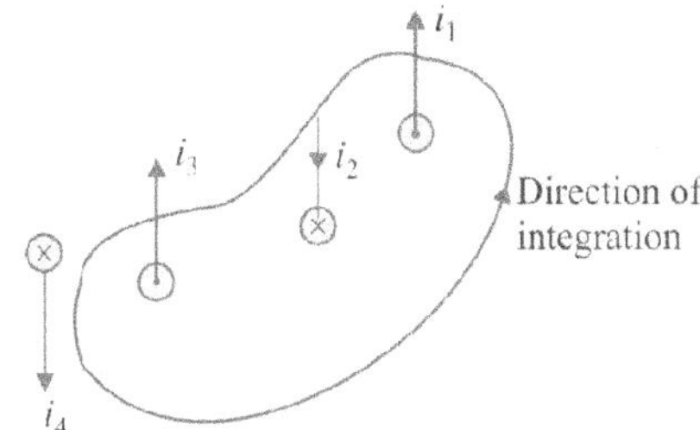

Fig. 6.31

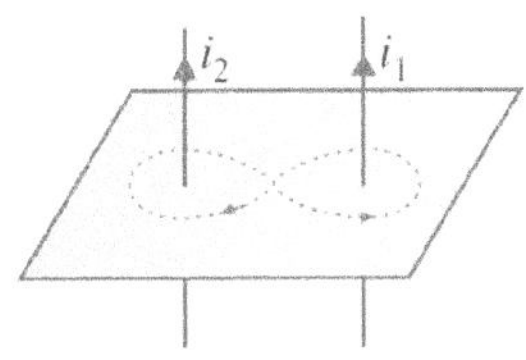

Fig. 6.32

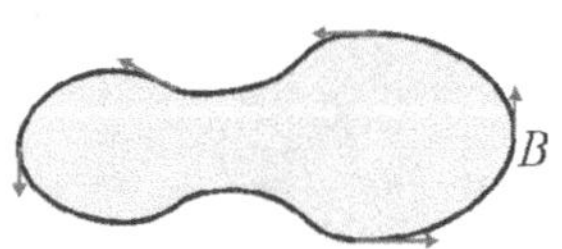

Fig. 6.33

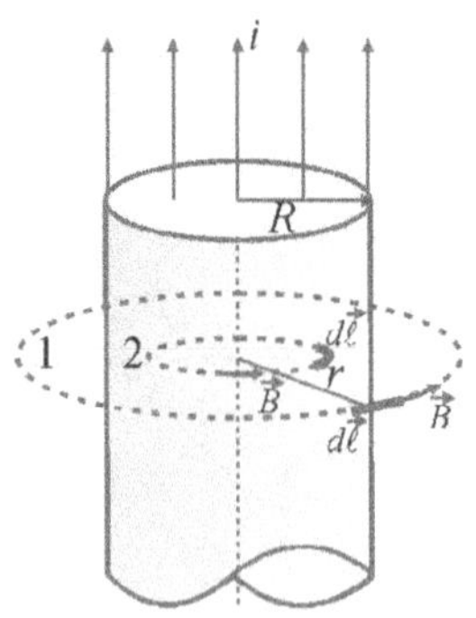

Fig. 6.34

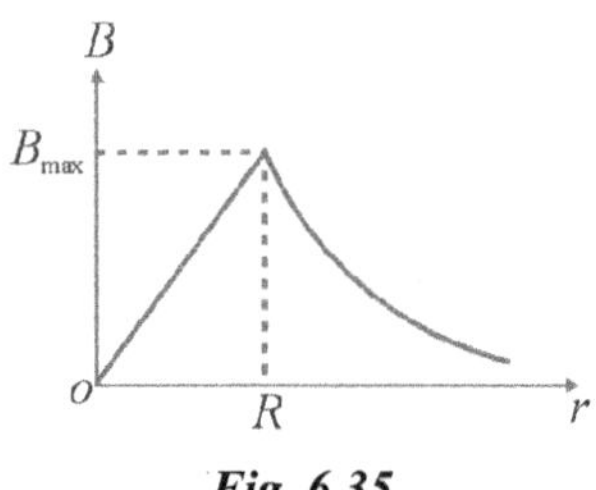

Fig. 6.35

Application of Ampere's law

In some cases of practical importance, symmetry considerations make it possible to use Ampere's law to compute the magnetic field caused by a certain current carrying conductor. Few guiding principles, analogous to those stated for Gauss's law are following.

1. If $\vec{B}$ is tangent to the integration path everywhere and has the same magnitude on each point of the path, then

$$B\ell \;=\; \mu_0 i .$$

Here ℓ is the length of the close path.

2. If $\vec{B}$ is everywhere perpendicular to the path or some portion of the path, then that portion of the path makes no contribution to the line integral.

3. In the integral $\oint \vec{B}.d\vec{\ell}$, $\vec{B}$ is always the resultant magnetic field at each point of the path. In general this field is caused partly by currents linked by the path and partly by currents outside. Even when no current is linked by the path the field at points on the path need not be zero. In case, however, $\oint \vec{B}.d\vec{\ell}$ is always zero.

4. Some judgement is required in choosing an integration path. Two useful guiding principles are that the point or points at which the field is to be determined must lie on the path, and that the path must have enough symmetry so that the integral can be evaluated.

Magnetic field due to long cylindrical wire

For $r \geq R$:

The magnetic field at each point of circular path surrounded the conductor is tangential. Therefore for circular path 1

$$\oint \vec{B}.d\vec{\ell} \;=\; \mu_0 i$$

or
$$\oint Bd\ell \cos 0° \;=\; \mu_0 i$$

or
$$B\oint d\ell \;=\; \mu_0 i$$

or
$$B \times 2\pi r \;=\; \mu_0 i$$

or
$$B \;=\; \frac{\mu_0}{2\pi}\frac{i}{r}$$

For $r < R$:

If the current is distributed uniformly through the cross-section of the wire, then the current inside the path is

$$i_{\text{in}} \;=\; \frac{i}{\pi R^2} \times \pi r^2 = \frac{ir^2}{R^2}$$

Now
$$\oint \vec{B}.d\vec{\ell} \;=\; \mu_0 i_{\text{in}}$$

or
$$B \times 2\pi r \;=\; \mu_0 \times \frac{ir^2}{R^2}$$

or
$$B \;=\; \frac{\mu_0}{2\pi}\frac{ir}{R^2}$$

For $r = R$
$$B_{\text{max}} \;=\; \frac{\mu_0}{2\pi}\frac{i}{R} .$$

Long solenoid

For the field at point inside the solenoid, let us consider a rectangular path $ABCDA$ as the path of integration. This path is particularly simple as :

(a) Outside the solenoid, along CD, we can assume field to be zero as it is many times weaker than that inside the solenoid

$$\therefore \qquad \int_{C}^{D} \vec{B}\cdot d\vec{\ell} = 0$$

(b) Along BC and DA, $\vec{B}$ is either zero (for outside parts of BC and DA) or perpendicular to $\vec{B}$ (for the parts inside the solenoid)

$$\therefore \qquad \int_{B}^{C} \vec{B}\bullet d\vec{\ell} = \int_{D}^{A} \vec{B}\bullet d\vec{\ell} = 0$$

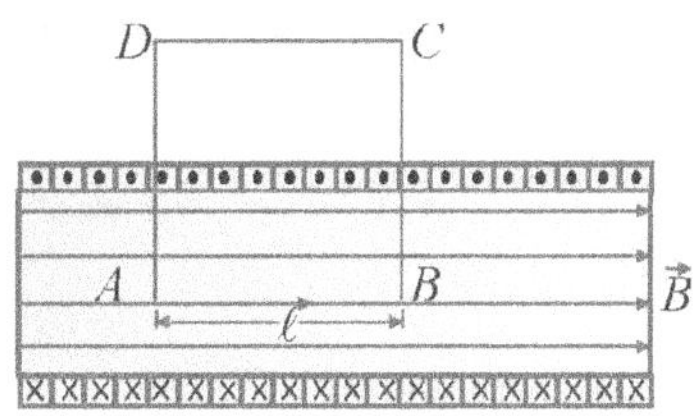

Fig. 6.36

(c) Inside the solenoid $\vec{B}$ is constant and is along AB.

$$\therefore \qquad \int_{A}^{B} \vec{B}\cdot d\vec{\ell} = B\ell$$

Now apply Ampere's Law for closed loop $ABCDA$, we get

$$\oint \vec{B}\bullet d\vec{\ell} = \mu_0 i_{in}$$

$$\text{or} \quad \int_{A}^{B} \vec{B}\bullet d\vec{\ell} + \int_{B}^{C} \vec{B}\bullet d\vec{\ell} + \int_{C}^{D} \vec{B}\bullet d\vec{\ell} + \int_{D}^{A} \vec{B}\bullet d\vec{\ell} = \mu_0 i_{in}$$

$$\text{or} \qquad B\ell = \mu_0 \left(n\ell i\right)$$

As $i_{in} = \left(n\ell\right)i$

$$\therefore \qquad B = \mu_0 ni.$$

Thin hollow current carrying tube

For $x \geq R$, $\qquad B_{max} = \dfrac{\mu_0}{2\pi}\cdot\dfrac{i}{r}$

For $x < R$, $\qquad i_{in} = 0,$

$\therefore \qquad\qquad B = 0.$

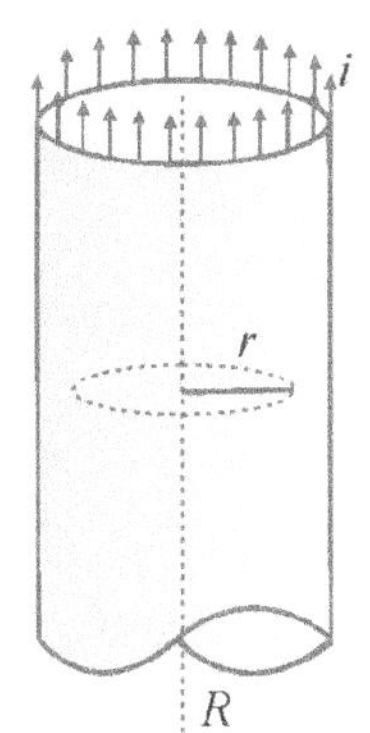

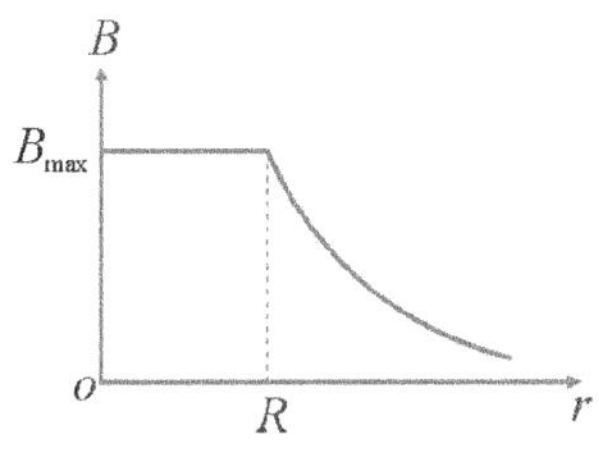

Fig. 6.37

Ex. 9 Each of the eight conductors in *fig. 6.38* carries 2.0 A of current into or out of the page. Two paths are indicated for the line integral $\oint \vec{B}.d\vec{\ell}$. What is the value of the integral for the path (a) at the left and (b) at the right ?

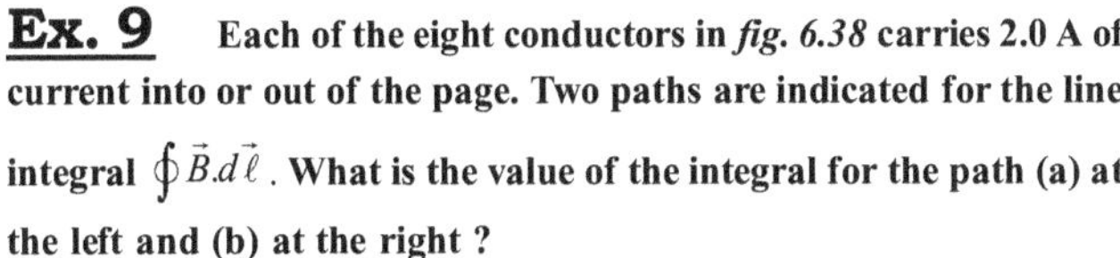

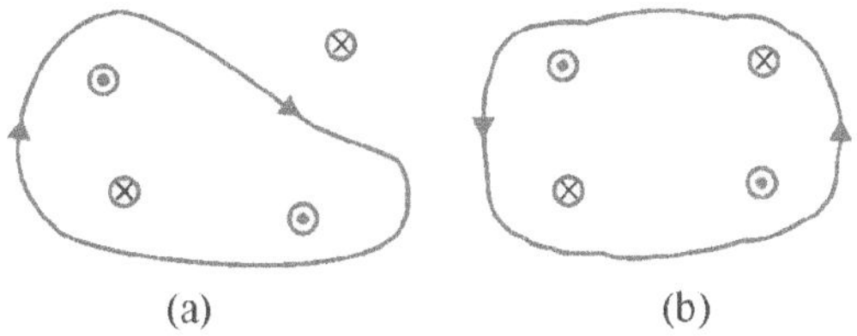

(a)   (b)

Fig. 6.38

Sol.

(a) By Ampere law $\oint \vec{B}.d\vec{\ell} = \mu_0 i_{in}$;

in close loop $i_{in} = (-2 + 2 - 2)\,A = -2A$

$$\therefore \qquad \oint \vec{B}.d\vec{\ell} = \mu_0 (-2) = -2\mu_0. \qquad \textit{Ans.}$$

(b) In this loop $i_{in} = (2 - 2 + 2 - 2) = 0,$

$$\therefore \qquad \oint \vec{B}.d\vec{\ell} = 0. \qquad \textit{Ans.}$$

Ex. 10 Eight wires cut the page perpendicularly at the points shown in *fig. 6.39*. A wire labeled with the integer k ($k = 1, 2, ...8$) carries the current $k\, i_0$. For those with odd k, the current is out of the page; for those with even k, it is into the page.

Evaluate $\oint \vec{B}\bullet d\vec{\ell}$ along the closed path in the direction shown.

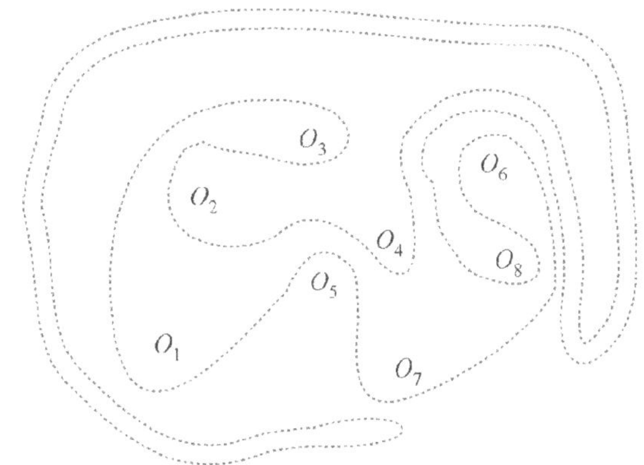

Fig. 6.39

Sol. In accordance with Ampere's law

$$\oint \vec{B}\cdot d\vec{\ell} = \mu_0 \left(i_{in}\right)$$

$$= -5\mu_0 i_0. \qquad \textit{Ans.}$$

Ex. 11 Inside a homogeneous long straight wire of circular cross-section, there is a circular cylindrical cavity whose axis is parallel to the conductor axis and displaced relative to it by a distance ℓ. A direct current of density $\hat{j}$ flows along the wire. Find magnetic induction $\vec{B}$ inside the cavity.

Sol. By the principle of superposition, the required quantity can be given by

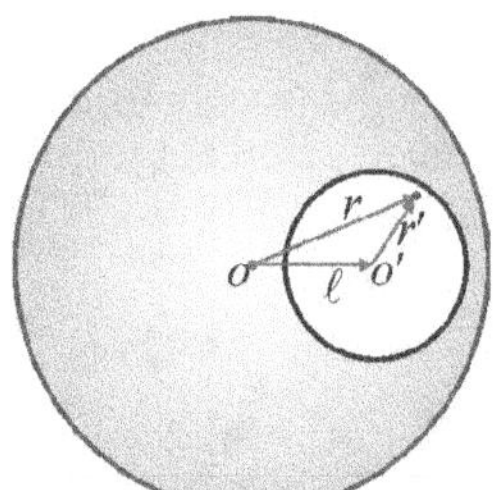

Fig. 6.40

$$\vec{B} = \vec{B}_0 - \vec{B}',$$

where B_0 is the magnetic field of the conductor without cavity, while $\vec{B}'$ is the magnetic field of the conductor which has removed.

Here $$\vec{B}_0 = \frac{\mu_0}{2\pi}\frac{ir}{a^2} = \frac{\mu_0}{2\pi}\frac{j(\pi a^2)r}{a^2} = \frac{\mu_0 r}{2}j$$

This expression can be represented in vector form

$$\vec{B}_0 = \frac{\mu_0}{2}(\hat{j} \times \vec{r}).$$

Similarly $$\vec{B}' = \frac{\mu_0}{2}(\hat{j} \times \vec{r}')$$

Thus $$\vec{B} = \vec{B}_0 - \vec{B}' = \frac{\mu_0}{2}[\hat{j} \times (\vec{r} - \vec{r}')]$$

From the figure $$\vec{r} = \vec{\ell} + \vec{r}', \quad \therefore \quad \vec{r} - \vec{r}' = \vec{\ell},$$

$$\therefore \qquad \vec{B} = \frac{\mu_0}{2}(\hat{j} \times \vec{\ell}). \qquad Ans.$$

Ex. 12 If current density in the conducting wire is proportional to the distance r from the axis of the conductor, then find magnetic field at the position $r < R$, where R is the radius of cross section of the conductor.

Sol. Let current density $j = kr$, where r is the distance from the axis of the wire. If current in the wire is i, then

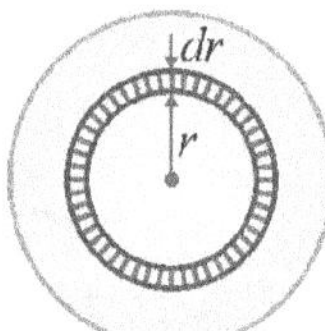

Fig. 6.41

$$i = \int_0^R j \times 2\pi r\, dr$$

$$= \int_0^R kr \times 2\pi r\, dr$$

$$= \frac{2\pi k R^3}{3}$$

And current inside the close path of radius r

$$i_{in} = \int_0^r j \times 2\pi r\, dr = \int_0^r kr \times 2\pi r\, dr$$

$$= \frac{2\pi k r^3}{3} = \frac{ir^3}{R^3}$$

For $r < R$: $$\oint \vec{B}.d\vec{\ell} = \mu_0 i_{in}$$

or $$B \times 2\pi r = \mu_0\left(\frac{ir^3}{R^3}\right),$$

which gives $$B = \frac{\mu_0 i}{2\pi}\frac{r^2}{R^3} \qquad Ans.$$

It is more useful to write Ampere's law as follows :
$$\oint \vec{B}.d\vec{\ell} = \mu_0 \int \vec{j}.d\vec{A}$$

Ex. 13 *Fig. 6.42 show a cross-section of a large metal sheet carrying an electric current along its axis. The current in a strip of width $d\ell$ is $kd\ell$ where k is constant. Find the magnetic field at a point P at a distance x from the metal sheet.*

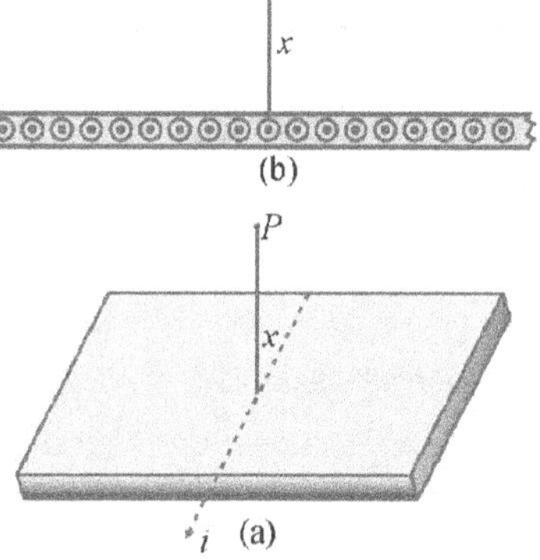

Fig. 6.42

Sol. Consider two strips R and S of the sheet situated symmetrically on the two sides of P. The magnetic field at P above sheet and below sheet is parallel to sheet as shown in figure. There is no field perpendicular to the sheet.

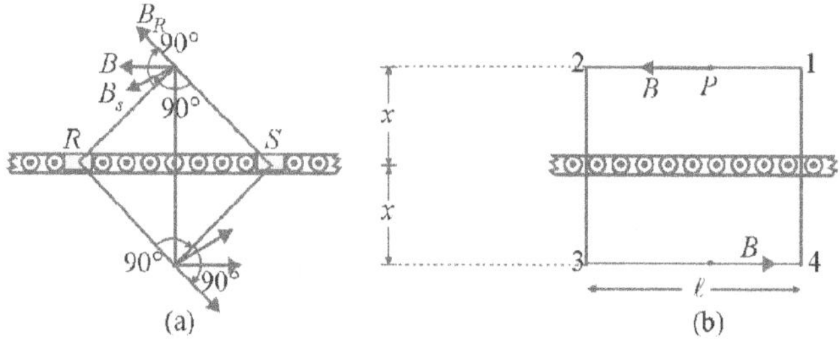

Fig. 6.43

Now applying Ampere's law to the close path 1-2-3-4-1 as shown in *fig. 6.43* ;

$$\oint \vec{B}.d\vec{\ell} = \mu_0\, i_{in}$$

$$\int_1^2 \vec{B}.d\vec{\ell} + \int_2^3 \vec{B}.d\ell + \int_3^4 \vec{B}.d\ell + \int_4^1 \vec{B}.d\ell = \mu_0(k\ell)$$

or $\qquad B\ell + 0 + B\ell + 0 = \mu_0 k\ell$

or $\qquad\qquad B = \dfrac{\mu_0 k}{2}$. $\qquad$ *Ans.*

1. Magnetic field in this case in independent of x.
2. Two large metal current carrying sheets: The magnetic field at different positions is shown in figure.

$$B_1 = B_2 = \dfrac{\mu_0 k}{2} \qquad\qquad B_1 = B_2 = \dfrac{\mu_0 k}{2}$$

$$B = B_1 + B_2 = \mu_0 k \qquad\qquad B = B_2 - B_1 = 0$$

$$B = B_1 - B_2 = 0 \qquad\qquad B = B_1 + B_2 = \mu_0 k$$

$$B = B_1 + B_2 = \mu_0 k \qquad\qquad B = B_1 - B_2 = 0$$

Ex. 14 *Fig. 6.44 shows a cross-section of a long thin ribbon of width b that is carrying a uniformly distributed total current i into the page. Calculate the magnitude and direction of the magnetic field $\vec{B}$ at a point P in the plane of the ribbon at a distance 'a' from its edge.*

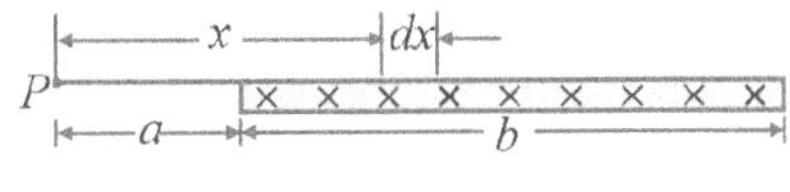

Fig. 6.44

Sol. Take a small element of thickness dx at a distance x from P, the current in the element

$$di = \dfrac{i}{b}dx ,$$

and magnetic field at P, $dB = \dfrac{\mu_0}{2\pi}.\dfrac{di}{x}$

$$= \dfrac{\mu_0}{2\pi}.\dfrac{idx/b}{x}$$

The total field $\qquad B = \dfrac{\mu_0}{2\pi}.\dfrac{i}{b}\int_a^{(a+b)}\dfrac{dx}{x}$

$$= \dfrac{\mu_0}{2\pi}.\dfrac{i}{b}|lnx|_a^{(a+b)}$$

$$= \dfrac{\mu_0}{2\pi}.\dfrac{i}{b}ln\dfrac{(a+b)}{a} . \qquad\qquad \textit{Ans.}$$

1. Unlike the gravitational and electric field, there is no scalar potential associated with the magnetic field.
2. $\mu_0 = 4\pi \times 10^{-7}$ Tm/A is an exact number and not an empirical constant.
3. Ampere's law is not independent of the Biot-Savart law. It can be derived from the Biot-Savart law. Its relationship to the Biot-Savart law is similar to the relationship between Gauss's law and Coulomb's law.

Ex. 15 Consider the current carrying loop shown in *fig. 6.45* formed of radial line and segments of circles whose centres are at point P. Find the magnitude and direction of $\vec{B}$ at point P.

Sol. Magnetic field by straight parts of the loop is zero because point P lies on their axis. The field produced by curved parts is

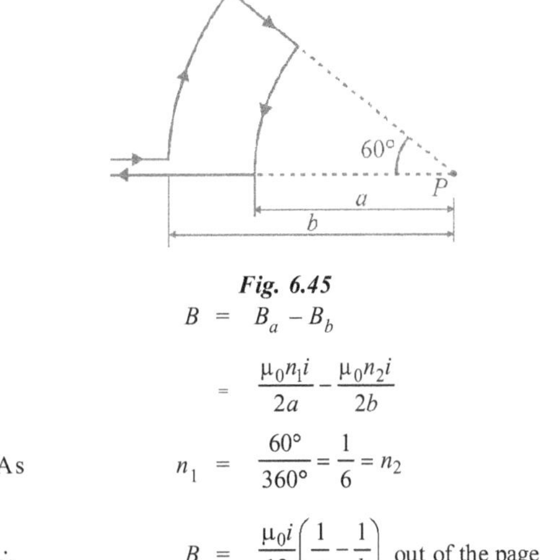

Fig. 6.45

$$B = B_a - B_b$$

$$= \dfrac{\mu_0 n_1 i}{2a} - \dfrac{\mu_0 n_2 i}{2b}$$

As $\qquad n_1 = \dfrac{60°}{360°} = \dfrac{1}{6} = n_2$

$\therefore \qquad B = \dfrac{\mu_0 i}{12}\left(\dfrac{1}{a} - \dfrac{1}{b}\right)$ out of the page $\quad$ *Ans.*

Ex. 16 A loop, carrying a current i, lying in the plane of the paper, is in the field of a long straight wire with constant current i_0 (inward) as shown in *fig. 6.46*. Find the torque acting on the loop.

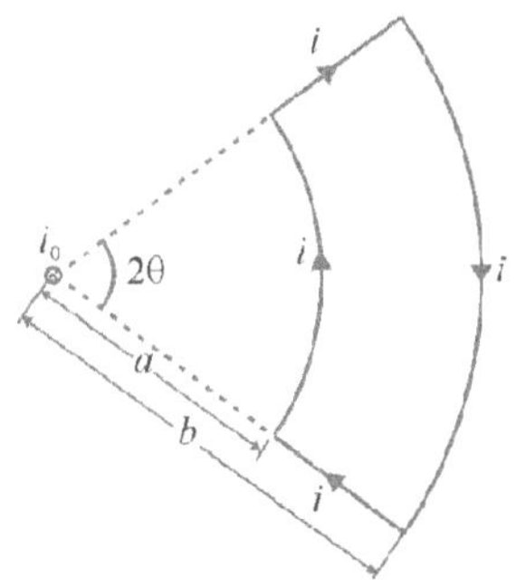

Fig. 6.46

Sol. The field due to current carrying wire is tangential to every point on the circular portion of the loop and hence the forces acting on these segments are zero.

Now consider two small elements of length dr at a distance r from the axis symmetrically as shown in *fig. 6.47.*

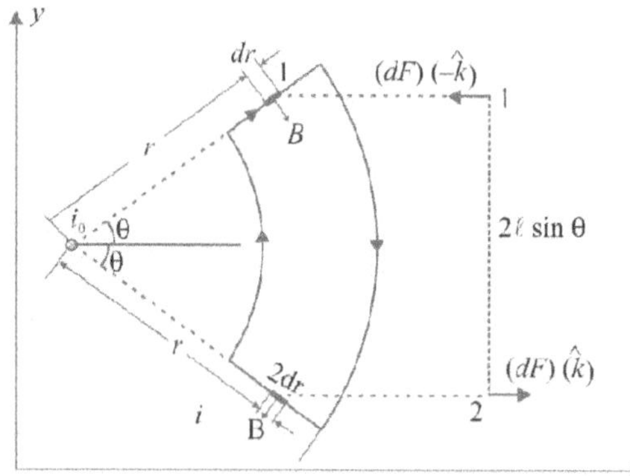

Fig. 6.47

The magnitude of the force experienced by each element is

$$dF = B\,i\,dr$$

$$= \left(\frac{\mu_0}{2\pi}\cdot\frac{i_0}{r}\right)i\,dr$$

On element 1 it is into the page and on 2 it is out of the page

$$\therefore \qquad d\tau = dF \times 2r\sin\theta$$

$$= \left(\frac{\mu_0 i_0 i}{2\pi r}dr\right)\times 2r\sin\theta$$

Now total torque,

$$\tau = \frac{\mu_0 i_0 i \sin\theta}{\pi}\int_a^b dr$$

$$= \frac{\mu_0 i_0 i}{\pi}\sin\theta(b-a). \qquad \textbf{\textit{Ans.}}$$

Ex. 17 A circular loop of radius R is bent along a diameter and given a shape as shown in the figure. One of the semicircles (KNM) lies in the xz- plane and other one (KLM) in the yz- plane with their centres at the origin current i is flowing through each of the semicircles as shown in *fig. 6.48.*

(a) A particle of charge q is released at the origin with a velocity $\vec{v} = -v_0\hat{i}$. Find the instantaneous force F on the particle. Assume that space is gravity free.

(b) If an external uniform magnetic field $B\hat{j}$ is applied, determine the forces F_1 and F_2 on the semicircles KLM and KNM due to this field and the net force F on the loop.

Sol. (a) The magnetic field due to the loop at the origin

$$\vec{B}_0 = \vec{B}_{KLM} + \vec{B}_{KNM}$$

$$= \left(\frac{\mu_0 i}{4R}\right)(-\hat{i}) + \left(\frac{\mu_0 i_0}{4R}\right)(\hat{j})$$

$$= \frac{\mu_0 i}{4R}(-\hat{i} + \hat{j})$$

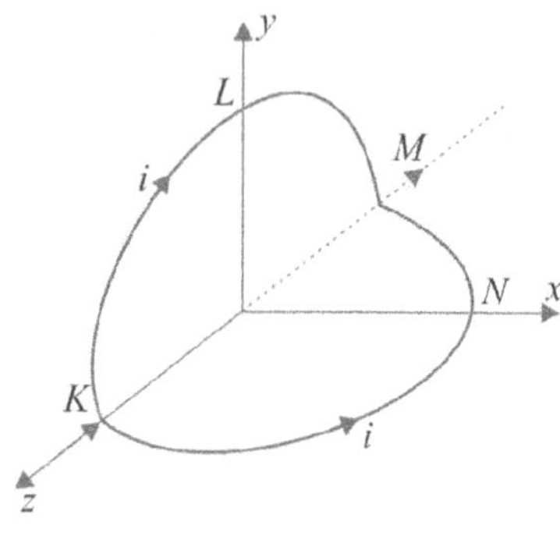

Fig. 6.48

Force on charge q at origin

$$\vec{F} = q(\vec{v}\times\vec{B})$$

$$= q\left[(-v_0\hat{i})\times\left(\frac{\mu_0 i}{4R}(-\hat{i}+\hat{j})\right)\right]$$

$$= \frac{\mu_0 q i v_0}{4R}[-\hat{i}\times(-\hat{i}+\hat{j})]$$

$$= -\frac{\mu_0 q i v_0}{4R}\hat{k} \qquad \textbf{\textit{Ans.}}$$

(b) In a uniform field the force on the curved loop is $\vec{F} = i(\vec{\ell}\times\vec{B})$, where $\vec{\ell} \to$ vector from one end of loop to the other end.

$$\therefore \qquad \vec{F}_{KLM} = i(\vec{KM}\times\vec{B}) = i[2R(-\hat{k})\times B\hat{j}] = 2BiR\hat{i}$$

$$\text{and} \qquad \vec{F}_{KNM} = i[2R(-\hat{k})\times B\hat{j}] = 2BiR\hat{i}$$

$$\therefore \qquad \vec{F} = \vec{F}_{KLM} + \vec{F}_{KNM}$$

$$= 4BiR\hat{j}. \qquad \textbf{\textit{Ans.}}$$

Ex. 18 A circular loop of radius r carrying a current i is held at the centre of another circular loop of radius $R\ (\gg r)$ carrying a current I. The plane of the smaller loop makes an angle $30°$ with that of the larger loop. If the smaller loop is held fixed in this position by applying a single force at a point on its periphery. What would be the minimum magnitude of this force ?

Sol. The magnetic field at the centre of the smaller loop, $B = \dfrac{\mu_0 I}{2R}$.

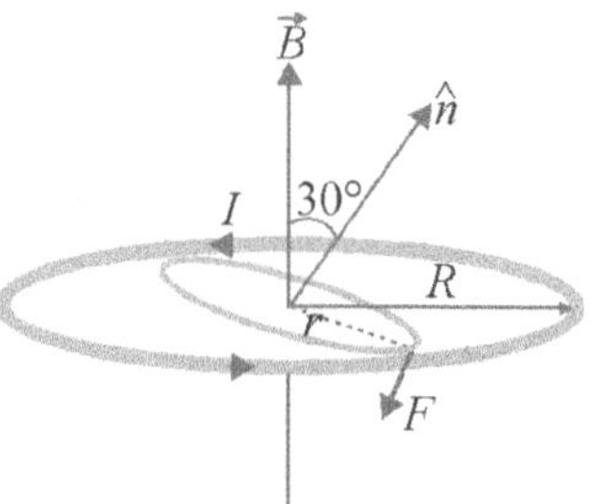

Fig. 6.49

According to right hand screw rule, it is along as shown in *fig. 6.50.* Since smaller loop is placed at its centre and assuming that field is uniform all over it, the torque exerted by magnitude field

$$\tau = MB\sin\theta$$

$$= (i\pi r^2) \times \frac{\mu_0 I}{2R}\sin 30°$$

$$= \frac{\mu_0 \pi i l r^2}{4R}$$

If F is the force at the periphery then, to keep the loop at its position

$$F \times r = \frac{\mu_0 \pi i l r^2}{4R}$$

or $$F = \frac{\mu_0 \pi i l r}{4R}. \qquad \textit{Ans.}$$

Ex. 19 A long straight wire carries a current i. A particle having a positive charge q and mass m, kept at a distance x_0 from the wire is projected towards it with a speed v. Find the minimum separation between the wire and the particle.

Sol. Let the particle be initially at P. The magnetic field $\vec{B}$ at any point to the right of the wire is along the negative z-axis. The magnetic force on the particle is, therefore, in the xy- plane. As there is no initial velocity along the z-axis, the motion will be in the xy- plane. Also its speed remain unchanged. As the field is not uniform, so the path of the particle not remain as circle.

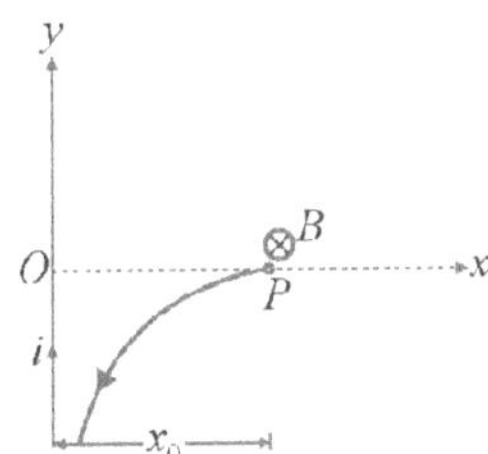

Fig. 6.50

We have, $$\vec{v} = v_x \hat{i} + v_y \hat{j}$$

and $$\vec{B} = \left(\frac{\mu_0}{2\pi} \cdot \frac{i}{x}\right)\left(-\hat{k}\right)$$

The force on the particle

$$\vec{F} = q\vec{v} \times \vec{B}$$

$$= q\left(v_x \hat{i} + v_y \hat{j}\right) \times \left(-\frac{\mu_0 i}{2\pi x}\hat{k}\right)$$

$$= -\left(\frac{qv_y\mu_0 i}{2\pi x}\right)\hat{i} + \left(\frac{qv_x\mu_0 i}{2\pi x}\right)\hat{j}$$

Thus $$a_x = \frac{F_x}{m} = -\frac{qv_y\mu_0 i}{2\pi m x}$$

$$= -k\frac{v_y}{x} \qquad ....(i)$$

where $$k = \frac{\mu_0 qi}{2\pi m}$$

Also $$a_x = \frac{dv_x}{dt} = \frac{dv_x}{dx}\cdot\frac{dx}{dt} = v_x\frac{dv_x}{dx} \qquad ...(ii)$$

As $$v_x^2 + v_y^2 = v^2 \text{ (constant)}$$

On differentiating

$$2v_x dv_x + 2v_y dv_y = 0$$

which gives $$v_x dv_x = -v_y dv_y \qquad ...(iii)$$

From equations (i), (ii) and (iii), we have

$$\frac{v_y dv_y}{dx} = -k\frac{v_y}{x}$$

or $$\frac{dx}{x} = \frac{dv_y}{k}$$

Initially at $$x = x_0, v_y = 0$$
At minimum separation from wire, $\vec{v_x} = 0, v_y = -v$

Thus $$\int_{x_0}^{x} \frac{dx}{x} = \int_{0}^{-v} \frac{dv_y}{k}$$

or $$\left|\ell nx\right|_{x_0}^{x} = \left|\frac{v_y}{k}\right|_{0}^{-v}$$

or $$\ell n\frac{x}{x_0} = \frac{-v}{k}$$

or $$x = x_0 e^{-\frac{v}{k}}$$

$$= x_0 e^{-\frac{2\pi m v}{\mu_0 qi}}. \qquad \textit{Ans.}$$

Ex. 20 A copper wire with cross-sectional area S, bent to make three sides of a square can turn about a horizontal axis OO'. The wire is located in uniform vertical field. Find the magnetic induction if on passing a current i through the wire the latter deflects by an angle θ.

Sol.

Let side of square is a. The magnetic field $\vec{B}$ makes $180°$ with OP and $0°$ with QO' therefore forces on these sides are zero. The force on side PQ $= Bia$, acts out of page and $\perp$ to the plane of the figure. The torque exerted by field

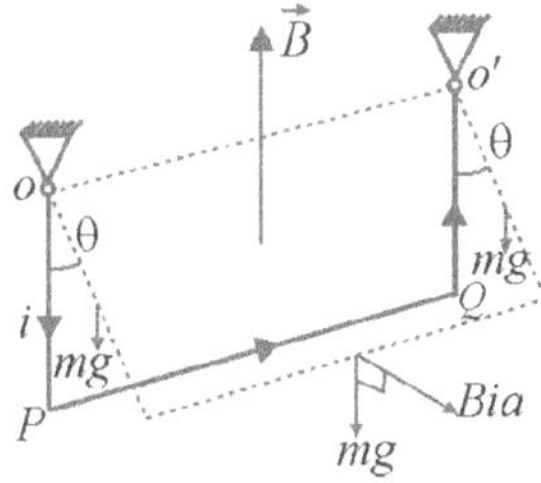

Fig. 6.51

$$\tau = \left(Bia\right) \times a\cos\theta$$

Let mass of each side is m, then restoring torque

$$\tau_{res} = mg \times \frac{a}{2}\sin\theta + mg \times a\sin\theta + mg \times \frac{a}{2}\sin\theta$$

$$= 2mg\,a\,\sin\theta$$

$$= 2\left(Sa\rho\right)a\sin\theta$$

For equilibrium,

$$Bia^2\cos\theta = 2S\rho ga^2\sin\theta$$

or

$$B = \frac{2S\rho g}{i}\tan\theta. \qquad \textit{Ans.}$$

Ex. 21 A current of 10A flows around a closed path in a circuit which is in the horizontal plane as shown in *fig. 6.52*. The circuit consists of eight alternating arcs of radii $r_1 = 0.08$ m and $r_2 = 0.12$ m each. Each arc subtends the same angle at the centre.

(a) Find the magnetic field produced by this circuit at the centre.

(b) An infinitely long straight wire carrying a current of 10A is passed through the centre of the above circuit vertically with the direction of the current being into the plane of the circuit. What is the force acting on the wire at the centre due to the current in the circuit ?

What is the force acting on the arc ACD and the straight segment CD due to the current at the centre ?

Sol. (a) The magnetic field due to straight parts of the loop is zero, because centre O lies on their axis.

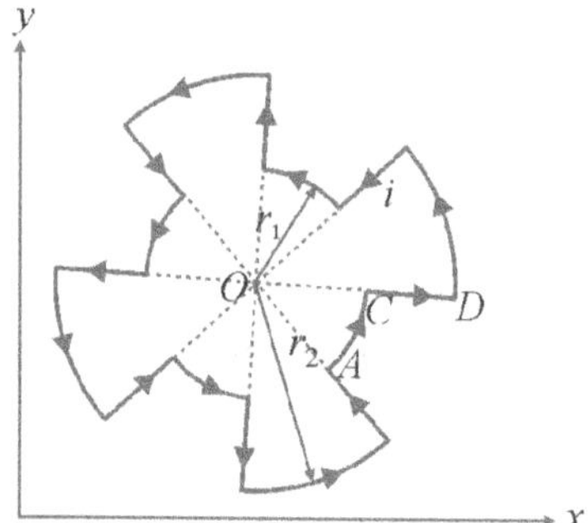

Fig. 6.52

The total field at the centre

$$B = B_1 + B_2$$

$$= \frac{\mu_0\left(\frac{1}{2}\right)i}{2r_1} + \frac{\mu_0\left(\frac{1}{2}\right)i}{2r_2}$$

$$= \frac{\mu_0 i}{4}\left(\frac{1}{r_1} + \frac{1}{r_2}\right),$$

the direction of the field is out of the page, i.e. along z-axis

$$= \left(\frac{4\pi \times 10^{-7}}{4}\right)\times 10\left(\frac{1}{0.08} + \frac{1}{0.12}\right)$$

$$= 65.45 \times 10^{-6}\ T. \qquad \textit{Ans.}$$

(b) As the field of the circuit at centre and conductor are anti parallel, therefore force on it is zero. Further, field due to current carrying conductor at centre will be tangentially to each point of AC. Therefore force of part AC is zero. While field is perpendicular to

part CD, but varies from C to D.

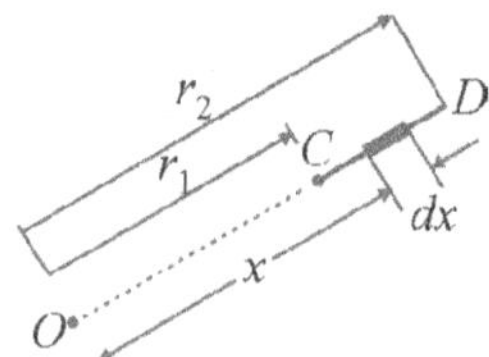

Fig. 6.53

Let at any distance x from the centre.

$$B = \frac{\mu_0}{2\pi}\frac{i}{x}$$

The force on length dx of CD

$$dF = Bi\,(dx)$$

$$= \left(\frac{\mu_0}{2\pi}\frac{i}{x}\right)i\,dx$$

Total force

$$F = \int_{r_1}^{r_2}\frac{\mu_0}{2\pi}\frac{i^2}{x}\,dx$$

$$= \frac{\mu_0}{2\pi}i^2\ell n\frac{r_2}{r_1}$$

or

$$= \left(2\times 10^{-7}\right)\times\left(10\right)^2\times\ell n\left[\frac{0.12}{0.08}\right]$$

$$= 8.1\times 10^{-6}\ N. \qquad \textit{Ans.}$$

Ex. 22 Two particles each having a mass m are placed at a separation d in a uniform magnetic field B as shown in *fig. 6.54*. They have opposite charges of equal magnitude q. At time $t = 0$, the particles are projected towards each other, each with a speed of v. Suppose the Coulomb force between charges is switched off.

(a) Find the maximum value of v_m of the projection speed so that the two particles do not collide.

(b) What would be the minimum and maximum separation between the particles if $v = \dfrac{v_m}{2}$?

(c) At what instant will a collision occur between the particles, if $v = 2v_m$?

(d) Suppose $v = 2v_m$ and collision between the particles is completely inelastic. Describe the motion after the collision.

Sol. (a)

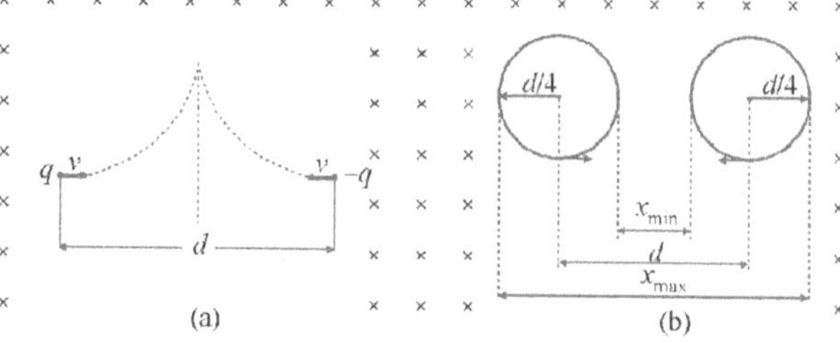

Fig. 6.54

They projected with such a speed v_m so that each moves in a path of radius $r = \dfrac{d}{2}$. If they will not collide, then

$$r = \frac{d}{2} = \frac{mv_m}{qB}$$

or $\qquad v_m = \dfrac{qBd}{2m}$ **Ans.**

(b) For $\qquad v = \dfrac{v_m}{2}$

$$= \frac{qBd}{4m},$$

$$r = \frac{mv}{qB} = \frac{m\left(\dfrac{qBd}{4m}\right)}{qB} = \frac{d}{4}$$

Both the particles move on the path of radius $\dfrac{d}{4}$.

From the figure $x_{\min} = \dfrac{d}{2}$

and $\qquad x_{\max} = d + \dfrac{d}{2} = \dfrac{3d}{2}$ **Ans.**

(c) When particle velocity

$$v = 2v_m = \frac{qBd}{m},$$

$$r = \frac{mv}{qB} = \frac{m\left(qBd\right)}{qB} = d$$

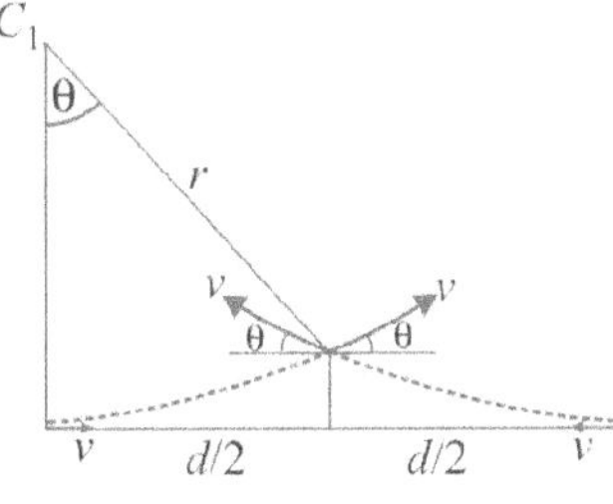

Fig. 6.55

They will collide at a horizontal distance $\dfrac{d}{2}$.

$$\therefore \qquad \sin\theta = \frac{\left(\dfrac{d}{2}\right)}{r} = \frac{\dfrac{d}{2}}{d} = \frac{1}{2}$$

or $\qquad \theta = \dfrac{\pi}{6}$ radian

Therefore each particle travel for time t before collision

$$\therefore \qquad t = \frac{T}{2\pi}\theta = \left(\frac{2\pi m}{qB}\right) \times \left(\frac{\dfrac{\pi}{6}}{2\pi}\right) = \frac{\pi m}{6qB}$$

Ans.

(d) When collision is perfectly inelastic, the particles stick together.

The resultant momentum of the combined mass in horizontal direction becomes zero. Therefore the combined mass moves along a straight line drawn upward in the plane of figure through the point of collision. Because magnetic field does not exert force on it, $q_{\text{net}} = 0$.

Momentum before collision = momentum after collision

$$mv\sin\theta + mv\sin\theta = (2m)v'$$

$$\therefore \qquad v' = v\sin\theta$$

$$= v \times \frac{1}{2} = \frac{v}{2}$$

$$= \frac{2v_m}{2} = v_m.$$ **Ans.**

Ex. 23 Given *fig. 6.56* shows a coil bent with all edges of length 1m and carrying a current of 1A. There exists in space a uniform magnetic field of $2T$ in the positive *y*-direction. Find the torque on the loop.

Sol. The forces on the edges FG and BC are zero. The forces on the other edges are :

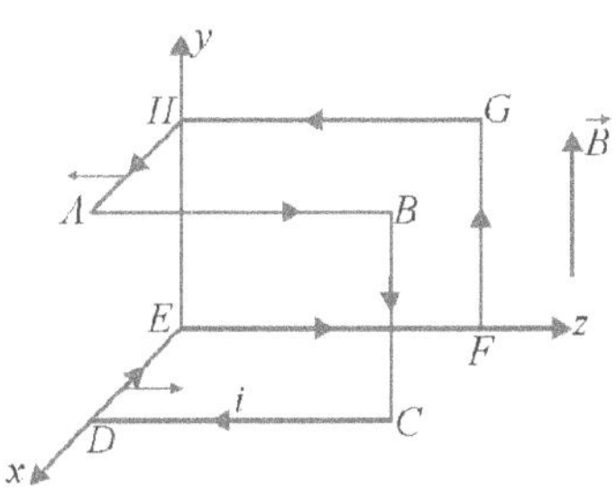

Fig. 6.56

$$F_{AB} = Bi\ell\left(\hat{i}\right),$$

$$F_{CD} = Bi\ell\left(-\hat{i}\right),$$

$$F_{HG} = Bi\ell\left(-\hat{i}\right),$$

$$F_{EF} = Bi\ell\left(\hat{i}\right).$$

The torque of the forces F_{AB} and F_{HG} is zero and that of F_{CD} and F_{EF} is zero.

The forces on edges AH and DE are equal and opposite and so constitutes a net torque. Thus

$$F_{AH} = Bi\ell\left(-\hat{k}\right) \text{ and } F_{DE} = Bi\ell\left(\hat{k}\right)$$

Torque, $\qquad \vec{\tau} = F_{AH}\,\ell\left(\hat{i}\right) = Bi\ell \times \ell\left(\hat{i}\right)$

$$= 2 \times 1 \times 1^2 = 2\hat{i} \text{ N-m.}$$

Ex. 24

(a) Current i enters into a loop as shown in figure. Find magnetic field at the centre of the loop.

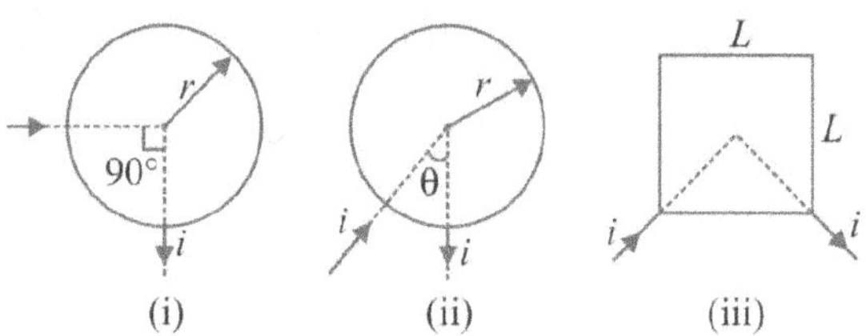

(i)   (ii)   (iii)

Fig. 6.57

(b) A circular current carrying circular loop of mass m and radius r is placed on horizontal surface in a uniform magnetic field B acts parallel to the plane of the ring. Find current in the loop, so that it will tilt about the edge.

(c) A long current carrying conductor carrying current i, is fixed on the surface. Another conductor of mass per unit length m is at a vertical distance h and parallel to first conductor. Find current i_2 in the second conductor so that it remains at rest.

(d) A conductor of length ℓ and mass m carrying current i is in on smooth inclined plane of inclination θ. A magnetic field B is acting vertically. Find value of current i, so that it remains in equilibrium on the plane.

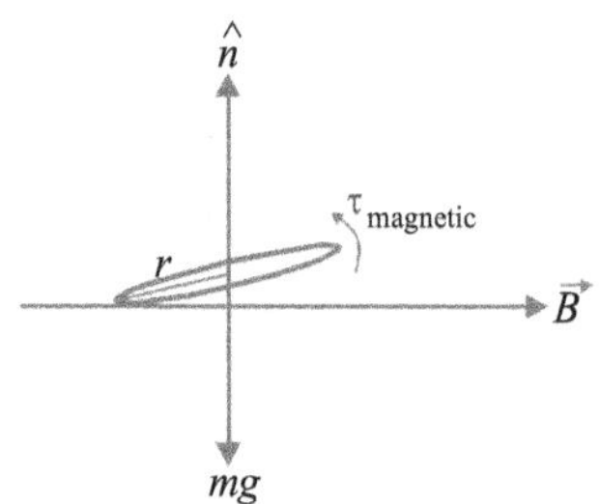

Fig. 6.58

Sol.

(a) The currents in two parts of the loop is shown in figure.

  (i) The magnetic field at the centre of the loop,

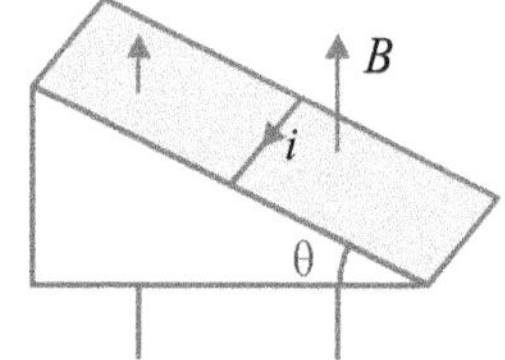

$$B = \frac{\mu_0 \left(\frac{3}{4}\right)\frac{i}{4}}{2r} - \frac{\mu_0 \left(\frac{1}{4}\right)\frac{3i}{4}}{2r}$$

$$= 0 \qquad \qquad \textit{Fig. 6.59} \qquad Ans.$$

  (ii) Solution is same as of part (i). $B = 0$

(b) The loop will tilt about the edge if,

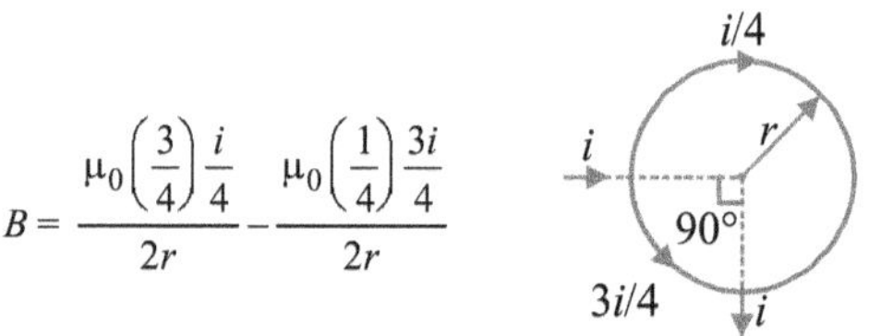

Fig. 6.60

$$\tau_{magnetic} = \tau_{weight}$$

or $\qquad iAB\sin 90° = mg \times r$

$$\therefore \qquad i = \left[\frac{mgr}{AB}\right]. \qquad\qquad Ans.$$

(c) For second conductor be at rest

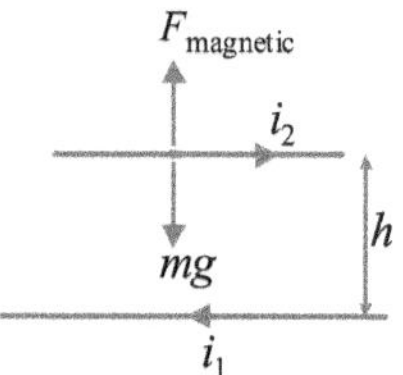

Fig. 6.61

Weight per unit length = magnetic force on unit length

or $\qquad mg = \dfrac{\mu_0}{2\pi}\cdot\dfrac{i_1 i_2}{h}$

$$\therefore \qquad i_2 = \frac{mgh}{\left(\dfrac{\mu_0}{2\pi}\right)i_1}. \qquad\qquad Ans.$$

(d) If i is the current in the conductor, then it experience a horizontal force of magnitude $B\,i\,\ell$. so for its equilibrium.

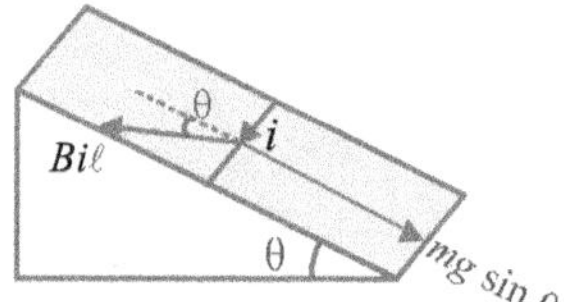

Fig. 6.62

$$Bi\ell\cos\theta = mg\sin\theta$$

or $\qquad i = \left(\dfrac{mg\tan\theta}{B\ell}\right). \qquad\qquad Ans.$

Ex. 25

A uniform constant magnetic field B is directed at an angle of 45° to the x-axis in xy-plane. PQRS is a rigid square wire frame carrying a steady current i_0, with its centre at the origin O. At time $t = 0$, the frame is at rest in the position shown in the figure, with its side parallel to x and y axis. Each side of the frame is of mass M and length L.

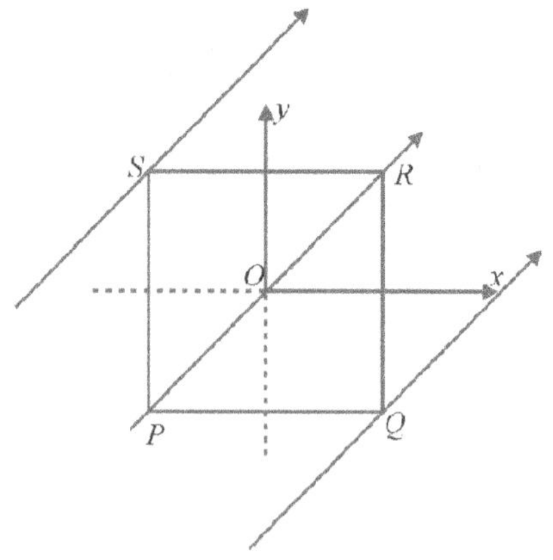

Fig. 6.63

(a) What is the torque $\vec{\tau}$ about O acting on the frame due to magnetic field ?

(b) Find the angle by which the frame rotates under the action of this torque in a short interval of time Δt, and the axis about which this rotation occurs (Δt is so short that any variation in the torque during this interval may be neglected).

Sol. (a) Given, magnetic field

$$\vec{B} = B\left(\cos 45°\,\hat{i} + \sin 45°\,\hat{j}\right) = \frac{B}{\sqrt{2}}\left(\hat{i} + \hat{j}\right)$$

$$\vec{A} = L^2\hat{k}$$

$$\therefore \quad \vec{\tau} = \vec{M} \times \vec{B}$$

$$= i\left(\vec{A} \times \vec{B}\right) = i_0\left[L^2\hat{k} \times \frac{B}{\sqrt{2}}\left(\hat{i} + \hat{j}\right)\right]$$

$$= \frac{i_0 L^2 B}{\sqrt{2}}\left(-\hat{i} + \hat{j}\right). \qquad \textit{Ans.}$$

(b) It is clear from above result that axis of rotation is $= \left(\dfrac{-\hat{i} + \hat{j}}{\sqrt{2}}\right)$

i.e., SQ.

Moment of inertia of the frame about axis of rotation SQ :
Moment of inertia of the frame about an axis passing through O and perpendicular to the plane of the frame.

$$I_O = 4\left[\frac{ML^2}{12} + M\left(\frac{L}{2}\right)^2\right] = \frac{4}{3}ML^2$$

By perpendicular axis theorem
$$2\,I_{SQ} = I.$$

$$\therefore \quad I_{SQ} = \frac{I_0}{2} = \frac{2}{3}ML^2$$

We know that $\quad \tau = I\alpha$

$$\therefore \quad \alpha = \frac{\tau}{I} = \frac{i_0 BL^2}{\frac{2}{3}ML^2} = \frac{3}{2}\frac{i_0 B}{M}$$

Thus angular rotation

$$\theta = \frac{1}{2}\alpha(\Delta t)^2$$

$$= \frac{1}{2}\left(\frac{3}{2}\frac{i_0 B}{M}\right)\Delta t^2$$

$$= \frac{3}{4}\frac{i_0 B}{M}\Delta t^2. \qquad \textit{Ans.}$$

Ex. 26 A rectangular loop **PQRS** made from a uniform wire has length a, width b and mass m. It is free to rotate about the arm PQ, which remains hinged along a horizontal line taken as the y-axis (see *fig. 6.64*). Take vertically upward direction as the z-axis. A uniform magnetic field $\vec{B} = \left(3\hat{i} + 4\hat{k}\right)B_0$ exists in the region. The loop is held in the xy-plane and a current I is passed through it. The loop is now released and is found to stay in the horizontal position in equilibrium.

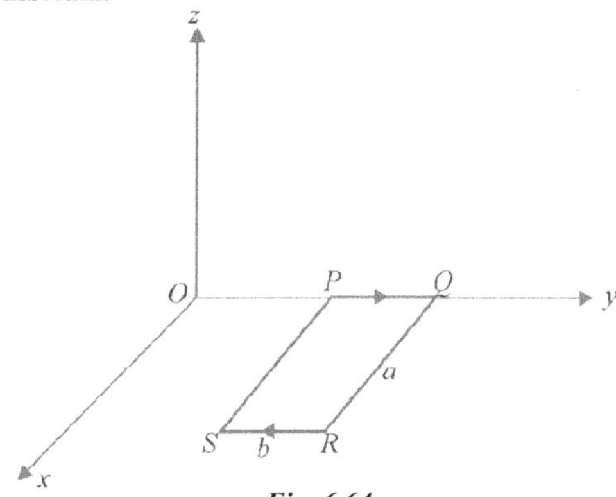

Fig. 6.64

(a) What is the direction of the current in PQ ?

(b) Find the magnetic force on the arm RS.

(c) Find the expression of I in terms of B_0, a, b and m.

Sol. (a) For the equilibrium of the loop in horizontal plane, the net torque on it must be zero. Thus if $\vec{\tau}_{mg}$ is the torque exerted by the weight and $\vec{\tau}_{mag}$ is the torque due to magnetic force, then

$$\vec{\tau}_{mg} + \vec{\tau}_{mag} = 0$$

$$\therefore \quad \vec{\tau}_{mag} = -\vec{\tau}_{mg} \qquad ...(i)$$

Here $\quad \vec{\tau}_{mg} = \left(mg\,\frac{a}{2}\,\hat{j}\right)$

and $\quad \vec{\tau}_{mag} = \vec{M} \times \vec{B}$

$$= I\,\vec{A} \times \vec{B}$$

$$= I\left[a\hat{i} \times \left(-b\hat{j}\right)\right] \times \left(3\hat{i} + 4\hat{k}\right)B_0$$

(Assuming direction of current in the loop clockwise.)

$$= I\left[ab\left(-\hat{k}\right)\right] \times \left(3\hat{i} + 4\hat{k}\right)B_0$$

$$= -3abI\,\hat{j}.$$

Substituting these values in equation (i), we get

$$-3abI\,\hat{j} = -\left(mg\,\frac{a}{2}\right)\hat{j}$$

$$\therefore \quad I = \frac{mg}{6bB_0} \qquad \textit{Ans.}$$

Positive sign with I indicates that direction of current in PQ is correctly assumed.

(b) Force on the arm RS is given by

$$\vec{F} = \left(I\vec{\ell} \times \vec{B}\right)$$

$$= I\left(-b\hat{j}\right) \times \left(3\hat{i} + 4\hat{k}\right)B_0$$

$$= I\,B_0\left(-4\hat{i} + 3\hat{k}\right) N \qquad \textit{Ans.}$$

(c) It has been obtained in part (a).

Ex. 27 Ring of radius R having uniformly distributed charge Q is mounted on a rod suspended by two identical strings as shown in *fig. 6.65*. The tension in strings in equilibrium is T_0. Now a vertical magnetic field is switched on and the ring is rotated at constant angular velocity ω. Find the maximum ω with which the ring can be rotated if the strings can withstand a maximum tension $\dfrac{3T_0}{2}$

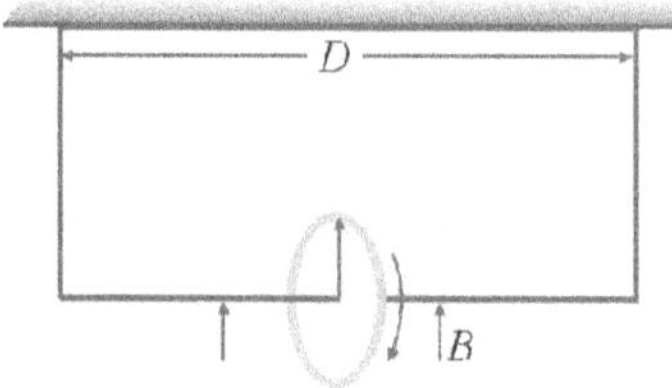

Fig. 6.65

Sol. Initially $\quad 2T_0 = mg \qquad\qquad ...(i)$

If ω be the frequency corresponding to the breaking of the string, then current in the ring

$$i = \frac{Q}{T} = \frac{Q}{\dfrac{2\pi}{\omega}} = \frac{Q\omega}{2\pi}$$

Magnetic moment of the loop

$$M = iA$$

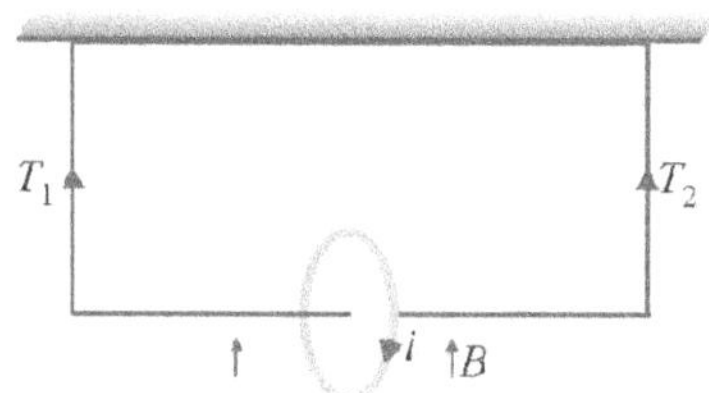

Fig. 6.66

The torque experiences now

$$\tau = MB\sin 90°$$
$$= iAB.$$

If T_1 and T_2 are the tensions in the strings now, then

$$\left(T_1 - T_2\right)\frac{D}{2} = iAB$$

or $\qquad T_1 - T_2 = \dfrac{2iAB}{D} \qquad ...(ii)$

Also $\qquad T_1 + T_2 = mg \qquad ...(iii)$

Solving equations (ii) and (iii), we get

$$T_1 = \frac{mg}{2} + \left(\frac{iAB}{D}\right)$$

and

$$T_2 = \frac{mg}{2} - \left(\frac{iAB}{D}\right)$$

As $T_1 > T_2$, $\therefore \qquad T_1 = \dfrac{3T_0}{2}$ (Given).

Hence $\qquad \dfrac{3T_0}{2} = \dfrac{2T_0}{2} + \dfrac{\omega Q}{2\pi D} \times \pi R^2 \times B$

or $\qquad T_0 = \dfrac{\omega QBR^2}{D}$

or $\qquad \omega = \dfrac{DT_0}{QBR^2}.$ **Ans.**

Review of formulae & Important Points

1. Magnetic field of moving charge :

$$B = \frac{\mu_0}{4\pi} \frac{qv\sin\theta}{r^2},$$

and its direction can be obtained by right hand screw rule.

2. The magnetic force between two moving charges q_1 and q_2 is given by

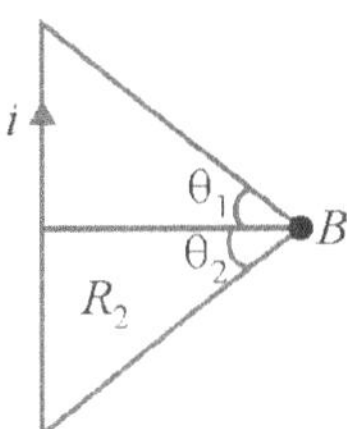

$$F_m = \frac{\mu_0}{4\pi} \cdot \frac{q_1 q_2 \, v_1 v_2}{r^2}$$

3. Biot-Savart law :

The magnetic field due to the current element $d\vec{\ell}$ at any point P at a distance $\vec{r}$ is given by

$$d\vec{B} = \frac{\mu_0}{4\pi} \frac{id\vec{\ell} \times \vec{r}}{r^3}.$$

4. Magnetic field due to a current carrying wire :

$$B = \frac{\mu_0}{4\pi} \frac{i}{r}\left(\sin\theta_1 + \sin\theta_2\right).$$

Magnetic field due to a long straight wire

$$B = \frac{\mu_0 i}{2\pi r},$$

at the middle region of the wire.

and $\qquad B = \frac{\mu_0 i}{4\pi r}$ at the end of the wire.

5. The force between two parallel current carrying wires :

$$\frac{dF}{d\ell} = \frac{\mu_0}{2\pi} \frac{i_1 i_2}{r}.$$

6. Magnetic field at the centre of the circular current carrying coil

$$B = \frac{\mu_0 Ni}{2a}$$

The magnetic field on the axis of the circular current carrying coil

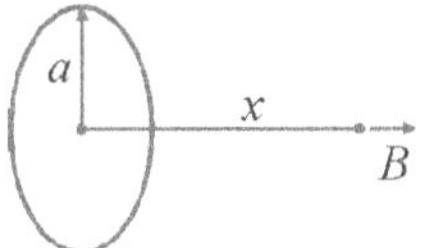

$$B = \frac{\mu_0 ia^2}{2\left(a^2 + x^2\right)^{3/2}}$$

7. Magnetic field due to a solenoid

$$B = \frac{\mu_0 ni}{2}\left[\cos\theta_1 - \cos\theta_2\right]$$

Magnetic field due to a long solenoid at its centre

$$B = \mu_0 ni.$$

Magnetic field of a toroid of radius R

$$B = \frac{\mu_0 Ni}{2\pi R}$$

8. Ampere's law : It states that

$$\oint \vec{B} \cdot d\vec{\ell} = \mu_0 \, i_{\text{in}}.$$

The line integral in this equation is evaluated around a closed loop called Amperian loop. The current i_{in} is the net current encircled by the loop.

9. The magnetic field inside a current carrying tube is zero.

10. The magnetic field due to a magnetic dipole on its axis

$$\vec{B} = \frac{\mu_0}{4\pi} \frac{2\vec{M}}{x^3}$$

★ ★ ★

LEVEL - 1

Only one option correct

1. The figure shows three long, straight, parallel, equally spaced wires with identical currents either into or out of the page. If F_A, F_B and F_C are the magnitudes of forces on them respectively, then

(a) $F_A > F_B > F_C$ (b) $F_A = F_B > F_C$

(c) $F_B > F_C > F_A$ (d) $F_C > F_A > F_B$

2. The figure shows three equal currents i (two parallel and one antiparallel) and four closed loops. Which loop has greatest value of $\oint \vec{B} \cdot d\vec{\ell}$?

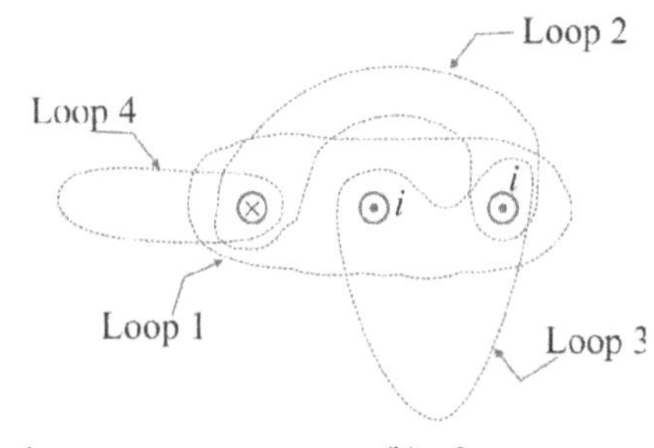

(a) 1   (b) 2

(c) 3   (d) 4

3. The figure shows four arrangements of circular loops of radius r or $2r$, centered on vertical axes (perpendicular to the loops) and carrying identical currents in the direction indicated, in which arrangement, the magnitude of the net magnetic field at the dot is the greatest :

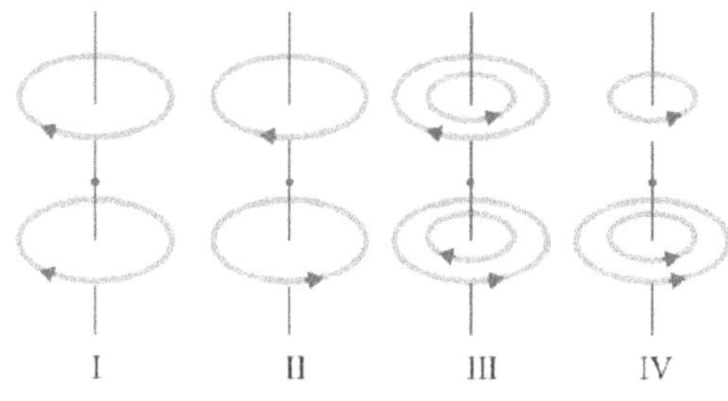

(a) I   (b) II

(c) III   (d) IV

4. In a coaxial, straight cable, the central conductor and the outer conductor carry equal currents in opposite directions. The magnetic field is zero

(a) inside the inner conductor

(b) inside the outer conductor

(c) in between the two conductor

(d) outside the cable.

5. A current-carrying straight wire is kept along the axis of a circular loop carrying a current. The straight wire

(a) will exert an inward force on the circular loop

(b) will exert an outward force on the circular loop

(c) will not exert any force on the circular loop

(d) will exert a force on the circular loop parallel to itself.

6. The magnetic field at the origin due to a current element $id\vec{\ell}$ placed at a position $\vec{r}$ is

(a) $-\dfrac{\mu_0}{4\pi} \dfrac{id\vec{\ell} \times \vec{r}}{r^3}$ (b) $\dfrac{\mu_0}{4\pi} \dfrac{id\vec{\ell} \times \vec{r}}{r^3}$

(c) $-\dfrac{\mu_0}{4\pi} \dfrac{\vec{r} \times id\vec{\ell}}{r^3}$ (d) none of these

7. Two infinitely long conducting wires carry currents, as shown in figure. If the horizontal wire carrying current produces a magnetic field B at the point $P(-2d,-d,0)$, then the resultant magnetic field at this point is

(a) $-2B\,\hat{k}$

(b) $-\sqrt{2}\,B\,\hat{k}$

(c) $\sqrt{2}\,B\,\hat{k}$

(d) zero

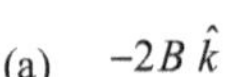

8. A length L of wire carries a steady current I. It is bent first to form a circular plane coil of one turn. The same length is now bent more sharply to give a double loop of smaller radius. The magnetic field at the centre caused by the same current is

(a) a quarter of its first value

(b) unaltered

(c) four times of its first value

(d) a half of its first value

9. A vertical straight conductor carries a current vertically upwards. A point P lies to the east of it at a small distance and another point Q lies to the west at the same distance. The magnetic field at P is

(a) greater than at Q

(b) same as at Q

(c) less than at Q

(d) greater or less than at Q depending upon the strength of the current

Answer Key	1	(c)	2	(c)	3	(d)	4	(d)	5	(c)
Sol. from page 437	6	(a)	7	(a)	8	(c)	9	(b)		

10. An infinitely long straight conductor is bent into the shape as shown in the figure. It carries a current of i ampere and the radius of the circular loop is r metre. Then the magnetic induction at its centre will be

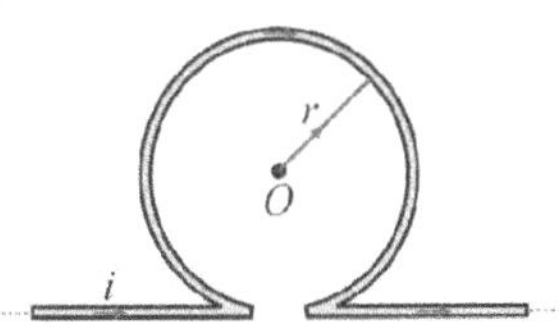

(a) $\dfrac{\mu_0}{\pi}\dfrac{2i}{r}(\pi+1)$

(b) $\dfrac{\mu_0}{4\pi}\dfrac{2i}{r}(\pi-1)$

(c) zero

(d) infinite

11. The magnetic induction at the centre O in the figure shown is

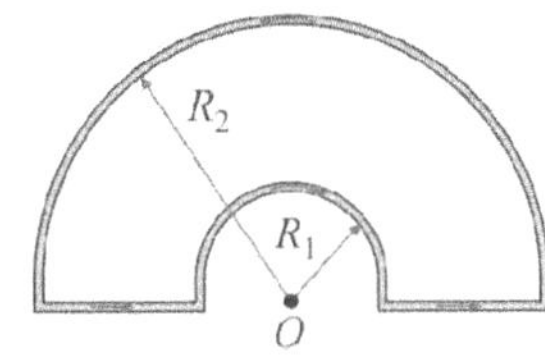

(a) $\dfrac{\mu_0 i}{4}\left(\dfrac{1}{R_1}-\dfrac{1}{R_2}\right)$

(b) $\dfrac{\mu_0 i}{4}\left(\dfrac{1}{R_1}+\dfrac{1}{R_2}\right)$

(c) $\dfrac{\mu_0 i}{4}\left(R_1-R_2\right)$

(d) $\dfrac{\mu_0 i}{4}\left(R_1+R_2\right)$

12. A vertical wire kept in zx-plane carries a current from Q to P (see figure). The magnetic field due to current will have the direction at the origin O along

(a) OX

(b) OX'

(c) OY

(d) OY'

13. An electron moving in a circular orbit of radius r makes n rotation per second. The magnetic field produced at the centre has a magnitude of

(a) $\dfrac{\mu_0 ne}{2r}$

(b) $\dfrac{\mu_0 n^2 e}{2r}$

(c) $\dfrac{\mu_0 ne}{2\pi r}$

(d) zero

14. Two long straight wires are set parallel to each other. Each carries a current i in the same direction and the separation between them is $2r$. The intensity of the magnetic field midway between them is

(a) $\mu_0 i/r$

(b) $4\mu_0 i/r$

(c) zero

(d) $\mu_0 i/4r$

15. A part of a long wire carrying a current i is bent into a circle of radius r as shown in figure. The net magnetic field at the centre O of the circular loop is

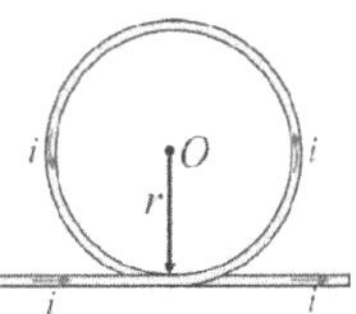

(a) $\dfrac{\mu_0 i}{4r}$

(b) $\dfrac{\mu_0 i}{2r}$

(c) $\dfrac{\mu_0 i}{2\pi r}(\pi+1)$

(d) $\dfrac{\mu_0 i}{2\pi r}(\pi-1)$

16. The earth's magnetic field at a given point is 0.5×10^{-5} Wb-m^{-2}. This field is to be annulled by magnetic induction at the center of a circular conducting loop of radius 5.0 cm. The current required to be flown in the loop is nearly

(a) 0.2 A

(b) 0.4 A

(c) 4 A

(d) 40 A

17. The magnetic field due to a current carrying circular loop of radius 3 cm at a point on the axis at a distance of 4 cm from the centre is 54 μT. What will be its value at the centre of the loop

(a) 250 μT

(b) 150 μT

(c) 125 μT

(d) 75 μT

18. Two concentric coils each of radius equal to 2π cm are placed at right angles to each other. 3 ampere and 4 ampere are the currents flowing in each coil respectively. The magnetic induction in weber / m^2 at the centre of the coils will be $\left(\mu_0 = 4\pi\times10^{-7}\ \text{Wb/A.m}\right)$

(a) 5×10^{-5}

(b) 7×10^{-5}

(c) 12×10^{-5}

(d) 10^{-5}

19. Wires 1 and 2 carrying currents i_1 and i_2 respectively are inclined at an angle θ to each other. What is the force on a small element $d\ell$ of wire 2 at a distance of r from wire 1 (as shown in figure) due to the magnetic field of wire 1

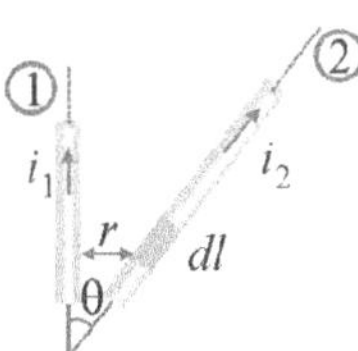

(a) $\dfrac{\mu_0}{2\pi r}i_1 i_2 d\ell \tan\theta$

(b) $\dfrac{\mu_0}{2\pi r}i_1 i_2 d\ell \sin\theta$

(c) $\dfrac{\mu_0}{2\pi r}i_1 i_2 d\ell \cos\theta$

(d) $\dfrac{\mu_0}{4\pi r}i_1 i_2 d\ell \sin\theta$

Answer Key	10	(b)	11	(a)	12	(d)	13	(a)	14	(c)
Sol. from page 437	15	(c)	16	(b)	17	(a)	18	(a)	19	(c)

20. Which of the following graphs shows the variation of magnetic induction B with distance r from a long wire carrying current

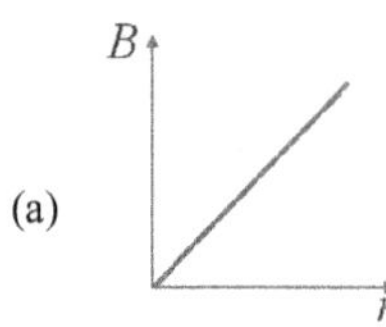

(a)

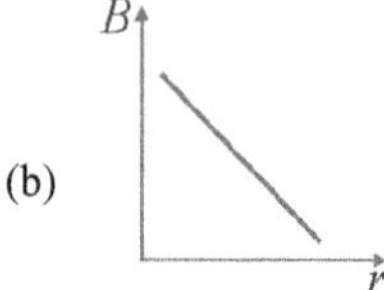

(b)

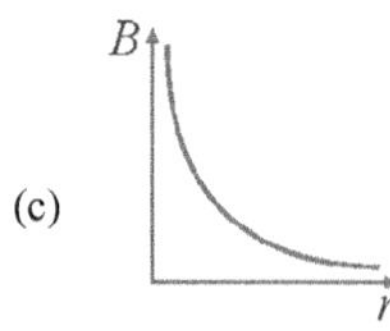

(c)

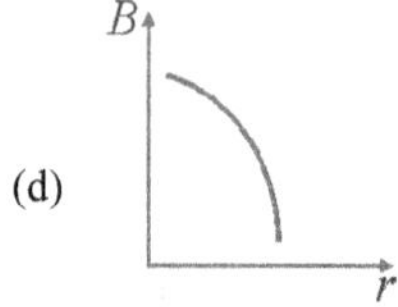

(d)

21. A wire of length L metre carries a current I ampere, is bent in the form of a circle. The magnitude of its magnetic moment in MKS units is :

(a) $4\pi IL^2$

(b) $\dfrac{2IL^2}{\pi}$

(c) $\dfrac{IL^2}{\pi}$

(d) $\dfrac{IL^2}{4\pi}$

22. Circular loop of a wire and a long straight wire carry currents I_c and I_e, respectively as shown in the figure. Assuming that these are placed in the same plane. The magnetic fields will be zero at the centre of the loop when the separation H is

(a) $\dfrac{I_e\,R}{I_c\,\pi}$

(b) $\dfrac{I_c\,R}{I_e\,\pi}$

(c) $\dfrac{\pi I_c}{I_e\,R}$

(d) $\dfrac{I_e\pi}{I_c\,R}$

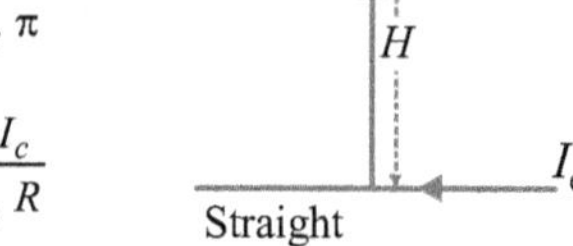

23. A charged particle moving in x-y plane enters a region of uniform magnetic field of intensity $\vec{B} = -B_0\hat{k}$ at $P(0, 0)$ with velocity $\vec{v}_1 = v\hat{i}$ and leaves the magnetic field at $Q(a, b)$ with velocity $\vec{v}_2 = v'\hat{i} + \sqrt{3}\,v'\hat{j}$. Choose the correct statement(s):

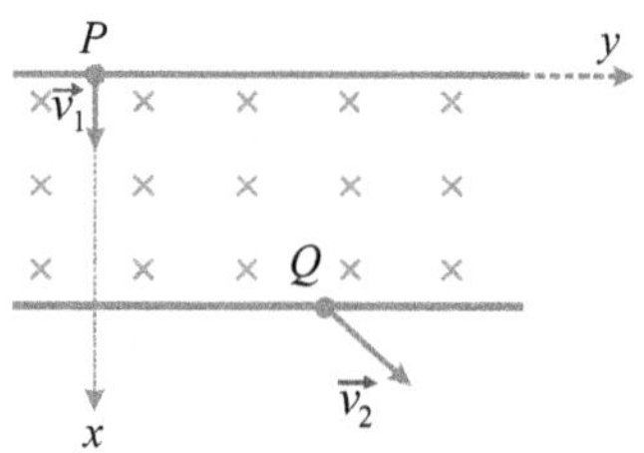

(a) The particle can't be positron

(b) Deviation suffered by the particle as it moves from P to Q equals 60°

(c) $\sqrt{3}\,a = b$

(d) $\vec{v}_1 = \vec{v}_2$

Answer Key	**20**	(c)	**21**	(d)	**22**	(a)	**23**	(b)
Sol. from page 437								

Only one option correct

1. Figure shows a uniform magnetic field $\vec{B}$ and four straight-line paths of equal lengths. Which path has the greatest value of

$$\oint \vec{B} \cdot d\ell$$

(a) I

(b) II

(c) III

(d) IV

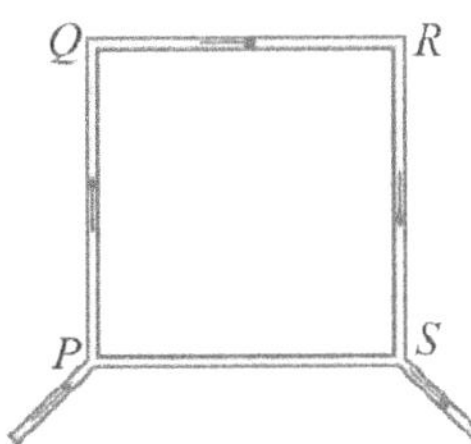

2. $PQRS$ is a square loop made of uniform conducting wire the current enters the loop at P and leaves at S. Then the magnetic field will be

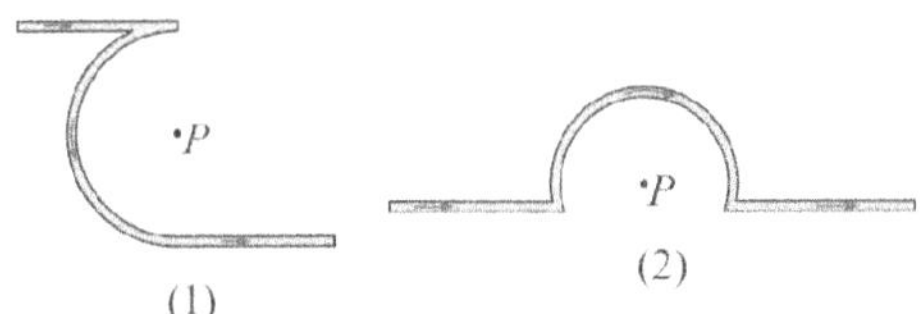

(a) maximum at the centre of the loop
(b) zero at the centre of loop
(c) zero at all points inside the loop
(d) zero at all points outside of the loop

3. The magnetic field at the centre of a circular coil of radius r is π times that due to a long straight wire at a distance r from it, for equal currents. Figure here shows three cases : in all cases the circular part has radius r and straight ones are infinitely long. For same current the B field at the centre P in cases 1, 2, 3 have the ratio

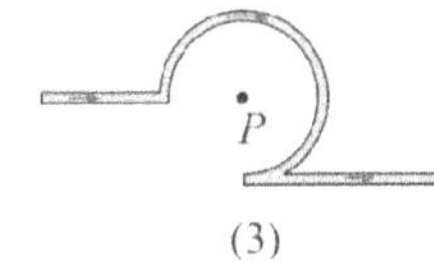

(a) $\left(-\dfrac{\pi}{2}\right) : \left(\dfrac{\pi}{2}\right) : \left(\dfrac{3\pi}{4} - \dfrac{1}{2}\right)$

(b) $\left(-\dfrac{\pi}{2} + 1\right) : \left(\dfrac{\pi}{2} + 1\right) : \left(\dfrac{3\pi}{4} + \dfrac{1}{2}\right)$

(c) $-\dfrac{\pi}{2} : \dfrac{\pi}{2} : 3\dfrac{\pi}{4}$

(d) $\left(-\dfrac{\pi}{2} - 1\right) : \left(\dfrac{\pi}{2} - \dfrac{1}{4}\right) : \left(\dfrac{3\pi}{4} + \dfrac{1}{2}\right)$

4. An infinitely long conductor PQR is bent to form a right angle as shown. A current I flows through PQR. The magnetic field due to this current at the point M is B_1. Now another infinitely long straight conductor QS is connected at Q so that the current is $I/2$ in QR as well as in QS, The current in PQ remaining unchanged. The magnetic field at M is now B_2. The ratio B_1 / B_2 is given by

(a) $\dfrac{1}{2}$

(b) 1

(c) $\dfrac{2}{3}$

(d) 2

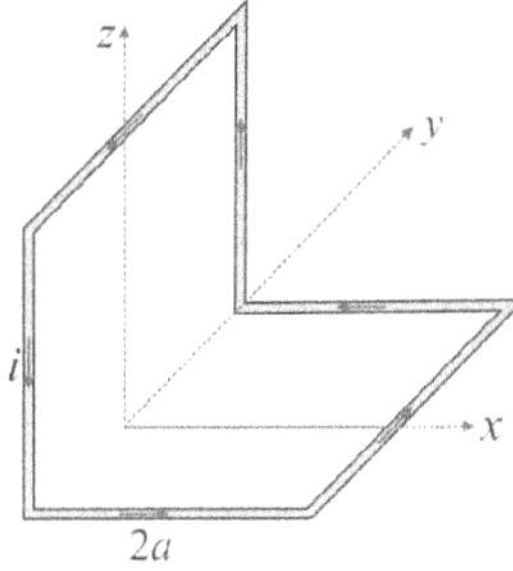

5. A non-planar loop of conducting wire carrying a current I is placed as shown in the figure. Each of the straight sections of the loop is of length $2a$. The magnetic field due to this loop at the point $P\,(a, 0, a)$ points in the direction

(a) $\dfrac{1}{\sqrt{2}}\left(-\hat{j} + \hat{k}\right)$

(b) $\dfrac{1}{\sqrt{3}}\left(-\hat{j} + \hat{k} + \hat{i}\right)$

(c) $\dfrac{1}{\sqrt{3}}\left(\hat{i} + \hat{j} + \hat{k}\right)$

(d) $\dfrac{1}{\sqrt{2}}\left(\hat{i} + \hat{k}\right)$

6. A long straight wire along the z-axis carries a current I in the negative z direction. The magnetic field vector $\vec{B}$ at a point having coordinates (x, y) in the $z = 0$ plane is

(a) $\dfrac{\mu_0 I \left(y\hat{i} - x\hat{j}\right)}{2\pi\left(x^2 + y^2\right)}$

(b) $\dfrac{\mu_0 I \left(x\hat{i} + y\hat{j}\right)}{2\pi\left(x^2 + y^2\right)}$

(c) $\dfrac{\mu_0 I \left(x\hat{j} - y\hat{i}\right)}{2\pi\left(x^2 + y^2\right)}$

(d) $\dfrac{\mu_0 I \left(x\hat{i} - y\hat{j}\right)}{2\pi\left(x^2 + y^2\right)}$

Answer Key	1	(a)	2	(b)	3	(a)	4	(c)
Sol. from page 438	5	(d)	6	(a)				

7. A steady current i flows in a small square loop of wire of side L in a horizontal plane. The loop is now folded about its middle such that half of it lies in a vertical plane. Let $\overrightarrow{M_1}$ and $\overrightarrow{M_2}$ respectively denote the magnetic moments due to the current loop before and after folding. Then

(a) $\overrightarrow{M_2} = 0$

(b) $\overrightarrow{M_1}$ and $\overrightarrow{M_2}$ are in the same direction

(c) $\dfrac{|\overrightarrow{M_1}|}{|\overrightarrow{M_2}|} = \sqrt{2}$

(d) $\dfrac{|\overrightarrow{M_1}|}{|\overrightarrow{M_2}|} = \left(\dfrac{1}{\sqrt{2}}\right)$

8. Two long parallel wires are at a distance $2d$ apart. They carry steady equal currents flowing out of the plane of the paper, as shown. The variation of the magnetic field B along the line xx' is given by

(a) 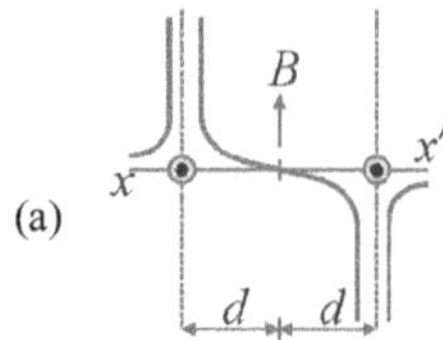
(b) 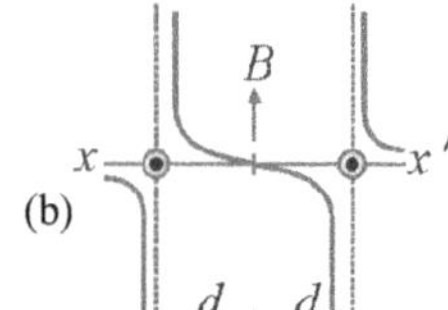

(c) 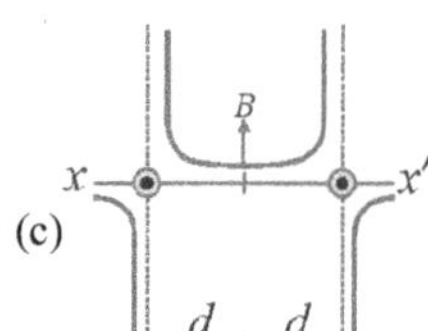
(d) 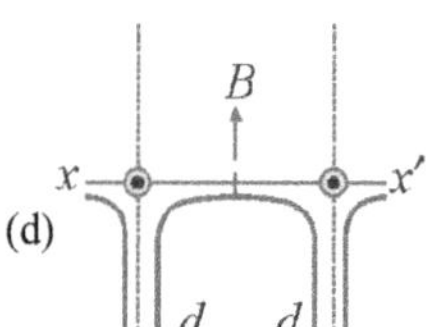

9. Two parallel beams of protons and electrons, carrying equal currents are fixed at a separation d. The protons and electrons move in opposite directions. P is a point on a line joining the beams, at a distance x from any one beam. The magnetic field at P is B. If B is plotted against x, which of the following best represents the resulting curve

(a) 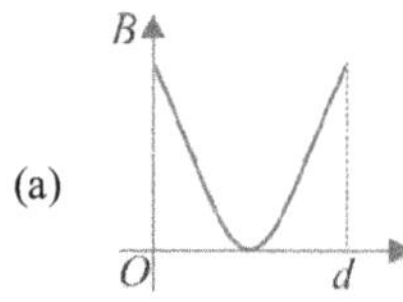
(b) 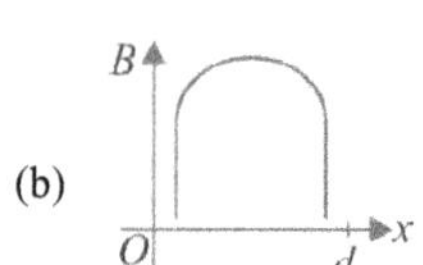

(c) 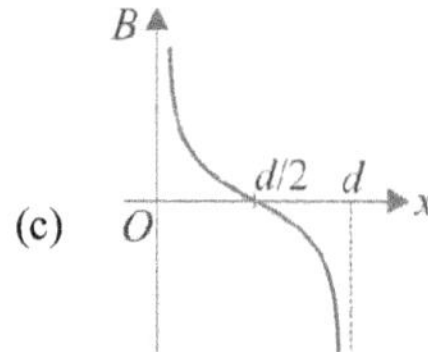
(d) 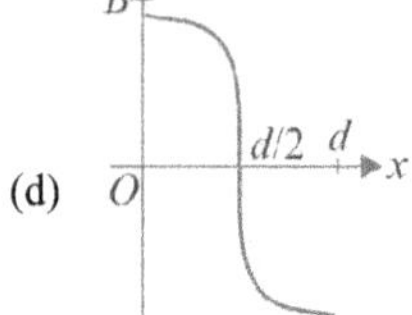

10. An infinitely long wire has a charge λ per unit length. The wire moves along its axis with a velocity v ($v \ll c$, the velocity of light). The ratio of the magnetic field to the electric field at a point r from the wire is :

(a)   proportional to r

(b)   inversely proportional to r

(c)   directly proportional to λ

(d)   independent of r

11. A thin uniform ring of radius R carrying uniform charge Q and mass M rotates about its axis with angular velocity ω. The ratio of its magnetic moment and angular momentum is :

(a) $\dfrac{Q}{M}$ (b) $\dfrac{M}{Q}$

(c) $\dfrac{Q}{2M}$ (d) $\dfrac{M}{2Q}$

12. A slab of resistance R is inserted between two parallel plates of a capacitor charged to Q_0. The capacitor is discharged through the solid. A magnetic field is present throughout and is out of the plane of the paper. The total momentum given to the slab after complete discharge is (given that the capacitance of the capacitor is C and the plates are separated by a distance d).

(a) CQ_0B

(b) dBQ_0

(c)   zero

(d)   in finity

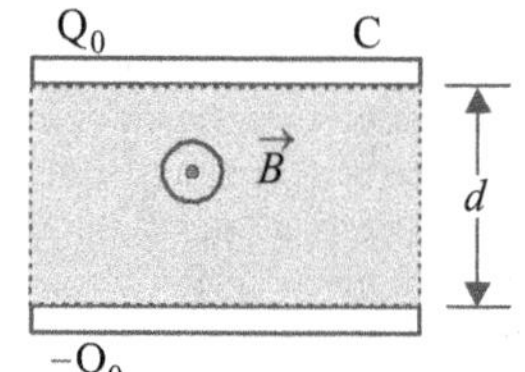

13. A charge q is moving with a velocity $\vec{v_1} = 1\hat{i}$ m/s at a point in a magnetic field and experiences a force $\vec{F_1} = q(-1\hat{j} + 1\hat{k})N$. If the charge is moving with a velocity $\vec{v_2} = 1\hat{j}$ m/s at the same point, it experiences a force $\vec{F_2} = q(1\hat{i} - 1\hat{k})N$. The magnetic induction B at that point is :

(a) $(1\hat{i} + 1\hat{j} + 1\hat{k})\text{Wb/m}^2$ (b) $(1\hat{i} - 1\hat{j} + 1\hat{k})\text{Wb/m}^2$

(c) $(-1\hat{i} + 1\hat{j} - 1\hat{k})\text{Wb/m}^2$ (d) $(1\hat{i} + 1\hat{j} - 1\hat{k})\text{Wb/m}^2$

14. A long wire carries a steady current. It is bent into a circle of one turn and the magnetic field at the centre of the coil is B. It is then bent into a circular loop of n turns. The magnetic field at the centre of the coil for same current will be

(a) nB (b) n^2B

(c) $2nB$ (d) $2n^2B$

Answer Key	7	(c)	8	(b)	9	(c)	10	(d)	11	(c)
Sol. from page 438	12	(b)	13	(a)	14	(b)				

15. Infinite number of straight wires each carrying current I are equally placed as shown in the figure. Adjacent wires have current in opposite direction. Net magnetic field at point P is

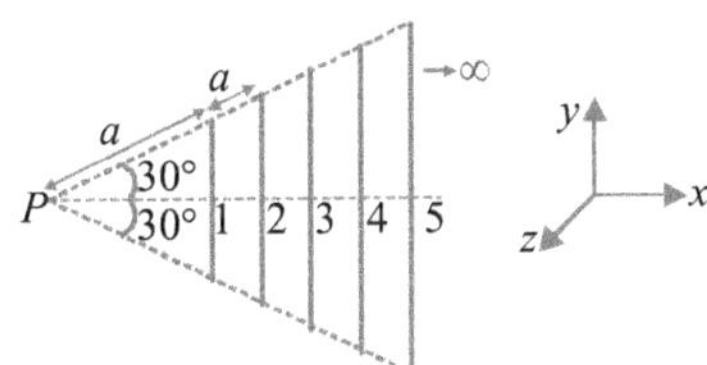

(a) $\dfrac{\mu_0 I}{4\pi}\dfrac{\ell n\,2}{\sqrt{3}}\dfrac{1}{a}\,\hat{k}$

(b) $\dfrac{\mu_0 I}{4\pi}\dfrac{\ell n\,4}{\sqrt{3}}\dfrac{1}{a}\,\hat{k}$

(c) $\dfrac{\mu_0 I}{4\pi}\dfrac{\ell n\,4}{\sqrt{3}}\dfrac{1}{a}\left(-\hat{k}\right)$

(d) zero

16. Find the magnetic field at P due to the arrangement shown

(a) $\dfrac{\mu_0 i}{\sqrt{2}\pi d}\left(1-\dfrac{1}{\sqrt{2}}\right)\otimes$

(b) $\dfrac{2\mu_0 i}{\sqrt{2}\pi d}\otimes$

(c) $\dfrac{\mu_0 i}{\sqrt{2}\pi d}\otimes$

(d) $\dfrac{\mu_0 i}{\sqrt{2}\pi d}\left(1+\dfrac{1}{\sqrt{2}}\right)\otimes$

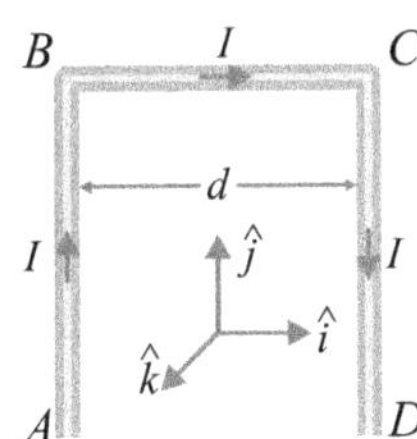

17. A hollow cylinder having infinite length and carrying uniform current per unit length λ along the circumference as shown. Magnetic field inside the cylinder is

(a) $\dfrac{\mu_0\lambda}{2}$

(b) $\mu_0\lambda$

(c) $2\mu_0\lambda$

(d) none

18. AB and CD are long straight conductors, distance d apart, carrying a current I. The magnetic field at the midpoint of BC is

(a) $\dfrac{-\mu_0 I}{2\pi d}\,\hat{k}$

(b) $\dfrac{-\mu_0 I}{\pi d}\,\hat{k}$

(c) $\dfrac{-\mu_0 I}{4\pi d}\,\hat{k}$

(d) $\dfrac{-\mu_0 I}{8\pi d}\,\hat{k}$

19. A disc (of radius r) carrying positive charge q is rotating with angular speed ω in a uniform magnetic field B about a fixed axis (as shown in figure), such that angle made by axis of disc with magnetic field is θ. Torque applied by axis on the disc is

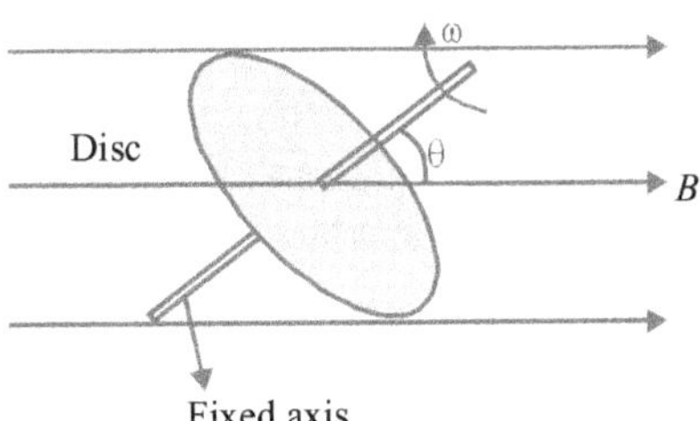

(a) $\dfrac{q\omega r^2 B\sin\theta}{2}$, clockwise

(b) $\dfrac{q\omega r^2 B\sin\theta}{4}$, anticlockwise

(c) $\dfrac{q\omega r^2 B\sin\theta}{2}$, anticlockwise

(d) $\dfrac{q\omega r^2 B\sin\theta}{4}$, clockwise

20. A current carrying ring is bent along its diameter such that its one half has magnetic moment $\vec{M}_1$ and other half has magnetic moment $\vec{M}_2$, then which of the following is incorrect?

(a) $\left|\vec{M}_1\right|=\left|\vec{M}_2\right|$

(b) $\vec{M}_1\cdot\left(\vec{M}_1\times\vec{M}_2\right)=\vec{0}$

(c) $\vec{M}_1\times\left[\left(\vec{M}_1\cdot\vec{M}_2\right)\vec{M}_2\right]$ may be zero

(d) $\vec{M}_1\cdot\vec{M}_2$ can never be zero

21. A coil having N turns is wound tightly in the form of a spiral with inner and outer radii a and b respectively. When a current I passes through the coil, the magnetic field at the centre is

(a) $\dfrac{\mu_0 NI}{b}$

(b) $\dfrac{2\mu_0 NI}{a}$

(c) $\dfrac{\mu_0 NI}{2(b-a)}\ell n\dfrac{b}{a}$

(d) $\dfrac{\mu_0 I}{2(b-a)}\ell n\dfrac{b}{a}$

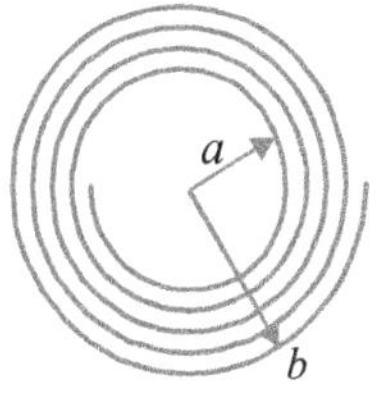

Answer Key	15	(b)	16	(a)	17	(b)	18	(b)
Sol. from page 438	19	(d)	20	(d)	21	(c)		

22. An infinite cylinder of radius r with surface charge density σ is rotated about its central axis with angular speed ω. What is the magnetic field at any point inside the cylinder?

(a) $\mu_0 \sigma \omega r^2$

(b) $\dfrac{\mu_0 \omega r}{\sigma}$

(c) $\mu_0 \sigma \omega r$

(d) $\mu_0 \sigma \omega^2 r$

23. A star shaped loop (with ℓ = length of each section) carries current i. Magnetic field at the centroid of the loop is

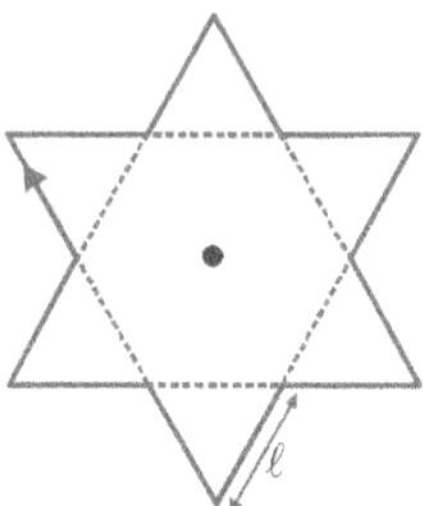

(a) $\dfrac{3\mu_0 i}{\pi \ell}$

(b) $\dfrac{3\mu_0 i}{2\pi \ell}$

(c) $\left(3 - \sqrt{3}\right)\dfrac{\mu_0 i}{\pi \ell}$

(d) $\left(3 + \sqrt{3}\right)\dfrac{\mu_0 i}{2\pi \ell}$

24. A conducting wire bent in the form of a parabola $y^2 = x$ carrying a current $i = 1$A as shown in the figure. This wire is placed in a magnetic field $\vec{B} = -2\hat{k}$ tesla. The unit vector in the direction of force is

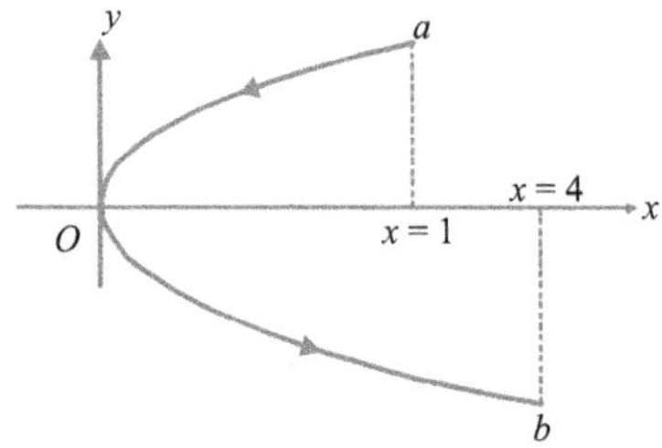

(a) $\dfrac{3\hat{i} + 4\hat{j}}{5}$

(b) $\dfrac{\hat{i} + \hat{j}}{\sqrt{2}}$

(c) $\dfrac{\hat{i} + 2\hat{j}}{\sqrt{5}}$

(d) none of these

25. Circular regions (1) and (2) have current densities J and $-J$ respectively, such that their region of intersection carries no current. Magnetic field in their region of intersection is

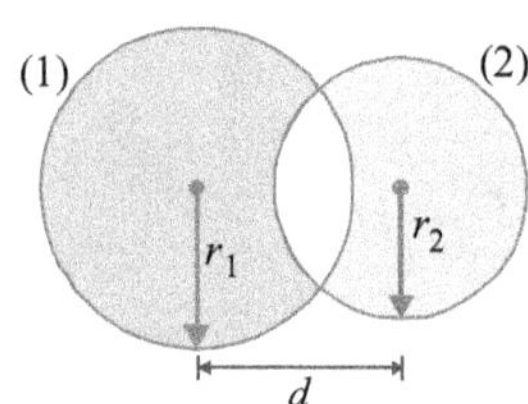

(a) uniform, proportional to $(r_1 + r_2) - d$
(b) uniform, proportional to d
(c) non-uniform
(d) zero

Answer Key	22	(c)	23	(c)	24	(b)	25	(b)
Sol. from page 438								

Magnetism

MCQ Type 2

Exercise 6.2

Multiple correct options

1. Two coaxial solenoids 1 and 2 of the same length are set so that one is inside the other. The number of turns per unit length are n_1 and n_2. The current i_1 and i_2 are flowing in opposite directions. The magnetic field inside the inner solenoid is zero. This is possible when

   (a) $i_1 \neq i_2$ and $n_1 = n_2$

   (b) $i_1 = i_2$ and $n_1 \neq n_2$

   (c) $i_1 = i_2$ and $n_1 = n_2$

   (d) $i_1 n_1 = i_2 n_2$

2. Consider the magnetic field produced by a finitely long current carrying wire. Then
   (a) the lines of field will be concentric circles with centres on the wire.
   (b) there can be two points in the same plane where magnetic fields are same
   (c) there can be large number of points where the magnetic field is same in magnitude.
   (d) the magnetic field at a point is inversely proportional to the distance of the point from the wire.

3. Consider three quantities $x = E/B$, $y = \sqrt{1/\mu_0 \varepsilon_0}$ and $z = \dfrac{\ell}{CR}$.

   Here l is the length of a wire, C is a capacitance and R is a resistance. All other symbols have standard meanings. Then :
   (a) x, y have the same dimensions
   (b) y, z have the same dimensions
   (c) z, x have the same dimensions
   (d) none of the three pairs have the same dimensions.

4. Two long thin, parallel conductors carrying equal currents in the same direction are fixed parallel to the x-axis, one passing through $y = a$ and the other through $y = -a$. The resultant magnetic field due to the two conductors at any point is B. Which of the following are correct?

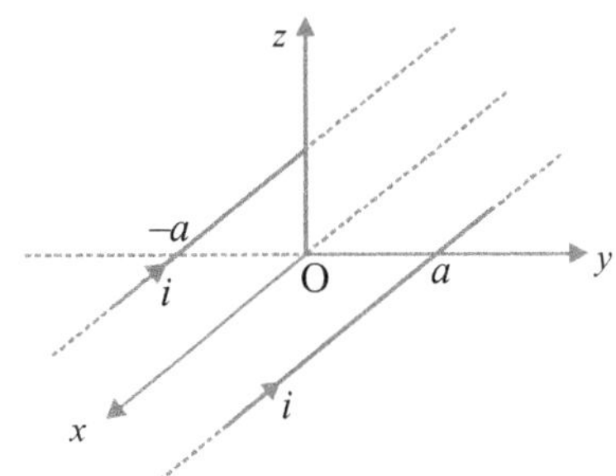

   (a) $B = 0$ for all points on the x-axis

   (b) At all points on the y-axis, excluding the origin, B has only a z-component.

   (c) At all points on the z-axis, excluding the origin, B has only a y-component.

   (d) B cannot have an x-component

5. An electron is moving along the positive x-axis. You want to apply a magnetic field for a short time so that the electron may reverse its direction and move parallel to the negative x-axis. This can be done by applying the magnetic field along,

   (a) y-axis   (b) z- axis

   (c) y-axis only   (d) z-axis only

6. Inside a region of non uniform magnetic field given by the formula $\vec{B} = -B_0 x \hat{k}$, a particle of mass M and charge q is projected horizontally as shown. It is given that $qB_0/M = 1$. At any instant the velocity vector of the particle is found to $(v/2)\hat{i} + a\hat{j} + b\hat{k}$. If the initial value of the velocity is v m/s, then

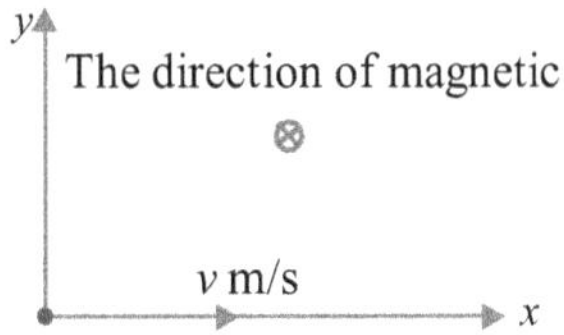

   (a) $a = v/2$ and $b = 0$

   (b) $a = \sqrt{3}\, v/2$ and $b = 0$

   (c) x coordinate of the particle at the instant when its velocity in the x-direction becomes equal to zero, is $\left(2v\right)^{1/2}$.

   (d) x coordinate of the particle at the instant when its velocity in the x-direction becomes equal to zero, is $\left(3v\right)^{1/2}$

Answer Key	1	(c, d)	2	(a, c, d)	3	(a, b, c)	4	(a, d)
Sol. from page 440	5	(a, b)	6	(b, c)				

Magnetism　　　# Statement Questions　　　*Exercise 6.3*

Read the two statements carefully to mark the correct option out of the options given below:
(a)　If both the statements are true and the *statement - 2* is the correct explanation of *statement - 1*.
(b)　If both the statements are true but *statement - 2* is not the correct explanation of the *statement - 1*.
(c)　If *statement - 1* true but *statement - 2* is false.
(d)　If *statement - 1* is false but *statement - 2* is true.

1.　*Statement - 1*

Alternating current shows no magnetic effect.

Statement - 2

The magnetic field produced by alternating current in complete cycle is zero.

2.　*Statement - 1*

A direct current flows through a thin conductor produces magnetic field only outside the conductor.

Statement - 2

There is no flow of charge carriers inside the conductor.

3.　*Statement - 1*

A current i flows along the long straight and thin walled pipe. Then magnetic field at any point inside the pipe is zero.

Statement - 2　It is according to $\oint \vec{B}.d\vec{\ell} = \mu_0 i$.

4.　*Statement - 1*

Ampere's law used for the closed loop shown in figure is written as $\oint \vec{B} \cdot d\vec{\ell} = \mu_0\left(i_1 - i_2\right)$. Right side of it does not include i_3, because it produces no magnetic field at the loop.

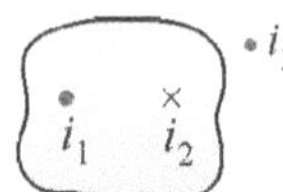

Statement - 2

The line integral of magnetic field produced by i_3 over the close loop is zero.

5.　*Statement - 1*

The magnetic field due to a very large current carrying loop is zero at its centre.

Statement - 2

Magnetic field at the centre of loop is, $B = \dfrac{\mu_0 i}{2R}$.

6.　*Statement - 1*

Figure shows cross-sections of two long straight wires; the left-hand wire carries current in directly out of the page. If the magnetic field due to the two currents is to be zero at P, the current i_2 must be into the page.

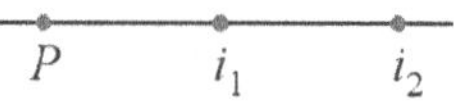

Statement - 2

$i_2 > i_1$.

7.　*Statement - 1*

Figure shows a current carrying circular loop. The magnetic field at the centre of loop is zero.

Statement - 2

Magnetic field at the centre of loop is given by

$$B = \dfrac{\mu_0 n i}{2R}.$$

8.　*Statement - 1*

Figure shows two identical currents i and a close path encircling them. For the close path $\oint \vec{B} \cdot d\vec{\ell} = 2i$.

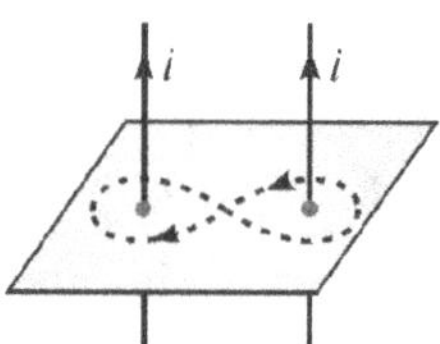

Statement - 2

For the close path $\oint \vec{B} \cdot d\vec{\ell} = 0$.

Answer Key	1	(d)	2	(c)	3	(a)	4	(d)
Sol. from page 441	5	(a)	6	(a)	7	(a)	8.	(d)

9. *Statement - 1*

The force between two parallel current carrying conductors carrying currents in same direction is attractive because there is no electrical interaction between them.

Statement - 2

The force between two electrons streams moving in the same direction repulsive because there is no magnetic interaction between them.

10. *Statement - 1*

Two square conducting loops carry currents 3A and 1A as shown in figure.

For the path 1, $\oint \vec{B} \cdot d\vec{\ell} = -2\mu_0$.

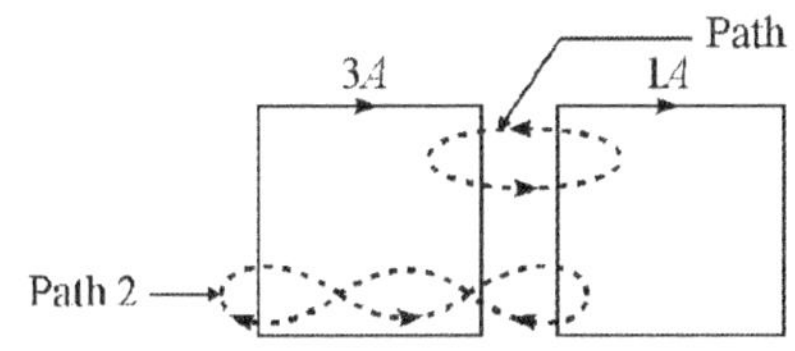

Statement - 2

For the path 2, $\oint \vec{B} \cdot d\vec{\ell} = -\mu_0$.

11. *Statement - 1*

Figure shows a current carrying conductor and a close path. For the close path $\oint \vec{B} \cdot d\vec{\ell} = 0$.

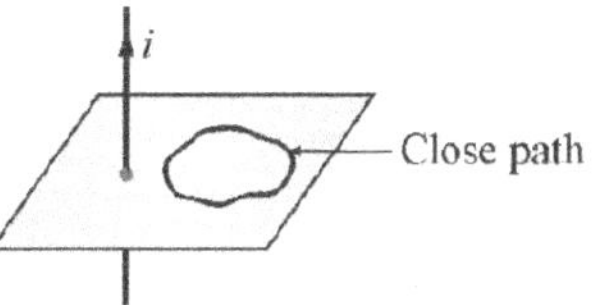

Statement - 2

For the close path, the magnetic field at each point on the path is zero.

12. *Statement - 1*

The magnetic field of a long solenoid is $\mu_0 ni$ at its centre.

Statement - 2

The magnetic field at any point outside the solenoid on its bisector is zero.

13. *Statement - 1*

Two long current carrying wires are placed perpendicular to each other. The net force exerted by one wire on the other is zero.

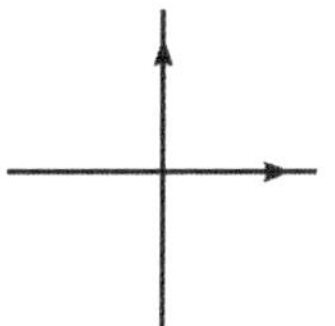

Statement - 2

The net torque exerted by one wire on the other is zero.

Answer Key	9	(c)	10	(b)	11	(c)	12	(b)
Sol. from page 441	13	(c)						

Passage & Matrix

PASSAGES

Passage for Q. 1 to Q. 3

A coaxial line carries the same current i up the inside conductor of radius a as down the outer conductor of inner radius b and outer radius c.

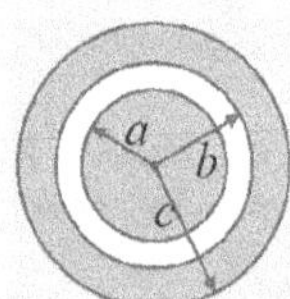

1. The magnetic field at a distance r from the axis, for $r < a$ is :

(a) zero

(b) $\dfrac{\mu_0}{2\pi}\dfrac{i\,r}{a^2}$

(c) $\dfrac{\mu_0}{4\pi}\dfrac{i\,a}{r^2}$

(d) $\dfrac{\mu_0}{2\pi}\dfrac{i}{r}$

2. The magnetic field at a distance r from the axis, for $a < r < b$ is :

(a) zero

(b) $\dfrac{\mu_0}{4\pi}\dfrac{i}{r}$

(c) $\dfrac{\mu_0}{2\pi}\dfrac{i}{r}$

(d) $\dfrac{\mu_0}{2\pi}\dfrac{i\,r}{a^2}$

3. The magnetic field at a distance r from the axis, for $b < r < c$ is :

(a) $\dfrac{\mu_0}{2\pi}\dfrac{i}{r}$

(b) $\dfrac{\mu_0}{2\pi}\dfrac{r^2-b^2}{c^2-b^2}$

(c) $\dfrac{\mu_0}{2\pi}\dfrac{i}{r}\left[1-\dfrac{r^2-b^2}{c^2-b^2}\right]$

(d) none of these

Passage for Q. 4 to Q. 6

Take a tightly-wound solenoid of radius a and length ℓ. The number of turns per unit length in it is n. It carries current i. Consider a small element of length dx of the solenoid at a distance x from one end. This contains ndx turns and can be assumed as a current carrying loop. The magnetic field due to whole solenoid will be the sum of magnetic field due to such elements.

4. The magnetic field due to this solenoid at the centre of its axis is :

(a) $\dfrac{\mu_0\,i}{2a}$

(b) $\dfrac{\mu_0\,n\,i}{2a}$

(c) $\dfrac{\mu_0\,ni}{\sqrt{1+\dfrac{a^2}{\ell^2}}}$

(d) $\dfrac{\mu_0 n\,i}{\sqrt{1+\dfrac{4a^2}{\ell^2}}}$

5. The magnetic field due to the solenoid at the centre of its axis in the situation $a \gg \ell$ is :

(a) $\dfrac{\mu_0 n\,i}{2}$

(b) $\mu_0 ni$

(c) $\dfrac{\mu_0 ni\ell}{2a}$

(d) $\dfrac{\mu_0 ni\ell}{a}$

6. The magnetic field due to the solenoid at the centre of its axis in the situation $a \ll \ell$ is :

(a) zero

(b) $\dfrac{\mu_0 n\,i}{2}$

(c) $\mu_0 ni$

(d) infinite

Passage for Q. 7 to Q. 9

A charge particle of mass m and charge q is projected on a rough horizontal xy-plane. Both electric and magnetic fields are given by $\vec{E} = -10\hat{k}\,N/C$ and magnetic field $\vec{B} = -5\hat{k}$ tesla are present in the region. The particle enters into the magnetic field at $(4, 0, 0)$ m with a velocity $50\hat{j}$ m/s. The particle starts into a curved path on the plane. If coefficient of friction $\mu = \dfrac{1}{3}$ between particle and plane, then $(qE = 2mg, g = 10$ m/s$^2)$:

7. Radius of curvature of the path followed by particle, initially, is

(a) 5 m

(b) 2.5 m

(c) 1.25 m

(d) 10 m

8. The time after which particle comes to rest, is

(a) 5 s

(b) 4 s

(c) 3 s

(d) 1 s

9. Total work done by electric force on the particle is

(a) 250 J

(b) zero

(c) 125 J

(d) none

Answer Key	1	(b)	2	(c)	3	(c)	4	(d)	5	(c)
Sol. from page 441	6	(c)	7	(a)	8	(a)	9	(b)		

Passage for Q. 10 to Q. 12

An electron is moving with velocity $v_1\hat{i} + v_2\hat{j}$ $(v_1 > 0, v_2 > 0)$ at the origin in the presence of electric and magnetic fields $E\hat{j}\ \&\ -B\hat{j}$ respectively.

10. The maximum value of the y-coordinate during the motion of the electron is

(a) $\dfrac{m\left(v_1^2 + v_2^2\right)}{2eE}$

(b) $\dfrac{mv_2^2}{2eE}$

(c) $\dfrac{mv_2^2}{eE}$

(d) $\dfrac{2mE}{eB^2}$

11. The condition such that the electron passes the origin again is (where n is a natural number)

(a) $v_2 = \dfrac{\pi n E}{B}$

(b) $v_2 = \dfrac{2\pi n E}{B}$

(c) $v_2 = \dfrac{\pi E}{nB}$

(d) $v_2 = \dfrac{nE}{\pi B}$

12. The number of revolutions the charge does before its y coordinate becomes negative is:

(a) $\dfrac{B\sqrt{v_1^2 + v_2^2}}{\pi E}$

(b) $\dfrac{B^2\left(v_1^2 + v_2^2\right)}{\pi E^2}$

(c) $\dfrac{\pi E}{Bv_2}$

(d) $\dfrac{Bv_2}{\pi E}$

MATRIX MATCHING

13. Six point charges, each of the same magnitude q, are arranged in different manners as shown in **Column-II**. In each case, a point M and line PQ passing through M are shown. Let E be the electric field and V be the electric potential at M (potential at infinity is zero) due to the given charge distribution when it is at rest. Now, the whole system is set into rotation with a constant angular velocity about the line PQ. Let B be the magnetic field at M and μ be the magnetic moment of the system in this condition. Assume each rotating charge to the equivalent to a steady current.

Column-I   **Column-II**

A. $E = 0$

B. $V \neq 0$

C. $B = 0$

D. $\mu \neq 0$

(p) 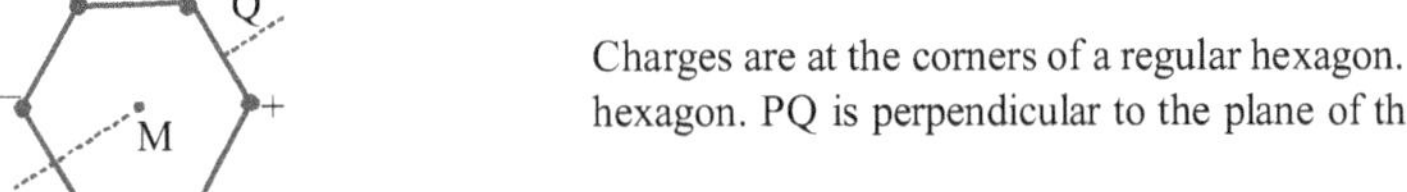

Charges are at the corners of a regular hexagon. M is at the centre of the hexagon. PQ is perpendicular to the plane of the hexagon.

(q) 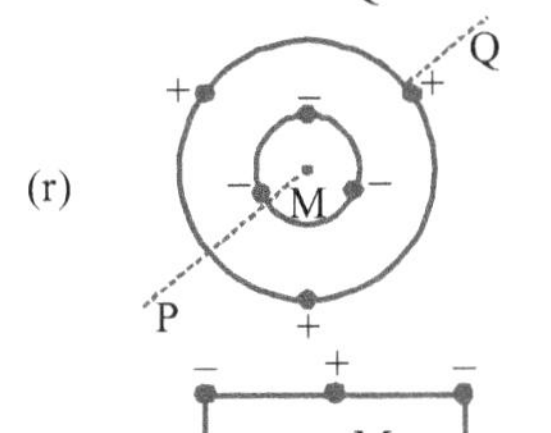

Charges are on a line perpendicular to PQ at equal intervals. M is the mid-point between the two innermost charges.

(r) 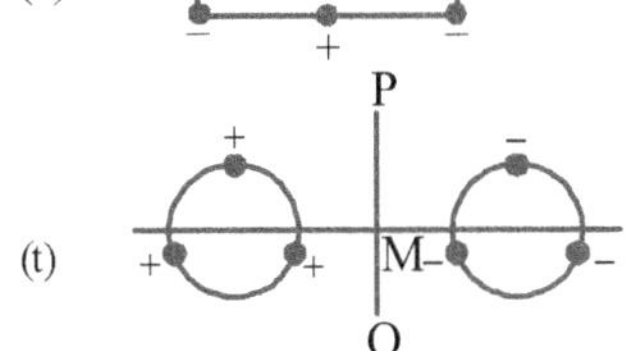

Charges are placed on two coplanar insulating rings at equal intervals. M is the common centre of the rings. PQ is perpendicular to the plane of the rings.

(s)

Charges are placed at the corners of a rectangle of sides a and $2a$ and at the mid points of the longer sides. M is at the centre of the rectangle. PQ is parallel to the longer sides.

(t)

Charges are placed on two coplanar, identical insulating rings at equal intervals. M is the mid-point between the centres of the rings. PQ is perpendicular to the line joining the centres and coplanar to the rings.

Answer Key	**10**	(b)	**11**	(a)	**12**	(d)
Sol. from page 441	**13**	A-p, r, s ; B - r, s ; C- p, q, t ; D- r, s				

14. Two wires each carrying a steady current I are shown in four configurations in Column I. Some of the resulting effects are described in Column II. Match the statements in Column I with the statements in column II and indicate your answer by darkening appropriate bubbles in the 4×4 matrix given in the ORS.

Column I

Column II

A. Point P is situated midway between the wires.

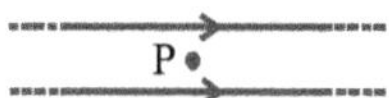

(p) The magnetic fields (B) at P due to the currents in the wires are in the same direction.

B. Point P is situated at the mid-point of the line joining the centers of the circular wires, which have same radii.

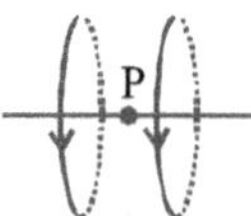

(q) The magnetic fields (B) at P due to the currents in the wires are in opposite directions.

C. Point P is situated at the mid-point of the line joining the centers of the circular wires, which have same radii.

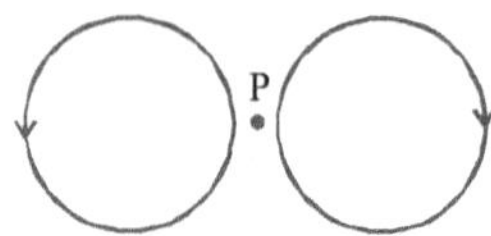

(r) There is no magnetic field at P.

D. Point P is situated at the common center of the wires.

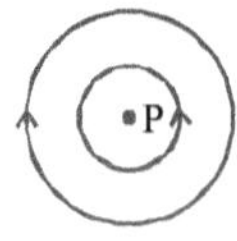

(s) The wires repel each other.

15. Match entries in Column I to all possible entries in Column II.

Column I

Column II

A. Motion of a free positively charged particle in uniform magnetic field only

(p) Uniform motion

B. Motion of a free negatively charged particle in electric field only

(q) Trajectory is circular

C. Motion of a particle for which velocity is given to be

$\vec{V} = k\sin t\,\hat{i} + \cos kt\,\hat{j} + k\hat{k}$. Here k is an integer

(r) Trajectory is helical

D. Superposition of simple harmonic motions given by :

$x = A\sin\omega t, \quad y = B\sin^2\omega t$. Here A and B are constants

(s) Trajectory is parabolic

(t) Trajectory is elliptical

Answer Key	14	A - q, r ; B - p ; C - p, r ; D- q, s		
Sol. from page 441	15	A-p, q, r ; B - q, r, s, t ; C- p, r ; D- s	16	A- r, t ; B - r, t ; C- r, s ; D- r, t

16. **Column – I**

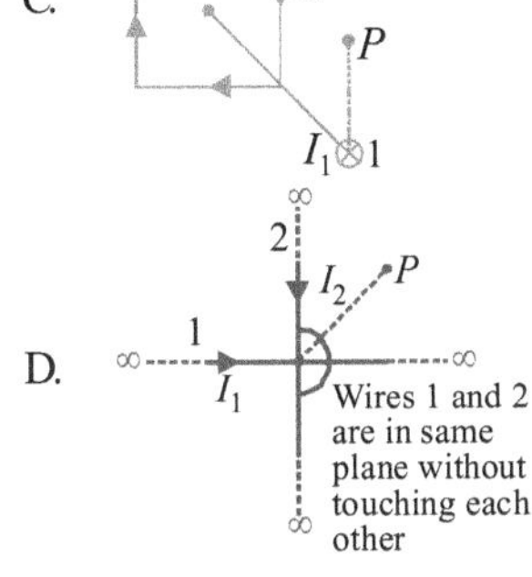

A.

B.

C.

D. Wires 1 and 2 are in same plane without touching each other

Column – II

(p) 1 and 2 attract each other

(q) 1 and 2 repel each other

(r) 1 and 2 do not exert any force on each other.

(s) Magnetic field at point P due to wires 1 and 2 are perpendicular to each other.

(t) Magnetic field at point P due to wires 1 and 2 are in same direction.

Answer Key	16	A- r, t ; B - r, t ; C- r, s ; D- r, t				
Sol. from page 441						

Magnetism Subjective Integer Type *Exercise 6.5*

Solution from page 444

1. A long, straight wire carries a current i. Let B_1 be the magnetic field at a point P at a distance d from the wire. Consider a section of length ℓ of this wire such that the point P lies on a perpendicular bisector of the section. Let B_2 be the magnetic field at this point due to this section only. Find the value of d/ℓ so that B_2 differs from B_1 by 1%. ***Ans :*** 0.07.

2. Four long copper wires are parallel to each other, their cross-sections forming the corners of a square with sides a = 20 cm. A 20 A current exists in each wire in the direction shown in figure. What are the magnitude and direction of $\vec{B}$ at the centre of the square ?

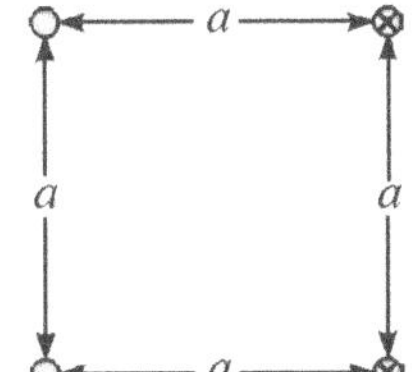

Ans : 80 µT up the page.

3. Two long parallel wires carrying current 2.5 and I ampere in the same direction (directed into plane of the paper) are held at P and Q respectively such that they are perpendicular to the plane of the paper. The points P and Q are located at a distance of 5 metre and 2 metre respectively from a collinear point R (fig.).

(i) An electron moving with a velocity of $4 \times 10^{+5}$ m/s along the positive x-direction experiences a force of magnitude 3.2×10^{-20} N at the point R. Find the value of I.

(ii) Find all the positions at which a third long parallel wire carrying a current of magnitude 2.5 A may be placed so that the magnetic induction at R is zero. ***Ans :*** (i) 4A (ii) ± 1m

4. A 200-turn solenoid having a length of 25 cm and a diameter of 10 cm carries a current of 0.30 A. Calculate the magnitude of the magnetic field $\vec{B}$ inside the solenoid. ***Ans :*** 0.30 mT.

5. A toroid having a square cross section, 5.00 cm on a side, and an inner radius of 15.0 cm has 500 turns and carries a current of 0.80 A. What is the magnetic field inside the toroid at

(a) the inner radius and (b) the outer radius of the toroid?

Ans : (a) 533 µT (b) 400 µT.

Magnetism

Subjective

Exercise 6.6

Solution from page 445

1. Consider a long, straight wire of cross-sectional area A carrying current i. Let there be n free electrons per unit volume. An observer places himself on a trolley moving in the direction to the current with a speed $v = \dfrac{i}{neA}$ and separated from the wire by a distance r. Find the magnetic field as seen by the observer.

$$\textit{Ans}: B = \frac{\mu_0 i}{2\pi r}.$$

2. In Bohr model of hydrogen atom, the electron circulates around nucleus on a path of radius 0.51Å at a frequency of 6.8×10^{15} rev/s. Calculate the magnetic field induction set up at the centre of the orbit. What is the effective dipole moment ?

$$\textit{Ans}: 14\frac{Wb}{m^2}, 9.0 \times 10^{-24}\ A - m^2.$$

3. At a certain position, earth's magnetic field of $39\ \mu T$ is horizontal and directed due north. Suppose the net field is zero exactly 8.0 cm above a long, straight, horizontal wire that carries a constant current. What are (a) the magnitude and (b) the direction of the current ?

$$\textit{Ans}: \text{(a) 16 A (b) west to east.}$$

4. A square loop of wire of edge length a carries current i. Show that, the magnetic field at the centre of loop is $B = \dfrac{2\sqrt{2}\ \mu_0 i}{\pi a}$.

5. A square loop of wire of edge length a carries current i. Show that the magnitude of the magnetic field produced at a point on the axis of the loop and a distance x from its centre is

$$B = \frac{4\mu_0\ ia^2}{\pi\left(4x^2 + a^2\right)\left(4x^2 + 2a^2\right)^{1/2}}.$$

6. In figure, a straight wire of length L carries current i. Show that the magnitude of magnetic field at P, a perpendicular distance R from one end of the wire is

$$B = \frac{\mu_0 i}{4\pi R}\ \frac{L}{\left(L^2 + R^2\right)^{1/2}}.$$

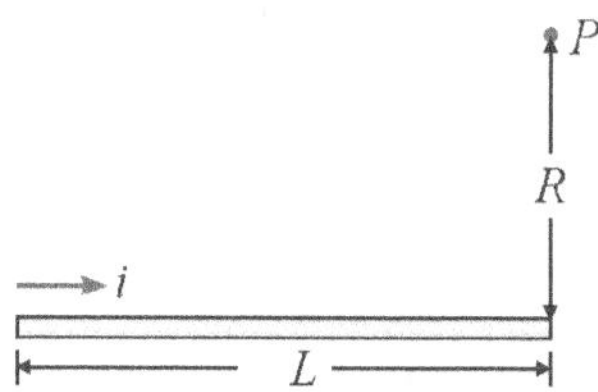

7. (i) A charge of 1 coulomb is placed at one end of a non-conducting rod of length 0.6 m. The rod is rotated in a vertical plane about a horizontal axis passing through the other end of the rod with angular frequency $10^4\ \pi$ rad/s. Find the magnetic field at a point on the axis of rotation at a distance of 0.8 m from the centre of the path.

    (ii) Now half the charge is removed from one end and placed on the other end. The rod is rotated in a vertical plane about

horizontal axis passing through the mid point of the rod with the same angular frequency. Calculate the magnetic field at a point on the axis at a distance of 0.4 m from the centre of rod.

$$\textit{Ans}: \text{(a) 11.3 gauss (b) 22.6 gauss.}$$

8. A pair of stationary and infinitely long bent wires are placed in the xy-plane as shown in figure. The wires carry currents of $i = 10\text{A}$ each as shown.

The segments L and M are along the x-axis. The segments P and Q are parallel to the y-axis such that $OS = OR = 0.02$ m. Find the magnitude and direction of the magnetic induction at the origin O.

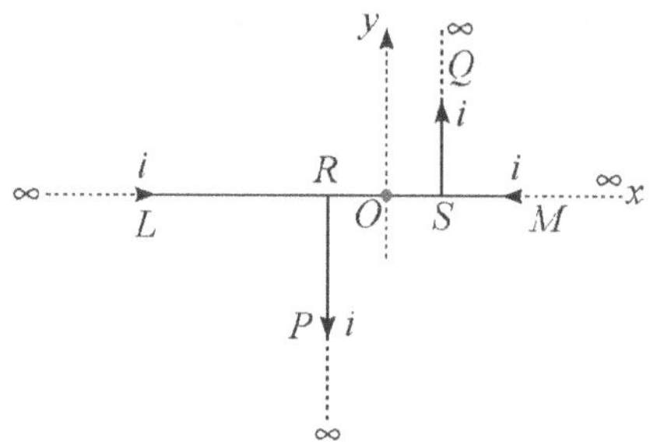

$$\textit{Ans}: 10^{-4}\ \text{Wb/m}^2.$$

9. In the circuit of figure, the curved segments are arcs of circles of radii a and b with common centre P. The straight segments are along radii. Find the magnetic field $\vec{B}$ at the point P, assuming a current i in the circuit.

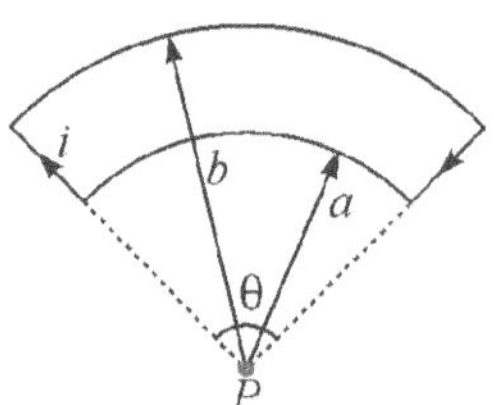

$$\textit{Ans}: \frac{\mu_0 i\theta}{4\pi}\left(\frac{1}{a} - \frac{1}{b}\right),\ \text{out of page.}$$

10. Figure shows the cross-section of a long conducting cylinder with inner radius $a = 2.0$ cm and outer radius $b = 4.0$ cm. The cylinder carries a current out of the page, and the current density in the cross-section is given by $J = cr^2$, with $c = 3.0 \times 10^6$ A/m^4 and r in metre. What is the magnetic field $\vec{B}$ at a point that is 3.0 cm from the central axis of the cylinder ?

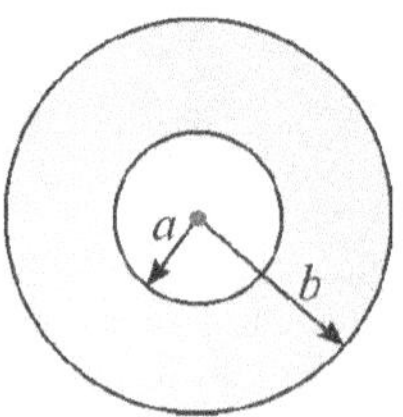

$$\textit{Ans}: B = 2.0 \times 10^{-5}\ \text{T}.$$

11. A long wire carrying a current i is bent to form a plane angle θ. Find the magnetic field B at a point on the bisector of this angle situated at a distance x from the vertex.

$$Ans: \frac{\mu_0 i}{2\pi x}\cot\frac{\theta}{4}$$

12. Find the magnitude and direction of magnetic field induction at point O due to current carrying wire shaped in figure. The current I = 5.0 A, R = 12.0 cm and angle $\theta = 90°$.

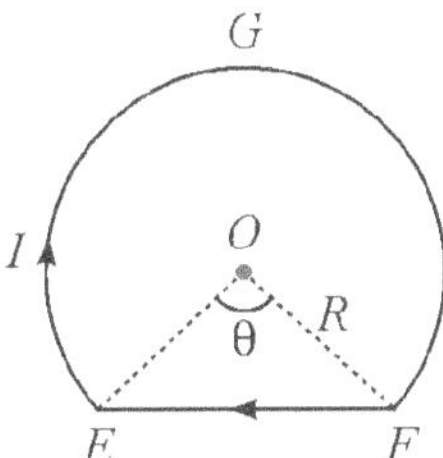

$$Ans: 2.8\times10^{-5}\ T.$$

13. The current density inside a long, solid cylindrical wire of radius a is in the direction of the central axis and varies linearly with radial distance r from the axis according to $J = J_0\dfrac{r}{a}$. Find the magnetic field inside the wire.

$$Ans: \frac{\mu_0 J_0 r^2}{3a}.$$

14. Figure shows a cross-section of a long cylindrical conductor of radius a containing a long cylindrical hole of radius b. The axes of the cylinder and hole are parallel and are a distance d apart; a current i is uniformly distributed over the shaded area.

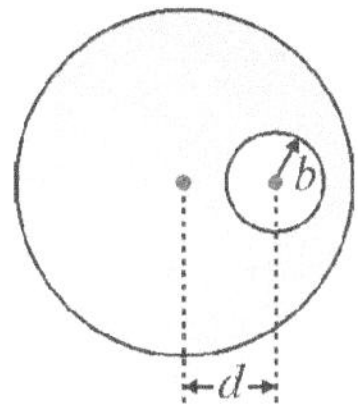

(a) Use superposition to show that the magnetic field at the centre of the hole is

$$B = \frac{\mu_0\ id}{2\pi\left(a^2 - b^2\right)}.$$

(b) Discuss the two special cases $b = 0$ and $d = 0$.
(c) Use Ampere's law to show that the magnetic field in the hole is uniform.

15. Figure shows a square loop of edge a made of a uniform wire. A current i enters the loop at the point A and leaves it at the point C. Find the magnetic field at the point P which is on the perpendicular bisector of AB at a distance $\dfrac{a}{4}$ from it.

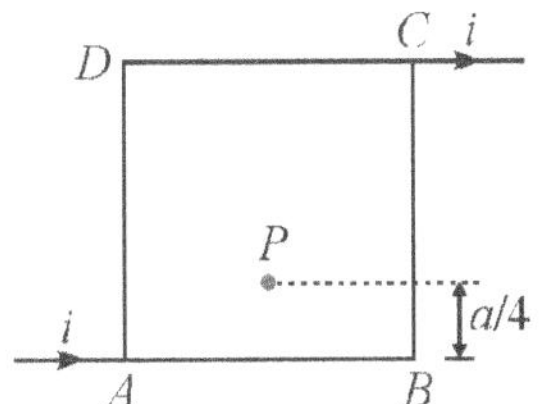

$$Ans: \frac{2\mu_0 i}{\pi\ a}\left(\frac{1}{\sqrt{5}} - \frac{1}{3\sqrt{13}}\right),\ \text{out of page.}$$

16. Four long, straight wires, each carrying a current of 5.0 A, are placed in a plane as shown in figure. The points of intersection form a square of side 5.0 cm.
(a) Find the magnetic field at the centre P of the square.
(b) Q_1, Q_2, Q_3 and Q_4 are points situated on the diagonals of the square and at a distance from P that is equal to the length of the diagonal of the square. Find the magnetic fields at these points.

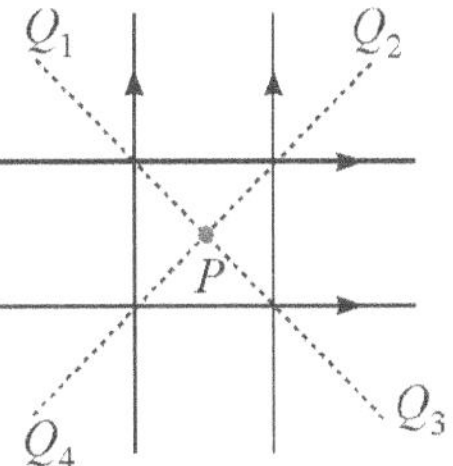

$Ans:$ (a) Zero (b) $Q_1 : 1.1\times10^{-4}\ T,\ \odot, Q_2$: zero; $Q_3 : 1.1\times10^{-4}\ T, \otimes$; and Q_4 : zero.

17. A long straight wire carries a current of 10 A directed along the negative y-axis, as shown in figure. A uniform magnetic field B_0 of magnitude $10^{-6}\ T$ is directed parallel to the x-axis. What is the resultant magnetic field at the following points ?
(a) $x = 0, z = 2m$;
(b) $x = 2m, z = 0$;
(c) $x = 0, z = -0.5$ m.

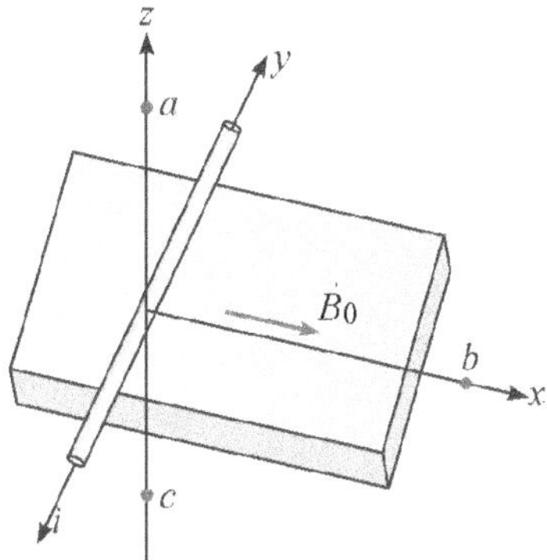

$Ans:$ (a) zero (b) 1.41×10^{-6} T, 45° in xy-plane (c) 5.00×10^{-6} T, $+x$-direction.

18. A long solenoid with 10.0 turns/cm and a radius of 7.00 cm carries a current of 20.0 mA. A current of 6.00 A exists in a straight conductor located along the central axis of the solenoid. (a) At what radial distance from the axis-will the direction of the resulting magnetic field be at 45.0° to the axial direction ? (b) What is the magnitude of the magnetic field there ?

$Ans:$ (a) 4.77 cm; (b) 35.5 μT.

19. A capacitor of capacitance 100 μF is connected to a battery of 20 volt for a long time and then disconnected from it. It is now connected across a long solenoid having 4000 turns per metre. It is found that the potential difference across the capacitor drops to 90% of its maximum value in 2.0 second. Estimate the average magnetic field produced at the centre of the solenoid during the period

$$Ans: 16\pi \times 10^{-8}\ T.$$

20. A current I flows along a lengthy thin-walled tube of radius R with longitudinal slit of width h. Find the induction of the magnetic field inside the tube under the condition $h \ll R$.

$$\textbf{\textit{Ans :}} \;\; B \simeq \frac{\mu_0 h I}{4\pi^2 R r}, \;\; \text{where } r \text{ is the distance from the cut.}$$

21. A current I flows in a long straight wire with cross-section having the form of a thin half-ring of radius R (figure). Find the induction of the magnetic field at the point O.

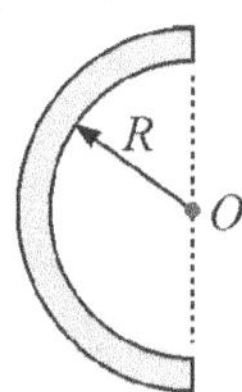

$$\textbf{\textit{Ans :}} \;\; B = \frac{\mu_0 I}{\pi^2 R}.$$

22. Find the current density as a function of distance r from the axis of a radially symmetrical parallel stream of electrons if the magnetic induction inside the stream varies at $B = br^\alpha$, where b and α are positive constant.

$$\textbf{\textit{Ans :}} \;\; j(r) = \left(\frac{b}{\mu_0}\right)(1+\alpha)r^{\alpha-1}.$$

23. Find the magnetic moment of a thin round loop with current if the radius of the loop is equal to R and the magnetic induction at its centre is equal to B.

$$\textbf{\textit{Ans :}} \;\; M = \frac{2\pi R^3 B}{\mu_0}.$$

24. A very long straight solenoid has a cross-section radius R and n turns per unit length. A direct current I flows through the solenoid. Suppose that x is the distance from the end of the solenoid, measured along its axis. Find :

(a) the magnetic induction B on the axis as a function of x; draw an approximate plot of B vs the ratio x/R;

(b) the distance x_0 to the point on the axis at which the value of B differs by $\eta = 1\%$ from that in the middle section of the solenoid.

$$\textbf{\textit{Ans :}} \;\; \text{(a)} \;\; B = \frac{\mu_0 n I}{2}\left[1 - \frac{x}{\sqrt{x^2 + R^2}}\right], \;\; \text{where } x > 0 \text{ outside the solenoid}$$

and $x < 0$ inside the solenoid.

$$\text{(b)} \quad x_0 = \frac{R(1-2\eta)}{2\sqrt{\eta(1-\eta)}} \simeq 5R.$$

$$\bigstar \; \bigstar \; \bigstar$$

Hints & Solutions

1. **(c)** If r is the separation between A and B or B and C, then force per unit length

$$F_A = \frac{\mu_0}{2\pi}\left[\frac{i^2}{r} - \frac{i^2}{2r}\right],\ F_B = \frac{\mu_0}{2\pi}\left[\frac{i^2}{r} + \frac{i^2}{r}\right],\ F_C = \frac{\mu_0}{2\pi}\left[\frac{i^2}{r} + \frac{i^2}{2r}\right]$$

Clearly, $F_B > F_C > F_A$.

2. **(c)** In loop 1 : $\oint \vec{B}.d\vec{\ell} = \mu_0(i - i + i) = \mu_0 i$

loop 2 : $\oint \vec{B}.d\vec{\ell} = \mu_0(i - i) = 0$

loop 3 : $\oint \vec{B}.d\vec{\ell} = \mu_0(i + i) = 2\mu_0 i$

loop 4 : $\oint \vec{B}.d\vec{\ell} = \mu_0(-i) = -\mu_0 i$

3. **(d)** If r is the distance of dot from centre of any coil, and B, B' are the fields due to larger and smaller coil respectively, then
$B_1 = B + B = 2B$, $B_2 = B - B = 0$, $B_3 = (B - B) + (B' - B') = 0$,
$B_4 = B + B' + B' = B + 2B'$.
Clearly the field is greatest in case of IV.

4. **(d)** Outside the cable,

$$\oint \vec{B}.d\vec{\ell} = \mu_0(i - i) = 0$$

or $B = 0$.

5. **(c)** The magnetic field of the straight wire is parallel to circular current and so force on it will be zero.

6. **(a)**

7. **(a)** Given $B = \frac{\mu_0}{2\pi}.\frac{(2)}{d}$.

Magnetic field due to 4 A wire, $B' = \frac{\mu_0}{2\pi}\frac{(4)}{2d} = B$.

So, resultant magnetic field $= B + B = 2B$ along $-$ve z-axis.

8. **(c)** If R and r are the radius of bigger and smaller loop respectively, then $2\pi R = 2 \times 2\pi r$, or $r = R/2$.

$$B_1 = \frac{\mu_0 i}{2R} \text{ and } B_2 = \frac{\mu_0(2)i}{2r} = \frac{\mu_0(2)i}{2R/2} = 4B_1.$$

9. **(b)** As the distance of the points P and Q is equal from the wire and so magnetic field is also equal.

10. **(b)** $B = \frac{\mu_0 i}{2r} - \frac{\mu_0}{2\pi}.\frac{i}{r}$

$$= \frac{\mu_0}{4\pi} \times \frac{2i}{r}[\pi - 1].$$

11. **(a)** $B = \frac{\mu_0\left(\frac{1}{2}\right)i}{2R_1} - \frac{\mu_0\left(\frac{1}{2}\right)i}{2R_2}$

$$= \frac{\mu_0 i}{4}\left(\frac{1}{R_1} - \frac{1}{R_2}\right).$$

12. **(d)** Using right hand screw rule, the direction of magnetic field is along OY'.

13. **(a)** $i = \frac{q}{T} = qn = en$

Now, $B = \frac{\mu_0 i}{2r} = \frac{\mu_0 en}{2r}$.

14. **(c)** $B = \frac{\mu_0}{2\pi}.\frac{i}{r} - \frac{\mu_0}{2\pi}.\frac{i}{r} = 0$

15. **(c)** $B = \left(\frac{\mu_0}{2\pi}.\frac{i}{r} + \frac{\mu_0 i}{2r}\right)$, out of plane of paper.

16. **(b)** $$B = \frac{\mu_0 i}{2r}$$

or $0.5 \times 10^{-5} = \frac{4\pi \times 10^{-7} \times i}{2 \times 0.05}$

$\therefore$ $i = 0.4$ A.

17. **(a)** $$B = \frac{\mu_0 i a^2}{2(a^2 + r^2)^{3/2}} \qquad \dots\dots (i)$$

and $B_{centre} = \frac{\mu_0 i}{2a} \qquad \dots\dots (ii)$

On dividing equation (ii) by (i), and putting the known values, we get

$$B_{centre} = 250 \times 10^{-6}\ T.$$

18. **(a)** $B = \sqrt{B_1^2 + B_2^2}$

$$= \sqrt{\left[\frac{\mu_0 \times 3}{2(2\pi)}\right]^2 + \left[\frac{\mu_0 \times 4}{2(2\pi)}\right]^2} = 5 \times 10^{-5}\ T.$$

19. **(c)** $F = \frac{\mu_0}{2\pi}.\frac{i_1 i_2}{r} \times \ell$

$$= \frac{\mu_0}{2\pi}.\frac{i_1 i_2}{r} \times (d\ell \cos\theta).$$

20. **(c)** As $B \propto \frac{1}{r}$, so it represents rectangular hyperbola.

21. **(d)** $L = 2\pi R$ or $R = \frac{L}{2\pi}$

Now $M = i A = I(\pi R^2) = I\pi\left(\frac{L}{2\pi}\right)^2 = \frac{IL^2}{4\pi}$.

22. **(a)** $B_{circular} = B_{straight}$

or $\frac{\mu_0 i_c}{2R} = \frac{\mu_0}{2\pi}.\frac{i_e}{H}$

$\therefore$ $H = \frac{i_e}{i_c}.\frac{R}{\pi}$

23. **(b)** $\tan\theta = \frac{v_y}{v_x} = \frac{\sqrt{3}}{1} = \sqrt{3}$

or $\theta = 60°$

Solutions **EXERCISE 6.1 LEVEL -2**

1. (a) For $\oint \vec{B}_1 d\vec{\ell}$ to be greatest, the projected length along magnetic field is greatest in case I.

2. (b) Magnetic field at the centre of the loop,

$$B = 3\left[\frac{\mu_0}{4\pi}.\frac{i/4}{r}(\sin 45° + \sin 45°)\right]$$

$$-\left[\frac{\mu_0}{4\pi}.\frac{3i/4}{r}(\sin 45° + \sin 45°)\right] = 0$$

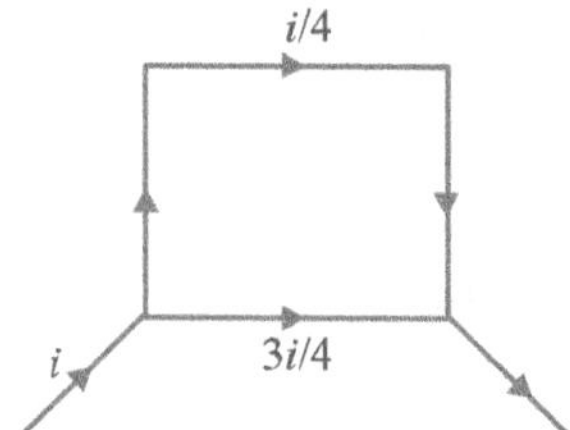

3. (a) If B is the magnetic field of straight conductor at P, then

$$B_1 = \frac{\pi B}{2}\odot, \quad B_2 = \frac{\pi B}{2}\otimes, \quad B_3 = \left(\frac{3\pi B}{4} - \frac{B}{2}\right)\otimes.$$

So $B_1 : B_2 : B_3 = \left(-\frac{\pi}{2}\right):\left(\frac{\pi}{2}\right):\left(\frac{3\pi}{4} - \frac{1}{2}\right).$

4. (c) $B_1 = \frac{\mu_0}{4\pi}.\frac{I}{r}, \quad B_2 = \frac{\mu_0}{2\pi}.\frac{(I/2)}{r} + \frac{\mu_0}{4\pi}.\frac{(I/2)}{r} = \frac{3}{2}\times\frac{\mu_0}{4\pi}.\frac{I}{r}$

$$\therefore \quad \frac{B_1}{B_2} = \frac{2}{3}.$$

5. (d) The equivalent loop is shown in figure. If B is the magnetic field of each loop, then

$$\vec{B}_{\text{resultant}} = B\hat{i} + B\hat{k} = B(\hat{i} + \hat{k})$$

So unit vector of resultant field $= \frac{\hat{i} + \hat{k}}{\sqrt{2}}.$

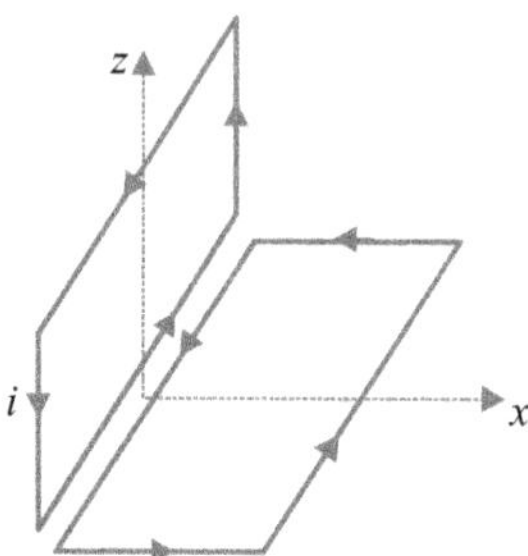

6. (a) Magnetic field due to long straight wire,

$$B = \frac{\mu_0}{2\pi}.\frac{I}{r}.$$

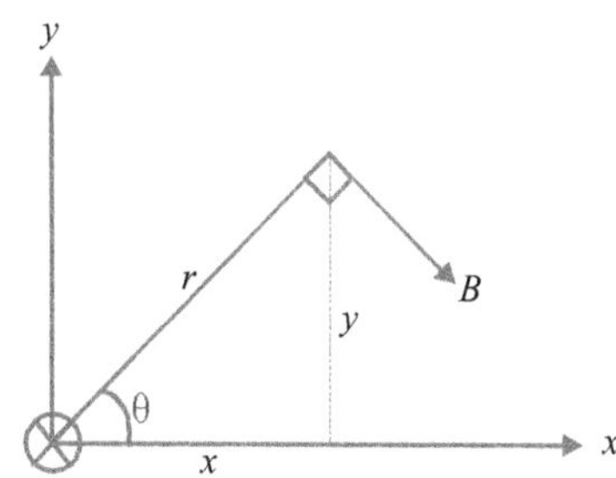

Now $\vec{B} = B\sin\theta\,\hat{i} - B\cos\theta\,\hat{j}$

$$= \frac{\mu_0}{2\pi}.\frac{I}{r}\left(\frac{y\hat{i}}{r} - \frac{x}{r}\hat{j}\right)$$

$$= \frac{\mu_0}{2\pi}.\frac{I}{r^2}(y\hat{i} - x\hat{j})$$

$$= \frac{\mu_0}{2\pi}I\frac{(y\hat{i} - x\hat{j})}{(x^2 + y^2)}.$$

7. (c) $M_1 = iA = iL^2$

$$M_2 = \sqrt{\left(i\frac{L^2}{2}\right)^2 + \left(i\frac{L^2}{2}\right)^2} = \frac{iL^2}{\sqrt{2}}.$$

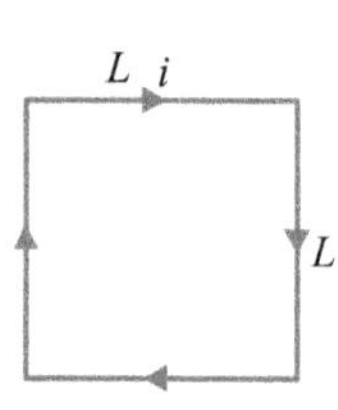
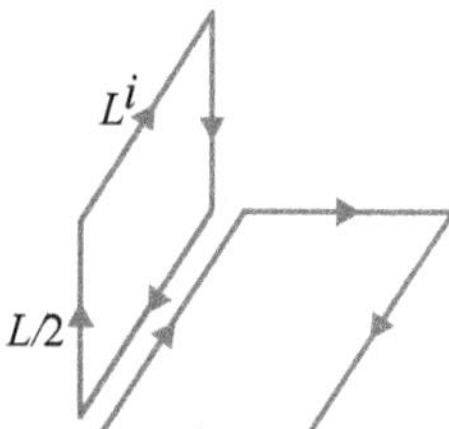

$$\therefore \quad \frac{M_1}{M_2} = \sqrt{2}.$$

8. (b) As $B = \frac{\mu_0}{2\pi}.\frac{i}{r}$, it represents a rectangular hyperbola. The combined graph is shown in figure.

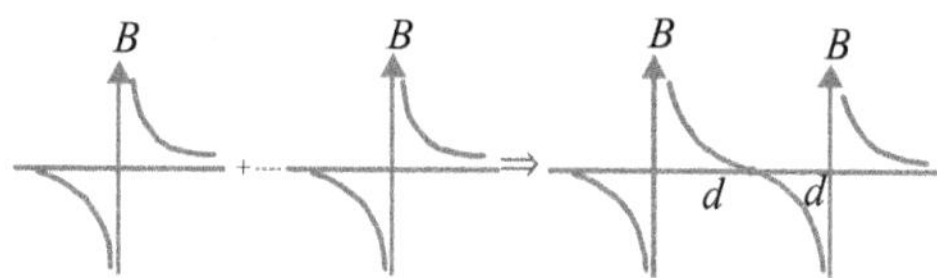

9. (c) Similar to Q. 8.

10. (d) $B = \frac{\mu_0}{2\pi}.\frac{i}{r}$ and $E = \frac{\lambda}{2\pi\epsilon_0 r}$

So, $\frac{B}{E} = k.r°.$

11. (c) $M = iA = \frac{Q}{T}A = \frac{Q\omega}{2\pi}\times\pi R^2 = \frac{Q\omega R^2}{2}.$

$L = I\omega = MR^2\omega$

$$\therefore \quad \frac{M}{L} = \frac{Q\omega R^2/2}{MR^2\omega} = \frac{Q}{2M}.$$

12. (b) Momentum,

$$P = \int F\,dt$$

$$= \int (Bid)\,dt$$

$$= Bd\int i\,dt$$

$$= BdQ_0.$$

13. (a) $\qquad \vec{F} = q(\vec{v}\times\vec{B})$

or $\quad q(-\hat{j} + \hat{k}) = q\left[\hat{i}\times(B_x\hat{i} + B_y\hat{j} + B_z\hat{k})\right]$ ..... (i)

and $\quad q(\hat{i} - \hat{k}) = q\left[\hat{j}\times(B_x\hat{i} + B_y\hat{j} + B_z\hat{k})\right]$ ..... (ii)

On simplifying above equations, we get

$$\vec{B} = (\hat{i} + \hat{j} + \hat{k}) \ Wb/m^2.$$

14. **(b)** $2\pi R = n(2\pi r), \ \therefore \ r = \dfrac{R}{n}.$

Now, $B = \dfrac{\mu_0 i}{2R}$ and $B' = \dfrac{\mu_0 ni}{r} = \dfrac{\mu_0 ni}{R/n} = n^2 B.$

15. **(b)** $\vec{B} = \dfrac{\mu_0}{4\pi} I(\sin 30° + \sin 30°)$

$$\left[\dfrac{1}{a\cos 30°} - \dfrac{1}{2a\cos 30°} + \dfrac{1}{3a\cos 30°} - .....\infty\right]\hat{k}$$

$$= \dfrac{\mu_0}{4\pi}.I\dfrac{2\sin 30°}{a\cos 30°}\left[1 - \dfrac{1}{2} + \dfrac{1}{3} - .....\infty\right]\hat{k}$$

$$= \dfrac{\mu_0}{4\pi}.I\dfrac{\ell n 4}{\sqrt{3}a}\hat{k}$$

16. **(a)** $B = 2\left[\dfrac{\mu_0}{4\pi}.\dfrac{i}{d\cos 45°}\{\sin(-45°) + \sin 90°\}\right]$

$$= \dfrac{\mu_0 i}{\sqrt{2}\pi d}\left[-\dfrac{1}{\sqrt{2}} + 1\right].\otimes$$

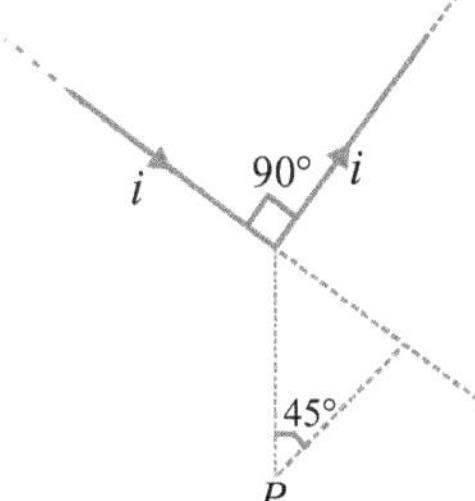

17. **(b)** The cylinder is cut into two equal halfs, as shown. Each half produces magnetic field inside is $\mu_0\lambda/2$. So,

$$B = \dfrac{\mu_0\lambda}{2} + \dfrac{\mu_0\lambda}{2} = \mu_0\lambda.$$

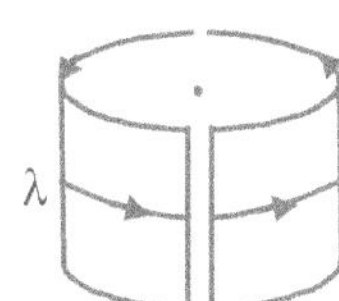

18. **(b)** $\vec{B} = 2\left(\dfrac{\mu_0}{4\pi}.\dfrac{I}{d/2}\right)(-\hat{k}) = \dfrac{-\mu_0 I}{\pi d}\hat{k}$

19. **(d)** The current, $di = \dfrac{dq}{dt} = \dfrac{(2\pi r dr)\sigma}{\left(\dfrac{2\pi}{\omega}\right)} = \sigma\omega r dr$

$$dm = (di) \times \pi r^2 = \pi\sigma\omega r^3 dr$$

$$\tau = \int_0^r (dM)B\sin\theta$$

$$= B\pi\sigma\omega \sin\theta \int_0^r r^3 dr$$

$$= B\pi\sigma\omega \sin\theta \dfrac{r^4}{4}$$

$$= (\sigma\pi r^2)\dfrac{\omega r^2 B\sin\theta}{4}$$

$$= \dfrac{q\omega r^2 B\sin\theta}{4}$$

20. **(d)** Both the half of equal area and so

$$\left|\vec{M_1}\right| = \left|\vec{M_2}\right|$$

Also their magnetic moment are perpendicular to each other, then $\vec{M_1}.\vec{M_2} = 0$

21. **(c)** $dN = \left(\dfrac{N}{b-a}\right)dr.$

Now $dB = \dfrac{\mu_0(dN)I}{2r}$

and $B = \displaystyle\int_a^b \dfrac{\mu_0\left(\dfrac{N}{b-a}\right)drI}{2r}$

$$= \dfrac{\mu_0 NI}{2(b-a)}\ell n\left(\dfrac{b}{a}\right).$$

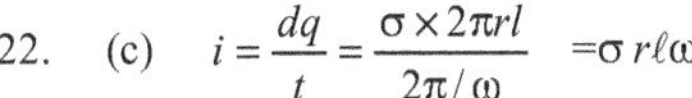

22. **(c)** $i = \dfrac{dq}{t} = \dfrac{\sigma \times 2\pi rl}{2\pi/\omega} = \sigma r l\omega$

Using Amphere's law, we can write

$$B\ell = \mu_0 i$$
or $\quad B\ell = \mu_0(\sigma r l\omega)$
$\therefore \quad B = \mu_0\sigma r\omega$

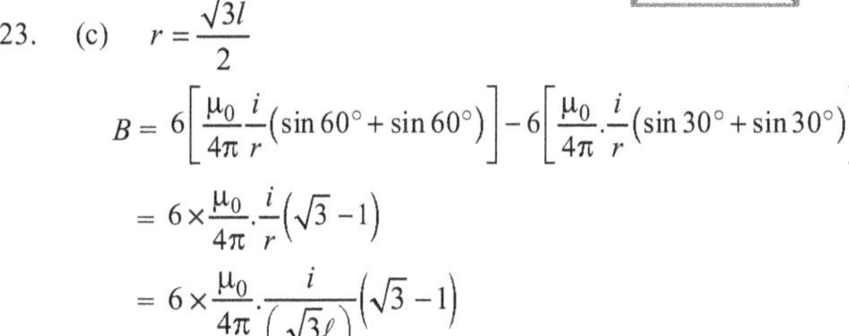

23. **(c)** $r = \dfrac{\sqrt{3}l}{2}$

$$B = 6\left[\dfrac{\mu_0}{4\pi}\dfrac{i}{r}\left(\sin 60° + \sin 60°\right)\right] - 6\left[\dfrac{\mu_0}{4\pi}.\dfrac{i}{r}\left(\sin 30° + \sin 30°\right)\right]$$

$$= 6\times\dfrac{\mu_0}{4\pi}.\dfrac{i}{r}\left(\sqrt{3} - 1\right)$$

$$= 6\times\dfrac{\mu_0}{4\pi}.\dfrac{i}{\left(\dfrac{\sqrt{3}\ell}{2}\right)}\left(\sqrt{3} - 1\right)$$

$$= \left(3 - \sqrt{3}\right)\dfrac{\mu_0 i}{\pi\ell}.$$

24. **(b)** At $x = 1, y = 1$ and at $x = 4, y = 2.$
The given wire can be replaced by a wire joining the two ends; a and b. So unit vector in the direction of force

$$= i\cos 45° + j\sin 45°$$

$$= \dfrac{\hat{i} + \hat{j}}{\sqrt{2}}.$$

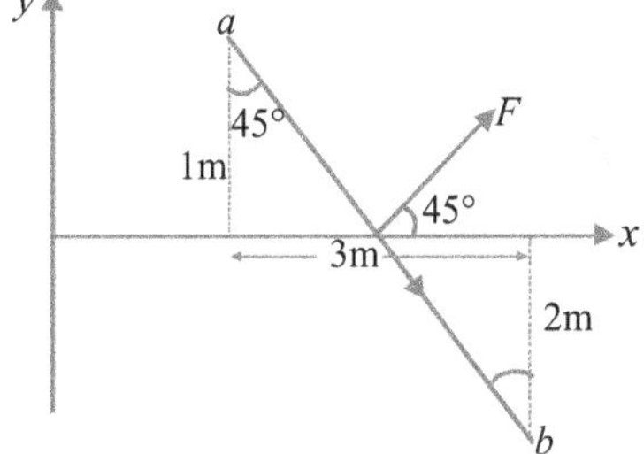

Alternative sol.

(b) $\vec{ab} = \vec{Ob} - \vec{Oa} = 4\hat{i} - 2\hat{j} - \hat{i} - \hat{j} = 3\hat{i} - 3\hat{j}$

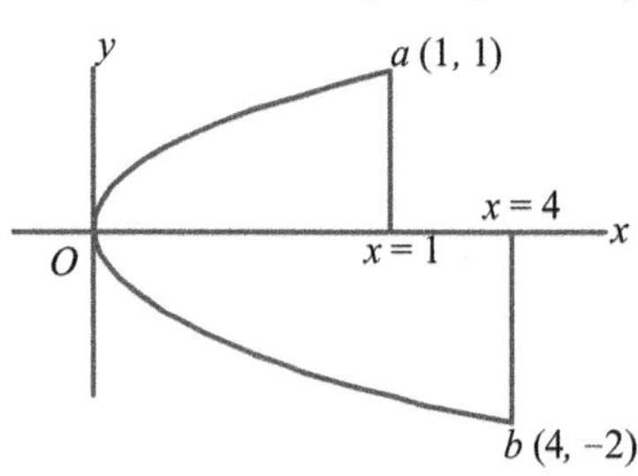

$\vec{F} = i(\hat{l} \times \vec{B}) = 1(3\hat{i} - 3\hat{j}) \times (-2\hat{k}) = (6\hat{j} + 6\hat{i})$

$\hat{F} = \dfrac{6\hat{j} + 6\hat{i}}{6\sqrt{2}} = \dfrac{\hat{i} + \hat{j}}{\sqrt{2}}$

25. (b)

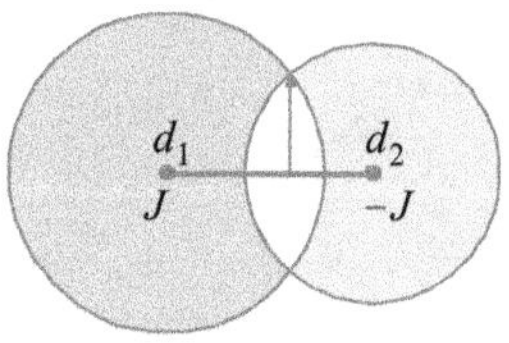

$$\oint \vec{B}.d\vec{i} = \mu_0 \hat{i}_{in}$$

or $\qquad B \times 2\pi r = \mu_0 (j \times \pi r^2)$

or $\qquad B = \dfrac{\mu_0 Jr}{2}$

If d_1 and d_2 are the distances from the centres of the regions, then

$$\vec{B} = \vec{B}_1 + \vec{B}_2$$

$$= \dfrac{\mu_0 J}{2}(\vec{d}_1 + \vec{d}_2)$$

$$= \dfrac{\mu_0 J}{2}\vec{d}$$

Solutions **EXERCISE-6.2**

1. **(c, d)** The magnetic field inside the inner solenoid is zero if,

$$B_{outer} = B_{inner}$$

or $\qquad \mu_0 n_1 i_1 = \mu_0 n_2 i_2$

or $\qquad n_1 i_1 = n_2 i_2$

Also if $i_1 = i_2$, then $n_1 = n_2$.

2. **(a, b, c)** See figure,

Also, $B \propto \dfrac{1}{r}$. points 1, 2, 3, ... have equal amount of magnetic field.

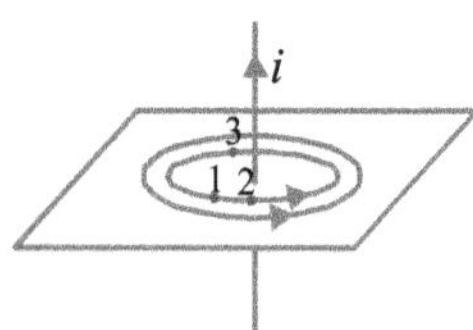

3. **(a, b, c)** E/B has dimensions of velocity. CR has dimensions of time and so $\dfrac{\ell}{CR}$ has dimensions of velocity. So x, y and z all the three have dimensions of velocity.

4. **(a, d)** On x-axis two conductors produce equal and opposite fields, so net field becomes zero.

5. **(a, b)** Electron stream can reverse the direction either through xy-plane of through xz-plane.

According to Fleming's left hand rule the magnetic field either along z-axis or along y-axis.

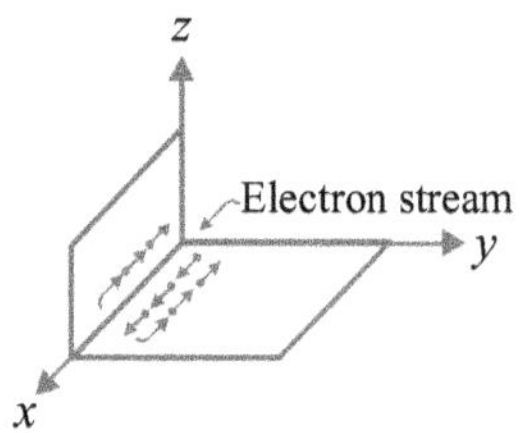

6. **(b, c)** As the magnetic field is acting along z-axis, and particle initial velocity is along x-axis, so particle will remain in xy-plane. Also its speed must be constant. Thus

$$b = 0, \text{ and } v = \sqrt{v_x^2 + v_y^2}$$

or $\qquad v^2 = \left(\dfrac{v}{2}\right)^2 + a^2$

$\therefore \qquad a = \dfrac{\sqrt{3}}{2}v$.

Now, $\qquad qvB = M\left(v\dfrac{dv}{dx}\right)$

or $\qquad qv \times (-B_0 x) = Mv\dfrac{dv}{dx}$

or $\qquad -\displaystyle\int_v^0 dv = \dfrac{qB_0}{M}\int_0^x x\,dx$

or $\qquad v = \left(\dfrac{qB_0}{M}\right)\dfrac{x^2}{2}$

or $\qquad v = 1 \times \dfrac{x^2}{2}$

$\therefore \qquad x = \sqrt{2v}$.

Solutions **EXERCISE-6.3**

1. (d) Current shows magnetic effect, but in one cmplete cycle the net magnetic field beocmes zero.

2. (c) The magnetic field inside conductor is given by

$$B = \frac{\mu_0}{2\pi} \cdot \frac{ir}{a^2}$$

For thin conductor, the point is on the axis of the conductor and so $r = 0$, $B = 0$.

3. (a) In thin walled tube, $i_{in} = 0$ and so

$$\oint \vec{B}.d\vec{\ell} = \mu_0 \times 0$$

or $B = 0$.

4. (d) The magnetic field at any point on the closed loop is due to all the three currents, but line integral of i_3 over the closed loop will be zero.

5. (a) Magnetic field at the centre of circular loop is given by

$$B = \frac{\mu_0 i}{2R}, \text{ as } R \to \infty, \text{ and so } B \to 0.$$

6. (a) For magnetic field to be zero at P

$$\frac{\mu_0}{2\pi} \cdot \frac{i_1}{r_1} = \frac{\mu_0}{2\pi} \cdot \frac{i_2}{r_2}$$

or $\dfrac{i_1}{r_1} = \dfrac{i_2}{r_2}$.

As $r_2 > r_1$, and so $i_2 > i_1$.

7. (a) The magnetic field of two equal halfs of the loop is equal and opposite and so $\vec{B} = 0$.

8. (d) For the given close path,

$$\oint \vec{B}.d\vec{\ell} = \mu_0(i - i) = 0.$$

9. (c) In case of two electron streams the electric repulsion is greater than magnetic attraction.

10. (b) For path 1, $\oint \vec{B}.d\vec{\ell} = \mu_0(-3+1) = -2\mu_0$.

For path 2, $\oint \vec{B}.d\vec{\ell} = \mu_0(3-3-1) = -\mu_0$.

11. (c) We know that , $\oint \vec{B}.d\vec{\ell} = \mu_0 i_{in}$. Since $i_{in} = 0$ and so $\oint \vec{B}.d\vec{\ell} = 0$. The magnetic field on any point on the close loop is zero.

12. (b) See theory of the chapter

13. (c) Each wire will experiences, equal and opposite forces and so net force on them becomes zero, but these forces constitues a couple whose torque is non zero.

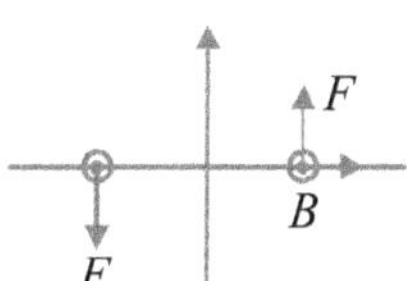

Solutions **EXERCISE-6.4**

Passage for Q. 1 to Q. 3

1. (b) $\oint \vec{B}.d\vec{\ell} = \mu_0 i_{in}$

or $B \times 2\pi r = \mu_0 \dfrac{i}{\pi a^2} \times \pi r^2$

$\therefore B = \dfrac{\mu_0}{2\pi} \cdot \dfrac{ir}{a^2}$.

2. (c) For $a < r < b$:

$B \times 2\pi r = \mu_0 i$

or $B = \dfrac{\mu_0}{2\pi} \cdot \dfrac{i}{r}$.

3. (c) For, $b < r < c$:

$$B \times 2\pi r = \mu_0 \left[i - \frac{i\pi(r^2 - b^2)}{\pi(c^2 - b^2)} \right]$$

or $B = \dfrac{\mu}{2\pi} \cdot \dfrac{i}{r} \left[1 - \dfrac{r^2 - b^2}{c^2 - b^2} \right]$

Passage for Q. 4 to Q. 6

4. (d) $dB = \dfrac{\mu_0(ndx)i}{2(a^2 + x^2)^{3/2}}$,

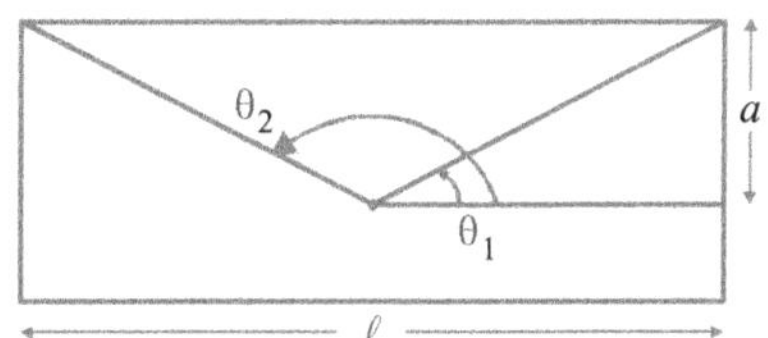

where $x = -a\cot\theta$

$$\therefore B = \frac{\mu_0 ni}{2} \int_{\theta_1}^{\theta_2} \sin\theta \, d\theta$$

$$= \frac{\mu_0 ni}{2}[\cos\theta_1 - \cos\theta_2]$$

Putting $\cos\theta_1 = \dfrac{\ell/2}{\sqrt{a^2 + (\ell/2)^2}}$

and $\cos\theta_2 = \dfrac{-\ell/2}{\sqrt{a^2 + (\ell/2)^2}}$,

we get $B = \dfrac{\mu_0 ni}{\sqrt{1 + 4a^2/\ell^2}} = \dfrac{\mu_0 ni\ell}{\sqrt{\ell^2 + 4a^2}}$

5.   (c)   In case $a \gg \ell$, $\sqrt{\ell^2 + 4a^2} \simeq 2a$ and so $B = \dfrac{\mu_0 ni\ell}{2a}$.

6.   (c)   For $a \ll \ell$, $\sqrt{\ell^2 + 4a^2} \simeq \ell$, and so $B = \mu_0 ni$.

Passage for Q. 7 to Q. 9

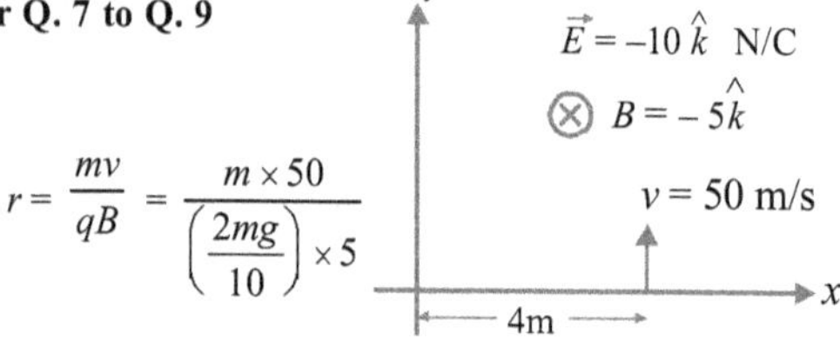

7.   (a) $r = \dfrac{mv}{qB} = \dfrac{m \times 50}{\left(\dfrac{2mg}{10}\right) \times 5}$

$\qquad = 5\ m$

8.   (a)   The retardation due to friction

$$a = \frac{f}{m} = \frac{\mu N}{m} = \frac{\mu(mg + Eq)}{m}$$

$$= \frac{\mu(mg + 2mg)}{m} = \mu \times 3g = \frac{1}{3} \times 3 \times 10 = 10 \text{m/s}^2$$

Now, $0 = u - at$,

or $\qquad t = \dfrac{u}{a} = \dfrac{50}{10} = 5s$.

9.   (b)   There is no displacement in the direction of electric force and so work done by it is equal to zero.

Passage for Q. 10 to Q. 12

10.   (b)   Using third equation of motion, we have

$$v_y^2 = u_y^2 + 2a_y y$$

or $0 = v_2^2 - 2\left(\dfrac{Ee}{m}\right)y$

$\therefore y = \left(\dfrac{mv_2^2}{2eE}\right)$.

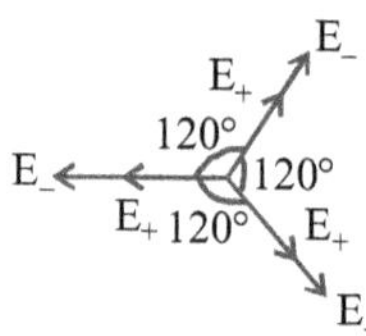

11.   (a)   Time period of revolution,

$$t = nT = n\frac{2\pi m}{eB} \quad \text{and} \quad 0 = v_2 t - \frac{1}{2}a_y t^2$$

or $t = \dfrac{2v_2}{a_y} = \dfrac{2v_2}{\left(\dfrac{Ee}{m}\right)}$

so $n \times \dfrac{2\pi m}{eB} = \dfrac{2v_2}{Ee/m}$

$\therefore v_2 = \dfrac{\pi nE}{B}$.

12.   (d)   We have, $v_2 = \pi nE/B$

and so $n = \dfrac{v_2 B}{\pi E}$

13.   (p)   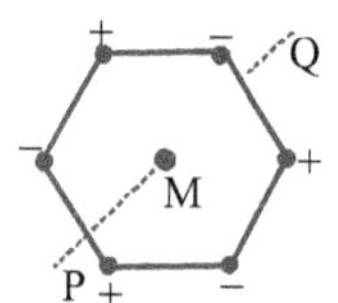

The electric field at M due to the charges at the corners of regular hexagon is as shown

Here $|E_+| = |E_-|$. The symmetry of the situation shows that $E = 0$ at M.

Therefore (A) is the correct option.

The electric potential due to all the charges at M is zero.

Therefore (B) is incorrect option.

When the system of charges is rotated about line PM, the net current will be zero.

Therefore the magnetic field at M is zero.

(C) is the correct option.

When magnetic field is zero, then $\mu = 0$

(D) is incorrect option.

(q)   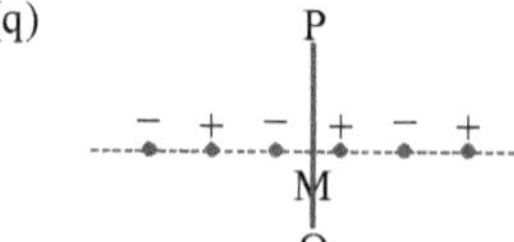

The electric field due to the inner most positive and negative charges at M is $E_1 = 2\left[k\dfrac{q}{r^2}\right]$ towards left. The electic field due to the

next positive and negative charges at M is $E_2 = 2\left[k\dfrac{q}{(2r)^2}\right]$ towards

right. The electric field due to the outermost positive and negative

charges at M is $E_3 = 2\left[k\dfrac{q}{(3r)^2}\right]$ towards left. Clearly the vector

sum of these three electric field is not zero.

(A) is incorrect option.

The electric potential due to the charges at M

$= k\left[\dfrac{+q}{r}\dfrac{-q}{r} + \dfrac{q}{2r} - \dfrac{q}{2r} + \dfrac{q}{3r} - \dfrac{q}{3r}\right] = 0$

(B) is incorrect option.

The net current due to the innermost positive and negative charges is zero. Similarly the net current due to other charges in pairs is zero. Therefore the magnetic field at M is zero. Also the magnetic moment is zero.

(C) is the correct option

(D) is incorrect option.

(r) 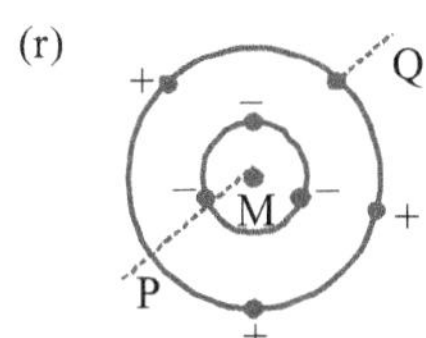

The net electric field due to negative charges in the inner circle is zero. Similarly the net electric field due to positive charges in the outercircle is zero.

(A) is the correct option.

The electric potential due to negative charges at M is different from the electric potential due to positive charges at M. Therefore the electric potential at M is not equal to zero.

(B) is the correct option.

When the system of charges rotate, we get a current I_1 due to negative charges and another current I due to positive charges. The magnitude of the magnetic at M due to the currents is different. Therefore $B \neq 0$ and $\mu \neq 0$.

(C) is incorrect option

(D) is the correct option.

(s) 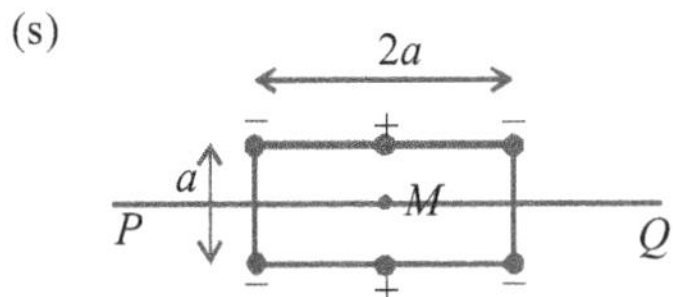

The electric field at M due to all the charges is zero because the electric field due to different charges cancel out in pairs.

(A) is the correct option.

The potential at M due to the charges is

$$V = k\left[\dfrac{+q}{a/2} + \dfrac{q}{a/2} - 4\left(\dfrac{q}{\dfrac{\sqrt{5a}}{4}}\right)\right] \neq 0$$

(B) is the correct option.

When the whole system is set into rotation with a constant angular velocity about the line PQ we get three loops in which current is flowing.

The magnetic field due to these currents produce a resultant magnetic field at M which is not equal to zero. Therefore a net magnetic dipole moment will be produced.

(C) is an incorrect option.

(D) is correct option.

(t) 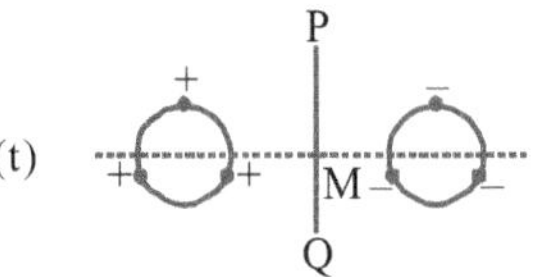

There will be a net electric field due to the arrangement of charges at M towards the right side.

(A) is an incorrect option.

The electric potential at M will can out in pairs by positive and negative charges, due to symmetrical arrangement of charges.

(B) is an incorrect option.

When the system of charges rotates about PQ, the net current is zero due to symmetrical arrangement of charges. Therefore $B = 0$ and $\mu = 0$

(C) is the correct option.

(D) is the incorrect option.

14. **A : q, r**

Statement -2 : The magnetic field at P due to current flowing in AB is perpendicular to the plane of paper acting vertically downward. And the magnetic field at P due to current flowing in CD is perpendicular to the plane of paper acting vertically upwards.

Therefore, q is correct.

As P is the mid point, the two magnetic fields, cancel out each other. Therefore, r is correct.

B : p

Statement -2 : The magnetic field at P due to current in loop A is along the axial line towards right. Similarly, the magnetic field at P due to current in loop B is also along the axial line towards right.

C : q, r

Statement -2 : The magnetic field due to current in loop A at P is equal and opposite to the magnetic field due to current in loop B at P.

D : q, s

Statement -2 : The direction of magnetic field at P due to current in loop A is perpendicular to the plane of paper directed vertically upwards.

The direction of magnetic field at P due to current in loop B is perpendicular to the plane of paper directed vertically downward.

Since the current are in opposite direction the wires repel each other.

15.   A-p, q, r : In uniform magnetic field, the motion of particle is uniform and circle of helical depend on the angle between $\vec{v}$ and $\vec{B}$.

B- q, r, s, t :

Electric field exerts the force on the charged particle so its motion no remains uniform. Depending on the nature of electric field, the path of the particle may be parabolic, etc.

C-p, r :

$$v = \sqrt{(k\sin t)^2 + (k\cos t)^2 + k^2} = \sqrt{2}\,k (\text{constant})$$

D- s :

Given; $y = B\sin^2 \omega t$ and $x = A\sin\omega t$

$$\therefore \quad y = B \times \left(\frac{x}{A}\right)^2$$

$$\text{or} \quad y = \frac{B}{A^2} x^2$$

$$\text{or} \quad x^2 = \frac{A^2}{B} y .$$

It represents a parabola.

16.   **A - r,t ; B - r,t ; C - r,s ; D - r,t**

Using right hand screw rule to get the direction of resultant field.

For A, B and C– Magnetic field at location of 1 due to 2 is parallel or antiparallel to current in 1, so force experienced by 1 due to magnetic field of 2 is zero. For D–Force experienced by upper half of 2 due to 1 is along left, while on lower half it is towards right. So, net force of interaction between the two is zero.

Direction of magnetic field at P can be found by using RHPR No. 1.

Solutions EXERCISE-6.5

1.

$$B_1 = \frac{\mu_0}{2\pi}\cdot\frac{i}{d}$$

and

$$B_2 = \frac{\mu_0}{4\pi}\cdot\frac{i}{d}[\sin\theta + \sin\theta]$$

$$= \frac{\mu_0}{4\pi}\cdot\frac{i}{d}\times 2\sin\theta$$

Here

$$\sin\theta = \frac{\ell/2}{\sqrt{(\ell/2)^2 + d^2}}$$

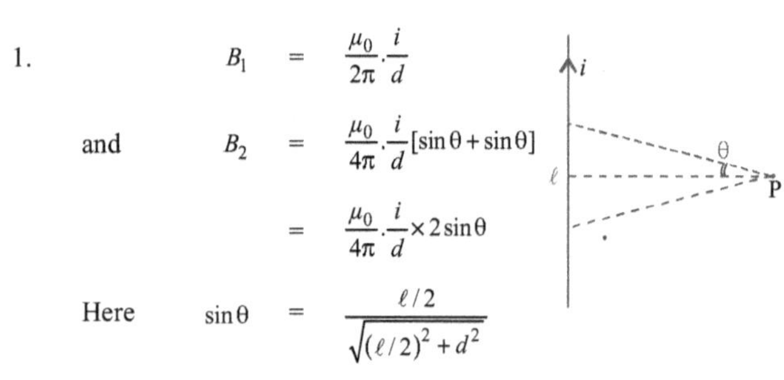

Given $\left[\dfrac{B_1 - B_2}{B_1}\right] = 0.01$

After substituting and simplifying, we get

$$d/\ell = 0.07 \qquad \textbf{Ans.}$$

2.   The magnetic field due to all the wire is shown in figure. So

$$B_{\text{total}} = 2\sqrt{2}B$$

$$= 2\sqrt{2}\left(\frac{\mu_0}{2\pi}\cdot\frac{i}{r}\right)$$

$$= 2\sqrt{2}\,\frac{\mu_0}{2\pi}\cdot\frac{i}{a/\sqrt{2}}$$

$$= 4\frac{\mu_0}{2\pi}\frac{i}{a}$$

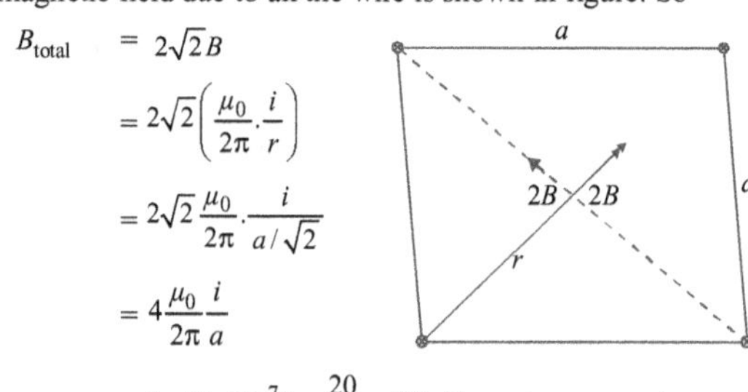

$$= 4\times(2\times 10^{-7})\times\frac{20}{0.20} = 80\mu T \text{ up the page.} \textbf{ Ans.}$$

3.   (i)   The magnetic field at point R,

$$\vec{B} = \frac{\mu_0}{2\pi}\left[\frac{I_1}{5} + \frac{I_2}{2}\right](-\hat{j})$$

$$\vec{v} = 4\times 10^{+5}\hat{i} \text{ m/s}$$

Force, $\vec{F} = (-e)[\vec{v}\times\vec{B}]$

After substituting the values and simplifying we get

$$I_2 = 4A .$$

(ii)

$$\vec{B} = \vec{B}_1 + \vec{B}_2 + \vec{B}_3 = 0$$

$$\text{or} \quad \frac{\mu_0}{2\pi}\left[\frac{I_1}{5} + \frac{I_2}{2} - \frac{I_3}{x}\right] = 0$$

Here, $I_1 = 2.5A$, $I_2 = 4A$ and $I_3 = 2.5A$

$$\therefore \qquad\qquad x = 1 \text{ m.} \qquad \textbf{Ans.}$$

4.   The magnetic field at the centre of the solenoid is given by

$$B = \frac{\mu_0 ni}{2}(\cos\theta_1 - \cos\theta_2)$$

Here $\cos\theta_1 = 0.93$, $\cos\theta_2 = \cos(180° - \theta_1) = -\cos\theta_1$

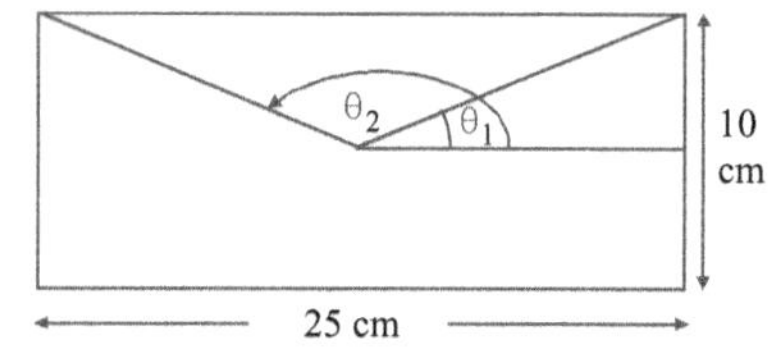

$$\therefore \quad B = \frac{4\pi\times 10^{-7}\times\left(\dfrac{200}{0.25}\right)\times 0.3\times(2\times 0.93)}{2}$$

$$= 0.3 \text{ mA} \qquad \textbf{Ans.}$$

5.   (a)   The inner radius is

$$r_i = 0.15m, \text{ so}$$

$$B = \frac{\mu_0 Ni}{2\pi r_i} = \frac{(4\pi\times 10^{-7})(500)(0.80)}{2\pi\times 0.25}$$

$$= 5.33\times 10^{-4}\text{T}$$

(b)

$$B = \frac{\mu_0 Ni}{2\pi r_0} = \frac{(4\pi\times 10^{-7})(500)(0.80)}{2\pi(0.15 + 0.05)}$$

$$= 4.00\times 10^{-4}\text{ T} \qquad \textbf{Ans.}$$

Solutions EXERCISE-6.6

1. Previously the magnetic field is due to the current causes due to movement of the free electrons. To an observer in a trolley moving in the direction of current the current is due to electrons becomes zero but it is now due to movement of positive ions. So magnetic field

$$B = \frac{\mu_0}{2\pi}\cdot\frac{i}{r}.$$

2. The current, $\quad i = \frac{q}{t} = \frac{e}{T} = ef.$

The magnetic field, $\quad B = \frac{\mu_0 i}{2r} = \frac{\mu_0(ef)}{2r}$

$$= 14 \text{ Wb/m}^2$$

Magnetic moment, $\quad M = iA = ef(\pi r^2)$

$$= 9\times10^{-24} \text{ A-m}^2 \qquad \textbf{Ans.}$$

3. The magnetic field of earth at that point becomes zero, when wire produces equal and opposite field. So

$$\frac{\mu_0}{2\pi}\cdot\frac{i}{r} = B_H$$

$$\therefore \qquad i = \frac{B_H r}{(\mu_0/2\pi)} = \frac{(39\times10^{-6})\times0.08}{2\times10^{-7}}$$

$$\approx 16 \text{ A from west to eas} \qquad \textbf{Ans.}$$

4. The magnetic field at the centre of the loop,

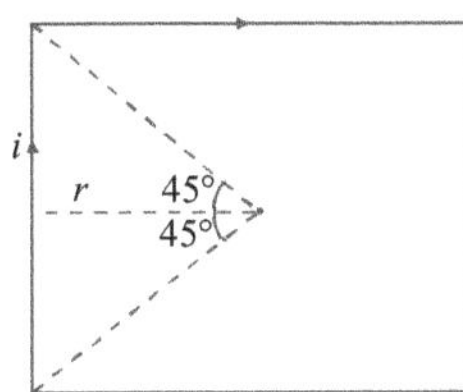

$$B = 4\left[\frac{\mu_0}{4\pi}\cdot\frac{i}{r}(\sin 45^\circ + \sin 45^\circ)\right]$$

Here, $r = a/2$,

After simplifying, we get $\quad B = \dfrac{2\sqrt{2}\mu_0 i}{\pi a}$

5. The magnetic field due to one side of the square can be calculated as:

$$dB = \frac{\mu_0}{4\pi}\cdot\frac{i}{r^2}\sin\theta dx$$

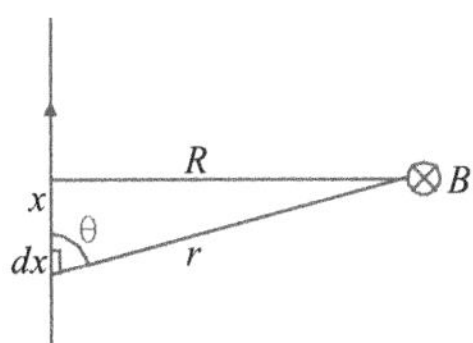

$$\therefore \qquad B = \int_{-a/2}^{a/2} \frac{\mu_0}{4\pi}\cdot\frac{i}{r^2}\sin\theta dx$$

$$= \frac{\mu_0 i}{2\pi R}\cdot\frac{a}{\sqrt{a^2+4R^2}} = \frac{\mu_0 i}{\pi\sqrt{4x^2+a^2}\sqrt{4x^2+2a^2}}.$$

Now magnetic field due to the all the four sides of the square can be calculated as :

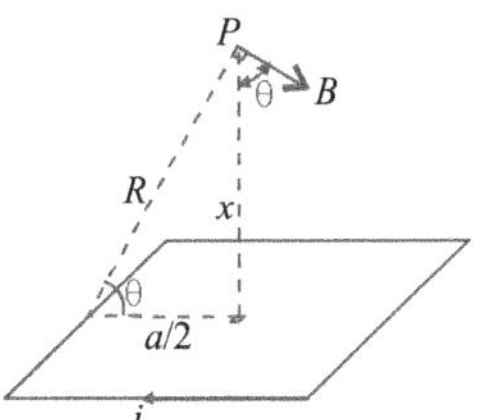

$$B_{\text{total}} = 4B\cos\theta$$

$$= \frac{4Ba}{2R} = \frac{4Ba}{\sqrt{4x^2+a^2}}$$

$$= \frac{4\mu_0 i a^2}{\pi(4x^2+a^2)(4x^2+2a^2)^{1/2}} \textbf{ Ans.}$$

6. The magnetic field due to a straight wire is given by

$$B = \frac{\mu_0}{4\pi}\cdot\frac{I}{r}(\sin\theta_1 + \sin\theta_2)$$

where, $r = R$, $\sin\theta_1 = \dfrac{L}{\sqrt{L^2+R^2}}$, $\sin\theta_2 = 0$

$$\therefore \qquad B = \frac{\mu_0}{4\pi R}i\frac{L}{\sqrt{L^2+R^2}}. \qquad \textbf{Ans.}$$

7. (i)

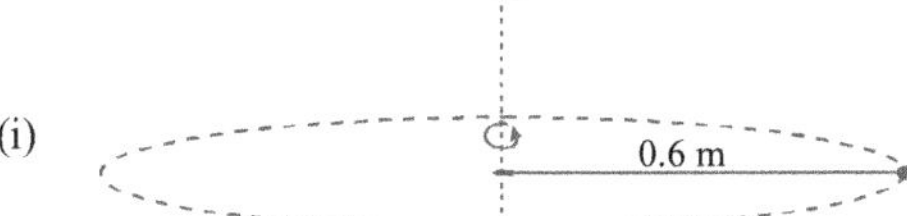

The equivalent current $i = \dfrac{q}{T} = \dfrac{q}{2\pi/\omega} = \dfrac{q\omega}{2\pi}$

The rotating rod with charge at its end behaves like a circular loop. So

$$B = \frac{\mu_0}{2}\frac{iR^2}{(R^2+x^2)^{3/2}}$$

Here, $R = 0.6$ m and $x = 0.8$ m.

After substituting the values and simplifying we get,

$$B = 11.3 \times 10^{-4} \text{ T}$$

(ii) In this case $i = q\omega/2\pi$, $R = 0.3\,\text{m}$, $x = 0.4\,\text{m}$

$$\therefore \qquad B = 22.6 \times 10^{-4} \text{ T} \qquad \textbf{\textit{Ans.}}$$

8. The magnetic field

$$B = B_L + B_P + B_Q + B_M$$

$$= 0 + \frac{\mu_0}{4\pi}\cdot\frac{i}{r} + \frac{\mu_0}{4\pi}\cdot\frac{i}{r} + 0$$

$$= \frac{\mu_0}{2\pi}\cdot\frac{i}{r} = 2\times10^{-7}\times\frac{10}{0.02}$$

$$= 10^{-4}\ \text{Wb/m}^2$$

9. Magnetic field due to segment of a circular loop is given by

$$B = \frac{\mu_0\theta i}{4\pi a}$$

$$\therefore \qquad B_{\text{net}} = \frac{\mu_0\theta i}{4\pi a}\left(\frac{1}{a}-\frac{1}{b}\right) \text{ out of page}$$

10. Using Ampere's law, we have

$$\oint \vec{B}.\overrightarrow{d\ell} = \mu_0 i_{\text{in}}$$

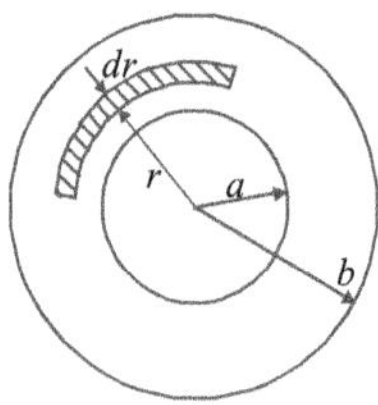

Here

$$i_{\text{in}} = \int_0^r i\,dA$$

$$= \int_{r_1}^{r_2} cr^2 \times 2\pi r\,dr$$

$$= 2\pi c\frac{(r_2^4 - r_1^4)}{4} = \frac{\pi c(r_2^4 - r_1^4)}{2}$$

$$\therefore \qquad B \times 2\pi r_1 = \mu_0\left[\frac{\pi c(r_2^4 - r_1^4)}{2}\right]$$

or

$$B = \frac{\mu_0 c}{4r_1}(r_2^4 - r_1^4)$$

$$= \frac{(4\pi\times10^{-7})(3\times10^6)[0.03^4 - 0.02^4]}{4\times0.03}$$

$$= 2.0 \times 10^{-5} \text{ T} \qquad \textbf{\textit{Ans.}}$$

11. Magnetic field is given by

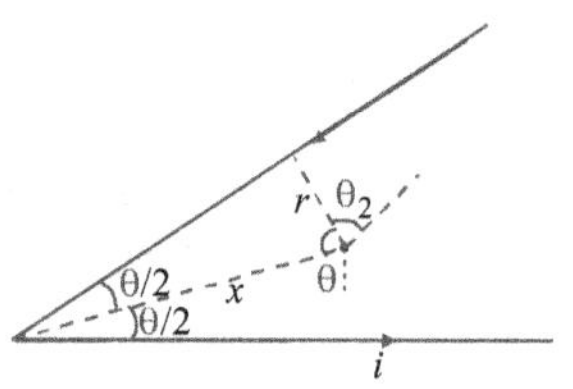

$$B = 2\left[\frac{\mu_0}{4\pi}\cdot\frac{i}{r}(\sin\theta_1 + \sin\theta_2)\right]$$

$$= 2\frac{\mu_0}{4\pi}\times\frac{i}{x\sin\theta/2}[\sin(90° - \theta/2) + \sin 90°]$$

$$= \frac{\mu_0 i}{2\pi x}\frac{[1+\cos\theta/2]}{\sin\theta/2} = \frac{\mu_0 i}{2\pi x}\cot\theta/4 \qquad \textbf{\textit{Ans.}}$$

12. $$B = B_{\text{curved}} + B_{\text{straight}}$$

$$= \frac{\mu_0\left(\dfrac{3}{4}\right)I}{2R} + \frac{\mu_0}{4\pi}\cdot\frac{I}{r}(\sin 45° + \sin 45°)$$

Here $\qquad r = R\cos 45°$

After substituting the values and solving, we get

$$B = 2.8\times10^{-5} \text{ T} \qquad \textbf{\textit{Ans.}}$$

13. Using Ampere's law, we have

$$\oint \vec{B}.\overrightarrow{d\ell} = \mu_0 i_{\text{in}}$$

or $\qquad B \times 2\pi r = \mu_0\displaystyle\int_0^r J\,dA$

$$= \mu_0\int_0^r\left(J_0\frac{r}{a}\right)\times 2\pi r\,dr$$

$$\therefore \qquad B = \frac{\mu_0 J_0 r^2}{3a}. \qquad \textbf{\textit{Ans.}}$$

14. (a) The area of shaded portion

$$A = \pi(a^2 - b^2)$$

$\therefore$ The current in whole cross-section of the conductor

$$I = \frac{i\pi a^2}{\pi(a^2 - b^2)} = \frac{ia^2}{(a^2 - b^2)}$$

The magnetic field due to cylindrical conductor at a distance r, inside

$$B = \frac{\mu_0}{2\pi}\cdot\frac{Ir}{a^2}$$

$$= \frac{\mu_0}{2\pi}\cdot\frac{\left[ia^2/(a^2-b^2)\right]d}{a^2}$$

$$= \frac{\mu_0 id}{2\pi(a^2-b^2)}.$$

(b) For the case b = 0; $B = \dfrac{\mu_0 id}{2\pi a^2}$, and for $d = 0$, $B = 0$.

15. The magnetic field of side AD and BC are equal and opposite so they cancel each other.

$$\therefore \quad B_{\text{net}} = B_{\text{AB}} - B_{\text{DC}}$$

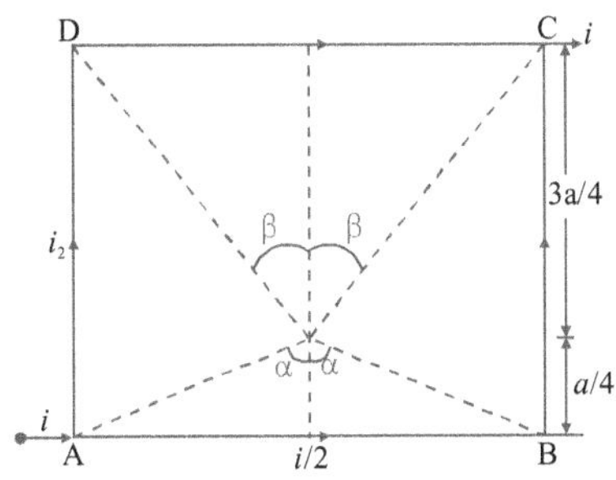

$$= \frac{\mu_0}{4\pi}\cdot\left[\frac{i/2}{a/4}(\sin\alpha+\sin\alpha)-\frac{i/2}{3a/4}(\sin\beta+\sin\beta)\right]$$

Here, $\sin\alpha = \dfrac{a/2}{\sqrt{(a/2)^2+(a/4)^2}}$, $\sin\beta = \dfrac{a/2}{\sqrt{(a/2)^2+(3a/4)^2}}$

After substituting the values, and simplifying, we get

$$B = \frac{2\mu_0 i}{\pi a}\left(\frac{1}{\sqrt{5}}-\frac{1}{3\sqrt{13}}\right), \text{ out of page } \textbf{\textit{Ans.}}$$

16. (a) The magnetic fields of parallel wires cancel each other, so net magnetic field at P will be zero.

(b) The magnetic field at

$$Q_1 = \frac{\mu_0}{2\pi}\left[\frac{i}{a/2}\times 2 + \frac{i}{3a/2}\times 2\right]$$

$$= \frac{8\mu_0 i}{3\pi a}$$

$$= 1.1\times 10^{-4}\text{ T, out of page}$$

Similarly at $Q_3 = 1.1\times 10^{-4}\,\text{T}$ into the page. It will be zero at Q_2 and Q_4.

17. The magnetic field at a distance of 2m from the wire

$$B = \frac{\mu_0}{2\pi}\cdot\frac{i}{r} = 2\times 10^{-7}\times\frac{10}{2} = 10^{-6}\text{T}$$

(a) The net magnetic field at $x = 0$, $z = 2m$

$$\vec{B} = B_1\hat{i} - B_2\hat{i}$$

$$= 10^{-6}\hat{i} - 10^{-6}\hat{i} = 0$$

(b) $$\vec{B} = 10^{-6}\hat{i} - 10^{-6}\hat{k}$$

$$= \sqrt{2}\times 10^{-6}\text{T} \qquad \textbf{\textit{Ans.}}$$

(c) Do this part similarly.

18. The field of the solenoid at the point is parallel to the solenoid axis and the field of the wire is perpendicular to the solenoid axis. The total field makes and angle of 45° with the axis if these two fields have equal magnitudes. Therefore

$$\mu_0 ni_{\text{solenoid}} = \frac{\mu_0}{2\pi}\cdot\frac{i_{\text{wire}}}{r}$$

$$\therefore \quad r = \frac{i_{\text{wrie}}}{2\pi ni_{\text{sol}}} = 4.77\times 10^{-2}\text{ m}$$

The resultant field, $B_{\text{resultant}} = \sqrt{2}B$

$$= \sqrt{2}\mu ni_{\text{solenoid}}$$

$$= 3.55\times 10^{-5}\text{ T}$$

19. We know that, $V = V_0 e^{-t/\tau}$

or $$0.90V_0 = V_0 e^{-2/\tau}$$

$$\therefore \quad \tau = 19.23\text{ s}$$

As $$\tau = CR$$

$$\therefore \quad R = \frac{\tau}{C} = \frac{19.23}{100\times 10^{-6}} = 19.23\times 10^4\,\Omega$$

$$i_0 = \frac{\Sigma}{R} = \frac{20}{19.23\times 10^4} = 1.04\times 10^{-4}\text{ A}$$

Magnetic field $$B = \mu_0 ni = \mu_0 n(ie^{-t/i})$$

$$B_{\text{av}} = \frac{\displaystyle\int_0^2 Bdt}{2} = 16\pi\times 10^{-8}\text{T} \quad \textbf{\textit{Ans.}}$$

20. The current in slit of width h (for h << R),

$$i = \frac{Ih}{2\pi R}$$

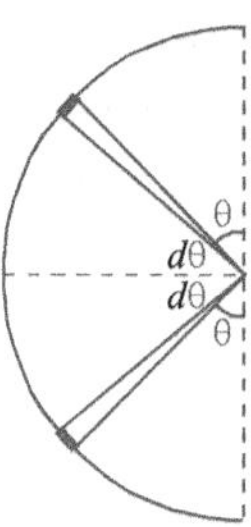

Magnetic field at a distance r from the slit,

$$B = \frac{\mu_0}{2\pi}\cdot\frac{I}{r} - \frac{\mu_0}{4\pi}\cdot\frac{(Ih/2\pi R)}{r}$$

$$= \frac{\mu_0 hI}{4\pi^2 Rr}. \qquad \textbf{\textit{Ans.}}$$

21. Take two elements, as shown in figure. The current in each element,

$$di = \frac{i}{\pi}d\theta$$

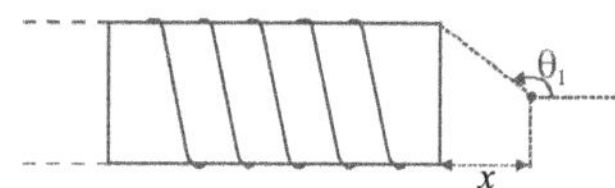

The resultant field

$$B = \int_0^{\pi/2} 2dB\sin\theta$$

$$= 2\int_0^{\pi/2}\left(\frac{\mu_0}{2\pi}\cdot\frac{i}{R}\right)\sin\theta\, d\theta$$

$$= \frac{\mu_0 i}{\pi^2 R} \qquad \textbf{\textit{Ans.}}$$

22. By Ampere's law $\oint \vec{B}.\vec{d\ell} = \mu_0 i_{in} = \mu_0 \int_0^r j(2\pi r\, dr)$

or $\qquad B\times 2\pi r = \mu_0 \int j(2\pi r\, dr)$

or $\qquad br^\alpha \times (2\pi r) = \mu_0 \int j(2\pi r\, dr)$

or $\qquad br^{(\alpha+1)} = \mu_0 \int jr\, dr$

On differentiation, we get

$$(\alpha+1)br^\alpha = \mu_0 jr$$

$$\therefore \qquad j = \frac{b(\alpha+1)r^{\alpha-1}}{\mu_0}. \qquad \textbf{\textit{Ans.}}$$

23. We know that, $\qquad B = \frac{\mu_0}{4\pi}\cdot\frac{2M}{R^3}$

$$\therefore \qquad M = \frac{2\pi R^3 B}{\mu_0} \qquad \textbf{\textit{Ans.}}$$

24. We know that, magnetic field due to a solenoid

(a) $\qquad B = \frac{\mu_0 ni}{2}(\cos\theta_1 - \cos\theta_2)$

Here, $\cos\theta_1 = -\dfrac{x}{\sqrt{x^2+R^2}}$, $\cos\theta_2 = 180°$

$$\therefore \qquad B = \frac{\mu_0 ni}{2}\left[-\frac{x}{\sqrt{x^2+R^2}} - \cos 180°\right]$$

$$= \frac{\mu_0 ni}{2}\left[1 - \frac{x}{\sqrt{x^2+R^2}}\right] \qquad \textbf{\textit{Ans.}}$$

(b) Do this part similarly.

$$\bigstar\ \bigstar\ \bigstar$$

7

Permanent Magnet & Magnetic Properties of Substance (449-484)

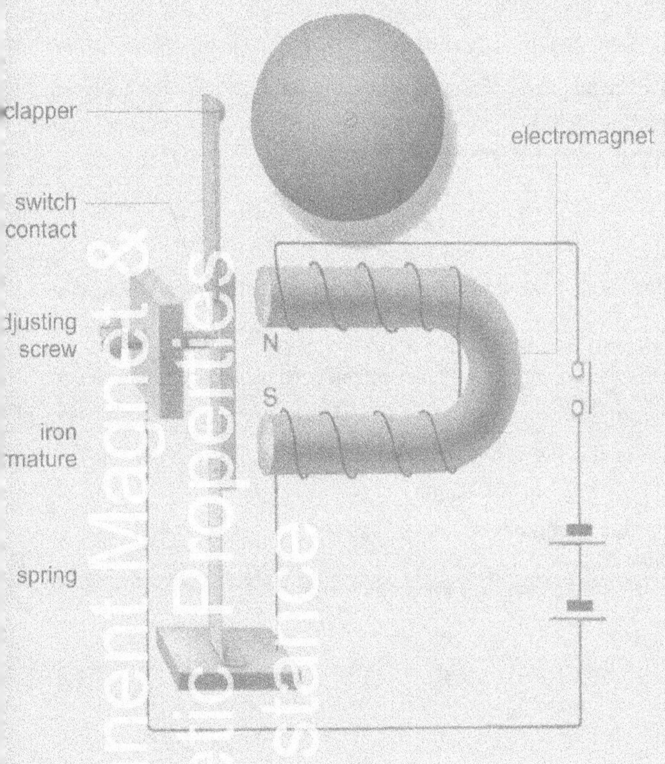

7.1 PERMANENT MAGNET : AN INTRODUCTION

In the previous chapter, we have seen that a current carrying loop, produces magnetic

field $\vec{B} = \dfrac{\mu_0}{4\pi}\dfrac{2\vec{M}}{r^3}$

at an axial point. Here $\vec{M} = i\vec{A}$ is the magnetic moment of the loop. Vector $\vec{A}$ represents the area vector of the current loop. Current loop in magnetic field experiences a

torque $\vec{\tau} = \vec{M} \times \vec{B}$. We also know that the electric field of the dipole is $\vec{E} = \dfrac{1}{4\pi \in_0}\dfrac{2\vec{P}}{r^3}$ on

the axis of the dipole and it experiences a torque $\vec{\tau} = \vec{P} \times \vec{E}$.

The above similarity of current loop with the electric dipole makes the following hypothetical model :

(1)   There are two types of charges; positive magnetic charge (+m) and negative

magnetic charge (–m). A magnetic charge m placed in a magnetic field $\vec{B}$ experiences a force

$$\vec{F} = m\vec{B} \qquad ...(1)$$

The force on a positive magnetic charge is along the field $\vec{B}$, and the force on negative charge is opposite to the field.

(2)   A magnetic charge m produces a magnetic field

$$B = \dfrac{\mu_0}{4\pi}\dfrac{m}{r^2} \qquad ...(2)$$

at a distance r from it.

(3)   A magnetic dipole is formed when two equal and opposite charges are placed at some separation.

Magnetic dipole moment, $M = m\ell$.

(4)   A current loop of area A carrying current i may be replaced by a magnetic dipole of

moment $\vec{M} = m\vec{\ell} = i\vec{A}$.

Bar magnet : Bar magnet is the permanent magnetic dipole.

(i)   Magnetic length $\simeq 0.84 \times$ geometric length

(ii) Magnetic charge or pole strength = m
SI unit of m is A-m or N/T.

(iii) Magnetic moment M = Pole strength $\times$ magnetic length

or $\vec{M} = m\vec{\ell}$

SI unit of M = A-m^2 or J/T.

Field of bar magnet is strong at its ends and negligibly small at its middle.

If we break a bar magnet, it seems, to isolate in a single pole or monopole. However, we cannot get an isolated pole even if we break the magnet down to its individual atoms and then to its electrons and nuclei. Each fragment has a north pole and south pole. Thus the simplest magnetic structure that can exist is a magnetic dipole. Magnetic monopoles do not exist.

7.2 COULOMB'S LAW IN MAGNETISM

According to Coulomb, the magnetic force between two magnetic charges m_1 and m_2 placed at a separation r is given by

$$F = \left(\dfrac{\mu_0}{4\pi}\right)\dfrac{m_1 m_2}{r^2}.$$

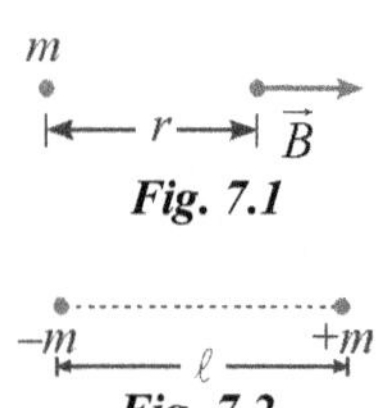

Fig. 7.1

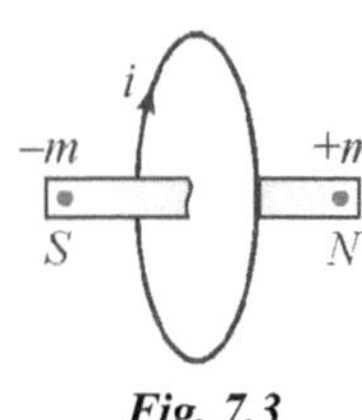

Fig. 7.2

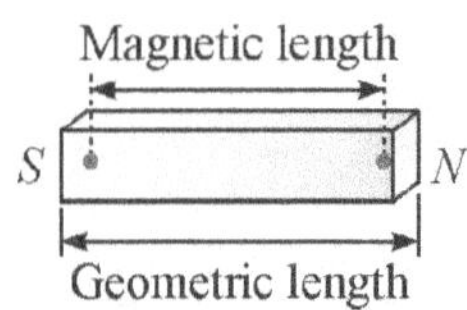

Fig. 7.3

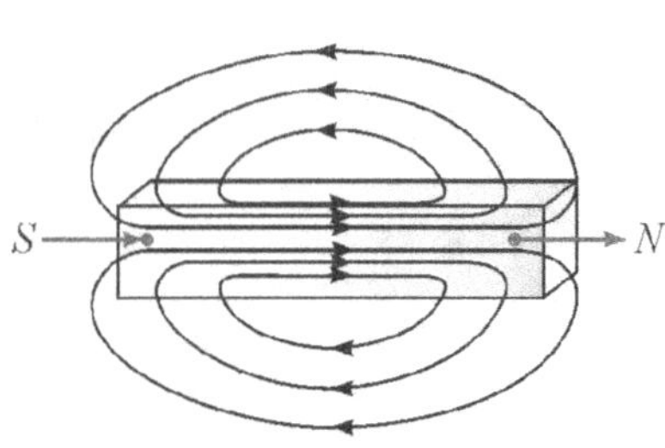

Fig. 7.4

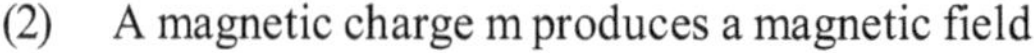
Fig.7.5 Magnetic field of bar magnet

Magnetic field due to a magnetic pole: If m_0 is the magnetic charge and F is the force exerted by another magnetic charge m, then magnetic field at a distance r from m can be defined as

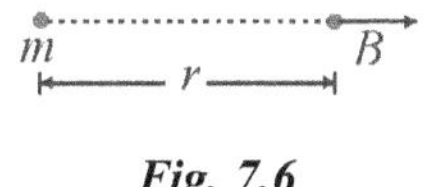

$$\vec{B} = \frac{\vec{F}}{m_0}$$

$$= \frac{\left(\dfrac{\mu_0}{4\pi}\dfrac{mm_0}{r^2}\right)}{m_0} = \frac{\mu_0}{4\pi}\frac{m}{r^2}.$$

Fig. 7.6

Magnetic potential

For a pole strength m, the field at a distance r is

$$B = \frac{\mu_0}{4\pi}\frac{m}{r^2},$$

and radially away from the pole. The potential at a distance r is given by,

$$V = -\int_{\infty}^{r} \vec{B}\, d\vec{r}$$

$$= -\int_{\infty}^{r} \frac{\mu_0}{4\pi}\frac{m}{r^2} \times dr$$

$$= \frac{\mu_0}{4\pi}\frac{m}{r}$$

Also

$$B = -\frac{dV}{dr}$$

Magnetic potential due to a dipole

Consider a magnetic dipole of moment M. If m is the pole strength and ℓ is the distance between the poles, then $M = m\ell$. If r_1 and r_2 are the distances of point P from the poles, then

$$r_1 = r - \frac{\ell}{2}\cos\theta$$

and

$$r_2 = r + \frac{\ell}{2}\cos\theta$$

Magnetic potential at P,

$$V = V_N + V_S$$

$$= \frac{\mu_0}{4\pi}\left[\frac{m}{r_1} - \frac{m}{r_2}\right]$$

$$= \frac{\mu_0 m}{4\pi}\left[\frac{1}{r - \dfrac{\ell}{2}\cos\theta} - \frac{1}{r + \dfrac{\ell}{2}\cos\theta}\right]$$

$$= \frac{\mu_0 m}{4\pi}\left(\frac{\ell\cos\theta}{r^2 - \dfrac{\ell^2}{4}\cos^2\theta}\right)$$

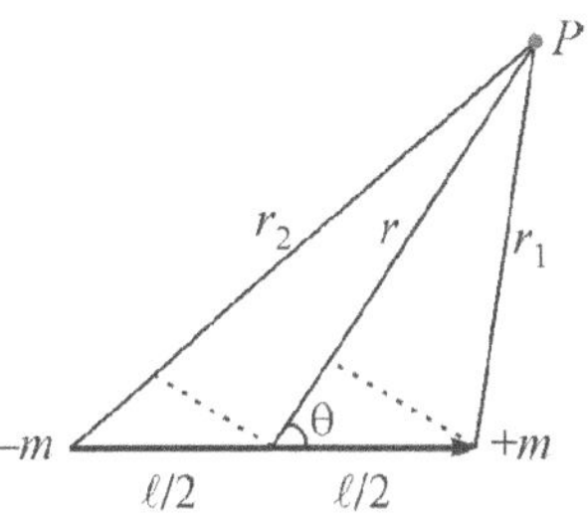

Fig. 7.7

Putting $m\ell = M$, and neglecting ℓ^2 in comparison to r, we get

$$V = \frac{\mu_0}{4\pi}\frac{M\cos\theta}{r^2}.$$

Magnetic field of a dipole

The magnetic field at any point P at an angular position θ at a distance r from the centre of the dipole can be obtained by resolving it in to two components. One component B_r which is along the radius vector and the other B_θ which is perpendicular to radius vector. The radial component of magnetic field

$$B_r = -\frac{dV}{dr}$$

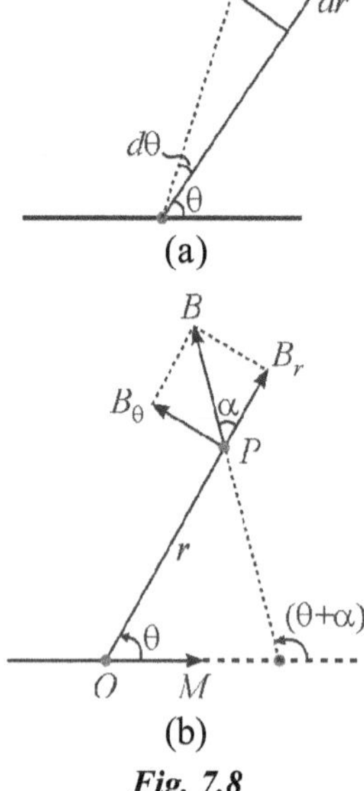

Fig. 7.8

$$= -\frac{d}{dr}\left[\frac{\mu_0}{4\pi}\frac{M\cos\theta}{r^2}\right] \qquad ...(1)$$

$$= \frac{\mu_0}{4\pi}\frac{2M\cos\theta}{r^3}$$

and

$$B_\theta = -\frac{dV}{dr} = -\frac{dV}{rd\theta}$$

$$= -\frac{1}{r}\left[\frac{dV}{d\theta}\right]$$

$$= -\frac{1}{r}\frac{d}{d\theta}\left[\frac{\mu_0}{4\pi}\frac{M\cos\theta}{r^2}\right]$$

$$= \frac{\mu_0}{4\pi}\frac{M\sin\theta}{r^3} \qquad ...(2)$$

The resultant magnetic field

$$B = \sqrt{B_r^2 + B_\theta^2}$$

On substituting the values of B_r and B_θ, we get

$$B = \frac{\mu_0}{4\pi}\frac{M\sqrt{3\cos^2\theta+1}}{r^3} \qquad ...(3)$$

If it makes angle α with $\vec{r}$, then

$$\tan\alpha = \frac{B_\theta}{B_r}$$

or

$$\tan\alpha = \frac{\tan\theta}{2}. \qquad ...(4)$$

Special cases :

Case 1: On the axis of dipole; $\theta = 0$,

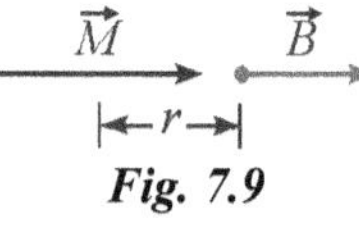

Fig. 7.9

$$\therefore \qquad V = \frac{\mu_0}{4\pi}\cdot\frac{M}{r^2},$$

$$B = \frac{\mu_0}{4\pi}\cdot\frac{2M}{r^3},$$

and $\qquad \alpha = 0$

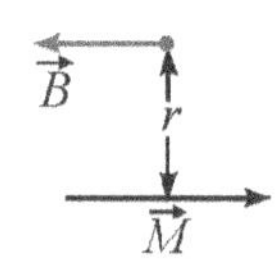

Fig. 7.10

Case 2 : On the equator of dipole, $\theta = 90°$,

$$\therefore \qquad V = 0$$

$$B = \frac{\mu_0}{4\pi} \frac{M}{r^3}$$

and $\qquad \alpha = 180^\circ.$

Field of a bar magnet

Case 1 : **On the axis of the magnet or end on position :** For a magnet of length ℓ, magnetic field on the axis of the magnet at a distance r from its centre.

$$B = \frac{\mu_0}{4\pi} \frac{2Mr}{\left[r^2 - \dfrac{\ell^2}{4}\right]^2},$$

for $\ell << r,\ B \simeq \dfrac{\mu_0}{4\pi} \dfrac{2M}{r^3}.$

Case 2 : **On the equator of the magnet or broad side on position :**

$$B = \frac{\mu_0}{4\pi} \frac{M}{\left[r^2 + \dfrac{\ell^2}{4}\right]^{\frac{3}{2}}},$$

for $\ell << r,\ B \simeq \dfrac{\mu_0}{4\pi} \dfrac{M}{r^3}$

Torque on a magnet in magnetic field

When a magnet is placed in an uniform magnetic field, its poles experience equal and opposite forces and so net force F_{net} on the magnet is zero. But the magnet experiences a torque given by,

$$\tau = mB \times \ell \sin\theta$$
$$= MB \sin\theta$$

In vector form, we can write $\qquad \vec{\tau} = \vec{M} \times \vec{B}$

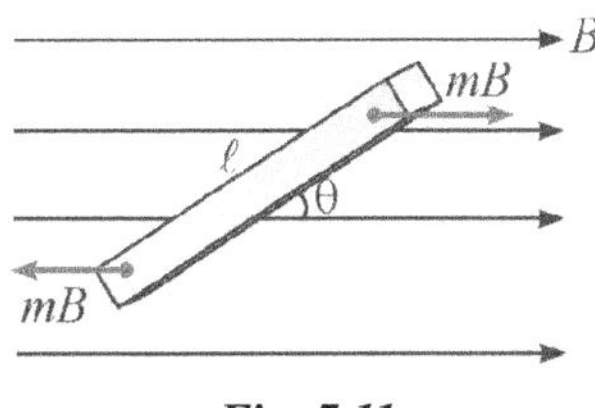

Fig. 7.11

Work done in rotating the magnet : The torque exerted by the agent for any angle θ is $MB \sin\theta$. Thus work done in rotating the magnet from θ_1 to θ_2,

$$W = \int_{\theta_1}^{\theta_2} \tau\, d\theta = \int_{\theta_1}^{\theta_2} M\,B \sin\theta\, d\theta$$

or $\qquad W = MB\left[\cos\theta_1 - \cos\theta_2\right].$

Potential energy in magnetic field

If we take potential energy at $\theta_1 = 90^\circ$ to be zero, then potential energy at $\theta_2 = \theta$,

$$U = MB\left[\cos 90^\circ - \cos\theta\right]$$

or $\qquad U = -MB\cos\theta$

Magnetic force between two short magnetic dipoles

(i) Consider two short dipoles $\vec{M_1}$ and $\vec{M_2}$ are placed on the same axis at a separation r. The force of interaction between them.

$$F = \frac{\mu_0}{4\pi} \frac{6M_1 M_2}{r^4}$$

(ii) When dipoles are placed on mutually perpendicular axes, the force of interaction between them

$$F = \frac{\mu_0}{4\pi} \frac{3M_1 M_2}{r^4}$$

Fig. 7.12

Fig. 7.13

Ex. 1   (a)   Indicate the positions and the nature of equilibrium of a number of magnetic needles arranged in a straight line at equal distances from one another.

(b)   A strong horseshoe magnet is closed by an iron plate *A* fig. (a). The weight of the plate corresponds to the lifting force of the magnet, and the magnet can easily hold the plate. If the poles of the magnet are now touched on the sides with a plate *B* made of soft iron, the plate *A* will drop at once. If the plate *B* is removed the magnet will again be capable of holding the plate *A*. Explain this phenomenon.

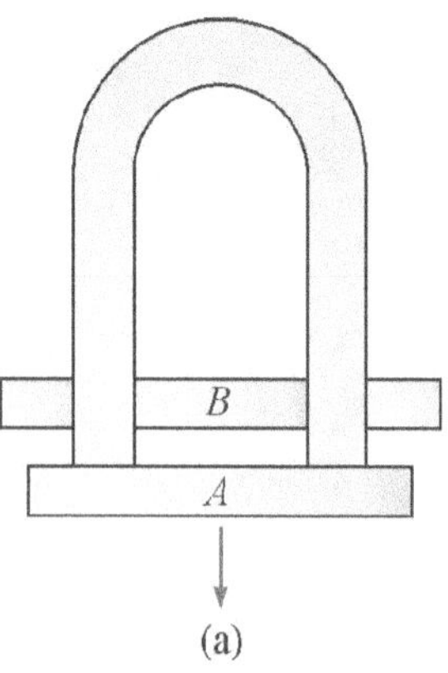

(a)

Fig. 7.14

(c)   A long rod made of soft iron is secured in a vertical position. If a strong magnet *A* is brought to the top of the rod as shown in *fig.7.14c*

   (i)   The rod will be magnetized so intensely as to retain at its other end several small pieces of iron. If the same magnet *A* is applied to the side of the rod near the bottom end *fig.7.14c*

   (ii)   the magnetization will be weak and the pieces of iron will fall. Explain why the magnet *A* acts differently in these two cases.

(d)   A strong magnet of magneto alloy can hold a chain consisting of several cylinders made of soft iron *fig.7.14*(d). What will happen to the cylinders if a similar magnet is brought up from below to this chain ? The magnets are arranged with their like poles facing. What will happen to the cylinders if the magnets have their opposite poles facing ?

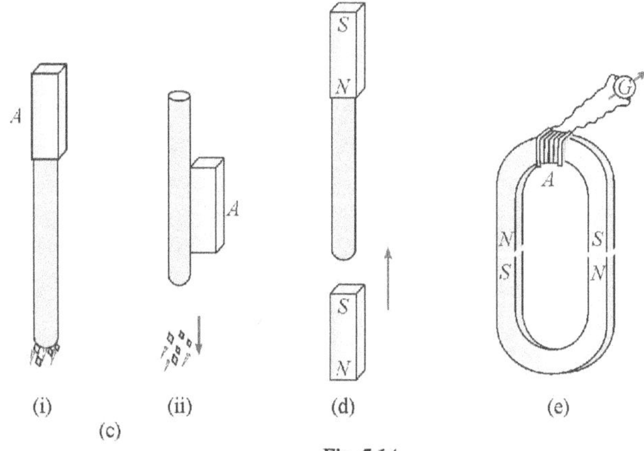

(i)   (ii)   (d)   (e)

(c)

Fig. 7.14

(e)   Two identical horseshoe magnets are linked by their opposite poles as shown in *fig.7.14*(e) One of the magnets has round it a coil *A* whose ends are connected to a galvanometer *G*. If the magnets are detached, the pointer of the galvanometer will be deflected at this instant through a certain angle. If the magnets are connected again the pointer of the galvanometer will also be deflected, but this time in the opposite direction.

Indicate the causes for the deflection of the pointer of the galvanometer.

(f)   Permalloy can be magnetized appreciably in the terrestrial magnetic field and does not possess residual magnetism, i.e., it is the softest material as far as magnetism is concerned.

How will a magnetic needle on a vertical axis near a long bar made of this alloy behave if :

   (i)   the bar is vertical *fig.7.15* (f);

   (ii)   the bar is horizontally placed along the magnetic meridian;

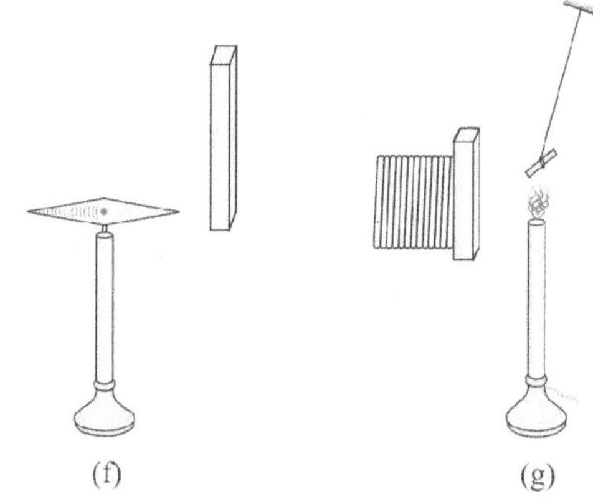

(f)   (g)

Fig. 7.15

(iii) the bar is in a horizontal plane perpendicular to the magnetic meridian.

     Will the behaviour of the needle change in these three cases when the bar is turned ?

(g)   A small thin iron nail is suspended from a light fire-proof thread. A strong electromagnet is placed near the nail *fig.7.15*(g). The flame from a powerful gas burner is directed precisely between the nail and the magnet and licks the nail when it is deflected by the magnet. If the windings of the electromagnet are energized the nail will be at once deflected into the flame and will then be ejected from it to assume its original position. After a lapse of time the nail will again be drawn to the magnet.

Explain what causes these periodic oscillations of the nail.

Sol.

(a)   The arrangement shown in Fig.(i) corresponds to the position of unstable equilibrium and that in Fig.(ii) corresponds to stable equilibrium.

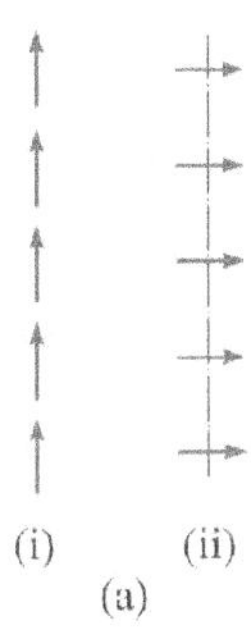

Fig. 7.16

(b) Upon contact with plate *B*, part of the magnetic lines of force are short-circuited through this plate (Fig. (b)). The number of the lines of force penetrating through plate A sharply decreases. As a result the interaction between the magnet and plate *A* also decreases and the latter drops.

(c) In the second case most of the magnetic lines of force are short-circuited inside the part of the rod adjoining the magnet (*Fig. 7.17. (c)*) and the rod cannot, therefore, be magnetized as intensely as in the first case.

(d) In the first case, as the lower magnet is brought nearer, the cylinders will be detached one after another from the chain and attracted to the lower magnet.

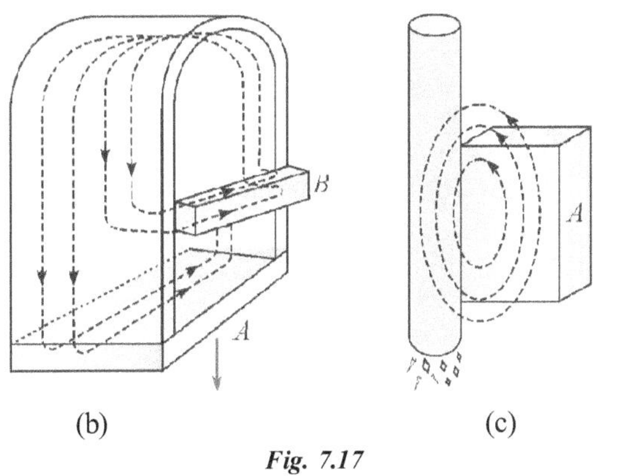

Fig. 7.17

7.3 EARTH'S MAGNETISM

It is a well known fact that freely suspended magnet or current carrying solenoid rests in specific direction, called magnetic meridian. It shows that earth has its own magnetic field. The modern theory about earth magnetic field is that, the earth rotates about an axis and has the surrounding ionised region due to interaction of cosmic rays. Due to rotation of earth the surrounding ionised region gives rise to strong electric current which causes magnetic field. Its value on earth surface is 1 gauss.

Elements of earth's magnetic field

To know about earth's magnetic field, we need three informations. They are :

(1) **Magnetic declination (ϕ):** Angle between geographical and magnetic meridian is known as angle of declination. It has an average value 17.5°.

In the second case, when the pole of the opposite sign is drawn closer, the "strength" of the chain will increase as the lower magnet is brought near. As soon as the second magnet comes in contact with the lower cylinder, the magnet will be attracted to the chain and will remain hanging on it.

(e) The magnets are detached owing to a sharp decrease in the number of the lines of force passing inside each magnet. At the moment of detachment an e.m.f. is induced in the coil due to the reduction in the number of the lines of force.

(f) (i) The bar will be magnetized due to the action of the vertical component of the terrestrial magnetic field and the magnetic needle will be attracted as it is brought near the ends of the bar.

   (ii) The bar will be magnetized by the action of the horizontal component of the terrestrial magnetic field. The magnetic needle will always turn towards the nearest end of the bar.

   (iii) The bar will not be magnetized by the magnetic field of the Earth and the needle will not change its position when the bar is brought close.

   It is assumed in all the three cases that when the needle is brought close to the bar the distance between them is still large enough for the additional magnetization of the bar due to the external magnetic field of the needle to be neglected.

   If the bar is turned, the behaviour of the needle will not change in any of the three cases.

(g) Iron loses its magnetic properties at quite a high temperature and behaves as any other non-magnetic substance (copper, glass, etc.). When the nail is heated in the flame of a burner to this temperature the interaction of the magnet and the nail abruptly decreases, the nail returns to the initial position, leaves the flame and gets cool. The magnetic properties of the nail thus cooled are regained, the forces of interaction between the nail and the magnet increase and the nail is again drawn to the magnet.

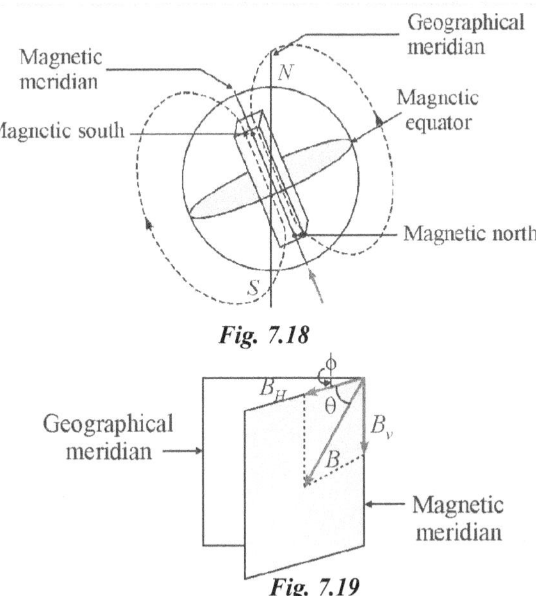

Fig. 7.18

Fig. 7.19

(2) **Angle of inclination or dip (θ) :** It is the angle between the magnetic field of earth and the horizontal at that place. It is zero at magnetic equator and 90° at poles.

In the magnetic northern hemisphere, the vertical component of earth's field points downward.

(3) **Horizontal component of earth's magnetic field (B_H) :** At any place other than magnetic poles, there is horizontal component of field.

$$B_H = B\cos\theta \qquad ...(i)$$

and vertical component $\qquad B_V = B\sin\theta \qquad ...(ii)$

By squaring and adding equations (i) and (ii), we get

$$B = \sqrt{B_H^2 + B_V^2} \qquad ....(1)$$

Dividing equation (ii) by (i), we get

$$\tan\theta = \frac{B_V}{B_H} \qquad ....(2)$$

True dip and apparent dip

The angle of dip in magnetic meridian plane is called true dip (θ), and angle of dip in different plane from magnetic meridian plane is called apparent dip.

We know that true dip

$$\tan\theta = \frac{B_V}{B_H} \qquad ...(i)$$

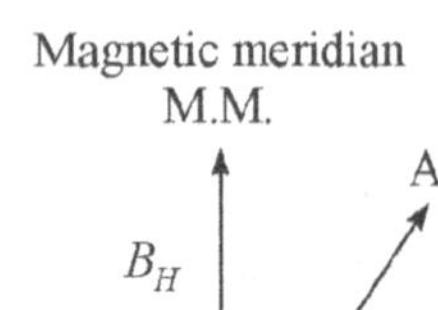
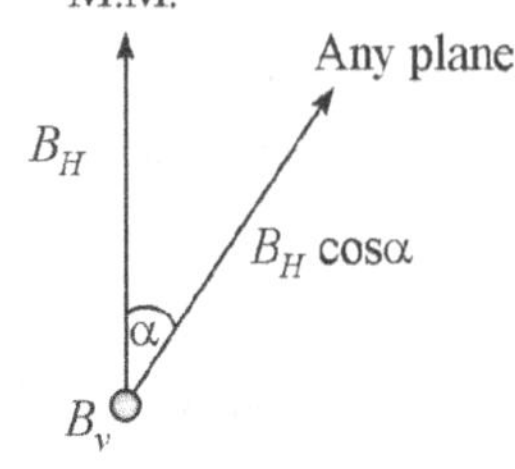

Fig. 7.20

On any other plane at an angle α from the meridian plane, the horizontal component of earth magnetic field will be $B_H \cos\alpha$ while vertical component remain as such. Thus apparent dip,

$$\tan\theta' = \frac{B_V}{B_H \cos\alpha} \qquad ...(ii)$$

From equations (i) and (ii), we get

$$\tan\theta' = \frac{\tan\theta}{\cos\alpha} \qquad ....(iii)$$

Compass needle and dip needle

Compass needle gives the direction of $\vec{B}_H$ and the dip needle gives direction of $\vec{B}$.

Magnetic map : It is found that many places have the same value of magnetic elements. The lines drawn by joining all places on the earth having same value of magnetic element form magnetic map.

Isogonic line : This is the line joining the places of equal angles of declination.

Agonic line : This is the line which passes through places having zero declination. Magnetic meridian itself is a agonic line.

Isoclinic line : This is the line joining the points of equal dip.

Aclinic line : This is the line joining the places of zero dip. Magnetic equator is an aclinic line.

Isodynamic line: This is the line joining the places of equal value of horizontal components of earth magnetic field.

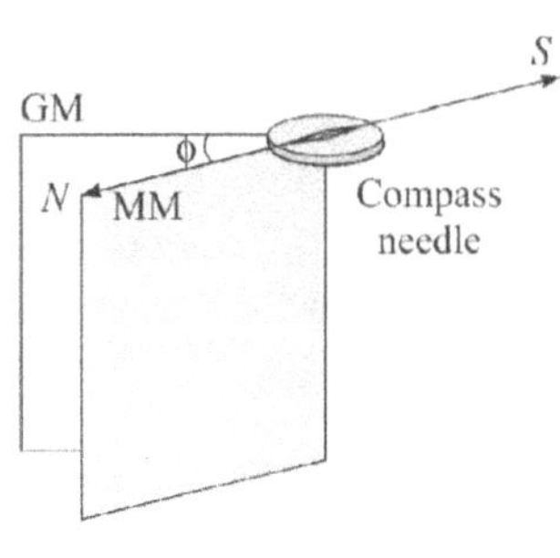

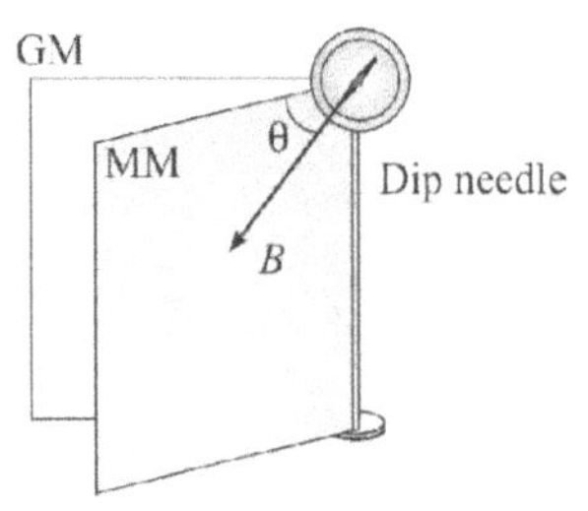

Fig. 7.21

Ex. 2 If θ_1 and θ_2 are the angles of dip observed in two vertical planes right angles to each other and θ be the true angle of dip, show that $\cot^2\theta = \cot^2\theta_1 + \cot^2\theta_2$.

Sol.

We have, $\qquad \tan\theta = \dfrac{B_V}{B_H} \qquad$ ...(i)

The value of vertical component remain same but horizontal component in two perpendicular planes are $B_H \cos\alpha$ and $B_H \sin\alpha$ as shown in fig. 7.22.

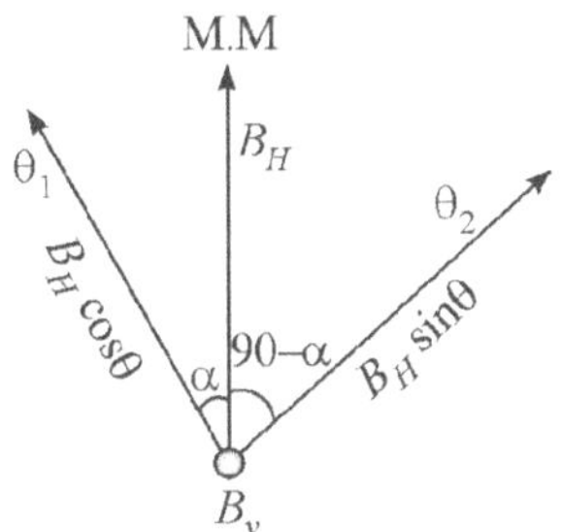

Fig. 7.22

$\therefore \qquad \tan\theta_1 = \dfrac{B_V}{B_H \cos\alpha} = \dfrac{\tan\theta}{\cos\alpha}$

or $\qquad \cos\alpha = \dfrac{\tan\theta}{\tan\theta_1} \qquad$ ...(ii)

and $\qquad \tan\theta_2 = \dfrac{B_V}{B_H \sin\alpha} = \dfrac{\tan\theta}{\sin\alpha}$

or $\qquad \sin\alpha = \dfrac{\tan\theta}{\tan\theta_2} \qquad$ ...(iii)

Squaring equations (ii) and (iii), and adding, we have

$$\cos^2\alpha + \sin^2\alpha = \tan^2\theta\left(\dfrac{1}{\tan^2\theta_1} + \dfrac{1}{\tan^2\theta_2}\right)$$

or $\qquad \dfrac{1}{\tan^2\theta} = \dfrac{1}{\tan^2\theta_1} + \dfrac{1}{\tan^2\theta_2}$

or $\qquad \cot^2\theta = \cot^2\theta_1 + \cot^2\theta_2. \qquad$ ***Proved***

Ex. 3 A bar magnet of length 8 cm and having a pole strength of 1.0 A-m is placed vertically on a horizontal table with the south pole on the table. A neutral point is found on the table at a distance 6.0 cm north of the magnet. Calculate the earth's horizontal magnetic field.

Sol.

The magnetic field at P due to south pole

$$B_S = \dfrac{\mu_0}{4\pi}\dfrac{m}{r^2}$$

and due to north pole

$$B_N = \dfrac{\mu_0}{4\pi}\dfrac{m}{\left(\ell^2 + r^2\right)} \text{ along } NP$$

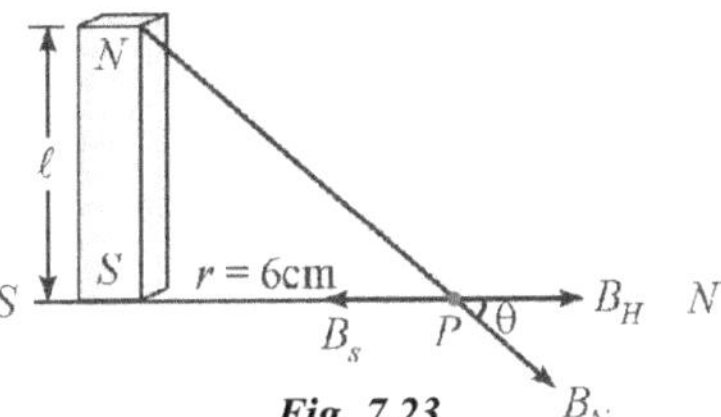

Fig. 7.23

Its component along north is $B_N \cos\theta$. On substituting the value of θ, it is

$$= \dfrac{\mu_0}{4\pi}\dfrac{m}{\left(\ell^2 + r^2\right)} \times \dfrac{r}{\sqrt{\ell^2 + r^2}}$$

$$= \dfrac{\mu_0}{4\pi}\dfrac{mr}{\left(\ell^2 + r^2\right)^{\frac{3}{2}}}$$

For neutral point at P, we have

$$B_H = B_S - B_N \cos\theta$$

$$= \dfrac{\mu_0}{4\pi}\left[\dfrac{m}{r^2} - \dfrac{mr}{\left(\ell^2 + r^2\right)^{\frac{3}{2}}}\right]$$

$$= 10^{-7} \times 1\left[\dfrac{1}{0.06^2} - \dfrac{0.06}{\left(0.08^2 + 0.06^2\right)^{\frac{3}{2}}}\right]$$

$$= 22 \times 10^{-6} \, T. \qquad \textbf{\textit{Ans.}}$$

Ex. 4 *Fig. 7.24* **shows some of the equipotential surfaces of the magnetic scalar potential. Find the magnetic field B at a point in the region.**

Sol.

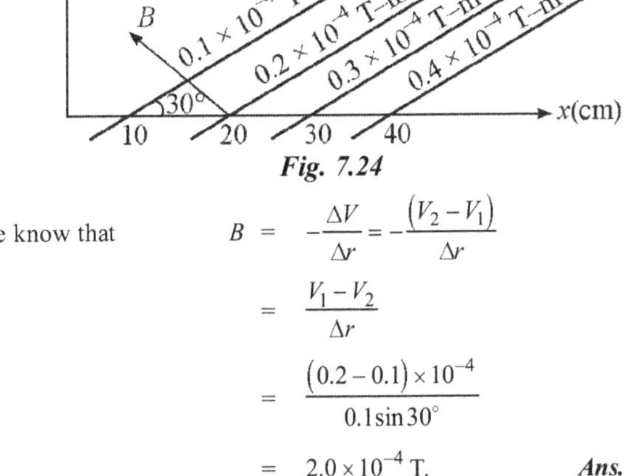

Fig. 7.24

We know that $\qquad B = -\dfrac{\Delta V}{\Delta r} = -\dfrac{\left(V_2 - V_1\right)}{\Delta r}$

$$= \dfrac{V_1 - V_2}{\Delta r}$$

$$= \dfrac{\left(0.2 - 0.1\right) \times 10^{-4}}{0.1 \sin 30°}$$

$$= 2.0 \times 10^{-4} \text{ T.} \qquad \textbf{\textit{Ans.}}$$

Ex. 5 A magnetic dipole of magnetic moment $0.72\sqrt{2}$ A-m^2 is placed horizontally with the north pole pointing towards east. Find the position of the neutral point if the horizontal component of the earth's magnetic field is 18 μT.

Sol.   Given $M = 0.72\sqrt{2}$ A-m

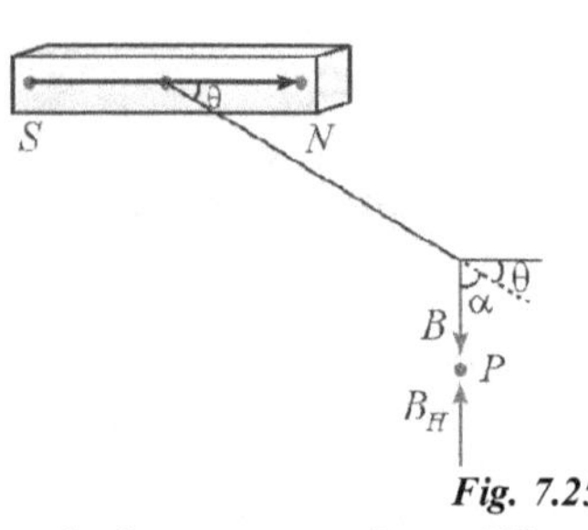

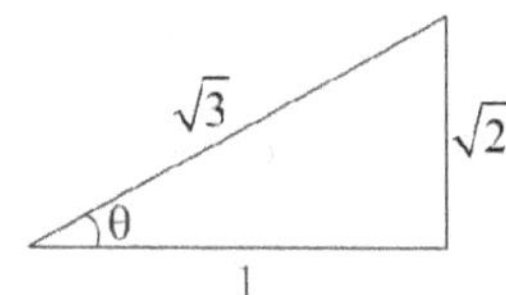

Fig. 7.25

From the figure $\qquad \alpha + \theta = 90^\circ$

$\therefore \qquad\qquad \alpha = (90^\circ - \theta)$

Fig. 7.26

We have, $\qquad\qquad \tan\alpha = \dfrac{\tan\theta}{2}$

or $\qquad \tan(90^\circ - \theta) = \dfrac{\tan\theta}{2}$

or $\qquad\qquad \cot\theta = \dfrac{\tan\theta}{2}$

or $\qquad\qquad \tan^2\theta = 2$

$\therefore \qquad\qquad\qquad \theta = \tan^{-1}\left(\sqrt{2}\right) \qquad\qquad$ *Ans.*

Let neutral point is at a distance r, then

$$B_H = B$$

$$= \frac{\mu_0}{4\pi}\,\frac{M\sqrt{3\cos^2\theta + 1}}{r^3}$$

or $\qquad 18\times 10^{-6} = \dfrac{10^{-7}\times 0.72\sqrt{2}\,\sqrt{3\left(\dfrac{1}{\sqrt{3}}\right)^2 + 1}}{r^3}$

On solving $\qquad r = 0.20$ m. $\qquad\qquad$ *Ans.*

Ex. 6   In order to keep the needle (see *fig. 7.28*) in a horizontal position a load P is suspended from its top end. Find the magnitudes of the horizontal and vertical components of the intensity of the terrestrial magnetic field. Calculate the total intensity of the terrestrial magnetic field. The dip angle is θ. The pole strength is m.

Sol.

The magnetic needle will be acted by two forces tending to turn it, their moments are : the moment of the force due to the terrestrial magnetic field acting on the poles of the needle

$$\tau = (mB_v)\ell$$

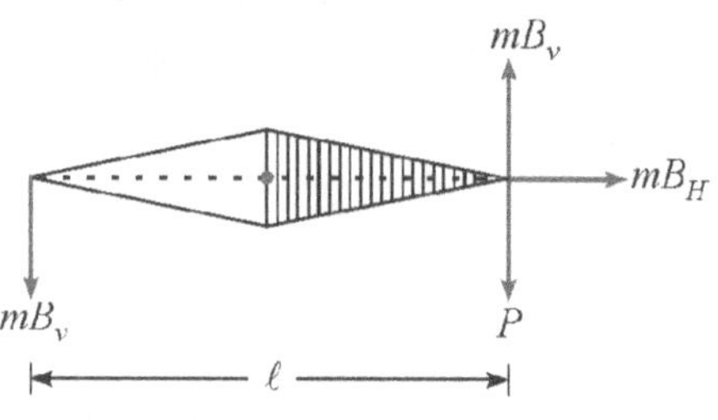

Fig. 7.28

and the moment produced by the load suspended from the needle and is equal to $P\dfrac{\ell}{2}$. Thus for the equilibrium of the needle

$$mB_v\ell = P\frac{\ell}{2}$$

Hence, $\qquad\qquad B_v = \dfrac{P}{2m} \qquad\qquad$ *Ans.*

The horizontal component of the terrestrial magnetic field

$$B_H = B_v\tan\theta,$$

and total field $\qquad B = \sqrt{B_H^2 + B_V^2}. \qquad$ *Ans.*

Ex. 7   **Two long equally magnetized needles are freely suspended by their like poles from a hook as shown in *fig. 7.29*. The length of each needle is ℓ cm and the weight is W. In equilibrium the needles make an angle α with each other. Determine the magnetic pole strength of the needles. The magnetic pole strength is concentrated at the ends of the needles.**

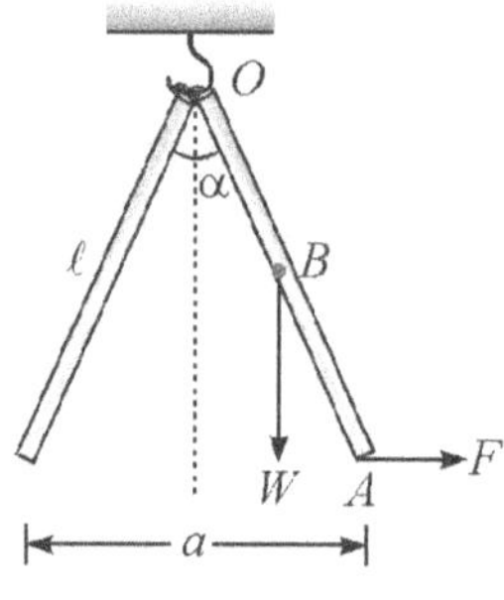

Fig. 7.29

Sol.

Let us consider one of the needles. It will be acted by the weight W, which acts through the centre of gravity B and the repulsive force between the poles $F = \dfrac{m^2}{a^2}$ acted through the point A. For the needle to be in equilibrium the sum of the moments of the forces acting on the needle should be equal to zero, i.e.,

$$P\frac{\ell}{2}\sin\frac{\alpha}{2} = F\ell\cos\frac{\alpha}{2}$$

Here $\qquad\qquad F = \dfrac{m^2}{a^2}$, where $a = 2\ell\sin\dfrac{\alpha}{2}$.

Thus
$$\frac{P}{2}\sin\frac{\alpha}{2} = \frac{m^2\cos\frac{\alpha}{2}}{4\ell^2\sin^2\frac{\alpha}{2}}$$

$$\therefore \qquad m = \ell\sin\frac{\alpha}{2}\sqrt{2P\tan\frac{\alpha}{2}}. \qquad \textit{Ans.}$$

Ex. 8

A magnetic needle with length ℓ and poles of pole strength $\pm m$ is attached to a wooden bar of length L (see *fig. 7.30*) and placed in a uniform magnetic field of intensity B. The bar and needle can revolve around point O. Find the magnitude of the moment of force that will cause the rotation of the bar around point O if the bar makes an angle α with the direction of the lines of force of the magnetic field.

Sol.

The moment of forces about O, acting upon each pole of the needle will be equal to $mB\,(\ell + L)\sin\alpha$ and $-mBL\sin\alpha$.

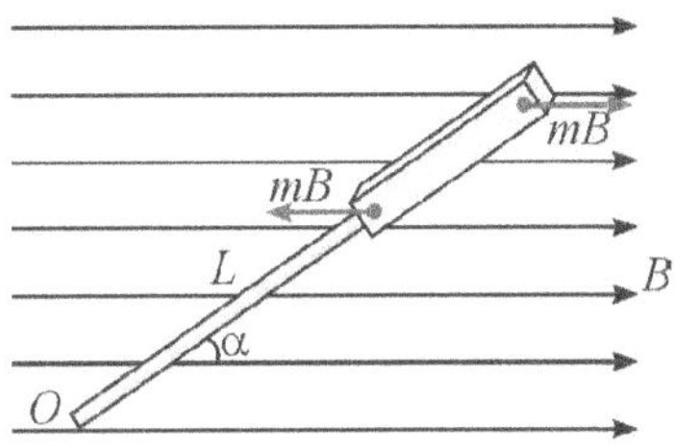

Fig. 7.30

Hence, the net moment of the force acting on the bar is

$$\tau = mB(\ell + L)\sin\alpha - mBL\sin\alpha$$
$$= mB\ell\sin\alpha = (m\ell)B\sin\alpha$$
$$= MB\sin\alpha. \qquad \textit{Ans.}$$

Note: The earth's magnetic field is not due to a large bar magnet inside it because the earth's core is hot and molten. It may be due to the convection currents around the equator. As to what dynamo effect sustains this current, and why the earth's field reverses polarity every million years or so, we do not know.

7.4 MOVING COIL GALVANOMETER

It is used to detect the direction of direct current. It is based on the interaction between current carrying loop with the magnetic field. In a moving coil galvanometer, the coil is suspended between the pole pieces of a strong magnet. The poles are made cylindrical and a soft iron cylindrical core is placed within the coil. This makes the field radial. In such a field the plane of the loop always remains parallel to the field, and $\theta = 90°$. The deflecting torque,

$$\tau_{\text{def}} = NiBA\sin90°$$
$$= NiBA \qquad ...(i)$$

This torque deflects the coil. As soon as coil starts rotating a restoring torque is set up in the suspension wire. If α is the angle of twist in the suspension wire and C is the torsional rigidity, then restoring torque

$$\tau_{\text{rest}} = C\alpha \qquad ...(ii)$$

From equations (i) and (ii), we have

$$NiBA = C\alpha$$

$$\Rightarrow \qquad i = \left(\frac{C}{NBA}\right)\alpha$$

or $$i = k\alpha, \qquad ....(1)$$

where $k = \dfrac{C}{NBA}$ is known as galvanometer constant.

Current sensitivity (s) : Current sensitivity is defined as

$$S = \frac{d\alpha}{di} \text{ or simply } \frac{\alpha}{i}$$

Therefore $$S = \frac{NBA}{C} \qquad .....(2)$$

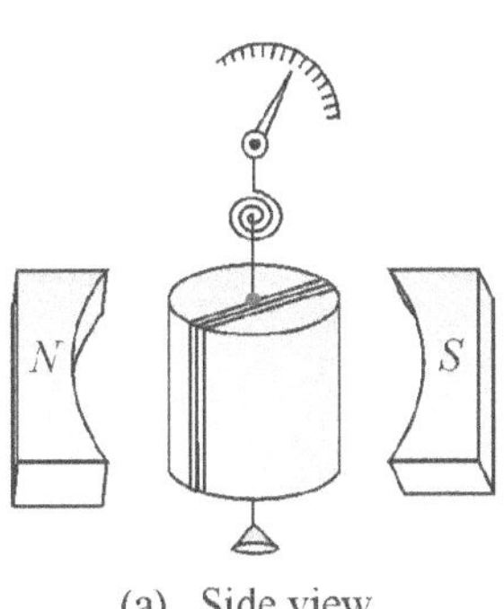

Fig. 7.31

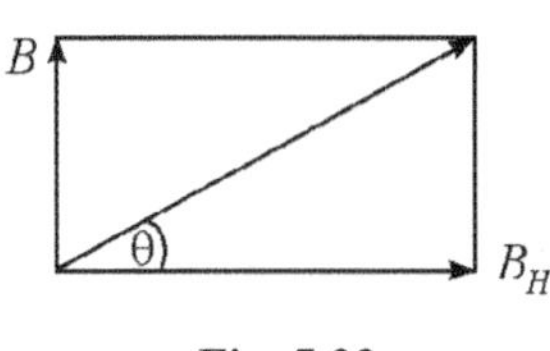

Fig. 7.32

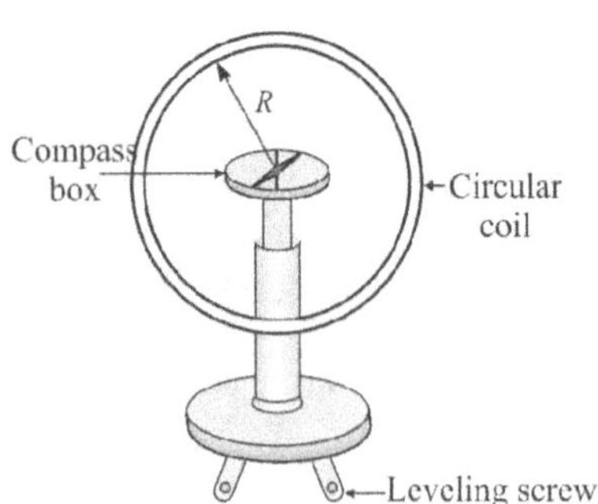

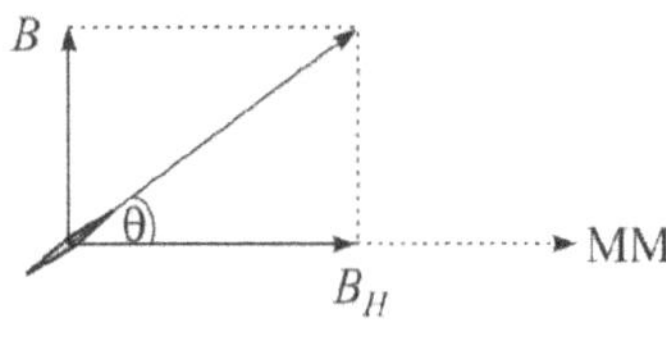

Fig. 7.33

7.5 Tangent law

When a compass needle is placed in two perpendicular fields, $\vec{B}$ and $\vec{B}_H$, the needle rests at an angle θ with $\vec{B}_H$. In equilibrium

$$\frac{B}{B_H} = \tan\theta$$

$$\Rightarrow \qquad B = B_H \tan\theta$$

This is known as the tangent law of perpendicular fields.

7.6 Tangent galvanometer

Tangent galvanometer is an instrument to measure direct current. It is based on tangent law.

The current to be measured is passed through coil set in M.M. produces a magnetic field at the centre that is perpendicular to the plane of the coil, $B = \dfrac{\mu_0 Ni}{2R}$. In addition to this field, there is earth magnetic field with horizontal component B_H, so the compass needle placed at the centre of the galvanometer, defects in the direction of resultant field. Thus

$$B = B_H \tan\theta$$

or

$$\frac{\mu_0 Ni}{2R} = B_H \tan\theta$$

$$\therefore \qquad i = \left(\frac{2RB_H}{\mu_0 N}\right)\tan\theta$$

$$\Rightarrow \qquad i = k\tan\theta$$

where $k = \dfrac{2RB_H}{\mu_0 N}$ is called reduction factor.

Sensitivity : Good sensitivity means that change in deflection is large for a given fractional change in current. We have

$$i = k\tan\theta$$

or

$$di = k\sec^2\theta \, d\theta$$

or

$$\frac{di}{i} = \frac{k\sec^2\theta \, d\theta}{k\tan\theta}$$

$$= \frac{d\theta}{\sin\theta\cos\theta}$$

$$= \frac{2d\theta}{\sin 2\theta}$$

or

$$\frac{d\theta}{di} = \frac{\sin 2\theta}{2i}.$$

For maximum sensitivity $\sin 2\theta = 1$, or $\theta = 45°$

So the tangent galvanometer is most sensitive when the deflection is around $45°$.

7.7 Vibration magnetometer

Vibration magnetometer is used for comparison of magnetic fields at different places and also to compare magnetic moments of the magnets. First of all set the magnetometer with its magnet along the meridian.

Then the experimental bar magnet is deflected from its mean position by external magnet and left free to oscillate in $\vec{B}_H$.

The restoring torque acts on the magnet for small angle θ

$$\tau \;=\; -MB_H \sin\theta$$

or $\qquad \alpha \;\simeq\; \dfrac{MB_H}{I}(-\theta) \quad$ [for small θ, $\sin\theta \simeq \theta$]

Compare with $\qquad \alpha \;=\; -\omega^2\theta$, we get

$$\omega \;=\; \sqrt{\dfrac{MB_H}{I}}$$

and $\qquad T \;=\; 2\pi\sqrt{\dfrac{I}{MB_H}} \qquad ....(1)$

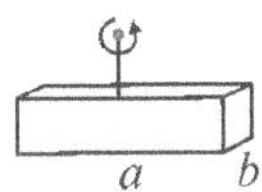

Fig. 7.34

where I is the moment of inertia of the magnet, which is given by

$$I \;=\; \dfrac{W}{12}\left(a^2 + b^2\right)$$

$W \rightarrow$ mass of the magnet.

Fig. 7.35

1. **Comparison of horizontal components of magnetic field at two places**

    If T_1 and T_2 are the time periods of motion of experimental magnet at two different places, then

    $$T_1 \;=\; 2\pi\sqrt{\dfrac{M}{B_{H_1}}} \quad \text{and} \quad T_2 = 2\pi\sqrt{\dfrac{M}{B_{H_2}}}$$

    $$\therefore \qquad \dfrac{B_{H_1}}{B_{H_2}} \;=\; \dfrac{T_2^{\,2}}{T_1^{\,2}} \qquad . \qquad ...(2)$$

2. **Comparison of magnetic moments of the magnets**

    Suppose M_1 and M_2 are the magnetic moments of the magnets. First place the magnets on the pan with like poles together, let time period is T_1 and then unlike poles together, let time period is T_2, then

    $$T_1 \;=\; 2\pi\sqrt{\dfrac{(I_1 + I_2)}{(M_1 + M_2)\,B_H}}$$

    and $\qquad T_2 \;=\; 2\pi\sqrt{\dfrac{(I_1 + I_2)}{(M_1 - M_2)\,B_H}}$

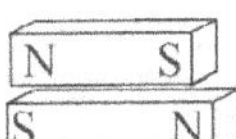

Fig. 7.36

    From above equations, we get

    $$\dfrac{M_1}{M_2} \;=\; \dfrac{T_2^{\,2} + T_1^{\,2}}{T_2^{\,2} - T_1^{\,2}} . \qquad ....(3)$$

7.8 DEFLECTION MAGNETOMETER

It is used to determine $\dfrac{M}{B_H}$ for a permanent bar magnet. Its working is based on tangent law. It consists of a small compass needle, which is pivoted at the centre of the magnetometer. The quantity $\dfrac{M}{B_H}$ can be measured in two standard positions of the magnetometer. One is called Tan-A position and the other is called Tan-B position.

1. **Tan-A position :**

In this position the magnetometer is set perpendicular to magnetic meridian, so that, magnetic field due to magnet is in axial position and perpendicular to earth's field. Hence by tangent law

$$B_H \tan\theta \;=\; B$$

or

$$B_H \tan\theta \;=\; \frac{\mu_0}{4\pi}\,\frac{2Mr}{\left(r^2-\dfrac{\ell^2}{4}\right)^2}$$

$\therefore$

$$\frac{M}{B_H} \;=\; \frac{4\pi}{\mu_0}\,\frac{\left(r^2-\dfrac{\ell^2}{4}\right)^2}{2r}\,\tan\theta \qquad ......(1)$$

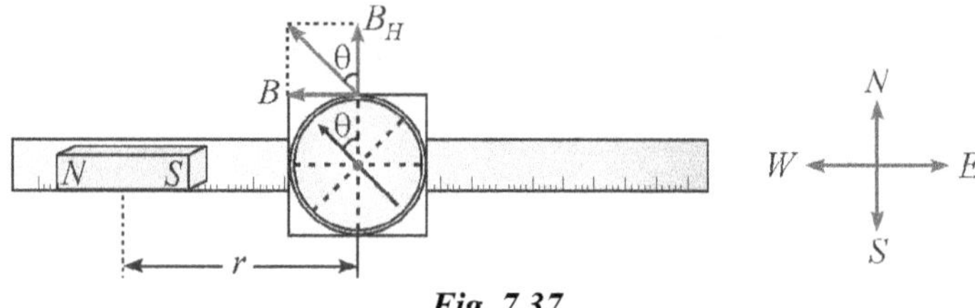

Fig. 7.37

2. **Tan B position :**

In this position the magnetometer is set in south north direction, so that the magnetic field due to magnet is at its equator. Hence by tangent law

$$B_H \tan\theta \;=\; B$$

or

$$B_H \tan\theta \;=\; \frac{\mu_0}{4\pi}\,\frac{M}{\left[r^2+\dfrac{\ell^2}{4}\right]^{\frac{3}{2}}}$$

$\therefore$

$$\frac{M}{B_H} \;=\; \frac{4\pi}{\mu_0}\left(r^2+\frac{\ell^2}{4}\right)^{\frac{3}{2}}\tan\theta \qquad .....(2)$$

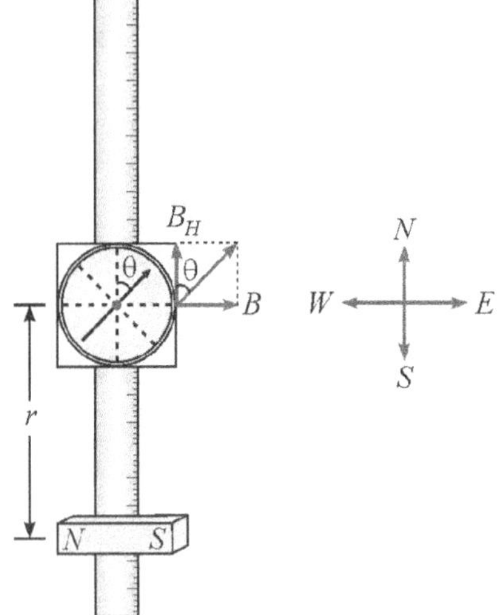

Fig. 7.38

7.9 GAUSS'S LAW IN MAGNETISM

In electrostatics, we have studied the Gauss's law for electric field, i.e.,

$$\oint \vec{E}\cdot d\vec{A} \;=\; \frac{q_{\text{inside}}}{\epsilon_0}$$

where $\oint \vec{E}\cdot d\vec{A}$ is the electric flux and q_{inside} is the net charge enclosed by the closed surface. On the similar way Gauss's law for magnetic field can be written as ;

$$\oint \vec{B}\cdot d\vec{A} \;=\; \mu_0 m_{\text{inside}}$$

where $\oint \vec{B}\cdot d\vec{A}$ is the magnetic flux and m_{inside} is the net 'magnetic charge' inside the closed surface. In any closed surface $m_{\text{inside}} = m - m = 0$, as isolated pole does not exist and so Gauss' law for magnetism, therefore states that

$$\oint \vec{B}\cdot d\vec{A} \;=\; 0.$$

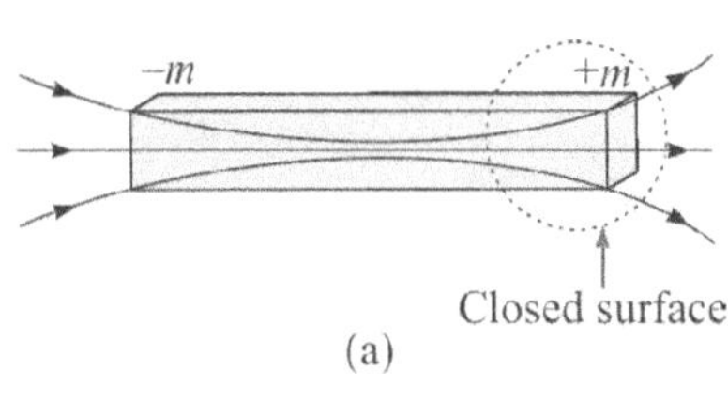

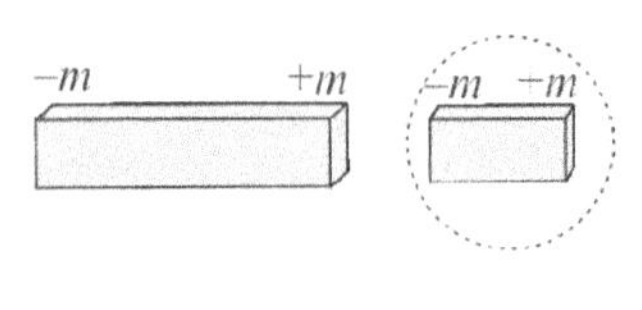

Fig. 7.39

Ex. 9 Two identical thin bar magnets, each of length ℓ and pole strength m are placed at right angles to each other with the north pole of one touching the south pole of the other. What is the resultant magnetic moment of the system ?

Sol.

If M is the magnetic moment of each bar magnet, then $M = m\ell$.

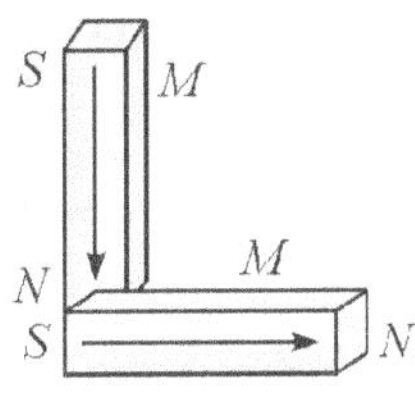

Fig. 7.40

The resultant magnetic moment

$$M' = \sqrt{2}\, M = \sqrt{2}\, m\ell.$$

Ex. 10 A magnetic needle is free to rotate in a vertical plane which makes an angle 60° with the magnetic meridian. If the needle stays in a direction making an angle of $\tan^{-1}\left(\dfrac{2}{\sqrt{3}}\right)$ with the horizontal, what would be the dip at that place ?

Sol.

Given, apparent dip

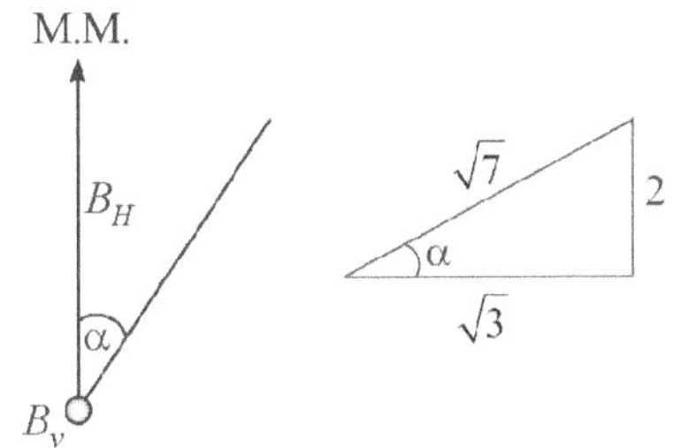

Fig. 7.41

$$\theta' = \tan^{-1}\left(\frac{2}{\sqrt{3}}\right)$$

and $\qquad \alpha = 60^\circ$

We have $\qquad \tan\theta' = \dfrac{\tan\theta}{\cos\alpha}$

or $\qquad \tan\theta = \tan\theta' \cos\alpha$

$$= \frac{2}{\sqrt{3}} \times \frac{1}{2} = \frac{1}{\sqrt{3}}$$

or $\qquad \theta = 30^\circ.$ *Ans.*

Ex. 11 The frequency of oscillation of the magnet in an oscillation magnetometer in the earth magnetic field is 40 oscillations per minute. A short bar magnet is placed to the north of the magnetometer, at a separation of 20 cm from the oscillating magnet, with its north pole pointing towards north. The frequency of oscillation is found to increase 60 oscillations per minute. Calculate the magnetic moment of the short bar magnet. Horizontal component of the earth's magnetic field is 24 μT.

Sol. Previously,

$$f = \frac{1}{2\pi}\sqrt{\frac{MB_H}{I}}$$

and then, $\qquad f' = \dfrac{1}{2\pi}\sqrt{\dfrac{M\left(B_H + B\right)}{I}}$

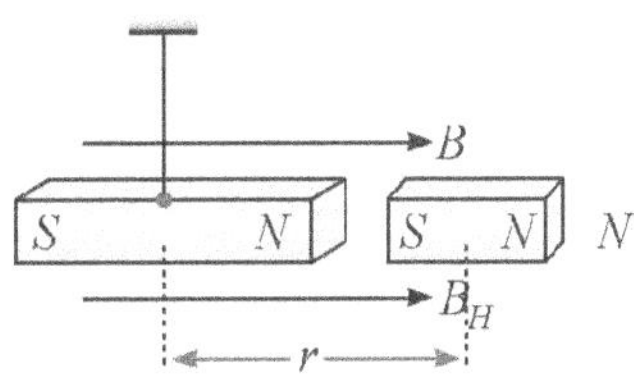

Fig. 7.42

$\therefore \qquad \dfrac{f'^2}{f^2} = \dfrac{B_H + B}{B_H}$

or $\qquad \left(\dfrac{60}{40}\right)^2 = \dfrac{B_H + B}{B_H}$

or $\qquad \dfrac{B}{B_H} = 1.25$

or $\qquad B = 1.25\, B_H$

$$= 1.25 \times 24\ \mu T = 30 \times 10^{-6} T$$

The oscillating magnet is in end- on position of the short magnet. Thus,

$$B = 30 \times 10^{-6} = \frac{\mu_0}{4\pi}\frac{2M'}{r^3}$$

or $\qquad M' = \dfrac{30 \times 10^{-6} \times r^3}{\left(\dfrac{\mu_0}{4\pi}\right) \times 2}$

$$= \frac{30 \times 10^{-6} \times \left(0.20\right)^3}{10^{-7} \times 2}$$

$$= 1.2\ \text{A-m}^2. \qquad \textit{Ans.}$$

Ex. 12 A long vertical wire carries a steady current of 10 A flowing upwards through it at a place where the horizontal component of earth magnetic field is 0.3 gauss. What is the resultant horizontal magnetic field at a point 5 cm from the wire due magnetic north of the wire ?

Sol.

The magnetic field due to current carrying conductor

$$B = \frac{\mu_0}{2\pi}\frac{i}{r} = \frac{2 \times 10^{-7} \times 10}{5 \times 10^{-2}}$$

$$= 0.4 \times 10^{-4} T = 0.4\ \text{gauss}$$

and $\qquad B_H = 0.3\ \text{gauss}$

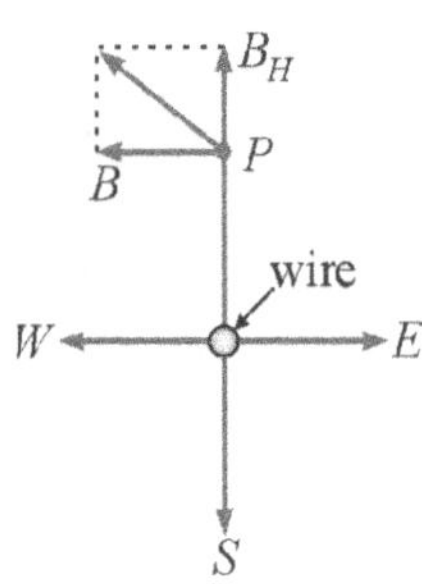

Fig. 7.43

$\therefore$ Net field at P $= \sqrt{B^2 + B_H^2}$

$$= \sqrt{0.4^2 + 0.3^2}$$

$$= 0.5 \text{ gauss} \qquad \textit{Ans.}$$

Ex. 13 A magnet is suspended in the magnetic meridian with an untwisted wire. The upper end of the wire is rotated through 180° to deflect the magnet by 30° from the magnetic meridian. Now this magnet is replaced by another magnet and the upper end of the wire has to be rotated through 270° to deflect the magnet by 30° from magnetic meridian. Compare magnetic moments of the two magnets.

Sol.

We know that,

$$\tau = C\alpha = MB_H \sin\theta$$

where α is the angle of twist and θ is the deflection of the magnet from the magnetic meridian.

For first magnet

$$C\left(180° - 30°\right) = M_1 B_H \sin 30° \qquad .....(i)$$

For the second magnet

$$C\left(270° - 30°\right) = M_2 B_H \sin 30° \qquad ....(ii)$$

Dividing equation (i) by (ii), we get

$$\frac{M_1}{M_2} = \frac{150}{240} = \frac{5}{8} \qquad \textit{Ans.}$$

Ex. 14 A thin magnet is cut into the equal parts by cutting it perpendicular to its length. What is the new magnetic moment of each part ? What is the time period of each part as compared to that of original magnet if vibrated in the same magnetic field.

Sol.

If ℓ is the initial length of the magnet, then magnetic moment $M = m\ell$ and its moment of inertia $I = \dfrac{\text{mass} \times \ell^2}{12}$. When the magnet is cut into two equal parts, the magnetic moment

$$M' = m\frac{\ell}{2} = \frac{M}{2} \text{ and}$$

$$I' = \frac{\left(\dfrac{\text{mass}}{2}\right)\left(\dfrac{\ell}{2}\right)^2}{12} = \frac{I}{8}.$$

If T and T' are the initial and final time periods, then

$$T = 2\pi\sqrt{\frac{I}{MB}} \text{ and } T' = 2\pi\sqrt{\frac{\dfrac{I}{8}}{\left(\dfrac{M}{2}\right)H}}$$

On comparing above equations, we get

$$T' = \frac{T}{2}.$$

7.10 MAGNETISM AND ELECTRON

Any material is magnetic because of the motions of electrons within it. There are two motions of electrons: spin and orbital, each involving a magnetic dipole moment that produces a magnetic field in the surrounding space. Explanation of these requires quantum physics which is beyond the scope of the book, so here we shall discuss only that part which can be understood by the previous knowledge of the subject.

Magnetic moment due to orbital motion of the electron

Suppose an electron moving at constant speed v in a circular path of radius r, counter clockwise as shown in *fig. 7.44*. The conventional current i will be clockwise. The magnitude of the orbital magnetic dipole moment of such a current loop

$$M_{\text{orbital}} = i A,$$

where A is the area enclosed by the loop, which is πr^2, and

$$i = \frac{\text{Charge}}{\text{time}} = \frac{e}{\left(\dfrac{2\pi r}{v}\right)}$$

$$= \frac{ev}{2\pi r}.$$

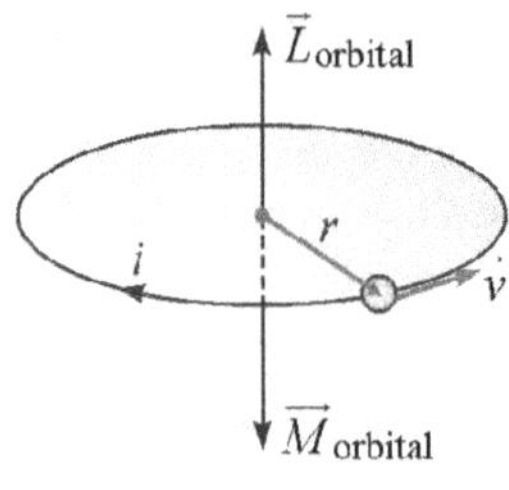

Fig. 7.44

Thus $\qquad M_{\text{orbital}} \quad = \quad \dfrac{ev}{2\pi r} \times \pi r^2 = \dfrac{evr}{2}$ ...(i)

The direction of this dipole moment is downward, by right-hand rule.
The angular momentum

$$\vec{L} \quad = \quad m\left(\vec{r} \times \vec{v}\right)$$

As $\vec{r}$ and $\vec{v}$ are perpendicular, so

$$L_{\text{orbital}} \quad = \quad mvr \sin 90^\circ = mvr \qquad \text{...(ii)}$$

$\vec{L}_{\text{orbital}}$ is directed upward.
From equations (i) and (ii), we get

$$\vec{M}_{\text{orbital}} \quad = \quad -\dfrac{e}{2m}\,\vec{L}_{\text{orbital}} \qquad \text{...(1)}$$

This result obtained by classical analysis is in agreement with that given by quantum physics.

Magnetic moment due to spin of the electron

An electron has an angular momentum due to its spin motion, is called spin angular momentum $\vec{S}$. The magnetic dipole moment due to the spin motion of the electron is given by

$$\vec{M}_{\text{spin}} \quad = \quad -\dfrac{e}{m}\,\vec{S}. \qquad \text{...(2)}$$

Here e is the elementary charge $\left(1.60 \times 10^{-19}\,\text{C}\right)$ and m is the mass of an electron $\left(9.11 \times 10^{-31}\,\text{kg}\right)$. The minus sign means that $\vec{M}_{\text{spin}}$ and $\vec{S}$ are oppositely directed.

The resultant magnetic dipole moment is the vector sum of these dipole moments. Thus

$$\vec{M} \quad = \quad \vec{M}_{\text{orbital}} + \vec{M}_{\text{spin}}$$

$$= \quad -\dfrac{e}{2m}\,\vec{L}_{\text{orbital}} - \dfrac{e}{m}\,\vec{S}$$

or $\qquad\qquad \vec{M} \quad = \quad -\dfrac{e}{2m}\left(\vec{L}_{\text{orbital}} + 2\vec{S}\right) \qquad \text{....(3)}$

Fig. 7.45. Magnetic dipole moment due to the spin motion of the electron

If the resultant magnetic dipole moment produces a magnetic field, then the material is magnetic. The types of magnetic material will be discuss little later in this chapter.

7.11 MAGNETIC PROPERTIES OF THE MATERIALS

Intensity of magnetisation

Each substance contains a large number of atoms. In general, the magnetic moments of these atoms are randomly oriented and there is no net magnetic moment in any volume of the material that contains thousands of atoms. However, when the material is kept in an external magnetic field, atomic dipoles try to align parallel to the field. The degree of alignment increases if the intensity of the applied field increases and also if the temperature is decreased. With sufficient strong field, the alignment is nearly perfect. We then say that the material is magnetically saturated.

When the atomic dipoles are aligned, partially or wholly, there is a net magnetic moment in the direction of the field in any small volume of the material. Thus magnetisation is defined as,

$$\vec{I} \quad = \quad \dfrac{\text{Magnetic dipole moment}}{\text{volume}}$$

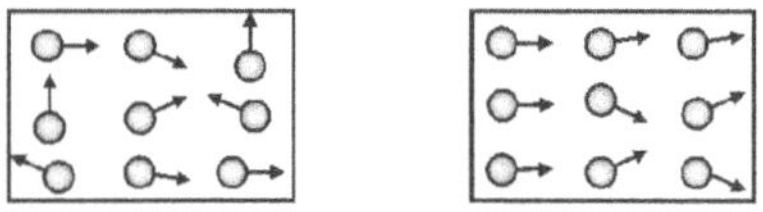

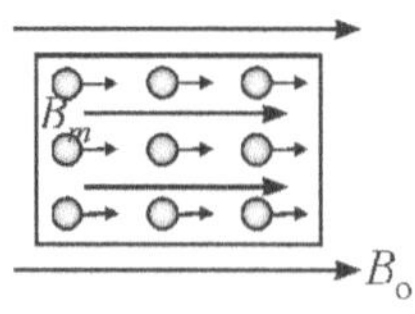

$$\vec{B} = 0, \vec{M} = 0 \qquad \vec{B} \neq 0, \vec{M} \neq 0$$

Fig. 7.46

Fig. 7.47

or
$$\vec{I} = \frac{\vec{M}}{V} \qquad \qquad ......(1)$$

Unit of magnetisation is A/m.

Consider a bar magnet of pole strength m, length ℓ and area of cross section A. The intensity of magnetisation

$$I = \frac{M}{V} = \frac{m\ell}{A\ell} = \frac{m}{A}.$$

Thus for a bar magnet, the intensity of magnetisation is defined as the pole strength per unit face area.

Intensity of magnetising field

When any material is placed in magnetic field, it gets magnetised. The actual magnetic field inside the material is the sum of the applied magnetic field and the magnetic field due to magnetisation of the material. Thus magnetic field inside the material

$$\vec{B} = \vec{B}_0 + \vec{B}_m,$$

where B_0 is the magnetic field in the vacuum produced by magnetising field, and equal to $\mu_0 \vec{H}$.

Here $\vec{H}$ is called intensity of magnetising field. Thus $\vec{H}$ can be defined as :

$$H = \frac{B_0}{\mu_0} = \frac{\mu_0 ni}{\mu_0} = ni.$$

$\vec{B}_m$ is the magnetic field due to magnetisation of material, which is, $\vec{B}_m = \mu_0 \vec{I}$.

Magnetic susceptibility

Magnetic susceptibility is defined as the intensity of magnetisation per unit magnetising field. Thus

$$\chi = \frac{I}{H}, \qquad \qquad ......(2)$$

where χ is a dimensionless quantity and may be positive or negative.

Magnetic permeability

Magnetic permeability of the material is the measure of degree to which the material can be permeated by magnetic field and is defined as the ratio of magnetic field in the material to the magnetising field. Thus

$$\mu = \frac{B}{H}$$

Also
$$\mu_0 = \frac{B_0}{H}, \text{ and } \frac{\mu}{\mu_0} = \mu_r.$$

Here μ_r is called relative permeability.

Relationship between μ_r and χ

We have,
$$\vec{B} = \vec{B}_0 + \vec{B}_m$$
or
$$B = \mu_0 H + \mu_0 I$$
or
$$B = \mu_0 H \left(1 + \frac{I}{H}\right)$$
or
$$\frac{B}{\mu_0 H} = 1 + \frac{I}{H}$$
As
$$B/H = \mu,$$

$$\therefore \qquad \frac{\mu}{\mu_0} = 1 + \frac{I}{H}$$

$$\text{or} \qquad \mu_r = 1 + \chi. \qquad \qquad ......(3)$$

Note :

The following points in regarding with $\vec{B}$ and $\vec{H}$ should be noted :

1. H is the cause and B is the effect. Both measure the intensity of the magnetic field and are vectors. B includes the presence of medium

$$B = \mu H \text{ and } B_0 = \mu_0 H.$$

2. B and H refer to external fields and not to magnet's own field.

3. The above magnetic phenomenon is analogous to electrostatic phenomenon, just as $\vec{P}, \vec{D}$ and $\vec{E}$ in electrostatics are related to bound charges, free charges and all charges respectively. Similarly I_m, H and B are related to bound currents, free currents and all currents. I_m is analogous to dielectric polarisation P.

Classification of magnetic materials

1. **Diamagnetic material :** Suppose a material in which individual atom does not have a net magnetic moment. When such a material is placed in a magnetic field, dipole moments are induced in the atoms by the applied field. The magnetic field due to induced magnetic moment opposes the original field. Thus the resultant field inside the material is smaller than the applied field. This type of material is called diamagnetic material.

   Magnetic moments are induced in all materials whenever a magnetic field is applied. Thus all materials have the property of diamagnetism. However, if there is a permanent atomic magnetic moment, then paramagnetism or ferromagnetism is much stronger than diamagnetism and the material does not show diamagnetic property.

2. **Paramagnetic material :** Now consider a material whose individual atoms have a net magnetic moment. When such a substance is placed in magnetic field, an extra magnetic field produces in the material in the direction of the field. The resultant magnetic field in the material is then greater than the applied field. The tendency to increase the magnetic field due to magnetisation of material is called paramagnetism, and material is called paramagnetic material.

3. **Ferromagnetic material :** In some materials, the permanent atomic magnetic moments have strong tendency to align themselves, even without any external field. These materials are called ferromagnetic materials. In every unmagnetised ferromagnetic material, the atoms form domains inside the material. Different domains, however, have different directions of magnetic moment and hence the materials remain unmagnetised. On applying an external field, these domains rotate and align in the direction of magnetic field.

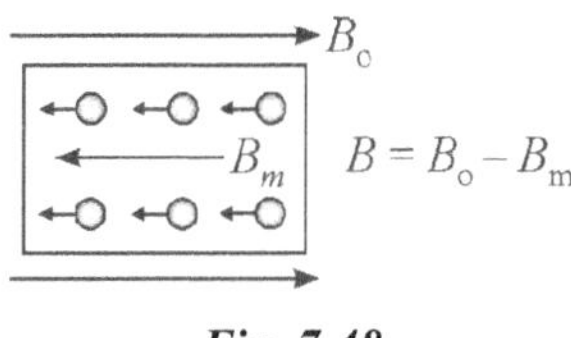

Fig. 7.48

Fig. 7.49

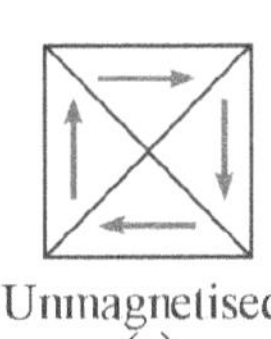
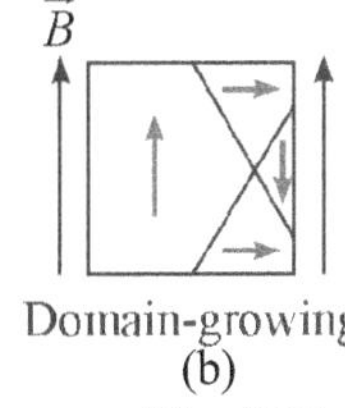
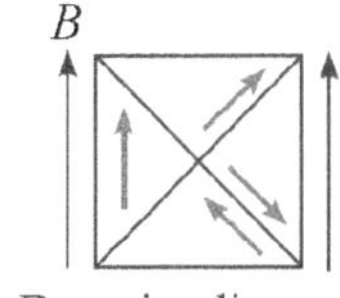

Fig. 7.50

Because of the domain character of ferromagnetic materials, even if a small magnetic field is applied, gives rise to large magnetisation. The resultant field is much larger than the applied field in such a material.

Curie's law : With the increase of temperature, the randomisation of atomic magnetic moments increases thereby decreasing the magnetisation I. The resultant magnetic field B decreases, which means χ decreases with temperature. The susceptibility of paramagnetic materials,

$$\chi \ = \ \frac{C}{T}, \qquad \text{(Curie's law)}$$

where C is Curie constant.

Curie temperature

The temperature at which ferromagnetic substance becomes paramagnetic is called Curie temperature.

At temperature above curie temperature the magnetic susceptibility of ferromagnetic materials is given by

$$\chi \ = \ \frac{C'}{T - T_c}.$$

Here $T_c \to$ Curie temperature, for iron it is 1043K.

Hysteresis

Hysteresis is shown only by ferromagnetic substances. In ferromagnetic materials, by removing external field, the magnetic moment of some domains remain aligned in the direction of previous applied magnetising field which results a residual magnetism. The laging of intensity of magnetisation (I) to magnetising field is (H) is known as hysteresis.

$OA \to$ Retentivity or residual magnetism

$OB \to$ Coercivity

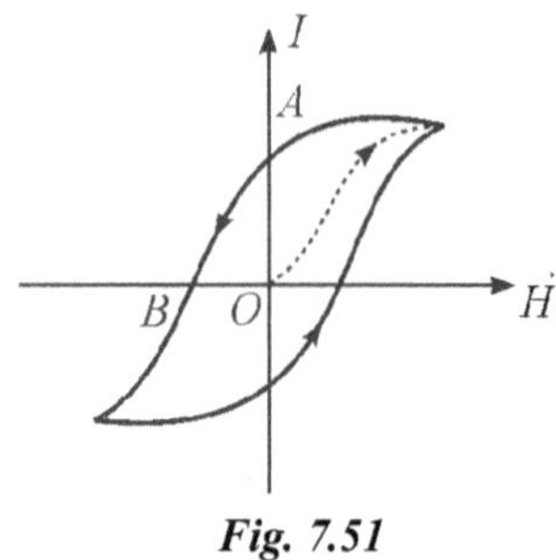

Fig. 7.51

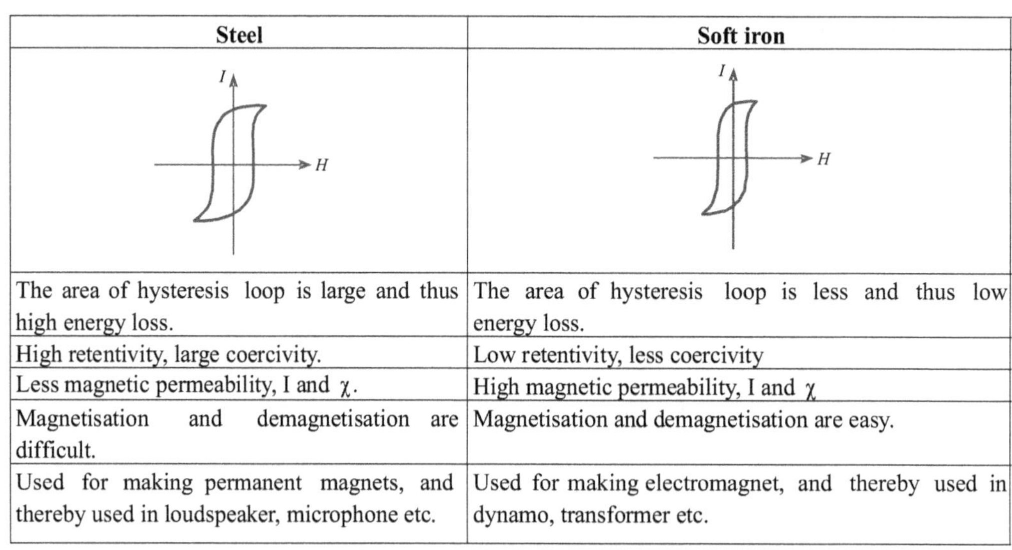

Steel	Soft iron
The area of hysteresis loop is large and thus high energy loss.	The area of hysteresis loop is less and thus low energy loss.
High retentivity, large coercivity.	Low retentivity, less coercivity
Less magnetic permeability, I and χ.	High magnetic permeability, I and χ
Magnetisation and demagnetisation are difficult.	Magnetisation and demagnetisation are easy.
Used for making permanent magnets, and thereby used in loudspeaker, microphone etc.	Used for making electromagnet, and thereby used in dynamo, transformer etc.

Note: 1. Diamagnetism is the universal property, it is present in all materials. But it is weak and hard to detect if the substance is para or ferromagnetic.

2. The phenomenon of magnetic hysteresis is similar to the elastic hysteresis : Strain may not be proportional to stress; here $\vec{H}$ and $\vec{I}$ are not linearly related.

3. Electrostatic shielding can be possible by any metal. But magnetic shielding can only possible by iron

Comparative study of magnetic properties of materials :

Diamagnetic substances	Paramagnetic substances	Ferromagnetic substances
Found in solids, liquids and gases.	Found in solids, liquids and gases.	Found normally in solids.
Examples : Ag, Au, Br, Cu, H_2O, NaCl, Sb etc.	Examples : Al, $CuCl_2$, Na, O_2 Mn, Pt etc.	Examples: Co, Fe, Ni, Cd, Fe_3O_4 etc.
Universal property	Not universal	Not universal
Can be explained on the basis of orbital motion of electrons	Can be explained on the basis of spin and orbital motion of electrons	On the basis of domain theory
When placed in strong magnetic field, magnetised weekly in the direction opposite of field $B = B_0 - B_m$	When placed in strong magnetic field, magnetised weekly in the direction of field $B = B_0 + B_m$	When placed in weak magnetic field, magnetised strongly in the direction of field. $B = B_0 + B_m$
Susceptibility χ low and negative $|\chi| \sim 1$	Susceptibility χ low but positive $\chi \simeq 1$	Susceptibility χ high and positive $\chi \sim 10^2$
Relative permeability $\mu_r < 1$	$\mu_r > 1$	$\mu_r \gg 1 \ (\mu_r \sim 10^3)$
	Dependence of χ on temperature	
Diamagnetic	**Paramagnetic**	**Ferromagnetic**

Ex. 15 Each atom of an iron bar $\left(5\,cm \times 1\,cm \times 1\,cm\right)$ has a magnetic moment $1.8 \times 10^{-23}\,A\text{-}m^2$. What will be the magnetic moment of bar in the state of magnetic saturation ?

Density of iron $= 7.78 \times 10^3\ kg/m^3$

Atomic weight of iron $A = 58$

Avogadro number, $N = 6.02 \times 10^{23}/g\text{-}mol.$

Sol.

The number of atoms per unit volume in a specimen

$$n = \frac{N}{V} = \frac{N}{\dfrac{A}{\rho}} = \frac{\rho N}{A}$$

$$= \frac{7.8 \times 10^3 \times 6.02 \times 10^{23}}{56}$$

$$= 8.38 \times 10^{28}/m^3$$

Total number of atoms in the bar

$$= nV = 8.38 \times 10^{28} \times \left(5 \times 1 \times 1\right) \times 10^{-6}$$

$$= 4.19 \times 10^{23}$$

$\therefore$ The saturated magnetic moment

$= $ Magnetic moment of each atom $\times$ total number of atoms in the bar

$$= 1.8 \times 10^{-23} \times 4.19 \times 10^{23}$$

$$= 7.54 \ \text{A-m}^2. \qquad \textbf{\textit{Ans.}}$$

Ex. 16 A toroid having 500 turns of wire and a mean circumferential length of 50 cm carries a current of 0.3A. The relative permeability of the core is 600.

(a)   What is the magnetic field in the core ?

(b)   What is the magnetic intensity ?

(c)   What part of the magnetic field is due to surface currents ?

Sol.

(a)   The magnetic field in the core of toroid

$$B = \left[\frac{\mu N i}{2\pi R}\right] = \mu_r \frac{\mu_0 N i}{2\pi R}$$

$$= \frac{600 \times \left(4\pi \times 10^{-7}\right) \times 500 \times 0.3}{0.50}$$

$$= 0.2262 \text{ T} \qquad \textit{Ans.}$$

(b) $$H = \frac{B}{\mu} = \frac{Ni}{2\pi R}$$

$$= \frac{500 \times 0.3}{0.50} = 300 \ Am^{-1} \qquad \textit{Ans.}$$

(c) $$B_0 = \mu_0 H$$

$$= 4\pi \times 10^{-7} \times 300$$

$$= 0.0003768 \text{ T}$$

We know that,

$$B = B_0 + B_m$$

$$\therefore \qquad B_m = B - B_0$$

$$= 0.2262 - 0.0003768$$

$$= 0.2258 \text{ T} \qquad \textit{Ans.}$$

Ex. 17 The current in the windings on a toroid is 2.0 A. There are 400 turns and the mean circumferential length is 40 cm. With the aid of a search coil and charge-measuring instrument, the magnetic field is found to be 1.0 T. Calculate

(a)   the magnetic intensity

(b)   the magnetisation

(c)   the magnetic susceptibility

(d)   the equivalent surface current, and

(e)   the relative permeability

Sol.

We have, $$B = \frac{\mu N i}{2\pi R}$$

or $$1.0 = \frac{\mu \times 400 \times 2.0}{0.40}$$

which gives $$\mu = 0.0005$$

$$\mu_r = \frac{\mu}{\mu_0} = \frac{0.0005}{4\pi \times 10^{-7}}$$

$$= 398 \qquad \textit{Ans (e)}$$

Magnetic intensity, $$H = \frac{B}{\mu} = \frac{1}{0.0005}$$

$$= 2000 \ Am^{-1} \qquad \textit{Ans (a)}$$

We know that $$I = \frac{B}{\mu_0} - H$$

$$= \left(\frac{1}{4\pi \times 10^{-7}}\right) - 2000$$

$$= 7.94 \times 10^5 \ A\text{-}m \qquad \textit{Ans (b)}$$

Magnetic susceptibility

$$\chi = \frac{I}{H} = \frac{7.94 \times 10^5}{2000} = 397 \qquad \textit{Ans (c)}$$

Ex. 18 A bar magnet has a coercivity of $4 \times 10^3 A/m$. It is desired to demagnetize by inserting it inside a solenoid 12 cm long and having 60 turns. What current should be carried by the solenoid ?

Sol.

We have

$$H = n i$$

$$\therefore \qquad i = \frac{H}{n} = \frac{4 \times 10^{-3}}{\left(\frac{60}{0.12}\right)}$$

$$= 8 \text{ A} \qquad \textit{Ans.}$$

Ex. 19 Find (a) the magnetisation I, (b) the magnetic intensity H and (c) magnetic field B at the centre of a bar magnet having pole strength 3.6 A-m, magnetic length 12 cm and cross-sectional area 0.90 cm².

Sol.

(a)

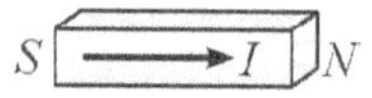

Fig. 7.52

Magnetisation, $$I = \frac{m}{A} = \frac{3.6}{0.90 \times 10^{-4}}$$

$$= 4 \times 10^4 \text{A}/\text{m} \qquad \textit{Ans.}$$

(b)   Magnetic intensity, due to north pole

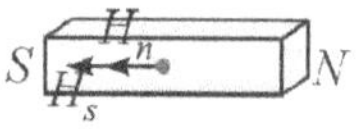

Fig. 7.53

$$H_n = \frac{B}{\mu_0} = \frac{1}{4\pi} \frac{m}{r^2}$$

$$= \frac{1}{4\pi} \frac{3.6}{\left(6 \times 10^{-2}\right)^2} = 79.6 \text{ A/m}$$

Similarly $$H_s = 76.6 \text{ A/m}$$

Resultant magnet intensity

$$H = H_n + H_s$$

$$= 159.2 \text{ A/m towards the south pole}$$

$$\textit{Ans.}$$

(c)   The magnetic field $\vec{B}$ at the centre is

Fig. 7.54

$$\vec{B} = \mu_0\left(\vec{I} + \vec{H}\right)$$

$$= \left(4\pi \times 10^{-7}\right)\left(4 \times 10^4 - 159.2\right)$$

$$= 5.0 \times 10^{-2} \ T \qquad \textit{Ans.}$$

The field is towards north pole

Ex. 20 A moving coil galvanometer has a coil of area A and number of turns N. A magnetic field B is applied on it. The torque acting on it is given by $\tau = k\,i$ where i is current through the coil. If moment of inertia of the coil is I about the axis of rotation

(a) Find the value of k in terms of galvanometer parameters (N, B, A).

(b) Find the value of torsional constant if current i_0 produce angular deflection of $\dfrac{\pi}{2}$ radian.

(c) If a charge Q is passed almost instantaneously through coil, find the maximum angular deflection in it.

Sol.

(a) The torque exerted by magnetic field on the coil of galvanometer

$$\tau = N\,i\,AB$$

Given $\qquad \tau = k\,i$

$\therefore \qquad k\,i = N\,i\,AB$

or $\qquad k = NBA \qquad$ **Ans.**

(b) If C is the torsional constant of the head, then

$$C\left(\frac{\pi}{2}\right) = N\,i_0\,AB$$

or $\qquad C = \dfrac{2NAB\,i_0}{\pi} \qquad$ **Ans.**

(c) If θ_0 is the maximum deflection, then by conservation of energy

$$\frac{1}{2}C\theta_0^2 = \frac{1}{2}I\,\omega^2$$

or $\qquad \theta_0 = \sqrt{\dfrac{I}{C}}\,\omega \qquad$ ...(i)

We know that $\qquad \tau = N\,i\,AB \qquad$ ...(ii)

If L is the angular momentum of the coil, then $L = I\,\omega$, and equation (ii) can be written as

$$\frac{dL}{dt} = N\frac{dQ}{dt}AB$$

or $\qquad dL = NAB\,dQ$

On integrating, we get

$$L = NABQ$$

or $\qquad I\omega = NABQ$

or $\qquad \omega = \dfrac{NABQ}{I}$

Substituting this value in (i), we get

$$\theta_0 = Q\sqrt{\dfrac{\pi NAB}{2i_0 I}}$$

Review of formulae & Important Points

1. **Bar magnet :** If m is the magnetic charge and ℓ is the length of the magnet, then magnetic moment of the magnet

$$\vec{M} = m\vec{\ell}$$

2. **Coulomb's law in magnetism :**

The magnetic force between two magnetic charges m_1 and m_2 placed at a separation r is given by

$$F = \frac{\mu_0}{4\pi}\frac{m_1 m_2}{r^2}$$

3. **Magnetic field due to a magnetic charge m at a distance r**

$$B = \frac{\mu_0}{4\pi}\frac{m}{r^2}$$

4. Magnetic field due to a short magnetic dipole M at a distance r

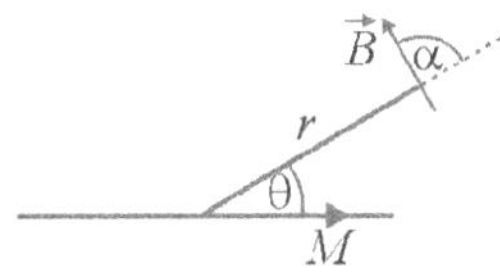

Fig. 10.23

$$B = \frac{\mu_0}{4\pi}\frac{M}{r^3}\sqrt{3\cos^2\theta + 1}$$

and $\qquad \tan\alpha = \dfrac{\tan\theta}{2}$

(i) On the axis of the dipole, $\theta = 0$

$$B = \frac{\mu_0}{4\pi}\frac{2M}{r^3}$$

(ii) On the equator, $\theta = 90°$

$$B = \frac{\mu_0}{4\pi}\frac{M}{r^3}$$

5. **Torque on a magnet in magnetic field**

$$\vec{\tau} = \vec{M}\times\vec{B}$$

6. **Work done in increasing angle from θ_1 to θ_2**

$$W = MB(\cos\theta_1 - \cos\theta_2).$$

7. **The potential energy of magnet in magnetic field**

$$U = -MB\cos\theta.$$

8. **Elements of earth magnetic field :**

(i) Angle of declination (ϕ) : Angle between geographical meridian and magnetic meridian is known as angle of declination.

(ii) Angle of dip (θ) : The angle made by dip needle with the horizontal is known as angle of dip. It is zero at the equator and 90° at the poles.

(iii) Horizontal component of earth magnetic field : If B is the resultant magnetic field at any place, then horizontal component

$$B_H = B\cos\theta.$$

9. **True dip and apparent dip :** If θ is the true dip and θ' is the apparent dip in a plane making angle α with the meridian plane, then

$$\tan\theta' = \frac{\tan\theta}{\cos\alpha}$$

10. **Moving coil galvanometer :** If i is the current in galvanometer, then

$$i = \frac{C}{NBA}\alpha$$

11. **Tangent galvanometer :** If θ is the reading of the galvanometer, then

$$i = \left(\frac{2RB_H}{\mu_0 N}\right)\tan\theta,$$

where $\left(\dfrac{2RB_H}{\mu_0 N}\right)$ is called reduction factor.

12. **Vibration magnetometer :** The time period of magnet of magnetometer

$$T = 2\pi\sqrt{\frac{I}{MB_H}}$$

For magnets of magnetic moments M_1 and M_2

$$\frac{M_1}{M_2} = \frac{T_2^2 + T_1^2}{T_2^2 - T_1^2}$$

13. **Gauss's law in magnetism :**

$$\oint \vec{B}\cdot d\vec{A} = 0$$

14. **Magnetic properties of materials :**

(i) Intensity of magnetisation

$$\vec{I} = \frac{\vec{M}}{V}$$

(ii) Intensity of magnetising field

$$\vec{H} = \frac{\vec{B}_0}{\mu_0}. \text{ Also } H = ni.$$

(iii) Magnetic permeability

$$\mu = \frac{B}{H} \text{ and } \mu_0 = \frac{B_0}{H}$$

Also relative permeability

$$\mu_r = \frac{\mu}{\mu_0}.$$

(iv) If χ is the susceptibility, then

$$\mu_r = 1 + \chi.$$

15. **Diamagnetic :** It is found in solids, liquids and gases. Ex. Ag, Au, Bi, Cu, H_2O, NaCl, Sb etc.

16. **Paramagnetic :** It is found in solids, liquids and gases. Ex. Al, $CuCl_2$, Na, O_2, Mn, Pt etc.

17. **Ferromagnetic :** It is normally found in solids. Ex. Co, Fe, Ni, Cd, Fe_3O_4 etc.

★ ★ ★

Magnetism

MCQ Type 1

Exercise 7.1

LEVEL - 1

Only one option correct

1. An electron in an external magnetic field $\vec{B}_{ext}$ has its angular momentum $\vec{L}$ antiparallel to $\vec{B}_{ext}$. If the electron undergoes a spin flip so that $\vec{L}$ is then parallel with $\vec{B}_{ext}$, then
   (a) energy is supplied to the electron
   (b) energy is lost by the electron
   (c) energy neither supplied nor lost
   (d) none of them.

2. The magnetic dipoles in a diamagnetic material are represented, for three situations. The three situations differ in the magnitude of a magnetic field applied to the material. In which situation the magnetisation of the material is the greatest :

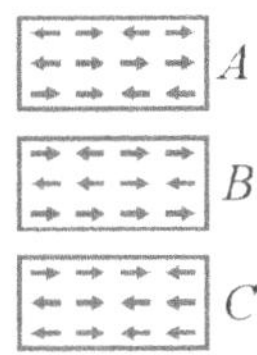

   (a) A
   (b) B
   (c) C
   (d) equal in A, B and C.

3. The magnetic susceptibility is negative for
   (a) diamagnetic substance
   (b) paramagnetic material
   (c) ferromagnetic material
   (d) all the above.

4. Electromagnets are made of soft iron because soft iron has
   (a) low retentively and low coercivity
   (b) low retentively and high coercivity
   (c) high retentively and low coerrity
   (d) high retentively and high coerrivity.

5. A compass which is allowed to move in a horizontal plane is taken to a geomagnetic pole. It
   (a) will stay in north-south direction only
   (b) will stay in east-west direction only
   (c) will stay in any position
   (d) none of these

6. A tangent galvanometer is connected directly to an ideal battery. If the number of turns in the coil is doubled, the deflection will
   (a) increase
   (b) decrease
   (c) remain same
   (d) any of these

7. An iron rod of length L and magnetic moment M is bent in the form of a semicircle. Now its magnetic moment will be
   (a) M
   (b) $\dfrac{2M}{\pi}$
   (c) $\dfrac{M}{\pi}$
   (d) $M\pi$

8. A magnetic needle lying parallel to a magnetic field requires W units of work to turn it through $60°$. The torque required to maintain the needle in this position will be
   (a) $\sqrt{3}W$
   (b) W
   (c) $\dfrac{\sqrt{3}}{2}W$
   (d) $2W$

9. A magnet of magnetic moment M is rotated through $360°$ in a magnetic field H, the work done will be
   (a) MH
   (b) $2MH$
   (c) $2\pi MH$
   (d) Zero

10. Force between two identical bar magnets whose centres are r metre apart is 4.8 N, when their axes are in the same line. If separation is increased to $2r$, the force between them is
    (a) 2.4 N
    (b) 1.2 N
    (c) 0.6 N
    (d) 0.3 N

11. A magnet of magnetic moment $50\hat{i}$ A-m^2 is placed along the x-axis in a magnetic field $\vec{B} = \left(0.5\hat{i} + 3.0\hat{j}\right)T$. The torque acting on the magnet is
    (a) $175\hat{k}$ N - m
    (b) $150\hat{k}$ N - m
    (c) $75\hat{k}$ N - m
    (d) $25\sqrt{37}\hat{k}$ N- m

12. The magnetic field lines due to a bar magnet are correctly shown in

    (a) 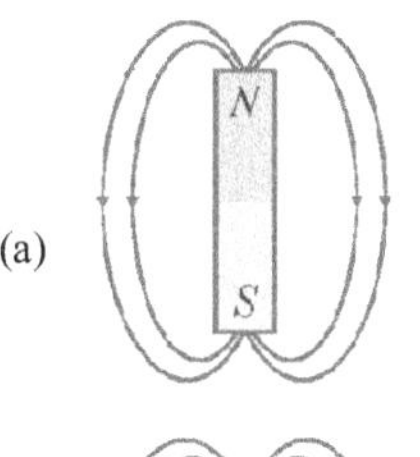
    (b) 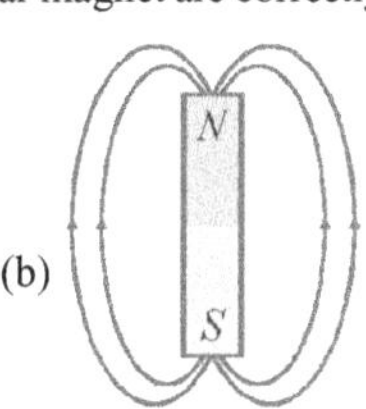
    (c) 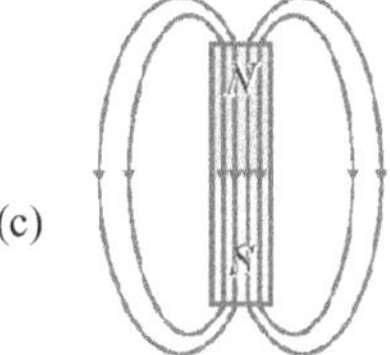
    (d) 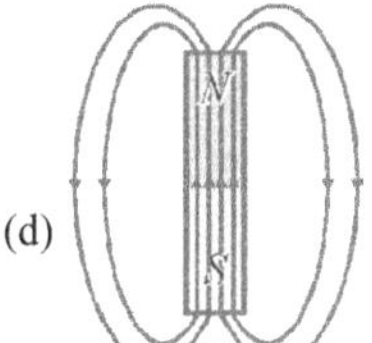

Answer Key	1	(a)	2	(b)	3	(a)	4	(a)	5	(c)	6	(c)
Sol. from page 481	7	(b)	8	(a)	9	(d)	10	(d)	11	(b)	12	(d)

13. A very small magnet is placed in the magnetic meridian with its south pole pointing north. The null point is obtained 20 cm away from the centre of the magnet. If the earth's magnetic field (horizontal component) at this point be 0.3 gauss, the magnetic moment of the magnet is

(a) 8.0×10^2 e.m.u. (b) 1.2×10^3 e.m.u.

(c) 2.4×10^3 e.m.u. (d) 3.6×10^3 e.m.u.

14. At a place, if the earth's horizontal and vertical components of magnetic fields are equal, then the angle of dip will be

(a) 30° (b) 90°

(c) 45° (d) 0°

15. Time period of a freely suspended magnet does not depend upon

(a) length of the magnet

(b) pole strength of the magnet

(c) horizontal component of earth's magnetic field

(d) length of the suspension thread

16. Two magnets of same size and mass make respectively 10 and 15 oscillations per minute at certain place. The ratio of their magnetic moments is

(a) $4 : 9$ (b) $9 : 4$

(c) $2 : 3$ (d) $3 : 2$

17. The period of oscillation of a magnet in vibration magnetometer is 2 sec. The period of oscillation of a magnet whose magnetic moment is four times that of the first magnet is

(a) 1 sec (b) 4 sec

(c) 8 sec (d) 0.5 sec

18. A magnetic needle suspended by a silk thread is vibrating in the earth's magnetic field. If the temperature of the needle is increased by 500°C, then

(a) the time period decreases

(b) the time period remains unchanged

(c) the time period increases

(d) the needle stops vibrating

19. The time period of oscillation of a bar magnet suspended horizontally along the magnetic meridian is T_0. If this magnet is replaced by another magnet of the same size and pole strength but with double the mass, the new time period will be

(a) $\dfrac{T_0}{2}$ (b) $\dfrac{T_0}{\sqrt{2}}$

(c) $\sqrt{2}T_0$ (d) $2T_0$

20. A magnet makes 40 oscillations per minute at a place having magnetic field intensity of $0.1 \times 10^{-5} T$. At another place, it takes 2.5 sec to complete one vibration. The value of earth's horizontal field at that place is

(a) $0.25 \times 10^{-6} T$ (b) $0.36 \times 10^{-6} T$

(c) $0.66 \times 10^{-8} T$ (d) $1.2 \times 10^{-6} T$

21. The magnetic needle of a tangent galvanometer is deflected at an angle 30° due to a magnet. The horizontal component of earth's magnetic field $0.34 \times 10^{-4} T$ is along the plane of the coil. The magnetic intensity is

(a) $1.96 \times 10^{-4} T$ (b) $1.96 \times 10^{-5} T$

(c) $1.96 \times 10^4 T$ (d) $1.96 \times 10^5 T$

22. Relative permeability of iron is 5500, then its mangetic susceptibility will be

(a) 5501 (b) 5499

(c) 5500×10^7 (d) none of these

(d) paramagnetic and ferromagnetic materials

23. Curie temperature is the temperature above which

(a) a paramagnetic material becomes ferromagnetic

(b) a ferromagnetic material becomes paramagnetic

(c) a paramagnetic material becomes diamagnetic

(d) a ferromagnetic material becomes diamagnetic

24. Liquid oxygen remains suspended between two poles faces of a magnet because it is

(a) diamagnetic (b) paramagnetic

(c) ferromagnetic (d) antiferromagnetic

25. A bar magnet is placed north south with its north pole due north. The points of zero magnetic field will be in which direction from the centre of the magnet

(a) north and south

(b) east and west

(c) north-east and south-west

(d) north-west and south-east.

26. Two identical magnetic dipoles of magnetic moments 1.0 A-m^2 each, placed at a separation of 2m with their axis perpendicular to each other. The resultant magnetic field at a point midway between the dipoles is

(a) $5 \times 10^{-7} T$ (b) $\sqrt{5} \times 10^{-7} T$

(c) 10^{-7} T (d) none of these

Answer Key	**13**	(b)	**14**	(c)	**15**	(d)	**16**	(a)	**17**	(a)	**18**	(c)	**19**	(c)
Sol. from page 481	**20**	(b)	**21**	(b)	**22**	(b)	**23**	(b)	**24**	(b)	**25**	(b)	**26**	(b)

27. A bar magnet of magnetic moment 3.0 A-m^2 is placed in a uniform magnetic field of 2×10^{-5} T. If each pole of the magnet experiences a force of 6×10^{-4} N, the length of the magnet is

(a) 0.5 m (b) 0.3 m

(c) 0.2 m (d) 0.1 m

28. A current carrying coil is placed with its axis perpendicular to N-S direction. Let horizontal component of earth's magnetic field be H_0 and magnetic field inside the loop be H. If a magnet is suspended inside the loop, it makes angle θ with H. Then $\theta =$

(a) $\tan^{-1}\left(\dfrac{H_0}{H}\right)$ (b) $\tan^{-1}\left(\dfrac{H}{H_0}\right)$

(c) $\operatorname{cosec}^{-1}\left(\dfrac{H}{H_0}\right)$ (d) $\cot^{-1}\left(\dfrac{H_0}{H}\right)$

29. Demagnetisation of magnets can be done by

(a) rough handling

(b) heating

(c) magnetising in the opposite direction

(d) all the above

30. If the angular momentum of an electron is $\vec{J}$ then the magnitude of the magnetic moment will be

(a) $\dfrac{eJ}{m}$ (b) $\dfrac{eJ}{2m}$

(c) $eJ\,2m$ (d) $\dfrac{2m}{eJ}$

31. When a ferromagnetic material is heated to temperature above its Curie temperature, the material

(a) is permanently magnetized

(b) remains ferromagnetic

(c) behaves like a diamagnetic material

(d) behaves like a paramagnetic material

32. Needles N_1, N_2 and N_3 are made of a ferromagnetic, a paramagnetic and a diamagnetic substance respectively. A magnet when brought close to them will

(a) attract N_1 strongly, N_2 weakly and repel N_3 weakly

(b) attract N_1 strongly, but repel N_2 and N_3 weakly

(c) attract all three of them

(d) attract N_1 and N_2 strongly but repel N_3.

33. Two identical short bar magnetics, each having magnetic moment M, are placed a distance of $2d$ apart with axes perpendicular to each other in a horizontal plane. The magnetic induction at a point midway between them is

(a) $\dfrac{\mu_0}{4\pi}\left(\sqrt{2}\right)\dfrac{M}{d^3}$ (b) $\dfrac{\mu_0}{4\pi}\left(\sqrt{3}\right)\dfrac{M}{d^3}$

(c) $\left(\dfrac{2\mu_0}{\pi}\right)\dfrac{M}{d^3}$ (d) $\dfrac{\mu_0}{4\pi}\left(\sqrt{5}\right)\dfrac{M}{d^3}$

Answer Key	27	(d)	28	(a)	29	(d)	30	(b)
Sol. from page 481	31	(d)	32	(a)	33	(d)		

Only one option correct

1. Figure (a) shows a pair of opposite spin orientations for an electron in an external magnetic field $\vec{B}_{ext}$. Figure (b) gives three choices for the graph of the potential energies associated with those orientation as a function of magnitude of $\vec{B}_{ext}$. Choices B and C consist of intersecting lines, choice A of parallel lines. Which is the correct choice

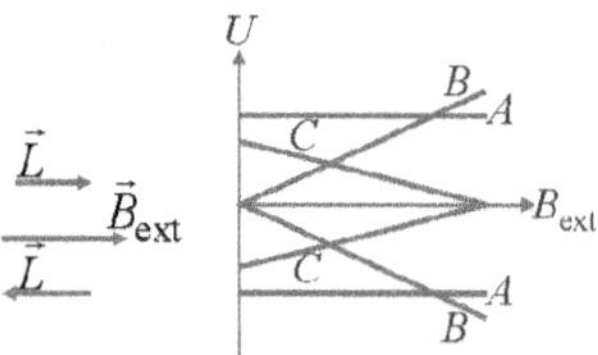

      (a)   (b)

(a) A, A (b) B, B

(c) C, C (d) $A, A; B, B.$

2. Two short magnets of equal dipole moment M are fastened perpendicularly at their centres. The magnitude of the magnetic field at a distance d from the centre of the bisector of the right angle is

(a) $\dfrac{\mu_0}{4\pi}\dfrac{M}{d^3}$

(b) $\dfrac{\mu_0}{4\pi}\dfrac{\sqrt{2}\,M}{d^3}$

(c) $\dfrac{\mu_0}{4\pi}\dfrac{2M}{d^3}$

(d) $\dfrac{\mu_0}{4\pi}\dfrac{2\sqrt{2}\,M}{d^3}$

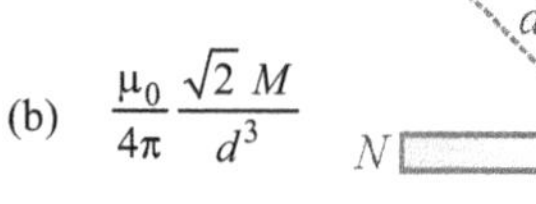

3. A very long bar magnet is placed with its north-pole coinciding with the centre of a circular loop carrying an electric current i. The magnetic field due to the magnet at a point on the periphery of the loop is B. The radius of the loop is a. The force on the loop is

(a) nearly $2\pi aiB$ perpendicular to the plane of the loop

(b) $2\pi aiB$ in the plane of the loop

(c) πaiB along the magnet

(d) zero.

4. The length of a magnet is large compared to its width and breadth. The time period of its oscillation in a vibration magnetometer is 2 s. The magnet is cut along its length into three equal parts and three parts are then placed on each other with their like poles together. The time period of this combination will be

(a) 2 s   (b) $2/3$ s

(c) $2\sqrt{3}$ s   (d) $2/\sqrt{3}s$

5. The true value of angle of dip at a place is $60°$, the apparent dip in a plane inclined at an angle of $30°$ with magnetic meridian is

(a) $\tan^{-1}\dfrac{1}{2}$ (b) $\tan^{-1}(2)$

(c) $\tan^{-1}\left(\dfrac{2}{3}\right)$ (d) None of these

6. A small coil C with $N = 200$ turns is mounted on one end of a balance beam and introduced between the poles of an electromagnet as shown in figure. The cross sectional area of coil is $A = 1.0$ cm^2, length of arm OA of the balance beam is $\ell = 30$ cm. When there is no current in the coil the balance is in equilibrium. On passing a current $I = 22$ mA through the coil the equilibrium is restored by putting the additional counter weight of mass $\Delta m = 60$ mg on the balance pan. Find the magnetic induction at the spot where coil is located.

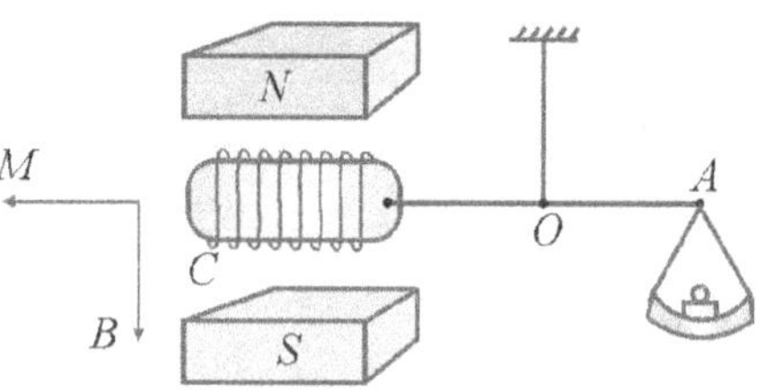

(a) 0.4 T   (b) 0.3 T

(c) 0.2 T   (d) 0.1 T

7. At a place on earth, horizontal component of earth's magnetic field is B_1 and vertical component of earth's magnetic field is B_2. If a magnetic needle is kept vertical, in a plane making angle α with the horizontal component of magnetic field, then square of time period of oscillation of needle when slightly distributed is proportional to

(a) $\dfrac{1}{\sqrt{B_1\cos\alpha}}$ (b) $\dfrac{1}{\sqrt{B_2}}$

(c) $\dfrac{1}{\sqrt{(B_1\cos\alpha)^2 + B_2^2}}$ (d) infinite

Answer Key	**1**	(b)	**2**	(d)	**3**	(a)	**4**	(b)
Sol. from page 482	**5**	(b)	**6**	(a)	**7**	(c)		

Magnetism   MCQ Type 2   *Exercise 7.2*

Multiple correct options

1. The figure shows two diamagnetic spheres located near the south pole of a bar magnet. Then

(a) the force on sphere 1 is directed towards the magnet
(b) the force on sphere 2 is directed away from the magnet
(c) the magnetic dipole moment of sphere is directed towards the magnet
(d) the magnetic dipole moment of sphere 2 is directed away from the magnet.

2. Figure shows a loop model (loop L) for a diamagnetic material.

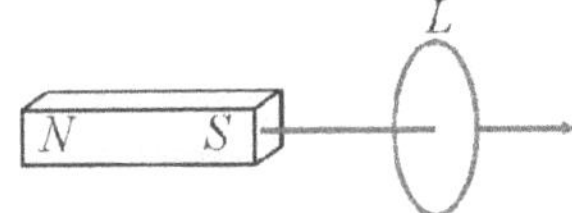

(a) The net dipole moment of the loop directed towards the magnet
(b) The net dipole moment of the loop directed away from the loop
(c) The loop gets attracted towards the magnet
(d) The loop gets repelled by the magnet.

3. A ferromagnetic material is placed in an external magnetic field. The magnetic domain
(a) may increase in size
(b) may decrease in size
(c) retain their size
(d) nothing can be said.

4. Mark out the correct options.
(a) Diamagnetism occurs in all materials
(b) Diamagnetism results from the partial alignment of permanent magnetic moment.
(c) The magnetizing field intensity H is always zero in free space.
(d) The magnetic field of induced magnetic moment is opposite to the applied field.

5. Which of the following statements are true about the magnetic susceptibility χ_m of paramagnetic substance

(a) value of χ_m is inversely proportional to the absolute temperature of the sample

(b) χ_m is positive at all temperature

(c) χ_m is negative at all temperature

(d) χ_m does not depend on the temperature of the sample

6. The current sensitivity of a moving coil galvanometer can be increased by
(a) increasing the magnetic field of the permanent magnet
(b) increasing the area of the deflecting coil
(c) increasing the number of turns in the coil
(d) increasing the restoring couple of the coil

Answer Key	1	(b, d)	2	(b, d)	3	(a, b)	4	(a, d)
Sol. from page 482	5	(a, b)	6	(a, b, c)				

Magnetism   # Statement Questions   *Exercise 7.3*

Read the two statements carefully to mark the correct option out of the options given below:
(a) If both the statements are true and the *statement - 2* is the correct explanation of *statement - 1*.
(b) If both the statements are true but *statement - 2* is not the correct explanation of the *statement - 1*.
(c) If *statement - 1* true but *statement - 2* is false.
(d) If *statement - 1* is false but *statement - 2* is true.

1. **Statement - 1**

   The poles of magnet can not be separated by breaking into two pieces.

   Statement - 2

   The magnetic moment will be reduced to half when a magnet is broken into two equal pieces.

2. **Statement - 1**

   When radius of a circular current carrying loop is doubled, its magnetic moment becomes four times.

   Statement - 2

   Magnetic moment is given by $M = iA$.

3. **Statement - 1**

   Gauss's law is not applicable in magnetism.

   Statement - 2

   Isolated pole does not exist.

4. **Statement - 1**

   We cannot think of magnetic field configuration with three poles.

   Statement - 2

   A bar magnet does not exert a torque on itself due to its own field.

5. **Statement - 1**

   The earth's magnetic field is due to iron present in its core.

   Statement - 2

   At a high temperature magnet losses its magnetism.

6. **Statement - 1**

   The tangent galvanometer can be made more sensitive by increasing the number of turns of its coil.

   Statement - 2

   Current through galvanometer is proportional to the number of turns of the coil.

7. **Statement - 1**

   Reduction factor (k) of a tangent galvanometer helps in reducing deflection to current.

   Statement - 2

   Reduction factor increases with increase of current.

8. **Statement - 1**

   Paramagnetic substances possess the property of diamagnetism.

   Statement - 2

   Diamagnetism is the universal property, it is present in all substances.

9. **Statement - 1**

   The ferromagnetic substance do not obey Curie's law.

   Statement - 2

   At Curie point a ferromagnetic substance start behaving as a paramagnetic substance.

10. **Statement - 1**

    For making permanent magnets, steel is preferred over soft iron.

    Statement - 2

    Steel possesses high retentivity.

11. **Statement - 1**

    Soft iron is used as transformer core.

    Statement - 2

    Soft iron has low hysteresis loss.

12. **Statement - 1**

    To protect any instrument from external magnetic field, it is put inside an iron body.

    Statement - 2

    Iron has high permeability.

13. **Statement - 1**

    The sensitivity of a moving coil galvanometer is increased by placing a suitable magnetic material as a core inside the coil.

    Statement - 2

    Soft iron has high magnetic permeability and cannot be easily magnetized or demagnetized.

Answer Key	1	(b)	2	(a)	3	(a)	4	(b)	5	(d)	6	(b)	7	(c)
Sol. from page 483	8	(a)	9	(b)	10	(a)	11	(a)	12	(a)	13	(c)		

Magnetism | # Subjective Integer Type | *Exercise 7.4*

Solution from page 483

1. At a certain place the horizontal component of earth's magnetic field is $\sqrt{3}$ times the vertical component. What is the angle of dip at that place ? ***Ans :*** 30°.

2. A bar magnet of magnetic moment 2.0 A-m^2 is free to rotate about a vertical axis passing through its centre. The magnet is released from rest from east-west position. Find the kinetic energy of the magnet as it takes north-south position. [Horizontal component of earth's field is 25 μT]. ***Ans :*** 50 μJ.

3. A magnetic needle is free to rotate in a vertical plane which makes an angle of 60° with the magnetic meridian. If the needle stays in a direction making an angle of $\tan^{-1}\left(\dfrac{2}{\sqrt{3}}\right)$ with the horizontal, what would be the dip at that place ? ***Ans :*** 30°.

4. An iron rod of volume 10^{-4} m^3 and relative permeability 1000 is placed inside a long solenoid wound with 5 turns/cm. If a current of 0.5 A is passed through the solenoid, find the magnetic moment of the rod. ***Ans :*** 25 A-m^2.

5. An ideal solenoid having 40 turns/cm has an aluminium core and carries a current of 2.0 A. Calculate the magnetisation I developed in the core and the magnetic field B at the centre. The susceptibility of aluminium = 2.3×10^{-5}. ***Ans :*** I = 0.18 A/m.

6. A tangent galvanometer shows a deflection of 45° when 10 mA of current is passed through it. If the horizontal component of the earth's magnetic field is $B_H = 3.6 \times 10^{-6}$ T and radius of coil is 10 cm, find the number of turns in the coil. ***Ans :*** 570.

Magnetism | # Subjective | *Exercise 7.5*

Solution from page 483

1. A magnet is suspended in such a way that it oscillates in the horizontal plane. If it makes 20 oscillations per minute at a place where dip angle is 30° and 15 oscillations per minute at a place where dip angle is 60°. Find the ratio of total earth magnetic field at the two places. ***Ans :*** $\dfrac{16}{9\sqrt{3}}$

2. Find the magnetic field due to a dipole of magnetic moment 1.2 A-m^2 at a point 1 m away from it in a direction making an angle of 60° with the dipole axis.

    Ans : 1.6×10^{-7} T at an angle α with the radial line where $\alpha = \tan^{-1}\left(\dfrac{\sqrt{3}}{2}\right)$.

3. A magnet is 10 cm long and its pole strength is 12 A-m. Find the magnitude of the magnetic field B at a point on its axis at a distance 20 cm from it. ***Ans :*** 3.4×10^{-5} T.

4. A dip circle shows an apparent dip of 60° at a place where the true dip is 45°. If the dip circle is rotated through 90°, what apparent dip will it show ? ***Ans :*** $\cot^{-1}(0.816)$.

5. The needle of a deflection galvanometer shows a deflection of 60° due to a short bar magnet at a certain distance in tan A position. If the distance is doubled, what will be the deflection ?

    Ans : $\tan^{-1}\left(\dfrac{\sqrt{3}}{8}\right)$

6. A moving-coil galvanometer has 100 turns and each turn has an area 2.0 cm^2. The magnetic field produced by the magnet is 0.01 T. The deflection in the coil is 0.05 radian when a current of 10 mA is passed through it. Find the torsional constant of the suspension wire. ***Ans :*** 4.0×10^{-5} N-m/rad.

7. Two long bar magnets are placed with their axes coinciding in such a way that the north pole of the first magnet is 2.0 cm from the south pole of the second. If both the magnets have a pole strength of 10 A-m, find the force exerted by one magnet on the other. ***Ans :*** 2.5×10^{-2} N.

8. A bar magnet has a length 8 cm. The magnetic field at a point at a distance 3 cm from the centre in the broad side-on position is found to be 4×10^{-6} T. Find the pole strength of the magnet. ***Ans :*** 6×10^{-5} A-m.

9. Assume that each iron atom has a permanent magnetic moment equal to 2 Bohr magnetons (1 Bohr magneton = 9.27×10^{-24} A-m^2). The density of atoms in iron is 8.52×10^{28} $atoms/m^3$.

    (a) Find the maximum magnetisation I in a long cylinder of iron.

    (b) Find the maximum magnetic field B on the axis inside the cylinder. ***Ans :*** (a) 1.58×10^6 A/m (b) 2.0 T.

10. The susceptibility of annealed iron at saturation is 5500. Find the permeability of annealed iron at saturation. ***Ans :*** 6.9×10^{-3}.

11. Imagine rolling a sheet of paper into a cylinder and placing a bar magnet near its end as shown in figure. (a) Sketch the magnetic field lines that pass through the surface of the cylinder.

(b) What can you say about the sign of $\vec{B}.d\vec{A}$ for every area $d\vec{A}$ on the surface ?

(c) Does this contradict Gauss's law for magnetism ?

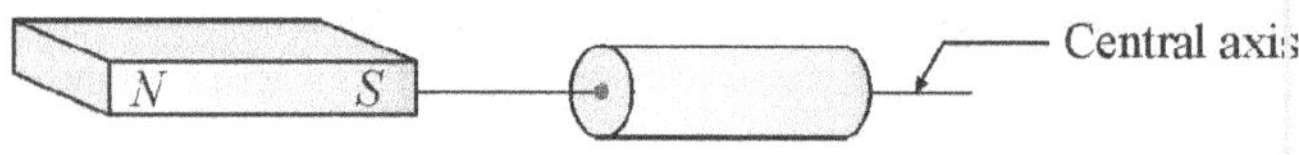

Ans : (b) sign is minus; (c) no, there is compensating positive flux through open end near magnet.

12. A compass needle made of pure iron (with density 7900 kg/m^3) has a length L of 3.0 cm, a width of 1.00 mm, and a thickness of 0.50 mm. The magnitude of the magnetic dipole moment of an iron atom is $M_{Fe} = 2.1 \times 10^{-23} \ J/T$. If the magnetisation of the needle is equivalent to the alignment of 10% of the atoms in the needle, what is the magnitude of the needle's magnetic dipole moment $\vec{M}$?

Ans : 2.7×10^{-3} J/T.

13. A short magnet oscillates in an oscillation magnetometer with a time period of 0.10s where the earth's horizontal magnetic field is 24 μT. A downward current of 18 A is established in a vertical wire placed 20 cm east of the magnet. Find the new time period.

Ans : 0.076 s.

14. A deflection magnetometer is placed with its arm in north-south direction. How and where should a short magnet having $\dfrac{M}{B_H} = 40$ A-m^2 be placed so that the needle can stay in any position ?

Ans : 2.0 cm from the needle, north pole pointing towards south.

★ ★ ★

Hints & Solutions

Solutions EXERCISE 7.1 LEVEL -1

1. (a)
$$U_i = -MB\cos 0° = -MB$$
and $$U_f = -MB\cos 180° = MB$$
$$\therefore \quad \Delta U = U_f - U_i = MB - (-MB)$$
$$= 2MB.$$

2. (b) The largest number of dipole moment is in case B and so greatest magnetisation is of B.

3. (a)

4. (a)

5. (c) At geomagnetic poles, there is no horizontal component of earth field and so compass needle may stay at any position.

6. (c)
$$i = \left(\frac{2RB_H}{\mu_0 N}\right)\tan\theta$$

or $$\frac{V}{R} = \left(\frac{2RB_H}{\mu_0 N}\right)\tan\theta \quad \ldots (i)$$

When number of turns are doubled, resistance of the coil is also doubled, so

$$\frac{V}{(2R)} = \left[\frac{2RB_H}{\mu_0(2N)}\right]\tan\theta' \quad \ldots (ii)$$

From (i) and (ii), $\theta' = \theta$.

7. (b) Given : $$M = m\ell$$

Now, $\ell = \pi R$ or $R = \dfrac{\ell}{\pi}$

$$\therefore \quad M' = m \times 2R = m \times 2\frac{\ell}{\pi}$$

$$= \frac{2M}{\pi}.$$

8. (a)
$$W = MB\cos 60°$$
and $$\tau = MB\sin 60°$$
$$\therefore \quad \tau = \sqrt{3}\,W .$$

9. (d)
$$U_i = -MB\cos 0° = -MB$$
and $$U_f = -MB\cos 360° = -MB$$
Now, $$W = U_f - U_i = -MB - (-MB) = 0.$$

10. (d) Force between two short bar magnets is given by

$$F = \frac{\mu_0}{4\pi}\frac{6M_1 M_2}{r^4}$$

$$\therefore \quad \frac{F_1}{F_2} = \frac{r_2^4}{r_1^4} = \left(\frac{2r}{r}\right)^4$$

or $$F_2 = \frac{F_1}{16} = \frac{4.8}{16} = 0.3\ N.$$

11. (b)
$$\vec{\tau} = \vec{M}\times\vec{B} = 50\hat{i}\times(0.5\hat{i}+3\hat{j}).$$
$$= 150\,\hat{k}\ N\text{-}m$$

12. (d) The field lines emerge from north pole and enters into magnet through south pole.

13. (b)

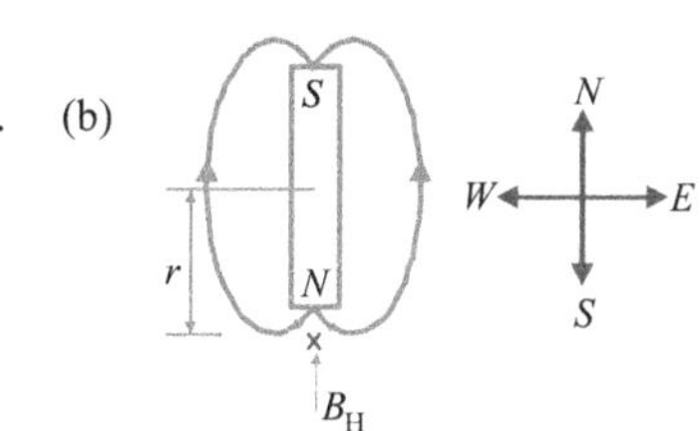

$$B = B_H$$

or $$\frac{\mu_0}{4\pi}\cdot\frac{2M}{r^3} = 0.3$$

or $$10^{-7}\times\frac{2M}{(20)^3} = 0.3$$

$$\therefore \quad M = 1.2\times10^3\ \text{emu}.$$

14. (c) $\tan\theta = \dfrac{B_V}{B_H} = 1$

$$\therefore \quad \theta = 45°$$

15. (d)

16. (a) $T_1 = \dfrac{60}{10} = 6\,s$ and $T_2 = \dfrac{60}{15} = 4\,s$

For identical magnets,

$$\frac{M_1}{M_2} = \frac{T_2^2}{T_1^2} = \frac{4^2}{6^2} = \frac{16}{36} = \frac{4}{9}.$$

17. (a)
$$\frac{T_1}{T_2} = \sqrt{\frac{M_2}{M_1}}$$

$$\therefore \quad T_2 = T_1\sqrt{\frac{M_1}{M_2}} = 2\sqrt{\frac{1}{4}} = 1\,\text{sec}.$$

18. (c) Due to change in temperature, magnetic moment of magnet decreases, and so time period of oscillations will increase.

19. (c)
$$I_1 = \frac{m\ell^2}{12} \text{ and } I_2 = \frac{(2m)\ell^2}{12} = 2I_1.$$

Now, $$\frac{T_1}{T_2} = \sqrt{\frac{I_1}{I_2}}$$

or $$\frac{T_0}{T_2} = \sqrt{\frac{1}{2}}$$

$$\therefore \quad T_2 = \sqrt{2}\,T_0.$$

20. (b) $T_1 = \dfrac{60}{40} = 1.5\,s$ and $T_2 = 2.5\,s$

We know that, $$\frac{T_1}{T_2} = \sqrt{\frac{B_2}{B_1}}$$

or $$B_2 = \frac{T_1^2}{T_2^2}\times B_1 = \left(\frac{1.5}{2.5}\right)^2\times(0.1\times10^{-5})$$

$$= 0.36\times10^{-6}\ \text{T}$$

21. (b) We know that

$$\frac{B}{B_H} = \tan\theta$$

or
$$B = B_H \tan\theta$$
$$= 0.34 \times 10^{-4} \tan 30°$$
$$= 1.96 \times 10^{-5} \text{ T}$$

22. (b) We know that,
$$\mu_r = 1 + x$$
or
$$x = \mu_{r-1}$$
$$= 5500 - 1 = 5499$$

23. (b)

24. (b

25. (b)

26. (b)
$$B_1 = \frac{\mu_0}{4\pi}.\frac{2M}{r^3} = 10^{-7} \times \frac{2 \times 1}{1^3} = 2 \times 10^{-7} \text{ T}$$

and
$$B_2 = \frac{\mu_0}{4\pi}.\frac{M}{r^3} = 10^{-7} \times \frac{1}{1^3} = 10^{-7} \text{ T}$$

Now, $B = \sqrt{B_1^2 + B_2^2} = \sqrt{5} \times 10^{-7} \text{ T}$.

27. (d)
$$F = mB$$
or $6 \times 10^{-4} = m \times 2 \times 10^{-5}$
$\therefore\quad m = 30 \text{ A-m}$

Now, $\ell = \dfrac{M}{m} = \dfrac{3}{30} = 0.1 \text{ m}$

28. (a) $\tan\theta = \dfrac{H_0}{H}$

29. (d)

30. (b) We know that,

$$\frac{M}{J} = \frac{q}{2m}$$

$\therefore\quad M = J \times \dfrac{e}{2m}$.

31. (d)

32. (a)

33. (d)
$$B_1 = \frac{\mu_0}{4\pi}.\frac{2M}{d^3} \text{ and } B_2 = \frac{\mu_0}{4\pi}.\frac{M}{d^3}.$$

Now, $B = \sqrt{B_1^2 + B_2^2} = \sqrt{5}\dfrac{\mu_0}{4\pi}.\dfrac{M}{d^3}$.

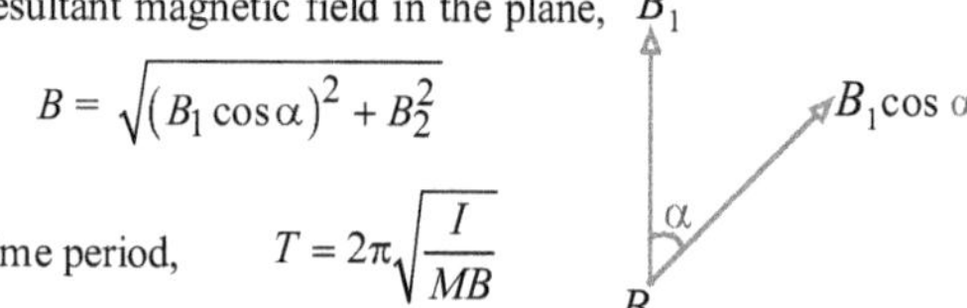

Solutions EXERCISE 7.1 LEVEL -2

1. (b)
$$U = -MB\cos\theta$$
For $\theta = 0$, $\quad U = -MB$
and for $\theta = 180°$, $\quad U = +MB$.
These represent straight inclined lines.

2. (d) The resultant magnetic moment $M' = \sqrt{2}\,M$

Magnetic field, $B = \dfrac{\mu_0}{4\pi}.\dfrac{2M'}{d^3}$

$$= \frac{\mu_0}{4\pi}.\frac{2\sqrt{2}M}{d^3}.$$

3. (a) The loop experiences the force due to north pole only. So,

$$F = Bi \int_0^{2\pi a} d\ell = Bi \times 2\pi a$$

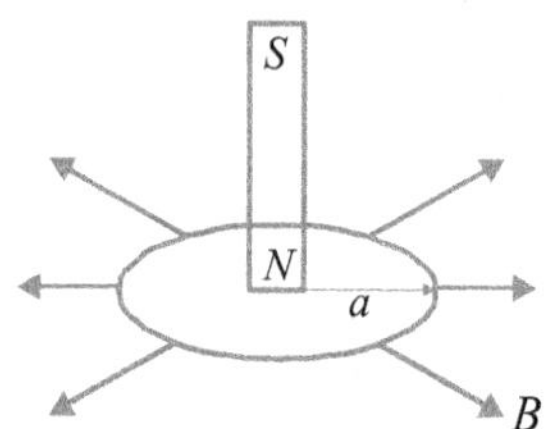

4. (b) The moment of inertia of original magnet $I = \dfrac{m\ell^2}{12}$

After dividing into three equal parts,

$$I' = 3(m/3).\frac{(\ell/3)^2}{12} = \frac{I}{9}.$$

Also magnetic moment, $M' = M$

Now, $\dfrac{T'}{T} = \sqrt{\dfrac{I'}{I} \times \dfrac{M}{M'}}$

$\therefore\quad T' = T \times \sqrt{\dfrac{I'}{I}} = 2 \times \sqrt{\dfrac{1}{9}} = \dfrac{2}{3}\text{ s}.$

5. (b) $\tan\theta' = \dfrac{\tan\theta}{\cos\alpha} = \dfrac{\tan 60°}{\cos 30°} = \dfrac{\sqrt{3}}{\sqrt{3}/2} = 2$

$\therefore\quad \theta' = \tan^{-1}(2)$.

6. (a) For equilibrium of the beam balance
$$mg \times \ell = NiAB$$

$\therefore\quad B = \dfrac{mg\ell}{NiA}$.

After substituting the given values and simplifying, we get
$B = 0.4 \text{ T}$.

7. (c) Resultant magnetic field in the plane, B_1

$$B = \sqrt{(B_1 \cos\alpha)^2 + B_2^2}$$

Time period, $T = 2\pi \sqrt{\dfrac{I}{MB}}$

Solutions EXERCISE 7.2

1. (b, d) Diamagnetic material gets repelled by magnet, and so both the spheres will be repelled by the magnet. The dipole moment of spheres also directed away from the magnet.

2. (b, d) The near face of the loop behaves like south pole and far face as north pole. So loop will be repelled by the magnet.

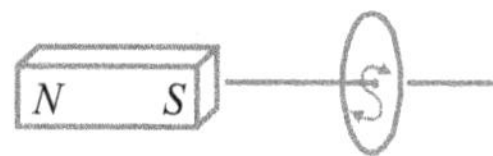

3. (a, b) The size of the domain may increase or decrease depending on the orientation of the domain w.r.t. magnetic field.

4. (a, d)

5. (a, b) $\chi_m = \dfrac{C}{(T - T_C)}$.

6. (a, b, c)

Solutions EXERCISE 7.3

1. (b) When a magnet is cut into pieces, each piece becomes new magnet. $M' = \dfrac{m\ell}{2} = \dfrac{M}{2}$.

2. (a)
$$M = iA = i \times \pi r^2$$
and
$$M' = i \times \pi(2r)^2 = 4M.$$

3. (a) The smallest element of the magnetism is dipole and so
$$m_{in} = m - m = 0, \text{ and Gauss's law}$$
$$\oint \vec{B}.d\vec{A} = \mu_0 m_{in} = 0.$$

4. (b)

5. (d) Magnetic field of earth is due to moving charged particles in the atmosphere. With increase in temperature, the magnetic moment of magnet decreases.

6. (b) In tangent galvanometer,
$$i = \left(\dfrac{2RB_H}{\mu_0 N}\right)\tan\theta, \text{ clearly } i \propto \tan\theta.$$
Sensitivity, $s = \dfrac{\theta}{i} \simeq \dfrac{\tan\theta}{i} = \dfrac{\mu_0 N}{2RB_H}$.

7. (c) Reduction factor of tangent galvanometer does not depend on current.

8. (a) Statement-2 is the explanation of statement-1.

9. (b) At Curie temperature, ferromagnetic substance changes into paramagnetic substance.

10. (a)

11. (a)

12. (a) Because of high permeability of the iron, the entire magnetic field will pass through iron, and so rest space becomes free from magnetic field.

13. (c) Sensitivity of galvanometer,
$$s = \dfrac{\theta}{i} \simeq \dfrac{\tan\theta}{i}$$
$$= \dfrac{\mu_0 N}{2RB_H}.$$
If a magnetic material is placed inside coil of galvanometer, then
$$s' = \dfrac{\mu_r \mu_0 N}{2RB_H}.$$

Solutions EXERCISE 7.4

1. Angle of dip, $\tan\theta = \dfrac{B_V}{B_H}$
$$= \dfrac{1}{\sqrt{3}}$$
$$\therefore \quad \theta = 30° \qquad \textbf{Ans.}$$

2.
$$W = \Delta K$$
or
$$\int_{90°}^{0} \tau d\theta = K_f - K_i$$
or
$$\int_{90}^{0} -MB\sin\theta d\theta = K_f - 0$$
or
$$K_f = -MB(-\cos 0° + \cos 90°)$$
$$= MB = 2 \times 25 = 50 \ \mu J \qquad \textbf{Ans.}$$

3. Given apparent dip, $\theta' = \tan^{-1}\left(2/\sqrt{3}\right)$
We know that, apparent dip
$$\tan\theta' = \dfrac{\tan\theta}{\cos\alpha}$$
$$\therefore \quad \tan\theta = \tan\theta' \times \cos\alpha$$
$$= \dfrac{2}{\sqrt{3}} \times \cos 60° = \dfrac{1}{\sqrt{3}}$$
or $\theta = 30°$ **Ans.**

4. We know that,
$$H = ni = (500) \times 0.5$$
$$= 250 \ A/m$$
$$\therefore \quad I = \mu_r H = 1000 \times 250$$
$$= 2.5 \times 10^5 \ A/m$$
We have
$$I = \dfrac{M}{V}$$
$$\therefore \quad M = IV$$
$$= (2.5 \times 10^5) \times (10^{-4})$$
$$= 25 \ A\text{-}m^2 \qquad \textbf{Ans}$$

5. We know that,
$$H = ni = (4000) \times (2)$$
$$= 8 \times 10^3 \ A/m$$
$$\therefore \quad I = \mu_r H = (2.3 \times 10^{-5}) \times (8 \times 10^3)$$
$$= 0.18 \qquad \textbf{Ans.}$$

6. We know that
$$i = \left[\dfrac{2RB_H}{\mu_0 N}\right]\tan\theta$$
After substituting, the values and simplifying, we get
$$N = 570. \qquad \textbf{Ans.}$$

Solutions EXERCISE 7.5

1. At place I,
$$T_1 = \dfrac{60}{20} = 2\pi\sqrt{\dfrac{I}{MB_{H_1}}} \quad \dots (i)$$
At place II,
$$T_2 = \dfrac{60}{15} = 2\pi\sqrt{\dfrac{I}{MB_{H_2}}} \quad \dots (ii)$$
From equations (i) and (ii), we have
$$\left(\dfrac{4}{3}\right)^2 = \dfrac{B_{H_1}}{B_{H_2}}$$
or
$$\dfrac{B_{H_1}}{B_{H_2}} = \dfrac{16}{9}$$
As
$$B = B_H / \cos\theta,$$
$$\therefore \quad \dfrac{B_1}{B_2} = \dfrac{B_{H_1}}{B_{H_2}} \times \dfrac{\cos 60°}{\cos 30°}$$
$$= \dfrac{16}{9} \times \dfrac{1/2}{\sqrt{3}/2} = \dfrac{16}{9\sqrt{3}} \qquad \textbf{Ans.}$$

2.

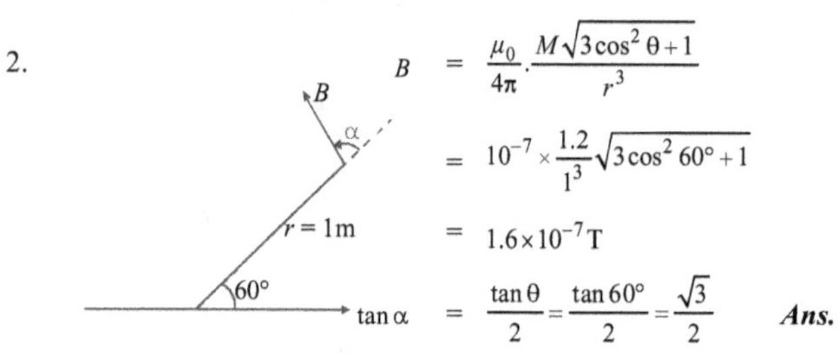

$$B = \frac{\mu_0}{4\pi}\cdot\frac{M\sqrt{3\cos^2\theta+1}}{r^3}$$

$$= 10^{-7}\times\frac{1.2}{1^3}\sqrt{3\cos^2 60°+1}$$

$$= 1.6\times10^{-7}\,\text{T}$$

$$\tan\alpha = \frac{\tan\theta}{2}=\frac{\tan 60°}{2}=\frac{\sqrt{3}}{2} \qquad \textbf{\textit{Ans.}}$$

3. The magnetic field at the axis of the magnet is given by,

$$B = \frac{\mu_0}{4\pi}\cdot\frac{2Mr}{\left[r^2-\dfrac{\ell^2}{4}\right]^2}$$

$$= 10^{-7}\times\frac{2\times(12\times0.1)\times0.20}{\left[(0.2)^2-\dfrac{(0.1)^2}{4}\right]^2}$$

$$= 3.4\times10^{-5}\,\text{T} \qquad \textbf{\textit{Ans.}}$$

4. Using the relation $\cot^2\theta = \cot^2\theta_1+\cot^2\theta_2$, we have

$$\cot^2 45° = \cot^2 60°+\cot^2\theta_2$$

$$\therefore\qquad \cot\theta_2 = 0.816 \qquad \textbf{\textit{Ans.}}$$

5. For deflection galvanometer, with short magnet, we can write

$$\frac{\tan\theta_1}{\tan\theta_2} = \frac{r_2^3}{r_1^3}$$

or

$$\frac{\tan 60°}{\tan\theta_2} = (2)^3$$

$$\therefore\qquad \tan\theta_2 = \frac{\sqrt{3}}{8} \qquad \textbf{\textit{Ans.}}$$

6. For moving coil galvanometer, we have

$$i = \left[\frac{C}{NBA}\right]\alpha$$

$$\therefore\qquad C = \frac{iNBA}{\alpha}$$

$$= \frac{(10\times10^{-3})\times(100)\times(0.01)\times(2\times10^{-4})}{0.05}$$

$$= 4.0\times10^{-5}\ \text{N-m/rad}$$

7. For long bar magnet, we can write,

$$F = \frac{\mu_0}{4\pi}\frac{m\times m}{r^2} = 10^{-7}\times\frac{(10)^2}{0.02^2}$$

$$= 2.5\times10^{-2}\ N \qquad \textbf{\textit{Ans.}}$$

8. Magnetic field due to a bar magnet in the broad-side on position is given by

$$B = \frac{\mu_0}{4\pi}\frac{M}{\left[r^2+\dfrac{\ell^2}{4}\right]^{3/2}} \quad ;\ M=m\ell.$$

After substituting the values and simplifying we get

$$B = 6\times10^{-5}\ \text{A-m}$$

9. (a) The total magnetic moment per unit volume. i.e., magnetisation

$$I = \frac{(8.52\times10^{28})\times(2\times9.27\times10^{-24})}{1}$$

$$= 1.58\times10^6\ \text{A/m}$$

(b) The magnetic field due to magnetisation

$$B_m = \mu_0 I$$

$$= (4\pi\times10^{-7})\times(1.58\times10^6)$$

$$= 2.0\ \text{T} \qquad \textbf{\textit{Ans.}}$$

10. We know that

$$\mu_r = 1+x$$

$$= 1+5500 = 5501$$

$$\therefore\qquad \mu = \mu_r\mu_0 = (5501)\times(4\pi\times10^{-7})$$

$$= 6.9\times10^{-3} \qquad \textbf{\textit{Ans}}$$

11. (b) The field is entering into the surface so flux is negative.
(c) Explanation is given in the answer.

12. The volume of the needle,

$$V = (3\times10^{-2})\times(1\times10^{-3})\times(0.5\times10^{-3})$$

$$= 1.5\times10^{-8}\ \text{m}^3$$

The mass of the needle

$$= \rho V$$

$$= 7900\times1.5\times10^{-8}$$

$$= 1.183\times10^{-4}\ \text{kg}$$

The number of atoms in the needle

$$= \left[\frac{1.185\times10^{-4}}{56\times10^{-3}}\right]\times6.02\times10^{23}$$

$$= 1.27\times10^{21}$$

The needle's dipole moment

$$M = \frac{1}{10}(1.27\times10^{21})\times(2.1\times10^{-23})$$

$$= 2.7\times10^{-3}\ \text{J/T} \qquad \textbf{\textit{Ans.}}$$

13. We know that

$$T_1 = 2\pi\sqrt{\frac{T}{MB_{H_1}}} \qquad \text{... (i)}$$

Where

$$B_{H_1} = 24\times10^{-6}\ \text{T}$$

The magnetic field produced by, wire

$$B = \frac{\mu_0}{2\pi}\cdot\frac{i}{r}$$

$$= (2\times10^{-7})\times\frac{(18)}{0.20}$$

$$= 1.8\times10^{-6}\ \text{T}$$

Now

$$B_{H_2} = B_{H_1}+B = 42\times10^{-6}\ \text{T}$$

$$T_2 = 2\pi\sqrt{\frac{I}{MBH_2}} \qquad \text{... (ii)}$$

Using equations (i) and (ii), and substituting the values, we get

$$T_2 = 0.076\ \text{s} \qquad \textbf{\textit{Ans.}}$$

14. For the needle to stay in any position

$$B = B_H$$

or

$$\frac{\mu_0}{4\pi}\cdot\frac{2M}{r^3} = B_H$$

$$\therefore\qquad r = \left[\frac{\mu_0}{4n}\cdot\frac{2M}{B_H}\right]^{1/3}$$

After substituting the values and simplifying we get,

$$r = 2.0\ \text{cm}$$

CHAPTER 8

Electromagnetic Induction (485 - 576)

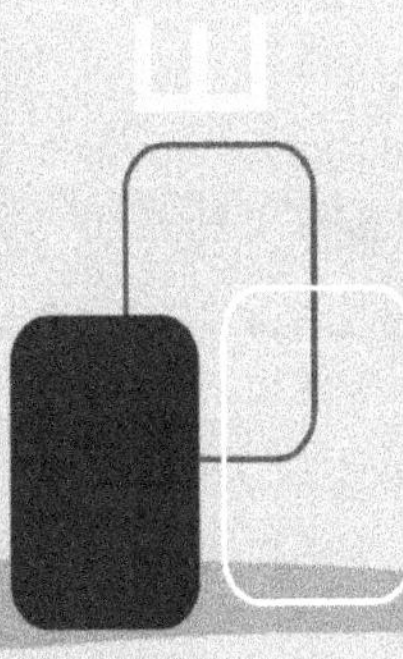

8.1 ELECTROMAGNETIC INDUCTION : AN INTRODUCTION

In 1831, **Michael Faraday** suggested that if electricity moving in a wire produces magnetism, then opposite might be true; a magnet moving near a wire could produce electricity. He moved a magnet in and out of a coil of wire, and electricity flowed in the coil. This is called **electromagnetic induction**. The electric current flows only while the magnetic field moves or varies. If the magnet and coil are still, no current flows in the coil. Electromagnetic induction is used in hundreds of machines and devices, like electric motors, generators etc. The energy needed to turn the magnet is provided by energy sources such as steam, moving water or the wind etc.

8.2 MAGNETIC FLUX

In fluid mechanics, we defined a quantity; rate of flow, $Q = vA\cos\theta$, in electrostatics; an electric flux, $\phi_e = EA\cos\theta$. On the same way here we can define magnetic flux. The magnetic flux through small element of surface $d\vec{A}$ is defined as;

$$d\phi_B = B_\perp dA$$
$$= (B\cos\theta)dA$$
$$= \vec{B}\cdot d\vec{A}$$

The total magnetic flux through the surface

$$\phi_B = \int \vec{B}\cdot d\vec{A}.$$

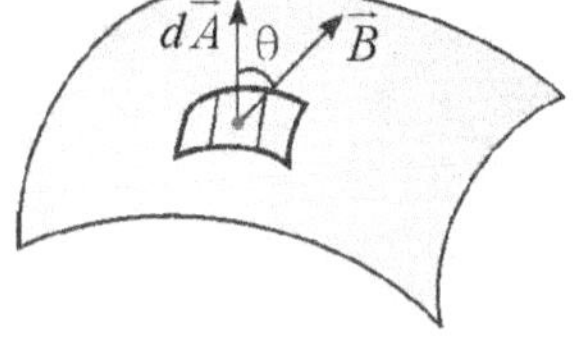

Fig. 8.1

When $\vec{B}$ is uniform over a plane surface with total area A,

$$\phi_B = B_\perp A = BA\cos\theta.$$

More about ϕ_B

1. We may take $d\vec{A}$ positive, pointing out of the surface.
2. Magnetic flux is a scalar quantity, but it may be negative.
3. Its SI unit is tesla-m^2, which is called the weber. Thus
$$1 \text{ weber} = 1\text{ Wb} = 1\text{T-m}^2.$$
4. If the elemental area of $d\vec{A}$ is right angles to the field lines, then

$$B = \frac{d\phi_B}{dA}$$

Thus, the magnetic field is equal to the flux per unit surface area at right angle to the magnetic field, and so it is also called magnetic flux density. Its unit is weber/m^2 (Wb/m^2).

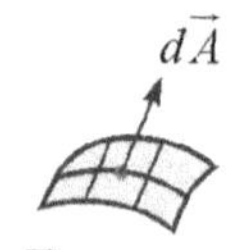

$d\vec{A}$ positive

(a)

$d\vec{A}$ positive

(b)

Fig. 8.2

5. 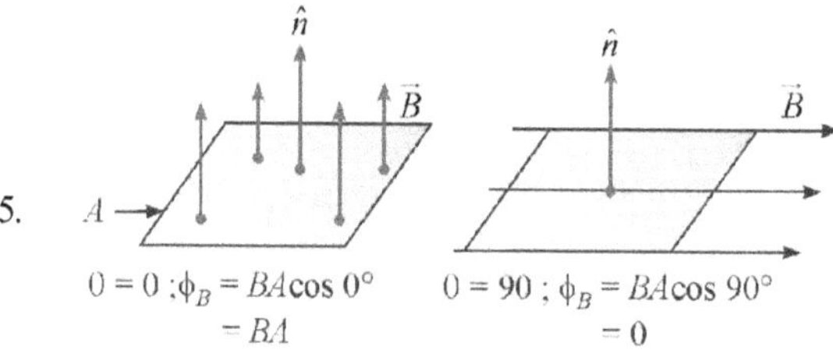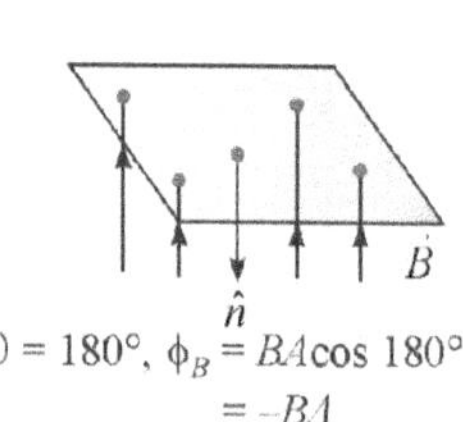

Fig. 8.3

8.3 FARADAY'S LAW OF EMI

According to Faraday, whenever there is change in magnetic flux linked with the circuit, there induces an emf in the circuit. The rate of change of magnetic flux is equal to the induced emf. Thus

$$e = -\frac{d\phi_B}{dt}.$$

Here negative sign indicates that induced emf opposes the change in flux.

Total magnetic flux (Magnetic-flux linkage)

If a closed loop in which an emf is induced contains not one but N turns, then induced emf e will be equal to the sum of the emfs induced in each turn. And if the magnetic flux associated by each turn is the same and equal to ϕ_B, the total flux ϕ_{Total} through the surface extended over such a complex loop can be represented by

$$\phi_{Total} = N\phi_B.$$

This quantity is called the total magnetic flux, or the magnetic flux-linkage. In this case, the emf induced in the loop is defined by the formula

$$e = -\frac{d\phi_{Total}}{dt} = -N\frac{d\phi_B}{dt}.$$

Note:

1. When the field $\vec{B}$ varies with time as well as the configuration or arrangement of the loop in the field, the induced emf should be calculated by taking in to consideration of two factors. So induced emf can be written as :

$$e = \oint \vec{E} \cdot d\vec{\ell} = -\frac{\partial \phi}{\partial t} + \oint \left[\vec{v} \times \vec{B}\right] \cdot d\vec{\ell}$$

   Here the first term is due to the time variation of the magnetic field, while the second is due to the motion of the loop.

2. When magnetic field changes with both time and space:

$$e = -\frac{d\phi_B}{dt} = -\left[\frac{\partial \phi_B}{\partial t} + \frac{\partial \phi_B}{\partial x}\frac{\partial x}{\partial t}\right] = -A\left[\frac{\partial B}{\partial t} + \frac{\partial B}{\partial x}v\right]$$

3. An emf is always induced whenever there is change in magnetic flux in the circuit. But current is induced only in closed circuit.

8.4 LENZ'S LAW

Lenz's law is used to get the direction of induced current. Which means that we can apply it directly only to a closed conducting loop. According to Lenz's law an induced current in a closed conducting loop will appear in such a direction that opposes the change which produces it.

More about Lenz's law

Whether we push the magnet towards the loop or pull it out from the loop, we shall always experience a resisting force and thus will have to do work. From the principle of conservation of energy, this work must exactly equal to the thermal energy that appears in the coil because there are only two energy transfer that take place in this isolated system. The faster we move the magnet, the more rapidly we do work, and thus greater the rate of production of thermal energy in the coil. If we cut the loop and then do experiment, there will be no induced current, no thermal energy, no resisting force on the magnet and no work requires to move it.

To understand Lenz's law, let us apply it to a specific case; namely, the first of Faraday's experiments.

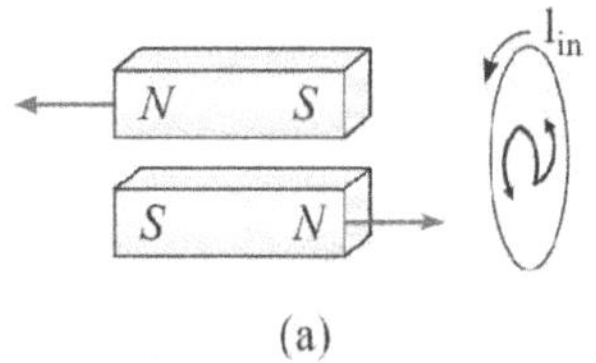

(a)

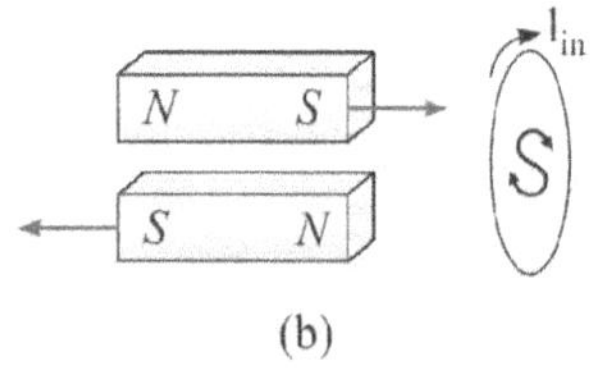

(b)

Fig. 8.4

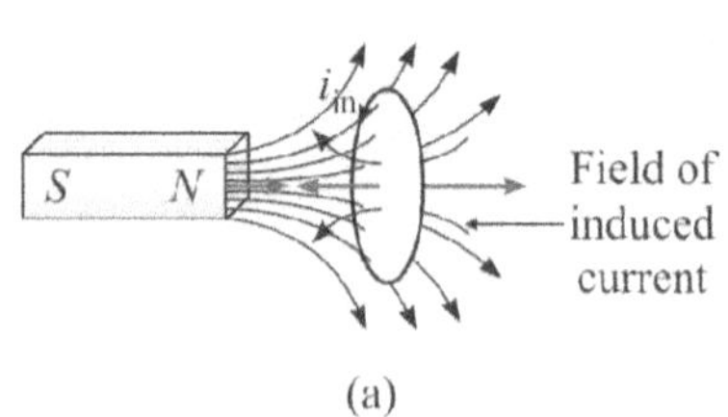

(a)

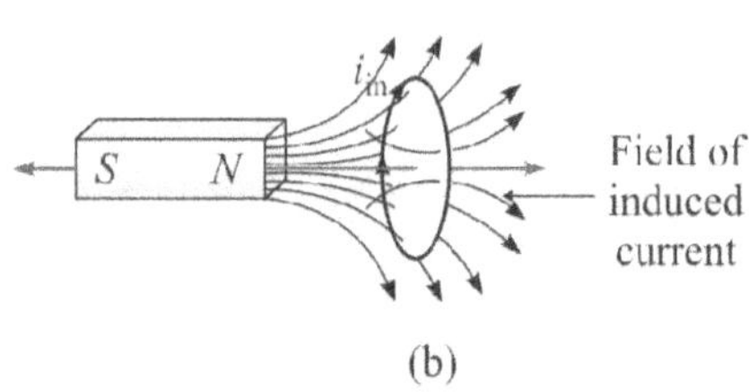

(b)

Fig. 8.5

Lenz's law 1 :

Let us consider a magnet with its north pole facing a closed conducting loop moves towards it or with the south face moves away from it.

When magnet moves towards the closed loop, the near face of loop becomes north, so that it repels the incoming magnet (according to Lenz's law), and therefore the induced current in the loop will induce in counter clockwise direction.

If the magnet moves away from the closed loop with its N-pole facing it, the facing side of the loop behaves like south pole and opposes the receding magnet. The direction of induced current in the loop will be clockwise.

Lenz's law 2 :

When the magnet moves with north pole towards the closed conducting loop, the flux through the loop increases, the induced current, therefore will be in such a direction; its magnetic field produces flux in opposite to the flux of the magnet.

When magnet with its north pole moves away from the loop, the flux through the loop decreases. The induced current in the loop, try to compensate this decrease in flux and therefore will be in the direction as shown in the figure.

Note :

1. In the experiment, we have moved the magnet, but the same effect will be observed if we move the loop and keep the magnet at rest.
2. The induced magnetic field does not oppose the magnetic field of the magnet but it opposes the change in this field.

Flux change and induced emf

The magnetic flux, $\phi = BA\cos\theta$ has three variables, and so flux will change if either of them changes. Thus :

(i) When B alone is changing, $\quad e = A\cos\theta\left(\dfrac{dB}{dt}\right).$

(ii) When A alone is changing, $\quad e = B\cos\theta\left(\dfrac{dA}{dt}\right).$

(iii) When θ alone is changing, $\quad e = BA\dfrac{d\cos\theta}{dt}.$

In case of closed loop, a current will induce. If R is the resistance of the loop, then induced current

$$i_{in} = \frac{e}{R} = \frac{\dfrac{d\phi}{dt}}{R}$$

The induced charge in the loop

$$dq = i_{in}\,dt = \left(\frac{\dfrac{d\phi}{dt}}{R}\right)dt = \frac{d\phi}{R}$$

or $\qquad \Delta q = \dfrac{\Delta\phi}{R}$

Ex. 1 A closed conducting loop is placed in a uniform magnetic field as shown in *fig. 8.6*. Find the direction of induced current in the loop when

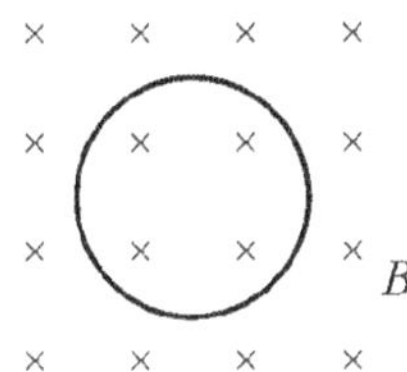

Fig. 8.6

(i)   magnetic field is increasing with time

(ii) magnetic field is decreasing with time.

Sol.

(i)   In case when field increases, the flux of which increases into the page and so the field of the induced current will be in upward direction. For this the current in the loop will be in counterclockwise direction.

(ii) The direction of induced current will be in clockwise.

Ex. 2 A closed conducting loop is placed in uniform magnetic field which points into the plane of the loop. What will be the direction of induced current when loop is expanding.

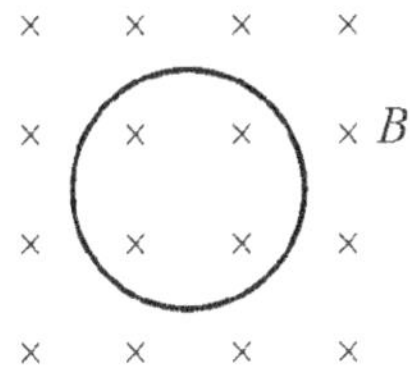

Fig. 8.7

Sol.

When area of the loop increases, the flux will increase into the page, and so the field of induced current must be out of the page. For this the direction of induced current will be counterclockwise.

Ex. 3 Two closed conducting loops are placed parallel to each other. The current in one of the loops starts increasing. Will the loops attract or repel ?

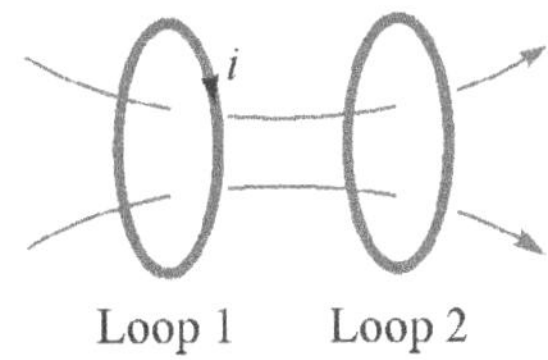

Fig. 8.8

Sol.

When current in first loop increases, the flux associated in second loop is also increases. To compensate this increase in flux the loops must move away from each other; means they will repel each other.

Ex. 4 In which case the flux changes and an emf induces?

Fig. 8.9

(i)   If magnet is rotated about its axis in the loop.

(ii) Loop is placed at rest in uniform field.

(iii) A closed loop moves in uniform field.

(iv) Loop is placed with its axis parallel to a current carrying conductor.

Sol.

The flux change in each case is zero, and so induced emf is zero.

Ex. 5 *Figure 8.10* shows a conducting loop consisting of a half circle of radius $r = 0.20$ m and three straight sections. The half-circles lies in a uniform magnetic field $\vec{B}$ that is directed out of the page; the field magnitude is given by $B = t^2 + 2t + 5$, with B in tesla and t in second. An ideal battery with emf $\xi = 2V$ is connected to the loop. The resistance of the loop is $2\,\Omega$.

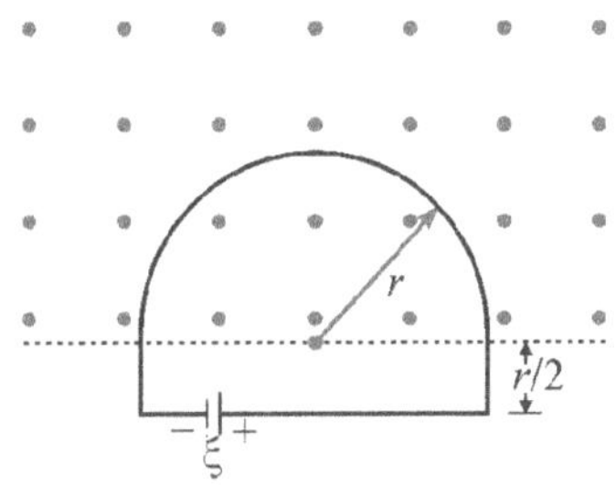

Fig. 8.10

(a)   What are the magnitude and direction of the emf induced around the loop by field at $t = 10$s ?

(b)   What is the current in the loop at $t = 10$s ?

Sol.

(a)   The flux of the field through the half loop (upto the field)

$$\phi = BA = \frac{\pi r^2}{2}\left(t^2 + 2t + 5\right)$$

According to Faraday's law

$$|e| = \frac{d\phi}{dt} = \frac{\pi r^2}{2}\frac{d}{dt}(t^2 + 2t + 5)$$

$$= \frac{\pi r^2}{2}\left(2t + 2\right)$$

$$= \frac{\pi(0.2)^2\left(2 \times 10 + 2\right)}{2}$$

$$= 1.38\ V. \qquad\qquad Ans.$$

(b) The induced emf causes the current in clockwise direction around the loop; the battery emf ξ tends to drive a current in counter clockwise direction. Because ξ_{bat} is greater than ξ_{ind}, and so the net emf ξ_{net} is counterclockwise. Thus

$$i = \frac{\xi_{net}}{R} = \frac{\xi_{bat} - \xi_{ind}}{R}$$

$$= \frac{2 - 1.38}{2}$$

$$= 0.31\,A \qquad \textbf{Ans.}$$

Ex. 6 Space is divided by the line *AD* into two regions. Region I is field free and region II has a uniform magnetic field *B* directed into the plane of the paper. *ACD* is a semicircular conducting loop of radius r with centre at *O*, the plane of the loop being in the plane of the paper. The loop is now made to rotate with a constant angular velocity ω about an axis passing through *O* and perpendicular to plane of paper. The effective resistance of the loop is *R*.

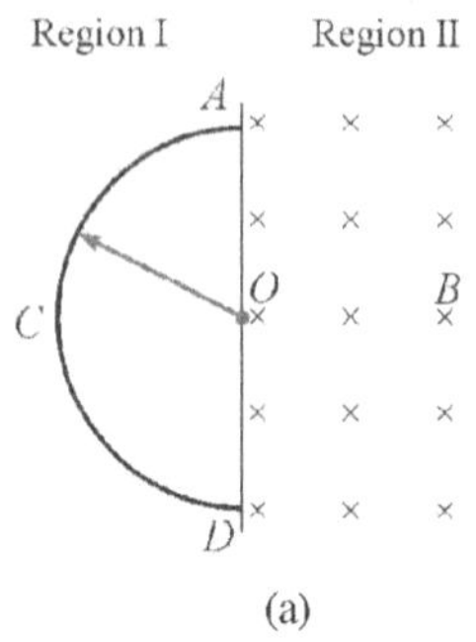
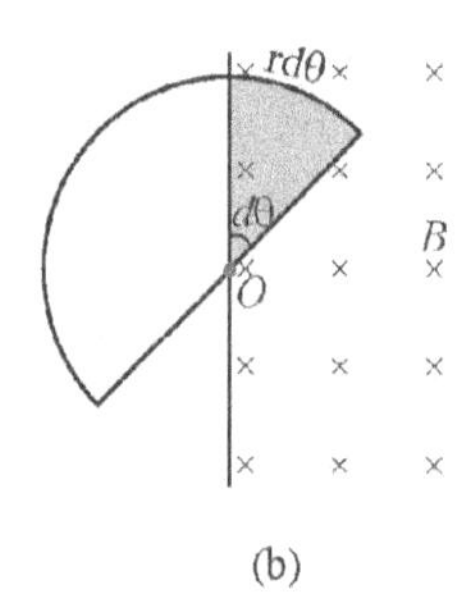

(a)   (b)

Fig. 8.11

(i) Obtain an expression for the magnitude of induced current in the loop.

(ii) Show the direction of current when the loop is entering into region II.

(iii) Plot a graph between the induced emf and the time of rotation for two periods of rotation.

Sol.

(i) Suppose the loop is rotated by small angle $d\theta$ in time dt. As it is rotated with constant angular velocity, so $d\theta = \omega dt$. The area of the loop into the field, $dA = \frac{1}{2}r\left(rd\theta\right) = \frac{r^2}{2}d\theta$. The magnetic flux through this area

$$d\phi = BdA$$

$$= B\frac{r^2}{2}d\theta$$

According to Faraday's law, induced emf

$$e = -\frac{d\phi}{dt} = -\frac{Br^2}{2}\frac{d\theta}{dt}$$

As $$\frac{d\theta}{dt} = \omega$$

$$\therefore \qquad |e| = \frac{Br^2}{2}\omega\,. \qquad \textbf{Ans.}$$

(ii) When loop enters into the magnetic field, the flux into it increases. By Lenz's law the induced current in the loop will be anticlockwise so as to compensate the increasing flux. After each $\frac{T}{2}$ the loop starts coming out from the magnetic field, and so the direction of current reverses, i.e., it becomes clockwise.

(iii) The magnitude of the induced emf $e = \frac{Br^2\omega}{2}$ is constant. It changes in sign each after $\frac{T}{2} = \frac{2\pi}{\omega}\frac{1}{2} = \frac{\pi}{\omega}$. The graph between induced emf and time is shown in *fig. 8.12*.

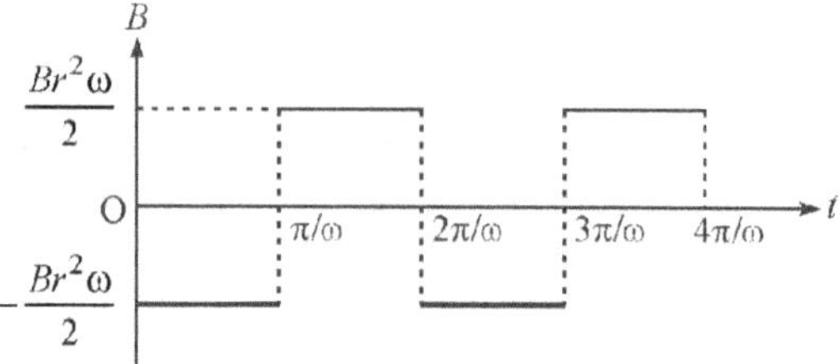

Fig. 8.12

Ex. 7 A plane loop shown in *fig. 8.13* is shaped as two squares with sides $a = 0.20$ m and $b = 0.10$ *m* and is introduced into a uniform magnetic field at right angles to the loop's plane.

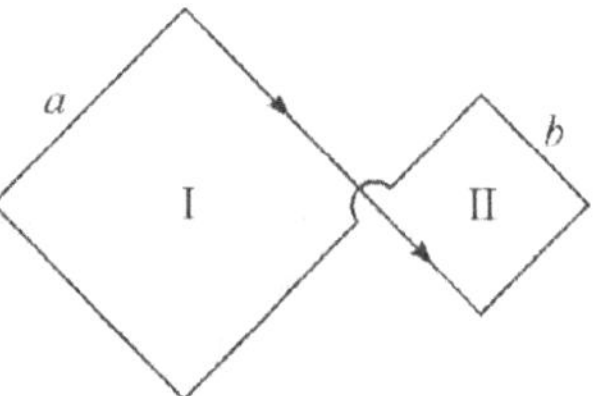

Fig. 8.13

The magnetic induction varies with time as $B = B_0 \sin\omega t$ where $B_0 = 10mT$ and $\omega = 100$ rad/s. Find the amplitude of current induced in the loop if the resistance per unit length is equal to $\rho = 50$ milli ohm/m. The inductance of the loop is negligible.

Sol.

The loops are connected in such a way that if the current is clockwise in I loop, then it will be anticlockwise in the II loop (see figure). The emf in loop I

$$e_1 = \frac{d\phi}{dt} = \frac{d\left(Ba^2\right)}{dt}$$

$$= a^2\frac{d}{dt}\left(B_0\sin\omega t\right)$$

$$= B_0 a^2\omega\cos\omega t$$

Similarly, the emf in the II loop,

$$e_2 = \frac{d\left(Bb^2\right)}{dt} = b^2 \frac{d}{dt}\left(B_0 \sin \omega t\right)$$

$$= B_0 b^2 \omega \cos \omega t$$

The net emf in the circuit

$$e_{net} = e_1 - e_2$$

$$= B_0\left(a^2 - b^2\right)\omega \cos \omega t.$$

Given resistance per unit length of the loop wire is ρ, thus total resistance

$$R = 4(a+b)\rho.$$

The induced current

$$i = \frac{e_{net}}{R}$$

$$= \frac{B_0\left(a^2 - b^2\right)\omega \cos \omega t}{4\left(a+b\right)\rho}$$

$$= \frac{B_0\left(a-b\right)\omega \cos \alpha}{4\rho}$$

The amplitude of the current

$$i_0 = \frac{B_0\left(a-b\right)\omega}{4\rho}$$

On substituting the values given, $i_0 = 0.5$ A. **Ans.**

Ex. 8 *Figure 8.14 illustrated plane figures made of thin conductors are located in a uniform magnetic field directed away from a reader beyond the plane of the drawing. The magnetic induction starts diminishing. Find how the currents induced in these loops are directed.*

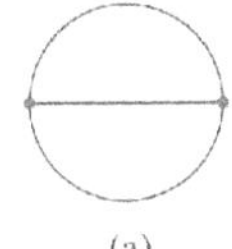  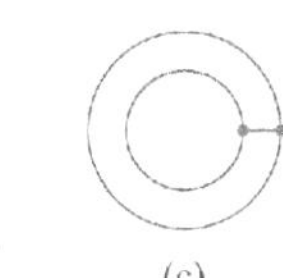 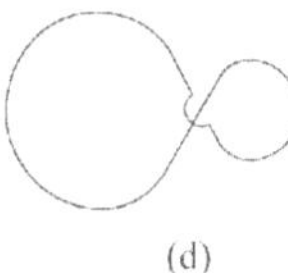

    (a)   (b)   (c)   (d)

Fig. 8.14

Sol.

As magnetic field is decreasing into the plane of the figure, so induced current will compensate this decrease by flowing in clockwise direction. Thus

(a) in round conductor the current flows clockwise, there is no current in the connector.

(b) in the outside conductor, clockwise;

(c) in both round conductors, clockwise : no current in the connector.

(d) in the left-hand of the figure eight, clockwise.

Ex. 9 A magnet falls into (a) closed conducting loop; (b) open conducting loop. Discuss the motion of the magnet.

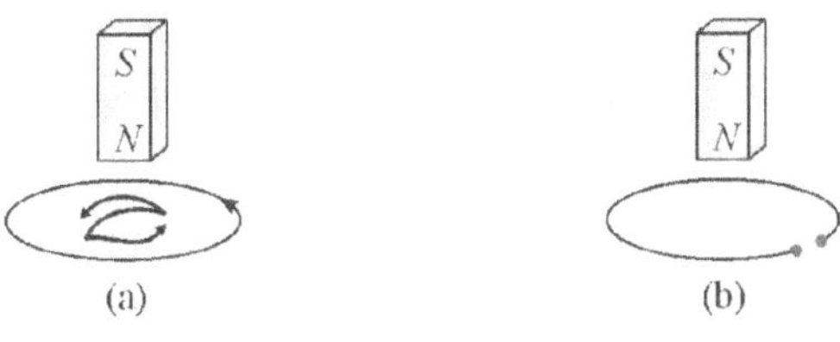

    (a)   (b)

Fig. 8.15

Sol.

(a) When magnet falls into the loop, the induced current in the loop will be in such a direction that the facing side of the loop opposes the incoming and outgoing magnet. So when north pole approaches towards the loop, the facing side of the loop becomes north and the acceleration of the magnet becomes less than g.

(b) If there is a cut in the loop and magnet falls into it, there will be no induced current in the loop and hence the acceleration of the magnet remains equal to g.

Ex. 10 Magnet falls into a long conducting tube. Discuss its motion.

Sol.

When magnet falls into the tube, the flux into it changes and so current will induce along its periphery. Because of the induced current the acceleration of falling magnet becomes less than g. The acceleration continuously decreases and becomes zero. There after magnet falls with constant velocity. This can be understand as; the tube can be assumed to be madeup of number of rings. Each ring decreases the acceleration of falling magnet and ultimately acceleration of magnet becomes zero. It means initially with the increasing of velocity of magnet, flux changes with increasing rate, and induced current increases in magnitude, which opposes the motion with greater force. After falling some distance the rate of change of flux becomes constant, which is enough to provide retarding force equal to weight of the magnet.

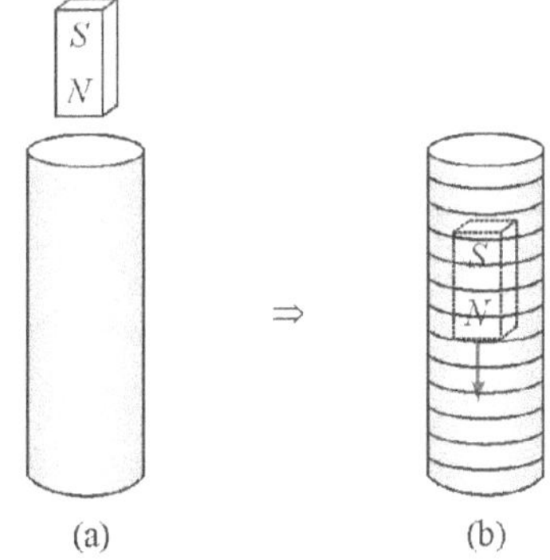

    (a)   (b)

Fig. 8.16

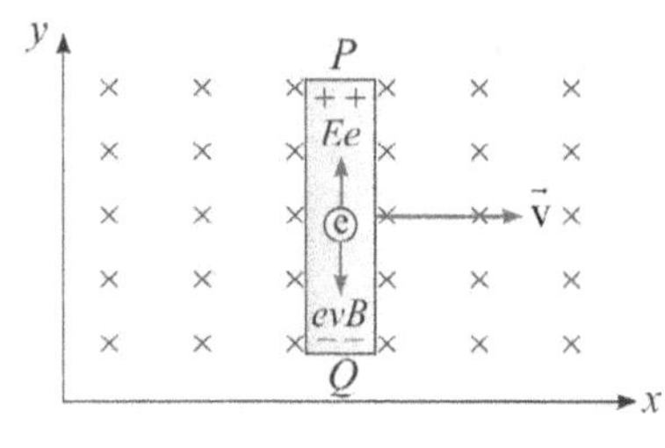

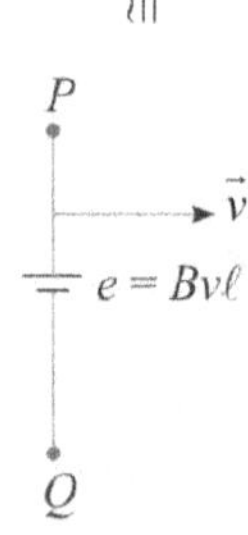

Fig. 8.17

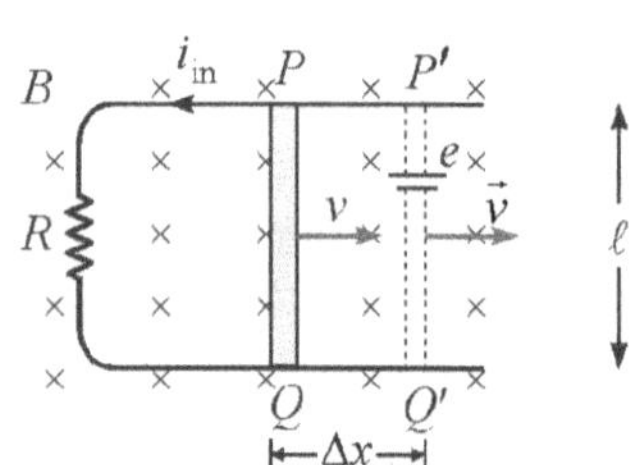

Fig. 8.18

8.5 Mechanism of EMI

Consider a conducting rod of length ℓ moving with constant velocity $\vec{v}$ which is perpendicular to a uniform magnetic field $\vec{B}$ directed into the plane of paper. Let the rod is moving toward right as shown in *fig. 8.17*. The free electrons also move to the right as they are trapped within the rod.

The magnetic field exerts force on the free electrons, $\vec{F}_m = -e\left(\vec{v} \times \vec{B}\right)$ so they move toward the end Q within the rod. The end P of the rod becomes positively charged while end Q becomes negatively charged, hence an electric field $\vec{E}$ is set up within the rod which exerts force on the free electrons in opposite to magnetic force. At equilibrium

$$\vec{F}_e + \vec{F}_m = 0$$

or

$$-e\vec{E} + \left(-e\right)\left(\vec{v} \times \vec{B}\right) = 0$$

or

$$\vec{E} = -\vec{v} \times \vec{B}$$

The induced emf across the rod

$$e = \int \vec{E} \cdot d\vec{\ell}$$

or

$$e = \int \left(\vec{v} \times \vec{B}\right) \cdot d\vec{\ell} \qquad \ldots(1)$$

In the case under consideration

$$e = \int \left[v\hat{i} \times B\left(-\hat{k}\right)\right] \cdot d\ell\,\hat{j}$$

$$\therefore \qquad e = vB\ell. \qquad \ldots(2)$$

Induced emf/current in moving conductor slides along a stationary U-shaped conductor

Method 1 : When conductor moves perpendicular to magnetic field, the charge carriers inside it experience magnetic force (qvB). When a charge q moves from Q to P through a distance ℓ, the work done by the force F is $W = F\ell = qvB\ell$

The emf is the work done per unit charge

$$\therefore \qquad e = \frac{W}{q} = vB\ell.$$

Method II : By Faraday's law

Let conductor PQ slides a distance Δx in time Δt, the change in magnetic flux in this time

$$\Delta \phi = B\Delta A = B(\ell \Delta x)$$

and

$$|e| = \frac{\Delta \phi}{\Delta t} = B\ell\left(\frac{\Delta x}{\Delta t}\right)$$

$$= B\ell v$$

1. Induced current

$$i_{in} = \frac{e}{R} = \frac{Bv\ell}{R}.$$

2. Magnetic force on the conductor : Conductor PQ experiences a force opposite to the direction of motion

$$F_m = Bi_{in}\ell = B\left(\frac{Bv\ell}{R}\right)\ell = \frac{B^2 v\ell^2}{R}$$

3.   Power dissipated in moving the conductor :

$$P_{\text{agent}} \;=\; \frac{dW}{dt} = \vec{F}_{\text{agent}} \cdot \vec{v} = \frac{B^2 v \ell^2}{R} \times v = \frac{B^2 v^2 \ell^2}{R}$$

4.   Electrical power : Electrical power dissipated through the resistance

$$P_{\text{thermal}} \;=\; i^2 R = \left(\frac{Bv\ell}{R}\right)^2 R = \frac{B^2 v^2 \ell^2}{R}$$

More about direction of induced current

Rule 1 :   The direction of induced current in a closed circuit with moving conductor can be obtained as follows : Place a positive charge on moving conductor, and then find direction of force on it by Fleming left hand rule. The charged particle will move in the direction of force, which will be the direction of induced current.

Rule 2 :   Direction of induced current can also be obtained by Fleming right hand rule. According to this, if middle finger, fore finger and thumb of right hand are held mutually perpendicular, then fore finger represents the direction of magnetic field, thumb represents the direction of velocity of the conductor; and middle finger will represent the direction of induced current.

Ex. 11 Find the induced emf across the ends of the conducting rod in the following situations. The length of the conductor is ℓ.

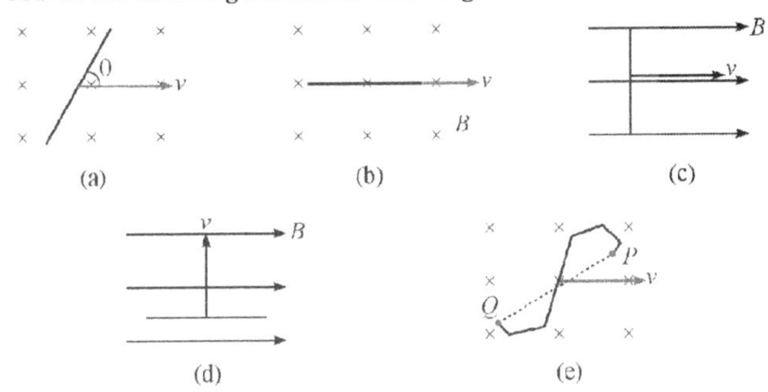

(a)   (b)   (c)

(d)   (e)

Fig. 8.19

Sol.

(a)   In this case we can make $\vec{v}$ perpendicular to length of the rod or $\vec{\ell}$ perpendicular to v. Thus

$$e \;=\; B(v\sin\theta)\,\ell \text{ or } Bv(\ell\sin\theta)$$

$$\;=\; Bv\ell\sin\theta \qquad\qquad Ans.$$

(b)   If we take the plane of motion of the rod as xy, then

$$e \;=\; \int\left[v\hat{i}\times\left(-B\hat{j}\right)\right]\cdot\left(\ell\hat{i}\right)$$

$$\;=\; -vB\ell\left(\hat{k}\cdot\hat{i}\right) = 0$$

(c) $$e \;=\; \int\left[v\hat{i}\times B\hat{i}\right]\cdot\left(\ell\hat{j}\right) = 0$$

(d) $$e \;=\; \int\left(v\hat{j}\times B\hat{i}\right)\cdot\ell\hat{i}$$

$$\;=\; vB\ell\left(-\hat{k}\cdot\hat{i}\right) = 0$$

(e)   If PQ line makes θ with the velocity vector, then

$$e \;=\; B(v\sin\theta)PQ.$$

Ex. 12   A closed loop of wire consists of a pair of equal semicircles, of radius 3.7 m, lying in mutually perpendicular planes. The loop was formed by folding a plane circular loop along a diameter until the two halves became perpendicular. A uniform magnetic field $\vec{B}$ of magnitude 76 mT is directed perpendicular to the fold diameter and makes equal angles (= 45°) with the planes of the semicircles as shown in *fig. 8.20*. The magnetic field is reduced to zero at a uniform rate during a time interval of 4.5 ms. Determine the magnitude of the induced emf and the direction of the induced current in the loop during this interval.

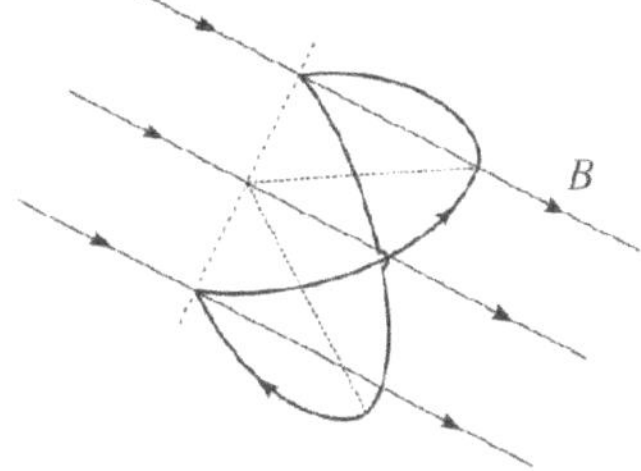

Fig. 8.20

Sol.

The change in flux in the given time interval Δt

$$\Delta\phi \;=\; \left(\pi r^2\right) B \cos 45°$$

By Faraday's law, the induced emf

$$e \;=\; \frac{\Delta\phi}{\Delta t} = \frac{\pi r^2 \, B\cos 45°}{\Delta t}$$

$$\;=\; \frac{\pi\left(3.7\right)^2 \times 76\times 10^{-3} \times \dfrac{1}{\sqrt{2}}}{4.5\times 10^{-3}}$$

$$\;=\; 51\times 10^{-3}\,\text{V} = 51\,\text{mV} \qquad Ans.$$

The direction of the current is clockwise (see figure).

Ex. 13 The dotted circle in *fig. 8.21* shows the region in which a permanent magnetic field $\vec{B}$ is localised (it is directed perpendicularly to the plane of the figure). This region in encircled by a fixed metallic ring R. By moving the sliding contacts to the other side of the ring, we introduce the magnetic flux ϕ into the closed contour containing a galvanometer G (1-initial position, 2-final position). Will the galvanometer show a current pulse ?

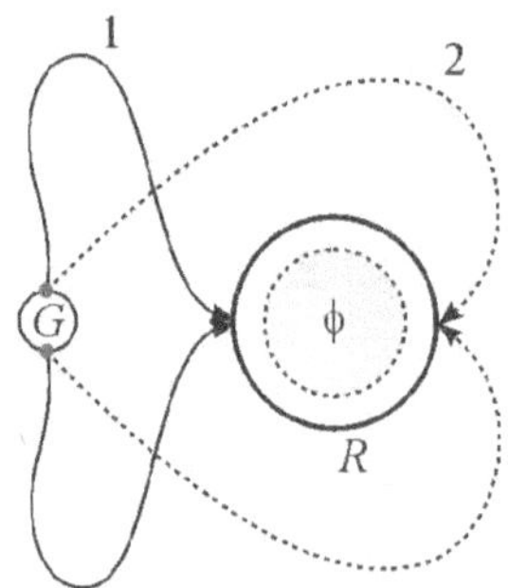

Fig. 8.21

Sol.

There will be no induced current. There is no current since in this case both $\dfrac{d\vec{B}}{dt}$ and Lorentz force are equal to zero : the magnetic field $\vec{B}$ is constant and the closed loop moves in the region where there is no magnetic field.

Ex. 14 (a) A small rectangular wire frame falls freely in the space between the wide poles of a sufficiently strong electromagnet fig. (a).

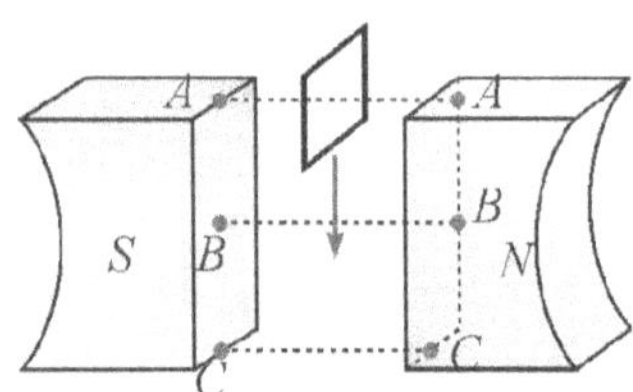

Fig. 8.22(a)

Show the direction of the currents induced in the frame when the middle of the frame passes through the positions A, B and C. How will the frame move in these sections ?

(b) A small pendulum consisting of a metal thread, a ball and a sharp point immersed in a cup of mercury fig. (b) makes part of an electric circuit. The pendulum is placed in the space between the broad poles of an electromagnet and swings in the plane perpendicular to the lines of force of the magnetic field. During the oscillations the sharp point of the pendulum point of the pendulum remains immersed in mercury.

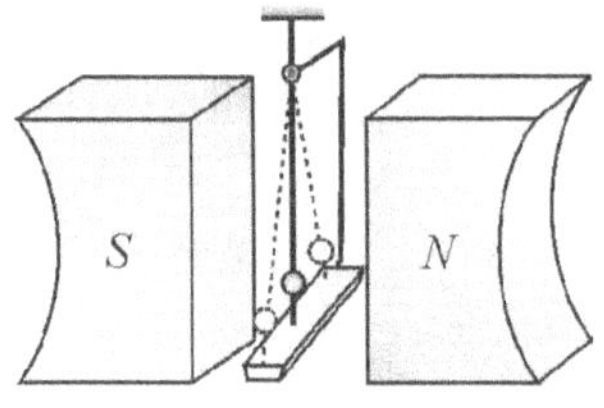

Fig. 8.22(b)

How will the magnetic field affect the motion of the pendulum ? What is the direction of the currents in the circuit of the pendulum ?

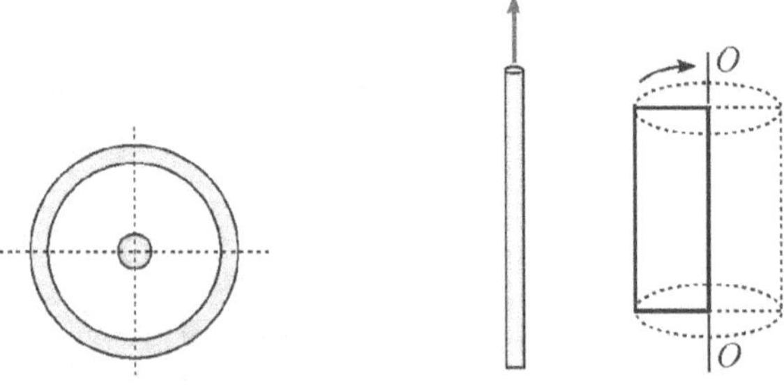

Fig. 8.22 (c)   *Fig. 8.22(d)*

(c) A copper wire connected to a closed circuit is surrounded by a thick iron shell fig. (c) and introduced together with the shell into the space between the poles of an electromagnet. The iron shell acts as a magnetic screen for the wire.

Will an e.m.f. be induced in the wire ?

(d) An aircraft flies along the meridian. Will the potentials at the ends of its wings be the same ?

Will the potential difference change if the aircraft flies in any other direction with the same velocity ?

(e) A rectangular wire frame rotates with a constant velocity around one of its sides parallel to a current carrying rectilinear conductor nearby fig. (e).

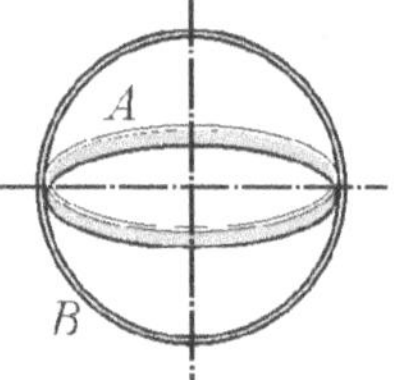

Fig. 8.22(e)

Indicate the positions in which the maximum and the minimum e.m.f.s will be induced in the frame.

(f) Two circular conductors are perpendicular to each other as shown in fig. (f).

Will a current be induced in the conductor A if the current is changed in the circuit B ?

Sol.

(a) As the frame passes through the position A the current will flow counterclockwise. When passing through the position B there is no change in flux through the coil and hence no induced current. In the position C the current will flow clockwise.

(b) As the pendulum oscillates, the periodic changes in the area enclosed by the circuit will induce currents in the latter. The induced currents will be directed so that their magnetic field compensates for the change in the flux of the magnetic lines of force penetrating the area of the circuit.

When the pendulum swings so as to increase the area enclosed by the circuit the current will flow counterclockwise, and if the motion is such as to decrease the area enclosed by the circuit, the current will be clockwise. The interaction of the magnetic field of induced currents with the field of a permanent magnet will further damp the oscillations of the pendulum.

(c) An emf will be induced because the introduction of the wire into the space between the poles of the magnet will change the flux passing through the area enclosed by the circuit.

(d) There will be p.d. across the ends of the wing. If B_v is the vertical component of earth field and v the horizontal velocity of the aircraft, then

$$e = B_v \, v\ell.$$

(e) The emf will be minimum when the frame arranges itself in the plane passing through the rectilinear conductor.

(f) There will be no induced current.

Ex. 15 Let us consider a closed conducting loop is moving in a uniform magnetic field, which is perpendicular to plane of the loop. Discuss about induced emf in the loop.

Sol.

Method I : (a)The magnetic flux through the loop is $\phi_B = BA$. Till the loop remain entirely inside the field, the flux will not change and so the net induced emf in the loop will be zero.

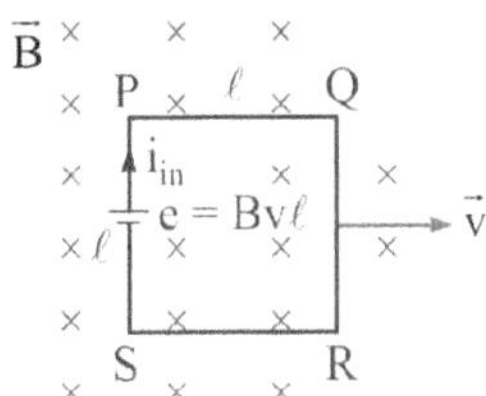

Fig. 8.23

Method II : We can split the loop into its four sides as shown in *fig. 8.24*. The induced emf across side PQ and SR is zero, while induced emf across PS and QR is $e = Bv\ell$. For the closed loop $PQRS$, the net emf becomes, $e - e = 0$.

Fig. 8.24

8.6 ROTATING CONDUCTOR

1. **Rod rotating in uniform magnetic field**

Consider a rod of length ℓ is rotating about an axis passing through one of its ends

with constant angular velocity ω in an uniform magnetic field $\vec{B}$ as shown in *fig. 8.27*.

Induced emf across the element

$$(de) = Bv_x (dx)$$
$$= B(\omega x)dx$$

Emf across the entire rod

$$e = \int_0^\ell B\omega \, x \, dx$$

$$e = V_P - V_Q = \frac{B\omega \ell^2}{2}$$

(b) Closed conducting loop coming out from the magnetic field.: When one of its sides QR comes out of the field, the emf across PQ, QR and RS are zero. But there is induced emf across PS, which is $e = Bv\ell$. So the net induced emf across the loop is also e. The direction of induced current in the loop will be clockwise.

(c) Closed conducting loop coming out of the uniform magnetic field, but velocity vector is perpendicular to one of its diagonals.

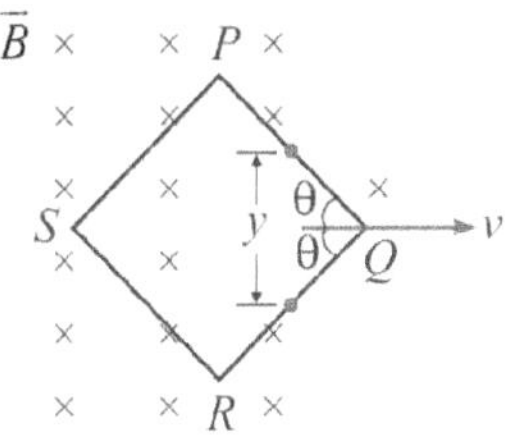

Fig. 8.25

The induced emf across the loop $e = Bvy$. As the loop is moving to the right, y increases and therefore induced emf increases and becomes maximum $e_{max} = Bv \times (PR)$. There after induced emf starts decreasing and becomes zero when entire loop comes out of the field.

(d) In the case shown in *fig. 8.26*, the induced emf across the ends of the conductor

$$e = Bv\left(\ell_1 \sin\theta_1 + \ell_2 \sin\theta_2\right)$$

Fig. 8.26

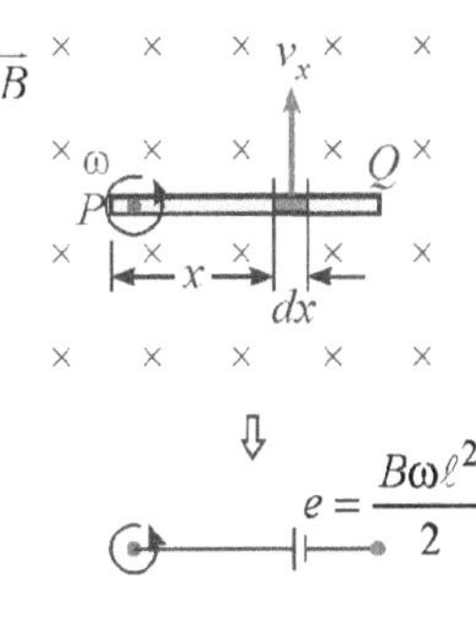

Fig. 8.27

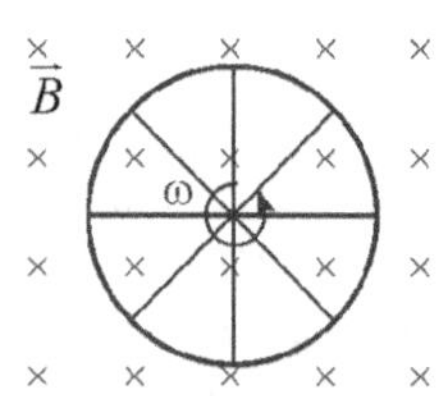

Fig. 8.28

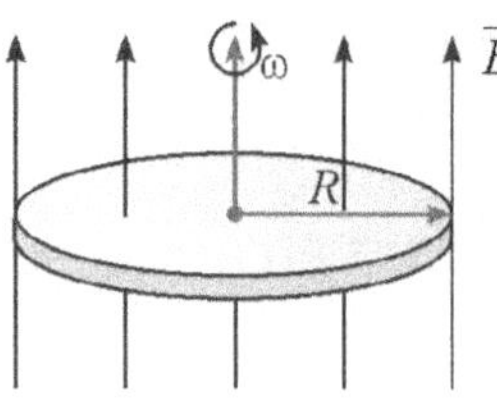

Fig. 8.29

2. **Cycle wheel**

Flux cutting by each metal spoke is same. Each spoke becomes cell of emf $e = \dfrac{B\omega\ell^2}{2}$. All such cells are in parallel fasnion, therefore $e_{net} = e$. Each point on the periphery of wheel has same potential.

3. **Faraday disc dynamo :** A metal disc can be assumed to be madeup of number of radial conductors. The emf induced across each conductor is $e = \dfrac{B\omega R^2}{2}$. All such conductors behave like a number of cells in parallel. Therefore

$$e_{net} \;=\; e = \frac{B\omega R^2}{2}.$$

Note: The induced emf in a rotating conductor does not depend on the shape of the conductor.

Ex. 16   A conducting rod PQ is rotated in a magnetic field about an axis passing through O. The one end of the rod is at a distance a and other end is at a distance b from O. Find induced emf across the ends of the rod.

Sol.

The induced emf across the element of length dx is

$$de \;=\; Bv_x\,dx = B(\omega x)\,dx.$$

Fig. 8.30

The emf across the whole rod

$$e \;=\; B\omega \int_a^b x\,dx$$

$$=\; \frac{B\omega\left(b^2 - a^2\right)}{2}. \qquad \textbf{Ans.}$$

Ex. 17   In *fig. 8.31* shows a bent rod rotating about its end O in a plane perpendicular to the magnetic field $\vec{B}$. The part OA of the rod is non-conducting while the part AB is conducting. Find the induced emf between the ends A and B.

Sol.   Suppose straight length of the rod is ℓ. The distance of the end B from O

$$OB^2 \;=\; OA^2 + \left(2R\right)^2 = \ell^2 + \left(2R\right)^2$$

Fig. 8.31

The potential difference between A and B can be calculated as :

$$V_A - V_B \;=\; \left(V_O - V_B\right) - \left(V_O - V_A\right) \qquad ...(i)$$

Here

$$V_O - V_B \;=\; \frac{B\omega\left(OB\right)^2}{2} = \frac{B\omega}{2}\left[\ell^2 + 4R^2\right]$$

and

$$V_O - V_A \;=\; \frac{B\omega}{2}\left(OA\right)^2 = \frac{B\omega\ell^2}{2}.$$

Substituting these values in equation (i), we get

$$V_A - V_B \;=\; \frac{B\omega}{2}\left[\left(\ell^2 + 4R^2\right) - \ell^2\right]$$

$$=\; \frac{B\omega}{2} \times 4R^2 = 2B\omega R^2. \qquad \textbf{Ans.}$$

The result obtained will remain same if conductor AB is straight.

Ex. 18 A uniform wire of resistance per unit length λ is bent into a semicircle of radius a. The wire rotates with angular velocity ω in a horizontal plane about a vertical axis passing through C. A uniform magnetic field B exists in space in a direction perpendicular to paper inwards.

(a)   Calculate potential difference between points A and D. Which point is at higher potential ?

(b)   If points A and D are connected by a conducting wire of zero resistance, then find the potential difference between A and C.

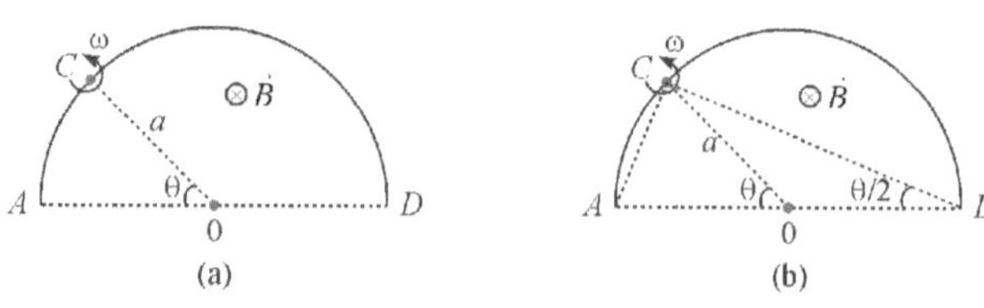

Fig. 8.32

Sol.

(a) The distance of end A from C,

$$AC = 2a\sin\frac{\theta}{2}$$

The distance of end D from C,

$$CD = 2a\cos\frac{\theta}{2}$$

The potential differences :

$$V_C - V_A = \frac{B\omega}{2}(AC)^2$$

and

$$V_C - V_D = \frac{B\omega}{2}(CD)^2$$

Thus $V_A - V_D$

$$= \left(V_C - V_D\right) - \left(V_C - V_A\right)$$

$$= \frac{B\omega}{2}\left[CD^2 - AC^2\right]$$

$$= \frac{B\omega}{2}\left[\left(2a\cos\frac{\theta}{2}\right)^2 - \left(2a\sin\frac{\theta}{2}\right)^2\right]$$

$$= \frac{B\omega \times (2a)^2}{2}\left[\cos^2\frac{\theta}{2} - \sin^2\frac{\theta}{2}\right]$$

$$= 2B\omega a^2 \cos\theta \qquad \textit{Ans.}$$

(b) When A and D are connected together, the current starts flowing from A towards B. The resistance of the loop

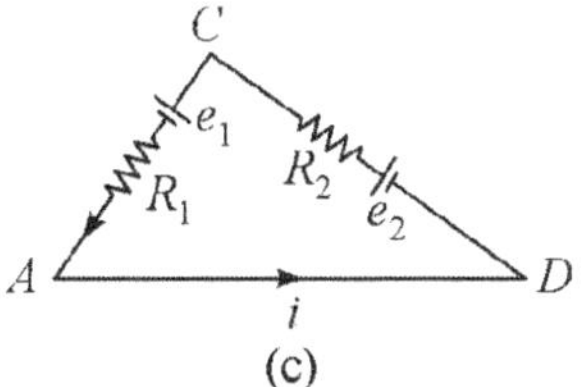

(c)

Fig. 8.33

$$R = (\text{length of wire } AD) \times \lambda$$
$$= \pi a \lambda.$$

Thus current in the closed loop,

$$i = \frac{V_A - V_D}{R}$$

$$= \frac{2B\omega a^2 \cos\theta}{\pi a \lambda} = \frac{2B\omega a \cos\theta}{\pi \lambda}. \quad \textit{Ans.}$$

The equivalent circuit is shown in *fig. 8.33* (c).
The resistance $R_1 = (a\theta)\lambda$.
The p.d. between A and C now becomes
$$V_A - V_C = e_1 + iR_1$$

$$= 2B\omega a^2 \sin^2\left(\frac{\theta}{2}\right) + \frac{2B\omega a \cos\theta}{\pi \lambda}(a\theta\lambda)$$

$$= 2B\omega a^2\left[\sin^2\frac{\theta}{2} + \frac{\theta}{\pi}\cos\theta\right] \quad \textit{Ans.}$$

8.7 INDUCED ELECTRIC FIELD

Consider a metal ring is placed in a uniform external magnetic field as shown in *fig. 8.34* (a). The field extends upto cylindrical region of radius R. If we increase the intensity of the field, the magnetic flux through the ring will then change and by Faraday's law an induced emf and thus induced current will flow in the ring. If there is a current in the metal ring, an electric field must be present at various points within the ring, and it must have been produced by the changing magnetic flux. This induced electric field E_n is just as real as an electric field by static charges. Thus we can say that changing magnetic field produces an electric field.

If we replace the metal ring by a hypothetical circular path of radius r and magnetic field is increasing at the constant rate dB/dt, the electric field induces at various points around the circular path. Due to symmetry it will be tangent to each point of the path (see *fig. 8.34* b).

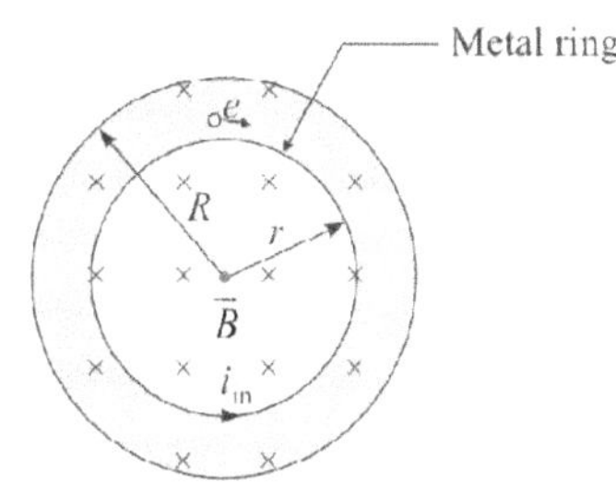

(a) If the magnetic field increases at a steady rate, a constant induced current appears in the metal ring.

Another form of Faraday's law

If $\vec{E}_n$ is the induced electric field, then work done by the force of this field in moving a test charge q_0 around the path is $(q_0 E)(2\pi r)$.

Suppose e is the induced emf, then work done on the test charge in one revolution is eq_0. Thus we can write

$$eq_0 = \left(q_0 E_n\right)\left(2\pi r\right)$$

or

$$e = E_n\left(2\pi r\right)$$

More generally $E_n(2\pi r)$ can be written as

$$e = \oint \vec{E}\cdot d\vec{\ell}$$

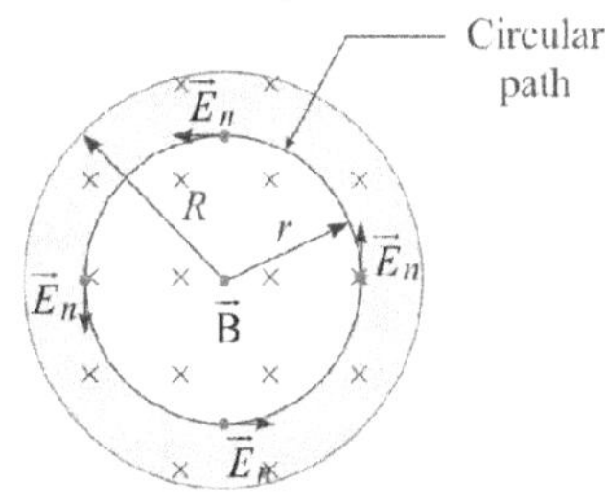

(b) Induced electric fields appear at various points even the ring is removed.

Fig. 8.34

According to the Faraday's law $\quad e = -\dfrac{d\phi_B}{dt},$

$$\oint \vec{E}_n \cdot d\vec{\ell} = -\dfrac{d\phi_B}{dt}$$

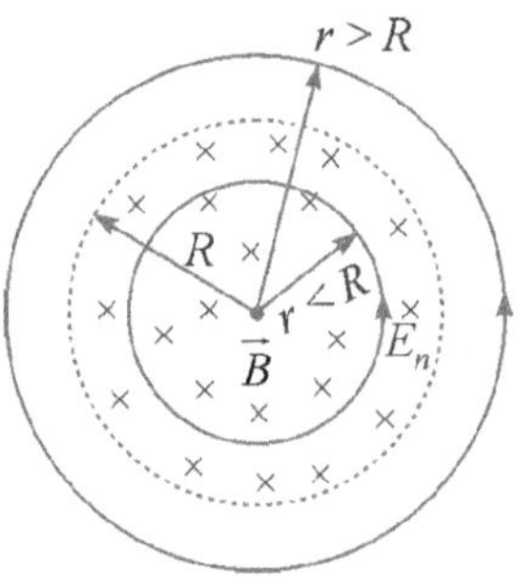

$r > R$

Fig. 8.35

Magnitude of $\vec{E}_n$

We have; $\qquad \oint \vec{E}_n \cdot d\vec{\ell} = -\dfrac{d\phi_B}{dt}$

(1)   **For $r < R$:**

$$E_n \times 2\pi r = -\dfrac{d\left(B \times \pi r^2\right)}{dt}$$

or $\qquad E_n = -\dfrac{r}{2}\dfrac{dB}{dt}$

(2)   **For $r \geq R$:**

$$E_n \times 2\pi r = -\dfrac{d\left(B \times \pi R^2\right)}{dt}$$

or $\qquad E_n = -\dfrac{R^2}{2r}\left(\dfrac{dB}{dt}\right).$

Difference between electric potential and induced emf

Electric field can be produced by static charge or by changing magnetic field. And electric field produced by any means exert forces on charged particles. The electric field produced by static charges never form closed loop, but induced electric fields form closed loop. The field produced by a static charge is of conservative nature while induced electric field is of non-conservative nature, and so its line integral over a closed path is not zero. Thus we can say that electric potential has meaning only for fields produced by static charges; it has no meaning for induced electric field.

Note :

1. Lenz's law is consistent with the principle of conservation of energy.
2. The induced emf in Faraday's law does not have a chemical or electrostatic origin. The work done in carrying a charge around the closed loop is not zero. If $\vec{E}_n$ is the induced electric field associated with an induced emf, then

$$\oint \vec{E} \cdot d\vec{\ell} \neq 0.$$ Thus here induced electric field is not a conservative field.

Ex. 19   A conducting rod is placed in a changing magnetic field as shown in *fig. 8.36*. Find induced emf across its length.

Sol.

Let us consider a rod of length ℓ is placed in magnetic field, which is perpendicular to the plane of paper and pointing into it. The field is changing at the constant rate of dB/dt.

Now consider a point A in the rod, it is at a distance $r = \dfrac{d}{\cos\theta}$ from the centre of field. The induced electric field at A,

$$E_n = -\dfrac{r}{2}\cdot\dfrac{dB}{dt} = -\dfrac{d}{2\cos\theta}\cdot\dfrac{dB}{dt}$$

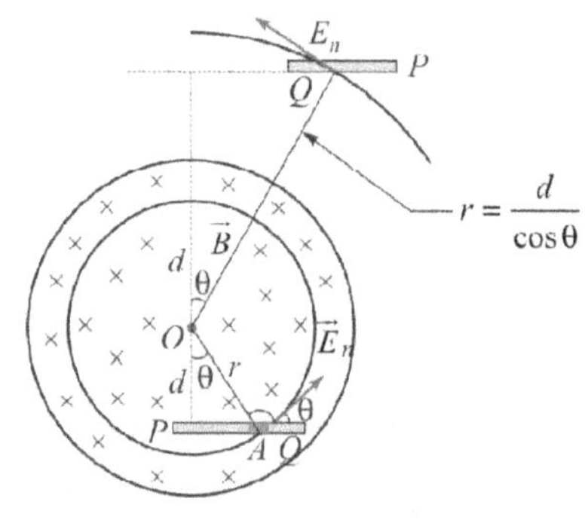

Fig. 8.36

The component of field along the rod

$$E = E_n \cos\theta = \frac{d}{2}\frac{dB}{dt}$$

∴ Potential difference between ends of the rod

$$e = E\ell = \frac{d}{2}\ell\frac{dB}{dt}$$

Case (1) : If rod is placed along the diameter

$$d = 0, \therefore e = 0.$$

Case (2) : If the rod is outside the changing field

$$E = \frac{R^2}{2d}\frac{dB}{dt}\cos\theta.$$

Ex. 20 *Figure 8.37* **shows a conducting loop** *a b c d e f a* **made of six segments** *ab, bc, cd, dc, ef* **and** *fa,* **each of length** ℓ**. Each segment makes a right angle with the next so that** *a b c* **is in the** *xy-* **plane,** *c d e* **in** *xy-* **plane and** *e f a* **in the** *yz-* **plane. A uniform magnetic field** *B* **exists along the** *x-***axis. If the magnetic field changes at a rate** $\frac{dB}{dt}$, **find the emf induced in the loop.**

Sol.

Since magnetic field is along *x*-axis, there is flux only across the face oafeo, $\phi_B = B \times \ell^2$. The flux across any other face is zero.

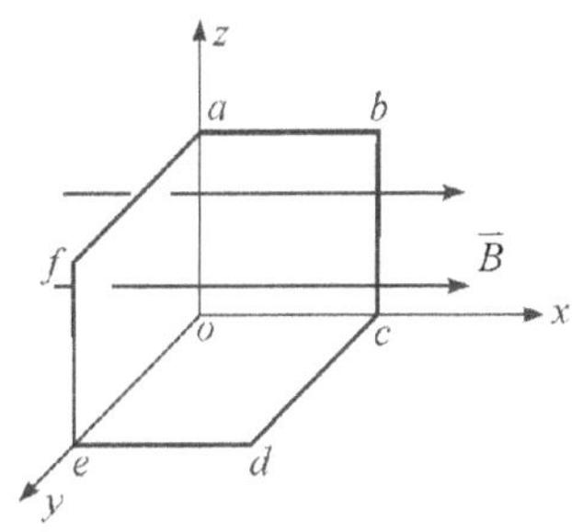

Fig. 8.37

The induced emf,

$$e = -\frac{d\phi_B}{dt} = -\frac{d\left(B\ell^2\right)}{dt}$$

$$= -\ell^2\left(\frac{dB}{dt}\right). \qquad Ans.$$

Ex. 21 **A square loop of edge 'a' having** *N* **turns is rotated with a uniform angular velocity** ω **about one of its diagonals which is kept fixed in a horizontal position. A uniform magnetic field** *B* **exists in the vertical direction. Find the emf induced in the coil.**

Sol. At any instant, θ = ω*t* and the flux through the loop

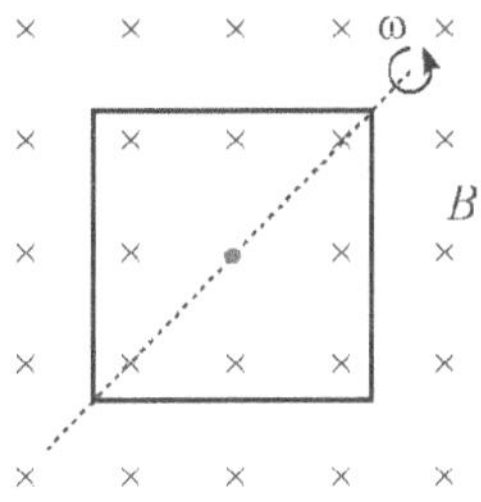

Fig. 8.38

$$\phi_B = NBA\cos\theta$$
$$= NBa^2\cos\omega t$$

Induced emf, $\qquad e = \frac{-d\phi_B}{dt}$

$$= -\frac{d\left[NBa^2\cos\omega t\right]}{dt}$$

$$= NBa^2\omega\sin\omega t \qquad Ans.$$

Note:

If the same loop is rotated about an axis parallel to one of its sides and passing through centre of square, the induced emf will be same. i.e.,

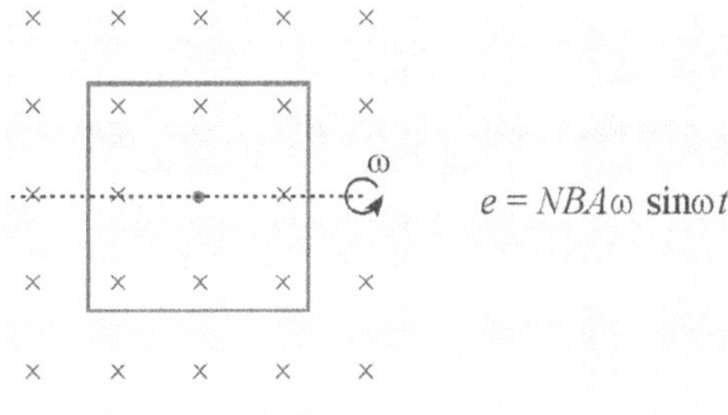

$$e = NBA\omega\sin\omega t$$

Fig. 8.39

Ex. 22 *Figure 8.40* **shows a straight, long wire carrying a current i and a rod of length** ℓ **coplanar with the wire and perpendicular to it. The rod moves with a constant velocity v in a direction parallel to the wire. The distance of the wire from the centre of the rod is** *x.* **Find the motional emf induced in the rod.**

Sol.

The magnetic field due to wire at a distance x from the wire,

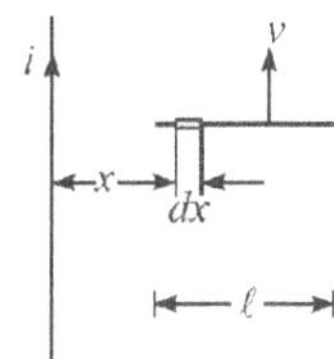

Fig. 8.40

$$B_x = \frac{\mu_0}{2\pi}\cdot\frac{i}{x}$$

The induced emf across the ends of the element dx,

$$de = B_x v\,dx$$

$$= \left(\frac{\mu_0}{2\pi}\cdot\frac{i}{x}\right)v\,dx$$

$\therefore$ Emf induced across whole length of the rod

$$e = \int\limits_{\left(x-\frac{\ell}{2}\right)}^{\left(x+\frac{\ell}{2}\right)} \frac{\mu_0}{2\pi}\frac{i_0 v}{x}\,dx$$

$$= \frac{\mu_0}{2\pi}iv \int\limits_{\left(x-\frac{\ell}{2}\right)}^{\left(x+\frac{\ell}{2}\right)} \frac{dx}{x}$$

$$= \frac{\mu_0}{2\pi}iv\left|\ell n\,x\right|_{x-\frac{\ell}{2}}^{x+\frac{\ell}{2}}$$

$$= \frac{\mu_0}{2\pi}iv\,\ell n\frac{\left(x+\dfrac{\ell}{2}\right)}{\left(x-\dfrac{\ell}{2}\right)}$$

$$= \frac{\mu_0}{2\pi}iv\,\ell n\left(\frac{2x+\ell}{2x-\ell}\right). \qquad Ans.$$

Ex. 23 A wire of mass m and length ℓ can freely slide on a pair of parallel, smooth, horizontal rails placed in a vertical magnetic field B (*fig. 8.41*). The rails are connected by a capacitor of capacitance C. The electric resistance of the rails and the wire is zero. If a constant force F acts on the wire as shown in the figure, find the acceleration of the wire.

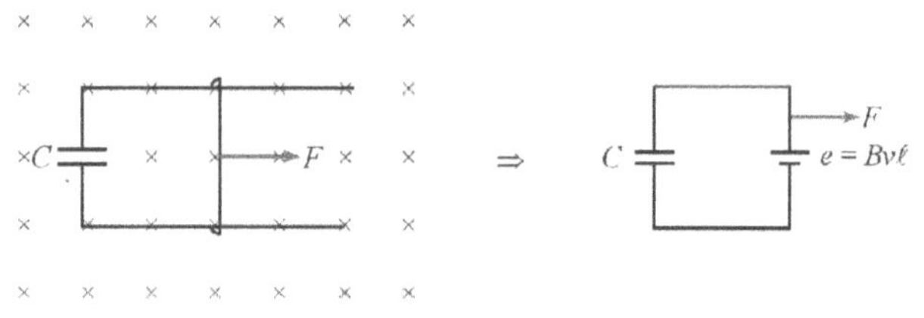

Fig. 8.41

Sol.

Let any instant the velocity of wire is v, the induced emf,

$$e = Bv\ell$$

and charge on capacitor

$$q = Ce$$
$$= CBv\ell,$$

and current in the wire

$$i = \frac{dq}{dt} = \frac{d}{dt}\left(CBv\ell\right)$$

$$= CB\left(\frac{dv}{dt}\right)\ell.$$

As $\dfrac{dv}{dt}$ is the acceleration a,

$$\therefore \qquad i = CBa\ell.$$

The resisting force on wire exerted by magnetic field

$$F_{res} = Bi\ell = B(CBa\ell)\ell$$
$$= B^2 Ca\ell^2$$

Now by Newton's second law

$$F-F_{rest} = m\,a$$

or $$F - B^2 Ca\ell^2 = m\,a$$

$$\therefore \qquad a = \left[\frac{F}{m+B^2 C\ell^2}\right]. \qquad Ans.$$

Ex. 24 *Figure 8.42 shows a rectangular conducting loop of resistance R, width L, and length b being pulled at constant speed is through a region of width d in which a uniform magnetic field $\vec{B}$ is set up by an electromagnet.*

(a) Plot the flux ϕ_B through the loop as a function of the position x of the right side of the loop. Assume that $L = 40$ mm, $b = 10$ cm, $d = 15$ cm, $R = 1.6$ Ω, $B = 2.0$ T, and $v = 1.0$ m/s.

(b) Plot the induced emf as a function of the position of the loop.

(c) Plot the rate of production of thermal energy in the loop as a function of the position of loop.

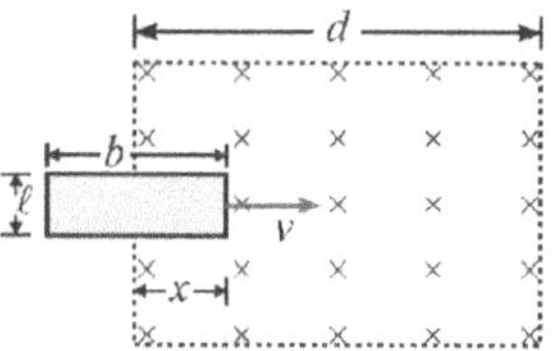

Fig. 8.42

Sol.

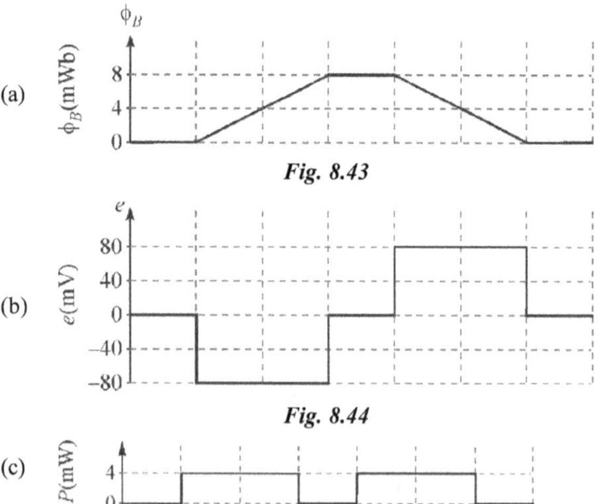

(a)

Fig. 8.43

(b)

Fig. 8.44

(c)

Fig. 8.45

(a) The magnet flux is zero when the loop is not in the field; it is $\phi_B = BL\,x$, when loop is entering into the field. It increases linearly and becomes maximum when $x = b$

i.e., $\phi_B = BL\,b = 2 \times \left(40 \times 10^{-3}\right) \times \left(10 \times 10^{-2}\right) = 8\,m$

When the loop is leaving the field, it is $\phi_B = BL\left[b - \left(x - d\right)\right]$

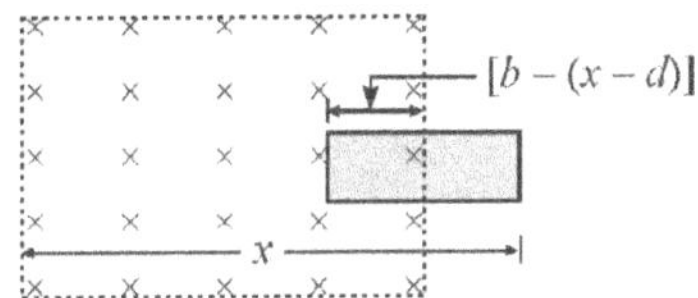

Fig. 8.46

(b) The induced emf is equal to $-\dfrac{d\phi_B}{dt}$, which can be written as

$$e = -\frac{d\phi_B}{dt} = -\frac{d\phi_B}{dx}\frac{dx}{dt} = -\frac{d\phi_B}{dx}\,v$$

where $\dfrac{d\phi_B}{dx}$ is the slope of curve (a).

From 0 to 10 cm

$$\frac{d\phi_B}{dx} = \frac{8}{0.10} = 80$$

$$\therefore \qquad e = -80 \times 1 = -80\,mV\,.$$

From 10 cm to 15 cm

$$\frac{d\phi_B}{dx} = 0$$

$$\therefore \qquad e = 0.$$

From 15 cm to 25 cm

$$\frac{d\phi_B}{dx} = -80$$

$$\therefore \qquad e = -\left(-80 \times 1\right) = +80\,mV$$

(c) We have $\qquad P = \dfrac{e^2}{R}$

$$\therefore \qquad P_{\max} = \frac{\left(80 \times 10^{-3}\right)^2}{1.6} = 4\,mW\,,$$

and $\qquad P_{\min} = 0.$ **Ans.**

Ex. 25 *Figure 8.47 shows a rectangular loop of wire immersed* in a non-uniform and varying magnetic field $\vec{B}$ that is perpendicular to and directed into the page. The field's magnitude is given by $B = 4t^2x^2$, with B in tesla, t in second, and x in metre. The loop has width $W = 3.0$ m and height $H = 2.0$ m. What are the magnitude and direction of the induced emf ξ around the loop at $t = 0.10$ s ?

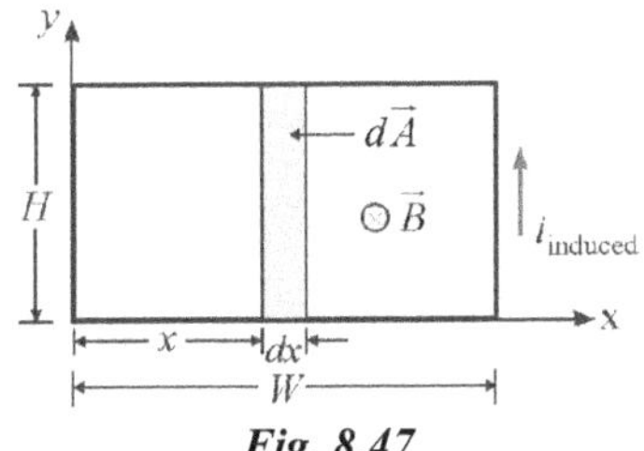

Fig. 8.47

Sol.

Take an element of thickness dx, its area $dA = Hdx$. The magnetic flux through this area

$$d\phi = \vec{B} \cdot d\vec{A} = BdA \cos 0° = BdA$$
$$= B(Hdx)$$
$$= 4t^2x^2\,Hdx$$

The total flux through the entire loop

$$\phi = \int d\phi = 4t^2 H \int_0^{3.0} x^2 dx$$

$$= 4t^2 H \left|\frac{x^3}{3}\right|_0^{3.0} = 72t^2 \quad (H = 2.0\text{ m})$$

Now by Faraday's law, the magnitude of induced emf

$$e = \frac{d\phi}{dt} = \frac{d\left[72t^2\right]}{dt}$$
$$= 144\,t$$

At $\qquad t = 0.10$ s,
$$e = 144 \times 0.10$$
$$= 14.4 \text{ V} \qquad \textbf{Ans.}$$

Direction of induced emf : The flux of $\vec{B}$ through the loop is into the page and is increasing in magnitude with time. According to Lenz's law, the field of the induced current must oppose this increase and so is directed out of the page. Therefore the direction of induced current or emf is counterclockwise in the loop (see figure).

Ex. 26 A square loop of side 12 cm with its side parallel to x and y axis is moved with a velocity of 8 cm/s in the positive x-direction in a magnetic field pointing towards positive z-direction. The field has a gradient of 10^{-3} T/cm. Find the magnitude of the induced emf if field changes at the rate of 0.1 T/s.

Sol.

We know that, the induced emf in this case is given by

$$|e| = A\left[\frac{\partial B}{\partial t} + v\frac{\partial B}{\partial x}\right]$$
$$= 144 \times 10^{-4}\left[0.1 + 8 \times 10^{-3}\right]$$
$$= 155 \text{ mV.} \qquad \textbf{Ans.}$$

Ex. 27 A wire PQ of length ℓ, mass m and resistance R slides on a smooth, thick pair of metallic rails joined at the bottom as shown in *fig. 8.48*. The plane of the rails makes an angle θ with the horizontal. A vertical magnetic field B exists in the region. If the wire slides on the rails at a constant speed v. Show that

$$B = \sqrt{\frac{mgR\sin\theta}{v\ell^2\cos^2\theta}}.$$

Fig. 8.48

Sol.

The induced emf across the wire PQ

$$e = Bv\ell \sin(90° + \theta)$$
$$= Bv\ell \cos\theta$$

The current in the wire,

$$i = \frac{e}{R} = \frac{Bv\ell \cos\theta}{R}$$

The magnetic force on the wire
$$F = Bi\ell,$$
its direction is as shown in *fig. 8.48*
The wire moves with constant velocity,

$$\therefore \quad mg\sin\theta = F\cos\theta$$
$$\text{or} \quad mg\sin\theta = Bi\ell\cos\theta$$

$$\text{or} \quad mg\sin\theta = B\left(\frac{Bv\ell\cos\theta}{R}\right)\ell\cos\theta$$

$$\therefore \quad B = \sqrt{\frac{mgR\sin\theta}{v\ell^2\cos^2\theta}}. \qquad \textbf{Proved.}$$

Ex. 28 *Figure 8.49* shows a metallic square frame of edge a in a vertical plane. A uniform magnetic field B exists in the space in a direction perpendicular to the plane of the figure. Two boys pull the opposite corners of the square to deform it into a rhombus. They start pulling the corners at $t = 0$ and displace the corners at a uniform speed u.

(a) Find the induced emf in the frame at the instant when the angles at these corners reduce to 60°.

(b) Find the induced current in the frame at this instant if the total resistance of the frame is R.

(c) Find the total charge which flows through a side of the frame by the time the square is deformed into a straight line.

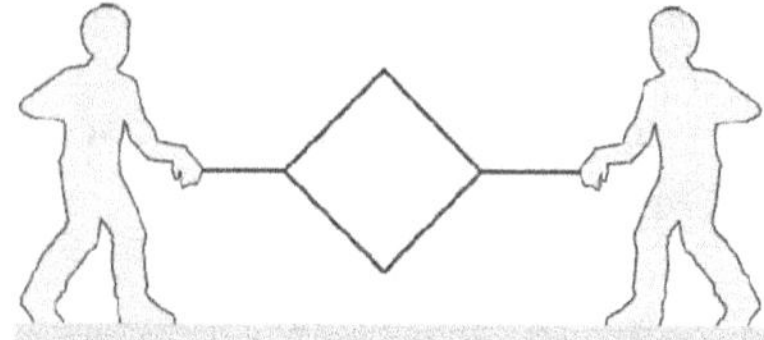

Fig. 8.49

Sol.

(a) The situation is shown in *fig. 8.50*.

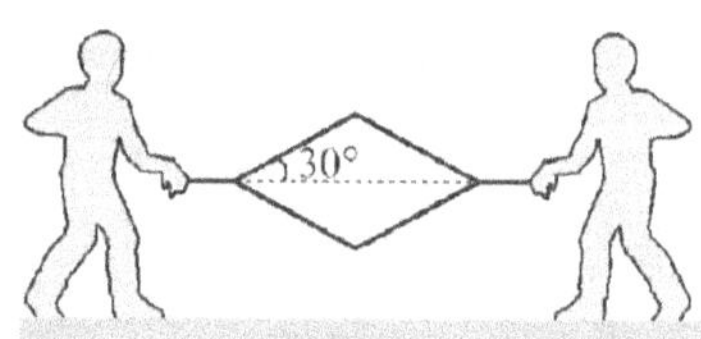

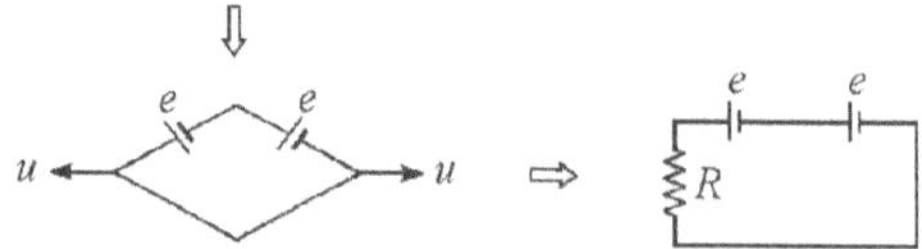

Fig. 8.50

The loop can be split into two identical parts. The emf across each part will be

$$e = B(a\sin30° \times 2)u$$
$$= B\,a\,u$$
$$\therefore \quad e_{\text{net}} = 2e = 2B\,a\,u \qquad \textbf{Ans.}$$

(b) The induced current in the frame

$$i = \frac{e_{\text{net}}}{R} = \frac{2Bau}{R} \qquad \textbf{Ans.}$$

(c) Total charge flows,

$$q = -\frac{\Delta\phi}{R} = \frac{\phi_1 - \phi_2}{R}$$

where,
$$\phi_1 = BA = B(a^2)$$
$$\phi_2 = 0$$

$$\therefore \quad q = \frac{Ba^2}{R}. \qquad \textbf{Ans.}$$

Ex. 29 The rectangular wire frame, shown in *fig. 8.51* has a width ℓ, mass m, resistance R and a large length. A uniform magnetic field B exists to the left of the frame. A constant force F starts pushing the frame into the magnetic field at $t = 0$.

(a) Find the acceleration of the frame when its speed has increased to v.

(b) Show that after some time the frame will move with a constant velocity till the whole frame enters into the magnetic field. Find the velocity

(c) Show that the velocity at time t is given by

$$v = v_0\left(1 - e^{-Ft/mv_0}\right)$$

Fig. 8.51

Sol.

(a) The induced emf in the loop, when its left side enters into the field

$e = Bv\ell$, and the induced current $i = \dfrac{e}{R}$, the restoring force exerted by magnetic field

$$F' = Bi\ell = B\left(\frac{e}{R}\right),$$

$$= B\left(\frac{Bv\ell}{R}\right)\ell = \frac{Bv\ell}{R}$$

Now by Newton's II law
$$F - F' = ma$$

$$\text{or} \quad F - \frac{B^2v\ell^2}{R} = ma$$

$$\therefore \quad a = \frac{FR - v\ell^2B^2}{mR} \qquad \textbf{Ans.}$$

(b) With the increase in speed, the acceleration of frame decreases. At a particular value of v_0 the acceleration of the frame becomes zero. There after frame will move with constant velocity

$$\therefore \qquad 0 = \frac{FR - v\ell^2 B^2}{mR}$$

which gives $\qquad v = v_0 = \dfrac{FR}{\ell^2 B^2}$

(c) We have,

$$\frac{dv}{dt} = \frac{FR - v\ell^2 B^2}{mR}$$

$$\int_0^v \frac{dv}{\left(\dfrac{FR - v\ell^2 B^2}{mR}\right)} = \int_0^t dt$$

or $\qquad \left| \dfrac{\ell n\left(\dfrac{FR - v\ell^2 B^2}{mR}\right)}{-\left(\dfrac{\ell^2 B^2}{mR}\right)} \right|_0^v = -t$

or $\quad \ell n\left[\dfrac{FR - v\ell^2 B^2}{mR}\right] - \ell n\left[\dfrac{FR}{mR}\right] = -\dfrac{\ell^2 B^2}{mR}t$

or $\quad \ell n\left[\dfrac{FR - v\ell^2 B^2}{mR}\right] = \dfrac{-\ell^2 B^2}{mR}t$

or $\ell n\left[\dfrac{FR\left(1 - v\dfrac{\ell^2 B^2}{FR}\right)}{FR}\right] = \dfrac{-\ell^2 B^2}{mR}t$

or $\qquad \ell n\left(1 - \dfrac{v}{v_0}\right) = -\dfrac{Ft}{mv_0}$

or $\qquad 1 - \dfrac{v}{v_0} = e^{-Ft/mv_0}$

or $\qquad v = v_0\left[1 - e^{\left(-Ft/mv_0\right)}\right]$ ***Proved***

Ex. 30 A wire bent as a parabola $y = c\,x^2$ is located in a uniform magnetic field of induction B, the vector B being perpendicular to the plane $-xy$. At the moment $t = 0$ a connector starts sliding translationwise from the parabola apex with a constant acceleration a. Find the emf of electromagnetic induction in the loop thus formed as a function of y.

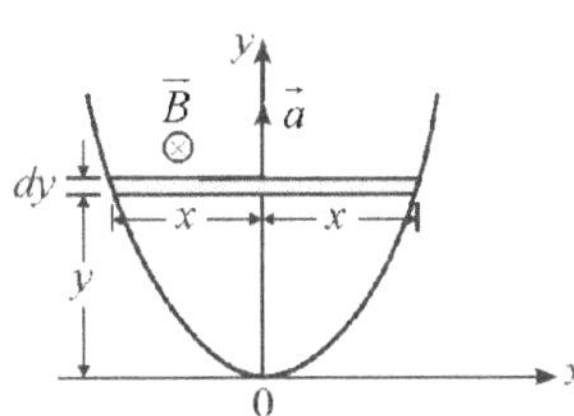

Fig. 8.52

Sol.

Let us consider an element of dy at a distance y from the apex. The magnetic flux associated

$$d\phi_B = B(2x \times dy) \qquad \text{...(i)}$$

We have $\qquad y = c\,x^2$

which gives $x \qquad = \sqrt{\dfrac{y}{c}}$

In time t_1 $\qquad y = \dfrac{1}{2}at^2$

or $\qquad t = \sqrt{\dfrac{2y}{a}} \qquad \text{...(ii)}$

From equation (i), we get

$$\frac{d\phi_B}{dt} = B\left(2x \times \frac{dy}{dt}\right)$$

or $\qquad = B \times 2x \times v$

where $\qquad v = at$

$\therefore \qquad \dfrac{d\phi_B}{dt} = B \times 2x \times at$

$$= B \times 2\sqrt{\frac{y}{c}} \times a \times \sqrt{\frac{2y}{a}}$$

or $\qquad |e| = By\sqrt{\dfrac{8a}{c}} \qquad$ ***Ans.***

Ex. 31 The magnetic field in the cylindrical region is shown in *fig. 8.53* increases at a constant rate of 20.0 mT/s. Each side of the square loop *abcd* and *defa* has a length of 1.00 cm and a resistance of 4.00 Ω. Find the current (magnitude and sense) in the wire *ad* if
(a) the switch S_1 is closed but S_2 is open
(b) S_1 is open but S_2 is closed,
(c) both S_1 and S_2 are open
(d) both S_1 and S_2 are closed.

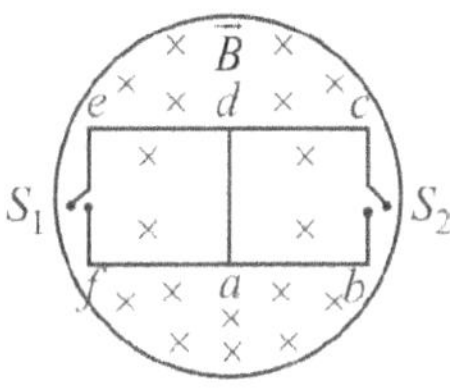

Fig. 8.53

Sol.

(a) Switch S_1 is closed and S_2 is open : The flux is confined in loop *adef*.

The induced emf in the loop

$$|e| = \frac{d\phi_B}{dt} = \frac{d(BA)}{dt}$$

$$= A\left(\frac{dB}{dt}\right)$$

$$= \left(1 \times 1 \times 10^{-4}\right) \times \left(20 \times 10^{-3}\right)$$

$$= 2 \times 10^{-6}\ V$$

The current in wire *ad*,

$$i = \frac{e}{R}$$

where R is the resistance of the loop $= 4 \times 4 = 16\,\Omega$

$$\therefore \quad i = \frac{e}{R} = \frac{2 \times 10^{-6}}{16}$$

$$= 1.25 \times 10^{-7}\,\text{A} \qquad \textbf{\textit{Ans.}}$$

The direction of current in ad is to oppose the increasing flux. Thus it is from *a* to *d*.

(b) S_1 is open but S_2 is closed.

Now flux is associated with closed loop *abcd* therefore induced emf will occur in it.

$$\therefore \qquad i = 1.25 \times 10^{-7}\,\text{A from } d \text{ to } a \quad \textbf{\textit{Ans.}}$$

(c) When both the switches are open : No flux is associated with any loop.

$$\therefore \qquad e = 0 \text{ and } i = 0.$$

(d) When both the switches are closed : The flux is associated with both the loops, and there is induced emf in both the loops. The equivalent circuit is as shown. Since $e_1 = e_2 = e$.

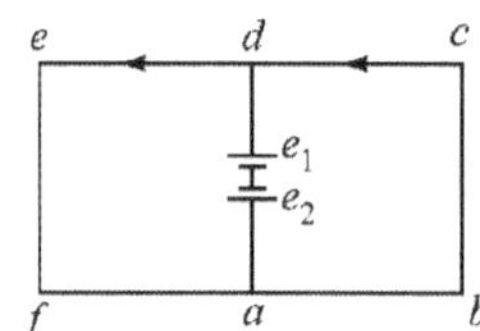

Fig. 8.54

The p.d. across *a* and *d* $= 0$

$\therefore$ Current in wire *ad*, $i = 0$.

Ex. 32 **The magnetic field in a region is given by $\vec{B} = \vec{k}\,\dfrac{B_0}{L}\,y$**

where L is a fixed length. A conducting rod of length L lies along y-axis between the origin and the point $(0, L, 0)$. If the rod moves with a velocity $\vec{v} = v_0\vec{i}$, find the emf induced between the ends of the rod.

Sol.

Consider a small element of width *dy* at a distance *y* from the origin. The induced emf across it

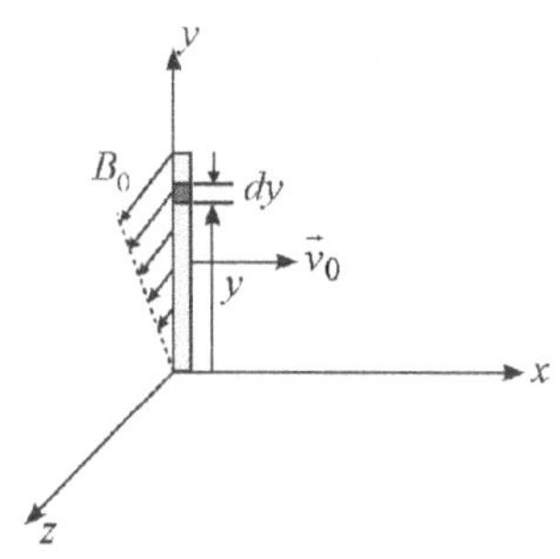

Fig. 8.55

$$de = B\,v\,(dy)$$

$$= \left(\frac{B_0\,y}{L}\right)v_0\,dy$$

The induced emf across whole length of the rod

$$e = \int_0^L \frac{B_0}{L}\,v_0\,y\,dy$$

$$= \frac{B_0 v_0 L}{2} \qquad \textbf{\textit{Ans.}}$$

Ex. 33 **A rectangular metallic loop of length ℓ and width b is placed coplanerly with a long wire carrying a current i. The loop is moved perpendicular to the wire with a speed v in the plane containing the wire and the loop. Calculate the emf induced in the loop when the rear end of the loop is at a distance a from the wire.**

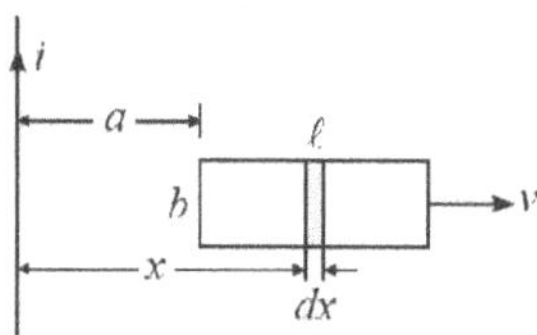

Fig. 8.56

Sol.

Method I : Consider an element of width dx in the loop. The magnetic flux across the element

$$d\phi_B = B_x\,(bdx)$$

$$= \frac{\mu_0}{2\pi}\,\frac{i}{x}\,bdx$$

The total flux across the loop

$$\phi_B = \frac{\mu_0}{2\pi}\,ib \int_x^{(x+\ell)} \frac{dx}{x}$$

$$= \frac{\mu_0}{2\pi}\,ib\,\big|\ell n\,x\big|_x^{(x+\ell)}$$

$$= \frac{\mu_0}{2\pi}\,ib\big[\ell n(x+\ell) - \ell n\,x\big]$$

Now,

$$e = -\frac{d\phi_B}{dt}$$

$$= -\frac{\mu_0 ib}{2\pi}\,\frac{d}{dt}\big[\ell n(x+\ell) - \ell n\,x\big]$$

$$= -\frac{\mu_0 ib}{2\pi}\,\frac{d}{dx}\big[\ell n(x+\ell) - \ell n\,x\big] \times \frac{dx}{dt}$$

$$e = -\frac{\mu_0 ib}{2\pi}\left[\frac{1}{x+\ell} - \frac{1}{x}\right] \times v$$

when $x = a, e$

$$= -\frac{\mu_0 ib}{2\pi}\left[\frac{1}{a+\ell} - \frac{1}{a}\right] \times v$$

$$= \frac{\mu_0 ib\ell v}{2\pi a(a+\ell)} \qquad \textbf{\textit{Ans.}}$$

Method II : When $x = a$, the position of the loop is shown in *fig. 8.57*. The magnetic field at left arm of the loop

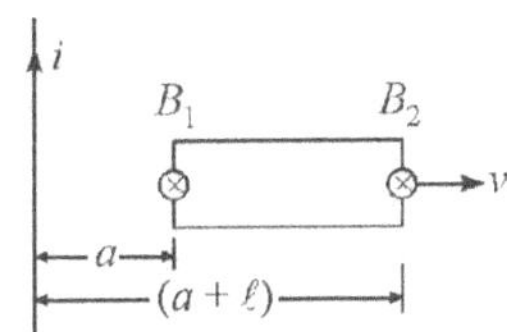

Fig. 8.57

$$B_1 = \frac{\mu_0}{2\pi} \frac{i}{a}$$

Similarly, magnetic field at right arm of the loop

$$B_2 = \frac{\mu_0}{2\pi} \frac{i}{(a+\ell)}$$

Now induced emf across left and right arms are

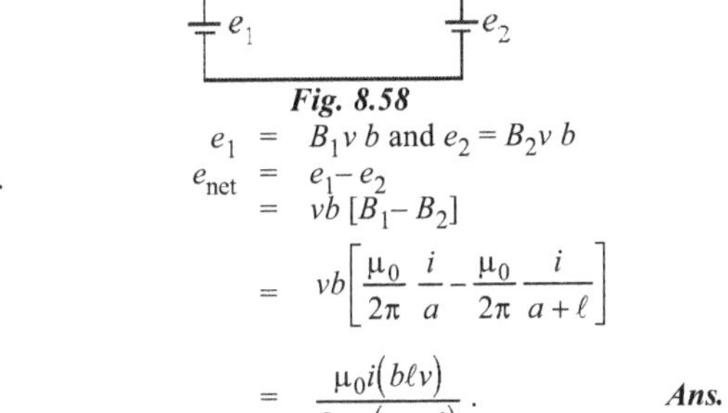

Fig. 8.58

$$e_1 = B_1 v\, b \text{ and } e_2 = B_2 v\, b$$

$$\therefore \quad e_{net} = e_1 - e_2$$

$$= vb\,[B_1 - B_2]$$

$$= vb\left[\frac{\mu_0}{2\pi} \frac{i}{a} - \frac{\mu_0}{2\pi} \frac{i}{a+\ell}\right]$$

$$= \frac{\mu_0 i\,(b\ell v)}{2\pi a\,(a+\ell)}. \qquad \textit{Ans.}$$

Ex. 34 (a) *Figure 8.59* shows a conducting circular loop of radius a placed in a uniform, perpendicular magnetic field B. A thick metal rod OA is pivoted at the centre O. The other end of the rod touches the loop at A. The centre O and a fixed point C on the loop are connected by a wire OC of resistance R. A force is applied at the middle point of the rod OA perpendicularly, so that the rod rotates clockwise at a uniform angular velocity ω. Find force.

(b) Suppose the wire connecting O and C has zero resistance but the circular loop has a resistance R uniformly distributed along its length. The rod OA is made to rotate with uniform angular speed ω as shown in the figure. Find the current in the rod when $\angle AOC = 90°$.

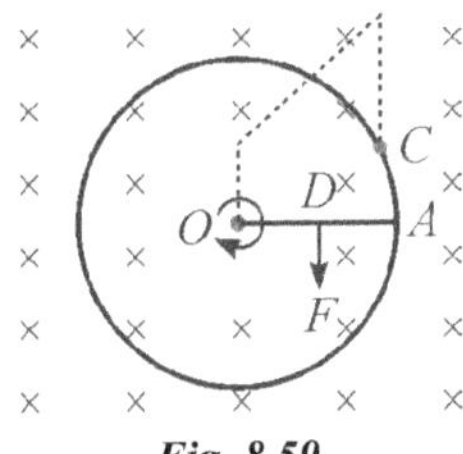

Fig. 8.59

Sol.

(a) When rod rotates with constant angular velocity, the induced emf across its ends

$$e = V_O - V_A = \frac{B\omega a^2}{2}$$

The current in the wire OC,

$$i = \frac{e}{R} = \frac{B\omega a^2}{2R}$$

The same current will flow across OA from A to O. Therefore the force exerted by magnetic field on the rod

$$F_m = B\,i\,a$$

$$= B\left(\frac{B\omega a^2}{2R}\right)a = \frac{B^2\omega a^3}{2R}$$

The rod is to be rotated with constant angular velocity so the torque of net force about centre of loop is equal to zero. i.e.,

$$(F - F_m) \times OD = 0$$

or $$F = F_m$$

$$= \frac{B^2\omega a^3}{2R}. \qquad \textit{Ans.}$$

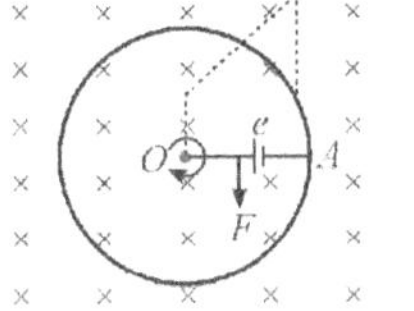

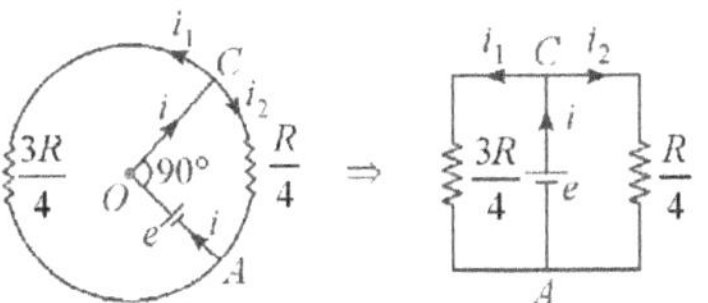

(a) The equivalent circuit.   (b) The equivalent circuit.

Fig. 8.60

(b) The effective resistance between A & C

$$R' = \frac{\left(\dfrac{3R}{4}\right) \times \left(\dfrac{R}{4}\right)}{\left(\dfrac{3R}{4} + \dfrac{R}{4}\right)} = \frac{3R}{16}$$

Now current in the rod OA

$$i = \frac{e}{R'} = \frac{\dfrac{B\omega a^2}{2}}{\left(\dfrac{3R}{16}\right)}$$

$$= \frac{8}{3} \frac{B\omega a^2}{R}. \qquad \textit{Ans.}$$

Ex. 35 A coil of N turns with the cross-sectional area A is placed inside a long solenoid. The coil is rotated at a constant angular velocity ω around the axis coinciding with its diameter and perpendicular to the axis of the solenoid. The magnetic field in the solenoid varies according to the law $B = B_0 \sin \omega t$. Find the emf induced in the coil, if at the instant $t = 0$ the coil axis coincided with the axis of the solenoid.

Sol. At any instant, the total magnetic flux through the coil is

$$\phi = NBA \cos \omega t$$

$$= N(B_0 \sin \omega t)\, A \cos \omega t$$

$$= \frac{1}{2} NB_0 A \sin 2\omega t$$

By Faraday's law $$e = -\frac{d\phi}{dt} = -\frac{d\left[\dfrac{1}{2} NB_0\, A \sin 2\omega t\right]}{dt}$$

$$= -\frac{1}{2} NB_0 A\,(2\omega) \cos 2\omega t$$

$$= -NB_0 A\omega \cos 2\omega t. \qquad \textit{Ans.}$$

Ex. 36 A wire frame of area 3.92×10^{-4} m^2 and resistance $20\,\Omega$ is suspended freely from a 0.392 m long thread. There is a uniform magnetic field of 0.784 tesla and the plane of wire-frame is perpendicular to the magnetic field. The frame is made to oscillate under gravity by displacing it through 2×10^{-2} m from its initial position along the direction of magnetic field. The plane of the frame is always along the direction of thread and does not rotate about it. What is the induced emf in wire frame as a function of time ? Also find the maximum current in the frame.

Sol.

At the intant, when thread makes an angle θ with the vertical, the magnetic flux through the frame

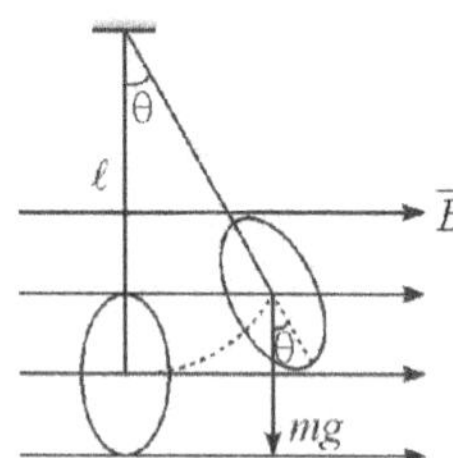

Fig. 8.61

$$\phi = B A \cos\theta$$

The induced emf

$$e = -\frac{d\phi}{dt} = BA\sin\theta\,\frac{d\theta}{dt} \quad ...(i)$$

For small θ, $\sin\theta \simeq \theta$.

The restoring torque on the frame

$$\tau = -mg(\ell \sin\theta)$$

or

$$\frac{d^2\theta}{dt^2} = \frac{mg\ell}{I}(-\theta)$$

$$= \frac{mg\ell}{m\ell^2}(-\theta)$$

$$= \left(\frac{g}{\ell}\right)(-\theta)$$

Putting $\left(\dfrac{g}{\ell}\right) = \omega^2$, we get

$$\frac{d^2\theta}{dt^2} + \omega^2\theta = 0 \qquad ...(ii)$$

This represents SHM, and so

$$\theta = \theta_0 \sin\omega t$$

Substituting value of θ in equation (i), we have

$$e = BA(\theta_0\sin\omega t)\frac{d}{dt}(\theta_0\sin\omega t)$$

$$= BA\,\theta_0\sin\omega t\,(\theta_0\omega\cos\omega t)$$

$$= \frac{1}{2}BA\omega\theta_0{}^2\sin 2\omega t$$

Here

$$\omega = \sqrt{\frac{g}{\ell}}$$

$$= \sqrt{\frac{9.8}{0.392}} = 5\,s^{-1},$$

$$\theta_0 = \frac{x_0}{\ell} = \frac{2 \times 10^{-2}}{0.392}$$

and

$$e = \frac{1}{2} \times (0.784) \times \left(3.92 \times 10^{-4}\right) \times 5 \times \left(\frac{2 \times 10^{-2}}{0.392}\right) \sin 10t$$

$$= 2 \times 10^{-6}\sin 10t.$$

Maximum induced emf

$$e_{max} = 2 \times 10^{-6}\,V$$

and

$$i_{max} = \frac{e_{max}}{R} = \frac{2 \times 10^{-6}}{20} = 10^{-7}\,A \textbf{ Ans.}$$

Ex. 37 An infinitesimally small bar magnet of dipole moment M is pointing and moving with the speed v in the x-direction. A small closed circular conducting loop of radius a and negligible self-inductance lies in the yz-plane with its centre at $x = 0$, and its axis coinciding with the x-axis. Find the force oppositing the motion of the magnet, if the resistance of the loop is R. Assume that the distance x of the magnet from the centre of the loop is much greater than a.

Sol.

Suppose magnet is at a distance x from the centre of the loop. The magnetic field due to the magnet at the centre of the loop

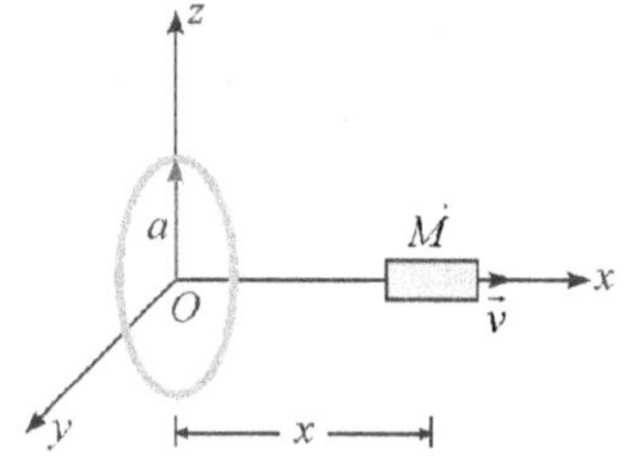

Fig. 8.62

$$B = \frac{\mu_0}{4\pi}\frac{2M}{x^3}.$$

The magnetic flux due to the magnet

$$\phi = BA = \frac{\mu_0}{4\pi}\frac{2M}{x^3}\left(\pi a^2\right)$$

Induced emf in the loop

$$e = -\frac{d\phi}{dt} = -\frac{d}{dt}\left[\frac{\mu_0}{4\pi}\frac{2M}{x^3}\left(\pi a^2\right)\right]$$

$$= \frac{\mu_0 Ma^2}{2}\left(\frac{3}{x^4}\frac{dx}{dt}\right)$$

As

$$\frac{dx}{dt} = v,$$

$$\therefore \qquad e = \frac{3\mu_0 Ma^2 v}{2x^4}$$

Induced current, $\qquad i = \dfrac{e}{R} = \dfrac{3\mu_0 Ma^2 v}{2x^4 R}$

If M_{loop} is the magnetic moment of the loop, then

$$M_{\text{loop}} = iA$$

$$= \dfrac{3\mu_0 Ma^2 v}{2x^4 R}\left(\pi a^2\right)$$

$$= \dfrac{3\pi\mu_0 Ma^4 v}{2x^4 R}$$

The opposing force $\qquad F = \dfrac{\mu_0}{4\pi}\,\dfrac{6\,M_{\text{magnet}}\,M_{\text{loop}}}{x^4}$

$$= \dfrac{\mu_0}{4\pi}\,\dfrac{6M}{x^4}\left[\dfrac{3\pi\mu_0 Ma^4 v}{2x^4 R}\right]$$

$$= \dfrac{9}{4}\,\dfrac{\mu_0^2}{R}\,\dfrac{M^2 a^4 v}{x^8}. \qquad \textbf{\textit{Ans.}}$$

Ex. 38 Two straight conducting rails from a right angle where their ends are joined. A conducting bar in contact with the rails starts at the vertex at time $t = 0$ and moves with a constant velocity of 5.20 m/s along them, as shown in *fig. 8.63*. A magnetic field with $B = 0.35$ T is directed out of the page. Calculate

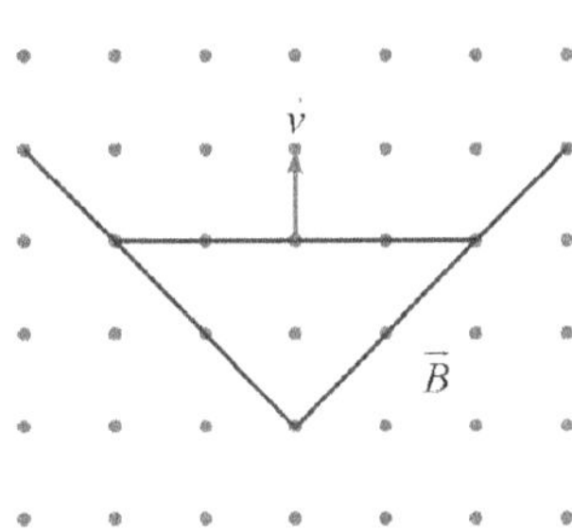

Fig. 8.63

(a) The flux through the triangle formed by the rails and bar at $t = 3.0$ s and
(b) the emf around the triangle at that time.
(c) If we write the emf $e = at^n$, where a and n are constants, what is the value of n ?

Sol.

Suppose joint of the rails is the origin of the coordinate axis. The distance moved by the bar in time t,

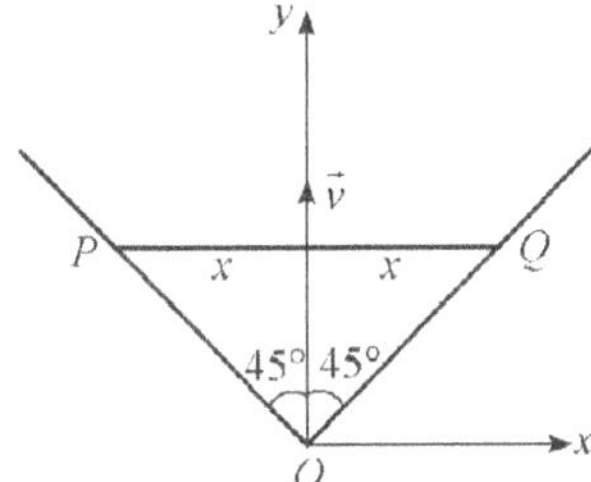

Fig. 8.64

$$y = vt.$$

The corresponding x value is

$$x = y\tan 45° = y.$$

The distance $\qquad PQ = 2x = 2y$

$$= 2vt.$$

(a) The area of the triangle $OPQ = \dfrac{1}{2}(2x)\,y = xy$

Thus the flux through the triangle

$$\phi_B = BA = B\,(xy)$$

or $\qquad \phi_B = B\,(vt)\times vt$

$$= Bv^2 t^2.$$

At $t = 3.0$ s, $\quad \phi_B = 0.35\times(5.20)^2\times 3^2.0 = 85.17\,Wb$

(b) The induced emf around the triangle

$$e = \dfrac{d\phi_B}{dt}$$

$$= \dfrac{d\left[Bv^2 t^2\right]}{dt}$$

$$= Bv^2\times 2t$$

$$= 2B\,v^2 t$$

$$= 2\times 0.35\times(5.20)^2\,t$$

$$= 18.93\,t$$

At $\quad t = 3\text{s}, \qquad e = 18.93\times 3 = 56.79\ V$

(c) Induced emf $\qquad e = 18.93\,t.$

On comparing with $e = at^n$, we get $n = 1$ $\quad$ *Ans.*

Ex. 39 A shaped as a semi-circle of radius a rotates about an axis OO' with an angular velocity ω in a uniform magnetic field of induction B (see *fig. 8.65*). The rotation axis is perpendicular to the field direction. The total resistance of the circuit is equal to R. Neglecting the magnetic field of induced current, find the mean amount of thermal power being generated in the loop during a rotation period.

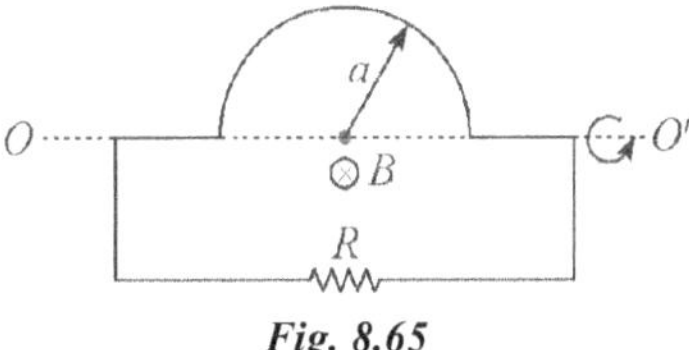

Fig. 8.65

Sol.

The area of the loop, $\qquad A = \dfrac{\pi a^2}{2}.$

If θ is the angle between magnetic field and normal to the loop at any time t, then

$$\theta = \omega t,$$

and flux $\qquad \phi = BA\cos\omega t$

$$= B\left(\dfrac{\pi a^2}{2}\right)\cos\omega t$$

According to Faraday's law

$$e = -\frac{d\phi}{dt}$$

$$= B\left(\frac{\pi a^2}{2}\right)\omega \sin\omega t$$

Induced current

$$i = \frac{e}{R} = \left(\frac{B\omega\pi a^2}{2R}\right)\sin\omega t$$

The intantaneous power generated

$$P = ei = \left(\frac{B\omega\,\pi a^2}{2}\right)^2 \frac{\sin^2\omega t}{R}$$

Thus mean power

$$P_{mean} = \frac{\int_0^T P\,dt}{T}$$

$$= \frac{\left(\frac{B\omega\pi a^2}{2}\right)^2 \frac{1}{R}\int_0^T \sin^2\omega t\,dt}{T}$$

$$= \left(\frac{B\omega\pi a^2}{2}\right)^2 \frac{1}{2R}\,.\,\textbf{\textit{Ans.}}$$

8.8 SELF INDUCTANCE

We can define an inductor as an arrangement that can be used to produce a known magnetic field. We can express the connection between capacitors and inductors as follows :

Capacitor is to electric field	**Inductor is to magnetic field**

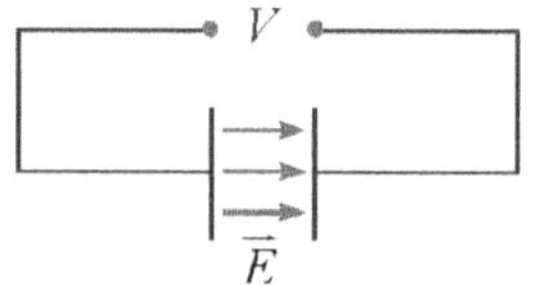

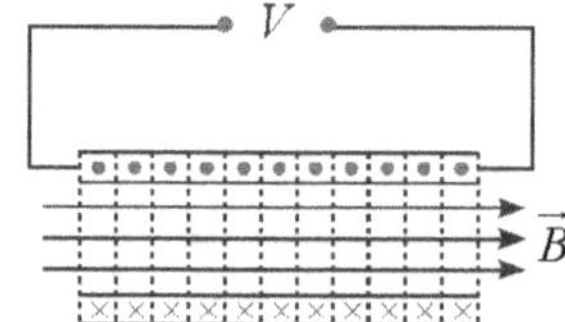

$$C = \frac{q}{V}$$

SI unit of C is C/V
linkage.

$1\ C/V = 1$ farad

Sumbol : —| |—

$$L = \frac{N\phi}{i}$$

The product $N\phi$ is called flux

SI unit of inductance is $T.\,m^2/A$.
We call this as the henry (H)

Symbol : —ⅬⲘ—

8.9 SELF INDUCTION

Whenever there is change in magnetic flux, electromagnetic induction will take place.

If there is a time varying current in a coil the magnetic field of this current will also change. And this leads to the variation of the magnetic flux through the coil, and hence to the appearance of an induced emf.

Thus, the variation of current in a circuit will cause an induced emf in this circuit. This phenomenon is called **self induction**.

In the absence of any ferromagnetics in the space surrounding the coil, the total flux through the coil are proportional to the current i, and we can write

$$N\phi_B = L\,i \qquad\qquad ...(1)$$

where L is called the coefficient of self induction of the circuit. The inductance L depends on the shape and size of the loop as well as on the magnetic properties of the surrounding medium. The unit of inductance is henry.

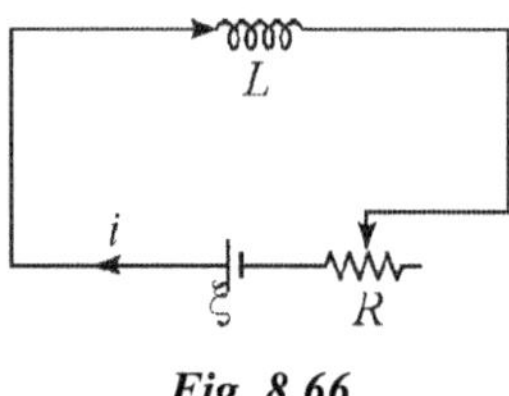

Fig. 8.66

Emf of self-induction

According to Faraday's law, a variation in the current of the circuit causes an induced emf. Thus on differentiating equation (1), we get

$$\frac{d(N\phi)}{dt} = L\frac{di}{dt}$$

or
$$e = -\frac{L\,di}{dt} \qquad \qquad ...(2)$$

Thus when current in the coil increases, the induced emf in the coil opposes the applied emf, and so net emf of the circuit

$$\xi_{net} = \xi - e = \xi - \frac{Ldi}{dt}$$

$$\xi_{net} = \xi - \frac{Ldi}{dt}$$

If current in the coil decreases, then the induced emf in the coil favours the applied emf, and so net emf of the circuit

$$\xi_{net} = \xi + e = \xi + \frac{L\,di}{dt}$$

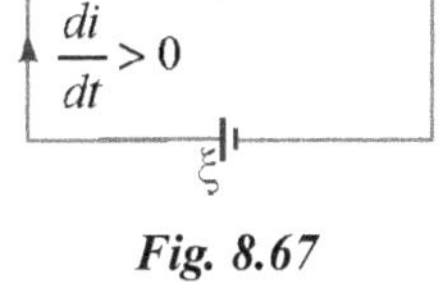

Fig. 8.67

Fig. 8.68

Steps for finding L

1. Assume current i in the coil.
2. Determine the magnetic field due to this current in the coil.
3. Obtain flux linkage $N\phi_B$.
4. Compare with $N\phi = Li$ to get L.

Calculation of self inductance

1. **Circular coil :**

   Let us consider a circular coil of radius r and containing N-turns. Suppose it carries a current i. The magnetic field due to this current

$$B = \frac{\mu_0 Ni}{2r}$$

And total flux
$$N\phi_B = NBA$$

$$= N\left(\frac{\mu_0 Ni}{2r}\right)\pi r^2$$

or
$$= \frac{\mu_0 \pi N^2 r\, i}{2}$$

Now compare with $N\phi_B = L\,i$, we get

$$L = \frac{\mu_0 \pi N^2 r}{2}$$

Note: Inductance may be viewed as electrical inertia. It is analogous to inertia in mechanics. It does not oppose the current, but it opposes the change in current.

2. **Solenoid :** Consider a long solenoid of cross-sectional area A. Take a length ℓ near the centre of this solenoid. The number of flux linkages for this section of the solenoid is

$$N\phi_B \;=\; (n\ell)(BA)$$
or
$$\qquad\;=\; n\ell\,(\mu_0 ni)\,A$$

Now compare with, $N\phi_B = Li$, we get

$$L \;=\; \mu_0\, n^2\, A\ell$$

Inductance per unit length for a long solenoid near its centre

$$\frac{L}{\ell} \;=\; \mu_0 n^2 A$$

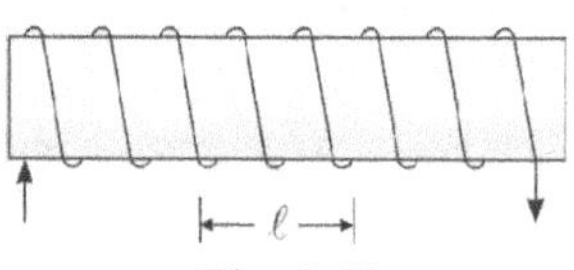
Fig. 8.69

3. **Toroid of circular cross-section :**

Consider an air-core toroid of cross-sectional area A and mean radius r is closely wound with N turns of wire. We neglect the variation of $\vec{B}$ across the cross-section, assuming its average value to the very nearly equal to be value at the centre of the cross-section. Then the flux linkage

$$N\phi_B \;=\; N(BA)$$

$$\qquad\;=\; N\!\left(\frac{\mu_0 Ni}{2\pi r}\right)\! A$$

Now compare with $N\phi_B = Li$, we get

$$L \;=\; \frac{\mu_0 N^2 A}{2\pi r}$$

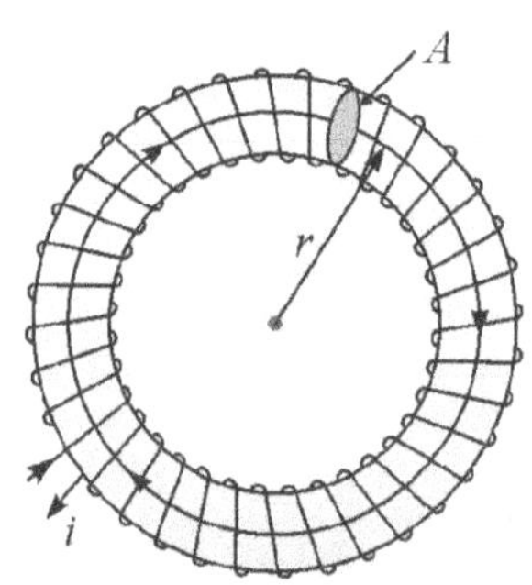

Fig. 8.70

4. **Inductance of toroid of rectangular cross-section :** The magnetic field (assuming uniform) at a distance r from the centre of toroid,

$$B \;=\; \frac{\mu_0 Ni}{2\pi r}$$

where i is the current in toroid. The flux ϕ_B over the entire cross-section must be found out by integration.

If $h(dr)$ is the area of the elementary strip shown, then we have,

$$\phi_B \;=\; \int \vec{B}\, d\vec{A}$$

$$\qquad\;=\; \int_a^b B\left(h\,dr\right)$$

$$\qquad\;=\; \int_a^b \frac{\mu_0 Ni}{2\pi r}\, h\, dr$$

$$\qquad\;=\; \frac{\mu_0 Nih}{2\pi}\int_a^b \frac{dr}{r}$$

$$\qquad\;=\; \frac{\mu_0 Ni\, h}{2\pi}\,\ell\mathrm{n}\,\frac{b}{a}$$

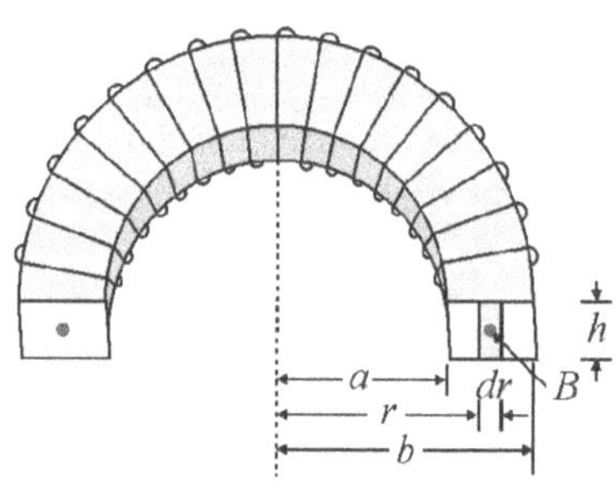

Fig. 8.71

Total flux linkage
$$N\phi_B \;=\; \frac{\mu_0 N^2 i\, h\, \ell\mathrm{n}\,\dfrac{b}{a}}{2\pi}$$

Therefore
$$\frac{N\phi_B}{i} \;=\; \frac{\mu_0 N^2 h\, \ell\mathrm{n}\,\dfrac{b}{a}}{2\pi}$$

or
$$L \;=\; \frac{\mu_0 N^2 h\, \ell\mathrm{n}\,\dfrac{b}{a}}{2\pi}$$

Energy in an inductor

A changing current in an inductor causes an emf, the source supplying the current must maintain a potential difference between its terminals and hence must supply energy to the inductor. When an inductor carries an instantaneous current i which is changing at

the rate $\dfrac{di}{dt}$, the induced emf is equal to $L\dfrac{di}{dt}$, and the power P supplied to the inductor is

$$P \;=\; ei = \;\; Li\frac{di}{dt}$$

The energy dU supplied in time dt is Pdt

or $$dU \;=\; Pdt = Li\,di$$

and the total energy supplied while the current increases from zero to a final value I is

$$U \;=\; L\int_0^I i\,di$$

or $$U \;=\; \frac{1}{2}LI^2.$$

Note : After the current has reached its final steady value, $\dfrac{di}{dt} = 0$, the power input

is zero. The energy that has been supplied to the inductor is used to establish the magnetic field in and around the inductor, where it is stored as a form of potential energy as long as the current is maintained. When current is reduced to zero, this energy is returned to the circuit which supplied it. If the current is suddenly interrupted by opening a switch, the energy may be dissipated in an arc across the switch contacts

The energy can be considered as associated with the magnetic field itself, and a relationship can be developed which is analogous to that obtained for electric field energy.

The self inductance of solenoid,

$$L \;=\; \mu_0 n^2\, A\ell$$

and $$U \;=\; \frac{1}{2}LI^2$$

$$=\; \frac{1}{2}\left(\mu_0 n^2\, A\ell\right)I^2$$

$$=\; \frac{\left(\mu_0 nI\right)^2}{2\mu_0}\,A\ell$$

$$=\; \frac{B^2}{2\mu_0}V$$

Thus the magnetic energy per unit volume

$$u \;=\; \frac{B^2}{2\mu_0}.$$

2. In case of AC of frequency f and amplitude i_0, the rate of change in current from i_0 to $-i_0$ will be ;

$$\frac{di}{dt} = \frac{2i_0}{T/2} = \frac{4i_0}{T} = 4fi_0$$

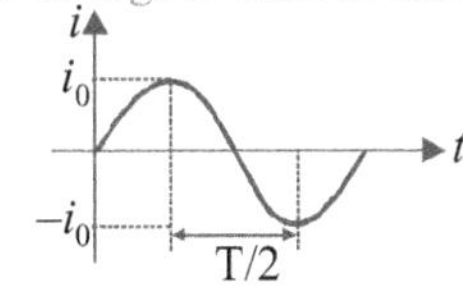

Electrical and magnetic quantities

		Electrical	Magnetic
1.	Definition	$C = \dfrac{q}{V}$	$L = \dfrac{N\phi_B}{i}$
2.	Dimensions	$C = \epsilon_0 \times a\ \text{length}$	$L = \mu_0 \times a\ \text{length}$
3.	Constants	$\epsilon_0 = 8.85\,pF/m$	$\mu_0 = 1.26\,\mu H/m$
4.	Energy stored	$U_e = \dfrac{1}{2}CV^2 = \dfrac{q^2}{2C}$	$U_B = \dfrac{1}{2}Li^2$
5.	Energy density	$u_e = \dfrac{1}{2}\epsilon_0 E^2$	$u_B = \dfrac{B^2}{2\mu_0}$
6.	Time constant	$\tau = RC$	$\tau = \dfrac{L}{R}$

Ex. 40   A 12 *H* inductor carries a steady current of 2.0 A. How can a 60 *V* self-induced emf be made to appear in the inductor ?

Sol. We know that $\quad |e| = L\dfrac{di}{dt}$

$$\therefore \qquad \dfrac{di}{dt} = \dfrac{|e|}{L} = \dfrac{60}{12} = 5\ \text{A/s.}$$

Thus current in the inductor should change at the rate of 5 A/s.

Ex. 41   A resistor of 1Ω and an inductor of 1 H are connected in series across a source of 10V. Suppose the current in the circuit is changing by the added device. Find the net emf of the circuit when

(a) $\dfrac{di}{dt} = +5\ \text{A/s,}$ **(b)** $\dfrac{di}{dt} = -5\ \text{A/s.}$

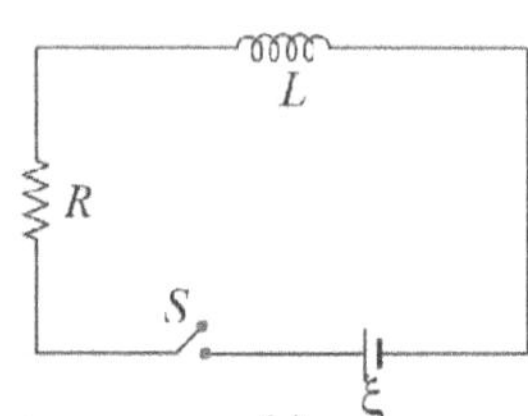

Fig. 8.72

Sol.

(a)   The induced emf in the inductor is given by

$$e = -L\dfrac{di}{dt}$$

For $\quad \dfrac{di}{dt} = +5\ \text{A/s,}$

$$e = -1 \times 5 = -5V.$$

The net emf of the circuit

$$\xi_{net} = 10 - 5 = 5\ V \qquad \textit{Ans.}$$

(b)   For $\quad \dfrac{di}{dt} = -5\ \text{A/s,}$

$$e = -1 \times (-5) = 5V$$

Thus the net emf of the circuit

$$\xi_{net} = 10 + 5 = 15\ V \qquad \textit{Ans.}$$

8.10 RL - DC CIRCUIT

Consider a circuit having inductor and resistor in series with a direct current source of emf ξ.

As soon as the switch S is closed, the current in the resistor starts increasing. If the inductor were not present, the current would rise rapidly to a steady value $\dfrac{\xi}{R}$. Because of the inductor, however, self induced emf $e = L\dfrac{di}{dt}$ appears in the circuit; from Lenz's law, this emf opposes the rise of the current, which means it opposes the battery emf. Therefore

$$e_{net} = \xi - L\dfrac{di}{dt}$$

Now by loop rule $\qquad \xi - L\dfrac{di}{dt} = iR \qquad \qquad \text{...(i)}$

or $\qquad L\dfrac{di}{dt} = \xi - iR$

or $\qquad \dfrac{di}{(\xi - iR)} = \dfrac{dt}{L}$

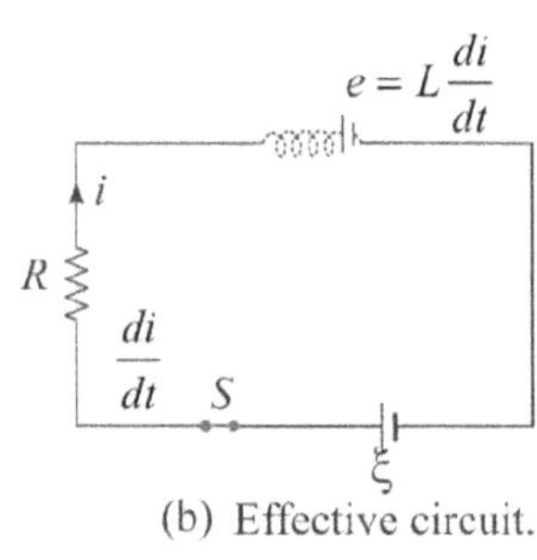

(a)

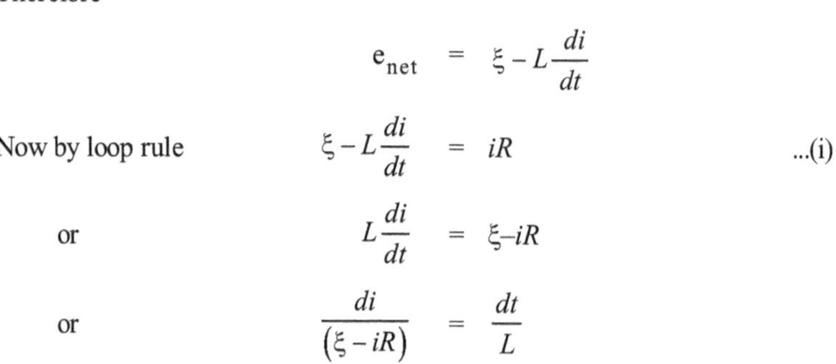

(b) Effective circuit.

Fig. 8.73

Integrating both sides of above equation, we get

$$\int_0^i \frac{di}{(\xi - iR)} = \int \frac{dt}{L}$$

or
$$\left. \frac{\ell n\,(\xi - iR)}{-R} \right|_0^i = \frac{t}{L}$$

or
$$\ell n(\xi - iR) - \ell n\,\xi = \frac{-t}{\left(\dfrac{L}{R}\right)}$$

or
$$\ell n\left(\frac{\xi - iR}{\xi}\right) = \frac{-t}{\left(\dfrac{L}{R}\right)}$$

or
$$\ell n\left(1 - \frac{i}{\dfrac{\xi}{R}}\right) = \frac{-t}{\left(\dfrac{L}{R}\right)} \qquad .....(ii)$$

Substituting
$$\xi / R = i_0, \text{ maximum current and}$$
$$L / R = \tau, \text{ time constant in equation (ii), we have}$$

$$\ell n\left(1 - \frac{i}{i_0}\right) = -\frac{t}{\tau}$$

or
$$i = i_0(1 - e^{-t/\tau}) \qquad ...(1)$$

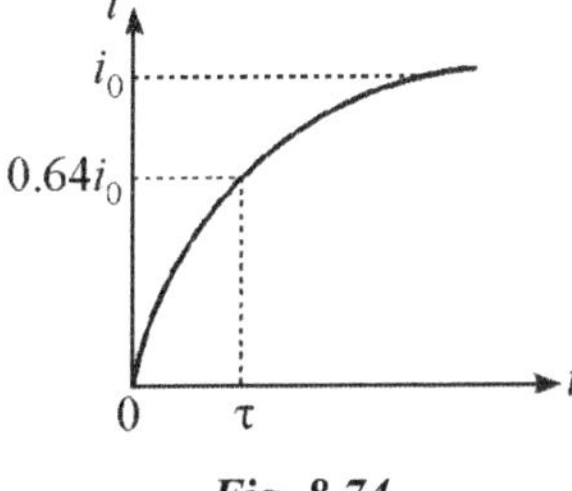

Fig. 8.74

Inductive time constant (t) :

For
$$t = \tau, \text{ we have}$$

$$i = i_0\left(1 - e^{-1}\right)$$

$$= 0.638\, i_0 \simeq 0.64\, i_0$$

Thus the inductive time constant can be defined as the time in which rising current in the circuit becomes 0.64 times the maximum current.

Energy stored

For any current i, the energy stored in the inductor is

$$U = \frac{1}{2}Li^2 = \frac{1}{2}L\left[i_0\left(1 - e^{-\frac{t}{\tau}}\right)\right]^2$$

$$= \frac{1}{2}L\, i_0^2\left(1 - e^{-\frac{t}{\tau}}\right)^2$$

or
$$U = U_0\left(1 - e^{\frac{-t}{\tau}}\right)^2 . \qquad ...(2)$$

Decay of current

After establishing current in the circuit ($i_0 = \xi / R$), the source is disconnected from the circuit. And the circuit is short circuited. The current in the circuit starts decaying. The energy stored in inductor will change into thermal energy. The equation for decaying current can be obtained by putting $\xi = 0$ in previous equation (i), we have

$$\therefore \qquad -L\frac{di}{dt} = i\,R$$

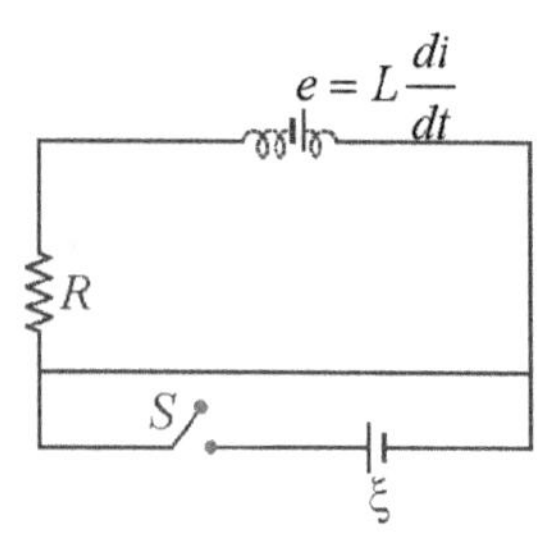

$$e = L\frac{di}{dt}$$

Fig. 8.75

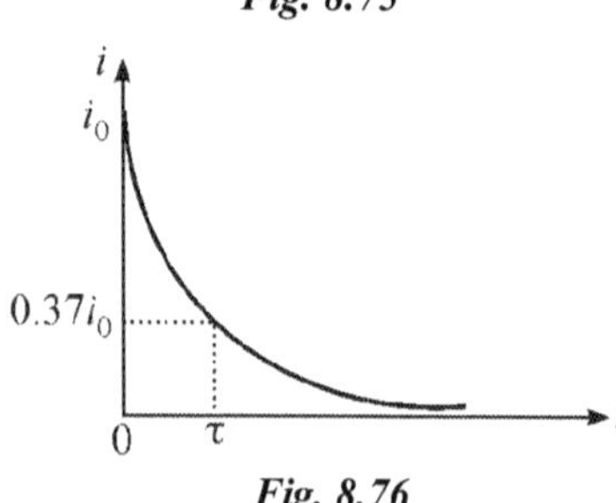

Fig. 8.76

or

$$\frac{di}{i} = -\frac{dt}{\left(\dfrac{L}{R}\right)}$$

Integrating above equation, we get $\displaystyle\int_{i_0}^{i}\frac{di}{i} = -\int\frac{dt}{\left(\dfrac{L}{R}\right)}$

or

$$\left|\ell n\, i\right|_{i_0}^{i} = -\frac{t}{\tau}$$

or

$$\ell n\, i - \ell n\, i_0 = -\frac{t}{\tau}$$

or

$$\ell n\frac{i}{i_0} = \frac{-t}{R}$$

or

$$i = i_0 e^{-\frac{t}{\tau}} \qquad \ldots(1)$$

For $t = \tau$, $i = i_0 e^{-1} \simeq 0.37\, i_0$. Thus the inductive time constant can also be defined as the time in which the decaying current becomes 0.37 times the maximum current.

Energy at any time :

$$U = \frac{1}{2}Li^2 = \frac{1}{2}L\left[i_0 e^{-\frac{t}{\tau}}\right]^2$$

$$= \left(\frac{1}{2}Li_0^2\right)e^{\frac{-2t}{\tau}}$$

$$U = U_0 e^{-\frac{t}{\tau'}} \; ; \tau' = \frac{\tau}{2} \qquad \ldots(2)$$

More about inductor

1. At $t = 0$, $i = i_0\left(1 - e^0\right) = 0$ and at $t = \infty$, $i = i_0\left(1 - e^{-\infty}\right) = i_0 = \dfrac{\xi}{R}$. It means inductor offers infinite resistance initially and zero resistance after very long time : It becomes ineffective when current becomes steady in the circuit.

2. Inductor does not oppose the current, but it opposes the change in current. It causes delay in growing or decaying of current. Therefore it also called electrical inertia.

Ex. 42 A coil has an inductance of 53 mH and a resistance of 0.35 Ω.

(a) If a 12 V emf is applied across the coil, how much energy is stored in the magnetic field after the current has built up to its maximum value ?

(b) After how many time constants will half the maximum energy be stored in the magnetic field ?

Sol. (a) The maximum current in the coil

$$i_0 = \frac{\xi}{R} = \frac{12}{0.35} = 34.3\,A$$

The maximum energy stored

$$U_0 = \frac{1}{2}Li_0^2 = \frac{1}{2}\left(53 \times 10^{-3}\right)\left(34.3\right)^2$$

$$= 31\,J \qquad \textit{Ans.}$$

(b) We know that, energy at any time in the coil is given by

$$U = U_0\left(1 - e^{-\frac{t}{\tau}}\right)^2$$

For $U = U_0/2$, we have

$$\frac{U_0}{2} = U_0\left(1 - e^{-\frac{t}{\tau}}\right)^2$$

or

$$e^{-\frac{t}{\tau}} = 1 - \frac{1}{\sqrt{2}} = 0.293$$

or

$$\frac{t}{\tau} = 1.23$$

$$\therefore \qquad t = 1.23\,\tau \qquad \textit{Ans.}$$

8.11 The LC-oscillations

Consider a LC- circuit shown in *fig. 8.77*, a resistanceless inductor is connected between the terminals of a charged capacitor. At the instant when connections are made, the capacitor starts to discharge through the inductor. At a later instant, the capacitor has completely discharged and the potential difference between its terminals has decreased to zero. The current in the inductor has meanwhile establishes a magnetic field in the space around it. This magnetic field now decreases, inducing an emf in the inductor in the same direction as the current. The current therefore persists, although with decreasing magnitude, until the magnetic field has disappeared and the capacitor has been charged in the opposite sense to its initial polarity. The process now repeats itself in the reverse direction, and in the absence of any energy losses, the charges on the capacitor surge back and forth indefinitely. This process is called **electrical oscillations**. From the energy state point, the oscillations of an electrical circuit consist of a transfer of energy back and forth from electric field of capacitor to the magnetic field of the inductor, the total energy associated with the circuit remaining constant. This is analogous to the transfer of energy in an oscillating mechanical system from kinetic to potential, and vice versa. Let a capacitor C is given an initial charge Q and, at $t = 0$ is connected to the inductor of

self inductance L. The magnetic energy of the inductor $\left(\dfrac{1}{2}Li^2\right)$ at any time corresponds to the kinetic energy of the oscillating mass-spring system. The potential energy of the

capacitor $\left(\dfrac{q^2}{2C}\right)$ corresponds to the potential energy of the spring $\left(\dfrac{1}{2}kx^2\right)$. The sum of

these energies of the system, is equal to initial energy, $\dfrac{Q^2}{2C}$. Therefore by conservation of energy

$$\frac{1}{2}Li^2 + \frac{q^2}{2C} = \frac{Q^2}{2C}.$$

Differentiating above equation w.r.t. time, we get

$$\frac{1}{2}L \times 2i \times \frac{di}{dt} + \frac{1}{2C} \times 2q \times \frac{dq}{dt} = 0$$

or

$$L\frac{di}{dt} + \frac{q}{C} = 0$$

As

$$i = \frac{dq}{dt},$$

∴

$$\frac{d^2q}{dt^2} + \frac{q}{LC} = 0 \qquad \qquad ...(1)$$

Compare above equation with differential equation of oscillations of mass-spring system, i.e.,

$$\frac{d^2x}{dt^2} + \omega^2 x = 0, \text{ we get}$$

$$\omega = \sqrt{\frac{1}{LC}}, \qquad \qquad ...(2)$$

This is called natural frequency of the LC circuit.

Time period $\qquad T = 2\pi\sqrt{LC}$

Also, $\qquad\qquad q = Q\cos(\omega t + \phi)$

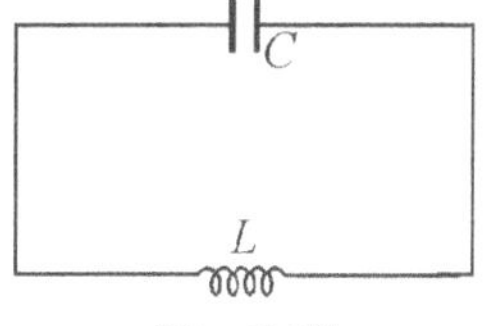

Fig. 8.77

Comparison between electrical oscillations with the oscillations of mass spring system

$t = 0$	$t = T/4$	$t = T/2$	$t = 3T/4$	$t = T$
$U_E = q^2/2C$ $U_B = 0$	$U_E = 0$ $U_B = 1/2\,Li^2$	$U_E = q^2/2C$ $U_B = 0$	$U_E = 0$ $U_B = 1/2\,Li^2$	$U_E = q^2/2C$ $U_B = 0$
P.E. $= 1/2kx^2$ K.E. $= 0$	P.E. $= 0$ K.E. $= 1/2mv^2$	P.E. $= 1/2kx^2$ K.E. $= 0$	P.E. $= 0$ K.E. $= 1/2mv^2$	P.E. $= 1/2kx^2$ K.E. $= 0$
Mean position	Mean position	Mean position	Mean position	Mean position

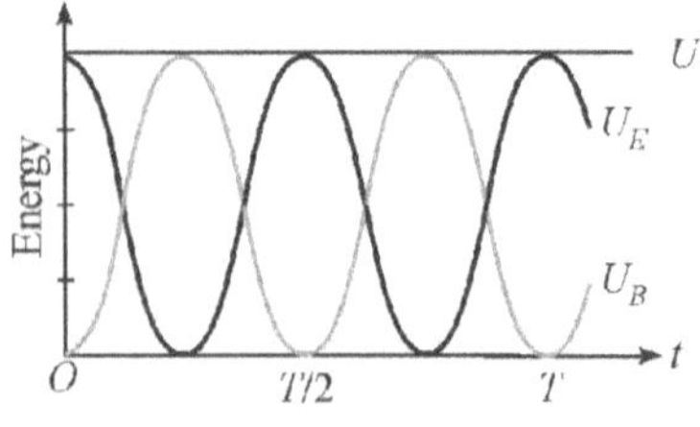

Fig. 8.78

$$U_E = \frac{q^2}{2C} = \frac{Q^2}{2C}\cos^2\left(\omega t + \phi\right)$$

and

$$U_B = \frac{1}{2}Li^2 = \frac{Q^2}{2C}\sin^2\left(\omega t + \phi\right)$$

8.12 DAMPED OSCILLATIONS IN AN RLC CIRCUIT

In the previous case we have assumed that the LC- circuit contains no resistance. This is an idealisation, of the circuit for every real inductor there is resistance associated with the windings, and there may be resistance in the connecting wires as well. The effect is to dissipate the electromagnetic energy and convert it to heat; thus, resistance in an electric circuit plays a role analogous to that of friction in the mechanical system.

Suppose an inductor of self-inductance L and a resistor of resistance R are connected in series with the capacitor. If the capacitor is initially charged, it starts discharging at the instant the connections are made, but because of i^2R losses in the resistor, the energy of the inductor when capacitor is completely discharged is less than the original energy of the capacitor. In the same way, the energy of the capacitor where the magnetic field has collapsed is still smaller, and so on. If the resistance R is relatively small, the circuit oscillates, but with damped harmonic motion. As R is increased, the oscillations die out more rapidly. At a sufficiently large value of R, the circuit no longer oscillates and is said to be critically damped. For still larger resistance it is overdamped.

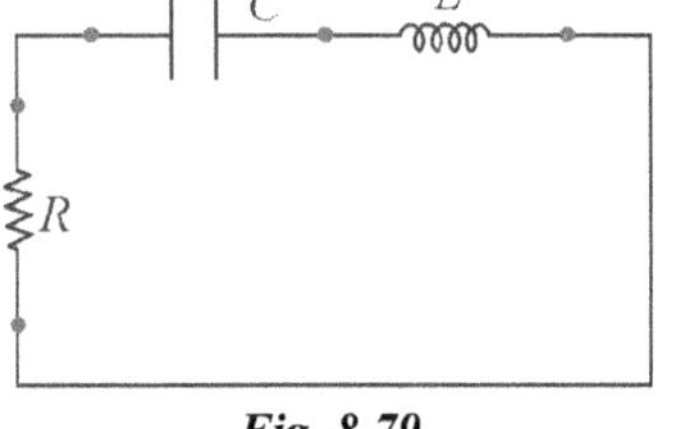

Fig. 8.79

Using loop rule to the circuit yields the equation :

Rate of dissipation of electromagnetic energy = power generated as heat

or

$$\frac{d}{dt}\left[\frac{q^2}{2C} + \frac{1}{2}L\,i^2\right] = -i^2R$$

or

$$\frac{2q}{2C}\frac{dq}{dt} + \frac{L}{2}\times 2i \times \frac{di}{dt} = -i^2R$$

or

$$\frac{q}{C}i + L\,i\,\frac{d^2q}{dt^2} = -i^2R$$

or

$$\frac{d^2q}{dt^2} + \frac{R}{L}\frac{dq}{dt} + \frac{q}{LC} = 0 \qquad\qquad ...(1)$$

The above equation is analogous to damped harmonic oscillator of mechanical system.
i.e.,

$$\frac{d^2x}{dt^2} + b\frac{dx}{dt} + kx = 0$$

The solution of equation (1) can be

$$q = Qe^{-\frac{Rt}{2L}}\cos\left(\omega_d t + \phi\right) \qquad ...(2)$$

Here, $\quad \omega_d = \sqrt{\dfrac{1}{LC} - \left(\dfrac{R}{2L}\right)^2}$, is called damed frequency

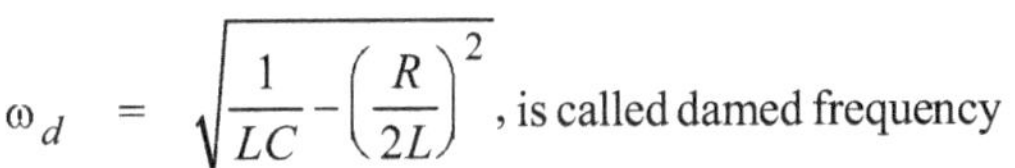

Critical damping

As R increases ω becomes smaller and smaller; when $R^2 = \dfrac{4L}{C}$ the quantity under the

underroot becomes zero, and the case is called critical damping.

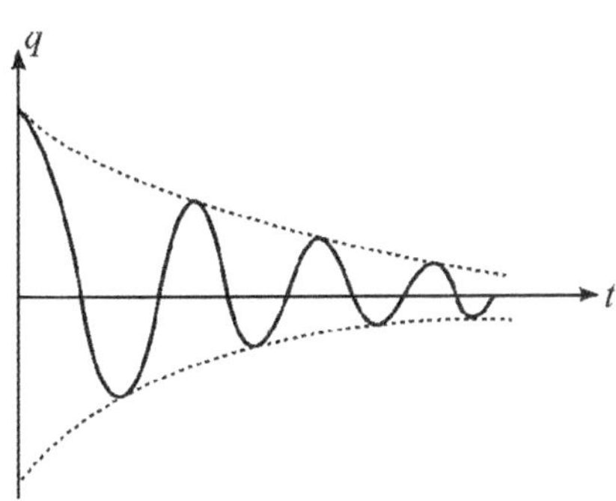

Fig. 8.80 Variation of charge of capacitor with time.

8.13 MUTUAL INDUCTION

Consider two coils placed close together, a steady current i in one coil will set up a magnetic flux ϕ_B linking with the other coil. If we change i with time, an emf will appear in the second coil. This is called **mutual induction**.

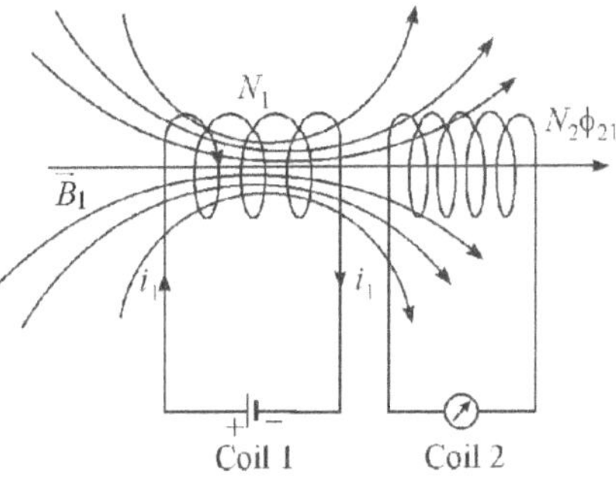

Note:

For ease of representation, the two coils shown in *fig. 8.81* are not actually drawn as close-packet : In close-packet coils the turns have the same flux through them.

Consider two circular closed packed coils are placed near each other and sharing a common central axis. There is steady current i_1 in coil 1, set up by the battery in the

external circuit. This current produces a magnetic field $\vec{B}_1$, which produces magnetic

flux $N_2\phi_{21}$ in coil 2, linked by its N_2 turns.
We can define the mutual inductance M_{21} of coil 2 with respect to 1 as

$$M_{21} = \frac{N_2\phi_{21}}{i_1}$$

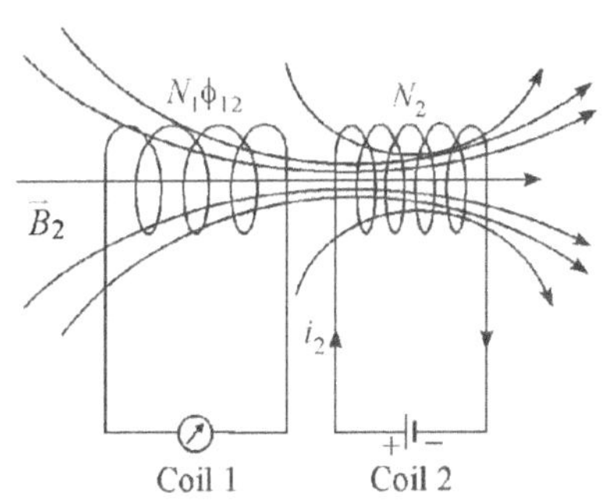

Fig. 8.81

or it can be written as

$$M_{21} i_1 = N_2\phi_{21}.$$

If i_1 changes with time, then

$$M_{21}\frac{di_i}{dt} = N_2\frac{d\phi_{21}}{dt}$$

According to Faraday's law, the right side of the equation is equal to $-e_2$. Thus

$$e_2 = -M_{21}\frac{di_i}{dt}$$

By doing similar treatment for first coil, we get

$$e_1 = -M_{12}\frac{di_2}{dt}$$

By experiments, $M_{12} = M_{21} = M$. Thus

$$e_1 = -M\frac{di_2}{dt} \qquad ...(1)$$

and

$$e_2 = -M\frac{di_1}{dt} \qquad\qquad ...(2)$$

The SI unit of M is henry.

The coefficient of mutual induction depends on the shape, size, and mutual arrangement of the coils, as well as the magnetic permeability of the medium surrounding the coils.

Reciprocity theorem

Calculations show (and experiments confirm) that in the absence of material medium between the coils, the coefficients M_{12} and M_{21} are equal :

$$M_{12} = M_{21}$$

This property of mutual inductance is called the reciprocity theorem. Because of this reason, we do not have to distinguish between M_{12} and M_{21} and can simply speak of the mutual inductance of two circuits.

Steps for finding M

1. Imagine current i_1 in the first coil.
2. Determine magnetic field due to i_1 in the second coil.
3. Obtain flux linkage, $N_2\,\phi_2 = N_2\,(B_1 A_2)$.
4. Compare with, $N_2\phi_2 = M\,i_1$ and find M.

Mutual induction between circular coils

Consider two circular close-packed coils, the smaller (radius R_2, with turns N_2) being coaxial with the larger (radius R_1, with N_1 turns) and in the same plane. Assuming $R_1 \gg R_2$. Imagine a current i_1 in the larger coil, the value of B_1 at the centre of coil,

$$B_1 = \frac{\mu_0 N_1 i_1}{2R_1}$$

Because we have assumed that $R_1 >> R_2$, we may take B_1 to the magnetic field at all points within the boundary of the smaller coil. Therefore the number of flux linkage for the smaller coil is

$$N_2\phi_{21} = N_2(B_1)\,(\pi R_2{}^2)$$

$$= N_2\left(\frac{\mu_0 N_1 i_1}{2R_1}\right)\pi R_2^2$$

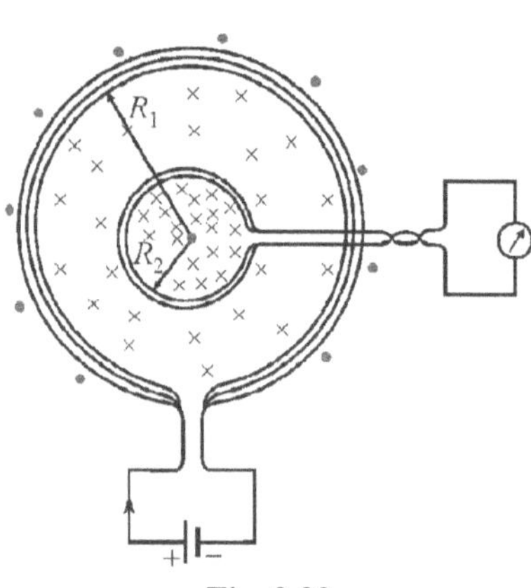

Fig. 8.82

Now compare with

$$N_2\phi_{21} = M\,i_1, \text{ we get}$$

$$M = \frac{\mu_0\pi\,N_1\,N_2\,R_2{}^2}{2R_1}$$

Mutual induction between solenoid and coil

A long solenoid of length ℓ and cross-sectional area A is closely wound with N_1 turns of wire. A small coil of N_2 turns surrounds at its centre. A current i_1 in the solenoid set up a magnetic field $\vec{B}$ at its centre of magnitude

$$B = \mu_0 n i_1 = \mu_0\frac{N_1\,i_1}{\ell}$$

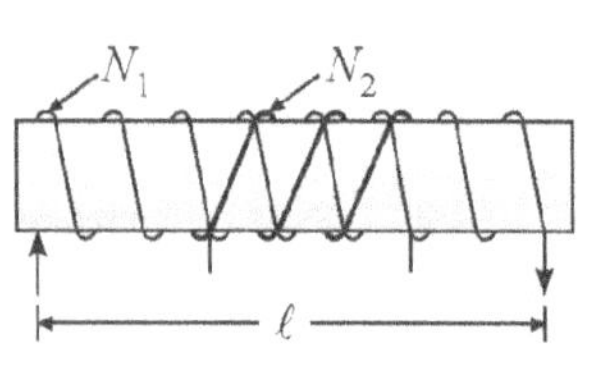

Fig. 8.83

The flux through the central section is equal to BA, and since all of this flux links with the small coil, then

$$N_2\phi_{21} = N_2(B_1 A_2)$$

$$= N_2\left(\frac{\mu_0 N_1\,i_1}{\ell}\right)A$$

Now compare with $N_2\phi_{21} = M\,i_1$, we get

$$M = \mu_0 \frac{N_1\,N_2\,A}{\ell}$$

Coefficient of coupling

Let us consider two coils placed close to each other. For them

$$M_{12} = \frac{N_1\phi_{12}}{i_2} \text{ and } M_{21} = \frac{N_2\phi_{21}}{i_1}$$

Similarly

$$L_1 = \frac{N_1\phi_1}{i_1} \text{ and } L_2 = \frac{N_2\phi_2}{i_2}$$

If coils are closely packed, that is, flux of coil 1 is completely associated with 2 and vice versa, then

$$\phi_{12} = \phi_{21}$$

Also

$$M_{12} = M_{21} = M$$

$$\therefore \quad M_{12}\,M_{21} = M^2 = \frac{N_1\,N_2\,\phi_1\,\phi_2}{i_1\,i_2}$$

$$= \left(\frac{N_1\phi_1}{i_1}\right)\left(\frac{N_2\,\phi_2}{i_2}\right)$$

$$= L_1\,L_2$$

or

$$M = \sqrt{L_1\,L_2}$$

If there is some leakage of flux between the coils, then

$$M < \sqrt{L_1\,L_2}$$

In general, we can write

$$M = k\sqrt{L_1\,L_2}$$

where k is called coefficient of coupling; $0 \le k \le 1$.
For tight coupling $k = 1$, for loose coupling $k < 1$

k can be defined as,

$$k = \frac{\text{Magnetic flux linked in secondary}}{\text{Magnetic flux linked in primary}}$$

8.14 COMBINATIONS OF INDUCTORS

Series : Let two inductors L_1 and L_2 are connected in series. Considering only self inductance of inductors, then total induced emf

$$e = e_1 + e_2$$

or

$$-L\frac{di}{dt} = -L_1\frac{di}{dt} - L_2\frac{di}{dt}$$

$$\therefore \quad L = L_1 + L_2$$

Parallel : At the junction

$$i = i_1 + i_2 \qquad \text{...(i)}$$

As the inductors are in parallel, so

$$e_1 = e_2 = e$$

or

$$-L_1\frac{di_1}{dt} = -L_2\frac{di_2}{dt} = -L\frac{di}{dt}$$

$$= K \qquad \text{...(ii)}$$

or

$$\frac{di_1}{dt} = \frac{K}{-L_1}, \frac{di_2}{dt} = \frac{-K}{L_2}$$

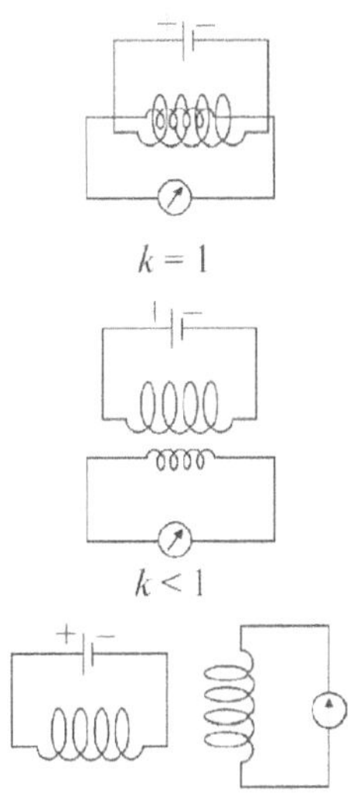

Fig. 8.84

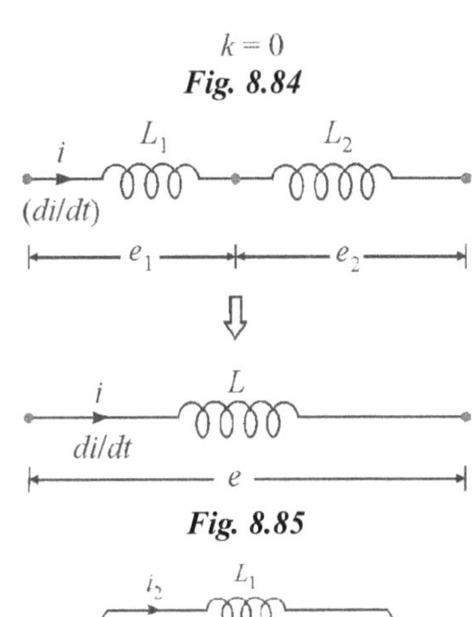

Fig. 8.85

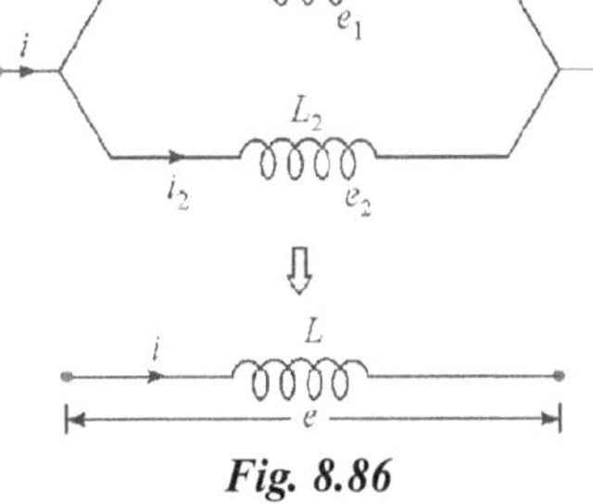

Fig. 8.86

and
$$\frac{di}{dt} = \frac{K}{-L}$$

From equation (i), we have

$$\frac{di}{dt} = \frac{di_1}{dt} + \frac{di_2}{dt}$$

or
$$\frac{K}{-L} = \frac{K}{-L_1} - \frac{K}{L_2}$$

or
$$\frac{1}{L} = \frac{1}{L_1} + \frac{1}{L_2}$$

Total inductance

When coils are connected together in a circuit, they offer both self induction and mutual induction. Their total induction will be the algebraic sum of self induction and mutual induction.

(i)   Suppose two coils of self inductances L_1 and L_2 are connected in series in such a way that their fluxes are additive.

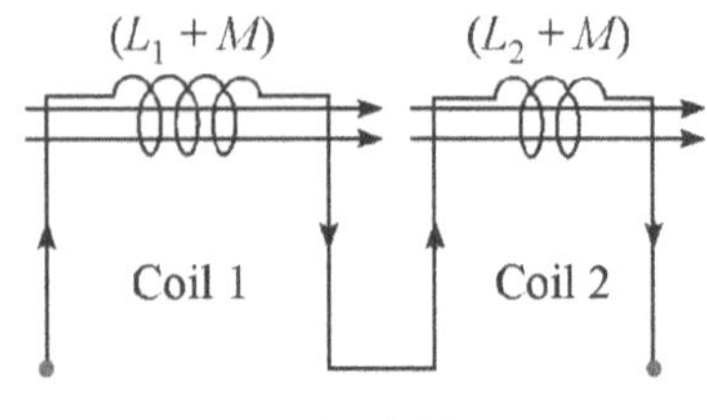

Fig. 8.87

If $\dfrac{di}{dt}$ is the rate of increase of current in the coils, then self induced emf in coil 1,

$$e_1 = -L_1 \frac{di}{dt}$$

Mutual induced emf in coil 1, due to change in current in coil 2

$$e_1' = -M \frac{di}{dt}$$

Self induced emf in coil 2,

$$e_2 = -L_2 \frac{di}{dt}$$

Mutual induced emf in coil 2, due to change in current in coil 1,

$$e_2' = -M \frac{di}{dt}$$

Total induced emf in the combination

$$e = \left(e_1 + e_1'\right) + \left(e_2 + e_2'\right)$$

$$= -\frac{di}{dt}\left(L_1 + L_2 + 2M\right) \qquad \text{...(i)}$$

If L_{Total} in the total or equivalent induced emf in that single coil, then

$$e = -L_{\text{Total}} \frac{di}{dt} \qquad \text{...(ii)}$$

On equating equations (1) and (2), we get
$$L_{\text{Total}} = L_1 + L_2 + 2M \qquad \text{...(1)}$$

(ii)   When the coils are so connected that their fluxes are in opposite directions.

If $\dfrac{di}{dt}$ is the rate of increase of current in the coils, then

$$e_1 = -L_1 \frac{di}{dt},$$

$$e_1' = +M\frac{di}{dt},$$

$$e_2 = -L_2\frac{di}{dt}$$

and

$$e_2' = +M\frac{di}{dt}$$

The total induced emf $= -\frac{di}{dt}\left(L_1 + L_2 - 2M\right)$

Thus total inductance $L_{Total} = L_1 + L_2 - 2M$ ....(2)

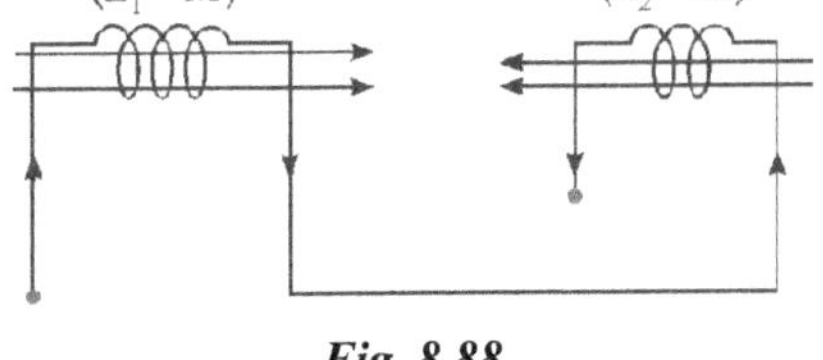

Fig. 8.88

Ex. 43 Two circular loops 1 and 2 whose centres coincide lie in a plane (see *fig. 8.89*). The radii of the loops are a_1 and a_2. Current i flows in loop 1. Find the magnetic flux ϕ_2 associated by loop 2, if $a_1 << a_2$.

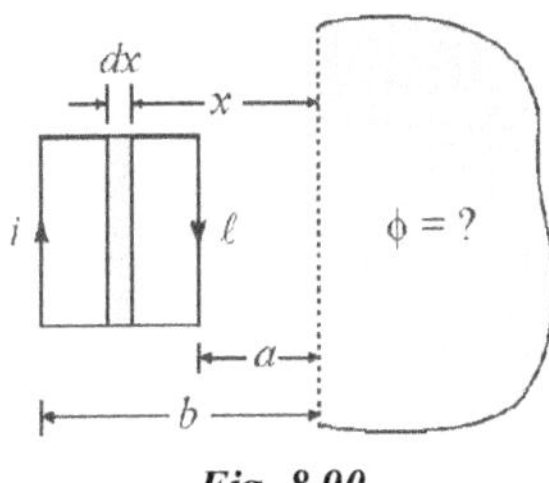

Fig. 8.89

Sol.

The direct calculation of the flux ϕ_2 is clearly a rather complicated problem since the configuration of the field itself is complicated. However, the application of the reciprocity theorem greatly simplifies the solution of the problem. Let us pass the same current i through loop 2. Then the magnetic flux ϕ_1 created by this current through loop 1 can be easily found, provided that $a_1 << a_2$: it is sufficient to multiply the magnetic field B at the centre of the loop $\left(B = \dfrac{\mu_0 i}{2a_2}\right)$ by the area πa_1^2 of the circle.

Thus

$$\begin{aligned}\phi_2 &= \phi_1 \\ &= B_2 A_1 \\ &= \frac{\mu_0 i}{2a_2}\pi a_1^2 . \qquad \textit{Ans.}\end{aligned}$$

Ex. 44 A loop with current *i* has the shape of a rectangle. Find the magnetic flux ϕ through the hatched half-plane (see *fig. 8.90*) whose boundary is at a given distance from the contour. Assume that this half-plane and the loop are in the same plane.

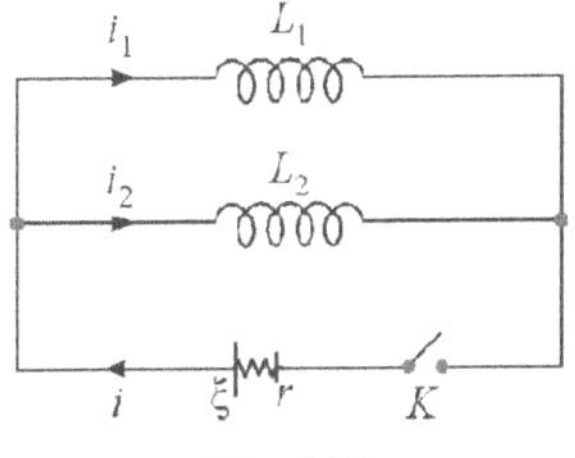

Fig. 8.90

Sol.

In this case, the magnetic field of current i has a complex configuration, and hence it is very difficult to calculate directly the flux ϕ in which we are interested. However, the solution can be considerably simplified by using the reciprocity theorem. Suppose that current i flows not around the rectangular contour but along the boundary of the half-plane, enveloping it at infinity. The magnetic field created by this current in the region of the rectangular loop has a simple configuration as this is the field of a straight current. Hence we can easily find the magnetic flux ϕ' through the rectangular contour

$$\begin{aligned}\phi &= \phi' \\ &= \int_a^{(a+b)} \frac{\mu_0}{2\pi}\frac{i}{x}\ell\,dx \\ &= \frac{\mu_0 i\ell}{2\pi}\ell n\left(\frac{a+b}{a}\right). \qquad \textit{Ans.}\end{aligned}$$

Ex. 45 In the circuit shown in *fig. 8.91*, the emf ξ of the source, its internal resistance r and the inductances L_1 and L_2 of superconducting coils are known. Find the currents established in the coils after key K has been closed.

Fig. 8.91

Sol. Suppose i_1 and i_2 are the currents in the respective coils and i is the current drawn from the battery, then

$$\begin{aligned}i &= \frac{\xi}{r} \\ &= i_1 + i_2 \qquad ...(i)\end{aligned}$$

Inductors L_1 and L_2 are in parallel, and so $e_1 = e_2$

or $\qquad L_1\dfrac{di_1}{dt} = L_2\dfrac{di_2}{dt}$

On integrating both sides, we have

$$L_1 i_1 = L_2 i_2 \qquad ...(ii)$$

Solving equations (i) and (ii), we get

$$i_1 = \frac{\xi}{r}\frac{L_2}{L_1 + L_2}$$

and $\qquad i_2 = \dfrac{\xi}{r}\dfrac{L_1}{L_1 + L_2}$ **Ans.**

Ex. 46
A small cylindrical magnet M is placed at the centre of a thin coil of radius a, containing N turns (see figure). The coil is connected to a galvanometer. The resistance of the circuit is R. After the magnet had been rapidly removed from the coil, a charge q passed through the galvanometer. Find the magnetic moment of the magnet.

Sol.   We know that, the charge flow

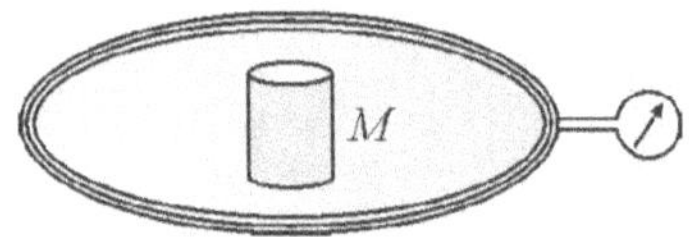

Fig. 8.92

$$q = \dfrac{|\Delta\phi|}{R},$$

where $\qquad |\Delta\phi| = |\phi_f - \phi_i| = |0 - \phi|$

$$= \phi, \qquad ...(i)$$

$$\therefore \qquad q = \dfrac{\phi}{R}$$

ϕ is the magnetic flux through the coil at the beginning of the process. The quantity ϕ can not be determined directly. This difficulty, however, can be overcome by using the reciprocity theorem. We mentally replace the magnet by a small current loop creating in the surrounding space the same magnetic field as that of the magnet. If the area of the loop is A and current in it is i, then its magnetic moment $M = iA$. According to reciprocity theorem $M_{12} = M_{21}$ and the problem is reduced to determine the magnetic flux through the area A of the loop, which creates the same current i, but flowing in the coil. Assuming the field to be uniform within the loop, we have

$$\phi = BA = \left(\dfrac{\mu_0 Ni}{2a}\right)A \quad ...(ii)$$

Substituting the value of ϕ in equation (i), we have

$$q = \dfrac{\mu_0 N}{2aR}(iA)$$

$$\therefore \qquad iA = \dfrac{2aqR}{\mu_0 N} \qquad \textbf{Ans.}$$

Ex. 47
Two coils, A of 12500 turns and B of 16000 turns lie in parallel planes so that 60% of flux produced in A links with B. It is found that a current of 5A in A produces a flux of 0.6 mWb while the same current in B produces 0.8 mWb. Determine (i) mutual induction, (ii) coefficient of coupling.

Sol.

For coil A, $\qquad L_A = \dfrac{N_A\phi_A}{i} = \dfrac{12500 \times \left(0.6 \times 10^{-3}\right)}{5}$

$$= 0.15 \text{ H}$$

For coil B, $\qquad L_B = \dfrac{N_B\phi_B}{i} = \dfrac{16000 \times \left(0.8 \times 10^{-3}\right)}{5}$

$$= 0.26 \text{ H}$$

For the mutual induction, we can write

$$M = \dfrac{N_B\phi_B}{i_A} = \dfrac{N_B\left(0.6\phi_A\right)}{i_A}$$

$$= \dfrac{\left(16000 \times 0.6 \times 0.6 \times 10^{-3}\right)}{5}$$

$$= 1.15 \text{ H}$$

Thus coefficient of coupling

$$k = \dfrac{M}{\sqrt{L_1 L_2}} = \dfrac{1.15}{\sqrt{0.15 \times 0.26}}$$

$$= 0.586 \qquad \textbf{Ans.}$$

Ex. 48
Two coils with terminals T_1, T_2 and T_3, T_4 respectively are placed side by side. When measured separately, the inductance of the first coil is 1200 mH and that of second is 800 mH. With T_2 joined to T_3, the inductance between T_1 and T_4 is 2500 mH. What is the mutual inductance between the two coils ? Also, determine the inductance between T_1 and T_3 when T_2 is joined to T_4.

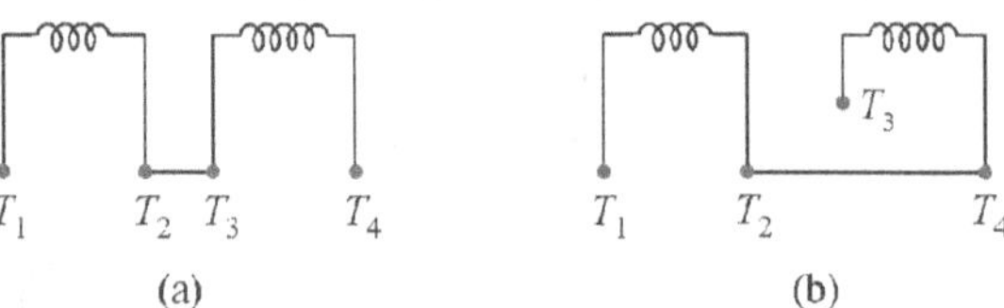

Fig. 8.93

Sol. Given, $\qquad L_1 = 1200 \text{ mH}, L_2 = 800 \text{ mH}.$

In *fig. 8.93* (a), $\qquad L_{\text{Total}} = 2500 \text{ mH. Thus}$

$$2500 = L_1 + L_2 + 2M$$

or $\qquad 2500 = 1200 + 800 + 2M$

$$\therefore \qquad M = 250 \text{ mH.}$$

In *fig. 8.93* (b)

$$L_{\text{Total}} = L_1 + L_2 - 2M$$

$$= 1200 + 800 - 2 \times 250$$

$$= 1500 \text{ mH} \qquad \textbf{Ans.}$$

Note:

In accordance with the total inductance, the total energy of the two coils is the sum of energies due to their self induction and mutual induction between them : Thus

$$U = \dfrac{1}{2}L_1 i_1{}^2 + \dfrac{1}{2}L_2\, i_2{}^2 + Mi_1 i_2,$$

when both the coils carrying currents in same direction, and

$$U = \dfrac{1}{2}L_1 i_1{}^2 + \dfrac{1}{2}L_2\, i_2{}^2 - Mi_1 i_2,$$

when current are in opposite directions.

Ex. 49 A rectangular conducting loop in the vertical xz-plane has length L, width W, mass M and resistance R. It is dropped lengthwise from rest. At $t = 0$ the bottom of the loop is at a height h above the horizontal x-axis. There is a uniform magnetic field B perpendicular to xz-plane, below the x-axis. The bottom and top of the loop cross this axis at $t = t_1$ and $t = t_2$ respectively. Obtain the expression for the velocity of the loop for the time $t_1 \leq t \leq t_2$.

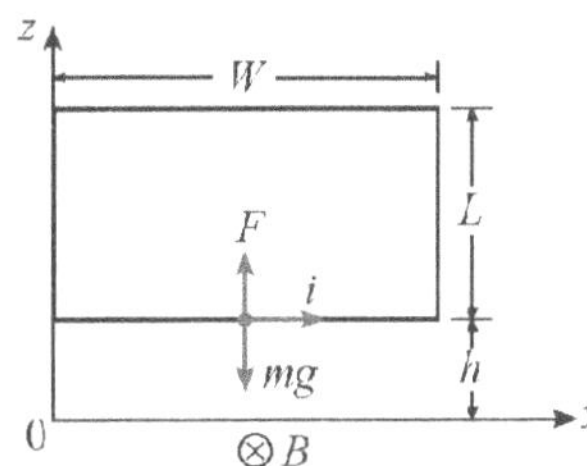

Fig. 8.96

Sol. For $0 \leq t \leq t_1$; there is no induced current and hence loop falls freely. Thus its velocity is given by

$$v_1 = gt_1 = \sqrt{2gh}$$

For $t_1 \leq t \leq t_2$; the emf induces across the bottom side of the loop, which is BvW, and induced current $i = \dfrac{BvW}{R}$ in counter clockwise direction. Due to this, it experiences an upward force,

$$F = BiW = B\left(\frac{BvW}{R}\right)W = \frac{B^2vW^2}{R}.$$

Now using Newton's second law for the motion of the loop, we have

$$mg - \frac{B^2vW^2}{R} = m\frac{dv}{dt}$$

or

$$\frac{dv}{\left[g - \dfrac{B^2vW^2}{mR}\right]} = dt$$

On integrating above expression, we have

$$\int_{v_1}^{v} \frac{dv}{\left[g - \dfrac{B^2vW^2}{mR}\right]} = \int_{t_1}^{t} dt$$

$$-\left(\frac{mR}{B^2W^2}\right)\left[\ell n\left(g - \frac{B^2vW^2}{mR}\right)\right]_{v_1}^{v} = t - t_1$$

or

$$\left[\ell n\left\{g - \frac{B^2vW^2}{mR}\right\} - \ell n\left\{g - \frac{B^2v_1W^2}{mR}\right\}\right] = \left[-(t - t_1)\frac{B^2W^2}{mR}\right]$$

or

$$\frac{\left[g - \left(\dfrac{B^2vW^2}{mR}\right)\right]}{\left[g - \left(\dfrac{B^2v_1W^2}{mR}\right)\right]} = e^{-\left[(t-t_1)\frac{B^2W^2}{mR}\right]}$$

or

$$v = \frac{mgR}{B^2W^2} + \left(v_1 - \frac{mgR}{B^2W^2}\right)e^{-\left[(t-t_1)\frac{B^2W^2}{mR}\right]} \quad \textbf{\textit{Ans.}}$$

Ex. 50 A thermocole vessel contains 0.5 kg of distilled water at 30°C. A metal coil of area 5×10^{-3} m^2, number of turns 100, mass 0.06 kg and resistance 1.6 Ω is lying horizontally at the bottom of the vessel. A uniform, time varying magnetic field is setup to pass vertically through the coil at time $t = 0$. The field is first increased from zero to 0.8 T at a constant rate between 0 and 0.2 s and then decreased to zero at the same rate between 0.2 and 0.4 s. This cycle is repeated 12000 times. Make sketches of the current through the coil and the power dissipated in the coil as functions of time for the first two cycles. Clearly indicate the magnitudes of the quantities on the axes. Assume that no heat is lost to the vessel or the surroundings. Determine the final temperature of the water under thermal equilibrium. Specific heat of the metal = 500 J/kg-K and specific heat of water = 4200 J/kg-K. Neglect the inductance of the coil.

Sol. The induced emf in the coil

$$e = -N\frac{d\phi}{dt} = -NA\left(\frac{dB}{dt}\right).$$

Induced current

$$i = \frac{e}{R} = -\frac{NA}{R}\left(\frac{dB}{dt}\right).$$

Given

$$\frac{dB}{dt} = \frac{0.8 - 0}{0.2 - 0} = 4\ T/s.$$

Thus for the time interval 0 to 0.2 s,

$$i = -\frac{100\left(5 \times 10^{-3}\right)}{1.6} \times 4$$

$$= -1.25\ \text{A}.$$

In the interval 0.2 to 0.4s, dB/dt is negative and so induced current will be +1.25 A.

Power dissipated $\quad P = i^2R = 1.25^2 \times 1.6$

$$= 2.5\ \text{W}$$

The total energy dissipated in 12000 cycles

$$E = Pt$$
$$= 2.5 \times (12000 \times 0.4)$$
$$= 12 \times 10^3\ \text{J}$$

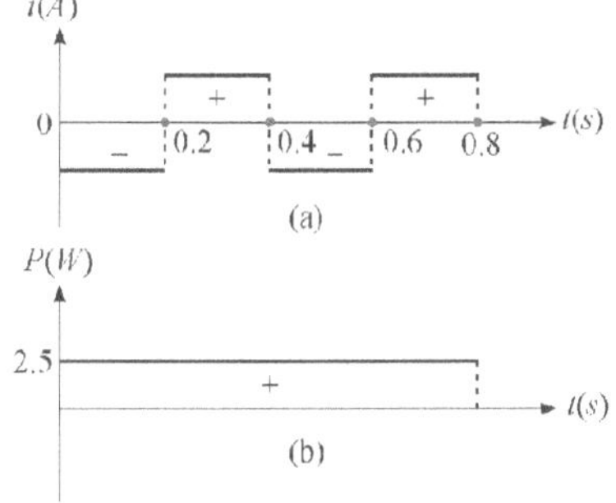

(a) Variation of current with time. (b) Variation of power with time.

Fig. 8.97

If ΔT is the change in temperature of water, then by conservation of energy

$$12 \times 10^3 = (m_1c_1 + m_2c_2)\,\Delta T$$

$$\therefore \qquad \Delta T = \frac{12 \times 10^3}{\left(m_1c_1 + m_2c_2\right)}$$

$$= \frac{12 \times 10^3}{\left(0.5 \times 4200 + 0.06 \times 500\right)}$$

$$= 5.6°C$$

Final temperature $= T_i + \Delta T$

$$= 30 + 5.6 = 35.6°C \qquad \textbf{\textit{Ans.}}$$

Ex. 51 A metal bar AB can slide on two parallel thick metallic rails separated by a distance ℓ. A resistance R and inductance L are connected to the rails as shown in *fig. 8.98*. A long straight wire carrying a constant current i_0 is passed in the plane of the rails and perpendicular to them as shown. The bar AB is held at rest at a distance x_0 from the long wire. At $t = 0$, it is made to slide on the rails away from the wire. Answer the following questions :

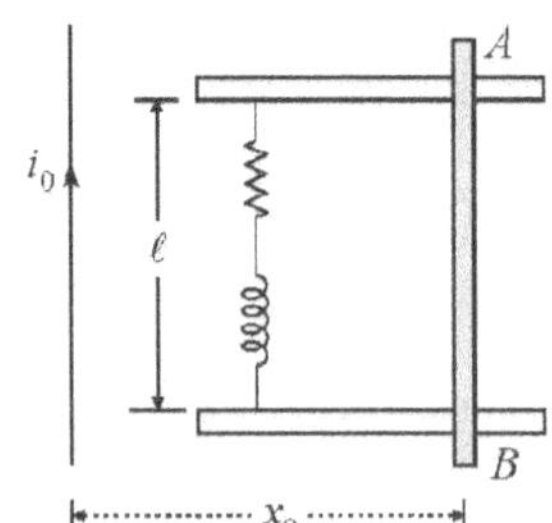

Fig. 8.98

(a) Find a relation among, i, $\dfrac{di}{dt}$ and $\dfrac{d\phi}{dt}$, where i is the current in the circuit and ϕ is the flux of the magnetic field due to the long wire through the circuit.

(b) It is observed that at time $t = T$, the metal bar AB is at a distance of $2x_0$ from the long wire and the resistance R carries a current i_1. Obtain an expression for the net charge that has flown through resistance R from $t = 0$ to $t = T$.

(c) The bar is suddenly stopped at time T. The current through resistance R is found to be $\dfrac{i_1}{4}$ at time $2T$. Find the value of $\dfrac{L}{R}$ in terms of the other given quantities.

Sol.

(a) If e is the induced emf and $\dfrac{di}{dt}$ is the rate of increase of current in the circuit, then by Kirchhoff's II law, we have

$$e - iR - L\frac{di}{dt} = 0$$

or $$e = iR + L\frac{di}{dt}$$

or $$\left|\frac{d\phi}{dt}\right| = iR + \frac{L\,di}{dt} \qquad ...(i)$$

Fig.8.99 The equivalent circuit.

(b) Equation (i) can be written as

$$d\phi = R(idt) + Ldi$$

or $$d\phi = R(dq) + Ldi$$

On integrating, we get

$$\int_{\phi_i}^{\phi_f} d\phi = R\int_{0}^{q} dq + L\int_{0}^{i_1} di$$

$$(\phi_f - \phi_i) = Rq + Li_1$$

∴ Charge flown during the time $t = 0$ to $t = T$ will be

$$q = \frac{\left(\phi_f - \phi_i\right)}{R} - \frac{Li_1}{R} \qquad ...(ii)$$

The change in flux can be obtained as

$$\phi_f - \phi_i = \int_{x_0}^{2x_0} B\,dA = \int_{x_0}^{2x_0} \frac{\mu_0 i_0}{2\pi x}\left(\ell dx\right)$$

$$= \frac{\mu_0 i_0 \ell}{2\pi}\ell n\,2.$$

On substituting this value in equation (ii), we get

$$q = \frac{\mu_0 i_0 \ell}{2\pi R}\ell n\,2 - \frac{L i_1}{R}$$

(c) When the bar is stopped, the induced emf becomes zero, and so from equation (i)

$$\frac{di}{i} = -\frac{R}{L}dt$$

On integrating, we have

$$\int_{i_1}^{\frac{i_1}{4}} \frac{di}{i} = -\frac{R}{L}\int_{T}^{2T} dt$$

or $$\left|\ell n\,i\right|_{i_1}^{\frac{i_1}{4}} = -\frac{R}{L}\left(2T - T\right)$$

or $$\ell n\left(\frac{1}{4}\right) = -\frac{RT}{L}$$

or $$\ell n\,4 = \frac{RT}{L}$$

∴ $$\frac{L}{R} = \frac{T}{\ell n\,4} \qquad \textbf{\textit{Ans.}}$$

Ex. 52 Two infinitely long parallel wires carrying current $i = i_0 \sin\omega t$ in opposite directions are placed at a distance $3a$ apart. A square loop of side a of negligible resistance with a capacitor of capacitance C is placed in the plane of wires as shown. Find the maximum current in the square loop. Also sketch the graph showing the variation of charge on the upper plate of the capacitor as a function of time for one complete cycle taking anticlockwise direction for the current in the loop as positive.

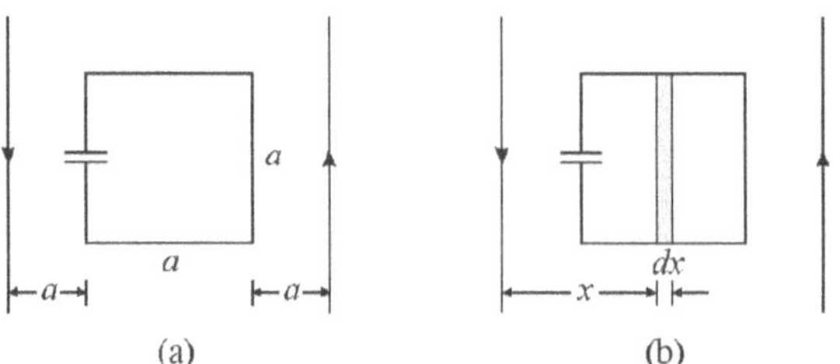

(a)   (b)

Fig. 100

Sol.

Take an element of thickness dx at a distance of x from left wire. The magnetic field at the position of element

$$B = \frac{\mu_0 i}{2\pi x} + \frac{\mu_0}{2\pi} \frac{i}{(3a-x)} \text{ upward}$$

$$= \frac{\mu_0 i}{2\pi}\left[\frac{1}{x} + \frac{1}{3a-x}\right]$$

The magnetic flux through the area of the element

$$d\phi = B(dA) = B(adx)$$

$$= \frac{\mu_0 i}{2\pi}\left[\frac{1}{x} + \frac{1}{3a-x}\right](ad.$$

The total magnetic flux through the loop

$$\phi = \frac{\mu_0 ia}{2\pi}\int_a^{2a}\left[\frac{1}{x} + \frac{1}{3a-x}\right]dx$$

$$= \frac{\mu_0 ia}{2\pi}\left[\ell n\, x - \ell n\,(3a-x)\right]_a^{2a}$$

$$= \frac{\mu_0 ia}{2\pi}\left[\left(\ell n\, 2a - \ell n\, a\right) - \left(\ell n\, a - \ell n\, 2a\right)\right]$$

$$= \frac{\mu_0 ia}{\pi}\ell n\, 2a$$

Given

$$i = i_0 i_0 \sin\omega t,$$

$$\therefore \quad \phi = \frac{\mu_0}{\pi}\left(i_0 \sin\omega t\right)a\,\ell n\, 2a$$

Induced emf

$$|e| = \frac{d\phi}{dt}$$

$$= \left[\frac{\mu_0 i_0 \omega a}{\pi}\ell n\, 2a\right]\cos\omega t$$

The maximum value of induced emf

$$e_0 = \left[\frac{\mu_0 i_0 a\omega \ell n\, 2a}{\pi}\right]$$

Impedance of the capacitor

$$Z = \frac{1}{\omega C}$$

$\therefore$ Maximum value of the current

$$I_0 = \frac{e_0}{Z} = \left[\frac{\mu_0 i_0 a\omega^2 C\,\ell n\, 2a}{\pi}\right] \quad \textit{Ans.}$$

The charge on the capacitor

$$q = Ce$$

$$= \left[\frac{\mu_0 i_0 a\omega C\,\ell n\, 2a}{\pi}\right]\cos\omega t$$

Thus maximum value of charge

$$q_0 = \left[\frac{\mu_0 i_0 a\omega C\,\ell n\, 2a}{\pi}\right]$$

According to the equation $i = i_0 \sin\omega t$, current and hence flux in the loop increases initially in upward direction, and so direction of induced current makes upper plate of the capacitor positive.

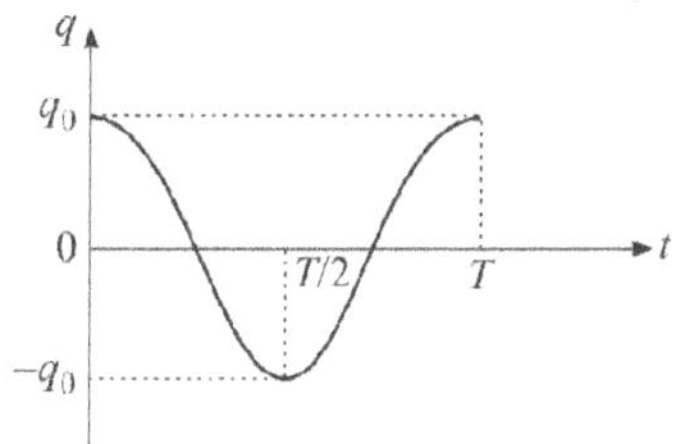

Fig.8.101 Variation of charge q with time.

Ex. 53 A thin wire ring of radius a and resistance r is located inside a long solenoid so that their axes coincide. The length of the solenoid is equal to ℓ, its cross-sectional radius to b. At a certain moment the solenoid was connected to a source of a constant voltage V. The total resistance of the circuit is equal to R. Assuming the inductance of the ring to be negligible, find the maximum value of the radial force acting per unit length of the ring.

Sol.

The self inductance of the solenoid

$$L = \mu_0 n^2 \pi b^2 \ell,$$

where n is the number of turns per unit length of the solenoid. When solenoid is connected to a source of a constant voltage V, a current is set-up. The current is given by

$$i = \frac{V}{R}\left(1 - e^{-\frac{tR}{L}}\right)$$

The flux through the coil

$$\phi_{coil} = B\, A_{coil}$$

$$= (\mu_0 ni)\,\pi a^2$$

$$\therefore \quad |e| = \frac{d\phi_{coil}}{dt} = \mu_0 n\pi a^2\left(\frac{di}{dt}\right)$$

The current in the coil

$$i' = \frac{e}{r} = \frac{\mu_0 n\pi a^2\left(\frac{di}{dt}\right)}{r}$$

The force on unit length on the ring

$$F = B\, i' \times 1 = (\mu_0 n\, i)i'$$

$$= \mu_0 n\left[\frac{V}{R}\left(1 - e^{-\frac{tR}{L}}\right)\times \frac{\mu_0 n\pi a^2}{r}\times \frac{Ve^{-\frac{tR}{L}}}{R}\times \frac{R}{L}\right]$$

$$= \left[\frac{\mu_0^2 \pi a^2 V^2 n^2}{rRL}\right]e^{-\frac{tR}{L}}\left(1 - e^{-\frac{tR}{L}}\right)$$

For maximum value of F, $\dfrac{dF}{dt} = 0$;

or $\quad \dfrac{d}{dt}\left[e^{-\frac{tR}{L}}\left(1 - e^{-\frac{tR}{L}}\right)\right] = 0.$

By doing this the maximum value of the term is found to be $\dfrac{1}{4}$. Thus

$$F_{max} = \frac{\mu_0^2 \pi a^2 V^2 n^2}{4rLR} = \frac{\mu_0^2 \pi a^2 V^2 n^2}{4r\left(\mu_0 n^2 \pi b^2 \ell\right)R}$$

$$= \frac{\mu_0 a^2 V^2}{4rRb^2 \ell} \quad \textit{Ans.}$$

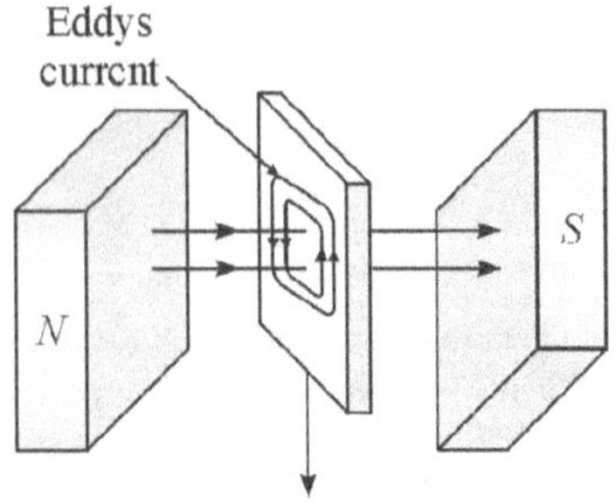

Fig. 8.102

8.15 EDDYS CURRENT

So far we have considered only instances in which currents resulting from induced emf's were confined to well-defined paths provided by the wires like coils or rings. However, one finds masses of metal located in changing magnetic field or moving in a magnetic field, with the result induced currents circulate throughout the volume of the metal. Because of their general circulatory nature, these are referred to as eddy currents. Consider a metal sheet entering into a magnetic field perpendicular to the plane of the sheet. The magnetic flux through the sheet increases. The current induced in the body of sheet in the form of eddys as shown in *fig. 8.102*.

The direction of eddy currents are such that, they compensate the increasing flux (by Lenz's law). Accordingly when metal sheet enters into the field, the direction of eddys are counterclockwise. When it is leaving the field the direction of eddys will be clockwise.

8.16 AC GENERATOR OR DYNAMO

It is used to convert mechanical energy into electrical energy.

Construction : The main components of ac generator are :

(i)   Armature coil : It consist of large number of turns of insulated copper wire wound over iron core.

(ii) Magnet : Strong permanent magnet (for small generator) or an electromagnet (for large generator) with cylindrical poles in shape.

(iii) Slip rings : The two ends of the armature coil are connected to two brass rings R_1 and R_2. These rings rotate along with the armature coil.

(iv) Brushes : Two carbon brushes (B_1 and B_2), are pressed against the slip rings. These brushes are connected to the load through which the output is obtained.

Principle : It works on the principle of electromagnetic induction. According to it when a coil is rotated in magnetic field, an emf is induced in the coil. The coil may be rotated by water energy, steam energy or oil energy. Let at any instant magnetic flux through armature coil,

$$N\phi_B = NBA\cos\theta = NBA\cos\omega t$$

The induced emf

$$e = -\frac{d\phi_B}{dt} = NBA\omega\sin\omega t$$

or

$$e = e_0\sin\omega t, \text{ where } e_0 = NBA\omega.$$

and induced current

$$i = \frac{e}{R} = \frac{e_0}{R}\sin\omega t = i_0\sin\omega t$$

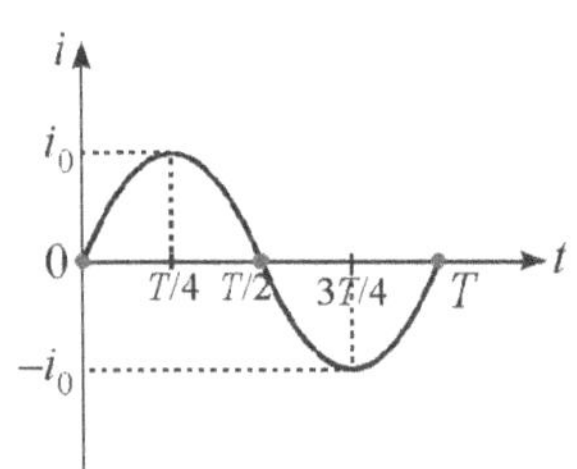

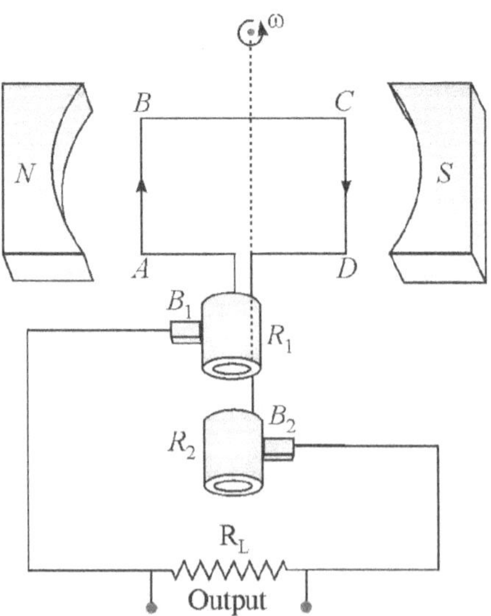

Fig. 8.103 AC Generator

8.17 DC GENERATOR

It produces direct current. It is possible by providing split rings or commutator in place of slip rings. DC generator consists of :
(i)   armature coil,
(ii) magnet,
(iii) split rings,
(iv) brushes.
For DC generator

$$\text{output current} \qquad i \;=\; |\,i_0 \sin \omega t\,|$$

8.18 DC MOTOR

It is an electrical machine which converts electrical energy into mechanical energy.
Principle : It is based on the fact that a current carrying coil placed in magnetic field experiences a torque. Because of this torque the coil starts rotating.
Construction : It consists of
(i)   strong magnet,
(ii) armature,
(iii) split rings,
(iv) brushes.

Back emf :

As soon as motor starts rotating, the flux changes in the coil, because of this change in flux, an emf is induced in the coil which opposes the emf of the battery. This induced emf is called back emf. The net emf of the circuit

$$e_{net} \;=\; \xi - e, \text{ where } e = NBA\omega \sin\omega t = k\omega$$

Armature current

$$i \;=\; \frac{e_{net}}{R} = \frac{\xi - e}{R}.$$

$$=\; \frac{\xi - k\omega}{R}$$

Armature current i will be maximum, when motor is just started i.e., $\omega = 0$, $i_{max} = \xi/R$. And minimum when motor picks full speed

$$i_{min} \;=\; \frac{\xi - k\omega_{max}}{R}$$

Efficiency of motor :

If ξ is the potential applied and i is the current in armature, then

$$\xi i \;=\; i^2 R + \text{mechanical power}$$

$$\therefore \quad \text{Mechanical power} \;=\; \xi i - i^2 R = i\,(\xi - iR)$$

$$=\; i e \qquad (e \text{ is the back emf})$$

$$\text{Efficiency} \qquad \eta \;=\; \frac{\text{Available mechanical power}}{\text{input electrical power}}$$

$$=\; \frac{e i}{\xi i} = \frac{e}{\xi}.$$

η is maximum, when $(e i)$ is maximum

$$\text{Let} \qquad x \;=\; ei = e\left(\frac{\xi - e}{R}\right)$$

$$\text{or} \qquad =\; \left(\frac{e\xi - e^2}{R}\right)$$

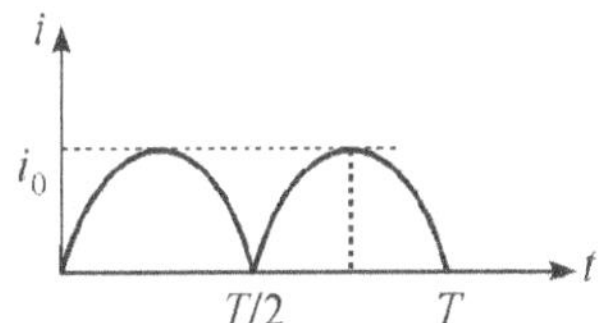

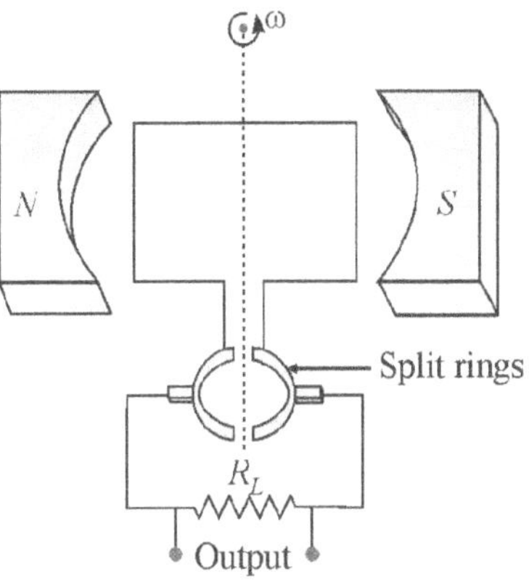

Fig. 8.104 DC Generator

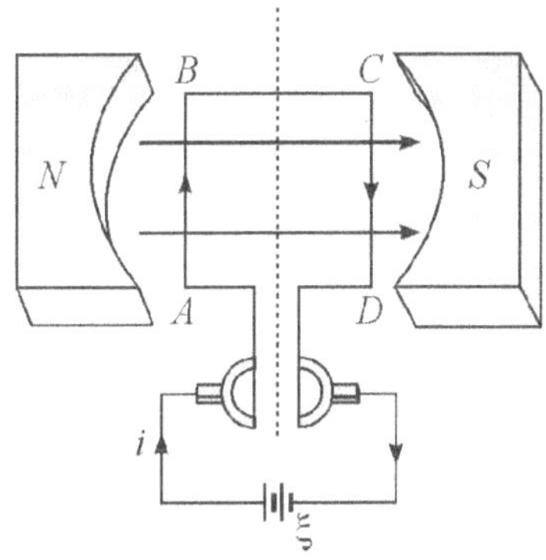

Fig. 8.105 DC Motor

x to be maximum, $\qquad \dfrac{dx}{de} = 0$

or $\qquad \xi - 2e = 0$

which gives $\qquad e = \dfrac{\xi}{2} \qquad \therefore \eta = 50\%.$

8.19 TRANSFORMER

Transformer is used to change the voltage in ac circuits.

(1) It is based on principle of mutual induction.

(2) It works with ac only.

(3) It can not change the voltage without change in current. There will inverse change in current. For ideal transformer

$$P_{out} = P_{in}$$

or $\qquad V_S i_S = V_P i_P$

$\Rightarrow \qquad \dfrac{V_S}{V_P} = \dfrac{i_P}{i_S} \qquad \qquad ...(i)$

(4) Same flux links in both primary and secondary, so the induced emf per turn is the same in each.

i.e., $\qquad \dfrac{d\phi_S}{dt} = \dfrac{d\phi_P}{dt}$

For primary coil $\qquad V_P = e_P = N_P \dfrac{d\phi_P}{dt},$

and for secondary coil $\qquad V_S = e_S = N_S \dfrac{d\phi_S}{dt}$

$\therefore \qquad \dfrac{V_S}{V_P} = \dfrac{e_S}{e_P} = \dfrac{N_S}{N_P} \qquad \qquad ...(ii)$

From equations (i) and (ii), we get

$$\dfrac{V_S}{V_P} = \dfrac{e_S}{e_P} = \dfrac{i_P}{i_S} = \dfrac{N_S}{N_P} = K \qquad \qquad ...(1)$$

where K is called transformer ratio. $K > 1$ for step-up transformer and $K < 1$ for step down transformer.

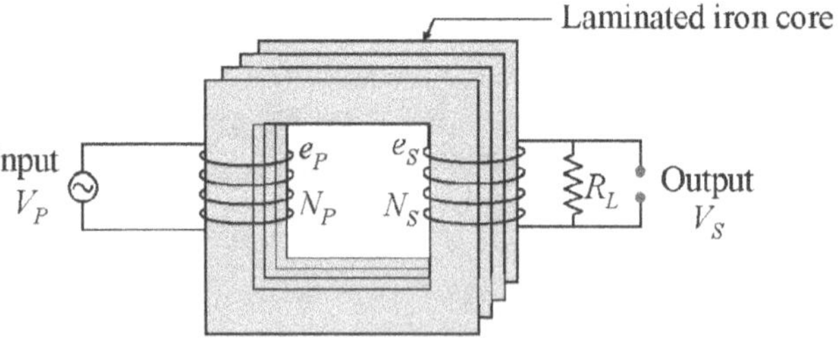

Fig. 8.106

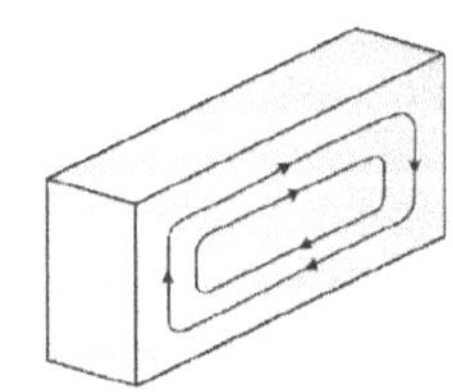

(a) Solid core with large eddys in whole volume of core.

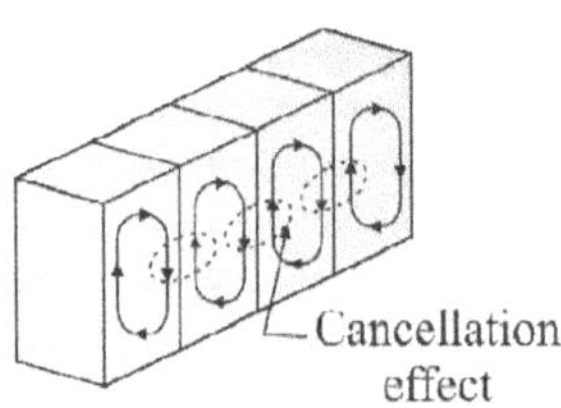

(b) Laminated core with small eddys.

(5) Symbol of transformer is ⎓⎓.

Losses in transformer

The output power of a transformer is necessarily less than the input power because of unavoidable losses. These losses consist of i^2R losses in the primary and secondary coils, and hysteresis and eddy losses in the core. Hysteresis losses are minimised by the use of iron core, and eddy losses are minimised by laminating the core. The electrical resistance between the surfaces of the laminations (by insulating varnish) effectively confines the eddy currents to individual laminae. The resulting path is greatly increased, with consequent increase in resistance. Hence, although the induced emf is not altered, but the currents and their heating effects are minimised.

Efficiency of a transformer (η)

$$\eta\,(\%) \;=\; \frac{P_{out}}{P_{in}} \times 100 = \frac{V_s\,i_s}{V_p\,i_p} \times 100 \qquad ...(2)$$

In practice η can be achieved from 90% to 99%.

Ex. 54 A transformer has 500 primary turns and 10 secondary turns.
(a) If V_p is 120 V (rms), what is V_s with an open circuit ?
(b) If the secondary now has a resistive load of 15 Ω, what are the currents in the primary and secondary ?

Sol.

Given, $N_P = 500$, $N_s = 10$, $V_P = 120$ V.
(a) For a transformer

$$\frac{V_s}{V_P} = \frac{N_s}{N_P}$$

$$\therefore \qquad V_s = V_P \frac{N_s}{N_P}$$

$$= 120\frac{10}{500} = 2.4\,V \qquad Ans.$$

(b) The current in secondary coil

$$i_s = \frac{V_s}{R_s} = \frac{2.4}{15}$$

$$= 0.16\,A$$

We know that

$$\frac{i_p}{i_s} = \frac{N_s}{N_P}$$

$$\therefore \qquad i_P = i_s\frac{N_s}{N_P}$$

$$= 0.16 \times \frac{10}{500}$$

$$= 3.2\,m\,A \qquad Ans.$$

Ex. 55 A toroidal solenoid has a mean radius of 0.12 m and a cross-sectional area 20×10^{-4} m^2. It is found that when the current is 20 A, the energy stored is 0.1 J. How many turns the winding have ?

Sol.

For toroidal solenoid energy stored

$$U = \frac{1}{2}Li^2$$

$$= \frac{1}{2}\left[\frac{\mu_0\,N^2\,A}{2\pi r}\right]i^2$$

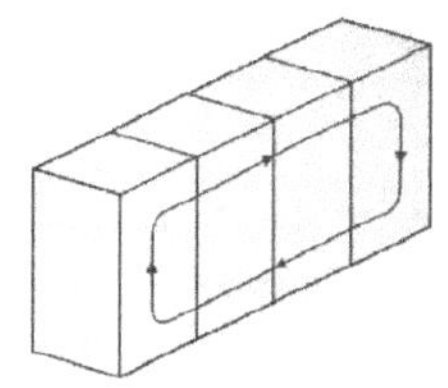

(c) Effective eddys current.
Fig. 8.107

$$\text{or} \qquad 0.1 = \frac{1}{2}\left[\frac{2 \times 10^{-7} \times N^2 \times 20 \times 10^{-4}}{0.12}\right] \times (20)^2$$

$$\therefore \qquad N = 387 \qquad Ans.$$

Ex. 56 An inductor of inductance 3H and resistance 6 Ω is connected to the terminals of a battery of emf 12 V and of negligible internal resistance. Find
(a) the initial rate of increase of current in the circuit,
(b) the rate of increase of current at the instant when the current is 1A,
(c) the current 0.2 s after the circuit is closed,
(d) the final steady state current.

Sol. Given; $H = 3\,H$, $R = 6\,\Omega$, $\xi = 12$ V,

(a) We know that $\quad i = i_0\left(1 - e^{-\frac{t}{\tau}}\right) \qquad ....(i)$

where $\qquad i_0 = \frac{\xi}{R} = \frac{12}{6} = 2\,A$

$$\frac{di}{dt} = \frac{i_0}{\tau}e^{-\frac{t}{\tau}} = \frac{\frac{\xi}{R}}{\frac{L}{R}}e^{-\frac{t}{\tau}} = \frac{\xi}{L}e^{-\frac{t}{\tau}}$$

At $t = 0$, $\quad \frac{di}{dt} = \frac{\xi}{L}e^{\circ} = \frac{\xi}{L} = \frac{12}{3} = 4\,A/s \qquad Ans.$

(b) The time of $i = 1$A:

$$\tau = \frac{L}{R} = \frac{3}{6} = \frac{1}{2}$$

From equation (i)

$$1 = 2\left(1 - e^{-\frac{t}{\tau}}\right)$$

$$\text{or} \qquad e^{-\frac{t}{\tau}} = \frac{1}{2}$$

$$\text{Now} \qquad \frac{di}{dt} = \frac{\xi}{L}e^{-\frac{t}{\tau}} = \frac{12}{3} \times \frac{1}{2}$$

$$= 2\,A/s \qquad Ans.$$

(c) $$i = i_0\left(1 - e^{-\frac{t}{\tau}}\right)$$

$$= 2\left[1 - e^{-\frac{0.2}{(1/2)}}\right]$$

$$= 2\left[1 - e^{-0.4}\right]$$

$$= 0.659\,A \qquad Ans.$$

(d)   Steady current i_0 = $\dfrac{\xi}{R} = \dfrac{12}{6} = 2A$ ***Ans.***

Ex. 57 Consider the circuit shown in *fig. 8.108*. With switch S_1 closed and the other two switches open, the circuit has a time constant τ_C. With switch S_2 closed and the other two switches open, the circuit has a time constant τ_L. With switch S_3 closed and other two switches open, the circuit oscillates with a period T. Find T.

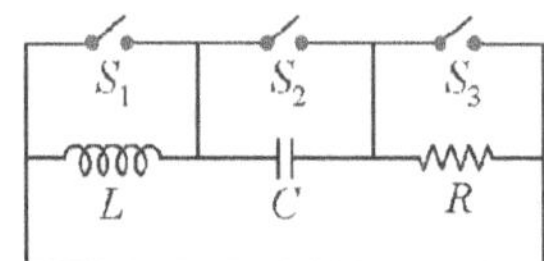

Fig. 8.108

Sol.

When only S_1 is closed, the circuit is active through C and R,

$$\therefore \quad \tau_C = CR$$

Similarly $\tau_L = L/R$

$$\therefore \quad \tau_C\,\tau_L = LC$$

Now when S_3 is closed, the circuit elements are L and C

$$\therefore \quad T = 2\pi\sqrt{LC}$$

$$= 2\pi\sqrt{\tau_C\,\tau_L} \qquad \textbf{\textit{Ans.}}$$

Ex. 58 In the given circuit containing an inductor and resistors. Find the time constant of the circuit.

Sol.

For the given circuit, the effective resistance across the inductor

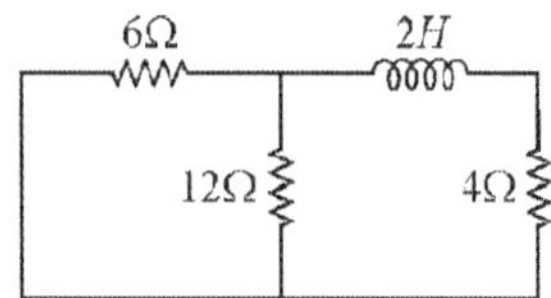

Fig. 8.109

$$R = \dfrac{6 \times 12}{6 + 12} + 4 = 8\ \Omega$$

$$\therefore \quad \tau = \dfrac{L}{R} = \dfrac{2}{8} = \dfrac{1}{4}\ \text{s} \qquad \textbf{\textit{Ans.}}$$

Ex. 59 Two parallel wires whose centres are at a distance d apart carry equal currents in opposite directions. Neglecting the flux within the wires themselves, find the inductance of a length of such pair of wires, given that the radius of the wires is a.

Sol.

The magnetic field at a distance x from left wire due to the current in the two wires is

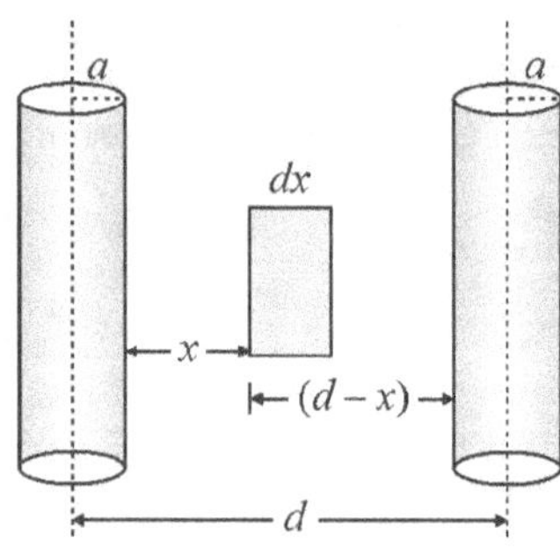

Fig. 8.110

$$B = \dfrac{\mu_0}{2\pi} \cdot i\left(\dfrac{1}{x} + \dfrac{1}{d-x}\right)$$

Now consider an element of width dx and length ℓ. The flux enclosed between wires

$$\phi_B = \int B(\ell\, dx) = \dfrac{\mu_0 i\ell}{2\pi}\int\limits_{a}^{d-a}\left[\dfrac{1}{x} + \dfrac{1}{d-x}\right]dx$$

$$= \dfrac{\mu_0}{2\pi}\, i\ell\left[\ell n\, x - \ell n(d-x)\right]_{a}^{d-a}$$

$$= \dfrac{\mu_0 i\ell}{2\pi}\left(\ell n\left(\dfrac{d-a}{a}\right) - \ell n\dfrac{a}{(d-a)}\right)$$

$$= \dfrac{\mu_0 i\ell}{2\pi}\,\ell n\left(\dfrac{d-a}{a}\right)^2$$

$$= \dfrac{\mu_0 i\ell}{\pi}\,\ell n\left(\dfrac{d-a}{a}\right)$$

The inductance $L = \dfrac{\phi_B}{i} = \dfrac{\mu_0 \ell}{\pi}\,\ell n\left(\dfrac{d-a}{a}\right)$ ***Ans.***

Ex. 60   For the given circuit here, find the
(a)   energy stored in C
(b)   energy stored in L
(c)   current in each circuit element and
(d)   voltage across each circuit element.

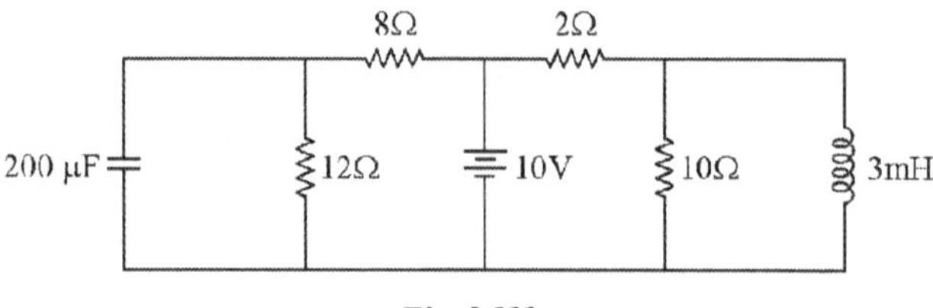

Fig. 8.111

Sol.

After reaching steady state, capacitor stops the current. While inductor offers zero resistance. The current in the right side of the battery will pass through inductor.

The above circuit can be reduced as follows :

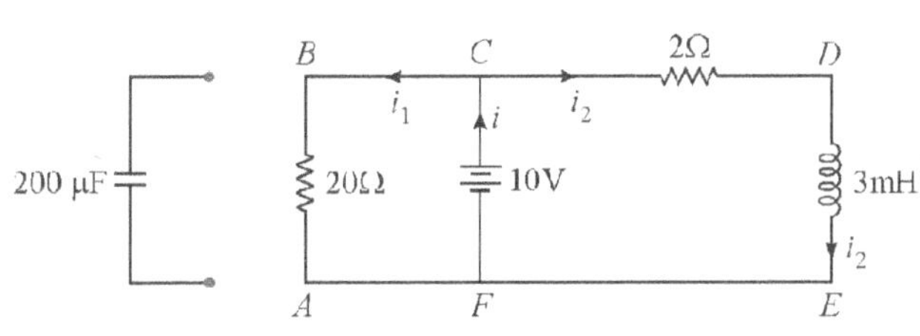

Fig. 8.112

In close loop *ABCFA*,

$$20\,i_1 = 10$$

$$\Rightarrow \quad i_1 = \frac{1}{2}\,A = 0.5\,A$$

and in close loop *FCDEF*,

$$2i_2 = 10$$
$$\Rightarrow \quad i_2 = 5\,A$$

(a) The p.d. across the capacitor

$$= \text{p.d. across } 12\ \Omega \text{ resistor}$$

$$= 12\,i_1 = 12 \times \frac{1}{2} = 6\,V$$

∴ Energy stored in capacitor

$$= \frac{1}{2}CV^2$$

$$= \frac{1}{2} \times 200 \times 10^{-6} \times 6^2$$

$$= 3.6\ mJ \qquad\qquad Ans.$$

(b) The energy stored in inductor

$$= \frac{1}{2}L\,i^2$$

$$= \frac{1}{2} \times \left(3 \times 10^{-3}\right) \times \left(5\right)^2$$

$$= 37.5\ m\,J \qquad\qquad Ans.$$

(c) The current in each circuit elements are shown as follows.

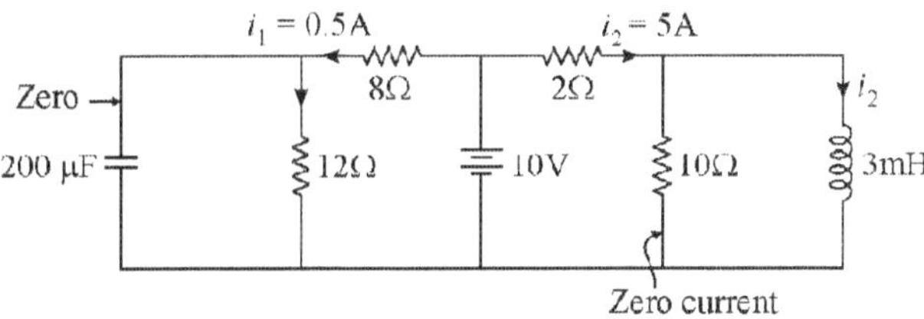

Fig. 8.113

(d) The p.d. across each circuit element are shown in *fig. 8.112*

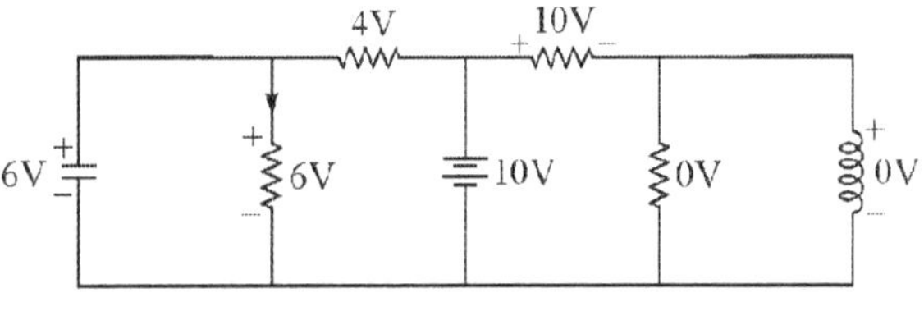

Fig. 8.114

Ex. 61 A voltage waveshape of the form $V(t) = Kt^3$ is applied to a circuit element at time $t = 0$. Find current through a resistor R, an inductor L and a capacitor C.

Sol. Current through resistor

$$i = \frac{V}{R} = \frac{Kt^3}{R} \qquad\qquad Ans.$$

To an inductor

$$\frac{L\,di}{dt} = Kt^3$$

or

$$\int_0^i di = \frac{K}{L}\int_0^t t^3 dt$$

or

$$i = \frac{Kt^4}{4L} \qquad\qquad Ans.$$

For capacitor,

$$q = CV$$
$$= C\,K\,t^3$$

Current

$$i = \frac{dq}{dt} = \frac{d\left(CKt^3\right)}{dt}$$

$$= 3CKt^2 \qquad\qquad Ans.$$

Ex. 62 In *fig. 8.115*, $\xi = 100$ V, $R_1 = 10.0\,\Omega$, $R_2 = 20.0\,\Omega$, $R_3 = 30.0\,\Omega$, and $L = 2.00$ H. Find the values of i_1 and i_2

(a) immediately after switch S is closed;
(b) a long time later;
(c) immediately after switch S is opened again
(d) a long time later.

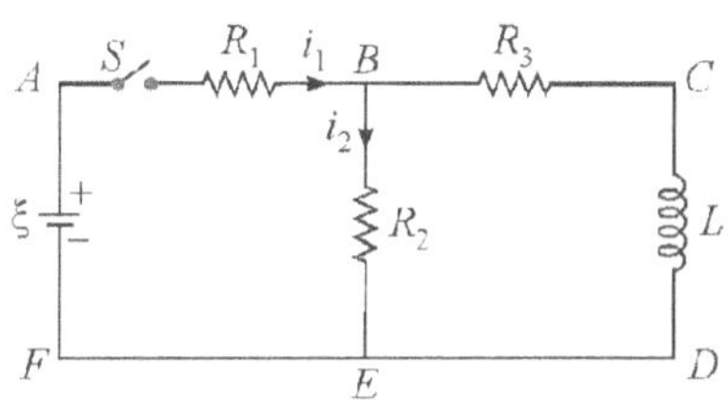

Fig. 8.115

Sol.

(a) Immediately after switch S is closed, inductor offers infinite resistance, therefore current in its arm will be zero. For closed loop *ABEFA*

$$i_1 = \frac{\xi}{R_1 + R_2} = \frac{100}{10+20} = 3.33\ A$$

(b) After a long time, inductor becomes ineffective. The effective circuit becomes

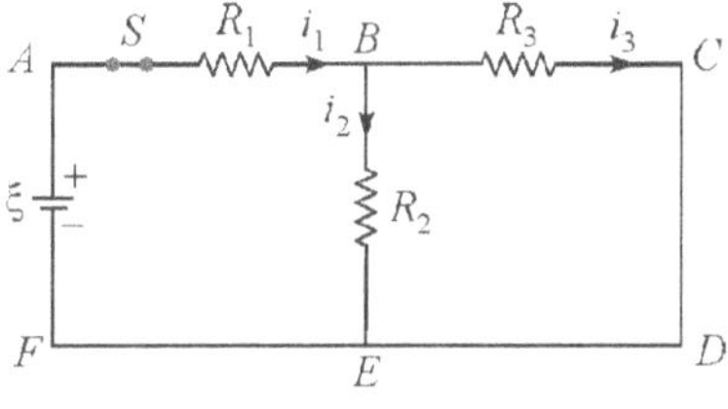

Fig. 8.116

$$i_1 = \frac{\xi}{R_1 + \dfrac{R_2 R_3}{R_2 + R_3}}$$

$$= \frac{100}{10 + \dfrac{20 \times 30}{20 + 30}}$$

$$= 4.55 \text{ A}$$

We have $i_1 = i_2 + i_3$ and $20\, i_2 = 30\, i_3 \Rightarrow i_3 = \dfrac{2}{3} i_2$

$\therefore \qquad 4.55 = i_2 + \dfrac{2i_2}{3}$

or $\qquad\qquad i_2 = 2.73 \text{ A}, \; i_3 = 1.82 \text{ A}$

(c) Immediately after switch S is opened, $i_1 = 0$
and $i_2 = i_3 = 1.82$ A

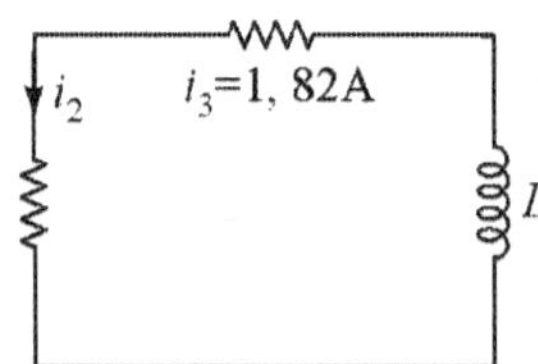

Fig. 8.117

(d) After a long time, the magnetic energy stored in inductor will change into heal and therefore $i_1 = i_2 = 0$.

Ex. 63 In the circuit diagram shown in *fig. 8.118*, $R = 10\,\Omega$, $L = 5H$, $\xi = 20$ V, $i = 2A$. This current is decreasing at a rate of 1.0 A/s. Find V_{ab} at this instant.

Fig. 8.118

Sol. The induced emf across inductor

Fig. 8.119

$$e = \frac{-Ldi}{dt}$$

$$= -5 \times (-1.0)$$

$$= 5 \text{ V}$$

As the current is decreasing the inductor can be replaced by a source of emf 5V in such a manner so that it compensate the decreasing current. It to be like as shown in *fig. 8.119*.
Now by loop rule

$$-Ri + e - \xi - V_{ab} = 0$$

or $\qquad V_{ab} = Ri + \xi - e$

$$= 10 \times 2 + 20 - 5$$

$$= 35 \text{ V} \qquad\qquad\qquad \textit{Ans.}$$

Ex. 64 Find the time dependence of the current flowing through the inductance L of the circuit shown in *fig. 8.120* after the switch S is shorted at the moment $t = 0$.

Sol. Let at any instant the current in the inductor is i_1 and increasing at the rate of $\dfrac{di_1}{dt}$. The induced emf across $L\left(e = L\dfrac{di_1}{dt}\right)$ opposes the increasing current. So it to be as shown in the circuit.

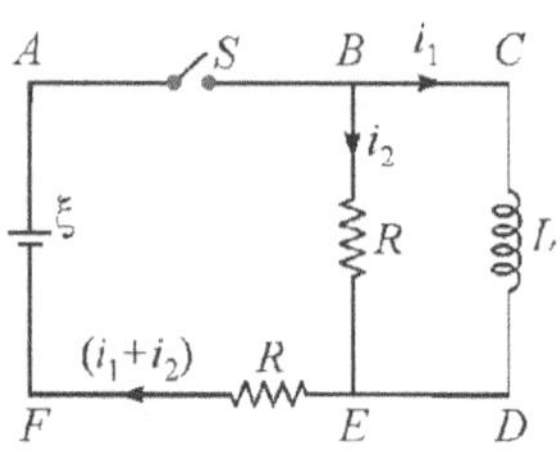

Fig. 8.120

In close loop $A\,B\,C\,D\,E\,F\,A$,

$$-e - (i_1 + i_2)R + \xi = 0 \qquad\qquad \text{...(i)}$$

In close loop $B\,C\,D\,E\,B$,

$$-e + i_2 R = 0 \qquad\qquad \text{...(ii)}$$

From equation (ii), we have

$$i_2 = e/R$$

substituting this value in equation (i), we get

$$-e - (i_1 + e/R)R + \xi = 0$$

or $\qquad -2e - i_1 R + \xi = 0$

or $\qquad 2L\dfrac{di_1}{dt} = (\xi - i_1 R)$

or $\qquad \displaystyle\int_0^{i_1} \frac{di_1}{(\xi - i_1 R)} = \int_0^{t} \frac{dt}{2L}$

$$\left|\frac{\ell n\,(\xi - i_1 R)}{(-R)}\right|_0^{i_1} = \frac{t}{2L}$$

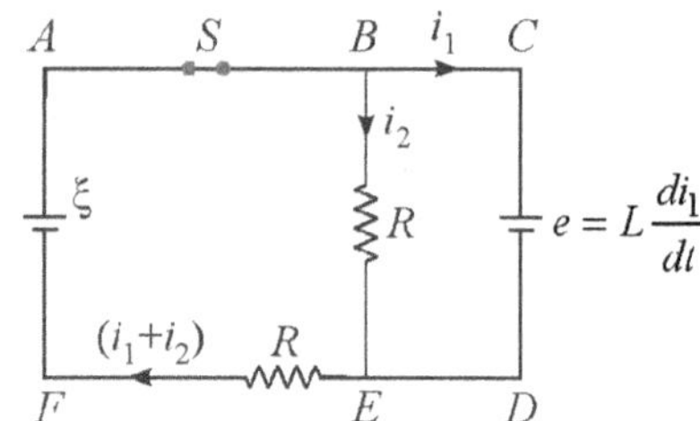

Fig. 8.121

or $\qquad \ell n(\xi - i_1 R) - \ell n\, \xi = -\dfrac{Rt}{2L}$

or $\qquad \ell n\left(1 - \dfrac{i_1}{\dfrac{\xi}{R}}\right) = -\dfrac{Rt}{2L}$

or $\qquad i_1 = \dfrac{\xi}{R}\left(1 - e^{-\frac{tR}{2L}}\right).$

Review of formulae & Important Points

1. **Magnetic flux :** Magnetic flux of the magnetic field $\vec{B}$ through the normal area A is

$$\phi_B = B_\perp A = BA\cos\theta$$

2. **Faraday's law :** Whenever there is change in magnetic flux linked with circuit, there induces an emf in the circuit. The rate of change of magnetic flux is equal to the induced emf. Thus

$$\xi = -\frac{d\phi_B}{dt},$$

here negative sign indicates that induced emf opposes the change in flux.

Induced charge in time Δt,

$$\Delta Q = \frac{\Delta\phi}{R}$$

3. **Motional emf :** When a metallic conductor moves in a magnetic field $\vec{B}$ with velocity $\vec{v}$, an emf induces across its ends. The induced emf

$$e = Bv\ell\sin\theta.$$

In general, it can be written as :

$$e = \int\left(\vec{v}\times\vec{B}\right)\cdot d\vec{\ell}$$

4. **When a metallic conductor is rotated in normal magnetic field about its one ends, the induced emf across the ends**

$$e = \frac{B\omega\ell^2}{2},$$

5. **Induced electric field :** If E_n is the induced electric field, then by Faraday's law

$$e = \oint\vec{E}\cdot d\vec{\ell} = -\frac{d\phi_B}{dt}$$

6. **Induced emf in a coil rotating in uniform magnetic field**

$$e = NBA\omega\sin\omega t$$

7. **Self induction :** The induced emf in the coil itself due to change in current in it is called self induction. For the coil of N turns

$$N\phi_B = Li,$$

where L is called self inductance.

8. **Self induction of circular coil of N turns and radius r**

$$L = \frac{\mu_0\pi N^2 r}{2}.$$

9. **Energy stored in an inductor :** Energy in the inductor stores due to magnetic field in it. For any current i in the inductor, the energy stored

$$U = \frac{1}{2}Li^2.$$

If B is the magnetic field in the coil, then

$$U = \frac{B^2}{2\mu_0}\times Vol.$$

10. **RL-DC circuit : For a circuit with time constant τ, the growing current i in circuit at any time t**

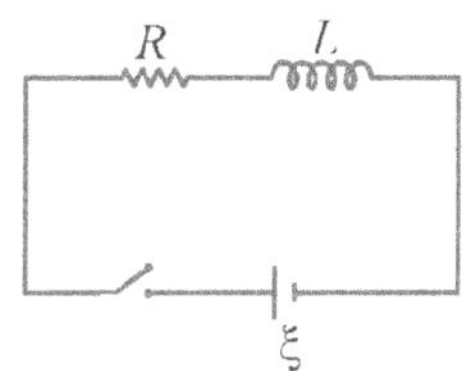

$$i = i_0\left(1-e^{-t/\tau}\right)$$

where $i_0 = \dfrac{\xi}{R}$ and $\tau = \dfrac{L}{R}$

The decay current in the circuit, with initial current i_0

$$i = i_0 e^{-t/\tau}$$

11. **LC-oscillations :** When a capacitor C with a charge q is connected to an inductor L, the energy of the circuit oscillates between C and L. If ω is the angular frequency of oscillations, then

$$\frac{d^2q}{dt^2}+\omega^2 q = 0,$$

where

$$\omega = \sqrt{\frac{1}{LC}}.$$

Also

$$T = 2\pi\sqrt{LC}.$$

Electrical energy of capacitor will store in inductor after time $T/4$ and vice-versa.

12. **Mutual inductance :** The induced emf in the second coil due to change in current in first coil, is called mutual induction. If M is the mutual inductance between the coils, then

$$N_2\phi_{21} = Mi_1,$$

or

$$N_1\phi_{12} = Mi_2.$$

13. **Mutual induction between two circular coils of radii R_1 and R_2 with turns N_1 and N_2 is**

$$M = \left[\frac{\mu_0 \pi N_1 N_2 R_2{}^2}{2R_1} \right]$$

14. If L_1 and L_2 are the self inductances of two coils, then mutual induction between them

$$M = \sqrt{L_1 L_2}$$

15. **Combination of inductors :**

(i) **In series :** $L = L_1 + L_2$

(ii) **In parallel :** $\dfrac{1}{L} = \dfrac{1}{L_1} + \dfrac{1}{L_2}$

16. **AC generator :** If i_0 be the maximum current (current amplitude), then

$$i = i_0 \sin \omega t,$$

where $\qquad i_0 = \dfrac{NBA\omega}{R}$

17. **Transformer :** For the transformer with the turns N_p and N_s in the primary and secondary coils, the ratio of output and input potentials

$$\frac{V_s}{V_P} = \frac{N_s}{N_P}$$

For the ideal transformer

$$V_P i_P = V_s i_s.$$

✮ ✮ ✮

LEVEL - 1

Only one option correct

1. The graph gives the magnitude $B(t)$ of a uniform magnetic field that exists throughout a conducting loop, perpendicular to the plane of the loop. In which region, the magnitude of induced emf will be greatest :

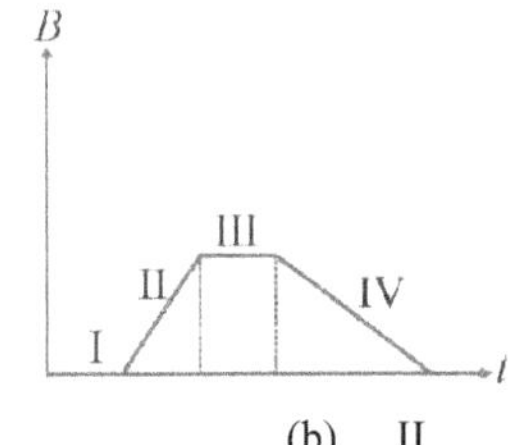

(a)   I
(b)   II
(c)   III
(d)   IV

2. The figure shows three circuits with identical batteries, inductor, and registers. In which circuit, the current through the battery is greatest just after closing of the switch

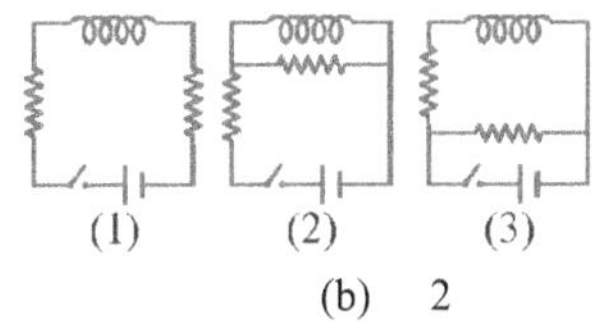

(a)   1
(b)   2
(c)   3
(d)   1, 3

3. Figure shows three circuits with identical batteries, inductors, and resistors. In which circuits the time taken to reach 50% of the maximum current is greatest :

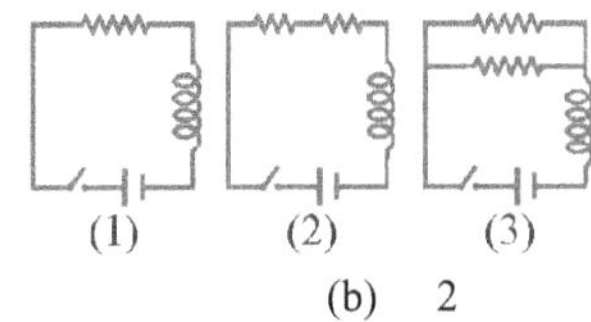

(a)   1
(b)   2
(c)   3
(d)   2, 3

4. If the circular conductor undergoes thermal expansion while it is in a uniform magnetic field, a current will be induced in clockwise around it. If B is the magnitude of the magnetic field, then its direction is :

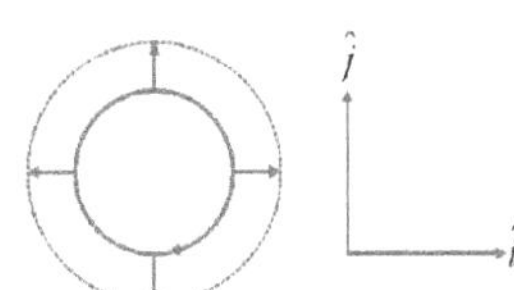

(a) $B\hat{i}$
(b) $B\hat{j}$
(c) $-B\hat{j}$
(d) $B\hat{k}$

5. A circular loop of resistance R and enclosing an area A is subjected to a magnetic field $B_0 e^{-bt}$ perpendicular to its plane, B_0 and b being constants, and t is the time. What is the induced current at $t = 0$?

(a) $\dfrac{AB_0 b}{R}$
(b) $\dfrac{B_0 bR}{A}$
(c) $\dfrac{AB_0 R}{b}$
(d) $\dfrac{B_0 bR}{2A}$

6. The magnetic field through a loop of area $1\,m^2$ and of resistance $10\,\Omega$, changes with time as shown in figure. The induced current in the loop at $t = 1s$

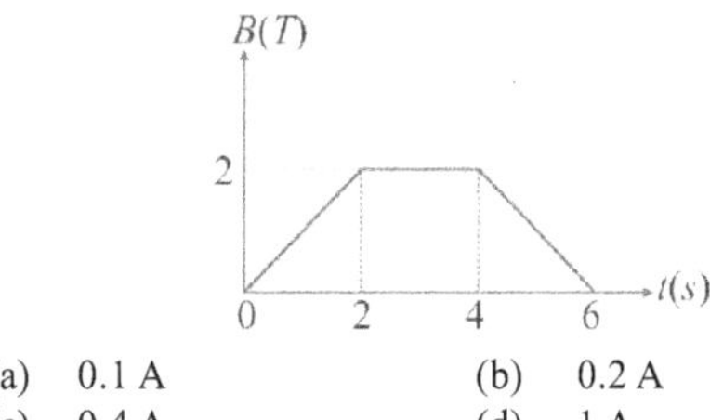

(a)   0.1 A
(b)   0.2 A
(c)   0.4 A
(d)   1 A

7. In figure, a circular loop of wire 10 cm in diameter is placed with its normal $\vec{N}$ at an angle $\theta = 30°$ with the direction of a uniform magnetic field $\vec{B}$ of magnetic 0.50 T. The loop is then rotated such that $\vec{N}$ rotates in a cone about the field direction at the constant rate of 100 rev/min; the angle θ remains unchanged during the process. The induced emf in the loop :

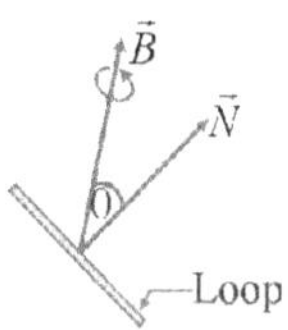

(a)   0 V
(b)   10 V
(c)   100 V
(d)   none

8. Transformers are used
(a)   in AC circuits only
(b)   in DC circuit only
(c)   in both AC and Dc circuits
(d)   neither in AC nor in DC circuits.

9. A generator supplies 100 V to the primary-coil of a transformer of 50 turns. If the secondary coil has 500 turns, then the secondary voltage is
(a)   100 V
(b)   500 V
(c)   550 V
(d)   1000 V

Answer Key	1	(b)	2	(c)	3	(c)	4	(d)	5	(a)
Sol. from page 561	6	(a)	7	(a)	8	(a)	9	(d)		

10. Consider the situation shown in figure. If the switch is closed and after some time it is opened again, the closed loop will show

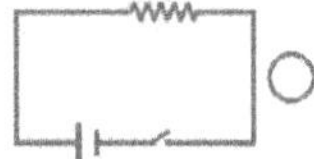

- (a) a clockwise current
- (b) an anticlockwise current
- (c) an anticlockwise current and then clockwise
- (d) a clockwise current and then an anticlock wise current.

11. In the circuit shown, $\otimes$ indicated a uniform magnetic field, which is directed into the page and decreasing in magnitude at the rate of 150 T/s. The reading of ammeter is :

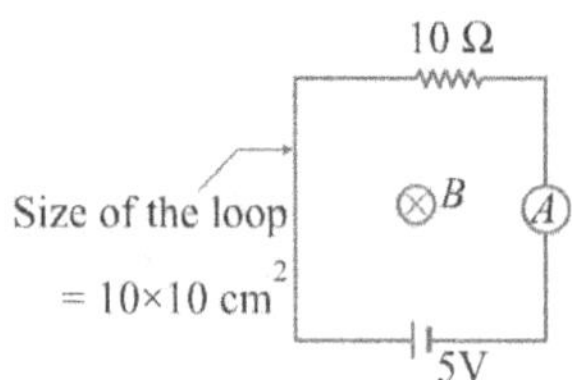

- (a) 0.15 A
- (b) 0.35 A
- (c) 0.50 A
- (d) 0.65 A

12. A circular wire loop of radius r is placed in a region of magnetic field B such that the plane of the loop makes an angle θ with the direction of $\vec{B}$. Consider the following in this regard :

1. Change in B with time
2. Change in r with time
3. B being non-uniform in space
4. Change in θ with time

The conditions for an induced emf in the loop would include

- (a) 1 and 4
- (b) 1, 2 and 4
- (c) 1 and 3
- (d) 2, 3 and 4

13. A series would dc motor has a total resistance of 1.5 ohm. When connected across a 115 volt and running at a certain speed it draws a current of 10 A. The back emf in the motor is

- (a) 100 V
- (b) 115 V
- (c) 15 V
- (d) 1.5 V

14. Which of the following can produce the maximum induced emf in an inductor ?

- (a) 50 A, DC
- (b) 50 A, 50 Hz AC
- (c) 50 A, 500 Hz AC
- (d) 100 A, DC.

15. Two circular loops of equal radii are placed coaxially at some separation. The first is cut and a battery is inserted in between to drive a current in it. The current changes slightly because of the variation in resistance with temperature. During this period, the two loops

- (a) attract each other
- (b) repel each other
- (c) do not interact
- (d) none of these

16. A metal rod is moved with a constant velocity v in a magnetic field. A potential difference appears across the two ends

- (a) if $\vec{v} \parallel \vec{\ell}$
- (b) if $\vec{v} \parallel \vec{B}$
- (c) if $\vec{\ell} \parallel \vec{B}$
- (d) none of these

17. A rod of length ℓ rotates with a uniform angular velocity ω about its perpendicular bisector. A uniform magnetic field B exists parallel to the axis of rotation. The potential difference between two ends of the rod is

- (a) $\dfrac{1}{2} B\omega^2 \ell$
- (b) $B\omega^2 \ell$
- (c) $2B\omega^2 \ell$
- (d) zero

18. A magnet NS is suspended from a spring and while it oscillates, the magnet moves in and out of the coil C. The coil is connected to a galvanometer G. Then as the magnet oscillates,

- (a) G shows deflection to the left and right with constant amplitude
- (b) G shows deflection on one side
- (c) G shows no deflection
- (d) G shows deflection to the left and right but the amplitude steadily decreases.

19. An infinitely long cylinder is kept parallel to an uniform magnetic field B directed along positive z axis. The direction of induced current as seen from the z axis will be

- (a) clockwise of the +ve z axis.
- (b) anticlockwise of the +ve z axis.
- (c) zero emf.
- (d) along the magnetic field.

20. An electric potential difference will be induced between the ends of the conductor as shown in the diagram, when the conductor moves in the direction

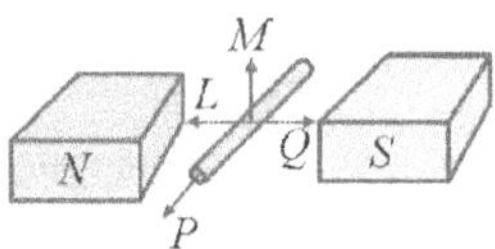

- (a) P
- (b) Q
- (c) L
- (d) M

Answer Key	**10**	(d)	**11**	(d)	**12**	(b)	**13**	(a)	**14**	(c)	**15**	(a)
Sol. from page 561	**16**	(d)	**17**	(d)	**18**	(d)	**19**	(c)	**20**	(d)		

21. A conducting square loop of side L and resistance R moves in its plane with a uniform velocity v perpendicular to one of its sides. A magnetic induction B constant in time and space, pointing perpendicular and into the plane of the loop exists everywhere. The current induced in the loop is

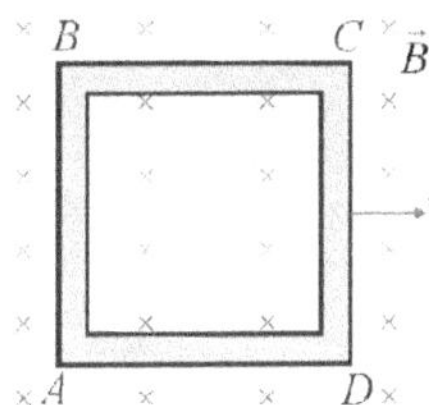

(a) $\dfrac{Blv}{R}$ clockwise

(b) $\dfrac{Blv}{R}$ anticlockwise

(c) $\dfrac{2Blv}{R}$ anticlockwise

(d) zero

22. The inductance of a closed-packed coil of 400 turns is 8 mH. A current of 5 mA is passed through it. The magnetic flux through each turn of the coil is

(a) $\dfrac{1}{4\pi}\mu_0\, Wb$

(b) $\dfrac{1}{2\pi}\mu_0\, Wb$

(c) $\dfrac{1}{3\pi}\mu_0\, Wb$

(d) $0.4\,\mu_0\, Wb$

23. The adjoining figure shows two bulbs B_1 and B_2 resistor R and an inductor L. When the switch S is turned off

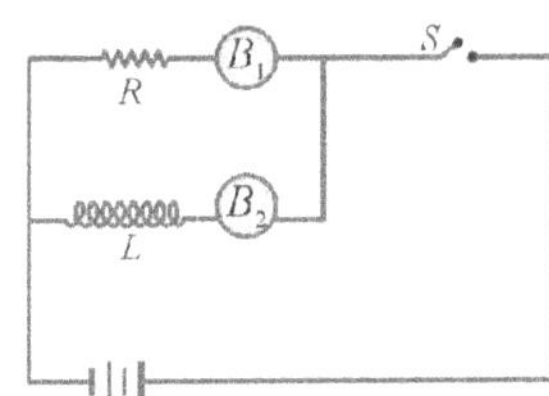

(a) both B_1 and B_2 die out promptly
(b) both B_1 and B_2 die out with some delay
(c) B_1 dies out promptly but B_2 with some delay
(d) B_2 dies out promptly but B_1 with some delay

24. An electron moves along the line AB, which lies in the same plane as a circular loop of conducting wires as shown in the diagram. What will be the direction of current induced if any, in the loop

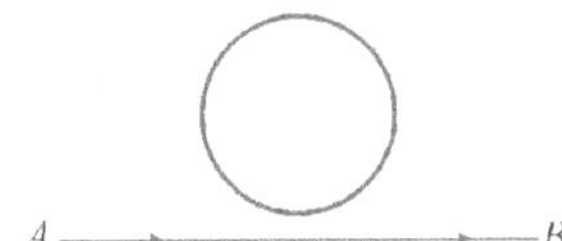

(a) no current will be induced
(b) the current will be clockwise
(c) the current will be anticlockwise
(d) the current will change direction as the electron passes by

25. A thin semicircular conducting ring of radius R is falling with its plane vertical in a horizontal magnetic induction B. At the position MNQ, the speed of the ring is V and the potential difference developed across the ring is

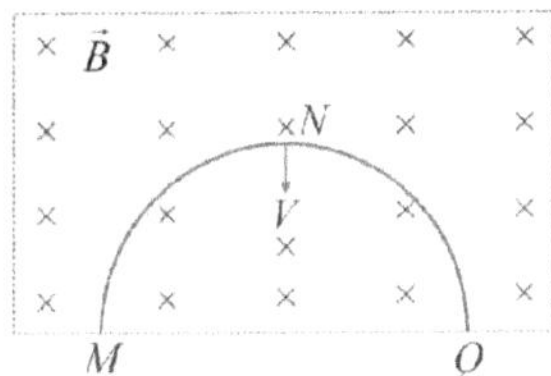

(a) zero
(b) $Bv\pi R^2 / 2$ and M is at higher potential
(c) πRBV and Q is at higher potential
(d) $2RBV$ and Q is at higher potential

26. A circular loop of radius R carrying current I lies in xy- plane with its centre at origin. The total magnetic flux through xz-plane is

(a) directly proportional to I
(b) directly proportional to R
(c) directly proportional to R^2
(d) zero

27. Two identical circular loops of metal wire are lying on a table without touching each other. Loop-A carries a current which increases with time. In response, the loop-B

(a) remains stationary
(b) is attracted by the loop-A
(c) is repelled by the loop-A
(d) rotates about its CM, with CM fixed (CM is the centre of mass)

28. A wire of length 1 m is moving at a speed of $2\,ms^{-1}$ perpendicular to its length and a homogeneous magnetic field of 0.5 T. The ends of the wire are joined to a circuit of resistance $6\,\Omega$. The rate at which work is being done to keep the wire moving at constant speed is

(a) $\dfrac{1}{12}W$

(b) $\dfrac{1}{6}W$

(c) $\dfrac{1}{3}W$

(d) $1\,W$

29. Two circular coils can be arranged in any of the three situations shown in the figure. Their mutual inductance will be

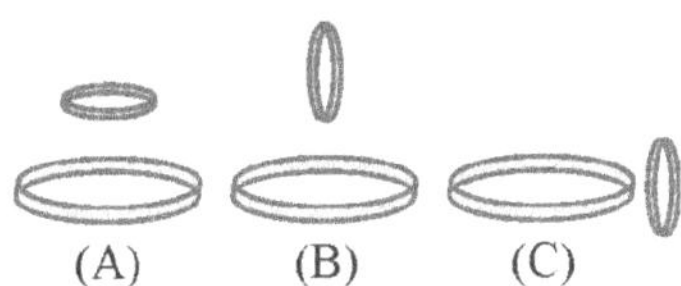

(a) maximum in situation (A)
(b) maximum in situation (B)
(c) maximum in situation (C)
(d) the same in all situations

Answer Key	21	(d)	22	(a)	23	(c)	24	(d)	25	(d)
Sol. from page 561	26	(d)	27	(c)	28	(b)	29	(a)		

30. As shown in the figure, P and Q are two coaxial conducting loops separated by some distance. When the switch S is closed, a clockwise current I_P flows in P (as seen by E) and an induced current I_{Q_1} flows in Q. The switch remains closed for a long time. When S is opened, a current I_{Q_2} flows in Q. Then the directions of I_{Q_1} and I_{Q_2} (as seen by E) are

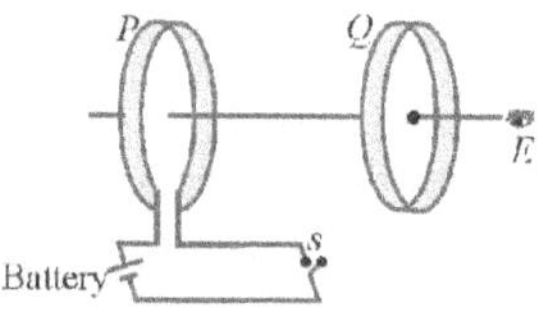

(a) respectively clockwise and anticlockwise
(b) both clockwise
(c) both anticlockwise
(d) respectively anticlockwise and clockwise

31. A short-circuited coil is placed in a time-varying magnetic field. Electrical power is dissipated due to the current induced in the coil. If the number of turns were to be quadrupled and the wire radius halved, the electrical power dissipated would be

(a) halved (b) the same
(c) doubled (d) quadrupled

32. A coil of inductance 8.4 mH and resistance $6\,\Omega$ is connected to a 12 V battery. The current in the coil is 1.0 A at approximately the time

(a) 500 sec (b) 20 sec
(c) 35 milli sec (d) 1 milli sec

33. A conducting wire frame is placed in a magnetic field which is directed into the paper. The magnetic field is increasing at a constant rate. The directions of induced current in wires AB and CD are

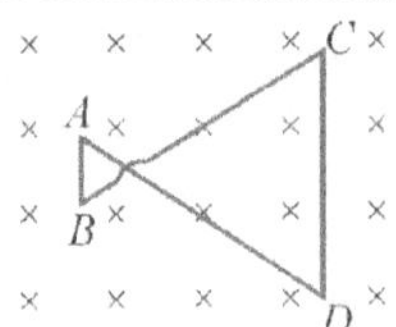

(a) B to A and D to C (b) A to B and C to D
(c) A to B and D to C (d) B to A and C to D

34. A conducting ring of radius 1 meter is placed in an uniform magnetic field B of 0.01 telsa oscillating with frequency 100 Hz with its plane at right angles to B. What will be the induced electric field

(a) π volt / m (b) 2 volt / m
(c) 10 volt / m (d) 62 volt / m

35. The variation of induced emf (E) with time (t) in a coil if a short bar magnet is moved along its axis with a constant velocity is best represented as

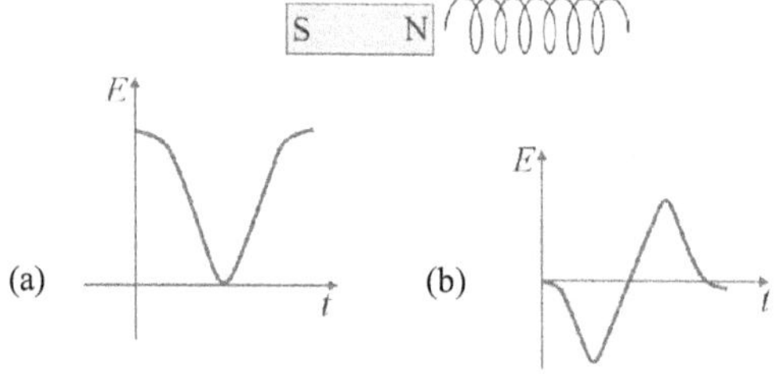

36. An alternating current of frequency 200 rad/sec and peak value 1 A as shown in the figure, is applied to the primary of a transformer. If the coefficient of mutual induction between the primary and the secondary is 1.5 H, the voltage induced in the secondary will be

(a) 300 V
(b) 191 V
(c) 220 V
(d) 471 V

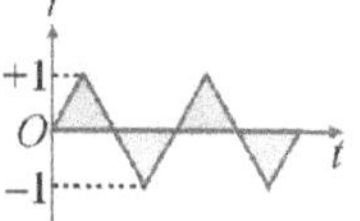

37. A horizontal loop abcd is moved across the pole pieces of a magnet as shown in fig. with a constant speed v. When the edge ab of the loop enters the pole pieces at time $t = 0$ sec, which one of the following graphs represents correctly the induced emf in the coil?

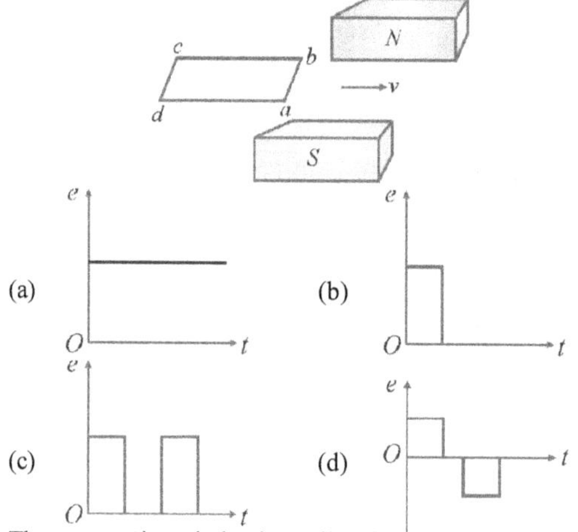

38. The current i in an induction coil varies with time t according to the graph shown in figure.

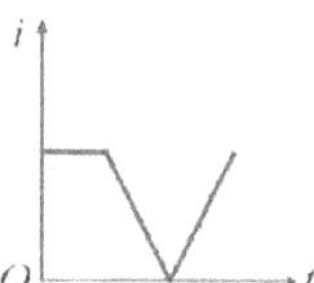

Which of the following graphs shows the induced emf (E) in the coil with time?

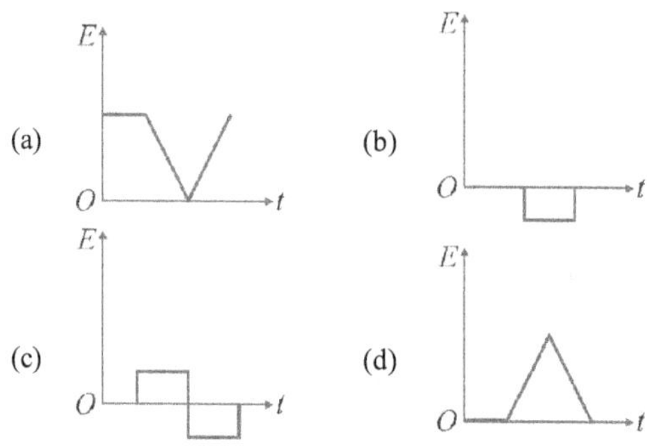

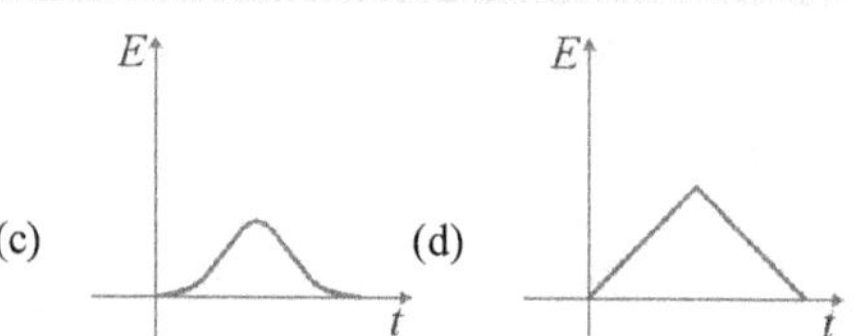

Answer Key	30	(d)	31	(b)	32	(d)	33	(a)	34	(b)
Sol. from page 561	35	(a)	36	(b)	37	(d)	38	(c)		

39. A magnet is made to oscillate with a particular frequency, passing through a coil as shown in figure. The time variation of the magnitude of e.m.f. generated across the coil during one cycle is

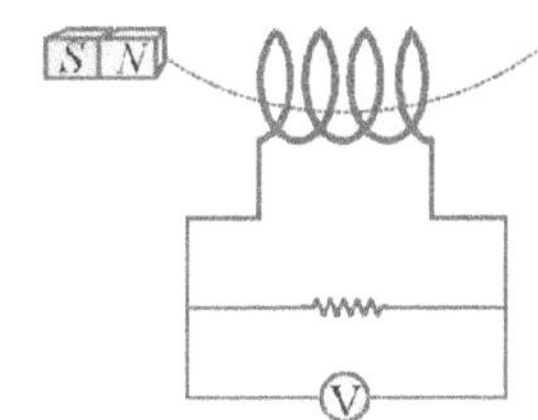

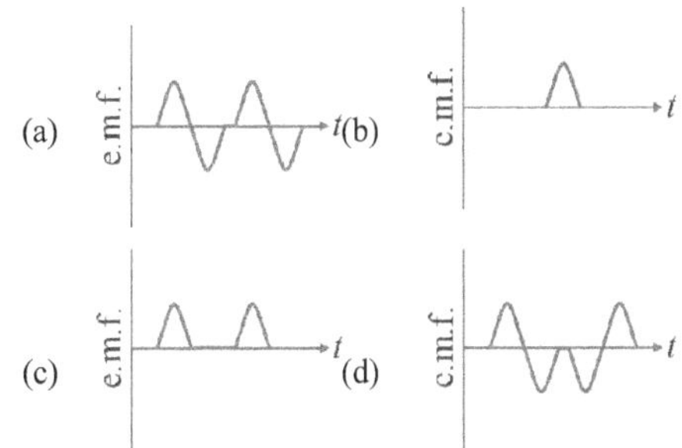

(a) 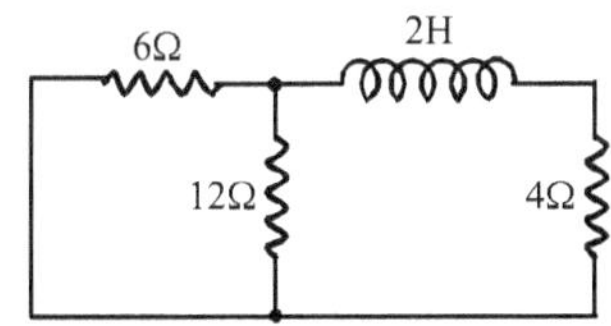

40. In the given circuit containing an inductor and resistors, the time constant of the circuit is :

(a) $\dfrac{1}{4}s$

(b) $\dfrac{1}{2}s$

(c) $\dfrac{1}{3}s$

(d) $\dfrac{1}{5}s$

41. A voltage wave shape of the form $V(t) = Kt^3$ is applied to a circuit element at time $t = 0$. The current through a resistor (R), an inductor (L) and a capacitor (C) respectively are :

(a) $\dfrac{K}{R}t^3,\ \dfrac{K}{L}\dfrac{t^3}{3}$ and $\dfrac{3CKt^4}{4}$

(b) $\dfrac{K}{4R}t^4,\ \dfrac{K}{L}\dfrac{t^4}{4}$ and $\dfrac{3KC^2t^2}{2}$

(c) $\dfrac{K}{R}t^3,\ \dfrac{K}{L}\dfrac{t^4}{4}$ and $3CKt^2$

(d) $\dfrac{K}{R}t^3,\ \dfrac{K}{L}\dfrac{t^3}{3}$ and CKt^3

42. A short magnet is allowed to fall along the axis of a horizontal metallic ring. Starting from rest, the distance fallen by the magnet in one second may be :
(a) 4.0 m   (b) 5.0 m
(c) 6.0 m   (d) 7.0 m

43. When a metallic plate swings between the poles of a magnet
(a) no effect on the plate
(b) eddy currents are set up inside the plate and the direction of the current is along the motion of the plate
(c) eddy currents are set up inside the plate and the direction of the current oppose the motion of the plate
(d) eddy currents are set up inside the plate

44. Pure inductance of 3.0 H is connected as shown below. The equivalent inductance of the circuit is

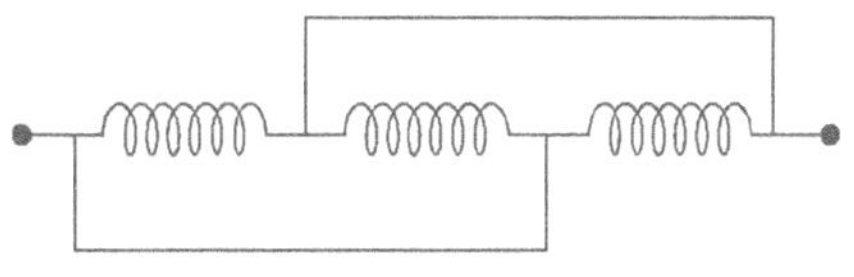

(a) $1\,H$ (b) $2\,H$
(c) $3\,H$ (d) $9\,H$

45. If the switch in the following circuit is turned off, then

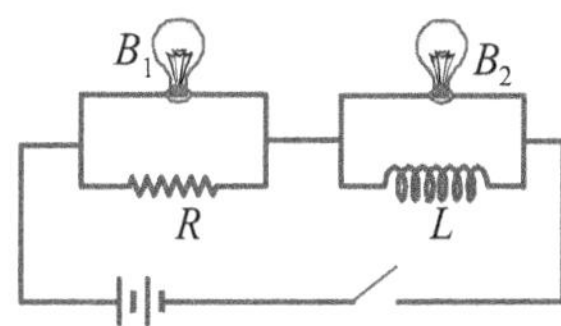

(a) the bulb B_1 will go out immediately whereas B_2 after sometimes
(b) the bulb B_2 will go out immediately whereas B_1 after sometime
(c) both B_1 and B_2 will go out immediately
(d) both B_1 and B_2 will go out after sometime

46. The figure shows certain wire segments joined together to form a coplanar loop. The loop is placed in a perpendicular magnetic field in the direction going into the plane of the figure. The magnitude of the field increases with time. I_1 and I_2 are the currents in the segments ab and cd. Then,

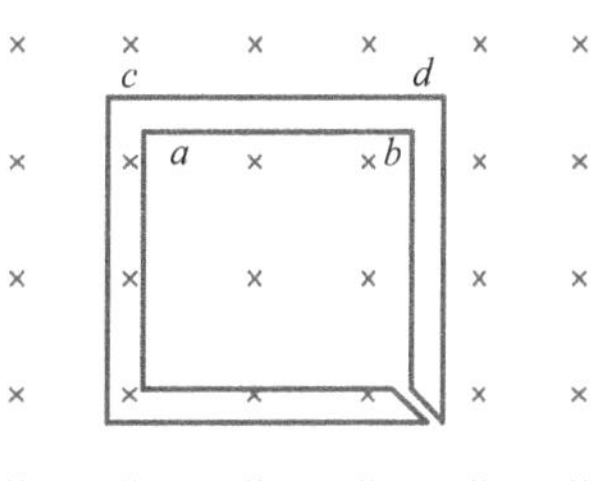

(a) $I_1 > I_2$
(b) $I_1 < I_2$
(c) I_1 is in the direction ba and I_2 is in the direction cd
(d) I_1 is in the direction ab and I_2 is in the direction dc

Answer Key	39	(a)	40	(a)	41	(c)	42	(a)	43	(c)
Sol. from page 561	44	(a)	45	(d)	46	(d)				

Only one option correct

1. The figure shows three situations in which identical circular conducting loops are in uniform magnetic fields that are either increasing or decreasing in magnitude at identical rates. In each, the dashes line coincides with a diameter. In which situation the magnitude of the induced current is maximum :

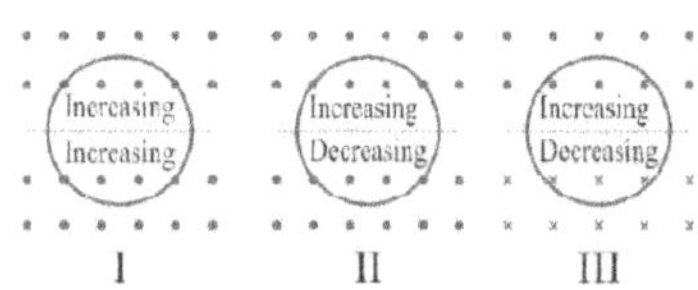

   (a) I   (b) I, II

   (c) II, III   (d) I, III

2. A square loop with 2.0 m sides is perpendicular to a uniform magnetic field, with half the area of the loop in the field is shown in figure. The loop contains a 20.0 V battery with negligible interval resistance. If the magnitude of the field varies with time according to $B = 0.042 - 0.87\,t$, with B in tesla and t in second. The net emf of the circuit is :

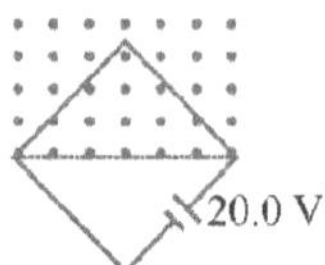

   (a) 20.0 V   (b) 18.26 V

   (c) 21.74 V   (d) none

3. Figure shows a circular region in which an increasing uniform magnetic field is directed out of the page, as well as a concentric circular path along which $\oint \vec{E}\cdot d\vec{\ell}$ is to be evaluated. The table gives the initial magnitude, and the time interval for the increase, in three situations. The situation according to the greatest magnitude of the electric field induced along the path :

Situation	Initial field	Increase	Time
A	B_1	ΔB_1	Δt_1
B	$2B_1$	$\Delta B_1 / 2$	Δt_1
C	$B_1 / 4$	ΔB_1	$\dfrac{\Delta t_1}{2}$

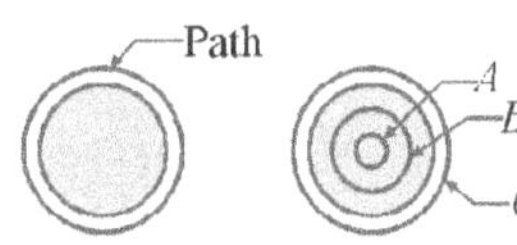

   (a) A (b) B

   (c) C (d) A and B

4. The switch in the circuit of figure has been closed for a very long time when it is then thrown to b. The resulting current through the inductor is indicated in the figure for four sets of values for the resistance R and inductance L : (1) R_0 and L_0 (2) $2\,R_0$ and L_0, (3) R_0 and $2L_0$. (4) $2R_0$, $2L_0$. Select the correct matching :

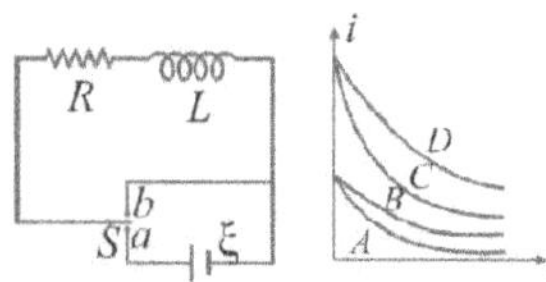

   (a) A-1, B-2, C-3, D-5   (b) A-4, B-3, C-2, D-1

   (c) A-2, B-4, C-1, D-3   (d) none

5. A coil having n turns and resistance $R\,\Omega$ is connected with a galvanometer of resistance $4R\,\Omega$. This combination is moved in time t second from a magnetic flux ϕ_1 weber to ϕ_2 weber. The induced current in the circuit is

   (a) $-\dfrac{\phi_2 - \phi_1}{5\,Rnt}$ (b) $-\dfrac{n\left(\phi_2 - \phi_1\right)}{5\,Rt}$

   (c) $-\dfrac{\left(\phi_2 - \phi_1\right)}{Rnt}$ (d) $-\dfrac{n\left(\phi_2 - \phi_1\right)}{Rt}$

6. One conducting U tube can slide inside another as shown in figure, maintaining electrical contacts between the tubes. The magnetic field B is perpendicular to the plane of the figure. If each tube moves towards the other at a constant speed v then the emf induced in the circuit in terms of B, ℓ and v where ℓ is the width of each tube, will be

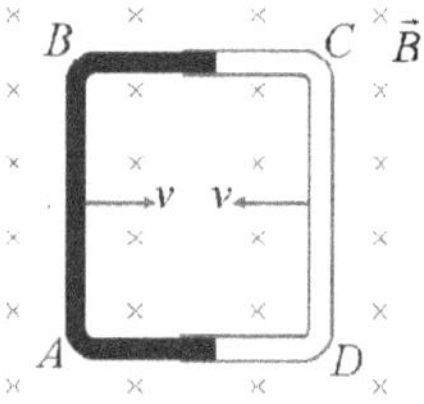

   (a) zero   (b) $2\,Blv$

   (c) Blv (d) $-B$

7. A small square loop of wire of side ℓ is placed inside a large square loop of wire of side L $(L > \ell)$. The loop are coplanar and their centre coincide. The mutual inductance of the system is proportional to

   (a) ℓ / L (b) ℓ^2 / L

   (c) L / ℓ (d) L^2 / ℓ

Answer Key	1	(d)	2	(c)	3	(c)	4	(c)
Sol. from page 562	5	(b)	6	(b)	7	(b)		

8. A uniform but time-varying magnetic field $B(t)$ exists in a circular region of radius a and is directed into the plane of the paper, as shown. The magnitude of the induced electric field at point P at a distance r from the centre of the circular region

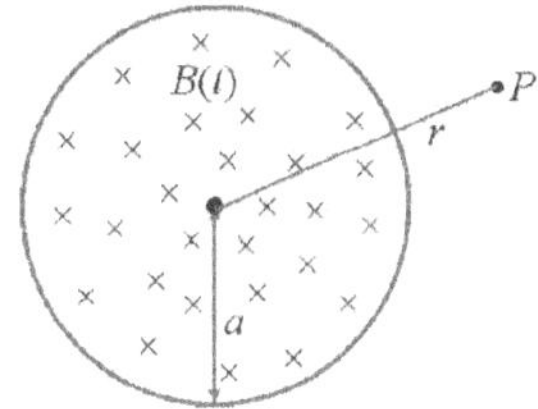

(a) is zero

(b) decreases as $\dfrac{1}{r}$

(c) increases as r

(d) decreases as $\dfrac{1}{r^2}$

9. A coil of wire having finite inductance and resistance has a conducting ring placed coaxially within it. The coil is connected to a battery at time $t = 0$, so that a time-dependent current $I_1(t)$ starts flowing through the coil. If $I_2(t)$ is the current induced in the ring and $B(t)$ is the magnetic field at the axis of the coil due to $I_1(t)$, then as a function of time $(t > 0)$, the product $I_2(t) \, B(t)$

(a) increases with time

(b) decreases with time

(c) does not vary with time

(d) passes through a maximum

10. Shown in the figure is a circular loop of radius r and resistance R.

A variable magnetic field of induction $B = B_0 e^{-t}$ is established inside the coil. If the key (K) is closed, the electrical power developed right after closing the switch is equal to

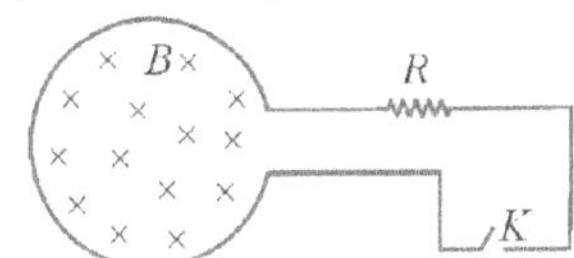

(a) $\dfrac{B_0^2 \pi r^2}{R}$

(b) $\dfrac{B_0 10 r^3}{R}$

(c) $\dfrac{B_0^2 \pi^2 r^4 R}{5}$

(d) $\dfrac{B_0^2 \pi^2 r^4}{R}$

11. A highly conducting ring of radius R is perpendicular to and concentric with the axis of a long solenoid as shown in fig. The ring has a narrow gap of width d in its circumference. The solenoid has cross sectional area A and a uniform internal field of magnitude B_0. Now beginning at $t = 0$, the solenoid current is steadily increased to so that the field magnitude at any time t is given by $B(t) = B_0 + \alpha t$ where $\alpha > 0$. Assuming that no charge can flow across the gap, the end of ring which has excess of positive charge and the magnitude of induced e.m.f. in the ring are respectively

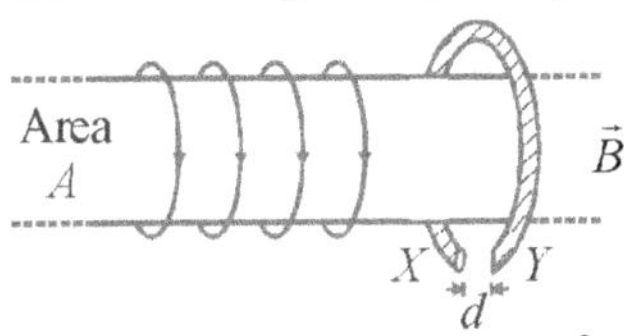

(a) $X, A\alpha$

(b) $X, \pi R^2 \alpha$

(c) $Y, \pi A^2 \alpha$

(d) $Y, \pi R^2 \alpha$

12. The current in a LR circuit builds up to $\dfrac{3}{4}th$ of its steady state value in 4s. The time constant of this circuit is

(a) $\dfrac{1}{\ell n\,2} s$

(b) $\dfrac{2}{\ell n\,2} s$

(c) $\dfrac{3}{\ell n\,2} s$

(d) $\dfrac{4}{\ell n\,2} s$

13. A rectangular loop is being pulled at a constant speed v, through a region of certain thickness d, in which a uniform magnetic field B is set up. The graph between position x of the right hand edge of the loop and the induced emf E will be

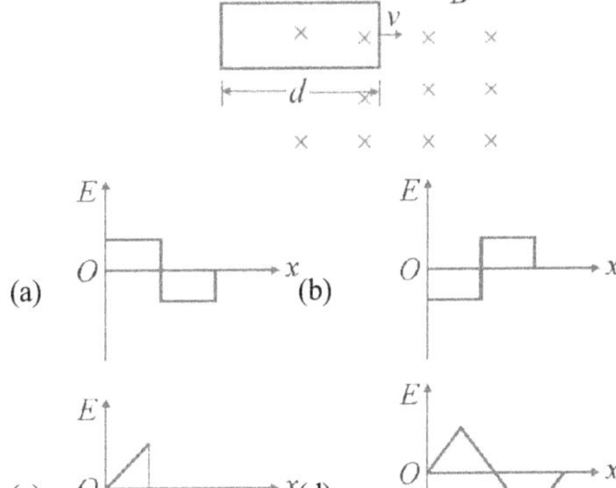

14. A flexible wire bent in the form of a circle is placed in a uniform magnetic field perpendicular to the plane of the coil. The radius of the coil changes as shown in figure. The graph of induced emf in the coil is represented by

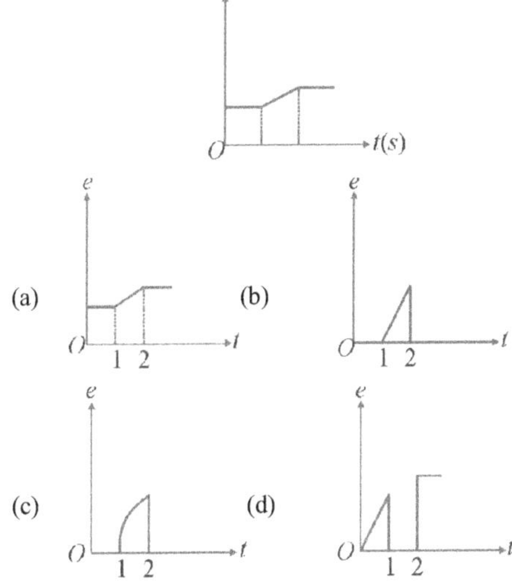

	8	(b)	**9**	(d)	**10**	(d)	**11**	(a)
Sol. from page 562	**12**	(b)	**13**	(b)	**14**	(b)		

15. A square loop of side 5 cm enters a magnetic field with 1 cms^{-1}. The front edge enters the magnetic field at $t = 0$ then which graph best depicts emf

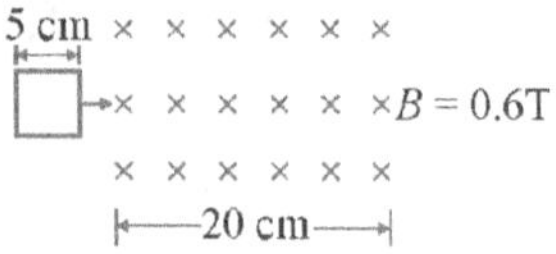

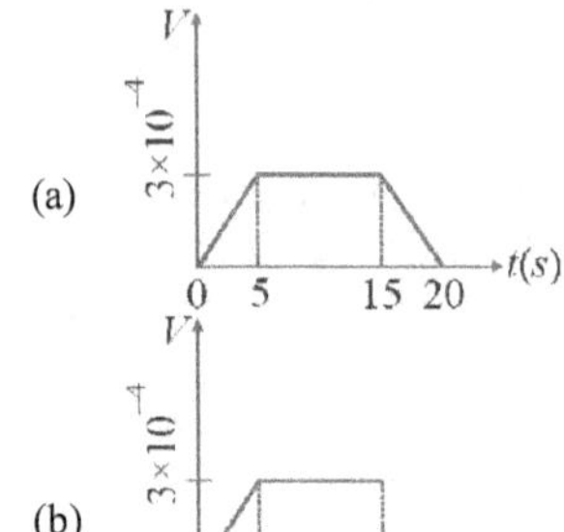

(a)

(b)

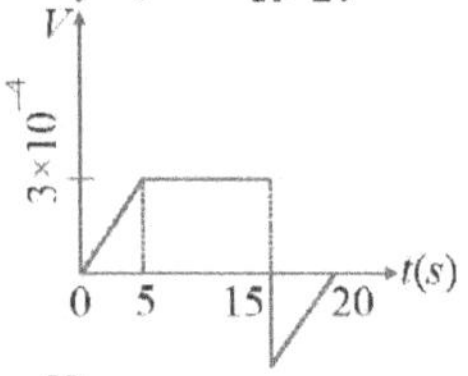

(c)

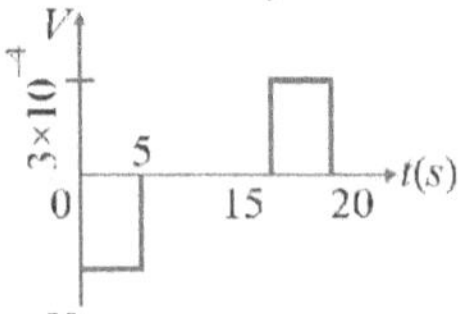

(d)

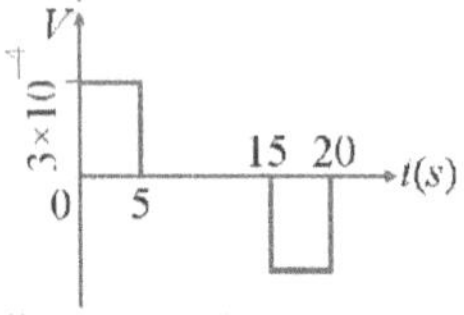

16. A sliding wire of length 0.25 m and having a resistance of 0.5 Ω moves along conducting guiding rails AB and CD with a uniform speed of 4 m/s. A magnetic field of 0.5 T exists normal to the plane of $ABCD$ directed into the page. The guides are short -circuited with resistances of 4 and 2 Ω as shown. The current through the sliding wire is :

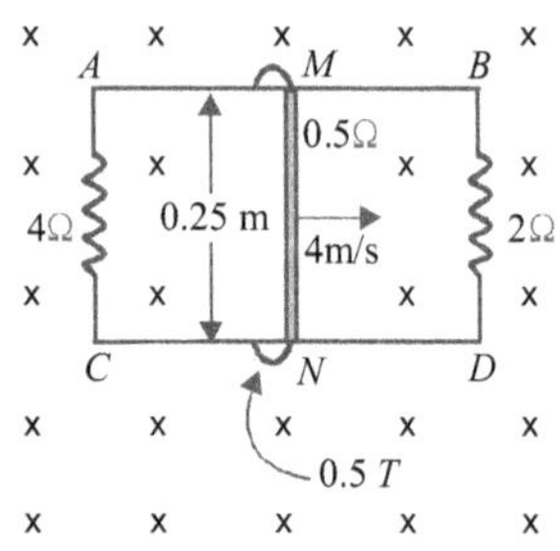

(a)   0.27 A   (b)   0.37 A

(c)   1.0 A   (d)   0.72 A

17. The magnetic field in a region is given by $B = B_0\left(1+\dfrac{x}{a}\right)\hat{k}$. A square loop of edge-length d is placed with its edges along the x and y-axes. The loop is moved with a constant velocity $v = v_0\,\hat{i}$. The emf induced in the loop is :

(a)   zero   (b) $v_0 B_0 d$

(c) $\dfrac{v_0 B_0 d^3}{a^2}$ (d) $\dfrac{v_0 B_0 d^2}{a}$

18. A circuit contains an inductance L, a resistance R and a battery of emf ξ. The circuit is switched off at $t = 0$. The charge flown through the battery in one time constant (τ) is :

(a) $\dfrac{2\xi\tau}{R.e}$ (b) $\dfrac{\xi}{R}.\dfrac{\tau}{e}$

(c) $\dfrac{\xi\tau}{2Re}$ (d)   zero

19. Two coils, one primary of 500 turns and one secondary of 25 turns, are wound on an iron ring of mean diameter 20 cm and cross-sectional area 12 cm^2. If the permeability of iron is 800, the mutual inductance is :

(a)   0.48 H   (b)   2.4 H

(c)   0.12 H   (d)   0.24 H

20. The current through an inductor of 1H is given by $i = 3t \sin t$. The voltage across the inductor of 1 H is :

(a) $3 \sin t + 3 \cos t$ (b) $3 \cos t + t \sin t$

(c) $3 \sin t + 3t \cos t$ (d) $3t \cos t + \sin t$

21. An L-shaped conductor rod is moving in transverse magnetic field as shown in the figure. Potential difference between ends of the rod is maximum if the rod is moving with velocity

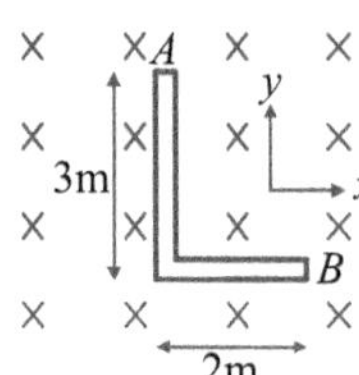

(a) $4\hat{i} - 6\hat{j}$ m/s   (b) $-4\hat{i} + 6\hat{j}$ m/s

(c) $3\hat{i} + 2\hat{j}$ m/s   (d) $\sqrt{13}\,\hat{i}$ m/s

22. A rectangular coil has a long straight wire passing through its centroid perpendicular to its plane as shown. If current through the wire varies as $i = i_0 \sin \omega t$, induced current in the coil will be (Given R = Resistance of the coil)

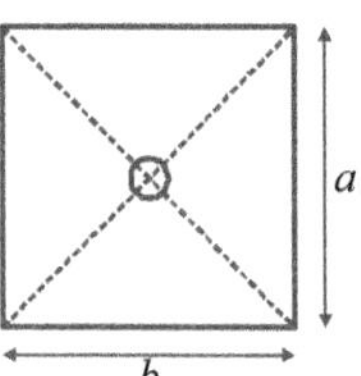

(a) $\dfrac{i_0 \sin \omega t}{R}$ (b) $\dfrac{\pi a \sin \omega t}{bR}$

(c) $\dfrac{\pi a \cos \omega t}{bR}$ (d)   zero

Answer Key	**15**	(c)	**16**	(a)	**17**	(d)	**18**	(b)
Sol. from page 562	**19**	(d)	**20**	(c)	**21**	(c)	**22**	(d)

23. The circuit shown here is in its steady state. Time constant of the circuit is

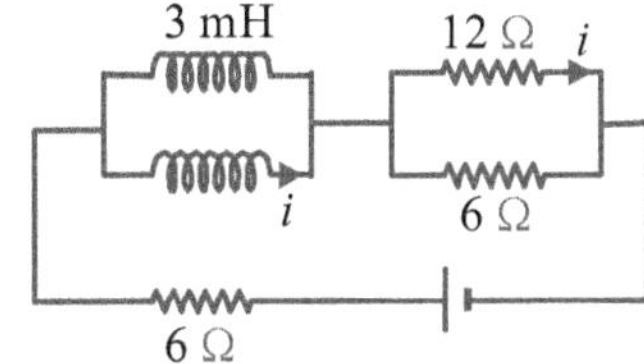

(a) 0.1 ms
(b) 0.2 ms
(c) 0.3 ms
(d) information is insufficient of determine time constant

24. Consider cylindrical region of the magnetic field shown in the figure. Region I and II have fields directed perpendicularly outward and inward respectively. Fields are varying with time as

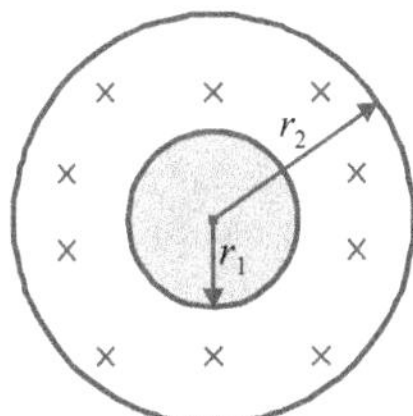

Region I   : $B = 3B_0 t$
Region II : $B = B_0 t$

$\dfrac{r_1}{r_2}$ such that there is no net induced electric field in the region outside the magnetic field is

(a) 0.5   (b) 0.6
(c) 0.8   (d) 0.2

25. Two conducting rings are moving on a smooth conducting horizontal surface as shown. There is a transverse uniform magnetic field of strength B in the region. Potential difference between highest points of the rings is zero in this case. Had the rings been moving in opposite direction with same speeds, potential difference between the highest points would be

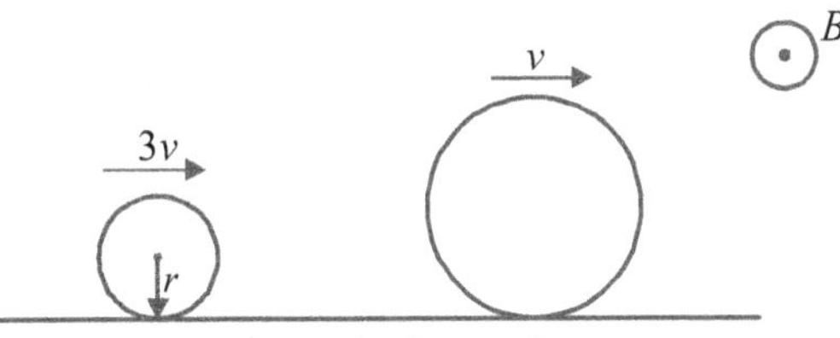

(a) $3\,Brv$
(b) $6\,Brv$
(c) $12\,Brv$
(d) zero, as the surface on which rings are moving is conducting and hence are equipotential

26. A nonconducting ring (of mass m, radius r, having charge Q) is placed on a rough horizontal surface (in a cylindrical region with transverse magnetic field). The field is increasing with time at the rate R and coefficient of friction between the surface and the ring is μ. For ring to remain in equilibrium μ should be greater than

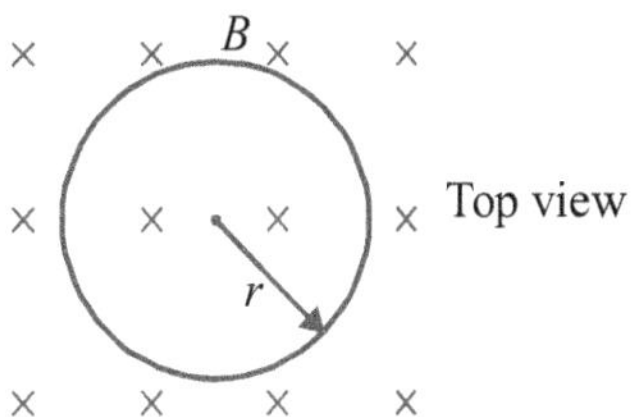

(a) $\dfrac{Qr^2 R^2}{2mg}$ (b) $\dfrac{QrR}{2mg}$

(c) $\dfrac{Qr^2 R}{2mg}$ (d) $\dfrac{QrR^2}{2mg}$

27. Consider a pair of smooth metallic rails joined at one of the ends. Rails are parallel and are inclined at 30° with horizontal. A jumper of mass m, length ℓ and resistance R slides down the rails with constant speed v. Magnetic field in the region is vertical. Strength of magnetic field is

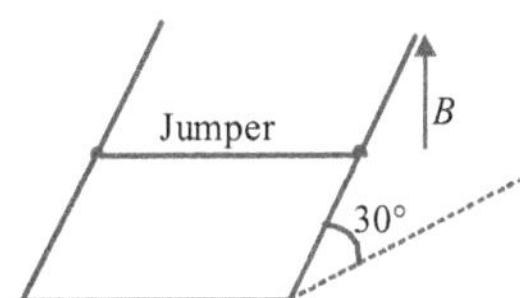

(a) $\sqrt{\dfrac{mgR}{3v\ell^2}}$ (b) $\sqrt{\dfrac{2mgR}{3v\ell^2}}$

(c) $\sqrt{\dfrac{3mgR}{v\ell^2}}$ (d) $\sqrt{\dfrac{\sqrt{3}mgR}{v\ell^2}}$

28. A conducting rod of mass m and ℓ is placed on a smooth horizontal surface in a region where transverse uniform magnetic field B exists in the region. At $t = 0$, constant force F starts acting on the rod at its mid point as shown. Potential difference between ends of the rod, $V_P - V_Q$ at any time t is

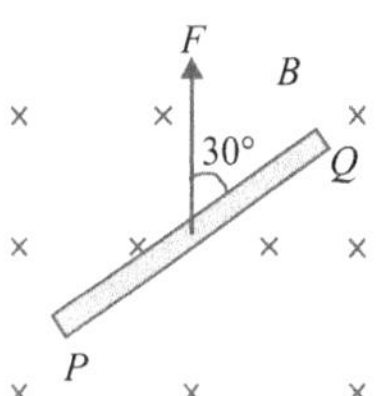

(a) $\dfrac{BF\ell t}{2m}$ (b) $\dfrac{BF\ell t}{4m}$

(c) $\dfrac{5BF\ell t}{8m}$ (d) $\dfrac{7BF\ell t}{8m}$

Answer Key	23	(b)	24	(a)	25	(c)	26	(b)
Sol. from page 562	27	(b)	28	(a)				

29. Consider a region of cylindrical magnetic field, changing with time at the rate x. A triangular conducting loop PQR is placed in the field such that mid point of side PQ coincides with axis of the magnetic field region. $PQ = 2\ell$, $PR = 2\ell$. E.m.f induced in the sides PQ, QR, PR of the loop are

(a) $x\ell^2, 0, x\ell^2$

(b) $0, \dfrac{x\ell^2}{2}, \dfrac{3x\ell^2}{2}$

(c) $0, x\ell^2, x\ell^2$

(c) $0, \dfrac{3}{2}x\ell^2, \dfrac{x\ell^2}{2}$

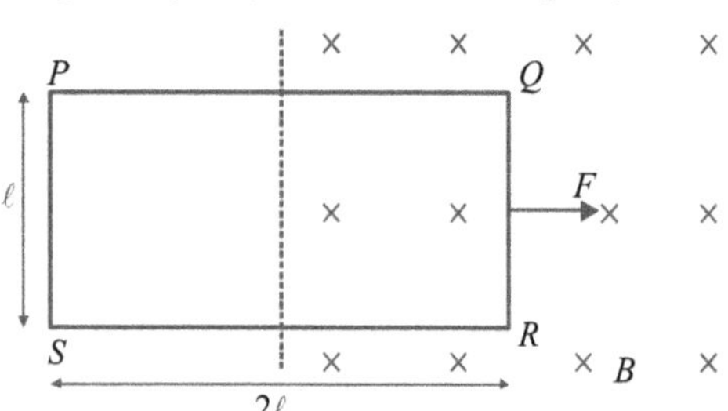

30. A conducting wire PQ of length ℓ, mass m and resistance r is sliding down a smooth, vertical, thick pair of rails (as shown) with constant speed. Choose the correct alternative, if the circuit is in steady state

(a) $i = \dfrac{mg}{B\ell}, q = +\dfrac{mgCR}{B\ell}$

(b) $i = -\dfrac{mg}{B\ell}, q = \dfrac{mgCR}{B\ell}$

(c) $i = -\dfrac{mg}{B\ell}, q = zero$

(d) $i = zero, q = -\dfrac{mgCR}{B\ell}$

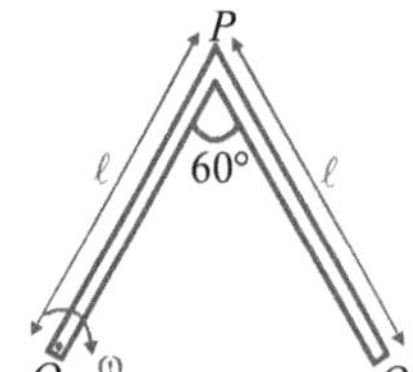

31. A rectangular loop $PQRS$, is pulled with constant speed into a uniform transverse magnetic field by a force F (as shown). E.m.f. induced in side PS and potential difference between points P and S respectively are (Resistance of the loop = r)

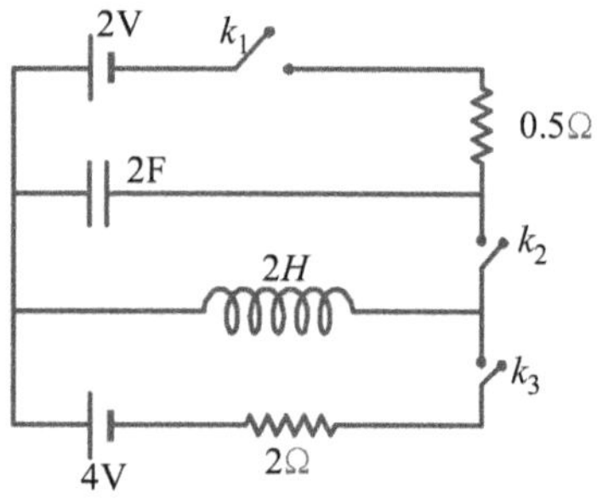

(a) zero, $\dfrac{Fr}{B\ell}$

(b) zero, zero

(c) zero, $\dfrac{Fr}{6B\ell}$

(d) $\dfrac{Fr}{6B\ell}, \dfrac{Fr}{6B\ell}$

32. A rod OPQ is rotating with angular speed ω about point O. A uniform magnetic field B exists perpendicular to the plane of the rod. Potential difference between point P and Q on the rod is

(a) $\dfrac{B\omega\ell^2}{2}$

(b) $B\omega\ell^2$

(c) zero

(d) $\dfrac{B\omega\ell^2}{8}$

33. A conducting loop is being pulled with speed v from region I of magnetic field to region II. If resistance of the loop is R, current induced in the loop at the instant shown is

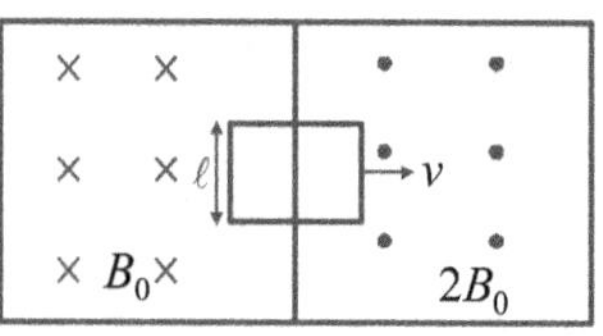

(a) $\dfrac{B_0\ell v}{R}$, clockwise

(b) $\dfrac{B_0\ell v}{R}$, anticlockwise

(c) $\dfrac{3B_0\ell v}{R}$, clockwise

(d) $\dfrac{3B_0\ell v}{R}$, anticlockwise

34. For the circuit shown here keys k_1 and k_3 are closed for 1 second. Key k_2 is closed at the instant k_1 and k_3 are opened. Maximum charge on the capacitor after key k_2 is closed is

(a) $4\left(1-\dfrac{1}{e}\right)C$

(b) $4\sqrt{2}\left(1-\dfrac{1}{e}\right)C$

(c) $8\left(1-\dfrac{1}{e}\right)C$

(d) zero

35. Potential difference across the capacitor is varying as $V = e^{-\frac{1}{2}}$ volt. Potential difference between points A and B, $V_A - V_B$ equals

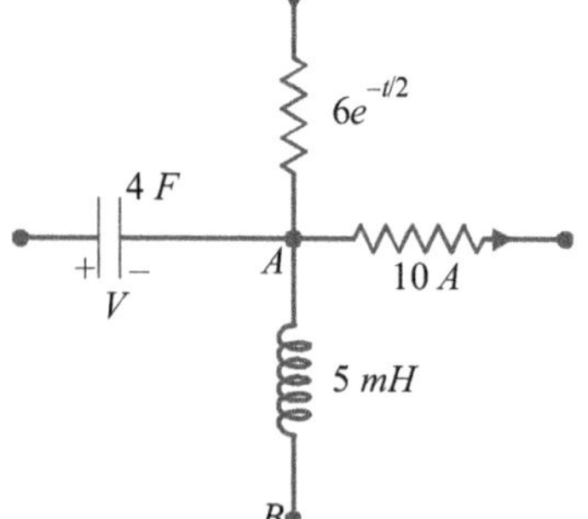

(a) $5e^{-\frac{t}{2}}mV$

(b) $-5e^{-\frac{t}{2}}mV$

(c) $10e^{-\frac{t}{2}}mV$

(d) $-10e^{-\frac{t}{2}}mV$

Answer Key	**29**	(c)	**30**	(a)	**31**	(c)	**32**	(c)
Sol. from page 562	**33**	(c)	**34**	(b)	**35**	(d)		

36. Two capacitors of capacitances $3C$ and $2C$ are connected in series with an inductor of inductance L. Potential differences across the capacitors are $V_P - V_Q = V_0$, $V_R - V_Q = \dfrac{7}{2}V_0$. Initial current in the circuit is zero. Energy in capacitor with capacitance $3C$ when current in the inductor is maximum is

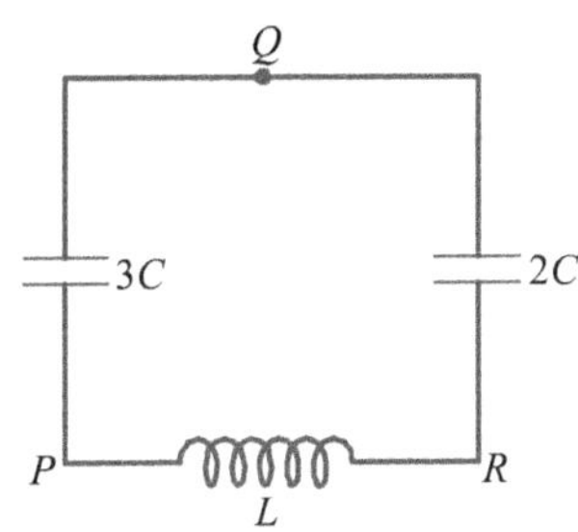

(a) $\dfrac{3}{2}CV_0^2$

(b) $3CV_0^2$

(c) $6CV_0^2$

(d)   zero

37. Key for the circuit shown is closed at time $t = 0$. Currents through the inductor and the capacitor are equal at time t (in ms) equal to

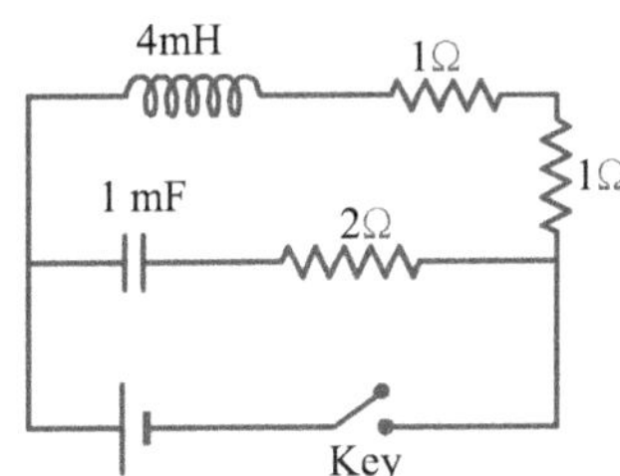

(a) $\ell n\,2$

(b) $\ell n\,4$

(c) $\ell n\,8$

(d) $\ell n\!\left(\dfrac{1}{2}\right)$

38. Regarding the given circuit, the correct statement is

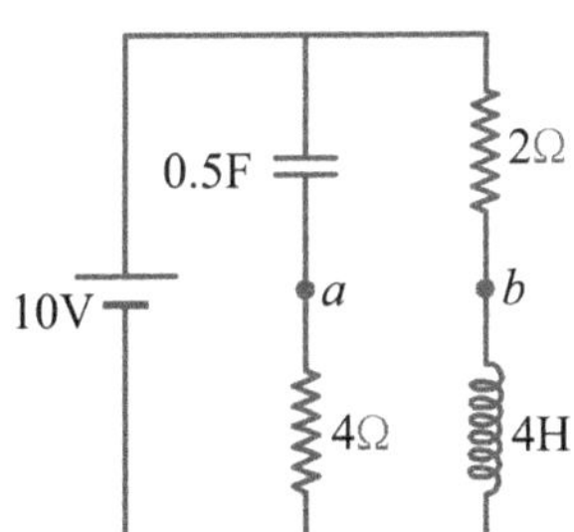

(a) $\left(V_a - V_b\right)$ is increasing with time

(b) $\left(V_a - V_b\right)$ is decreasing with time

(c) $\left(V_a - V_b\right) = 10\,\text{V}$

(d) $\left(V_a - V_b\right) =$ zero

39. A cylindrical region of radius 1 m has instantaneous homogenous magnetic field of 5T and it is increasing at a rate of 2T/s. A regular hexagonal loop ABCDEFA of side 1 m is being drawn in to the region with a constant speed of 1 m/s as shown in the figure. What is the magnitude of emf developed in the loop just after the shown instant when the corner A of the hexagon is coinciding with the centre of the circle ?

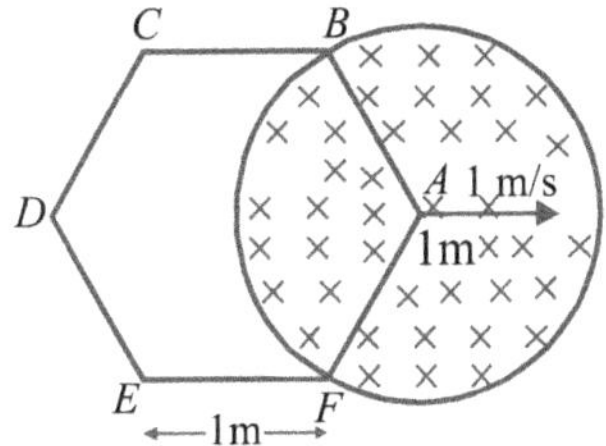

(a) $5/\sqrt{3}V$

(b) $2\pi/3\ V$

(c) $\left(5\sqrt{3} + 2\pi/3\right)V$

(d) $\left(5\sqrt{3} + \pi\right)V$

40. In given figure, a wire loop has been bent so that it has three segments: segment ab (a quarter circle), bc (a square corner), and ca (straight). Here are three choices for a magnetic field through the loop:

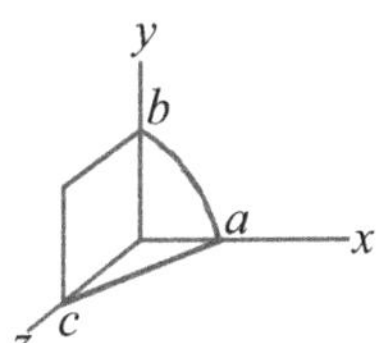

(1) $\vec{B}_1 = 3\hat{i} + 7\hat{j} - 5t\hat{k}$

(2) $\vec{B}_2 = 5t\hat{i} - 4\hat{j} - 15\hat{k}$

(3) $\vec{B}_3 = 2\hat{i} - 5t\hat{j} - 12\hat{k}$

where $\vec{B}$ is in milliteslas and t is in seconds. If the induced current in the loop due to $\vec{B}_1$, $\vec{B}_2$ and $\vec{B}_3$ are i_1, i_2 and i_3 respectively then

(a) $i_1 > i_2 > i_3$

(b) $i_2 > i_1 > i_3$

(c) $i_3 > i_2 > i_1$

(d) $i_1 = i_2 = i_3$

Answer Key	**36**	(c)	**37**	(b)	**38**	(d)	**39**	(c)
Sol. from page 562	**40**	(b)						

Multiple correct options

1. The figure shows four wire loops, with edge lengths of either ℓ or 2ℓ. All four loops will move through a region of uniform magnetic field $\vec{B}$ at the same constant velocity. In which loop the emf induced is maximum :

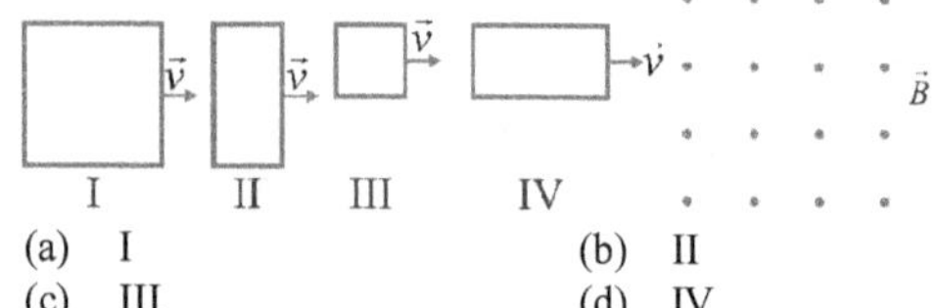

(a) I   (b) II
(c) III   (d) IV

2. Figure shows a circuit with two resistors and an ideal inductor.

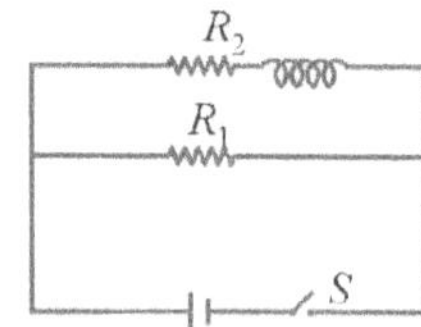

(a) The current in R_1 is zero just after closing the switch S.
(b) The current in R_1 is maximum just after closing the switch S.
(c) The current in R_2 is zero just after closing of the switch S.
(d) The currents in the resistors are maximum of their values a long time after closing the switch S.

3. L, C and R represent inductance, capacitance and resistance respectively. Which of the following have dimensions of frequency ?

(a) $\dfrac{L}{C}$ (b) $\dfrac{1}{\sqrt{LC}}$

(d) $\dfrac{R}{L}$ (d) $\dfrac{1}{RC}$

4. A conducting loop is placed in a uniform magnetic field with its plane perpendicular to the field. An emf is induced in the loop if
(a) it is translated
(b) it is rotated about its axis
(c) it is rotated about axis through bisector
(d) it is expanded

5. Two different coils have self-inductance $L_1 = 8$ mH, $L_2 = 2$mH. The current in one coil is increased at a constant rate. The current in the second coil is also increased at the same rate. At a certain instant of time, the power given to the two coils is the same. At that time the current, the induced voltage and the energy stored in the first coil are i_1, V_1 and W_1 respectively. Corresponding values for the second coil at the same instant are i_2, V_2 and W_2 respectively. Then

(a) $\dfrac{i_1}{i_2} = \dfrac{1}{4}$ (b) $\dfrac{i_1}{i_2} = 48$

(c) $\dfrac{W_2}{W_1} = 4$ (d) $\dfrac{V_2}{V_1} = \dfrac{1}{4}$

6. Two metallic rings A and B, identical in shape and size but having different resistivities ρ_A and ρ_B, are kept on top of two identical solenoids as shown in the figure. When current I is switched on in both the solenoids in identical manner, the rings A and B jump to heights h_A and h_B, respectively, with $h_A > h_B$. The possible relation(s) between their resistivities and their masses m_A and m_B is(are)

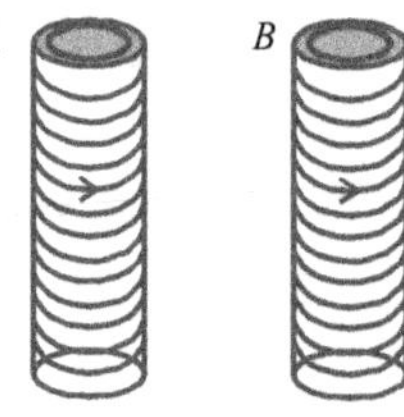

(a) $\rho_A > \rho_B$ and $m_A = m_B$ (b) $\rho_A < \rho_B$ and $m_A = m_B$
(c) $\rho_A > \rho_B$ and $m_A > m_B$ (d) $\rho_A < \rho_B$ and $m_A < m_B$

7. Figure shown plane figure made of a conductor located in a magnetic field along the inward normal to the plane of the figure. The magnetic field starts diminishing. Then the induced current

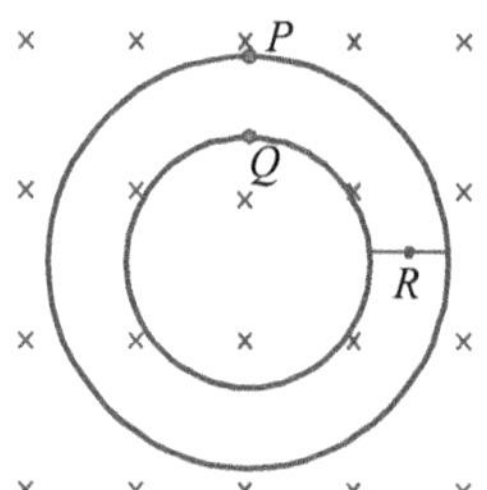

(a) at point P is clockwise
(b) at point Q is anticlockwise
(c) at point Q is clockwise
(d) at point R is zero

8. Two circular coils P & Q are fixed coaxially & carry currents I_1 and I_2 respectively

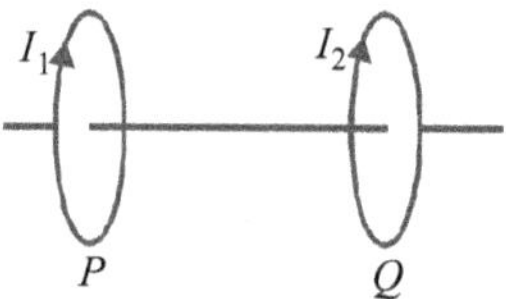

(a) if $I_2 = 0$ & P moves towards Q, a current in the same direction as I_1 is induced in Q
(b) if $I_1 = 0$ & Q moves towards P, a current in the opposite direction to that of I_2 is induced in P.
(c) when $I_1 \neq 0$ and $I_2 \neq 0$ are in the same direction then the two coils tends to move apart.
(d) when $I_1 \neq 0$ and $I_2 \neq 0$ are in opposite direction then the coils tends to move apart.

Answer Key	1	(a, b)	2	(b, c, d)	3	(b, c, d)	4	(c, d)
Sol. from page 567	5	(a, c, d)	6	(b, d)	7	(a, c, d)	8	(b, d)

9. A semicircle conducting ring of radius R is placed in the xy plane, as shown in the figure. A uniform magnetic field is set up along the x-axis. No net emf, will be induced in the ring if

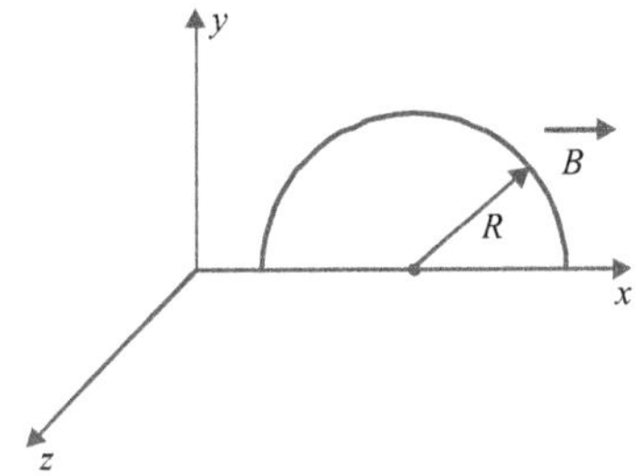

(a) it moves along the x-axis   (b) it moves along the y-axis
(c) it moves along the z-axis   (d) it remains stationary

10. Current growth in two-L-R circuits (b) and (c) as shown in figure (a). Let L_1, L_2 R_1 and R_2 be the corresponding values in two circuits. Then

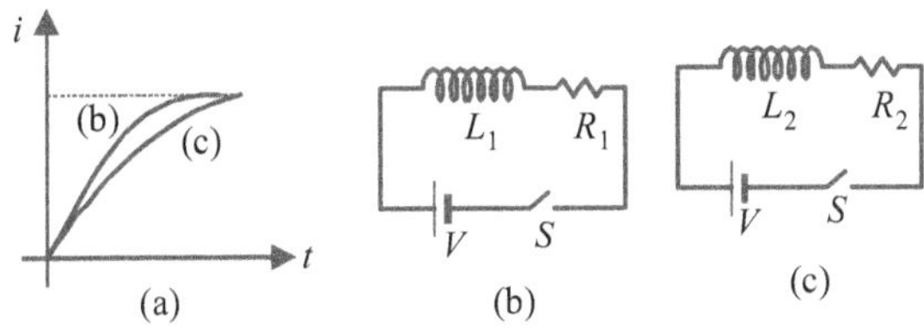

(a) $R_1 > R_2$ (b) $R_1 = R_2$
(c) $L_1 > L_2$ (d) $L_1 < L_2$.

11. The arrangement shown which is confined in a vertical plane has two rails inclined at angle θ with horizontal. A horizontal rod of length ℓ moves on the rails with constant speed v, in the region with transverse field B. Choose the correct alternative(s). The rod starts moving at time $t = 0$

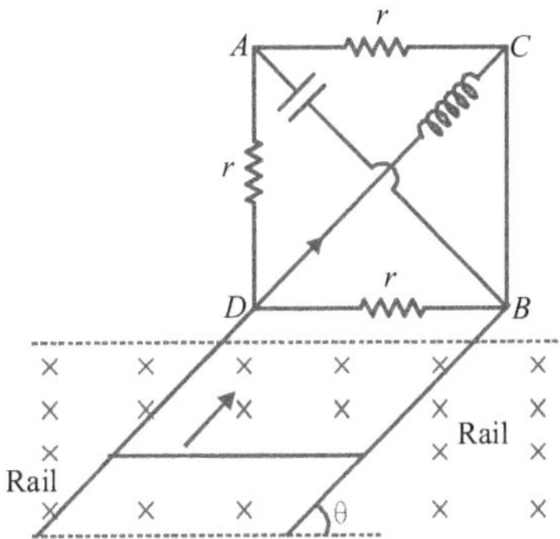

(a) At $t = 0$, current in the circuit is $\dfrac{2BVl\sin\theta}{r}$

(b) At $t = \infty$, current in the circuit is $\dfrac{Blv\sin\theta}{r}$

(c) At any time t (except at $t = 0$) point A is at higher potential than point B

(d) At any time t (except at $t = 0$) point D is at lower potential than C

12. Keys K_1 and K_2 are simultaneously closed at $t = 0$. At any time t current through K_1 is i and current in inductor is increasing at the rate x. Current in the resistor is zero. Choose the correct alternative

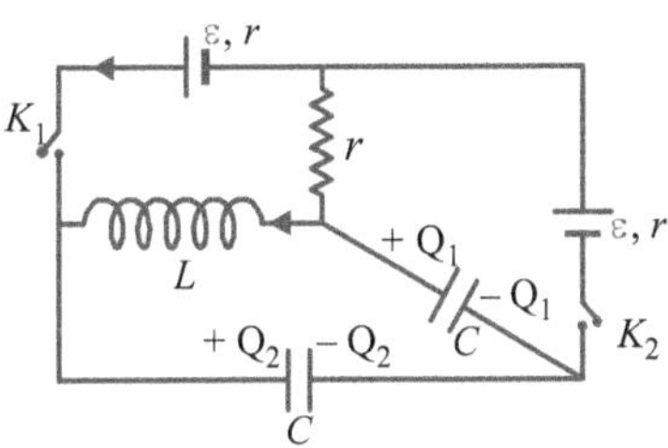

(a) $\varepsilon - ir = Lx$ (b) $\varepsilon + ir = \dfrac{Lx}{2}$

(c) $Q_2 = 2Q_1$ (d) $\dfrac{Q_1}{C} = Lx$

13. Key is in position 2 for time t. Thereafter, it is in position 1. Resistances of the bulb and inductance of inductor are marked in the figure choose the correct alternative

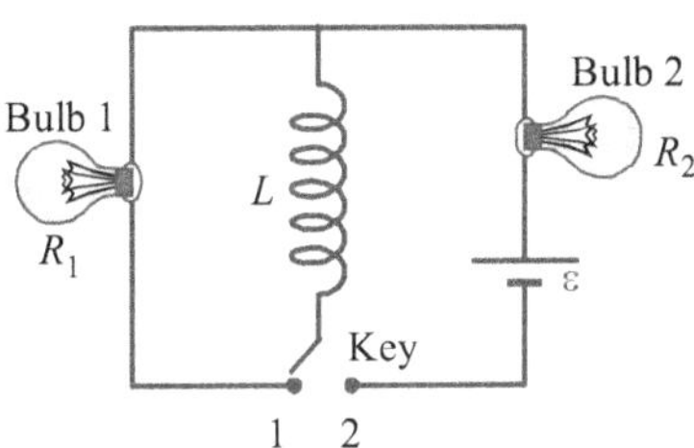

(a) Bulb 2 dies as soon as key is switched into position 1
(b) Time in which brightness of bulb 1 becomes half its maximum brightness does not depend on t.

(c) If $t = \infty$, total heat produced in bulb 1 is $\dfrac{L\varepsilon^2}{2R_2^2}$

(d) Ratio of maximum power consumption of bulbs depends on time

14. Consider the circuit shown with respective specifications of elements marked in the figure. Capacitor-1 is charged such that charge on it is Q_0 and it's left plate is positively charged. While capacitor-2 is uncharged. The switch is closed at $t = 0$

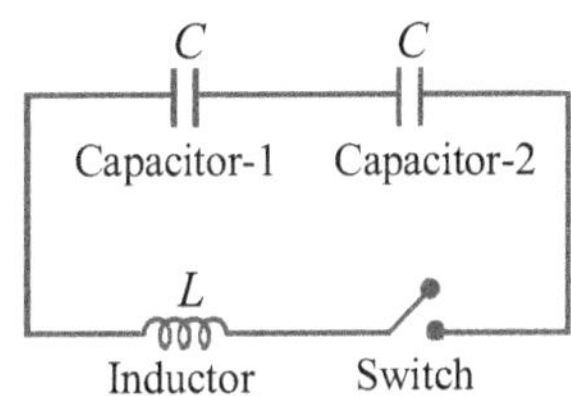

(a) Frequency of oscillation of charge on left plate of capacitor-1 is $\dfrac{1}{\pi\sqrt{2LC}}$

(b) Frequency of oscillation of charge on left plate of capacitor-1 is $\dfrac{1}{\pi}\sqrt{\dfrac{2}{LC}}$

(c) Maximum current through the inductor is $\dfrac{Q_0}{\sqrt{2LC}}$

(d) Maximum current through the inductor is $\dfrac{Q_0}{\sqrt{LC}}$

Answer Key	**9**	(a, b, c, d)	**10**	(b, d)	**11**	(a, b)	**12**	(a, c, d)
Sol. from page 567	**13**	(a, b, c)	**14**	(a, c)				

15. A rod OA of length l is rotating (about end O) over a conducting ring in crossed magnetic field B with constant angular velocity ω as shown in figure

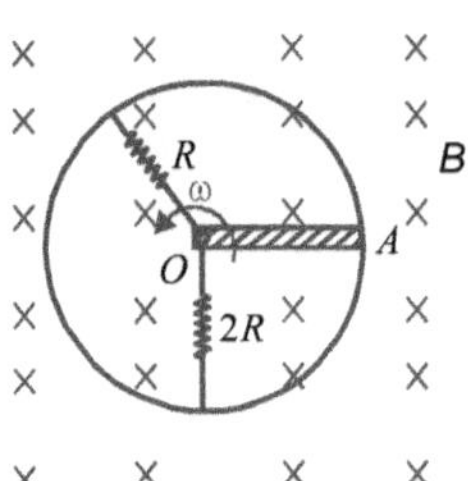

(a) Current flowing through the rod is $\dfrac{3B\omega l^2}{4R}$

(b) Magnetic force acting on the rod is $\dfrac{3B^2\omega l^3}{4R}$

(c) Torque due to magnetic force acting on the rod is $\dfrac{3B^2\omega l^4}{8R}$

(d) Magnitude of external force that acts perpendicularly at the end of the rod to maintain the constant angular speed is

$$\dfrac{3B^2\omega l^3}{8R}$$

16. In the figure shown the key is switched on at $t = 0$. Let I_1 and I_2 be the currents through inductors having self inductances L_1 & L_2 at any time t respectively. The magnetic energy stored in the inductors 1 and 2 be U_1 and U_2. Then U_1/U_2 at any instant of time is

(a) L_1/L_2

(b) L_2/L_1

(c) I_1/I_2

(d) I_2/I_1

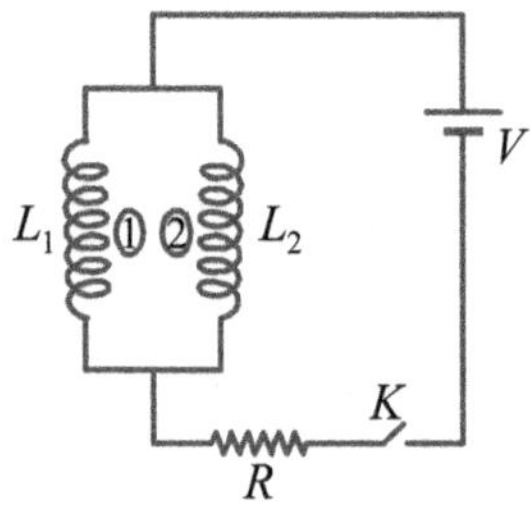

	15	(a, b, c, d)	16	(b, c)				
Sol. from page 567								

Magnetism

Statement Questions

Exercise 8.3

Read the two statements carefully to mark the correct option out of the options given below:
(a)   If both the statements are true and the *statement - 2* is the correct explanation of *statement - 1*.
(b)   If both the statements are true but *statement - 2* is not the correct explanation of the *statement - 1*.
(c)   If *statement - 1* true but *statement - 2* is false.
(d)   If *statement - 1* is false but *statement - 2* is true.

1.   Statement - 1
Induced emf will always occur whenever there is change in magnetic flux.
Statement - 2
Current always induces whenever there is change in magnetic flux.

2.   Statement - 1
An emf can be induced by moving a conductor in a magnetic field.
Statement - 2
An emf can be induced by changing the magnetic field.

3.   Statement - 1
Figure shows a closed conducting loop and two axes of rotation. The magnetic fields is acted towards right. The emf in the loop will induce when the loop is rotated about axis-1

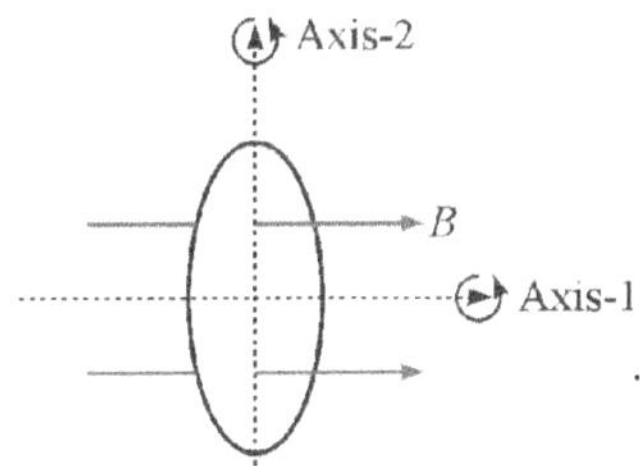

Statement - 2
The emf in the loop will induce when the loop is rotated about the axis-2.

4.   Statement - 1
Lenz's law violates the principle of conservation of energy.
Statement - 2
Induced current always opposes the change in magnetic flux responsible for its production.

5.   Statement - 1
An aeroplane flies along the meridian, the potential at the ends of its wings will be non zero.
Statement - 2
Whenever there is change in magnetic flux, emf induces.

6.   Statement - 1
Faraday's laws are consequence of conservation of energy.
Statement - 2
In a purely resistive ac circuit, the current legs behind the emf in phase.

7.   Statement - 1
Only a change in magnetic flux will maintain an induced current in the coil.
Statement - 2
The presence of large magnetic flux through a coil maintain a current in the coil of the circuit is continuous.

8.   Statement - 1
An artificial satellite with a metal surface is moving above the earth in a circular orbit. A current will be induced in satellite if the plane of the orbit is inclined to the plane of the equator.
Statement - 2
The induced emf across the ends of the moving conductor is given by $e = Bv\ell \sin\theta$.

9.   Statement - 1
Figure shows an emf e induced in a coil. It happens due to rightward decreasing current.

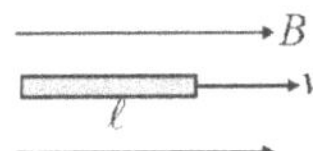

Statement - 2
In the coil self induced emf $e = -L\dfrac{di}{dt}$.

10.   Statement - 1
Figure shows a metallic conductor moving in magnetic field. The induced emf across its ends is zero.

$$\xrightarrow{} B$$
$$\xrightarrow{} v$$
$$\ell$$

Statement - 2
The induced emf across the ends of a conductor is given by $e = Bv\ell\sin\theta$.

11.   Statement - 1
In the phenomenon of mutual induction, self induction of each of the coil persists.
Statement - 2
Self induction arises due to change in current in the coil itself. In mutual induction current changes in both the individual coil.

12.   Statement - 1
A transformer cannot work in *dc* supply.
Statement - 2
There is no change in flux due to *dc*.

Answer Key	1	(c)	2	(b)	3	(d)	4	(d)	5	(a)	6	(c)
Sol. from page 568	7	(c)	8	(a)	9	(a)	10	(a)	11	(a)	12	(a)

13. *Statement - 1*

Eddy currents are produced in any metallic conductor when magnetic flux is changed around it.

Statement - 2

Electric potential determines the flow of charge.

14. *Statement - 1*

The quantity L/R possesses dimensions of time.

Statement - 2

To reduce the rate of increases of current through a solenoid should increase the time constant $\left(\dfrac{L}{R}\right)$.

15. *Statement - 1*

Acceleration of a magnet falling through a long solenoid decreases.

Statement - 2

The induced current produced in a circuit always flow in such direction that it opposes the change to the cause that produced it.

16. *Statement - 1*

An inductor is connected to a battery through a switch. The emf induced in the inductor is much larger when the switch is opened as compared to the emf induced when the switch is closed.

Statement - 2

Induced emf in an inductor, $e = -\dfrac{L\,di}{dt}$.

17. *Statement - 1*

Figure shows a horizontal solenoid connected to a battery and a switch. A copper ring is placed on a smooth surface, the axis of the ring being horizontal. As the switch is closed, the ring will move away from the solenoid.

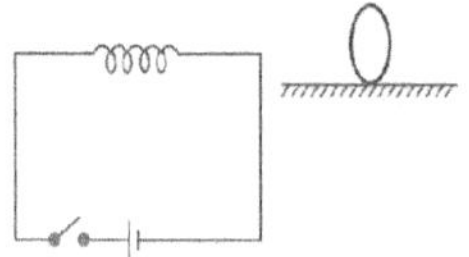

Statement - 2

Induced emf in the ring, $e = -\dfrac{d\phi}{dt}$.

18. *Statement - 1*

Consider the situation shown in figure. When switch is closed, a clockwise current will flow in the loop.

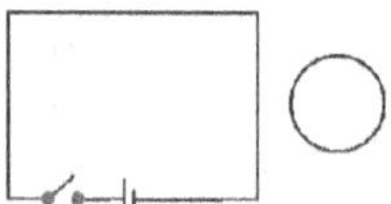

Statement - 2

Direction of the current in the loop is according to the Fleming's left hand rule.

19. *Statement - 1*

A flat, railroad car with a wooden base moves to the right with a constant velocity. A voltmeter V_1 is connected across the rails of the car and another voltmeter V_2 is connected across the axle of the car and in the car. The reading of V_1 is V volt.

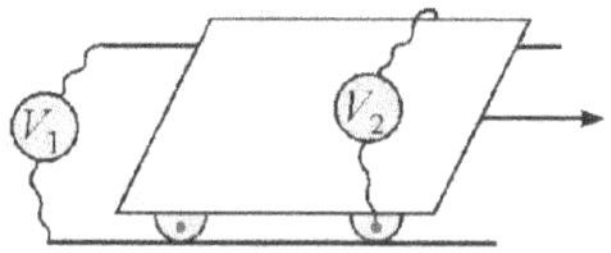

Statement - 2

The reading of V_2 will be $2V$ volt.

<table>
<tr><td rowspan="2">*Answer Key*
Sol. from page 568</td><td>**13**</td><td>(b)</td><td>**14**</td><td>(b)</td><td>**15**</td><td>(a)</td><td>**16**</td><td>(a)</td></tr>
<tr><td>**17**</td><td>(a)</td><td>**18**</td><td>(a)</td><td>**19**</td><td>(c)</td><td>**20**</td><td>(c)</td></tr>
</table>

| Magnetism | Passage & Matrix | Exercise 8.4 |

Passage for Q. 1 to Q. 3

Two capacitors of capacitances $2F$ and $1F$ are connected in series with an inductor of inductance L. Initially capacitors have charge such that $V_B - V_A = 4$ volt and $V_C - V_D = 1$ volt. Initial current in the circuit is zero. Find :

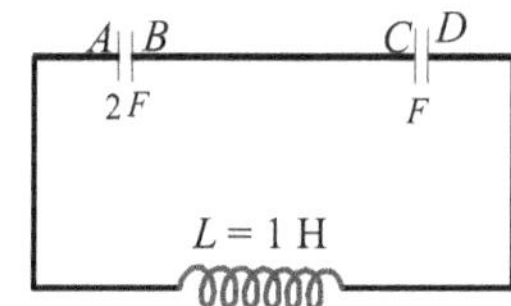

1. Maximum current that will flow in the circuit

(a) $\sqrt{3}\,A$ (b) $\sqrt{6}\,A$

(c) $\sqrt{9}\,A$ (d) $\sqrt{12}\,A$

2. Potential difference across AB capacitor at that instant (maximum current)

(a) $2\,V$ (b) $3\,V$

(c) $4\,V$ (d) $5\,V$

3. Frequency of oscillation

(a) $\sqrt{0.5}$ rad/s   (b) $\sqrt{0.66}$ rad/s

(c) $\sqrt{1.5}$ rad/s   (d) $\sqrt{2.5}$ rad/s

Passage for Q. 4 to Q. 6

The mobile side of the triangular conducting frame made of uniform wire as shown in the figure is slid symmetrically at a uniform speed of $v = 0.1$ m/s along the two other sides. The horizontal frame is in a vertical homogeneous magnetic field with an induction of $B = 0.4\,T$. At a certain instant, the length of each side is $l = 1$ m and combined resistance of all three sides is $1\,\Omega$.

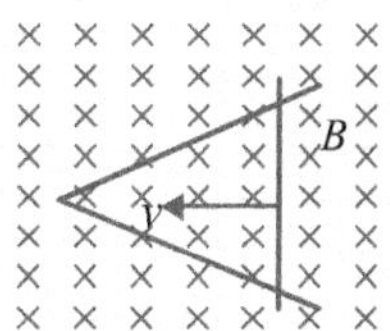

4. How much is the electromotive force induced in the circuit at the moment shown ?

(a) $0.04\,V$ (b) $0.12\,V$

(c) $0.06\,V$ (d) $0.4\,V$

5. How does the current change with time ?

(a) it increases

(b) it remains constant

(c) it decreases

(d) first increases then remains constant

6. How much power is required for sliding at the instant shown if friction is negligible?

(a) $\dfrac{8}{15}\,mW$ (b) $1.6\,mW$

(c) $\dfrac{4}{3}\,mW$ (d) $1.6\,W$

Passage for Q. 7 to Q. 9

A circular coil P of 1000 turns and radius 2 cm is placed coaxially at the centre of another circular coil Q of 100 turns and radius 20 cm.

7. The mutual induction between the coils is :

(a) $8.94 \times 10^{-4}\,H$ (b) $6.08 \times 10^{-4}\,H$

(c) $4.49 \times 10^{-4}\,H$ (d) $3.94 \times 10^{-4}\,H$

8. The induced emf in coil P when current in the coil Q decreases from 5A to 3A in 0.04 s :

(a) $10.28 \times 10^{-3}\,V$ (b) $15.75 \times 10^{-3}\,V$

(c) $19.72 \times 10^{-3}\,V$ (d) $21.72 \times 10^{-3}\,V$

9. Charge passing through coil P if its resistance is 8 ohm :

(a) $9.86 \times 10^{-5}\,C$ (b) $12.48 \times 10^{-5}\,C$

(c) $14.29 \times 10^{-5}\,C$ (d) $18.86 \times 10^{-5}\,C$

Answer Key	1	(b)	2	(b)	3	(c)	4	(a)	5	(b)
Sol. from page 568	6	(b)	7	(d)	8	(c)	9	(a)		

Passage for Q. 10 to Q. 12

A thin non-conducting ring of mass m radius a carrying a charge q rotates freely about its own axis which is vertical. At the initial moment, the ring was at rest and no magnetic field was present. At instant $t = 0$, a uniform magnetic field is switched on which is vertically downwards and increases with time according to the law $B = B_0 t$. Neglecting magnetism emf induced due to rotational motion of the ring.

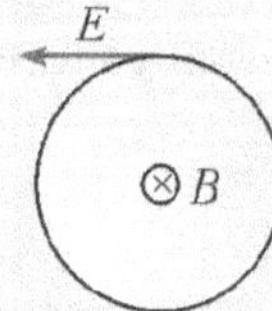

10. The magnitude of electric field at any point of the ring is :

(a) $E = \dfrac{a\,B_0}{2}$

(b) $E = aB_0$

(c) $E = \dfrac{\pi B_0}{2}$

(d) zero

11. The angular acceleration of the ring and its direction of rotation as seen from above

(a) $\dfrac{B_0 q}{m}$

(b) $\dfrac{B_0 q}{2m}$

(c) $\dfrac{2B_0 q}{m}$

(d) $\dfrac{\pi\,B_0\,q}{m}$

12. Power developed by the forces acting on the ring as a function of time is :

(a) $\dfrac{q^2\,B_0^2 a^2 t}{2m}$

(b) $\dfrac{q^2 B_0^2 a^2 t}{4m}$

(c) $\dfrac{\pi\,q^2 B_0^2 a^2 t}{m}$

(d) none of these

Passage for Q. 13 to Q. 15

A magnetic field $\vec{B} = \left(\dfrac{B_0 y}{a}\right)\hat{k}$ is into the paper in the $+z$ direction. B_0 and a are positive constants. A square loop $EFGH$ of side a and mass m and resistance R, in xy-plane, start falling under the influence of gravity. Note the directions of x and y axes in figure.

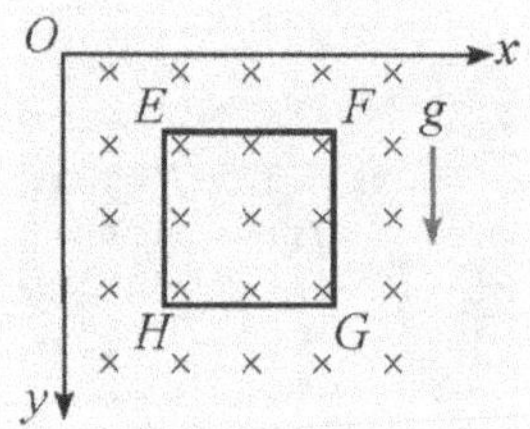

13. If v is the speed of the loop at any time, the induced current in the loop is :

(a) $\dfrac{B_0 av}{R}$ anticlockwise

(b) $\dfrac{2B_0 av}{R}$ anticlockwise

(c) $\dfrac{2B_0 av}{R}$ clockwise

(d) $\dfrac{B_0 av}{R}$ anticlockwise

14. The total Lorentz force acting on the loop in

(a) $\vec{F} = \dfrac{B_0^2 av}{2R}\left(-\hat{j}\right) N$

(b) $\vec{F} = \dfrac{B_0 a^2 v}{R}\left(+\hat{j}\right) N$

(c) $\vec{F} = \dfrac{B_0^2 a^2 v}{R}\left(-\hat{j}\right) N$

(d) none of these

15. The terminal speed of the loop is

(a) $\dfrac{mgR}{B_0^2 a^2}$

(b) $\dfrac{mgR}{B_0 a}$

(c) $\dfrac{2mgR}{B_0^2 a^2}$

(d) $\dfrac{mgR}{2B_0^2 a^2}$

16.

Column I	Column II
(A) Dielectric ring uniformly charged	(p) Constant electrostatic field out of system
(B) Dielectric ring uniformly charged rotating with angular velocity ω	(q) Magnetic field strength
(C) Constant current in ring i	(r) Electric field (induced)
(D) $i = i_0 \cos\omega t$	(s) Magnetic dipole moment

Answer Key	**10**	(a)	**11**	(b)	**12**	(b)	**13**	(a)
Sol. from page 568	**14**	(c)	**15**	(a)	**16**	A-p ; B -p, q, s ; C-q, s ; D- r		

17. Consider a uniform transverse magnetic field confined to a cylindrical region (with axis passing through O) as shown in the figure. Also shown is an imaginary rectangualr loop $abcd$, with midpoint of its side cd at O. Magnetic field in the region is increasing at a constant rate. Match the entries in Column I to the all possible entries in Column II.

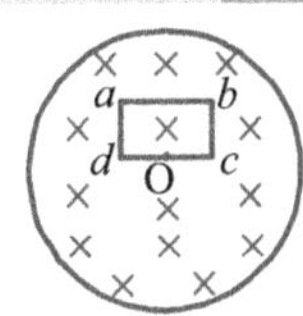

Column I	Column II
A. Potential difference between points a and c, $V_a - V_c$	(p) Zero
B. Work done in carrying charge q from point c to a	(q) Positive
C. Component of electrostatic field at point a along side ad, assuming direction from a towards d to be positive	(r) Negative
D. Component of induced electric field at point c and cb, assuming direction from c towards b to be positive	(s) Not defined
	(t) May have non-zero value

18. Column I gives some incomplete statements. Column II gives some completing statement. Match appropriately.

Column I
A. A rod rotates in a uniform transverse magnetic field as shown, about hinge at O. Potential difference between points A and B.

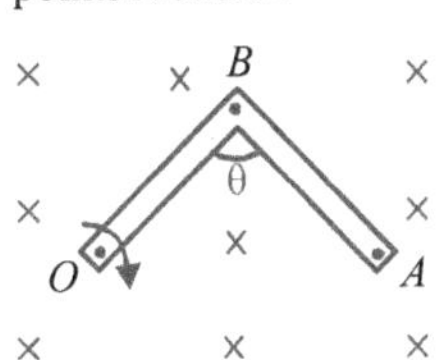

Column II
(p) May be zero

B. A conducting loop is moved in a region of transverse magnetic field, downward the plane of paper, as shown. Value of induced current i __________

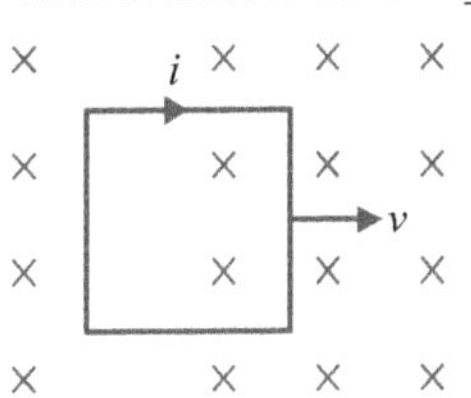

(q) Must be zero

C. If a constant force F is acting on the wire, rate of charge q stored by the capacitor, $\dfrac{dq}{dt}$ __________

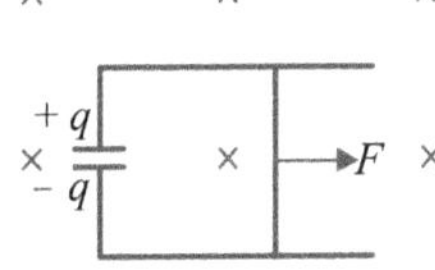

(r) is/may be non-negative

D. A square loop is rotated about diagonal in a region of uniform magnetic field as shown. Value of i at an instant __________

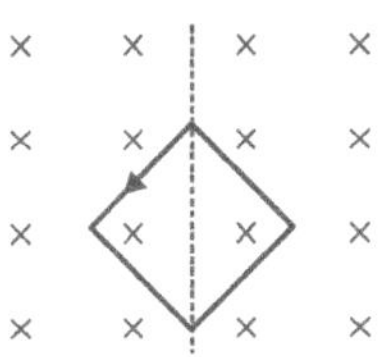

(s) is/may be non-positive

(t) May have non-zero value

Answer Key	17	A- p ; B- p, q, r, t ; C-p ; D-q, t
Sol. from page 568	18	A-p, r, s,t ; B-p, r, s, t; C- r, s, t; D -p, r, s, t

Subjective Integer Type

Exercise 8.5

Solution from page 569

1. The magnetic flux through the loop shown in figure increases according to the relation $\phi_B = 7.0\,t + 6.0\,t^2$, where ϕ_B is in milliweber and t in second.
(a) What is the magnitude of emf induced in the loop when $t = 2.0$ s ?
(b) What is the direction of the current through R ?

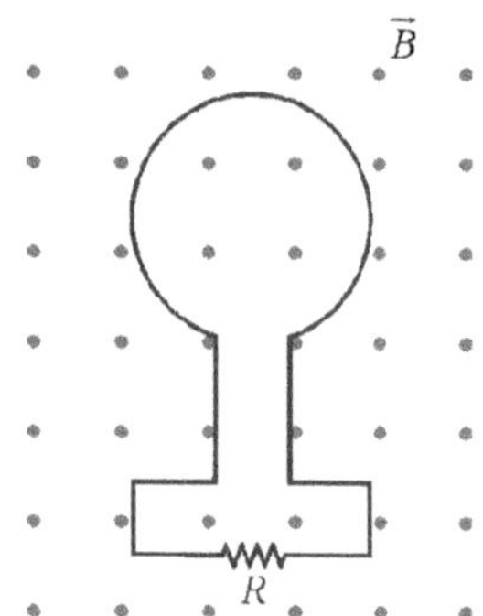

Ans : (a) 31 mV (b) right to left.

2. Two concentric coplanar circular loops made of wire, with resistance per unit length $10\,\Omega/\mathrm{m}$ have diameters 0.2 m and 2 m. A time varying potential difference $(4 + 2.5\,t)$ volt is applied to the larger loop. Calculate the current in the smaller loop.

Ans : 1.25 A

3. Consider the situation shown in figure. The wires P_1Q_1 and P_2Q_2 are made to slide on the rails with the same speed 5 cm/s. Find the electric current in the $19\,\Omega$ resistor if :
(a) both the wires move towards right and
(b) if P_1Q_1 moves towards left but P_2Q_2 moves towards right.

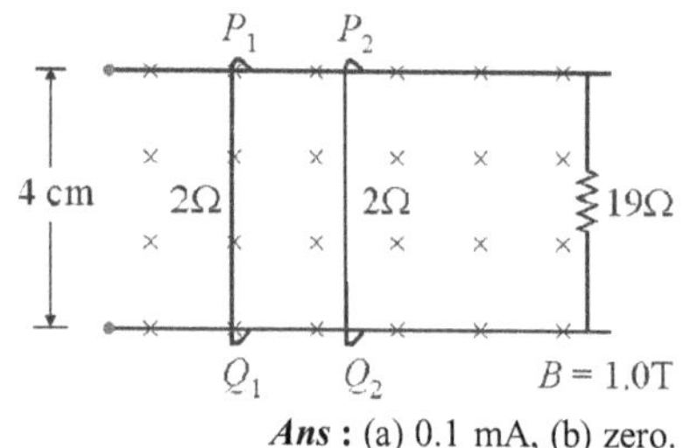

Ans : (a) 0.1 mA, (b) zero.

4. In figure a 120-turn coil of radius 1.8 cm and resistance $5.3\,\Omega$ is placed outside a solenoid. The current in the solenoid is 1.5 A and it reduces to zero at a steady rate in 25 ms. What current appears in the coil ? The number of turns per unit length of the solenoid is 220 turns/cm and its diameter $D = 3.2$ cm.

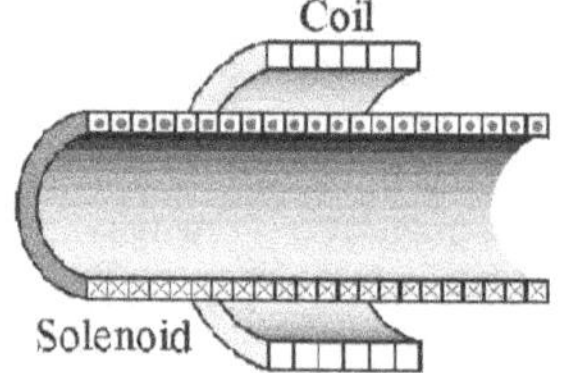

Ans : 30 mA

5. In figure, the square loop of wire has sides of length 2.0 cm. A magnetic field is directed out of the page; its magnitude is given by $B = 4.0\,t^2 y$, where B is in tesla, t in second, and y in metre. Determine the emf around the square at $t = 2.5$ s and give its direction.

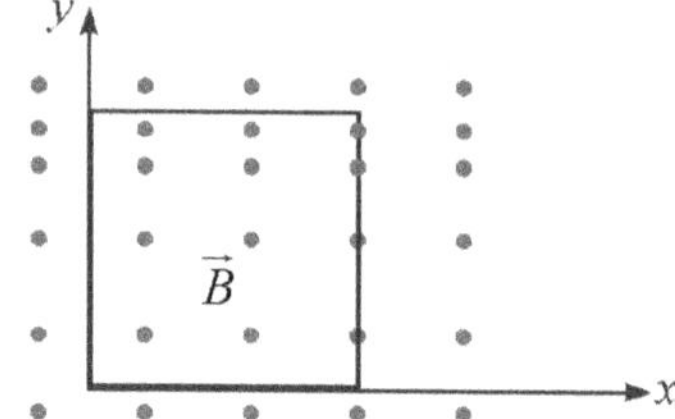

Ans : 80 μV, clockwise.

6. The current in a coil of self-induction 2.0 henry is increasing according to $i = 2 \sin t^2$ ampere. Find the amount of energy spent during the period when the current changes from 0 to 2 ampere.

Ans : 4 J

7. The current in an RL circuits drops from 1.0 A to 10 mA in the first second following removal of the battery from the circuit. If L is 10 H, find the resistance R in the circuit.

Ans : 46 Ω

Subjective

Exercise 8.6

Solution from page 570

1. A small loop of area A is inside of, and has its axis in the same direction as, a long solenoid of n turns per unit length and current i. If $i = i_0 \sin\omega t$, find the emf induced in the loop.

   Ans : $e = \mu_0 n i_0 A \omega \cos\omega t$.

2. A uniform magnetic field B exists in a direction perpendicular to the plane of a square frame made of copper wire. The wire has a diameter of 2 mm and a total length of 40 cm. The magnetic field changes with time at a steady rate $\dfrac{dB}{dt} = 0.02 \dfrac{T}{s}$. Find the current induced in the frame. Resistivity of copper $= 1.7 \times 10^{-8}$ W-m.

   Ans : 9.3×10^{-2} A.

3. A conducting circular loop having a radius of 5.0 cm, is placed perpendicular to a magnetic field of 0.50 T. It is removed from the field in 0.50 s. Find the average emf produced in the loop during this time. *Ans :* 7.8×10^{-3} V.

4. (a) The magnetic field in a region varies as shown in figure. Calculate the average induced emf in a conducting loop of area 2.0×10^{-3} m^2 placed perpendicular to the field in each of the 10 ms intervals shown.

   (b) In which intervals is the emf not constant ? Neglect the behaviour near the ends of 10 ms intervals.

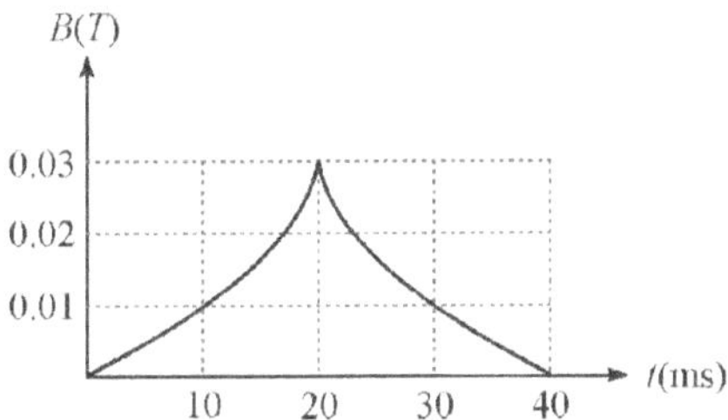

   Ans : (a)–2.0 mV, –4.0 mV, 4.0 mV, 2.0 mV; (b) 10 ms to 20 ms and 20 ms to 30 ms.

5. In figure let the flux through the loop be $\phi_B(0)$ at time $t=0$. Then let the magnetic field $\vec{B}$ vary in continuous but unspecified way, in both magnitude and direction, so that at time t the flux is represented by $\phi_B(t)$.

(a) Show that the net charge $q\,(t)$ that has passed through resistor R in time t is $q(t) = \dfrac{1}{R}\left[\phi_B(0) - \phi_B(t)\right]$ and is independent of the way $\vec{B}$ has changed.

(b) If $\phi_B(t) = \phi_B(0)$ in a particular case, we have $q(t) = 0$. Is the induced current necessarily zero throughout the interval from 0 to t ? *Ans :* (b) no.

6. A conducting loop of area 5.0 cm^2 is placed in a magnetic field which varies sinusoidally with time as $B = B_0 \sin\omega t$ where $B_0 = 0.20$ T and $\omega = 300$ s^{-1}. The normal to the coil makes an angle of $60°$ with the field. Find (a) the maximum emf induced in the coil, (b) the emf induced at $t = \left(\dfrac{\pi}{900}\right) s$ and (c) the emf induced at $t = \left(\dfrac{\pi}{600}\right) s$. *Ans :* (a) 0.015 V (b) 7.5×10^{-3} V (c) zero.

7. Figure shows a horizontal magnetic field which is uniform above the dotted line and is zero below it. A long, rectangular, conducting loop of width L, and mass m and resistance R is placed partly above and partly below the dotted line with the lower edge parallel to it. With what velocity should it be pushed downwards so that it may continue to fall without any acceleration ?

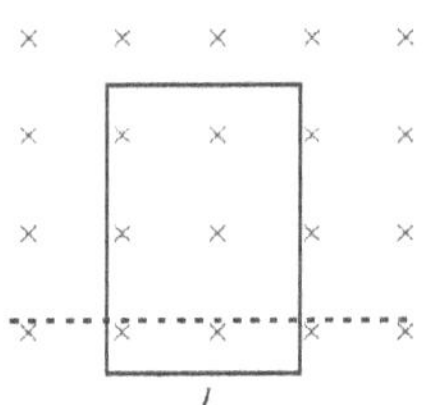

   Ans : $V = \dfrac{mgR}{B^2 L^2}$

8. An air plane, with a 20 m wing spread is plying at 250 m/s straight south parallel to earth's surface. The earth's magnetic field has a horizontal component of 2×10^{-5} Wb/m^2 and angle of dip is $60°$. Calculate the induced emf between the plane tips. *Ans :* 0.173 V.

9. Figure shows a square loop of side 5 cm being moved towards right at a constant speed of 1 cm/s. The front edge enters the 20 cm wide magnetic field at $t = 0$. Find the emf induced in the loop at (a) $t = 2$s, (b) $t = 10$ s, (c) $t = 22$ s and (d) $t = 30$ s.

   Ans : (a) 3×10^{-4} V, (b) zero, (c) 3×10^{-4} V and (d) zero.

10. Figure shows a circular wheel of radius 10.0 cm whose upper half, shown dark in the figure, is made of iron and the lower half of wood. The two junctions are joined by an iron rod. A uniform magnetic field B of magnitude 2.00×10^{-4} T exists in the space above the central line as suggested by the figure. The wheel is set into pure rolling on the horizontal surface. If it takes 2.00 second for the iron part to come down and the wooden part to go up, find the average emf induced during this period.

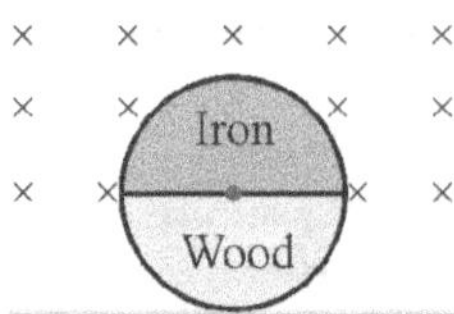

Ans : 1.57×10^{-6} V.

11. A pair of parallel horizontal conducting rails of negligible resistance shorted at one end is fixed on a table. The distance between the rails is L. A conducting massless rod of resistance R can slide on the rails frictionlessly. The rod is tied to a massless string passes over a pulley fixed to the edge of the table. A mass m tied to the other end of the string hangs vertically. A constant magnetic field B exists perpendicular to the table. If the system is released from rest, calculate

(a) the terminal velocity achieved by the rod and

(b) the acceleration of the mass at the instant when the velocity of the rod is half the terminal velocity.

$$Ans : \text{(a)} \; V_T = \frac{mg\,R}{B^2 L^2} \quad \text{(b) } g/2.$$

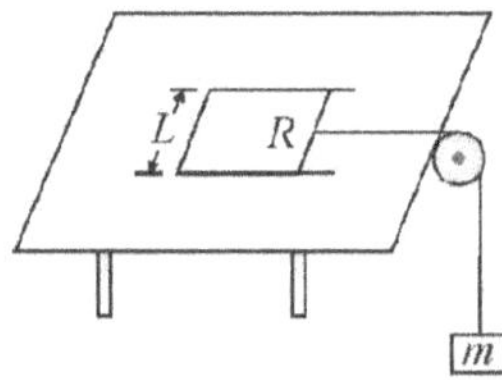

12. A current $i = 3.36\left(1+2t\right)\times10^{-2}\,A$ increases at a steady rate in a long straight wire. A small circular loop of radius 10^{-3} m has its plane parallel to the wire and is placed at a distance of 1 m from the wire. The resistance of the loop is $8.4\times10^{-4}\,\Omega$. Find the magnitude and the direction of the induced current in the loop.

Ans : 5.0×10^{-11}, anticlockwise.

13. The rectangular loop is figure, of area A and resistance R, rotates at uniform angular velocity ω about the y-axis. The loop lies in a uniform magnetic field $\vec{B}$ in the direction of the x-axis. Sketch the following graph :

(a) the flux ϕ through the loop as function of time (let $t = 0$ in the position shown);

(b) the induced emf in the loop.

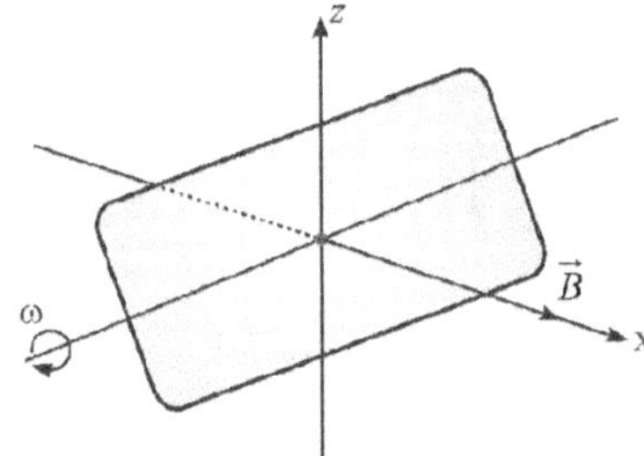

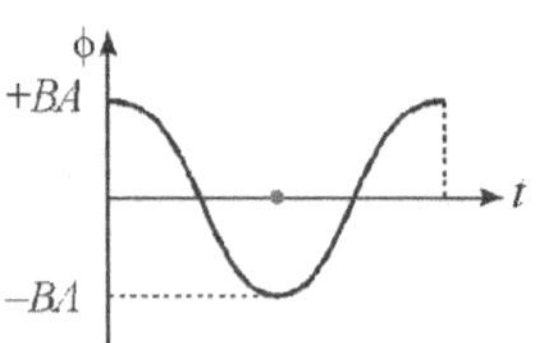
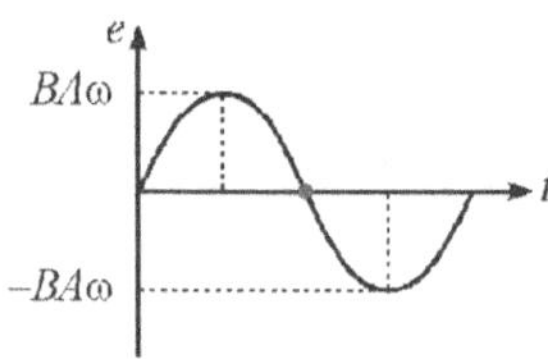

Ans : (a) $\phi = BA\cos\omega t$ (b) $e = BA\,\omega\sin\omega t$

14. A flexible circular loop 10 cm in diameter lies in a magnetic field 1.2 T, directed into the plane of the diagram in figure. The loop is pulled at the points indicated by the arrows, forming a loop to zero area in 0.2 s.

(a) Find the average induced emf in the circuit.

(b) What is the direction of the current in R ?

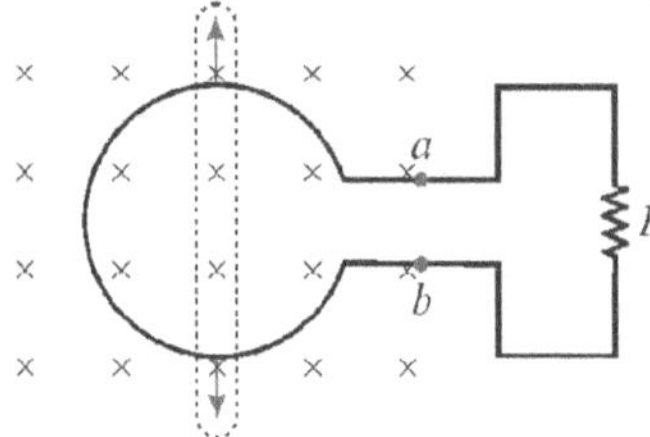

Ans : (a) 0.0471 V (b) From a to b.

15. The cube is figure, 1 m on a side, is in uniform magnetic field of 0.2 T, directed along the positive y-axis. Wires A, C, and D move in the direction indicated, each with a speed of 0.5 m/s.

(a) What is the motional emf in each wire ?

(b) What is the potential difference between the terminals of each ?

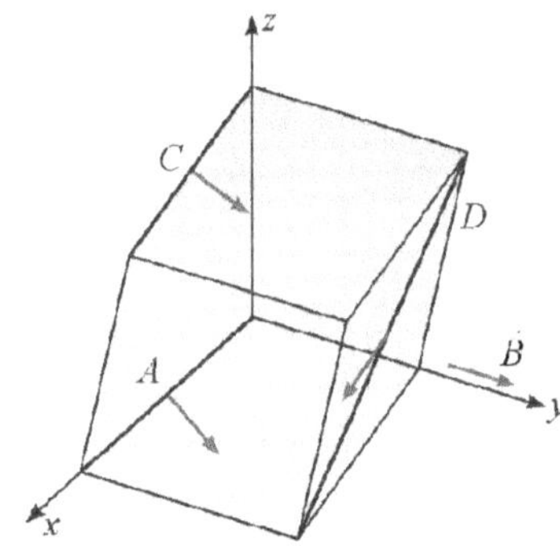

Ans : (a) 0, 0.0707, 0.141 V (b) 0, 0.0707, 0.141 V

16. The magnetic field within a long, straight solenoid of circular cross section and radius R is increasing at a rate $\dfrac{dB}{dt}$.

(a) What is the rate of change of flux through a circle of radius r_1 inside the solenoid, normal to the axis of the solenoid, and with centre of the solenoid ?

(b) Find the induced electric field $\vec{E}_n$ inside the solenoid, at a distance r_1 from its axis. Show that the direction of this field in a diagram.

(c) What is the induced electric field outside the solenoid at a distance r_2 from the axis ?

(d) What is the induced emf in a circular turn of radius $\dfrac{R}{2}$?

(e) of radius R ?

(f) of radius $2\,R$?

Ans : (a) $\pi r_1^2 \left(\dfrac{dB}{dt}\right)$ (b) $\left(\dfrac{r_1}{2}\right)\left(\dfrac{dB}{dt}\right)$ (c) $\dfrac{R^2}{2r_2}\left(\dfrac{dB}{dt}\right)$

(d) $\dfrac{\pi R^2}{4}\left(\dfrac{dB}{dt}\right)$ (e) $\pi R^2\left(\dfrac{dB}{dt}\right)$ (f) $\pi R^2\left(\dfrac{dB}{dt}\right)$

17. The magnetic field B at all points within the shaded circle of figure is 0.5 T. It is directed into the plane of the diagram and is decreasing at the rate of 0.1 T/s.

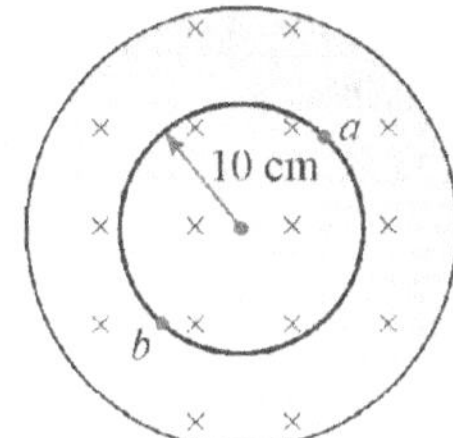

(a) What is the shape of the field lines of the induced $\vec{E}_n$-field within the shaded circle ?

(b) What are the magnitude and direction of this field at any point of the circular conducting ring of radius 10 cm, and what is the emf in the ring ?

(c) What is the current in the ring, if its resistance is $2\,\Omega$?

(d) What is the potential difference between points a and b of the ring ?

Ans : (a) Circles, clockwise (b) 0.005 V/m, 3.14 mV (c) 1.57 mA (d) zero

18. A square conducting loop, 20 cm on a side, is placed in the magnetic field 0.5 T, directed into the plane of the diagram and decreasing at the rate of 0.1 T/s.

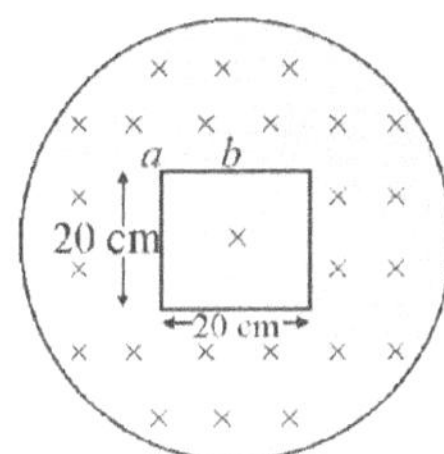

(a) Prove that the component of $\vec{E}_n$ along the loop has the same value at every point of the loop and is equal to that at the ring of previous problem.

(b) What is the current in the loop, if its resistance is $2\,\Omega$?

(c) What is the potential difference between points a and b ?

Ans : (b) 2.00mA (c) zero

19. A square conducting loop, 20 cm on a side, is placed in the magnetic field 0.5 T, directed into the plane of the diagram with the side ac along the diameter and b at the centre of the field and decreasing at the rate of 0.1 T/s.

(a) What is the induced emf in side ac ?

(b) What is the induced emf in the loop ?

(c) What is the current in the loop, if its resistance is $2\,\Omega$?

(d) What is the potential difference between points a and c ? Which is the higher potential ?

(e) Find the induced field $\vec{E}_n$ in each side of the square loop.

(f) Find the induced emf in each side

(g) Find the electrostatic field $\vec{E}_e$ in each side.

(h) Find the potential differences V_{ac}, V_{ce}, V_{eg}, and V_{ga}. What should be the sum of these potential differences ?

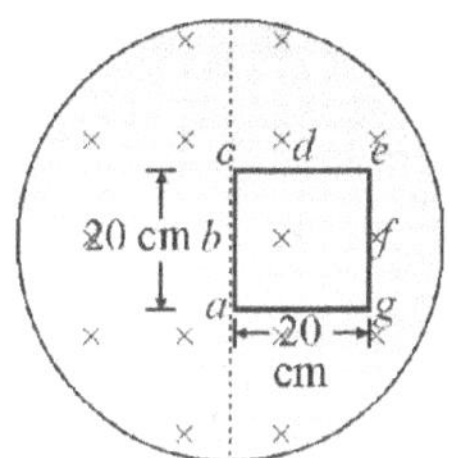

Ans : (a) zero (b) 4 mV (c) 2 mA (d) zero (e) 5.00 mV/m (f) 1.00 mV (g) zero (h) zero

20. A wire is bent into three circular segments, each of radius $r = 10$ cm, as shown in figure. Each segment is a quadrant of a circle, ab lying in the xy-plane, bc lying in the yz-plane, and ca lying in the zx-plane. (a) If a uniform magnetic field $\vec{B}$ points in the positive x-direction, what is the magnitude of the emf developed in the wire when B increases at the rate of 5.0 mT/s ? (b) What is the direction of the current in segment bc ?

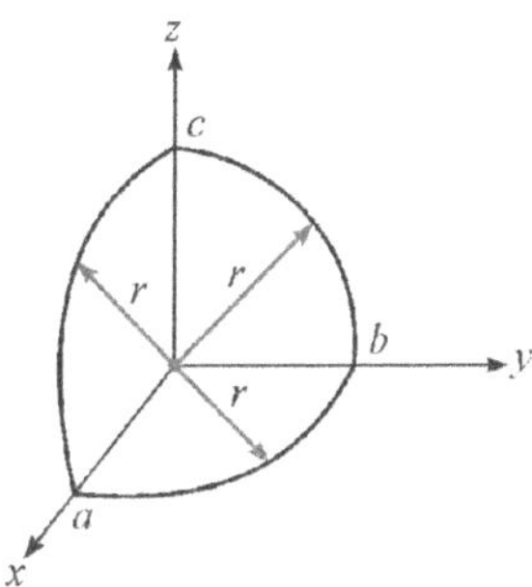

Ans : (a) 39.25 μV, (b) from c to b.

21. A rectangular coil of N turns and of length a and width b is rotated at frequency f in a uniform magnetic field $\vec{B}$, as indicated in figure. The coil is connected to co-rotating cylinders, against which metal brushes slide to make contact.

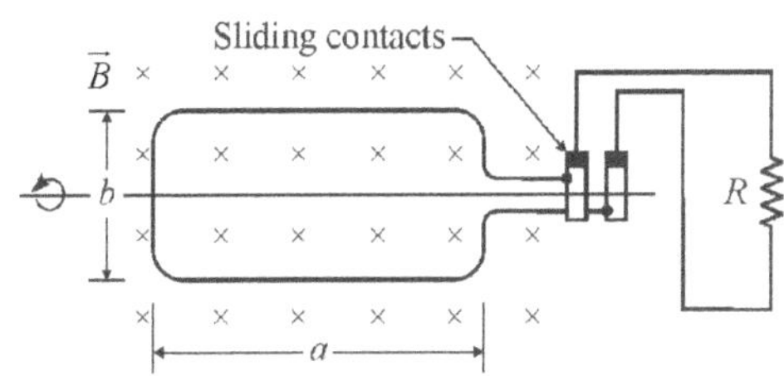

(a) Show that the emf induced in the coil is given (as a function of time t) by $e = e_0 \sin(2\pi ft)$,

where $e_0 = 2\pi f\, NabB$. This is the principle of the commercial alternating-current generator.

(b) Design a loop that will produce an emf with $e_0 = 150$ V when rotated at 60.0 rev/s in a uniform magnetic field of 0.500 T.

Ans : (b) $Nab = \left(\dfrac{5}{2\pi}\right) m^2$

22. A wire loop enclosing a semi-circle of radius a is located on the boundary of a uniform magnetic field of induction B (figure). At the moment $t = 0$ the loop is set into rotation with a constant angular acceleration α about an axis O coinciding with a line of vector $\vec{B}$ on the boundary. Find the emf induced in the loop as a function of time t. Draw the approximate plot of this function. The arrow in the figure shows the emf direction taken to be positive.

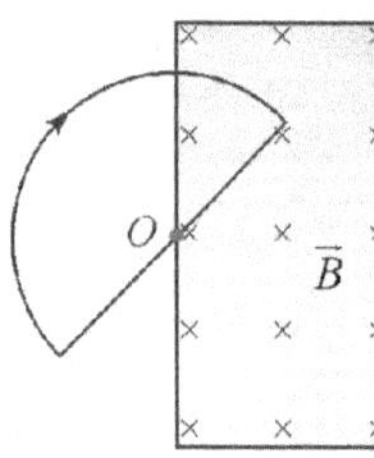

Ans : $e_i = \dfrac{1}{2}(-1)^n Ba^2\alpha t$, where $n = 1, 2, \ldots\ldots$ is the number of the half-revolution that the loop performs at the given moment t.

The plot $e_i(t)$ is shown in figure where $t_n = \sqrt{\dfrac{2\pi n}{\alpha}}$.

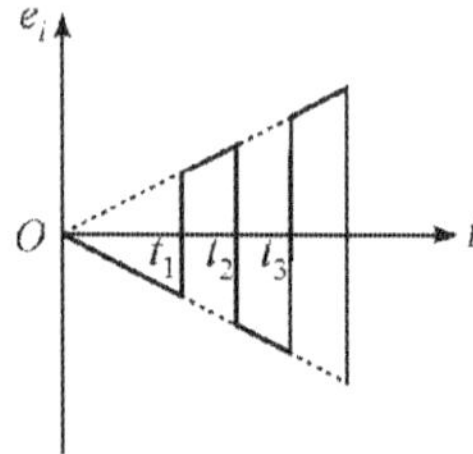

23. Consider the situation shown in figure. The wire PQ has a negligible resistance and is made to slide on the three rails with a constant speed of 5 cm/s. Find the current in the $10\ \Omega$ resistor when the switch S is thrown to (a) the middle rail (b) the bottom rail.

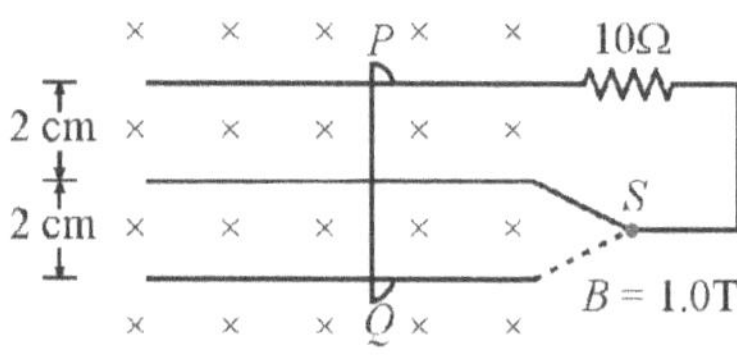

Ans : (a)0.1 mA, (b) 0.2 mA.

24. A very small circular loop of area 5×10^{-4} m^2, resistance 2 ohm and negligible inductance is initially coplanar and concentric with a much larger fixed circular loop of radius 0.1 m. A constant current of 1 ampere is passed in the bigger loop and the smaller loop is rotated with angular velocity ω rad/s about a diameter. Calculate (i) the flux linked with the smaller loop, (ii) induced emf and (iii) induced current in the small loop, as a function of time.

Ans : (i) $\pi \times 10^{-9} \cos\omega t$ (ii) $\pi \times 10^{-9}\omega \sin\omega t$ V

(iii) $1.57\times10^{-9} \omega \sin\omega t$ ampere.

25. Two long parallel wires of zero resistance are connected to each other by a battery of 1.0 V. The separation between the wires is 0.5 m. A metallic bar, which is perpendicular to the wires and of resistance $10\ \Omega$, moves on these wires when a magnetic field of 0.02 T is acting perpendicular to the plane containing the bar and the wires. Find the steady state velocity of the bar. If the mass of bar is 0.002 kg, find its velocity as a function of time

Ans : $V = 100(1 - e^{-0.005t})$

26. At a given instant the current and self-induced emf in an inductor are directed as indicated in figure.

(a)   Is the current increasing or decreasing ?

(b)   The induced emf is 25 V and the rate of change of the current is 25 kA/s; find the inductance.

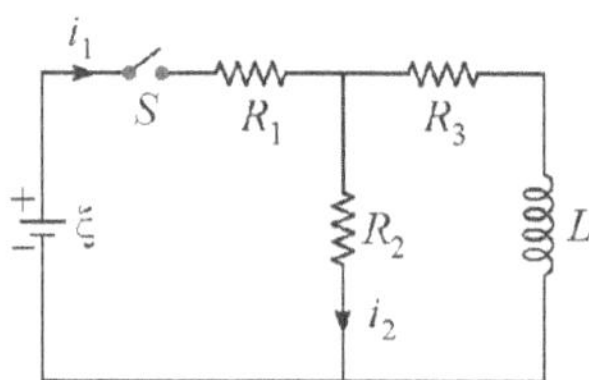

Ans : (a) The current in the inductor decreasing. (b) 1 mH.

27. A coil of inductance 1 H and resistance $10\ \Omega$ is connected to a resistanceless battery of emf 50 V at time $t = 0$. Calculate the ratio of the rate at which magnetic energy is stored in the coil to the rate at which energy is supplied by the battery at t = 0.1 s.

Ans : 0.36

28. The current (in ampere) in an inductor is given by $I = 5 + 16t$, where t is in second. The self-induced emf in it is 10 mV. Find

(a)   the self-inductance and

(b)   the energy stored in the inductor and the power supplied to it at $t = 1$s.

Ans : (a) 6.25×10^{-4} H (b) 210 mW.

29. A solenoid having an inductance of 6.30 μH is connected in series with a 1.20 $k\ \Omega$ resistor.

(a)   If a 14.0 V battery is switched across the pair, how long will it take for the current through the resistor to reach 80.0 % of its final value ?

(b)   What is the current through the resistor at time t = 1.0 τ_L ?

Ans : (a) 8.45 ns (b) 7.37 mA.

30. In figure $\xi = 100$ V, $R_1 = 10.0\ \Omega$, $R_2 = 20.0\ \Omega$, $R_3 = 30.0\ \Omega$ and $L = 2.00$ H. Find the values of i_1 and i_2

(a)   immediately after the closing of switch S,

(b)   a long time later, (c) immediately after reopening of switch S, and (d) a long time after the reopening.

Ans : (a) $i_1 = i_2 = 3.33\ A$; (b) $i_1 = 4.55\ A$, $i_2 = 2.73\ A$;

(c) $i_1 = 0$, $i_2 = 1.82$ (reversed); (d) $i_1 = i_2 = 0$.

31. In the circuit shown in figure, switch S is closed at time $t = 0$. Thereafter, the constant current source, by varying its emf, maintains a constant current i out of its upper terminal. (a) Derive an expression for the current through the inductor as a function of time (b) Show that the current through the resistor equals the current through the inductor at time $t = \left(\dfrac{L}{R}\right)\ell n\, 2$.

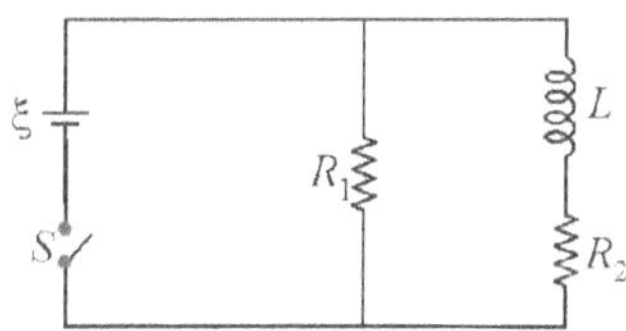

Ans : (a) $i\left(1 - e^{-Rt/L}\right)$

32. An inductor of inductance $L = 400$ mH and resistors of resistances $R_1 = 2\,\Omega$ and $R_2 = 2\,\Omega$ are connected to a battery of emf $\xi = 12$ V as shown in the figure. The internal resistance of the battery is negligible. The switch S is closed at $t = 0$.
What is the potential drop across L as a function of time ? After the steady state is reached, the switch is opened. What is the direction and the magnitude of current through R_1 as a function of time ?

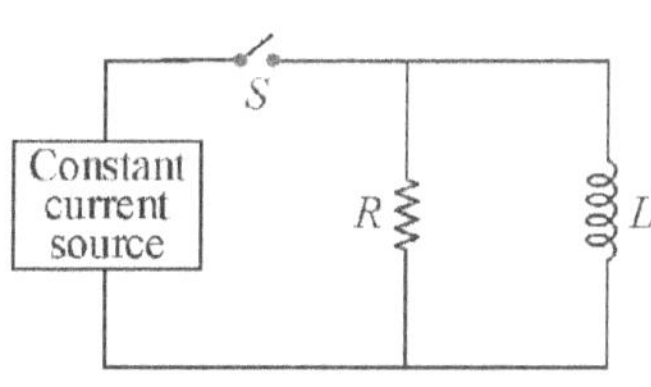

Ans : $V_L = \xi\, e^{-R_2 t/L}$, $i = 6\, e^{-10t}$.

33. In a circuit shown A and B are two cells of same emf ξ but different internal resistances r_1 and r_2 $(r_1 > r_2)$ respectively. Find the value of R such that the potential difference across the terminals of cell A is zero a long time after the key K is closed.

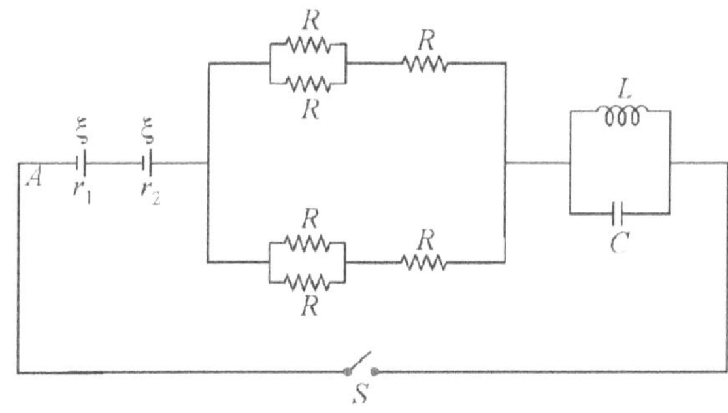

Ans : $R = \dfrac{4}{3}\left(r_1 - r_2\right)$

34. A circuit containing a two position switch S is shown in figure.
(a) The switch S is in position 1. Find the potential difference $V_A - V_B$ and the rate of production in joule heat in R_1.
(b) If now the switch S is put in position 2 at $t = 0$, find
(i) Steady current in R_4 and
(ii) the time when the current R_4 is half the steady value. Also calculate the energy stored in the inductor L at that time.

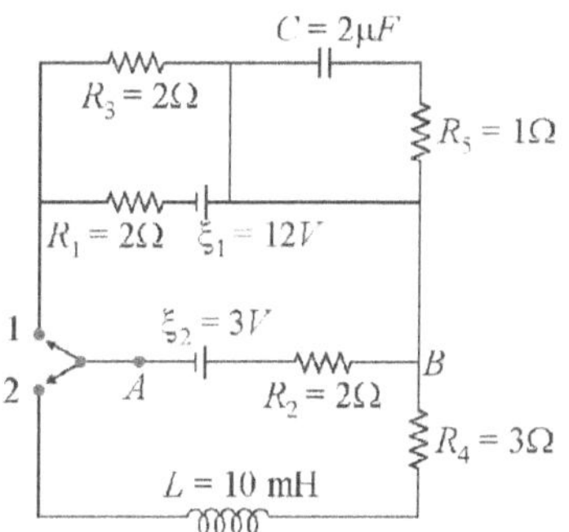

Ans : (a) $V_A - V_B = -5$V.
(b) (i) $i_0 = 0.6$ A, (ii) 1.386×10^{-3} s, 4.5×10^{-4} J.

35. An inductor of inductance 2.0 mH is connected across a charged capacitor of capacitance 5.0 μF and the resulting LC circuit is set oscillating at its natural frequency. Let Q denote the instantaneous charge on the capacitor and I the current in the circuit. It is found that the maximum value of charge Q is 200 μC.

(a) When $Q = 100$ μC, what is the value of $\left|\dfrac{dI}{dt}\right|$?

(b) When $Q = 200$ μC, what is the value of I ?
(c) Find the maximum value of I.
(d) When I is equal to one-half its maximum value, what is the value of $|Q|$

Ans : (a) 10^4 A/s (b) $I = 0$ (c) $I_{max} = 2$A (d) $Q = 173.2$ μC.

36. A metal rod OA of mass m and length r is kept rotating with a constant angular speed ω in a vertical plane about a horizontal axis at the end O. The free and A is arranged to slide without friction along a fixed conducting circular ring in the same plane as that of rotation. A uniform and constant magnetic induction B is applied perpendicular and into plane of rotation as shown in figure. An inductor L and an external resistance R are connected through a switch S between the point O and the point C on the ring so as to form an electrical circuit. Neglect the resistance of the ring and the rod. Initially the switch is open.
(a) What is the induced emf across the terminals of the switch ?
(b) The switch S is closed at time $t = 0$.
(i) Obtain an expression for the current as a function of time.
(ii) In the steady state obtain the time-dependence of the torque required to maintain the constant angular speed, given that the rod OA was initially along the positive x-axis at time $t = 0$.

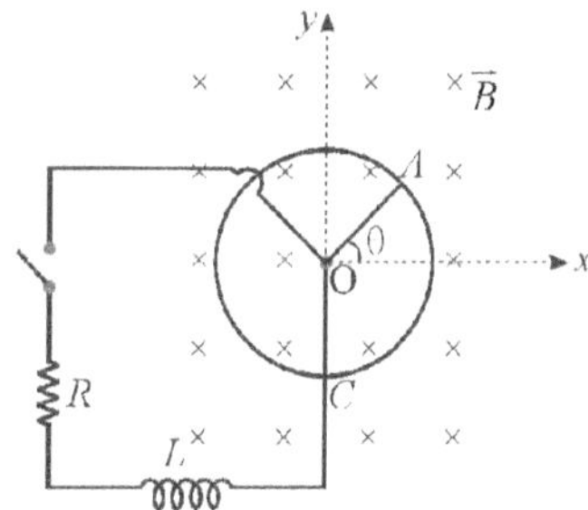

Ans : (a) $\dfrac{B\omega r^2}{2}$ (b) (i) $i = \dfrac{B\omega r^2}{2R}\left(1 - e^{-Rt/L}\right)$

(ii) $\tau = \dfrac{B^2\omega r^4}{4R} + \dfrac{mgr}{2}\cos\omega t.$

37. Figure shows, in cross-section, two coaxial solenoids. Show that the mutual inductance M for a length ℓ of this solenoid-solenoid combination is given by $M = \pi R_1^{\,2} \ell \mu_0 n_1 n_2$ in which n_1 and n_2 are the respective numbers of turns per unit length and R_1 is the radius of the inner solenoid. Why does M depend on R_1 and not on R_2 ?

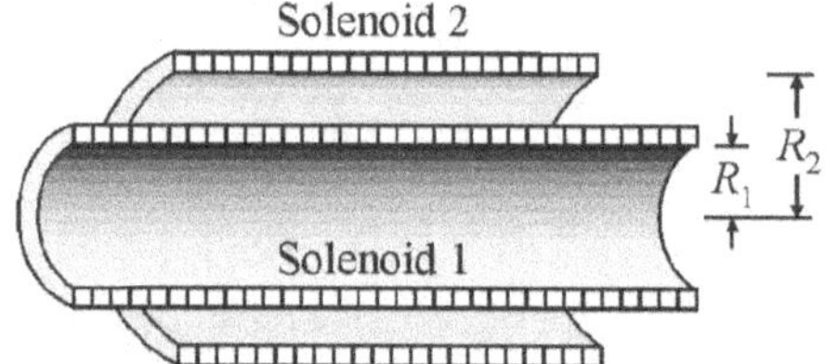

38. A rectangular loop of N close-packed turns is positioned near a long straight wire as shown in figure. What is the mutual inductance M for the loop-wire combination ?

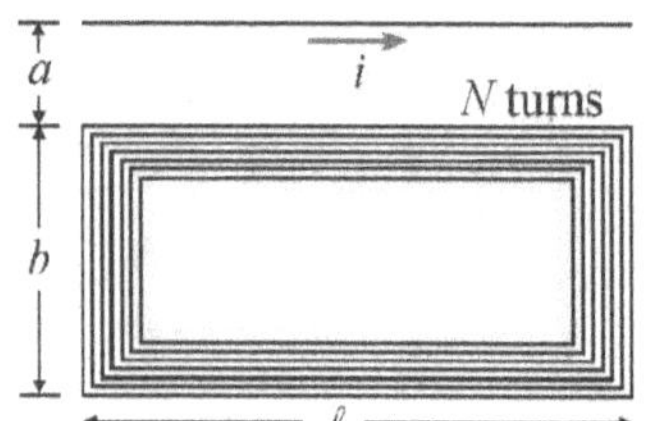

$$\textit{Ans}: \frac{\mu_0\, N\ell}{2\pi}\, \ell n\!\left(1+\frac{b}{a}\right)$$

39. Figure shows a coil of N_2 turns wound as shown around part of a toroid of N_1 turns. The toroid's inner radius is a, its outer radius is b, and its height is h. Show that the mutual inductance M for the toroid-coil combination is $M = \dfrac{\mu_0 N_1 N_2 h}{2\pi}\, \ell n \dfrac{b}{a}$.

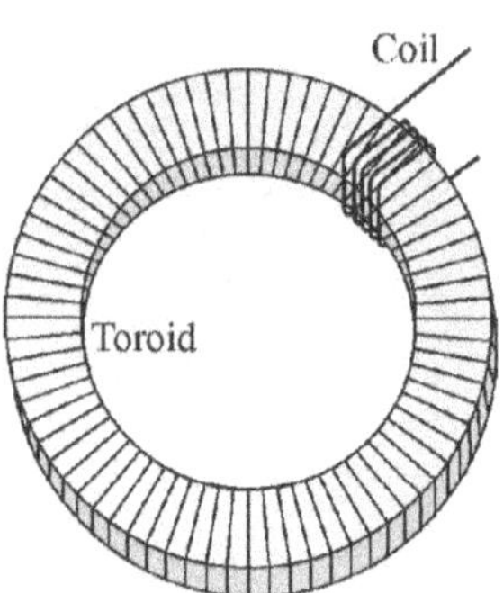

40. A transformer on a utility pole operate at $V_P = 8.5\ kV$ on the primary side and supplies electrical energy to a number of nearby houres at $V_s = 120$ V, both quantities being rms values. Assume an ideal step-down transformer, a purely resistive load, and a power factor of unity.

(a) What is the turns ratio N_P/N_s of the transformer ?

(b) The average rate of consumption in the houres served by the transformer is 78 kW. What are the rms currents in the primary and secondary of the transformer ?

(c) What is the resistive load R_s in the secondary circuit ? What is the corresponding relative load R_P in the primary ?

$$\textit{Ans}: \text{(a)} \approx 71 \text{ (b) } 9.2\,\text{A}, 650\,\text{A (c) } R_P = 926\,\Omega\ \ R_s = 0.18\ \Omega .$$

★ ★ ★

Hints & Solutions

1. (b) $|e| = \dfrac{d\phi}{dt} = A\left(\dfrac{dB}{dt}\right)$

   As the slope $\left(\dfrac{dB}{dt}\right)$ is greatest in II, and so $|e|$ is greatest in this region.

2. (c) Just after closing of the switch, inductor offers infinite resistance and so,

   $i_1 = 0$, $i_2 = \dfrac{\varepsilon}{2R}$, and $i_3 = \dfrac{\varepsilon}{R}$.

   Clearly $i_3 > i_2 > i_1$.

3. (c) Time constant of the circuits are ;

   $\tau_1 = \dfrac{L}{R}$, $\tau_2 = \dfrac{L}{2R}$ and $\tau_3 = \dfrac{L}{R/2} = \dfrac{2L}{R}$.

   As τ_3 is greatest, and so it takes greatest to reach any specific value.

4. (d) By right hand screw rule the direction of magnetic field will be out of the plane of the conductor. i.e., $\vec{B} = B\hat{k}$.

5. (a) $\phi = BA = AB_0 e^{-bt}$

   Induced emf, $|e| = \dfrac{d\phi}{dt} = AB_0 b e^{-bt}$

   At $t = 0$, $|e| = AB_0 b$, and current, $i = \dfrac{|e|}{R} = \dfrac{AB_0 b}{R}$.

6. (a) $e = A\dfrac{dB}{dt} = 1 \times \left(\dfrac{2}{2}\right) = 1\,V$

   $\therefore$ $i = \dfrac{e}{R} = \dfrac{1}{10} = 0.1\,A$.

7. (a) There is no change in the flux and so $e = 0$.

8. (a)

9. (d) $V_s = V_p\left(\dfrac{N_s}{N_p}\right) = 100\left(\dfrac{500}{50}\right) = 1000\,V$.

10. (d) According to Lenz's law, when switch is closed, the flux in the loop increases out of plane of paper, so induced current will be clockwise.

11. (d) $|e| = \dfrac{d\phi}{dt} = A\left(\dfrac{dB}{dt}\right) = 100 \times 10^{-4} \times 150 = 1.5$ V.

   For decreasing flux into the plane of paper, this emf must be added to battery emf, so $e_{net} = 5 + 1.5 = 6.5$ V, and

   $i = \dfrac{6.5}{10} = 0.65\,A$.

12. (b)

13. (a) If e_b is the back emf in the motor, then

$i = \dfrac{\varepsilon - e_b}{R}$

or $10 = \left(\dfrac{115 - e_b}{1.5}\right)$

$\therefore$ $e_b = 100$ V.

14. (c) In inductor,

   $e = L\left(\dfrac{di}{dt}\right)$.

   For maximum emf, $\dfrac{di}{dt}$ is to be maximum. In case (c) it is ;

   $\dfrac{di}{dt} = \dfrac{2i}{T/2} = \dfrac{4i}{(1/f)} = 4fi = 4 \times 500 \times 50 = 10^5\,A/s$

15. (a) Due to the heating effect of current, the resistance of loop increases and so current in the first loop decreases, whose flux in second loop decreases. To compensate this flux the second loop will come towards first loop.

16. (d) For enduced emf across the ends of the rod, one component of the velocity must be perpendicular to ℓ ; also $\vec{\ell}$ must be perpendicular to $\vec{B}$.

17. (d) The two ends of the rod are at the same potential and so $e = 0$.

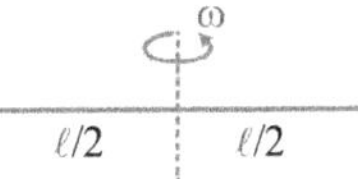

18. (d) Due to the change in flux in the coil enduced current starts flowing alternatively in it, which opposes the motion of the magnet.

19. (c) As there is no change in flux in the cylinder and so induced emf in it will be zero.

20. (d) The velocity component of conductor must be perpendicular to $\vec{\ell}$ and $\vec{B}$.

21. (d) Till loop remains completely inside the magnetic field, the flux will not change and hence induced emf/current will be zero.

22. (a) We know that, $N\phi = Li$

   $\therefore$ $\phi = \dfrac{Li}{N} = \dfrac{8 \times 10^{-3} \times 5 \times 10^{-3}}{400} = 10^{-7}\,Wb$

   $= \dfrac{\mu_0}{4\pi}Wb$.

23. (c) Because of inductor in bulb B_2, current decreases slowly.

24. (d) When electron approaches nearby the loop flux inside loop will increase and when electron recedes from the loop the flux inside loop decreases and so current change in direction.

25. (d) The induced emf, $e = Bv \times (PQ)\sin 90°$
   $= Bv \times 2R$,
   $= 2\,RvB$.

26.   (d)   The magnetic field of the loop will lie parallel to xy-plane and so there is no flux in this plane.

27.   (c)   With the increase in current in loop A, flux in loop B will increase, so to compensate this flux loop B will be repelled.

28.   (b)   The induced emf, $e = Bv\ell = 0.5 \times 2 \times 1 = 1$ V.

       The rate of work done, $= e^2 / R = \dfrac{1^2}{6} = \dfrac{1}{6} W.$

29.   (a)   Magnetic field of one coil passes through other coil in case A is maximum, and so mutual induction is also maximum.

30.   (d)

31.   (b)   Resistance of coil $R = \dfrac{\rho \ell}{\pi r^2}$. With the quadrupled turns and

       half radius, $R' = \dfrac{\rho(\ell/4)}{\pi (r/2)^2} = R$, and so power dissipated

       remains same.

32.   (d) $i = i_0(1 - e^{-t/\tau})$; $\tau = \dfrac{L}{R} = \dfrac{8.4 \times 10^{-3}}{6} = 1.4 \times 10^{-3} s$

       or $1 = \dfrac{12}{6}(1 - e^{-t/1.4 \times 10^{-3}})$

       $\therefore$ $t = 1 \times 10^{-3}$s.

33.   (a)   As the magnetic field increases, its flux also increases into the page and so induced current in bigger loop will be anticlockwise. i.e., from D to C in bigger loop and then from B to A in smaller loop.

34.   (b) $\dfrac{\Delta B}{\Delta t} = \dfrac{2 B_0}{T/2} = 4 B_0 f$

       Now $|e| = E \times 2\pi r = \dfrac{d\phi}{dt}$

       or $E \times 2\pi r = \pi r^2 \times \dfrac{dB}{dt}$

       $\therefore$ $E = \dfrac{r}{2} \times 4 B_0 f$

       $= \dfrac{1 \times 4 \times 0.01 \times 100}{2}$

       $= 2$ volt/m

35.   (a)   When magnet enters through the coil, the rate of change of magnetic flux starts decreasing and when magnet emerges out from the coil, the rate of change of magnetic flux again starts increasing, so(a) is the correct option.

36.   (b) $e = M\left(\dfrac{\Delta i}{\Delta t}\right)$

       $= 1.5 \times \dfrac{2I}{T/2} = 4 \times \dfrac{1.5\,I}{T}$

       $= \dfrac{6 \times 1}{2\pi/200} = 191\ V$

37.   (b)

38.   (c)   Induced emf in the coil, $e = -L\left(\dfrac{di}{dt}\right).$

       Initialy, $\dfrac{di}{dt} = 0$, then $\dfrac{di}{dt} = -ve$ and finally $\dfrac{di}{dt} = +ve$

       Accordingly $e = 0$, $e = +ve$, and finally $e = -ve$.

39.   (a)

40.   (a) $R_{\text{total}} = \dfrac{6 \times 12}{6 + 12} + 4 = 8\Omega$

       $C = \dfrac{L}{R_{total}} = \dfrac{2}{8} = \dfrac{1}{4} s.$

41.   (c)   Given, $V = Kt^3$,

       $i_R = \dfrac{V}{R} = \dfrac{Kt^3}{R},$

       $i_L = \int\limits_0^t \dfrac{Kt^3}{L} dt = \dfrac{Kt^4}{4L},$

       and $i_C = \dfrac{dq}{dt} = \dfrac{d(CV)}{dt} = \dfrac{d(CKt^3)}{dt} = 3CKt^2$.

42.   (a)   The distance falls by an object in 1 second under gravity

       $y = \dfrac{1}{2} gt^2 = \dfrac{1}{2} \times 10 \times 1^2 = 5m$

       The acceleration of magnet will be less than g $(a < g)$ and so distance falls will be less than 5 m.

43.   (c)

44.   (a)   The given inductors are in parallel in the circuit, and so

       $L_{\text{eq}} = \dfrac{L}{3} = \dfrac{3}{3} = 1\ H.$

45.   (d)   The presence of inductor will cause slow in decay of current in both the bulbs.

46.   (d)   The flux in outer loop will increases into the plane of paper and so induced current will be anticlockwise in outer loop. i.e, from d to c. This current flows into the smaller loop from a to b.

Solutions **EXERCISE 8.1 LEVEL -2**

1.   (d)   In I and III case the rate of change of flux is equal. But in II case, it is zero.

2.   (c)   Induced emf. $|e| = \dfrac{d\phi}{dt} = A\left(\dfrac{dB}{dt}\right)$

       $= \dfrac{2 \times 2}{2} \times \dfrac{d}{dt}(0.042 - 0.87t)$

       $= 2 \times 0.87 = 1.74$ V

       The net induced emf $= 20 + 1.74 = 21.74$ V

3.   (c)   Induced electric field is given by

       $E = \dfrac{r}{2}\left(\dfrac{dB}{dt}\right)$

       In situation A : $E = r_A \times \dfrac{\Delta B_1}{\Delta t_1}$

       B : $E = r_B \times \dfrac{\Delta B_1}{2\Delta t_1}$

$$C : E = r_C \times \left(\frac{\Delta B_1}{\Delta t_1 / 2} \right)$$

Clearly induced electric field is greater in case C.

4. (c) The decay of current in RL-circuit is given by

$$i = i_0 \, e^{-t/\tau} = \frac{\varepsilon}{R} e^{-\frac{tR}{L}} .$$

(1) $\quad i = \frac{\varepsilon}{R_0} e^{-tR_0 / L_0}$

(2) $\quad i = \frac{\varepsilon}{2R_0} e^{\frac{-t \times 2R_0}{L_0}}$

(3) $\quad i = \frac{\varepsilon}{R_0} e^{-\frac{tR_0}{2L_0}}$

(4) $\quad i = \frac{i}{2R_0} e^{-t \times \frac{2R_0}{2L_0}}$

Amplitude in case (1) and (3) are equal and in case (2) and (4) are equal.

5. (b) The change in flux $= n(\phi_2 - \phi_1)$

Total resistance of the circuit $= 4R + R = 5R$

Thus induced current, $i = \frac{\Delta\phi / \Delta t}{R} = \frac{n(\phi_2 - \phi_1)}{5RT}$.

6. (b) The induced emf across the sides AB and CD are shown in figure and so net emf of the device becomes, $= 2Bv\ell$

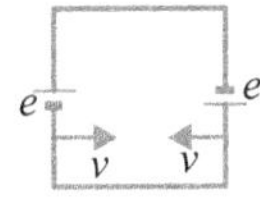

7. (b) $\quad \phi_{total} = B_{large} A_{small}$

$$= \frac{\mu_0}{4\pi} \frac{i}{L/2} (2 \sin 45°) \times \ell^2$$

On comparing with $\phi_{total} = Mi$, we get $M \propto \frac{\ell^2}{L}$

8. (b) $\quad E_n \times 2\pi r = -\pi R^2 \left(\frac{dB}{dt} \right)$

$$\therefore \quad E_n \propto \frac{1}{r} .$$

9. (d) Till current in coil changes, the induced current I_2 will occur in the ring and the magnetic field in the ring increases so product $I_2 B$ increases. When I_1 becomes steady, I_2 becomes zero and so product $I_2 B$ becomes zero.

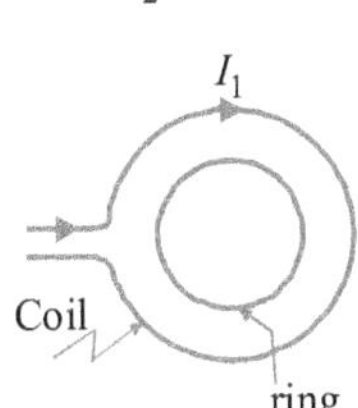

10. (d) $\quad e = -\frac{d\phi}{dt} - -A\frac{dB}{dt} = -\pi r^2 \frac{d}{dt}(B_0 e^{-t})$

$$= \pi r^2 B_0 e^{-t}$$

At $t = 0$, $e = \pi r^2 B_0$.

Power developed, $P = \frac{e^2}{R} = \frac{(\pi r^2 B_0)^2}{R} = \frac{\pi^2 r^4 B_0^2}{R}$ /

11. (a) $\quad |e| = \frac{d\phi}{dt} = A\frac{dB}{dt} = A\frac{d(B_0 + \alpha t)}{dt}$

$$= A\alpha.$$

12. (b) We know that, $i = i_0(1 - e^{-t/\tau})$

or $\quad \frac{3}{4} i_0 = i_0(1 - e^{-4/\tau})$

or $\quad e^{-4/\tau} = \frac{1}{4}$

or $\quad e^{4/\tau} = 4$

$\therefore \quad \frac{4}{\tau} = \ln 4$

or $\quad \tau = \frac{2}{\ln 2} s$

13. (b) Till front side of the loop moves into the field the emf induced $e = Bv\ell$ across it. When rear side comes in the field, the emf is induced across it.

14. (b) The flux through the coil is given by

$$\phi = BA \cos 0°$$
$$= (B \times \pi r^2)$$

Now $|e| = \frac{d\phi}{dt} = 2\pi Br \left(\frac{dr}{dt} \right)$.

Initially $\frac{dr}{dt} = 0$, and so $e = 0$. After that $\left(\frac{dr}{dt} \right)$ is of constant value, also r increases, so e is also increases. Finally $\left(\frac{dr}{dt} \right)$ becomes zero and so e becomes zero.

15. (c) From $t = 0$ to 5s : Emf will induced across the front edge. From $t = 5$ to 15s flux changes will be zero. Finally from 15 to 20s, emf is induced across rear edge of the loop.
$e = Bv\ell = 0.6 \times 0.01 \times 0.05 = 3 \times 10^{-4}$V.

16. (a) The induced emf across the sliding wire
$e = Bv\ell = 0.5 \times 4 \times 0.25 = 0.5$ V
The effective circuit is shown in figure.

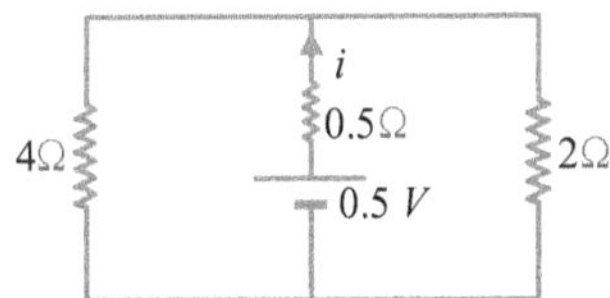

The equivalent resistance of the circuit

$$r = \frac{4 \times 2}{4 + 2} + 0.5 = 1.83 \ \Omega$$

Now, $i = \dfrac{V}{R} = \dfrac{0.5}{1.83} = 0.27 A$

17.   (d)   At $x = 0$, $B = B_0$, so $e_1 = B_0 v_0 d$

At, $x = d$, $B = B_0 \left(1 + \dfrac{d}{a}\right)$, so $e_2 = B_0 \left(1 + \dfrac{d}{a}\right) v_0 d$

Now $e_{net} = e_2 - e_1 = \dfrac{B_0 v_0 d^2}{a}$

18.   (b)   The current in the circuit, $i = i_0 e^{-t/\tau}$

$$\therefore \quad q = \int_0^\tau i\, dt = \int_0^\tau i_0 e^{-t/\tau} dt$$

$$= -i_0 \tau \left| e^{-t/\tau} \right|_0^\tau$$

or $\quad q = \dfrac{\varepsilon}{R} \dfrac{\tau}{e}.$

19.   (d) $M = \dfrac{\mu_0 \mu_r N_1 N_2}{2 R_1} A$

$$= \frac{4\pi \times 10^{-4} \times 800 \times 500 \times 25 \times 12 \times 10^{-4}}{2 \times 0.1}$$

20.   (c) $V = L \dfrac{di}{dt}$

$$= 1 \times \frac{d(3t \sin t)}{dt}$$

$$= 3\, t \cos t + 3 \sin t.$$

21.   (c)   For maximum potential difference the velocity must be perpendicular to the line AB, and so

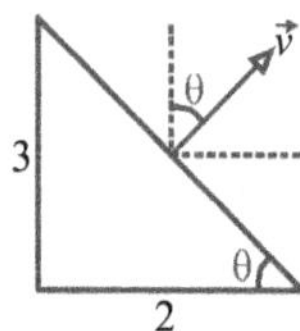

$$\vec{v} = v \sin\theta\, \hat{i} + v \cos\theta\, \hat{j}$$

$$= v \left[\frac{3}{\ell} \hat{i} + \frac{2}{\ell} \hat{j}\right]$$

$$= \frac{v}{\ell}\left[3\hat{i} + 2\hat{j}\right]$$

22.   (d)   The magnetic flux through the coil will be zero, and so induced emf in it will be zero.

23.   (b)   The inductance, $L_1 = 3mH$ and so $L_2 = 6mH$

$$L = \frac{L_1 L_2}{L_1 + L_2} = \frac{3 \times 6}{3 + 6} = 2mH$$

and $R = 6 + \dfrac{12 \times 6}{12 + 6} = 10\Omega$

Now $\tau = \dfrac{L}{R} = \dfrac{2}{10} = 0.2$ ms

24.   (a) $\oint \vec{E} . \vec{dl} = -\dfrac{d\phi_B}{dt}$

or $E \times 2\pi r = -\left[\dfrac{d\phi_1}{dt} + \dfrac{d\phi_2}{dt}\right]$

or $\quad 0 = -\left[\pi r_1^2 \times 3 B_0 - \pi\left(r_2^2 - r_1^2\right) \times B_0\right]$

$\therefore \quad \dfrac{r_1}{r_2} = \dfrac{1}{2}$

25.   (c) $e = \dfrac{B\omega \ell^2}{2} = Bv\ell$

$\therefore \quad e_1 = B(3v)(2r) = 6Bvr$

and $e_2 = B(v) \times 2r_2 = 2Bvr_2$

Given $\quad e_1 \sim e_2 = 0$

or $6Bvr - 2Bvr_2 = 0$

$\therefore \qquad\qquad r_2 = 3r$

Now, $e = e_1 + e_2 = 6Bvr + 6Bvr = 12Bvr$

26.   (b)   Induced electric field

$$E = \frac{r}{2}\left(\frac{dB}{dt}\right)$$

$$= \frac{rR}{2}.$$

This electric field exerts tangentive force on each part of the ring. So net force,

$$F = EQ = \frac{rRQ}{2}.$$

For ring to be in equilibrium,

$$F \leq F_{friction}$$

or $\quad r\dfrac{RQ}{2} \leq \mu mg$

$\therefore \qquad \mu \geq \dfrac{rRQ}{2mg}$

27.   (b)   The induced emf across the jumper, $e = B\, u\, \ell \cos 30°$

Current, $\quad i = \dfrac{B u \ell \cos 30°}{R}$

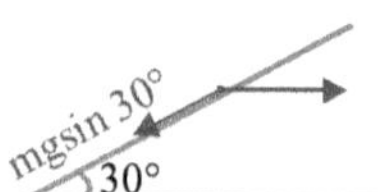

As jumper is moving with constant velocity, so

$$mg \sin 30° = B\, i\, \ell \cos 30°$$

or $\quad mg \sin 30° = B\left[\dfrac{Bu\ell \cos 30°}{R}\right]\cos 30°$

$$\therefore \quad B = \sqrt{\frac{2mgR}{3u\ell^2}}$$

28. (a) Velocity at any time t,

$$v = a\,t = \frac{F}{m}t$$

Now, $e = V_P - V_Q = Bv\ell\sin 30°$

$$= B\left(\frac{Ft}{m}\right)\ell \times \frac{1}{2} = \frac{BF\ell t}{2m}$$

29. (c) $e = \frac{d}{2}\ell\left(\frac{dB}{dt}\right)$

For PQ, $\quad d = 0, e_{PQ} = 0$

For QR, $\quad d = \ell, ePR = \frac{\ell}{2}\times 2\ell \quad x = x\,\ell^2$

In close loop,

$$e_{QP} + e_{PR} + e_{RQ} = 0$$
$$\text{or} \quad 0 + e_{PR} + e_{RQ} = 0$$
$$\therefore \quad e_{RQ} = -e_{PR}$$
$$= e_{RP}$$
$$\text{or} \quad = xl^2$$

30. (a) At steady state

$$Bil = mg, \qquad\qquad \therefore \ i = \frac{mg}{Bl}$$

Charge on the capacitor

$$q = C\,V = C \times iR = \frac{mgCR}{B\ell}$$

31. (c) There is no charge in flux through PS and so induced emf will be zero. But
$$V_P - V_B = V_Q - V_R$$
Also, $F = Bil$

$$\text{or} \quad i = \frac{F}{B\ell}$$
$$\therefore \ V_P - V_B = V_Q - V_R$$
$$= ir_{QR}$$
$$= \frac{F}{B\ell}\times\frac{r}{6} = \frac{Fr}{6B\ell}$$

32. (c) $V_0 - V_P = \dfrac{B\omega\ell^2}{2}$

and $V_0 - V_Q = \dfrac{B\omega\ell^2}{2}$

$$\therefore \ V_P - V_Q = 0$$

33. (c)

$$e = e_1 + e_2$$
$$= B_0v\ell + 2B_0v\ell$$
$$= 3B_0v\ell$$

$$\therefore \ i = \frac{e}{R} = \frac{3B_0v\ell}{R}$$

34. (b) At $t = 1$s, the potential of the capacitor

$$V = V_0\left(1 - e^{-\frac{t}{\tau}}\right); \tau = CR = 2 \times 0.5 = 1\text{s}$$

$$\text{or } V = 2\left(1 - e^{-\frac{t}{\tau}}\right)$$

$$= 2\left(1 - \frac{1}{e}\right)$$

$$q = CV = 2 \times 2\left(1 - \frac{1}{e}\right)$$

$$= 4\left(1 - \frac{1}{e}\right)$$

If q be the charge on the capacitor at any instant, then for LC oscillations, we can write

$$\frac{d^2q}{dt^2} + \frac{q}{LC} = 0$$

Here, $q = q_0\sin\omega t$

$$\therefore \quad q_0 = q\sqrt{2}$$

$$= 4\sqrt{2}\left(1 - \frac{1}{e}\right)$$

35. (d) Charge on the capacitor
$$q = CV$$

$$= 4e^{-\frac{t}{2}}$$

$$\therefore \ i = \frac{dq}{dt} = -2e^{-\frac{t}{2}}$$

Total current at junction A,

$$I = -2e^{-\frac{t}{2}} + 6e^{-\frac{t}{2}}$$

$$= 4e^{-\frac{t}{2}}$$

Now, $V_A - V_B = L\dfrac{dI}{dt}$

$$= 5\frac{d}{dt}\left[4e^{-\frac{t}{2}}\right] = -10e^{-\frac{t}{2}}mV$$

36. (c) Current in the inductor flows till the potentials of the capacitors become equal. So common potential

$$V = \frac{3C \times V_0 + 2C \times \frac{7V_0}{2}}{3C + 2C} = 2V_0$$

Now energy stored on the capacitor of $3C$

$$U = \frac{1}{2}(3C)(2V_0)^2$$
$$= 6CV_0^2$$

37. (b)

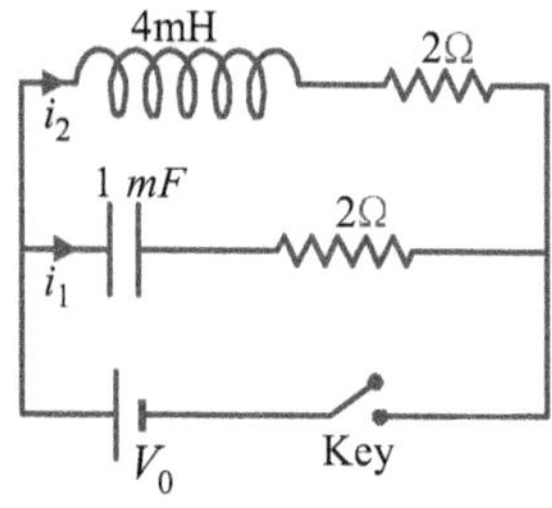

$$i_1 = \frac{V_0}{2}e^{-\frac{t}{1\times 2}} = \frac{V_0}{2}e^{-\frac{t}{2}}$$

and $\quad i_2 = \frac{V_0}{2}\left(1 - e^{-\frac{t\times 2}{4}}\right)$

For $\quad i_1 = i_2$

$$\frac{V_0}{2}e^{-\frac{t}{2}} = \frac{V_0}{2}\left(1 - e^{-\frac{t}{2}}\right)$$

or $\quad e^{-\frac{t}{2}} = \frac{1}{2}$

or $\quad e^{\frac{t}{2}} = 2$

or $\quad e^t = 4$

$\therefore \quad t = \ell n 4$

38. (d) Charge on capacitor $q = 5(1 - e^{-t/2})$

Current through inductor $I = 5(1 - e^{-t/2})$

Now, $\quad V_a + \dfrac{q}{0.5} - I \times 2 = V_b$

$\therefore \quad (V_a - V_b) = 0$

39. (c) The induced emf across the ends B and F due to motion of the loop,

$e_1 = Bv(BF) = 5 \times 1 \times 2 \sin 60° = 5\sqrt{3}\ V$.

The induced emf across the loop due to change in magnetic field

$$e_2 = A\frac{dB}{dt} = \frac{\pi R^2}{3}\left(\frac{dB}{dt}\right)$$

$$= \frac{\pi(1)^2}{3} \times 2 = \frac{2\pi}{3}\ V.$$

So $e = e_1 + e_2 = \left(5\sqrt{3} + \dfrac{2\pi}{3}\right)\ V$.

40. (b) If a ℓ is the side of the square, then

area of square, $\quad A_1 = \ell^2$

area of triangle, $\quad A_2 = \dfrac{\ell^2}{2}$

area of quarter circle, $\quad A_3 = \dfrac{\pi \ell^2}{4}$

Total area of the loop

$$\vec{A} = A_1\hat{i} + A_2\hat{j} + A_3\hat{k}$$

$$= \left(\ell^2\hat{i} + \frac{\ell^2}{2}\hat{j} + \frac{\pi\ell^2}{4}\hat{k}\right)$$

Now, $\phi_1 = \vec{B}_1.\vec{A}$

$$= (3\hat{i} + 7\hat{j} - 5t\hat{k}).\left(\ell^2\hat{i} + \frac{\ell^2}{2}\hat{j} + \frac{\pi\ell^2}{4}\hat{k}\right)$$

$$= \left(3\ell^2 + \frac{7\ell^2}{2} - \frac{5}{4}\pi\ell^2 t\right)$$

$\therefore \quad |e_1| = \dfrac{d\phi_1}{dt} = \dfrac{5}{4}\pi\ell^2$.

$\phi_2 = \vec{B}_2.\vec{A}$

$$= (5t\hat{i} - 4\hat{j} - 15\hat{k}).\left(\ell^2\hat{i} + \frac{\ell^2}{2}\hat{j} + \frac{\pi\ell^2}{4}\hat{k}\right)$$

$$= \left(5\ell^2 t - 2\ell^2 - \frac{15\pi}{4}\ell^2\right)$$

$\therefore \quad |e_2| = \dfrac{d\phi_2}{dt} = 5\ell^2$.

$\phi_3 = \vec{B}_3.\vec{A}$

$$= (2\hat{i} - 5t\hat{j} - 12\hat{k}).\left(\ell^2\hat{i} + \frac{\ell^2}{2}\hat{j} + \frac{\pi\ell^2}{4}\hat{k}\right)$$

$$= \left(2\ell^2 - \frac{5}{2}\ell^2 t - 3\pi\ell^2\right)$$

$\therefore \quad |e_3| = \dfrac{5\ell^2}{2}$.

Clearly, $e_2 > e_1 > e_3$

$\therefore \quad i_2 > i_1 > i_3$.

Solutions EXERCISE 8.2

1. (a, b) In case I and II, the induced emf, $e = Bv(2\ell)$.
   In case III and IV, the induced emf, $e = Bv\ell$.

2. (b, c, d) At $t = 0$, inductor offers infinite resistance, and so current in R_2 is zero and in R_1 is maximum. After a long time inductor offers zero resistance and so both the resistors will get their maximum values.

3. (b, c, d) $\dfrac{L}{R}$, CR and $\sqrt{LC}$ have dimensions of time and so

   $\dfrac{R}{L}, \dfrac{1}{CR}$ and $\dfrac{1}{\sqrt{LC}}$ have dimensions of frequency.

4. (c, d)

5. (a, c, d) For $P_1 = P_2$, we have $V_1 i_1 = V_2 i_2$

   or $\left(L_1 \dfrac{di}{dt}\right) i_1 = \left(L_2 \dfrac{di}{dt}\right) i_2$

   $\therefore \quad \dfrac{i_1}{i_2} = \dfrac{L_2}{L_1}$

   $\qquad = \dfrac{2}{8} = \dfrac{1}{4}.$

   Now $\dfrac{V_2}{V_1} = \dfrac{L_2(di/dt)}{L_1(di/dt)} = \dfrac{2}{8} = \dfrac{1}{4}$

   $\dfrac{W_2}{W_1} = \dfrac{\frac{1}{2}L_2 i_2^2}{\frac{1}{2}L_1 i_1^2} = \dfrac{2}{8} \times \left(\dfrac{4}{1}\right)^2 = 4$

6. (b, d) Current in first ring must be greater and so $\rho_A < \rho_B$.

   Height attained $h = \dfrac{v^2}{2g}$, so it does not depend on mass of the ring.

7. (a, c, d) When magnetic field decreases, the flux of which in loops decreases downwards and so induced current in the loops will be clockwise. And no current in the connecting wire.

8. (b, d) Use Lenz's law to get the answer.

9. (a, b, c, d) In all the given cases, there is no flux and change of flux across the semicircular ring.

10. (b, d) As steady current in both the cases in same and so

    $\dfrac{V}{R_1} = \dfrac{V}{R_2}$ or $R_1 = R_2$. Also $L_1 < L_2$.

11. (a,b) 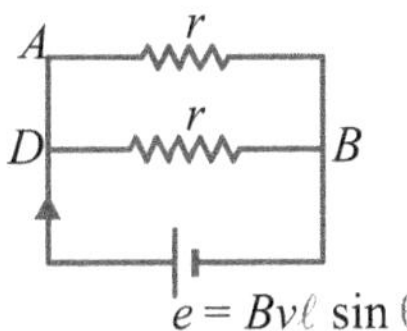
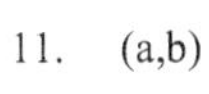

    $e = Bv\ell \sin\theta$

    The induced emf across the rod,
    $e = Bv\ell\sin\theta$

    The equivalent resistance between B and D is $= \dfrac{r}{2}$

    $\therefore$ current, $i = \dfrac{e}{r/2} = \dfrac{2Bv\ell\sin\theta}{r}$

    Also $V_A > V_B$.

12. (a,c,d) 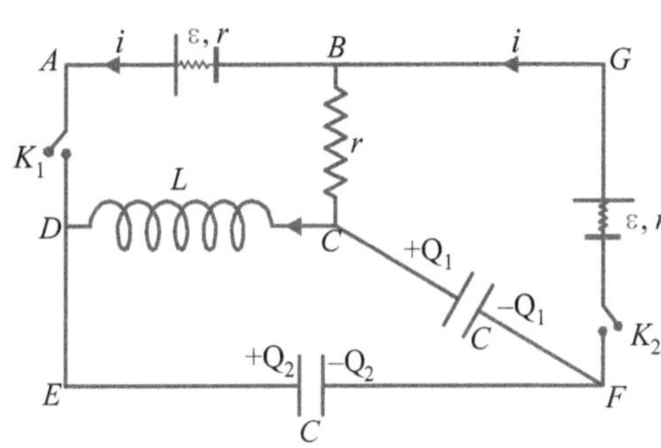

    In close loop ABCDA
    $\varepsilon - ir = Lx$ ...(i)
    In close loop, ABGFCDA

    $-\varepsilon + ir - \varepsilon + ir + \dfrac{Q_1}{C} + Lx = 0$

    or $-2(\varepsilon - ir) + \dfrac{Q_1}{C} + Lx = 0$

    or $-2Lx + \dfrac{Q_1}{C} + Lx = 0$

    or $\dfrac{Q_1}{C} = Lx$ ...(ii)

    Now in close loop ABGFEA,

    $-\varepsilon + ir - \varepsilon + ir + \dfrac{Q_2}{C} = 0$

    or $\dfrac{Q_2}{C} = 2(\varepsilon - ir) = 2\,Lx = 2\,\dfrac{Q_1}{C}$

    $\therefore \quad Q_2 = 2Q_1$

13. (a,b,c) The maximum current in the inductor

    $i_0 = \dfrac{\varepsilon}{R_2}$

    Energy stored in the inductor

    $U = \dfrac{1}{2}Li_0^2$

    $\qquad = \dfrac{1}{2}L\left(\dfrac{\varepsilon}{R_2}\right)^2 = \dfrac{L\varepsilon^2}{2R_2^2}$

    When key is in position 1, this energy will convert into heat energy through resistor.

14. (a, c) $f = \dfrac{1}{2\pi\sqrt{LC_{eq}}} = \dfrac{1}{\pi\sqrt{2LC}}$

    When i is max, $\dfrac{di}{dt} = 0$.

    $\Rightarrow$ Charge on two capacitors is same

    $\dfrac{1}{2}Li_0^2 = 2 \times \dfrac{\left(\dfrac{Q_0}{2}\right)^2}{2C} = \dfrac{Q_0^2}{4C}$

    $\Rightarrow \quad i_0 = \dfrac{Q_0}{\sqrt{2LC}}$.

15. (a, b, c, d) $I = \dfrac{\varepsilon}{\dfrac{2R}{3}} = \dfrac{3\varepsilon}{2R}$

$$= \dfrac{3}{2R} \times \dfrac{1}{2} B\omega l^2 = \dfrac{3B\omega l^2}{4R}$$

Magnetic force $F = \dfrac{3B\omega l^2}{4R} \times l \times B = \dfrac{3B^2\omega l^3}{4R}$

$$\tau = \dfrac{3B^2\omega l^3}{4R} \times \dfrac{l}{2} = \dfrac{3B^2\omega l^4}{8R}$$

$\therefore$ Force to be applied at the end $= \dfrac{3B^2\omega l^3}{8R}$.

16. (b, c)   As inductors are in parallel, so

$$e_1 = e_2 \ \text{ or } \ L_1\dfrac{di_1}{dt} = L_2\dfrac{di_2}{dt} \Rightarrow L_1 i_1 = L_2 i_2$$

Now $\dfrac{V_1}{V_2} = \dfrac{e_1 i_1}{e_2 i_2} = \dfrac{i_1}{i_2}$,

$$= \dfrac{L_2}{L_1}.$$

$\mathcal{S}olutions$ EXERCISE 8.3

1. (c)   Emf will always induces whenever, there is change in magnetic flux. The current will induced only in closed loop.
2. (b)   In both the cases, the magnetic flux will change, and so there is an induced current.
3. (d)   The magnetic flux changes only in case when loop is rotated about axis-2.
4. (d)   Lenz's is law is based on conservation of energy.
5. (a)
6. (c)   In purely resistive circuit, the current and emf are in the same phase.
7. (c)
8. (a)   In case when orbit of satellite inclined with the plane of equator there is a component of magnetic field, which is perpendicular to the velocity vector.
9. (a)
10. (a)   In the given case, there is no component of velocity, perpendicular to the magnetic field and so $e = Bvl \sin 0°$.

11. (a)
12. (a)
13. (b)   Both the statements are independently correct.
14. (b)   The quantity L/R is inductive time constant and so it possesses the dimensions of time.
15. (a)
16. (a)   The rate of change of current in case of opening of switch in much greater than the closing of the switch, and so induced emf is greater.
17. (a)   When switch is closed , the magnetic flux through the ring will increase and so ring will move away form the solenoil so as to compensate this flux. This is according to Lenz's law.
18. (c)   The direction of induced current in the loop is according to Lenz's law.
19. (c)   The reading of voltmeter V_2 will be zero.

$\mathcal{S}olutions$ EXERCISE 8.4

Passage Q.1 to Q.3

1. (b)   The equivalent circuit is shown in figure. The equivalent capacitance,

$$C = \dfrac{2 \times 1}{2 + 1} = \dfrac{2}{3} F$$

If i_0 is the maximum current, then

$$\dfrac{1}{2} L i_0^2 = \dfrac{1}{2} C V^2$$

or $\dfrac{1}{2} \times 1 \times i_0^2 = \dfrac{1}{2} \times \dfrac{2}{3} \times 3^2$

$\therefore \quad i_0 = \sqrt{6} \ A$

2. (b)   P. d across the capacitor, $= 3V$.

3. (c) $\omega = \sqrt{\dfrac{1}{LC}} = \sqrt{\dfrac{1}{1 \times 2/3}} = \sqrt{\dfrac{3}{2}} = \sqrt{1.5} \ rad/s$

Passage of Q.4 to Q.6

4. (a) $e = Bvl = 0.4 \times 0.1 \times 1 = 0.04$ V

5. (b) $i = \dfrac{Bvx}{R} = \dfrac{Bvx}{\rho \dfrac{x}{A}} = \dfrac{BvA}{\rho}$ (constant)

6. (b)   Power $P = \dfrac{e^2}{R} = \dfrac{0.04^2}{1} = 16 \times 10^{-4} = 1.6 \times 10^{-3} \ W$

Passage of Q.7 to Q.9

7. (d) $M = \dfrac{\mu_0 N_1 N_2 A_1}{2R_2} = \dfrac{4\pi \times 10^{-7} \times 1000 \times 100 \times \pi \times 0.02^2}{2 \times 0.20}$

$$= 3.94 \times 10^{-4} \ H.$$

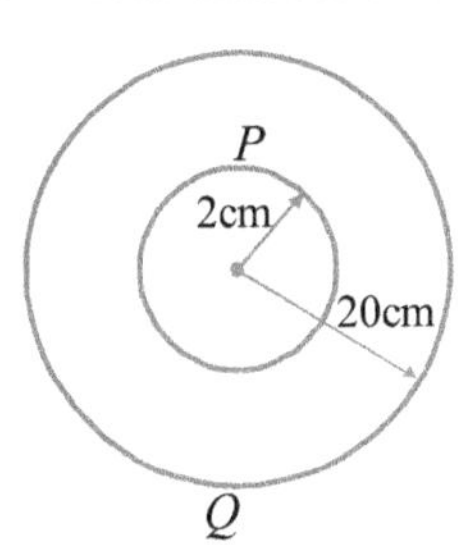

Passage of Q.13 to Q.15

13. (a) For simplicity we can take the moment when side EF of he loop is at $y = 0$, so
$$B_1 = 0 \; ; \; e_1 = 0$$

and at y = a, $B_2 = \dfrac{B_0 \times a}{a} = B_0 \; ; \; e_2 = B_0 va$.

The induced emf $e = e_1 + e_2 = B_0 v_a$.

Thus induced current, $i = \dfrac{e}{R} = \dfrac{B_0 va}{R}$, anticlockwise.

8. (b) $e = M\dfrac{di_2}{dt} = 3.94 \times 10^{-4} \times \dfrac{(5-3)}{0.04} = 19.72 \times 10^{-3} V$

9. (a) $q = it = \dfrac{e}{R}t = \dfrac{19.72 \times 10^{-3}}{8} \times 0.04 = 9.86 \times 10^{-5} C$

Passage of Q.10 to Q.12

10. (a) $\oint \vec{E}.d\vec{\ell} = \dfrac{d\phi}{dt}$

or $E \times 2\pi a = A\dfrac{dB}{dt}$

or $E \times 2\pi a = na^2 \times \dfrac{d(B_0 t)}{dt}$

$\therefore \quad E = \dfrac{B_0 a}{2}$.

11. (b) $\tau = F \times a = Eqa = \dfrac{B_0 a}{2} \times q \times a = \dfrac{B_0 qa^2}{2}$

Angular acceleration, $\alpha = \dfrac{\tau}{I} = \dfrac{B_0 qa^2/2}{ma^2} = \dfrac{B_0 q}{2m}$.

12. (b) Angular velocity at any time

$\omega = \alpha t = \dfrac{B_0 qt}{2m}$

Power developed, $P = \tau\omega$

$= \left(\dfrac{B_0 qa^2}{2}\right) \times \left(\dfrac{B_0 qt}{2m}\right)$

$= \dfrac{q^2 B_0^2 a^2 t}{4m}$.

14. (c) Power generated, $P = \dfrac{e^2}{R} = \dfrac{(B_0 va)^2}{R}$

So Lorentz force acting on the loop

$$F = \dfrac{P}{v} = \dfrac{B^2.va^2}{R} .$$

15. (a) For ternminal speed (constant speed), net force on the loop is zero, and so

$$mg = \dfrac{B_0^2 va^2}{R}$$

or $v = \dfrac{mgR}{B_0^2 a^2}$.

16. A - p ; A charged ring can produced electric field out of the centre.
B - p, q, s ; A charged rotating ring can produce electric field out of centre, magnetic and dipole moment.
C- q, s ; Current carrying produces magnetic field at the centre.
D- r ; Alternating current can produce induced electric field .

17. See example.

18. A-p, r, s, t ; Depending on value of q, the potential difference between A and B may be zero, positive or negative.
B-p, r, s, t ; When loop enters into the magnetic field, the direction of induced current is anticlockwise, when lop moves into the magnetic field, induced current is zero. When loop comes out of the field, the induced current will be clockwise.

C-r, s, t ; The induced current, $i = B^2 C\ell^2 \left[\dfrac{F}{m + B^2 C\ell^2}\right]$.

Depending on the direction of force, the current may be positive or negative.

D- p, r, s, t ; The induced current, $i = i_0 \sin\omega t$, and so it may be zero, positive or negative.

Solutions **EXERCISE-8.5**

1. Given, $\phi_B = 7.0t + 6.0t^2$

(a) Induced emf, $|e| = \dfrac{d\phi}{dt} = 7 + 12t$

$= 7 + 12 \times 2 = 31$ mV. *Ans.*

(b) Right to left.

2. The resistance of the loops, $R_1 = 2\pi r_1 \times 10 = 2\pi \times 0.1 \times 10$

$= 6.28\Omega$.

and $R_2 = 2\pi r_2 = 2\pi \times 1 \times 10$

$= 62.8\Omega$.

Flux in the smaller loop, $\phi = B_2 A_1$

$= \dfrac{\mu_0 i_2}{2r_2} \pi r_1^2$

$= \dfrac{\mu_0 \left[\dfrac{V}{R_2}\right] \pi r_1^2}{2r_2}$

$= \dfrac{\mu_0 \dfrac{[4 + 2.5t]}{R_2} \pi r_1^2}{2r_2}$

The induced current, $i_1 = \dfrac{e}{R_1} = \dfrac{[d\phi/dt]}{R_1}$

After substituting the value and simplifying we get

$$i = 1.25 \text{ A}. \qquad \textbf{\textit{Ans.}}$$

3.   (a)   The emf induced across each of the wire

$$e = Bv\ell = 1 \times 0.05 \times 0.04$$
$$= 2 \text{ mV}$$

The total emf, $\quad e_{net} = 2\text{mV} \text{ and } r = \dfrac{2 \times 2}{2 + 2} = 1\Omega$

The current, $\quad i = \dfrac{e_{net}}{R} = \dfrac{2}{19 + 1} = 0.1 \text{mA}$.

(b)   In this case, $\quad e_{net} = 0, \; \therefore \; i = 0.$

4.   The induced emf, $\quad |e| = A\left(\dfrac{\Delta B}{\Delta t}\right)$

$$= (\pi R)^2 \mu_0 n\left(\dfrac{\Delta i}{\Delta t}\right)$$

$$= \pi(1.8 \times 10^{-2})^2 \times (4\pi \times 10^{-7}) \times 220 \times 10^2 \times \left(\dfrac{1.5}{25 \times 10^{-3}}\right) = 68.6 \text{ mV}$$

Current, $\quad i = \dfrac{e}{R} = 30 \text{ mA} \qquad \textbf{\textit{Ans.}}$

5.   The magnetic flux through the strip of area (ℓdy) ,

$$d\phi = (4t^2 y)\ell dy$$

The total flux through the square

$$\phi = \int_0^\ell 4t^2 \ell y dy$$

$$= 4t^2 \ell \left|\dfrac{y^2}{2}\right|_0^\ell = 2t^2 \ell^3$$

The induced emf, $\quad |e| = \dfrac{d\phi}{dt} = 4t\ell^3$.

At $t = 2.5$ s, $\quad |e| = 4 \times 2.5 \times (0.02)^3$
$$= 8 \times 10^{-6} \text{ V} \qquad \textbf{\textit{Ans.}}$$

6.   For $\quad\quad 0 = 2\sin t^2 \Rightarrow t = 0$

and $\quad\quad 2 = 2\sin^2 t \Rightarrow t^2 = \dfrac{\pi}{2},$

$\therefore \quad\quad t = \sqrt{\dfrac{\pi}{2}}$

The energy spent, $\quad E = \dfrac{1}{2}Li^2$

$$= \dfrac{1}{2}L(2\sin t^2)^2$$

$$= 2L\sin^2 t$$

$$= 2 \times 2\sin^2 \pi/2 = 4J.$$

7.   We have, $\quad\quad i = i_0 e^{-tR/L}$

or $\quad\quad 10^{-3} = 1 \times e^{-1R/10}$

$\Rightarrow \quad\quad R = 46 \; \Omega$

$\mathcal{S}olutions$ EXERCISE-8.6

1.   The magnetic flux through the loop

$$\phi_B = BA$$
$$= \mu_0 niA$$
$$= \mu_0 n(i_0 \sin \omega t)A$$

Induced emf, $\quad |e| = \dfrac{d\phi_B}{dt} = \mu_0 ni_0 A\omega \cos\omega t \qquad \textbf{\textit{Ans.}}$

2.   The resistance of the wire $R = \dfrac{\rho\ell}{\pi r^2} = \dfrac{(1.7 \times 10^{-8}) \times (0.40)}{\pi(10^{-3})^2}$

$$= 2.16 \times 10^{-3} \Omega$$

The area of the loop $= 0.10 \times 0.10 = 10^{-2} \text{ m}^2$.

The induced emf, $\quad |e| = A\left(\dfrac{dB}{dt}\right)$

$$= 10^{-2} \times (0.02) = 2 \times 10^{-4} \text{ V}$$

The induced current, $\quad i = \dfrac{e}{R} = \dfrac{2 \times 10^{-4}}{2.16 \times 10^{-3}}$

$$= 9.3 \times 10^{-2} \text{ A}.$$

3.   The magnetic flux, $\quad \phi_B = BA = B \times \pi r^2$

The induced emf, $\quad |e| = \dfrac{\Delta\phi_B}{\Delta t} = \dfrac{B \times \pi r^2}{\Delta t}$

$$= \dfrac{0.50 \times \pi(0.05)^2}{0.50}$$

$$= 7.85 \times 10^{-2} \text{ V} \qquad \textbf{\textit{Ans.}}$$

4.   (a)   The induced emf, $\quad e = -\dfrac{d\phi_B}{dt} = -A\left(\dfrac{dB}{dt}\right)$

$$= -(2.0 \times 10^{-3}) \times \left(\dfrac{0.01}{10 \times 10^{-3}}\right)$$

$$= -2.0 \text{ mV}.$$

Do the other part similarly

(b)   From 10 ms to 20 ms and 20 ms to 30 ms, the rate of change of magnetic field is not constant and so emf is not constant in these intervals

5.   (a)   The charge flows in any interval Δt ,

$$\Delta q = -\dfrac{\Delta\phi}{R} = \left[\dfrac{\phi_i - \phi_f}{R}\right]$$

$$= \dfrac{[\phi_B(0) - \phi_B(t)]}{R}$$

(b)   If $\phi_B(t) = \phi_B(0)$, then $\Delta q = 0$,

6.   (a)   The magnetic flux, $\quad \phi_B = BA\cos 60°$

$$= (B_0 \sin \omega t)A \times \dfrac{1}{2}$$

$$= \dfrac{0.20}{2} \times (5 \times 10^{-4})\sin\omega t$$

$$= 5 \times 10^{-5} \sin\omega t$$

The induced emf, $\quad |e| \ = \ \dfrac{d\phi_B}{dt} = 5 \times 10^{-5}\,\omega\cos\omega t$

The maximum, value of emf,

$$e_0 \ = \ 5 \times 10^{-5}\,\omega$$
$$= \ (5 \times 10^{-5}) \times 300$$
$$= \ 0.015\ \text{V} \qquad \textbf{\textit{Ans.}}$$

(b) The emf, at $t = \dfrac{\pi}{900}$

$$e = 5 \times 10^{-5} \times 300\cos 300 \times \dfrac{\pi}{900}$$
$$= \ 7.5 \times 10^{-3}\ \text{V} \qquad \textbf{\textit{Ans.}}$$

(c) At $t = \dfrac{\pi}{600}$,

$$e = 5 \times 10^{-5} \times 300\cos 300 \times \dfrac{\pi}{600} = 0$$

7. If V is the velocity of the loop, then induced emf

$$e \ = \ VBL,$$

and induced current, $\quad i \ = \ \dfrac{e}{R} = \dfrac{VBL}{R}$

The force on the loop $\quad = \ BiL \ = \dfrac{B[VBL]L}{R}$

$$= \ VB^2L^2/R$$

For no acceleration $\quad mg \ = \ VB^2L^2/R$

$\therefore \qquad\qquad\qquad V \ = \ mgR/B^2L^2 \qquad \textbf{\textit{Ans.}}$

8. We have, $\qquad\qquad \tan\theta = \dfrac{B_V}{B_H}$

$\therefore \qquad\qquad B_V \ = \ B_H \tan\theta$
$$= \ 2 \times 10^{-5} \times \tan 60°$$
$$= \ 2\sqrt{3} \times 10^{-5}\ \text{T}$$

The induced emf, $\qquad e \ = \ B_v v\ell$
$$= \ (2\sqrt{3} \times 10^{-5}) \times 250 \times 20$$
$$= \ 0.173\ \text{V} \qquad \textbf{\textit{Ans.}}$$

9. (a) At $t = 2$s, the length of the loop inside magnetic field,
$$x \ = \ 1 \times 2 \ = 2\ \text{cm. so emf will}$$
induce due to right side of the loop,

$\therefore \qquad\qquad e \ = \ Bv\ell \ = \ 0.6 \times 0.01 \times 0.20$
$$= \ 3 \times 10^{-4}\ \text{V}$$

(b) At $t = 10$ s, $\qquad x \ = \ 1 \times 10 = 10$ cm. The entire loop is inside magnetic field and so
$$e \ = \ 0$$

(c) At $t = 22$ s, $\qquad x \ = \ 1 \times 22 = 22$ cm. The emf is induced due to left side of the loop, so
$$e \ = \ 3 \times 10^{-4}\ \text{V}.$$

(d) At $t = 20$ s, the loop will out of the field so, $e = 0$

10. The magnetic flux through the iron part

$$\phi_i \ = \ B \times \dfrac{\pi r^2}{2}$$

When iron part comes down, the final flux

$$\phi_t \ = \ 0$$

$\therefore \qquad\qquad |e| \ = \ \dfrac{\Delta\phi}{\Delta t} = \dfrac{\pi B r^2}{2\Delta t} = 1.57 \times 10^{-6}\ \text{V}$

Ans.

11. The induced emf across the rod
$$e \ = \ BvL$$

The induced current, $\qquad i \ = \ \dfrac{e}{R} = \dfrac{BvL}{R}$

The force on the rod, $\qquad F \ = \ BiL$
$$= \ B\left(\dfrac{BvL}{R}\right)L$$
$$= \ \dfrac{vB^2L^2}{R}$$

(a) Thus for terminal velocity,
$$mg \ = \ F$$
$$= \ \dfrac{vB^2L^2}{R}$$

$\therefore \qquad\qquad v \ = \ \dfrac{mgR}{B^2L^2} \qquad \textbf{\textit{Ans.}}$

(b) If a be the acceleration, then

$$mg - \dfrac{mg}{2} \ = \ ma$$

$\therefore \qquad\qquad a \ = \ g/2 \qquad \textbf{\textit{Ans.}}$

12. The magnetic flux through the loop,
$$\phi \ = \ BA$$
$$= \ \left(\dfrac{\mu_0 i}{2\pi r}\right)A$$

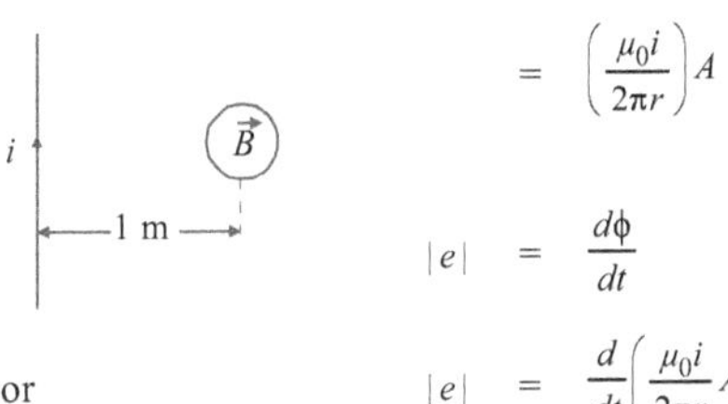

$|e| \ = \ \dfrac{d\phi}{dt}$

or $\qquad |e| \ = \ \dfrac{d}{dt}\left(\dfrac{\mu_0 i}{2\pi r}A\right)$
$$= \ 5 \times 10^{-11}\ \text{A, anticlockwise}$$

13. (a) The magnetic flux through the loop,
$$\phi \ = \ BA\cos\theta = BA\cos\omega t$$

(b) The induced emf, $\qquad e \ = \ -\dfrac{d\phi}{dt} = \dfrac{-d(BA\cos\omega t)}{dt}$
$$= \ BA\omega\sin\omega t \qquad \textbf{\textit{Ans.}}$$

14. (a) The initial flux through the loop,
$$\phi_i \ = \ BA$$

and $\qquad\qquad \phi_f \ = \ 0$

The average induced emf,

$|e| \ = \ \dfrac{\Delta\phi}{\Delta t} = \dfrac{\phi_f - \phi_i}{\Delta t}$
$$= \ \dfrac{BA}{\Delta t} = \dfrac{1.2 \times \pi(0.05)^2}{0.2}$$
$$= \ 0.0471\ \text{V}.$$

(b) From a to b.

15. (a, b) For wire A : $e = v = Bv\ell\sin\theta = 0$

     For wire C : $e = Bv\ell\sin 45° = 0.0707V$

     For wire D : $e = Bv\sqrt{2}\,\ell\sin 90° = 0.141V$ **Ans.**

16. (a) The magnetic flux through the circle of radius r_1,

$$\phi = BA\cos 0° = B\pi r_1^2$$

Thus $$\frac{d\phi}{dt} = \pi r_1^2\left(\frac{dB}{dt}\right).$$

(b) We have $$\oint \vec{E}_n.\vec{d\ell} = -\frac{d\phi}{dt}$$

or $$E_n \times 2\pi r_1 = -\pi r_1^2\left(\frac{dB}{dt}\right)$$

$$\therefore \qquad E_n = -\frac{r_1}{2}\left(\frac{dB}{dt}\right)$$

(c) For $r_2 > R$: $$E_n \times 2\pi r_2 = -\pi R^2\left(\frac{dB}{dt}\right)$$

$$\therefore \qquad E_n = -\frac{R^2}{2r_2}\left(\frac{dB}{dt}\right) \qquad \textbf{Ans.}$$

Do other parts similarly

17 (b) $$E_n = -\frac{r}{2}\left(\frac{dB}{dt}\right)$$

$$= -\frac{0.1}{2}\times 0.1 = -0.005 \ \text{V/m}$$

The induced emf, $$e = \pi r^2\left(\frac{dB}{dt}\right) = \pi(0.1)^2 \times 0.1$$

$$= 3.14 \times 10^{-3} \ \text{V} \qquad \textbf{Ans.}$$

(c) The induced current, $$i = \frac{e}{R} = \frac{3.14}{2} = 1.57 \times 10^{-3} \ A$$

(d) Zero.

18. (a) Induced emf $$\oint \vec{E}_n.\vec{dl} = -\frac{d\phi}{dt}$$

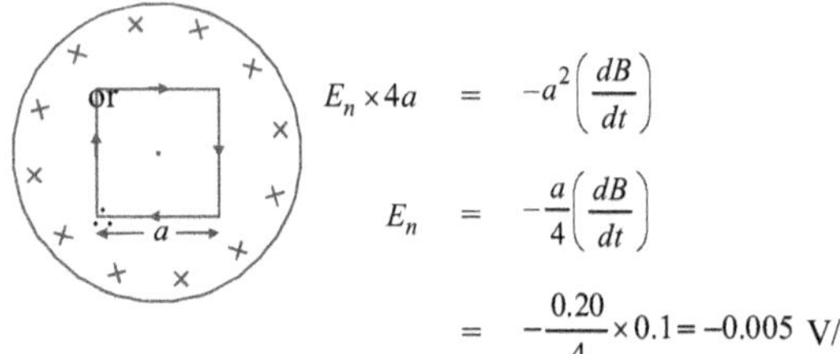

$$E_n \times 4a = -a^2\left(\frac{dB}{dt}\right)$$

$$E_n = -\frac{a}{4}\left(\frac{dB}{dt}\right)$$

$$= -\frac{0.20}{4}\times 0.1 = -0.005 \ \text{V/m}$$

(b) Induced emf, $$|e| = \frac{d\phi}{dt} = a^2 \times \frac{dB}{dt}$$

$$= (0.20)^2 \times 0.1 = 4\times 10^{-3}\,\text{V}$$

Induced current, $$i = \frac{e}{R} = \frac{4\times 10^{-3}}{2} = 2\times 10^{-3}\ \text{A}.$$

19. (a) The induced emf in any side of the loop is given by

$$e = -\frac{d}{2\cos\theta}\left(\frac{dB}{dt}\right)$$

where d is the distance of the side from the centre of the field. Here $d = 0$, $\therefore$ $e = 0$

(b) The induced emf, $$|e| = a^2\left(\frac{dB}{dt}\right)$$

$$= (0.20)^2 \times 0.1 = 4\times 10^{-3} \ \text{V}$$

Do the other parts accordingly.

20. The magnetic flux through the structure

$$\phi = BA = B\frac{\pi r^2}{4}$$

$$\therefore \qquad |e| = \frac{d\phi}{dt} = \frac{\pi r^2}{4}\left(\frac{dB}{dt}\right)$$

$$= \frac{\pi(0.1)^2}{4}\times(5\times 10^{-3})$$

$$= 39.25 \ \mu V \qquad \textbf{Ans.}$$

21. The flux through the coil at any instant

$$\phi = NBA\cos\omega t$$

Induced emf, $$e = -\frac{d\phi}{dt} = NBA\sin\omega t$$

$$= NB(ab)\times 2\pi f \sin 2\pi f t$$

22. The flux through the small area,

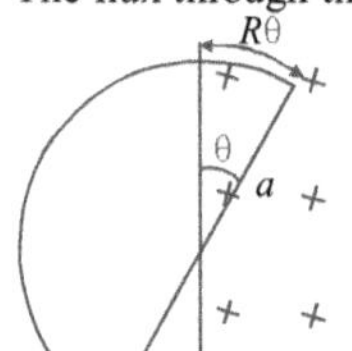

$$\phi = BA = B\left(\frac{a\theta \times a}{2}\right)$$

$$= \frac{Ba^2}{2}\theta$$

Induced emf, $$e = -\frac{d\phi}{dt} = -\frac{Ba^2}{2}\left(\frac{d\theta}{dt}\right)$$

$$= -\frac{Ba^2}{2}\omega$$

In time t, $$\omega = \alpha t$$

$$\therefore \qquad e = -\frac{Ba^2\alpha t}{2}$$

Time taken to complete half rotation

$$\theta = \pi = \frac{1}{2}\alpha t^2$$

$$\therefore \qquad t = \sqrt{\frac{2\pi}{\alpha}}$$

In general $$t = \sqrt{2\pi n/\alpha}$$

23. (a) The induced emf, $$e = Bv\ell$$
$$= 1 \times 0.05 \times 0.02$$
$$= 1\times 10^{-3} \ \text{V}$$

Thus current, $$i = \frac{e}{R} = \frac{1\times 10^{-3}}{10}$$
$$= 0.1 \ \text{mA} \qquad \textbf{Ans.}$$

(b) The induced emf, $$e = Bv\ell$$
$$= 1 \times 0.05 \times 0.04$$
$$= 2\times 10^{-3} \ \text{V}$$

Thus current, $$i = \frac{e}{R} = \frac{2\times 10^{-3}}{10}$$
$$= 0.2 \ \text{mA} \qquad \textbf{Ans.}$$

24. (i) The flux through the smaller loop

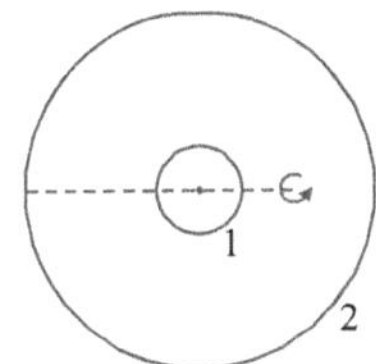

$$\phi = B_2 A_1 \cos\omega t$$

$$= \left(\frac{\mu_0 i}{2R_2}\right) A_1 \cos\omega t$$

$$= \frac{(4\pi\times10^{-7})\times1\times(5\times10^{-4})}{2\times0.1}\cos\omega t$$

$$= \pi\times10^{-9}\cos\omega t$$

(ii) The induced emf, $|e| = \dfrac{d\phi}{dt} = \pi\times10^{-9}\,\omega\sin\omega t$

(iii) The induced current, $i = \dfrac{e}{R} = 1.57\times10^{-9}\,\omega\sin\omega t$

25. Suppose field acts into the page. The force on the bar due to current i, $F = Bi\ell = B\left(\dfrac{e}{R}\right)\ell$

As soon as bar starts moving it experiences a retarding force,

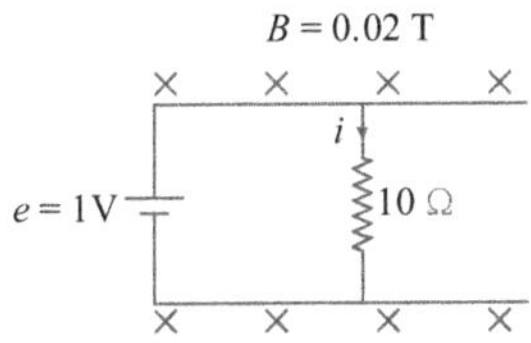

$$F' = Bi\ell = B\frac{(Bv\ell)}{R}\ell$$

$$= \frac{B^2 v\ell^2}{R}$$

By Newton's second law, we have

$$F - F' = ma$$

or $\left[\dfrac{Be\ell}{R} - \dfrac{B^2 v\ell^2}{R}\right] = m\left(\dfrac{dv}{dt}\right)$

After simplify and substituting the values, we get

$$v = 100\,(1 - e^{-0.005t}) \quad \textbf{\textit{Ans.}}$$

26. (b) We have $e = L\dfrac{di}{dt}$

$$\therefore \quad L = \frac{e}{(di/dt)} = \frac{25}{25\times10^3} = 1\times10^{-3}\,A$$

27. The required ratio, $\dfrac{E_{\text{stored}}}{E_{\text{Supplied}}} = \dfrac{V^2/R}{V_0^2/R}$

$$= \frac{V^2}{V_0^2} = \frac{V_0^2(1-e^{-t/\tau})}{V_0^2}$$

$$= (1-e^{-t/\tau})^2$$

$$= \left[1 - e^{-\left(\frac{0.1\times10}{1}\right)}\right]^2$$

$$= 0.36 \qquad \textbf{\textit{Ans.}}$$

28. (a) We have, $|e| = L\dfrac{di}{dt}$

$$\therefore \quad L = \frac{(e)}{(di/dt)} = \frac{10\times10^{-3}}{\dfrac{d}{dt}(5+16t)}$$

$$= 6.25\times10^{-4}\,H$$

(b) The power supplied $P = ei$

$$= 10\times10^{-3}\times(5+16t)$$

$$= 10\times10^{-3}\times(5+16)$$

$$= 210\,mW. \qquad \textbf{\textit{Ans.}}$$

29. (a) We have $i = i_0(1-e^{-t/\tau})$

or $0.8\,i_0 = i_0(1-e^{-t/\tau})$; $\tau = \dfrac{L}{R}$

After substituting the values and simplifying, we get

$$t = 8.45\,ns.$$

(b) $\qquad i = i_0(1-e^{-\tau/\tau}) = 7.37\,mA$ **Ans.**

30. (a) Immediately after closing of switch, inductor offers infinite resistance, so

$$i_1 = i_2 = \frac{100}{10+20} = 3.33\,A$$

(b) After long time, inductor offers zero resistance so

$$i_1 = \frac{V}{10+\dfrac{20\times30}{20+30}} = 4.55\,A$$

and $\qquad i_2 = 2.73\,A$ and $i_3 = 1.82A$

(c) After opening of the switch,

$$i_1 = 0,\; i_2 = -i_3 = -1.82\,A$$

(d) $i_1 = i_2 = 0$

31. (a) The direction of currents may be as shown in figure.

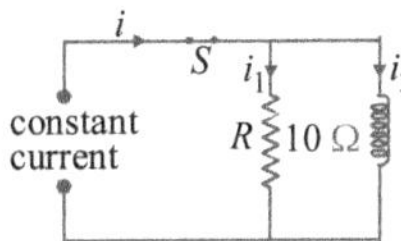

By junction rule

$$i = i_1 + i_2 \qquad \text{... (i)}$$

By loop rule, we have

$$i_1 R - L(di_2/dt) = 0 \qquad \text{... (ii)}$$

Since $\dfrac{di}{dt} = 0,$ $\qquad \therefore \left(\dfrac{di_1}{dt}\right) = \left(\dfrac{di_2}{dt}\right)$

Thus from equation (ii), we have

$$i_1 R + L\left(\dfrac{di_1}{dt}\right) = 0 \qquad \text{... (iii)}$$

After simplifying equations (i) and (iii), we get

$$i_1 = ie^{-Rt/L}$$

and $\qquad i_2 = i - i_1 = i\left[1 - e^{-Rt/L}\right]$

(b) When $\qquad i_1 = i_2$

or $\qquad ie^{-Rt/L} = i[1 - e^{-Rt/L}]$

$\therefore \qquad t = \dfrac{L}{R}\ln 2.$

32. By loop rule, we have

$$\xi - i_1 R_1 = 0 \qquad \ldots(i)$$

and $\qquad \xi - L\dfrac{di_2}{dt} - i_2 R_2 = 0 \qquad \ldots(ii)$

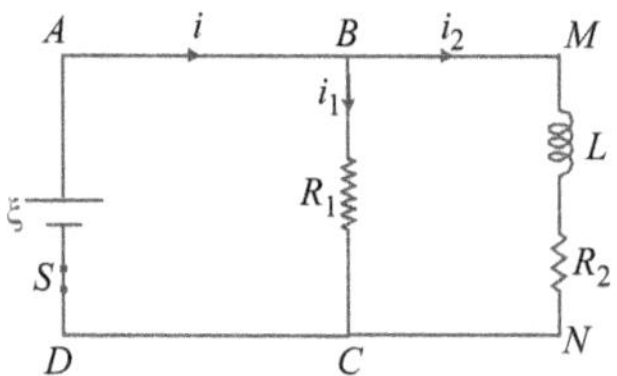

After simplifying equations (i) and (ii), we get

$$i_2 = \dfrac{\xi}{R_2}(1 - e^{-R_2 t/L}).$$

The potential difference across inductor

$$V_L = -L\dfrac{di_2}{dt}$$

$$= -L\dfrac{d}{dt}\left[\dfrac{\xi}{R_2}(1 - e^{-R_2 t/L})\right]$$

$$= \xi e^{-R_2 t/L} \qquad \textbf{Ans.}$$

At steady state, $\qquad i_1 = \dfrac{\xi}{R_1} = \dfrac{12}{2} = 6\,A$

and $\qquad i_2 = \dfrac{\xi}{R_2} = \dfrac{12}{2} = 6\,A$

When switch S is opened, the inductor opposes the decay of current, so direction of current in R_2 remains same while the direction of current in R_1 is reversed. If i_3 be the current then

$$L\dfrac{di_3}{dt} + i_3 R_1 + i_3 R_2 = 0$$

After simplifying, we get

$$i_3 = i_3 e^{-t(R_1 + R_2)/L}$$

$$= 6e^{-t(R_1 + R_2)/L}$$

$$= 6e^{-t(2+2)/0.4}$$

$$= 6e^{-10t} \qquad \textbf{Ans.}$$

33. After a long time steady state will reach and inductor offers zero resistance and capacitor offers infinite resistance, The effective circuit is shown in figure.

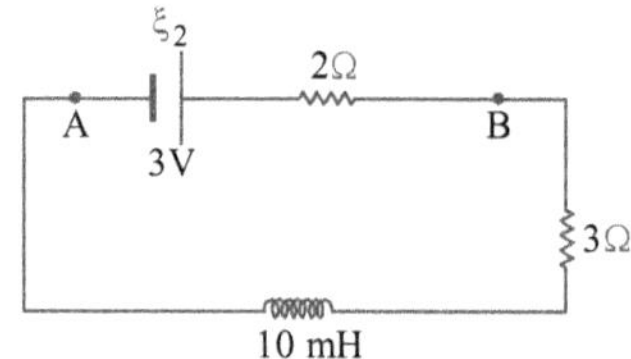

The current in the circuit $\quad i = \dfrac{2\xi}{\left(\dfrac{3R}{4} + r_1 + r_2\right)}$

For potential difference across the terminals of cell A is zero,

or $\qquad \xi - ir_1 = 0$

or $\qquad \xi - \dfrac{2\xi}{\left(\dfrac{3R}{4} + r_1 + r_2\right)}r_1 = 0$

$\therefore \qquad R = \dfrac{4}{3}(r_1 - r_2) \qquad \textbf{Ans.}$

34. (a) At steady state, the capacitor offers infinite resistance, and the effective circuit is shown in figure.

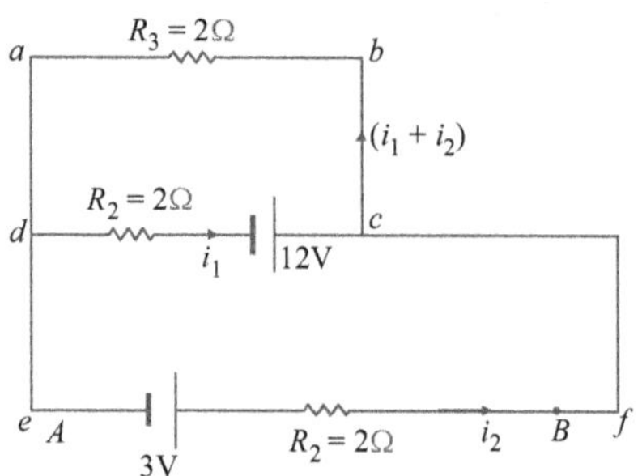

By loop rule, we can write

$$2i_1 + 2(i_1 + i_2) - 12 = 0$$

and $\qquad 2i_2 + 2(i_1 + i_2) - 3 = 0$

After simplifying above equation, we have

$$i_1 = 3.5\,A, \quad i_2 = -1\,A$$

$\therefore \qquad V_B - V_A = \varepsilon_2 - i_2 R_2 = 3 - (-1) \times 2 = 5\,V$

(b) When the switch is put in position 2, the equivalent circuit is

:

The steady current

$$i_0 = \dfrac{3}{5} = 0.6\,A$$

The current at any time is given by

$$i_0 = i_0(1 - e^{-Rt/L})$$

or $\qquad 0.5 = \dfrac{i_0}{(1 - e^{\frac{-5t}{10 \times 10^{-3}}})}$

$\therefore \qquad t = 1.386 \times 10^{-3}\,s \qquad \textbf{Ans.}$

The current at the instant

$$i = \dfrac{i_0}{2} = 0.3\,A$$

$\therefore$ Energy stored, $\quad U = \dfrac{1}{2}Li^2 = 4.5 \times 10^{-4}\,J\ \textbf{Ans.}$

35. (a) If $\dfrac{di}{dt}$ is the rate of change of current, then by Kirchoff's second law

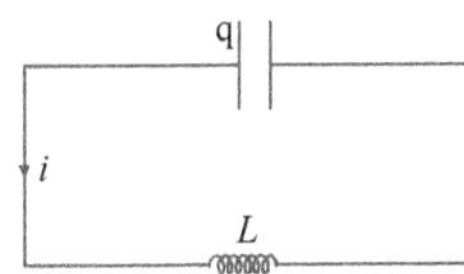

$$\frac{Q}{C} + L\frac{di}{dt} = 0$$

or

$$\frac{di}{dt} = \frac{Q}{LC}$$

$$= \frac{100 \times 10^{-6}}{2 \times 10^{-3} \times 5 \times 10^{-6}} = 10^4 \text{ A/s}$$

(b) When $Q = 200\mu C$, there is no energy stored in inductor, so $i = 0$.

(c)

$$\frac{1}{2}Li_{max}^2 = \frac{Q_{max}^2}{2C}$$

$$\therefore \quad i_{max} = \frac{Q_{max}}{\sqrt{LC}} = 2\text{A}.$$

(d) Given

$$i = \frac{i_{max}}{2} = 1\text{A}$$

From conservation of energy, we can write

$$\frac{1}{2}Li^2 + \frac{Q^2}{2C} = \frac{Q_{max}^2}{2C}$$

After substituting the value, and simplifying, we get

$$Q = 173.2 \ \mu C \qquad \textbf{\textit{Ans.}}$$

36. (a) The induced emf across the whole rod

$$e = \frac{B\omega r^2}{2}$$

(b) The effective circuit is shown in figure.

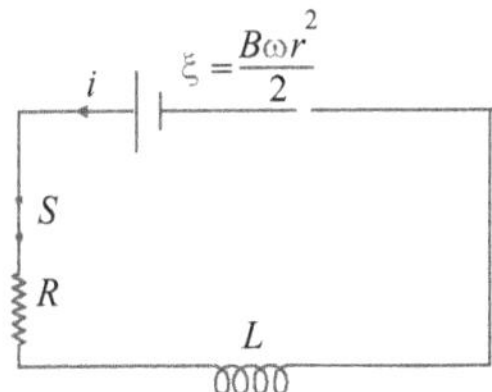

If i is the current and $\dfrac{di}{dt}$ is the increase in current in the circuit then

$$\xi - iR - \frac{Ldi}{dt} = 0$$

After simplifying, we get

$$i = \frac{\xi}{R}(1 - e^{-Rt/L})$$

(i) or

$$i = \frac{B\omega r^2}{2R}(1 - e^{-Rt/L}) \quad \textbf{\textit{Ans.}}$$

(ii) Torque,

$$\tau = \text{force} \times \text{moment arm}$$

$$= \tau_{magnetic} + \tau_{weight}$$

$$= \left[F_{magnetic} + F_{weight}\right] r/2$$

$$= [Bir + mg\cos\omega t]r/2$$

$$= \frac{B^2\omega r^4}{4R} + \frac{mgr\cos\omega t}{2} \ .\textbf{\textit{Ans.}}$$

37. The flux across first solenoid

$$\phi_2 = N_1 B_2 A_1$$

$$= n_1\ell(\mu_0 n_2 i_2)\pi R_1^2$$

$$\therefore \quad M = \mu_0 \pi \ell R_1^2 n_1 n_2$$

38. Magnetic field due to current carrying wire at a distance, x from wire

$$B = \frac{\mu_0}{2\pi}\cdot\frac{i}{x}$$

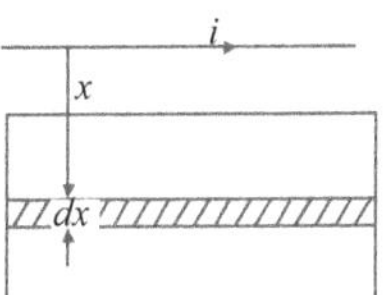

The flux through the area (ℓdx),

$$d\phi = NB(\ell dx)$$

$$\therefore \quad \phi_{total} = \int_a^b NB\ell dx$$

$$= N\ell\frac{\mu_0}{2\pi}\int_a^b \frac{i}{x}dx$$

$$= \frac{\mu_0 N\ell i}{2\pi}|\ell n\, x|_a^{(a+b)}$$

$$= \frac{\mu_0 N\ell i}{2\pi}\ell n\left(\frac{a+b}{a}\right)$$

On comparing with, $\phi_{total} = Mi$, we get

$$M = \frac{\mu_0 N\ell}{2\pi}.\ell n\left(1 + \frac{b}{a}\right) \quad \textbf{\textit{Ans.}}$$

39. The magnetic field of the toroid a distance r from the centre,

$$B = \frac{\mu_0 N_1 i}{2\pi r}.$$

The total flux through the area (hdr)

$$\phi_{total} = \int_a^b N_2 B(2\pi r dr)$$

$$= N_2 \int_a^b \frac{\mu_0 N_1 i}{2\pi r}(h\,dr)$$

$$= \frac{\mu_0 N_1 N_2 h}{2\pi} \ell n\left(\frac{b}{a}\right) i$$

$\therefore \qquad M = \frac{\mu_0 N_1 N_2 h}{2\pi} \ell n\left(\frac{b}{a}\right)$

40. (a) $\dfrac{N_p}{N_s} = \dfrac{V_p}{V_s}$

$$= \frac{8500}{120} \simeq 71$$

(b) $i_p = \dfrac{P}{V_P} = \dfrac{78000}{8500} = 9.2\,\text{A}$

and $i_s = \dfrac{P}{V_s} = \dfrac{78000}{120} = 650\,\text{A}$

(c) $R_P = \dfrac{V_P}{i_P} = \dfrac{8500}{9.2} \simeq 926\,\Omega$

and $R_s = \dfrac{V_P}{i_s} = \dfrac{120}{650} \simeq 0.18\,\Omega$ ***Ans.***

✵ ✵ ✵

35. (a) If $\dfrac{di}{dt}$ is the rate of change of current, then by Kirchoff's second law

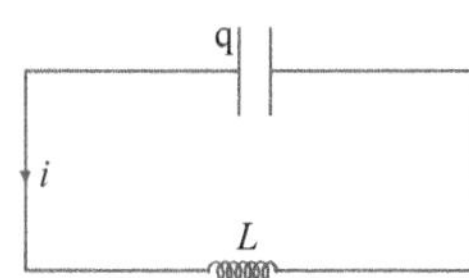

$$\frac{Q}{C} + L\frac{di}{dt} = 0$$

or

$$\frac{di}{dt} = \frac{Q}{LC}$$

$$= \frac{100 \times 10^{-6}}{2 \times 10^{-3} \times 5 \times 10^{-6}} = 10^4 \text{ A/s}$$

(b) When $Q = 200\mu C$, there is no energy stored in inductor, so $i = 0$.

(c)

$$\frac{1}{2}Li_{max}^2 = \frac{Q_{max}^2}{2C}$$

$\therefore$

$$i_{max} = \frac{Q_{max}}{\sqrt{LC}} = 2A.$$

(d) Given

$$i = \frac{i_{max}}{2} = 1A$$

From conservation of energy, we can write

$$\frac{1}{2}Li^2 + \frac{Q^2}{2C} = \frac{Q_{max}^2}{2C}$$

After substituting the value, and simplifying, we get

$$Q = 173.2 \ \mu C \qquad \textbf{Ans.}$$

36. (a) The induced emf across the whole rod

$$e = \frac{B\omega r^2}{2}$$

(b) The effective circuit is shown in figure.

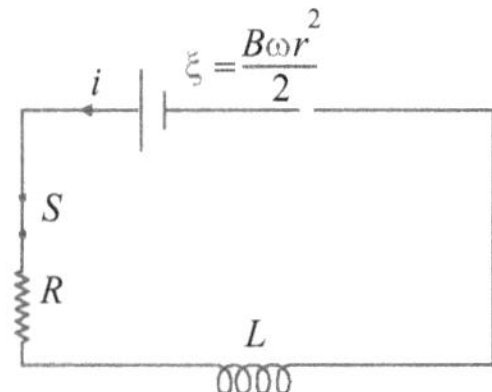

If i is the current and $\dfrac{di}{dt}$ is the increase in current in the circuit then

$$\xi - iR - \frac{Ldi}{dt} = 0$$

After simplifying, we get

$$i = \frac{\xi}{R}(1 - e^{-Rt/L})$$

(i) or

$$i = \frac{B\omega r^2}{2R}(1 - e^{-Rt/L}) \qquad \textbf{Ans.}$$

(ii) Torque, $\quad \tau \quad = \quad$ force $\times$ moment arm

$$= \tau_{magnetic} + \tau_{weight}$$

$$= \left[F_{magnetic} + F_{weight}\right]r/2$$

$$= \left[Bir + mg\cos\omega t\right]r/2$$

$$= \frac{B^2\omega r^4}{4R} + \frac{mgr\cos\omega t}{2} \ .\textbf{Ans.}$$

37. The flux across first solenoid

$$\phi_2 = N_1 B_2 A_1$$

$$= n_1\ell(\mu_0 n_2 i_2)\pi R_1^2$$

$\therefore \qquad M = \mu_0\pi\ell R_1^2 n_1 n_2$

38. Magnetic field due to current carrying wire at a distance, x from wire

$$B = \frac{\mu_0}{2\pi}\cdot\frac{i}{x}$$

The flux through the area (ℓdx),

$$d\phi = NB(\ell dx)$$

$\therefore$

$$\phi_{total} = \int_a^b NB\ell dx$$

$$= N\ell\frac{\mu_0}{2\pi}\int_a^b \frac{i}{x}dx$$

$$= \frac{\mu_0 N\ell i}{2\pi}|\ell n\, x|_a^{(a+b)}$$

$$= \frac{\mu_0 N\ell i}{2\pi}\ell n\left(\frac{a+b}{a}\right)$$

On comparing with, $\phi_{total} = Mi$, we get

$$M = \frac{\mu_0 N\ell}{2\pi}.\ell n\left(1 + \frac{b}{a}\right) \quad \textbf{Ans.}$$

39. The magnetic field of the toroid a distance r from the centre,

$$B = \frac{\mu_0 N_1 i}{2\pi r}.$$

The total flux through the area (hdr)

$$\phi_{total} = \int_a^b N_2 B(2\pi r dr)$$

$$= N_2 \int_a^b \frac{\mu_0 N_1 i}{2\pi r}(h\,dr)$$

$$= \frac{\mu_0 N_1 N_2 h}{2\pi}\ell n\!\left(\frac{b}{a}\right)i$$

$\therefore \qquad M = \dfrac{\mu_0 N_1 N_2 h}{2\pi}\ell n\!\left(\dfrac{b}{a}\right)$

40. (a)

$$\frac{N_p}{N_s} = \frac{V_p}{V_s}$$

$$= \frac{8500}{120} \simeq 71$$

(b) $\qquad i_p = \dfrac{P}{V_P} = \dfrac{78000}{8500} = 9.2\,\text{A}$

and $\qquad i_s = \dfrac{P}{V_s} = \dfrac{78000}{120} = 650\,\text{A}$

(c) $\qquad R_P = \dfrac{V_P}{i_P} = \dfrac{8500}{9.2} \simeq 926\,\Omega$

and $\qquad R_s = \dfrac{V_P}{i_s} = \dfrac{120}{650} \simeq 0.18\,\Omega$ ***Ans.***

★ ★ ★

CHAPTER

9

AC & EM-Waves

(577-619)

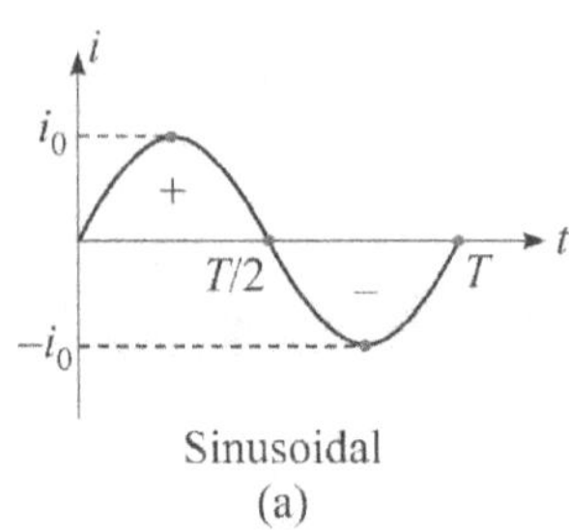

Sinusoidal
(a)

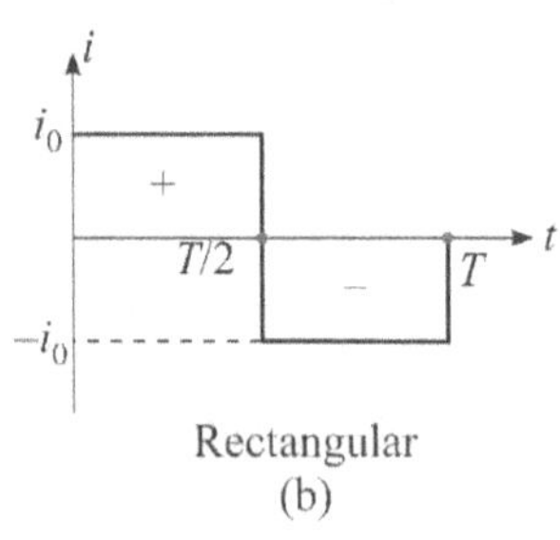

Rectangular
(b)

Fig. 9.1

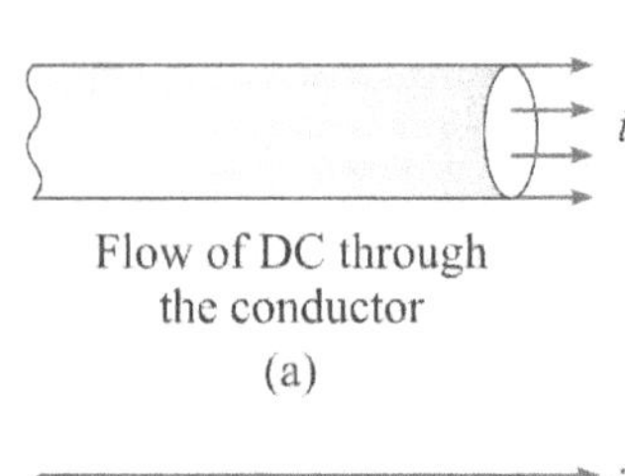

Flow of DC through
the conductor
(a)

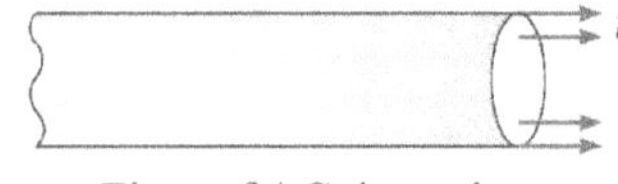

Flow of AC through
the conductor
(b)

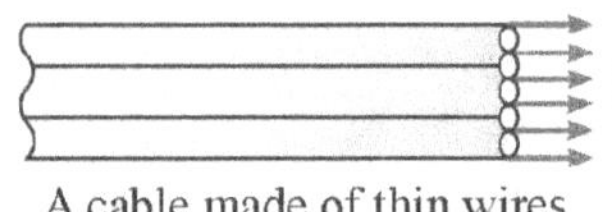

A cable made of thin wires
(c)

Fig. 9.2

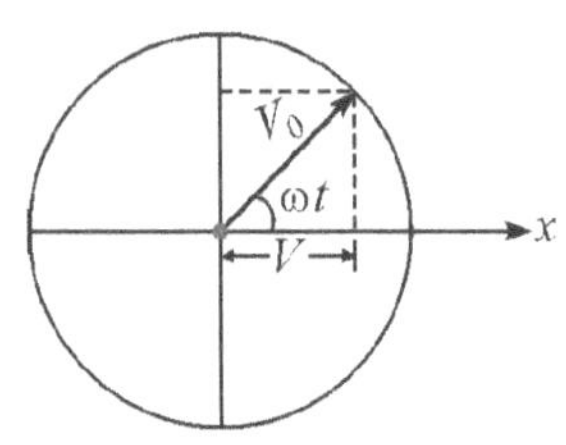

Fig. 9.4

9.1 ALTERNATING CURRENT (AC)

Definition : The current which we use commonly in our houses is alternating current. Alternating current or potential is one whose direction changes periodically, often in a sinusoidal manner. Figure shows two alternating currents; one sinusoidal and other square/rectangular.

Skin effect : A direct current flows uniformly throughout the cross-section of the conductor, while an alternating current, flows mainly along the surface of the conductor. This is know as skin effect.

By increasing surface area, we can decrease the resistance for ac. It can be possible by making a cable which made of number of thin wires having same amount of metal as in the case of a single wire cable.

Why alternating current used in practice?

1. AC potential can very easily be changed by using transformer according to the requirement.
2. We can minimise transmission losses (i^2R) by providing cable made of a number of thin wires.
3. AC is more readily adaptable in rotating machinery such as generators and motors.

Alternating current and potential : Figure 9.3 (a) and (b) represent alternating current and potential respectively. They can be represently by the equations $i = i_0 \sin \omega t$ and $V = V_0 \sin \omega t$.

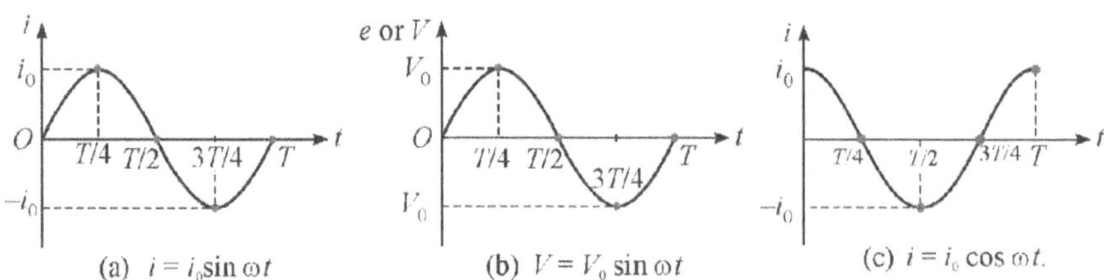

(a) $i = i_0 \sin \omega t$ (b) $V = V_0 \sin \omega t$ (c) $i = i_0 \cos \omega t.$

where i_0 is peak value of current   where V_0 is the peak of potential.
ω is angular frequency in rad/s.

Fig. 9.3

The circuit symbol for an ac source is ⊝.

Phasor diagram

Analysis of alternating current circuit is facilitated by the use of vector diagrams similar to those used in the study of SHM. In such diagrams, the instantaneous value of a quantity that varies sinusoidally with time is represented by the projection onto a horizontal or vertical axis of a vector of length corresponding to the amplitude of the quantity and rotating anticlockwise with angular velocity w. In the context of ac-circuit analysis, these rotating vectors are often called phasors, and diagram containing them are called phasor diagrams.

From the diagram, the projection on x-axis diameter gives
$$V = V_0 \cos \omega t,$$
and projection on y-axis gives $V = V_0 \sin \omega t.$

9.2 AVERAGE AND ROOT MEAN SQUARE (RMS) VALUES

Average value :

The average value x_{av} of any quantity $x(t)$ that varies with time over a time interval t_1 to t_2, is defined as

$$x_{av} \text{ or } \overline{x} = \frac{\int_{t_1}^{t_2} x(t)\,dt}{\int_{t_1}^{t_2} dt} = \frac{1}{(t_2 - t_1)} \int_{t_1}^{t_2} x(t)\,dt$$

Let us now calculate average value of sinusoidally varying quantity, $i = i_0 \sin\omega t$.

(i) Average over half cycle :

$$i_{av} = \frac{i_0 \displaystyle\int_0^{T/2} \sin\omega t \, dt}{\left(\dfrac{T}{2}\right)}$$

$$= \frac{i_0 \displaystyle\int_0^{T/2} \sin\left(\dfrac{2\pi}{T}\right)t \, dt}{\left(\dfrac{T}{2}\right)}$$

$$= \frac{2i_0}{T} \left|\frac{-\cos\left(\dfrac{2\pi t}{T}\right)}{\left(\dfrac{2\pi}{T}\right)}\right|_0^{\frac{T}{2}}$$

$$= \frac{i_0}{\pi}\left[-\cos\pi - (-\cos 0)\right]$$

$$= \frac{2i_0}{\pi}$$

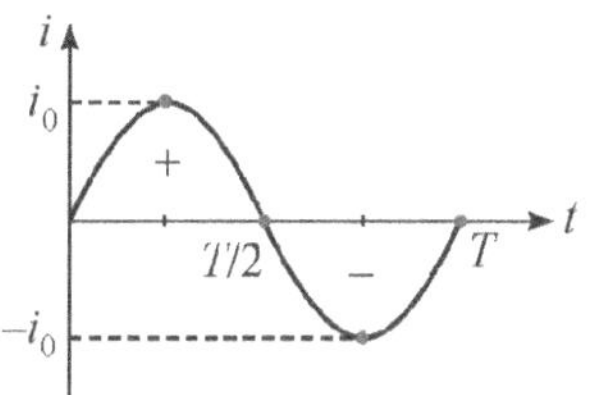

Fig. 9.5

(ii) Average over complete cycle :

$$i_{av} = i_0 \int_0^T \frac{\sin\omega t \, dt}{T}$$

$$= \frac{i_0}{T} \int_0^T \sin\left(\frac{2\pi}{T}t\right) dt$$

$$= \frac{i_0}{T} \left|\frac{-\cos\dfrac{2\pi t}{T}}{\left(\dfrac{2\pi}{T}\right)}\right|_0^T$$

$$= \frac{i_0}{2\pi}\left[-\cos 2\pi - (-\cos 0)\right]$$

$$= 0$$

(iii) Average of half rectified wave :

$$i_{av} = \frac{1}{T} \int_0^{\frac{T}{2}} \sin\omega t \, dt$$

$$= \frac{i_0}{\pi}$$

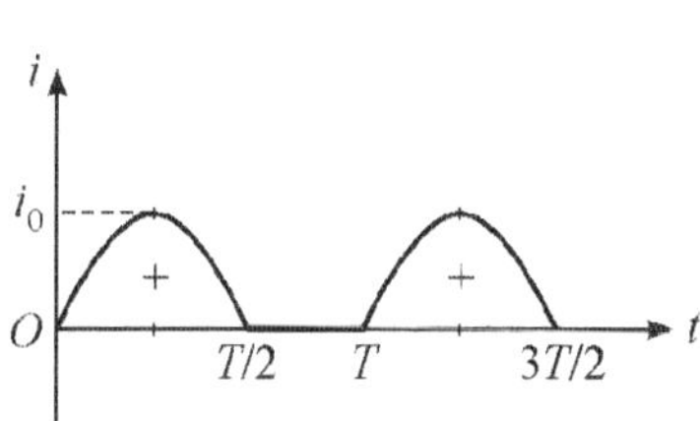

Fig. 9.6

(iv) Average of full rectified wave :

$$i_{av} = \frac{1}{T} \int_0^T \sin\omega t \, dt$$

$$= \frac{2i_0}{\pi}$$

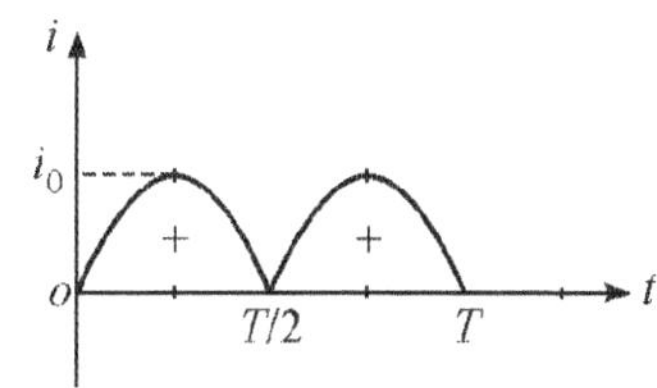

Fig. 9.7

RMS value :

1. Mathematically rms of numerous values $i_1, i_2, ..., i_n$ is defined as

$$i_{rms} = \sqrt{\frac{i_1^2 + i_2^2 + ... + i_n^2}{n}}$$

For a quantity changes continuously, we can write

$$i_{rms} = \sqrt{\frac{\int_0^T i^2\, dt}{\int_0^T dt}} = \sqrt{\frac{\int_0^T i^2\, dt}{T}}$$

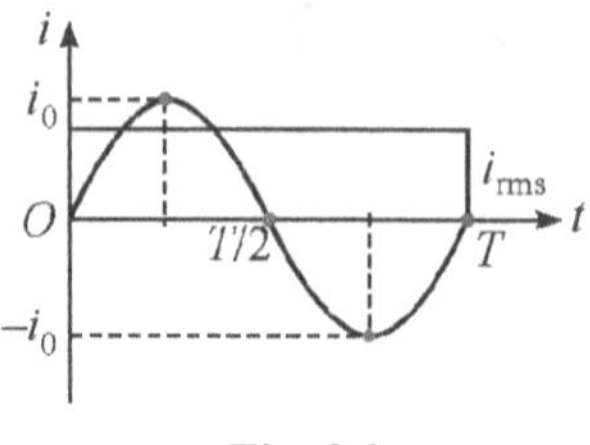

Fig. 9.8

2. **RMS value of $i = i_0 \sin\omega t$:** we can write

$$i_{rms}^2 = \frac{\int_0^T i^2\, dt}{T}$$

$$= \frac{i_0^2}{T} \int_0^T \sin^2 \omega t\, dt$$

$$= \frac{i_0^2}{T} \int_0^T \left[\frac{1 - \cos 2\omega t}{2} \right] dt$$

$$= \frac{i_0^2}{2T} \int_0^T \left[1 - \cos \frac{2 \times 2\pi t}{T} \right] dt$$

$$= \frac{i_0^2}{2T} \left| t - \frac{\sin \frac{4\pi t}{T}}{\frac{4\pi}{T}} \right|_0^T$$

$$= \frac{i_0^2}{2T} \left[(T - 0) - 0 \right]$$

$$= \frac{i_0^2}{2}$$

$$\therefore \qquad i_{rms} = \frac{i_0}{\sqrt{2}} = 0.707\, i_0 \qquad\qquad ....(1)$$

Similarly $\qquad V_{rms} = \frac{V_0}{\sqrt{2}} = 0.707\, V_0. \qquad\qquad ....(2)$

Remember :

1. $\quad \dfrac{1}{T} \displaystyle\int_0^T \sin \omega t\, dt = 0 \qquad ; \qquad \dfrac{1}{T} \displaystyle\int_0^T \cos \omega t\, dt = 0$

2. $\quad \dfrac{1}{T} \displaystyle\int_0^T \sin^2 \omega t\, dt = \dfrac{1}{2} \qquad ; \qquad \dfrac{1}{T} \displaystyle\int_0^T \cos^2 \omega t\, dt = \dfrac{1}{2}$

Where average and RMS values are used ?

The usual moving-coil galvanometer, however, has very large moment of inertia to follow the instantaneous values of current. It average out the fluctuating torque on its coil, and its deflection is proportional to the average current.

RMS values of voltage and current are useful in finding power or energy loss in ac circuits.

Most ac meters are calibrated to read not the maximum value of the current or voltage, but the rms value of current or voltage.

$$\text{Form factor } \left(R_f \right) = \frac{\text{rms value}}{\text{average value}}.$$

Ex. 1 An alternating current is given by the equation $i = i_1 \sin \omega t + i_2 \cos \omega t$. Find its *rms* value.

Sol.
$$i^2 = \left(i_1 \sin\omega t + i_2 \cos\omega t \right)^2$$

$$= i_1^2 \sin^2 \omega t + i_2^2 \cos^2 \omega t + 2 i_1 i_2 \sin\omega t \cos\omega t$$

or
$$i^2 = i_1^2 \sin^2 \omega t + i_2^2 \cos^2 \omega t + i_1 i_2 \sin 2\omega t$$

and
$$\overline{i^2} = i_1^2 \times \frac{1}{2} + i_2^2 \times \frac{1}{2} + i_1 i_2 \times 0$$

$$= \left(\frac{i_1^2 + i_2^2}{2} \right)$$

$$\therefore \quad i_{rms} = \sqrt{\overline{i^2}} = \sqrt{\frac{i_1^2 + i_2^2}{2}} \qquad \textit{Ans.}$$

In our country the power supply for domestic purpose is 220 V and 50 Hz. That is,

$$V_{rms} = 220\,V, \text{ or } V_0 = \sqrt{2} \times 220 \approx 311\,V$$

and $f = 50$ Hz, or $\omega = 2\pi \times 50 = 100\,\pi$ rad

$$\therefore \quad V = V_0 \sin \omega t = 311 \sin 100\pi t.$$

Ex. 2 The current in a discharging *LR* circuit is given by $i = i_0 e^{-\frac{t}{\tau}}$ where τ is the time constant of the circuit. Calculate the rms current for the period $t = 0$ to $t = \tau$.

Sol. Given, $i = i_0 e^{-\frac{t}{\tau}}$

$$\therefore \quad i^2 = i_0^2 e^{-\frac{2t}{\tau}}$$

and
$$\overline{i^2} = \frac{i_0^2}{\tau} \int_0^\tau e^{-\frac{2t}{\tau}}\, dt$$

$$= \frac{i_0^2}{\tau} \left| \frac{e^{-\frac{2t}{\tau}}}{\left(-\frac{2}{\tau} \right)} \right|_0^\tau$$

$$= \frac{i_0^2}{\tau} \times \frac{\tau}{(-2)} \left[e^{-2} - e^0 \right]$$

$$= \frac{i_0^2}{2} \left[1 - \frac{1}{e^2} \right]$$

$$\therefore \quad i_{rms} = \sqrt{\overline{i^2}} = \frac{i_0}{e} \sqrt{\frac{\left(e^2 - 1 \right)}{2}} \qquad \textit{Ans.}$$

Ex. 3 Find the average and effective values of the saw-tooth wave form as shown in *fig. 9.9*.

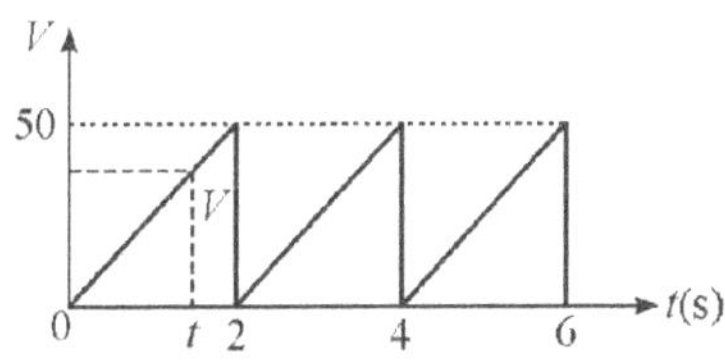

Fig. 9.9

Sol. Since voltage increases linearly, so

$$V_{av} = \frac{0 + 50}{2} = 25\,V \qquad \textit{Ans.}$$

Let V is the instantaneous value of voltage between 0 to 2s, then

$$V = \frac{50}{2} t = 25t$$

The rms or effective value of the voltage is

$$V_{rms}^2 = \frac{1}{T} \int_0^T V^2 dt$$

$$= \frac{1}{2} \int_0^2 (25t)^2 dt$$

$$= \frac{625}{2} \int_0^2 t^2 dt$$

$$= \frac{625}{2} \left| \frac{t^3}{3} \right|_0^2 = 833.3\,V$$

$$\therefore \quad V_{rms} = 28.9\,V \qquad \textit{Ans.}$$

Ex. 4 Determine the rms value of a semicircular wave which has a maximum value I_0.

Sol.   The equation of a semicircular wave is

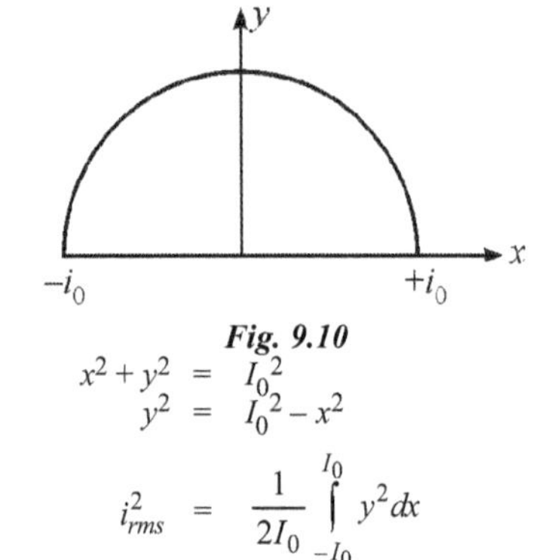

Fig. 9.10

$$x^2 + y^2 = I_0^2$$

or

$$y^2 = I_0^2 - x^2$$

$$\therefore \quad i_{rms}^2 = \frac{1}{2I_0} \int_{-I_0}^{I_0} y^2\, dx$$

$$= \frac{1}{2I_0} \int_{-I_0}^{I_0} \left(I_0^2 - x^2\right) dx$$

$$= \frac{1}{2I_0} \left| I_0^2 x - \frac{x^3}{3} \right|_{-I_0}^{I_0}$$

$$= \frac{1}{2I_0} \left[\left(I_0^3 - \frac{I_0^3}{3} \right) - \left(-I_0^3 + \frac{I_0^3}{3} \right) \right]$$

$$= \frac{2I_0^2}{3}$$

or

$$I_{rms} = \sqrt{\frac{2I_0^2}{3}} = \sqrt{\frac{2}{3}} I_0 \quad Ans.$$

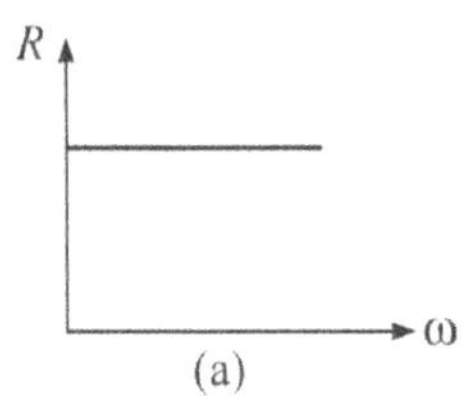

(a)

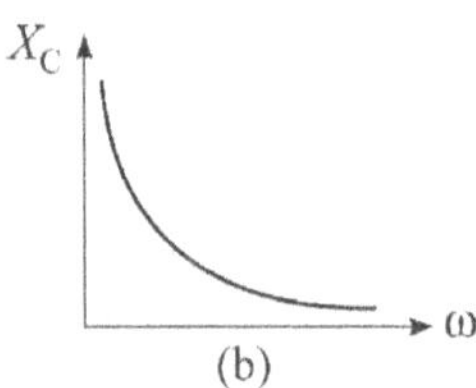

(b)

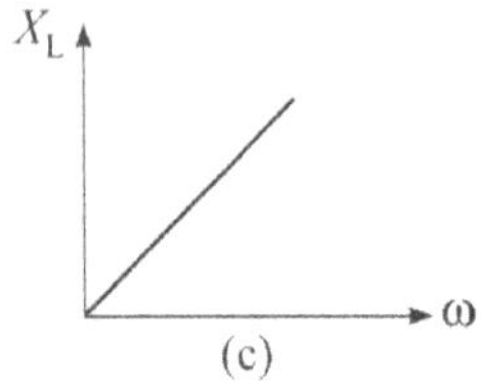

(c)

Fig. 9.11

Circuit elements :

In circuits, we have three circuit-elements : resistor, capacitor and inductor. All these three offer resistance for ac. The resistance of resistor is real while the resistance offers by capacitor and inductor is virtual.

Resistance :

The opposition offered by the resistor is called resistance. It is independent of frequency of ac.

Capacitive reactance (X_C) :

The opposition offered by the capacitor in an ac circuit is called capacitive reactance. It is a virtual resistance. It is given by

Its unit is ohm.
$$X_C = \frac{1}{\omega C} = \frac{1}{2\pi f C}.$$

For dc, $\omega = 0$, $X_C = \infty$.

Inductive reactance (X_L) :

It is the resistance offered by the inductor in an ac circuit. It is also a virtual resistance. Its unit is ohm. It is given by

$$X_L = \omega L.$$

For dc, $\omega = 0$, $X_L = 0$

Impedance (Z) :

The total resistance of ac circuit is called impedance.

Admittance (A) :

Reciprocal of impedance is known as admittance; i.e., $A = \dfrac{1}{Z}$. It's unit is mho.

9.3 THREE SIMPLE CIRCUITS

1. **A resistive circuit :** Suppose that an alternating potential difference $V = V_0 \sin\omega t$ is applied to resistance R, then current in resistor

$$i_R = \frac{V}{R} = \frac{V_0}{R} \sin\omega t$$

or

$$i_R = i_0 \sin\omega t, \qquad \qquad ...(1)$$

where $i_0 = \dfrac{V_0}{R}$, is the amplitude of the current.

Current and voltage both vary with $\sin\omega t$, hence they are in same phase.

2. **A capacitive circuit :** If a capacitor of capacitance C is connected across alternating source, the charge at any instant,

$$q = CV_0$$
$$= CV_0 \sin\omega t$$

Current
$$i_C = \frac{dq}{dt} = CV_0\omega\cos\omega t$$

$$= \frac{V_0}{\left(\dfrac{1}{\omega C}\right)}\sin\left(\omega t + \frac{\pi}{2}\right) = \frac{V_0}{X_C}\sin\left(\omega t + \frac{\pi}{2}\right)$$

or
$$i_C = i_0 \sin\left(\omega t + \frac{\pi}{2}\right) \qquad ...(2)$$

where $\dfrac{1}{\omega C} = X_C$, is called capacitive reactance.

3. **An inductive circuit :** Suppose that an alternating potential $V = V_0 \sin\omega t$ is applied across a pure inductor of self inductance L. From the definition of inductance, we can write

$$V_L = L\frac{di_L}{dt}$$

or
$$V_0\sin\omega t = \frac{Ldi_L}{dt}$$

or
$$di_L = \frac{V_0}{L}\sin\omega t\, dt$$

or
$$i_L = \int di_L = \frac{V_0}{L}\int \sin\omega t\, dt$$

$$= \frac{V_0}{\omega L}\cos\omega t + c$$

The value of the constant over complete cycle will be zero, $X_L = \omega L$, is called inductive reactance.

$$\therefore \qquad i_L = \frac{V_0}{X_L}\sin\left(\omega t - \frac{\pi}{2}\right)$$

or
$$i_L = i_0 \sin\left(\omega t - \frac{\pi}{2}\right) \qquad ...(3)$$

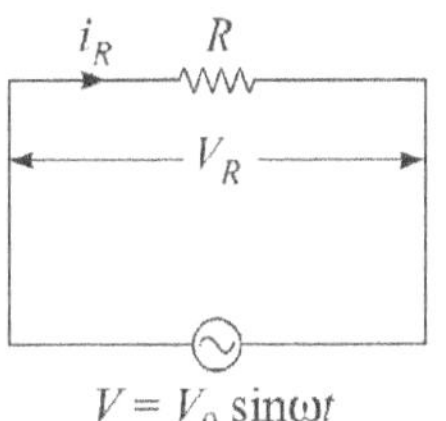

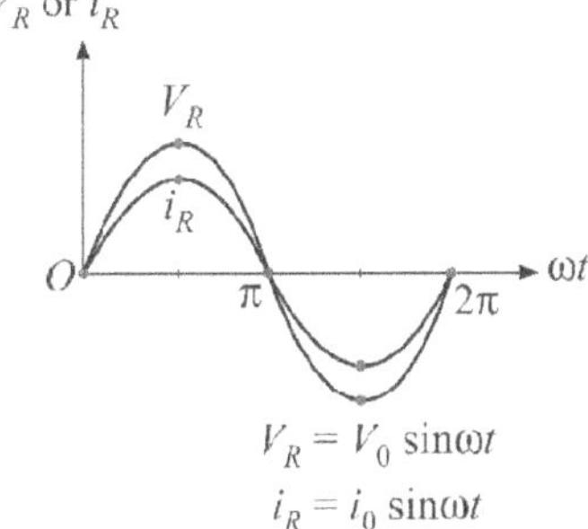

Fig. 9.12

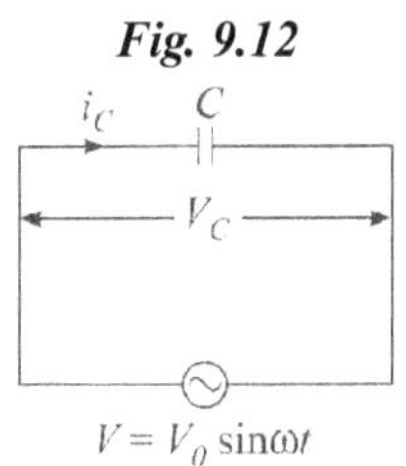

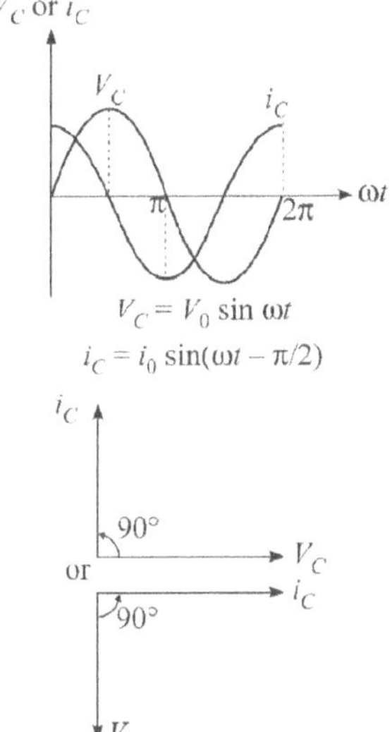

Fig. 9.13

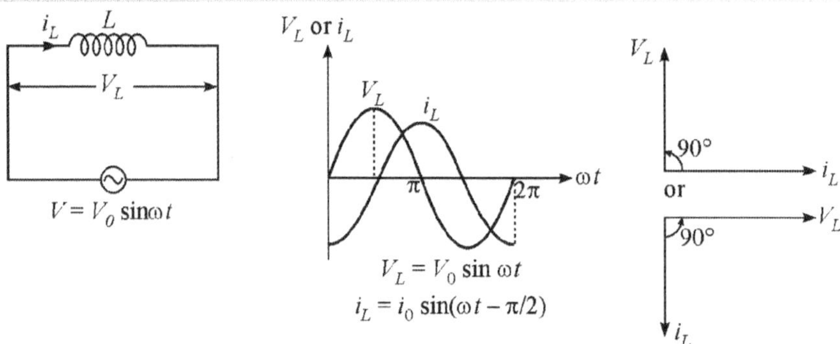

Fig. 9.14

Phase and amplitude relations for alternating currents and voltage

Circuit element	Symbol	Impedance	Phase of the current	Phase angle ϕ	Amplitude relation
Resistor	R	R	In phase with V_R	$0°$	$V_R = i_R\, R$
Capacitor	C	X_C	Lead V_C by $\dfrac{\pi}{2}$	$+\dfrac{\pi}{2}$	$V_C = i_C\, X_C$
Inductor	L	X_L	Lags V_L by $\dfrac{\pi}{2}$	$-\dfrac{\pi}{2}$	$V_L = i_L\, X_L$

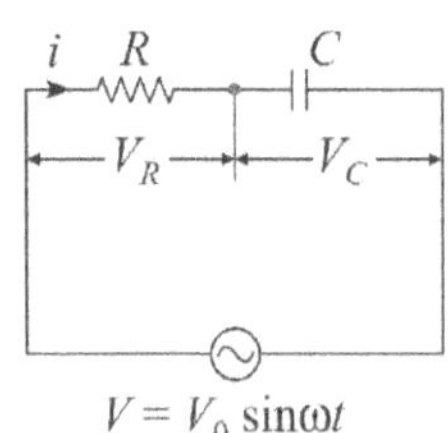

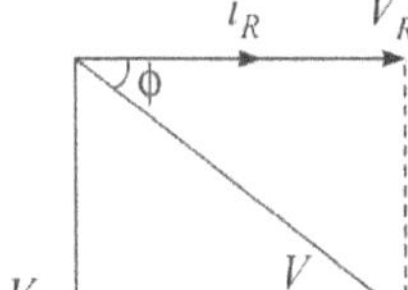

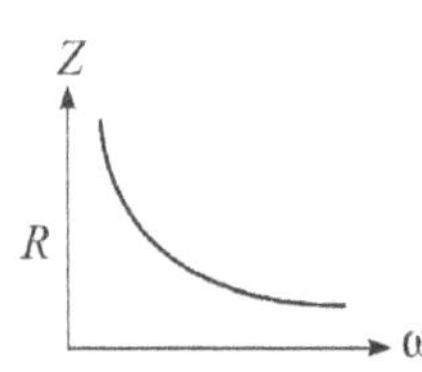

Fig. 9.15

9.4 RC-CIRCUIT

Consider a circuit with resistor R and capacitor C, connected in series with an alternating source of potential V. If V_R and V_C are the p.d. across resistor and capacitor respectively, then

(i)   Supply voltage

$$V = \sqrt{V_R{}^2 + V_C{}^2} = \sqrt{(iR)^2 + (iX_C)^2}$$

(ii)   Impedance

$$Z = \frac{V}{i} = \sqrt{R^2 + X_C{}^2} = \sqrt{R^2 + \left(\frac{1}{\omega C}\right)^2}$$

(iii)   Current

$$i = i_0 \sin(\omega t + \phi)$$

where

$$\tan\phi = \frac{X_C}{R} = \frac{1}{\omega CR}$$

(iv)   Peak current

$$i_0 = \frac{V_0}{Z} = \frac{V_0}{\sqrt{R^2 + X_C{}^2}}$$

9.5 LR-CIRCUIT

Consider a circuit with a resistor R and an inductor L connected in series with an alternating source of potential V. If V_R and V_L are the p.d. across resistor and inductor respectively, then

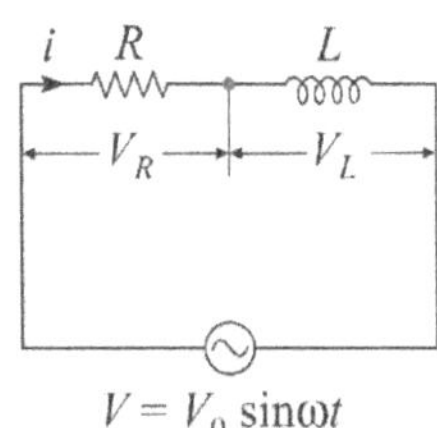

Fig. 9.16

(i)   Supply voltage

$$V = \sqrt{V_R{}^2 + V_L{}^2} = \sqrt{(iR)^2 + (iX_L)^2}$$

(ii)   Impedance

$$Z = \frac{V}{i} = \sqrt{R^2 + X_L{}^2} = \sqrt{R^2 + (\omega L)^2}$$

(iii)   Current

$$i = i_0 \sin(\omega t - \phi)$$

where

$$\tan\phi = \frac{X_L}{R} = \frac{\omega L}{R}$$

(iv) Peak current $i_0 = \dfrac{V_0}{Z} = \dfrac{V_0}{\sqrt{R^2 + X_L^2}}$

9.6 LC-CIRCUIT

Consider a circuit with inductor L and capacitor C connected in series with an alternating potential V. If V_L and V_C are the p.d. across inductor and capacitor respectively, then

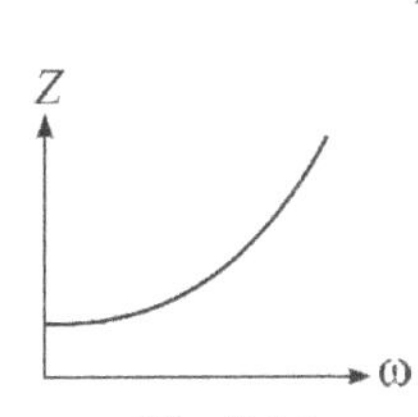

Fig. 9.16

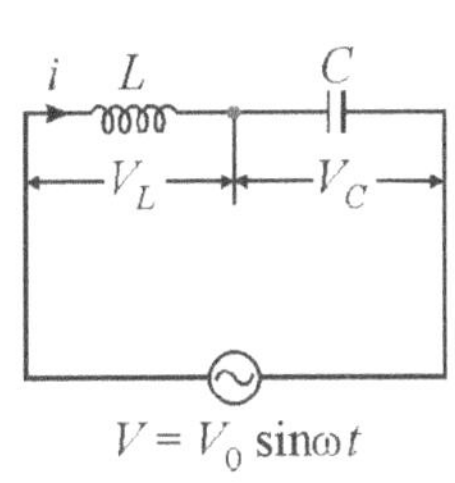

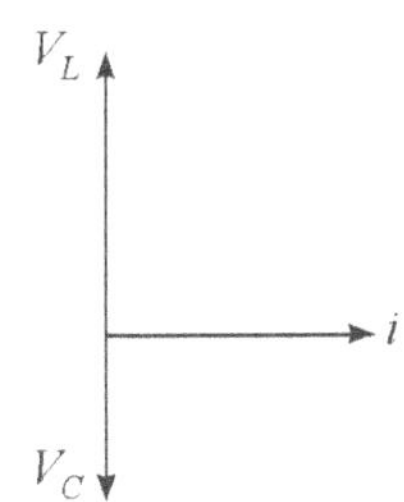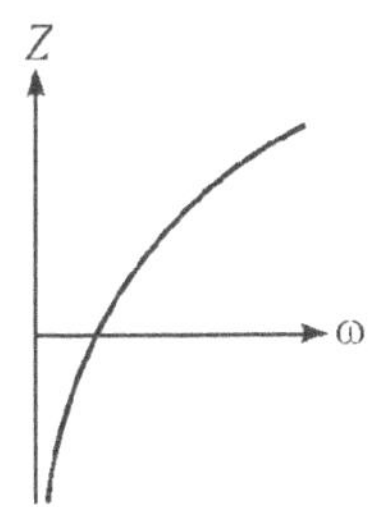

Fig. 9.17

(i)   Supply voltage $V = V_L \sim V_C = i\left(X_L - X_C\right)$

(ii) Impedance $Z = \dfrac{V}{i} = X_L - X_C = \omega L - \dfrac{1}{\omega C}$

(iii) Current $i = i_0 \sin\left(\omega t \pm \dfrac{\pi}{2}\right)$

(iv) Peak current $i_0 = \dfrac{V_0}{Z} = \dfrac{V_0}{X_L - X_C} = \dfrac{V_0}{\omega L - \dfrac{1}{\omega C}}$

9.7 SERIES RLC-CIRCUIT

Consider a RLC- series circuit shown in *fig. 9.18*. If V_R, V_L and V_C are the p.d. across the resistor, inductor and capacitor respectively, then

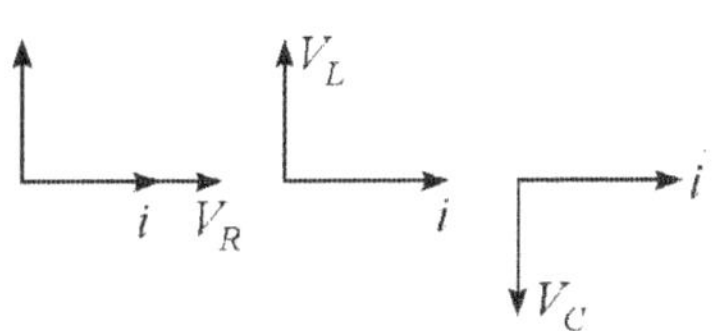

(i)   Supply voltage $V = \sqrt{V_R^2 + \left(V_L - V_C\right)^2}$

$= \sqrt{\left(iR\right)^2 + \left(iX_L - iX_C\right)^2}$

(ii) Impedance $Z = \dfrac{V}{i} = \sqrt{R^2 + \left(X_L - X_C\right)^2}$

$= \sqrt{R^2 + \left(\omega L - \dfrac{1}{\omega C}\right)^2}$

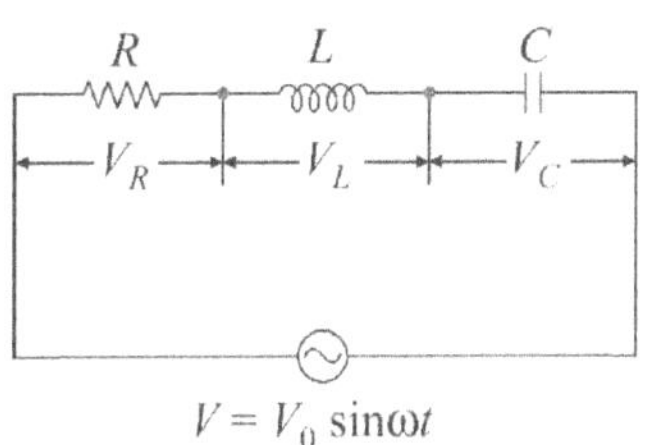

(iii) Current $i = i_0 \sin\left(\omega t \pm \phi\right)$

where $\tan\phi = \dfrac{X_L - X_C}{R} = \dfrac{\omega L - \dfrac{1}{\omega C}}{R}$

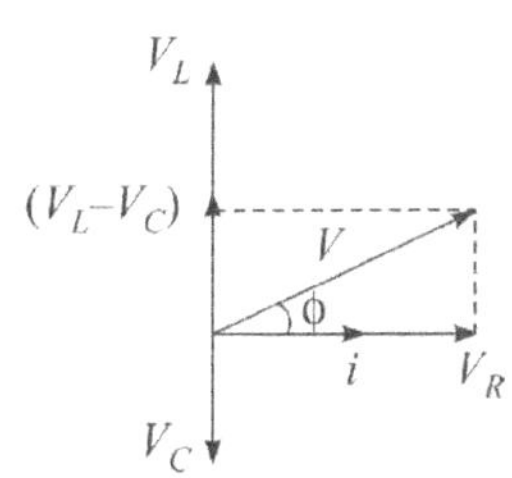

9.8 RLC, RESONANCE CIRCUIT

Resonance will occur when oscillating quantities, here i and V are in same phase, i.e.

$$\phi = 0$$

$\therefore \qquad X_L - X_C = 0$

or $\qquad \omega L = \dfrac{1}{\omega C}$

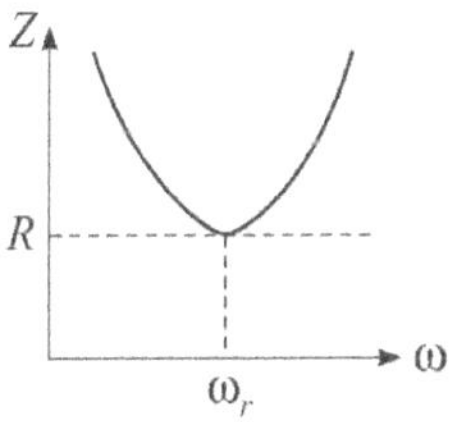

Fig. 9.18

or
$$\omega = \omega_0 = \sqrt{\frac{1}{LC}}$$

where ω_0 is called resonance frequency.

At resonance, $Z_{min} = R$.

Current :
$$i = \frac{V}{Z}$$

$$= \frac{V}{\sqrt{R^2 + \left(\omega L - \dfrac{1}{\omega C}\right)^2}}$$

at $\omega = 0, i = 0$

at $\omega = \omega_0, i_0 = \dfrac{V}{R}$

at $\omega = \infty, i = 0$

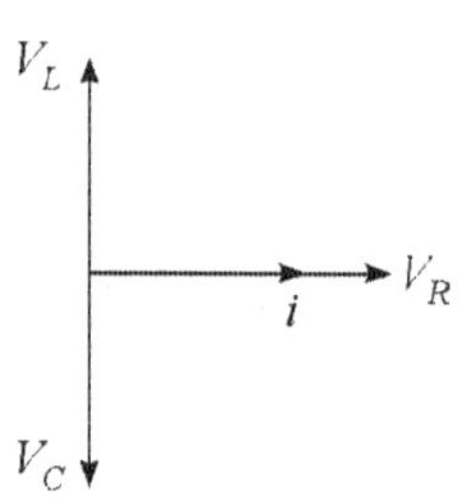

Fig. 9.19

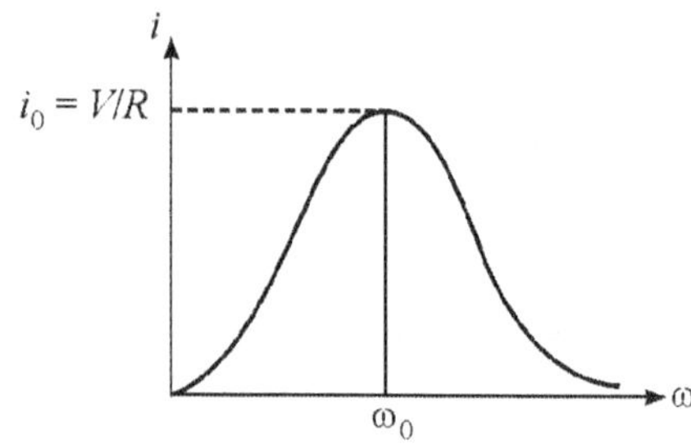

Fig. 9.20. Variation of current i with ω.

Remember :

$$\omega = \omega_0, \omega L = \frac{1}{\omega C} \qquad \omega < \omega_0, \omega L < \frac{1}{\omega C} \qquad \omega > \omega_0, \omega L > \frac{1}{\omega C}$$

$\phi = 0$, current in phase   current leads potential   current lags potential
with potential

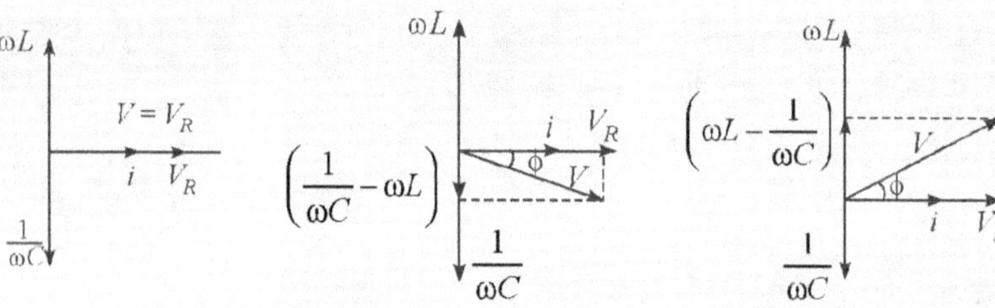

Fig. 9.21

Ex. 5 A 60 Hz voltage of 230 V effective value is impressed on an inductance of 0.265 H.

(i) Write the time equation for the voltage and the resulting current. Let the zero axis of the voltage wave be at $t = 0$.

(ii) Find the maximum energy stored in the inductance.

Sol.
$$V_0 = \sqrt{2}\,V_{rms} = \sqrt{2} \times 230\,V;$$

$$f = 60\,Hz,$$

$$\therefore \omega = 2\pi f = 2\pi \times 60 = 120\,\pi$$

$$X_L = \omega L = 120\pi \times 0.265 = 100\,\Omega$$

(i) The time equation for voltage

$$V = 230\sqrt{2}\,\sin 120\pi t.$$

$$i_0 = \frac{V_0}{X_L} = \frac{230\sqrt{2}}{100} = 2.3\sqrt{2}\,A$$

$$\therefore \quad i = 2.3\sqrt{2}\,\sin\left(120\pi t - \frac{\pi}{2}\right)$$

$$= -2.3\sqrt{2}\,\cos 120\pi t. \qquad \textit{Ans.}$$

(ii) Energy stored, $E_0 = \dfrac{1}{2}Li_0^2$

$$= \frac{1}{2} \times 0.265 \times \left(2.3\sqrt{2}\right)^2$$

$$= 1.4\,J \qquad \textit{Ans.}$$

Ex. 6 The voltage applied to a purely inductive coil of self inductance 15.9 mH is given by the equation

$$V = 100 \sin 314t + 75 \sin 942\,t + 50 \sin 1570\,t.$$

Find the equation of the resulting current wave.

Sol. The standard equation of the voltage can be written as :

$$V = V_{01}\sin \omega_1 t + V_{02}\sin \omega_2 t + V_{03}\sin \omega_3 t$$

On comparing this with the given equation, we have

$$\omega_1 = 314\frac{rad}{s},$$

$$X_{L1} = \omega_1 L = 314 \times 15.9 \times 10^{-3} = 5\,\Omega$$

$$\omega_2 = 942\frac{rad}{s},$$

$$X_{L2} = \omega_2 L = 942 \times 15.9 \times 10^{-3} = 15\,\Omega$$

and

$$\omega_3 = 1570\frac{rad}{s},$$

$$X_{L3} = \omega_3 L = 1570 \times 15.9 \times 10^{-3} = 25\,\Omega$$

Hence :

$$i_{01} = \frac{V_{01}}{X_{L1}} = \frac{100}{5} = 20\,A,$$

$$i_{02} = \frac{V_{02}}{X_{L2}} = \frac{75}{15} = 5\,A,$$

and

$$i_{03} = \frac{V_{03}}{X_{L3}} = \frac{50}{25} = 2\,A.$$

Thus

$$i = i_{01}\sin\omega_1 t + i_{02}\sin\omega_2 t + i_{03}\sin\omega_3 t$$

$$= 20\sin\left(314t - \frac{\pi}{2}\right) + 5\sin\left(942t - \frac{\pi}{2}\right) + 2\sin\left(1570t - \frac{\pi}{2}\right)$$

Ans.

9.9 POWER IN AC CIRCUITS

Consider a circuit in which there is a phase difference ϕ between i and V. Current i can be resolved into two mutually perpendicular components; $i\cos\phi$ along the direction of applied voltage V, and $i\sin\phi$ which is perpendicular to V.

The power consumed by the circuit is given by the product of V and that component of the current i which is in phase with V.

So

$$[P]_{true} = V \times i\cos\phi$$

and

$$[P_{true}]_{av} = V_{rms} \times i_{rms} \times \cos\phi$$

$$= \frac{V_0}{\sqrt{2}}\frac{i_0}{\sqrt{2}}\cos\phi = \frac{V_0 i_0}{2}\cos\phi$$

where $\cos\phi$ is called power factor.

This power consumed is called true power or active power.

$$\cos\phi = \frac{R}{Z}$$

where

$$\cos\phi \leq 1.$$

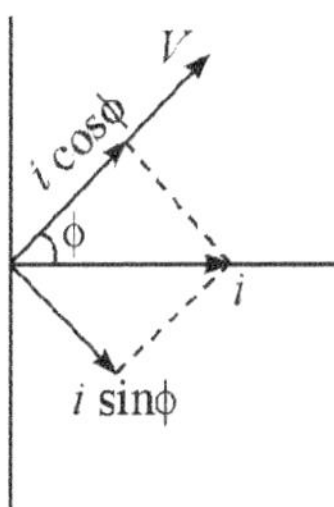

Fig. 9.22

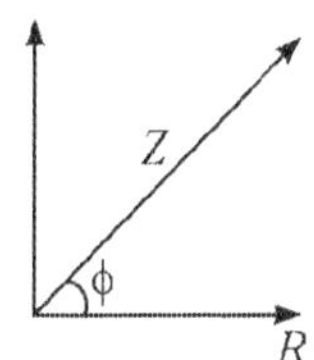

Fig. 9.23

In an ac circuit the product of rms voltage and rms current gives apparent power

$$[P_{av}]_{app} = V_{rms} \times i_{rms}$$

(i) When circuit has resistor only,

$$\phi = 0;\ \cos\phi = 1$$

and

$$P_{av} = V_{rms}\,i_{rms}$$

(ii) When circuit has inductor or capacitor only,

$$\phi = \frac{\pi}{2},\ \cos\phi = 0 \text{ and } P_{av} = 0$$

Current in such a circuit is called **wattless current**.

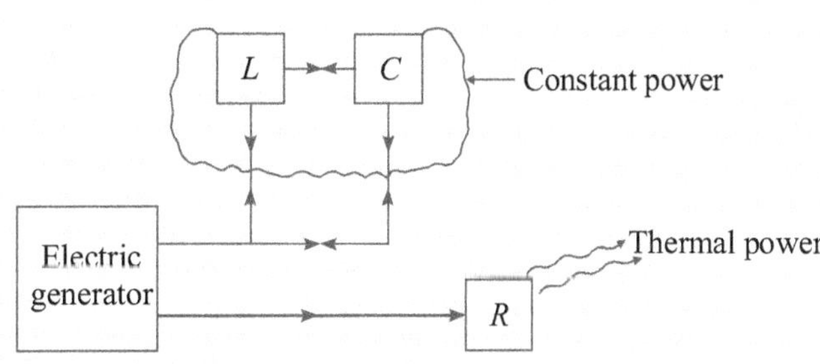

Fig. 9.24

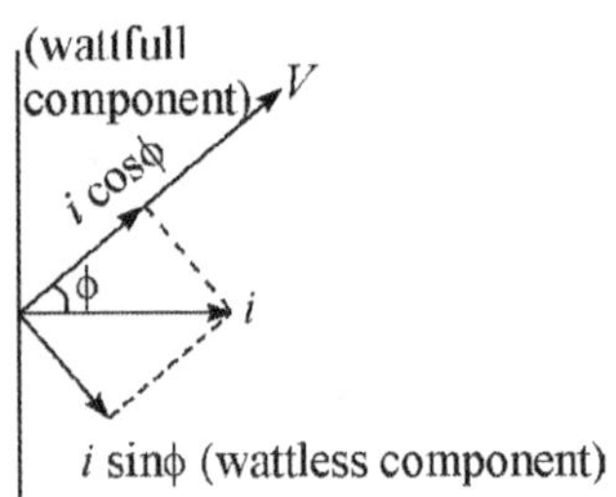

Fig. 9.25

Active and reactive components of circuit current

Active component is that which is in phase with the applied voltage V, i.e., $i\cos\phi$. It is also known as wattfull component. Reactive component is that component which is perpendicular to V, i.e., $i\sin\phi$. It is also known as wattless or idle component.

Instantaneous power and average power

Consider the most general case, in which current and voltage differ in phase by an angle ϕ. The instantaneous power

$$P_{inst} = Vi$$

$$= \left[V\sin\omega t\right]\left[i_0\sin(\omega t-\phi)\right]$$

$$= V_0 i_0 \sin\omega t\left[\sin\omega t\cos\phi - \cos\omega t\sin\phi\right]$$

$$= V_0 i_0 \left[\sin^2\omega t\cos\phi - \sin\omega t\cos\omega t\sin\phi\right]$$

$$P_{inst} = V_0 i_0\left[\sin^2\omega t\cos\phi - \frac{\sin 2\omega t\sin\phi}{2}\right]\quad \left[\begin{array}{l}\frac{1}{T}\int_0^T \sin^2\omega t\,dt = \frac{1}{2},\\ \frac{1}{T}\int_0^T \sin 2\omega t\,dt = 0\end{array}\right]$$

or $$P_{av} = V_0 i_0\left[\left(\frac{1}{2}\right)\cos\phi - 0\right] = \frac{V_0 i_0}{2}\cos\phi$$

or $$P_{av} = V_{rms}\, i_{rms}\,\cos\phi. \qquad .....(1)$$

Half power points and band width

We know that $$P_{av} = \frac{V_0 i_0}{2}\cos\phi$$

$$= \frac{V_0}{2}\times\frac{V_0}{Z}\times\frac{R}{Z}$$

$$= \frac{V_0^2 R}{2Z^2}$$

For RLC series circuit, $$Z = \sqrt{R^2 + \left(\omega L - \frac{1}{\omega C}\right)^2},$$

$$\therefore\quad P_{av} = \frac{V_0^2 R}{2\left[R^2 + \left(\omega L - \frac{1}{\omega C}\right)^2\right]}$$

At $\omega = \omega_0 = \sqrt{\dfrac{1}{LC}}$, $$P_{av} = P_0$$

$$= \frac{V_0^2}{2R}$$

$$\therefore\quad P_{av} = \frac{P_0 R^2}{\left[R^2 + \left(\omega L - \frac{1}{\omega C}\right)^2\right]} \qquad .....(2)$$

At $$\omega = 0, P_{av} = 0$$

At $$\omega = \infty, P_{av} = 0$$

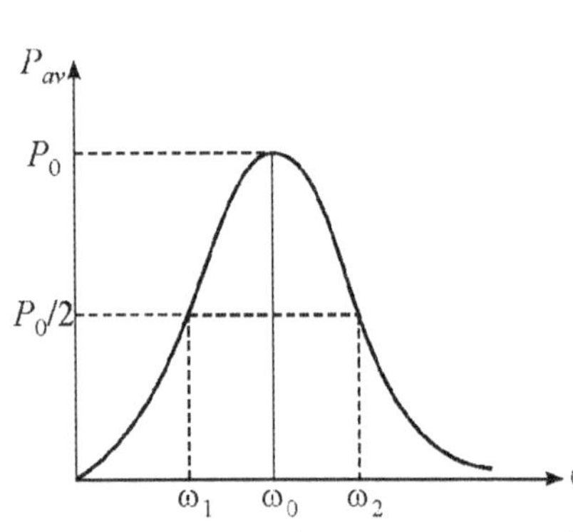

Fig. 9.26 variation of average power with ω.

For,
$$P_{av} = \frac{P_0}{2}, \text{ we have}$$

$$\frac{P_0}{2} = \frac{P_0 R^2}{\left[R^2 + \left(\omega L - \frac{1}{\omega C} \right)^2 \right]}$$

or
$$\left(\omega L - \frac{1}{\omega C} \right)^2 = R^2$$

or
$$\omega L - \frac{1}{\omega C} = \pm R$$

The above equation will have two values of ω, difference of which gives band width.

$$\omega L - \frac{1}{\omega C} = + R \qquad\qquad \omega L - \frac{1}{\omega C} = -R$$

or
$$\omega^2 - \omega \frac{R}{L} - \frac{1}{LC} = 0 \qquad\qquad \omega^2 + \omega \frac{R}{L} - \frac{1}{LC} = 0$$

$$\therefore \ \omega = \frac{+\frac{R}{L} \pm \sqrt{\left(\frac{R}{L}\right)^2 + 4\left(\frac{1}{LC}\right)}}{2} \qquad\qquad \omega = \frac{-\frac{R}{L} \pm \sqrt{\left(\frac{R}{L}\right)^2 + 4\left(\frac{1}{LC}\right)}}{2}$$

ω always be positive, therefore

$$\omega_2 = \frac{\frac{R}{L} + \sqrt{\left(\frac{R}{L}\right)^2 + \frac{4}{LC}}}{2} \qquad\qquad \omega_1 = \frac{-\frac{R}{L} + \sqrt{\left(\frac{R}{L}\right)^2 + \frac{4}{LC}}}{2}$$

B and width $\Delta\omega = \omega_2 - \omega_1 = \frac{R}{L}$

The current corresponds to half power, $i_{rms} = \frac{i_0}{\sqrt{2}} = 0.707\, i_0$

Quality factor or Q-factor

The characteristics of a series resonant circuit is determined by the Q-factor of the circuit. It can be defined as

$$Q\text{-factor} = 2\pi \frac{\text{maximum energy stored}}{\text{energy dissipated per cycle}}$$

$$= \frac{\text{Resonance frequency}}{\text{band width}} = \frac{\omega_0}{\Delta\omega}$$

$$= \frac{\sqrt{\frac{1}{LC}}}{\left(\frac{R}{L}\right)}$$

or
$$Q\text{-factor} = \frac{1}{R}\sqrt{\frac{L}{C}} \qquad\qquad ....(3)$$

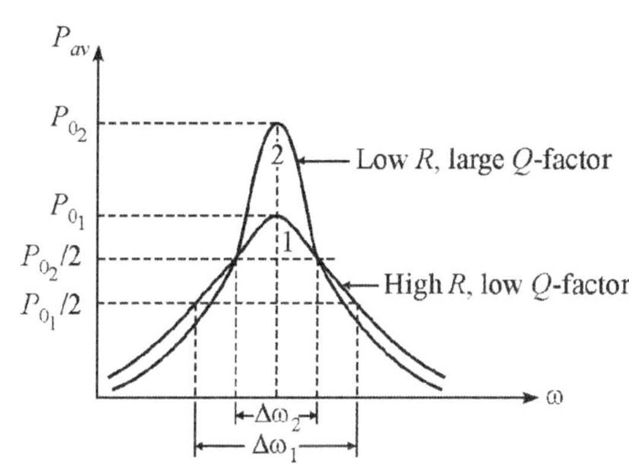

Fig. 9.27

Acceptor circuit

If the frequency of ac supply is varied, the series RLC circuit passes a maximum current and power output for $\omega = \omega_0$. This is the procedure by which a radio or television receiving set may be tuned to receive the signal from a desired station which is sending signals at a particular frequency. The circuit is thus known as an acceptor circuit.

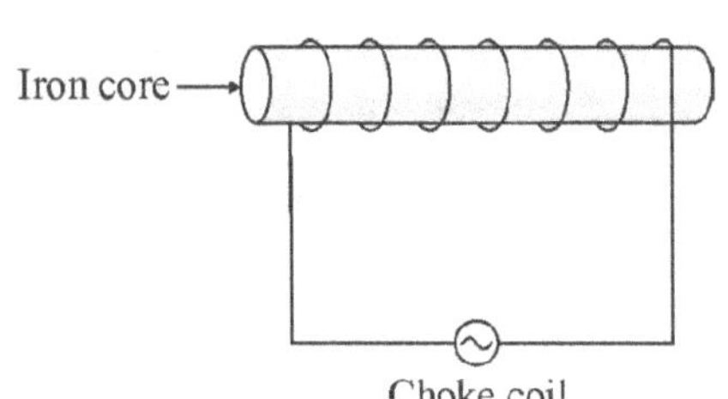

Choke coil

Fig. 9.28

Choke coil

Choke coil is a device having high inductance and negligible resistance. It is used to control ac in the circuit as rheostat is used for dc. Ideal choke coil has no power loss. But practical choke coil has some power loss because of resistance of inducting coil. Practical choke coil is in LR circuit as discussed earlier.

Parallel LCR circuit

Consider parallel LCR parallel circuit as shown in *fig. 9.29*.

We have,

$$i_R = \frac{V_0}{R}$$

$$i_L = \frac{V_0}{X_L}$$

$$i_C = \frac{V_0}{X_C}$$

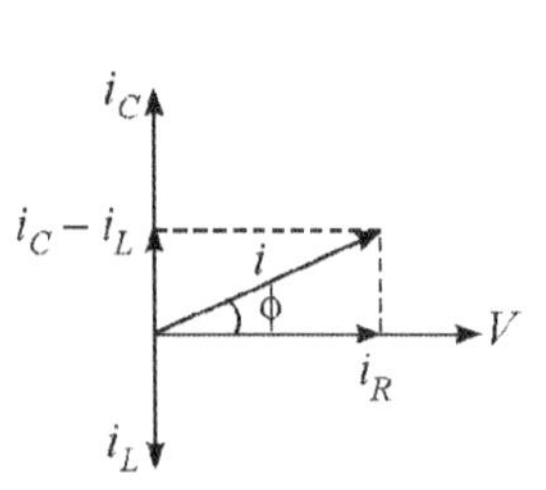

Phasor diagram

From phasor diagram

$$i = \sqrt{i_R^2 + (i_C - i_L)^2}$$

and

$$\tan\phi = \left(\frac{i_C - i_L}{i_R}\right)$$

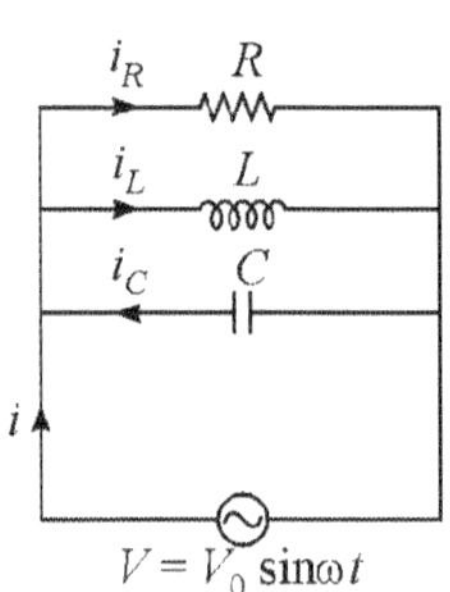

Fig. 9.29

Admittance (A) :

$$\frac{V_0}{Z} = \sqrt{\left(\frac{V_0}{R}\right)^2 + \left(\frac{V_0}{X_C} - \frac{V_0}{X_L}\right)^2}$$

or

$$\frac{1}{Z} = \sqrt{\left(\frac{1}{R}\right)^2 + \left(\omega C \sim \frac{1}{\omega L}\right)^2}$$

Current

$$i = \frac{V}{Z} = V\sqrt{\left(\frac{1}{R}\right)^2 + \left(\omega C - \frac{1}{\omega L}\right)^2}$$

At,

$$\omega = 0, i = \infty$$

$$\omega = \omega_0, \ i_{min} = \frac{V}{R}$$

$$\omega = \infty, i = \infty$$

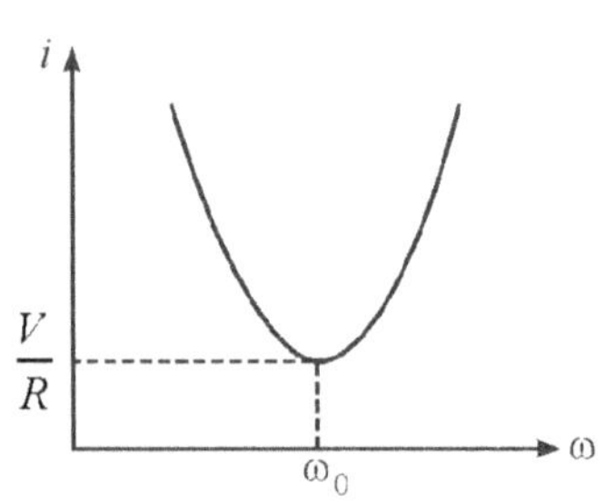

Fig. 9.30

Power

$$P = \frac{V^2}{Z} = V^2\left[\sqrt{\left(\frac{1}{R}\right)^2 + \left(\omega C - \frac{1}{\omega L}\right)^2}\right]$$

At,

$$\omega = 0, P = \infty$$

$$\omega = \omega_0, \ P_{min} = \frac{V^2}{R}$$

$$\omega = \infty, P = \infty$$

Resonance :

$$\phi = 0$$

$$i_C = i_L \text{ gives } i_{min} = i_R$$

or

$$\omega C = \frac{1}{\omega L}$$

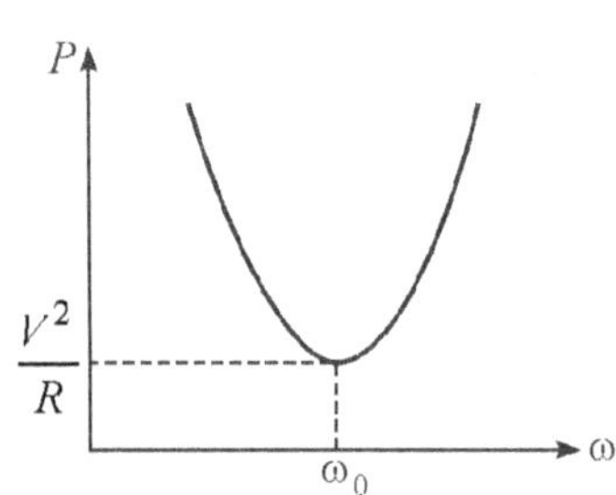

Fig. 9.31

$$\Rightarrow \quad \omega = \sqrt{\frac{1}{LC}} = \omega_0$$

or

$$f = \frac{1}{2\pi}\sqrt{\frac{1}{LC}}.$$

Use of operator j in AC circuits

In complicated ac circuits, the use of the operator j is of very great importance. In Cartesian form, a phasor A can be written as,

$$A = a + jb$$

where a is the x-component and b is the y-component of phasor $\vec{A}$.

The value of

$$j = \sqrt{-1}, \therefore j^2 = -1, j^3 = -j, \text{ and } j^4 = 1$$

From the geometry

$$A = \sqrt{a^2 + b^2}$$

and

$$\tan\phi = \frac{b}{a}$$

By using j operator we can write X_L and X_C in the following manner.

$$X_L = j\omega L$$

and

$$X_C = -j\left(\frac{1}{\omega C}\right)$$

$$= \frac{-j \times j}{j}\left(\frac{1}{\omega C}\right)$$

or

$$X_C = \frac{1}{j\omega C}$$

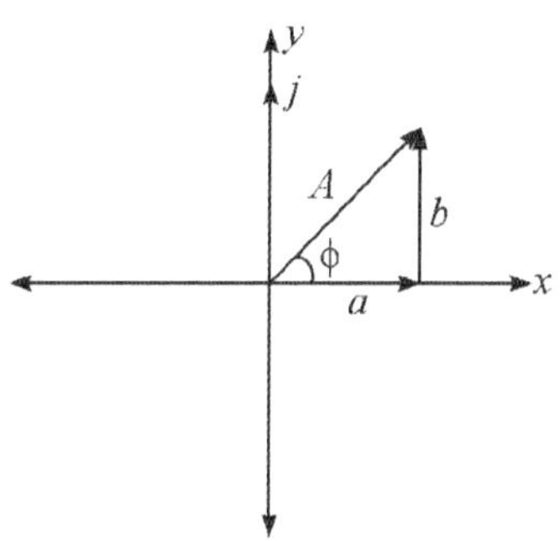

Fig. 9.32

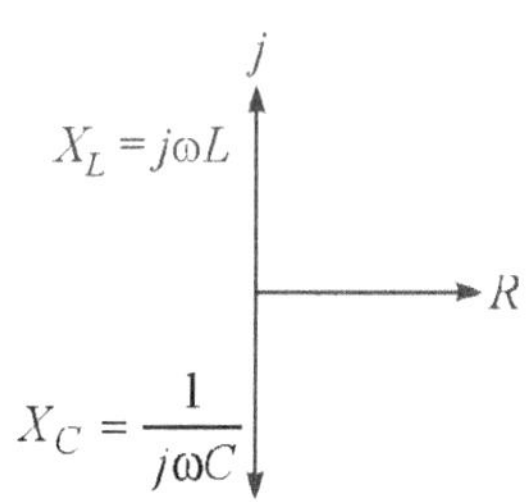

Fig. 9.33

Parallel circuit (Rejector circuit)

Let us consider an ac source is connected across an inductance L in parallel with C. The resistance in series with the inductance is R. Let the instantaneous value of potential be V and the corresponding current be i, the current through the inductance be i_L and through the capacitance be i_C. These currents i_L and i_C will be almost in opposite phase if R is very small. The total current,

$$i = i_L + i_C$$

or

$$\frac{V}{Z} = \frac{V}{(R + j\omega L)} + \frac{V}{\dfrac{1}{j\omega C}}$$

or

$$\frac{1}{Z} = \frac{1}{(R + j\omega L)} + j\omega C$$

or

$$A = \frac{1}{Z} = \frac{(R - j\omega L)}{(R + j\omega L)(R - j\omega L)} + j\omega C$$

$$= \frac{(R - j\omega L)}{(R^2 + \omega^2 L^2)} + j\omega C$$

$$= \frac{R + j\left(\omega CR^2 + \omega^3 L^2 C - \omega L\right)}{R^2 + \omega^2 L^2}$$

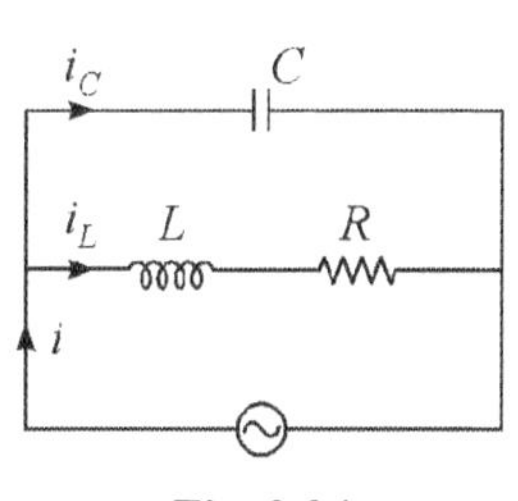

Fig. 9.34

$\therefore$ The magnitude of the admittance

$$A = \frac{1}{Z} = \frac{\sqrt{R^2 + \left(\omega CR^2 + \omega^3 L^2 C - \omega L\right)^2}}{R^2 + \omega^2 L^2}$$

For resonance, i will be in phase with V, if j component of A becomes zero. i.e.,

$$\omega CR^2 + \omega^3 L^2 C - \omega L = 0$$

or

$$\omega = \omega_0 = \sqrt{\frac{1}{LC} - \frac{R^2}{L^2}}$$

At resonance, Z will be maximum. It will be

$$Z = \frac{R^2 + \omega^2 L^2}{R}, \text{ is called dynamic resistance}$$

$$= \frac{R^2 + L^2\left(\frac{1}{LC} - \frac{R^2}{L^2}\right)}{R} = \frac{L}{CR}$$

At resonance the peak current from supply is, known as make up current, which is

$$i = \frac{V_0}{Z} = \frac{V_0}{\left(\dfrac{L}{CR}\right)}$$

or

$$i = \frac{CRV_0}{L}$$

For the values of L, C, R and ω satisfying the equation $\omega = \sqrt{\left(\dfrac{1}{LC} - \dfrac{R^2}{L^2}\right)}$, the reactive

component of A is real. At such a maximum impedance, the current in the circuit is minimum. Thus the parallel circuit does not allow this frequency from the source to pass through the circuit. Due to this reason the circuit with such a frequency is known as a **rejector circuit**.

Ex. 7 (a) In a circuit containing a capacitor and an AC source, the current is zero at the instant the source voltage is maximum. It is consistent with ohm's law ?

(b) Can you have an AC series circuit in which there is a phase difference of 180° between potential and current.

(c) Is rms value of alternating current can equal to peak value of current ?

Sol.

(a) No. (b) No. (c) Yes, in a square wave.

Ex. 8 A series circuit contains a resistance of 4Ω, an inductance of 0.5 H and a variable capacitor across a 100 V, 50 Hz supply. Find
(a) the capacitance for getting resonance,
(b) p.d. across inductance and capacitance
(c) the Q-factor of the series circuit.

Sol.

(a) For resonance $X_L = X_C$

or

$$\omega L = \frac{1}{\omega C}$$

$\therefore$

$$C = \frac{1}{\omega^2 L} = \frac{1}{(2\pi f)^2 L}$$

$$= \frac{1}{(2 \times \pi \times 50)^2 \times 0.5} = 20.3 \times 10^{-6} \, F$$

Ans.

(b) Current at resonance $= \dfrac{100}{4} = 25 \, A$

P.d. across inductor or capacitor

$$V_L = V_C = iX_L = 25 \, (2\pi \times 50 \times 0.5)$$
$$= 3925 \, V \qquad \qquad Ans.$$

(c) Q-factor $= \dfrac{\omega_0 L}{R}$

$$= \dfrac{(2\pi \times 50) \times 0.5}{4}$$

$$= 39.25 \qquad \textit{Ans.}$$

Ex. 9 An ac source of angular frequency ω is fied across a resistor R and a capacitor C is series. The current registered is i. If now the frequency of the source is changed to $\omega/3$ (but maintaining the same voltage), the current in the circuit is found to be halved. Calculate the ratio of reactance to resistance at the original frequency.

Sol. At angular frequency ω, the current in CR-circuit is given by

$$i_{rms} = \dfrac{V_{rms}}{\sqrt{R^2 + \left(\dfrac{1}{\omega C}\right)^2}} \qquad ...(i)$$

When frequency becomes $\omega/3$,

$$\dfrac{i_{rms}}{2} = \dfrac{V_{rms}}{\sqrt{R^2 + \left(\dfrac{1}{\dfrac{\omega C}{3}}\right)^2}} \qquad ...(ii)$$

From equations (i) and (ii), we get

$$3R^2 = \dfrac{5}{(\omega C)^2}$$

The ratio $\quad \dfrac{1/\omega C}{R} = \sqrt{\dfrac{3}{5}} \qquad \textit{Ans.}$

Ex. 10 In inductor-coil, a capacitor an AC source of rms voltage 24V are connected in series. When the frequency of the source is varied, a maximum rms current of 6.0 A is observed. If the inductor coil is connected to a battery of emf 12 V and internal resistance 4.0 Ω, what will be the current ?

Sol.

The maximum current will occur at resonance in series circuit, which is

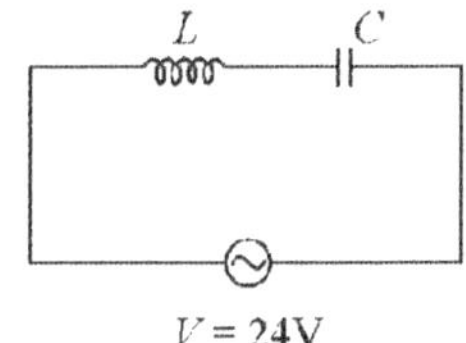

Fig. 9.35

$$i = \dfrac{V}{Z}$$

or $\quad Z = \dfrac{V}{i} = \dfrac{24}{6} = 4\,\Omega$

The impedance of the circuit = $4\,\Omega$. Now if this coil is connected to a battery of 12 V and internal resistance $4\,\Omega$, the impedance of circuit become, $Z' = 4 + 4 = 8\,\Omega$

$$\therefore \quad i' = \dfrac{V'}{Z'} = \dfrac{12}{8} = 1.5\,A \qquad \textit{Ans.}$$

Ex. 11 A circuit draws a power of 550 watt from a source of 220 volt, 50 hertz. The power factor of the circuit is 0.8 and the current lags in phase behind the potential difference. To make the power factor to the circuit as 1.0, what capacitance will have to be connected with it ?

Sol. The impedance of the circuit

$$Z = \dfrac{V^2}{P} = \dfrac{220^2}{550} = 88$$

or $\quad R^2 + (\omega L)^2 = 88^2$

or $\quad R^2 + (100\pi L)^2 = 88^2 \qquad ...(1)$

and $\quad \cos\phi = \dfrac{R}{Z}$

or $\quad 0.8 = \dfrac{R}{88}$

$\therefore \quad R = 70.4\,\Omega$

From (1), we get

$$\omega L = 42.2\,\Omega$$

For power factor to be 1, the resistor remain effective

$\therefore \quad \cos\phi = 1$

which gives $\quad \omega L = \dfrac{1}{\omega C}$

$$C = \dfrac{1}{\omega(\omega L)}$$

$$= \dfrac{1}{(2\pi \times 50) \times 42.2}$$

$$= 7.5 \times 10^{-5}\,F$$

$$= 75\,\mu F \qquad \textit{Ans.}$$

So capacitor of capacitance $75\,\mu F$ should be connected in series in the circuit.

Ex. 12 A box contains L, C and R. When 250 dc is applied to the terminals of the box, a current of 1.0 A flows in the circuit. When an ac source of 250 V rms at 2250 rad/s is connected, a current of 1.25 A rms flows. It is observed that the current rises with frequency and becomes maximum at 4500 rad/s. Find the values of L, C and R. Draw the circuit diagram.

Sol. When dc is used in the circuit, only resistor remain effective

$$\therefore \quad R = \dfrac{V}{i} = \dfrac{250}{1} = 250\,\Omega \qquad ...(i)$$

When dc is used, there is current in the circuit it means capacitor must not be in series. It may be in parallel to resistor together with inductor.

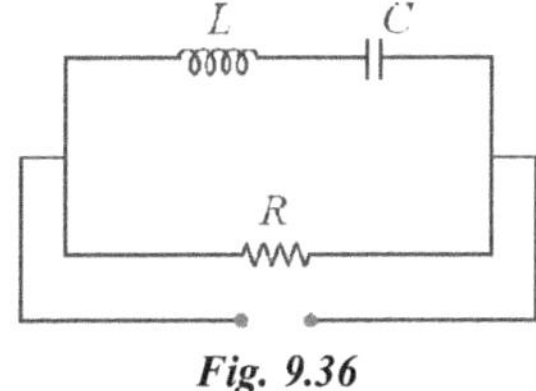

Fig. 9.36

When ac source is used in the circuit, all the circuit element remain effective.

$$\therefore \qquad Z = \frac{V}{i} = \frac{250}{1.25} = 200 \, \Omega$$

or

$$\frac{1}{R^2} + \frac{1}{\left(\omega L - \dfrac{1}{\omega C}\right)^2} = \frac{1}{Z^2} = \frac{1}{200^2} \qquad ...(ii)$$

With increase of frequency, current increases and becomes maximum at ω = 4500 rad/s. It means Z must be minimum. It will when

$$\omega L - \frac{1}{\omega C} = 0$$

or

$$\omega^2 = \frac{1}{LC}$$

or

$$LC = \frac{1}{\omega^2} = \frac{1}{(4500)^2} \qquad ...(iii)$$

After solving equations (i), (ii) and (iii), we get

$$L = \frac{4}{81} H$$

and $\qquad C = 1 \, \mu F \qquad\qquad$ *Ans.*

Ex. 13 In *RLC* series circuit, assume $R = 500 \, \Omega$, $L = 60.0$ mH, $f = 60.0$ Hz, and $V_0 = 30.0$ V. For what values of the capacitance would the average rate at which energy is dissipated in the resistor be (a) a maximum and (b) a minimum ? (c) what are these maximum and minimum energy dissipation rates ? What are (d) the corresponding phase angles and (e) the corresponding power factor ?

Sol. (a) In series *RLC* circuit maximum power is dissipated at resonance.

At resonance $\quad \omega_0 = \sqrt{\dfrac{1}{LC}}$

or $\qquad C = \dfrac{1}{\omega^2 L} = \dfrac{1}{(2\pi \times 60)^2 \times \left(60 \times 10^{-3}\right)}$

$$= 117 \, \mu F$$

and $\qquad P_0 = \dfrac{V_0^2}{2R} = \dfrac{30^2}{2 \times 5} = 90 \, W \qquad$ *Ans.*

(b) We have, $\quad P_{av} = \dfrac{P_0 \, R^2}{R^2 + \left(\omega L - \dfrac{1}{\omega C}\right)^2}$

P_{av} will be minimum, when C is zero that is $P_{av} = 0$ *Ans.*

(c) $P_0 = 90$ W, and $P_m = 0$ $\qquad\qquad$ *Ans.*

(d) Phase angles :

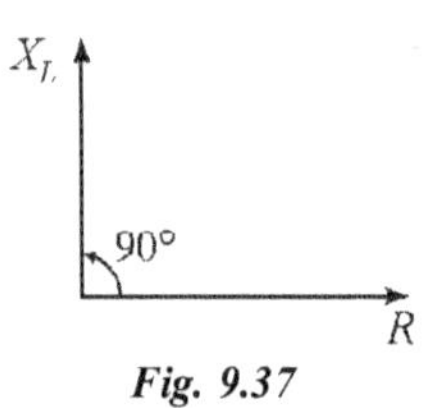

Fig. 9.37

At resonance, $\qquad \phi = 0$

At min^m P_{av}, $\qquad \phi = 90°$

(e) Power factor :

for $\qquad\qquad \phi = 0, \cos\phi = 1$

for $\qquad\qquad \phi = 90°, \cos\phi = 0$

Ex. 14 A circuit with $R = 70 \, \Omega$ in series with a parallel combination of $L = 1.5$ H and $C = 30 \, \mu F$ is driven by a 230 V supply of angular frequency 300 rad/s.

(i) Find the impedance of the circuit.

(ii) What is the rms value of total current ?

(iii) What are the current amplitudes in the L and C arms of the circuit ?

(iv) Find the total power input to the circuit and power factor.

(v) How will the circuit behave if $\omega = \dfrac{1}{\sqrt{LC}}$?

Sol. 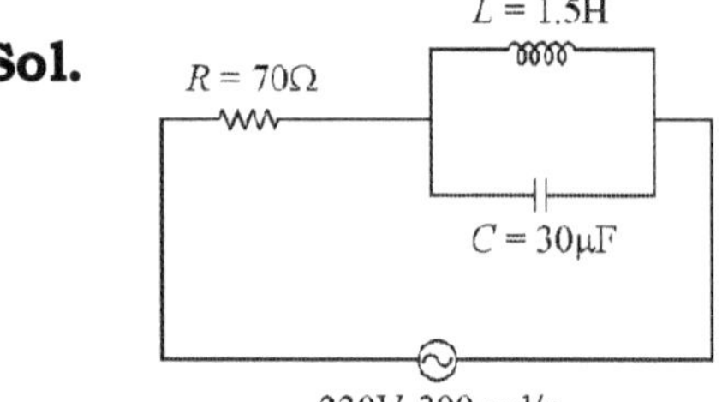

Fig. 9.38

The resultant impedance of L and C in parallel

$$\frac{1}{Z_1} = \frac{1}{X_L} + \frac{1}{X_C}$$

$$= \frac{1}{j\omega L} + \frac{1}{\left(\dfrac{1}{j\omega C}\right)} = \frac{1}{j\omega L} + j\omega C$$

$$= \frac{1 - \omega^2 LC}{j\omega L}$$

$$\therefore \qquad Z_1 = \frac{j\omega L}{1 - \omega^2 LC}$$

The total impedance of the circuit

$$Z = R + Z_1 = R + \frac{j\omega L}{\left(1 - \omega^2 LC\right)}$$

$$\therefore \qquad |Z| = \sqrt{R^2 + \left(\frac{\omega L}{1 - \omega^2 LC}\right)^2}$$

(i) Given, $R = 70 \, \Omega$, $L = 1.5$ H, $C = 30 \times 10^{-6} \, F$ and $\omega = 300$ rad/s.

$$\therefore \qquad Z = \sqrt{70^2 + \left(\frac{300 \times 1.5}{1 - 300^2 \times 1.5 \times 30 \times 10^{-6}}\right)^2}$$

$$= 163.3 \, \Omega \qquad\qquad \text{\textit{Ans.}}$$

(ii) $\qquad i_{rms} = \dfrac{V_{rms}}{Z} = \dfrac{230}{163.3} = 1.41\,A$ *Ans.*

(iii) If i_L and i_C are the currents in inductor and capacitor respectively, then

$$i_L + i_C = i_{rms} \qquad ...(i)$$

and $\qquad X_L\, i_L = X_C\, i_C \qquad ...(ii)$

On solving above equations, we have

$$i_L = \dfrac{X_C}{X_L + X_C}\, i_{rms}$$

and $\qquad i_C = \dfrac{X_L}{X_L + X_C}\, i_{rms}$

Again $\qquad i_L = \dfrac{\left(\dfrac{1}{j\omega C}\right)}{j\omega L + \dfrac{1}{j\omega C}}\, i_{rms} = \dfrac{i_{rms}}{1 - \omega^2 LC}$

$$= \dfrac{1.41}{1 - 300^2 \times 1.5 \times 30 \times 10^{-6}} = 0.46\,A$$

$$i_C = \dfrac{j\omega L}{\left(j\omega L + \dfrac{1}{j\omega C}\right)} = \dfrac{\left(\omega^2 LC\right) i_{rms}}{\omega^2 LC - 1}$$

$$= \dfrac{\left(300^2 \times 1.5 \times 30 \times 10^{-6}\right) \times 1.41}{300^2 \times 1.5 \times 30 \times 10^{-6} - 1}$$

$$= 1.87\,A$$

(iv) Power factor $\quad \cos\phi = \dfrac{R}{Z} = \dfrac{70}{163.3} = 0.43$ *Ans.*

(v) When $\qquad \omega = \dfrac{1}{\sqrt{LC}};\ \text{or}\ \omega^2 LC = 1$

Now $\qquad Z = \dfrac{j\omega L}{1 - \omega^2 LC} = \dfrac{j\omega L}{1 - 1} = \infty,\ \text{and so, } i = 0$

    Ans.

Ex. 15 In the circuit shown in *fig. 9.39*, the voltage applied is 100 V. Find the current in each branch, voltage drop across each branch, the power factor and the power supplied by the line to the circuit.

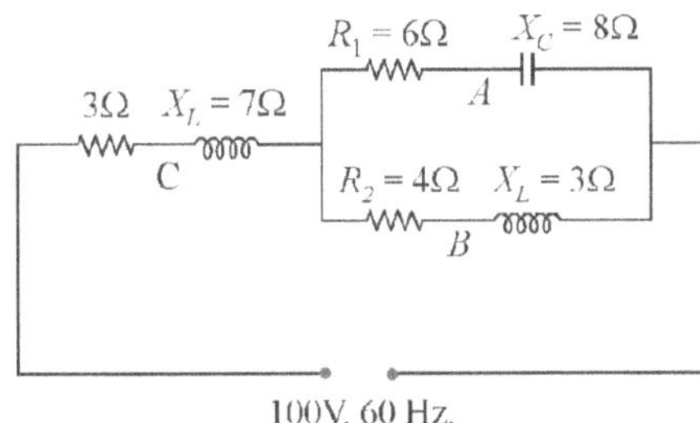

Fig. 9.39

Sol. If Z_A and Z_B are the impedances of the branches A and B respectively, then their combined impedance

$$Z_{AB} = \dfrac{Z_A Z_B}{Z_A + Z_B}$$

Here $\qquad Z_A = (6 - 8j)$ and $Z_B = 4 + 3j$

$\therefore \qquad Z_{AB} = \dfrac{(6-8j)(4+3j)}{(6-8j)+(4+3j)} = \dfrac{48 - 14j}{10 - 5j}$

$$= \dfrac{(48-14j)}{(10-5j)}\dfrac{(10+5j)}{(10+5j)} = \dfrac{550 + 100j}{125}$$

$$= 4.4 + 0.8j$$

The impedance of the branch C,

$$Z_C = 3 + 7j$$

Thus total impedance of the circuit

$$Z = Z_{AB} + Z_C$$
$$= (4.4 + 0.8j) + (3 + 7j)$$
$$= 7.4 + 7.8j$$

$$|Z| = \sqrt{(7.4)^2 + (7.8)^2}$$

Total current $\qquad i_0 = \dfrac{V_0}{Z}$

$$= \dfrac{100}{(7.4 + 7.8j)}$$

$$= \dfrac{100(7.4 - 7.8j)}{(7.4 + 7.8j)(7.4 - 7.8j)}$$

$$= \dfrac{740 - 780j}{54.76 + 60.84} = \dfrac{740 - 780j}{115.6}$$

$$= 6.4 - 6.74j$$

Current lags behind the applied voltage by

$$\tan\phi = \dfrac{6.74}{6.4}\ or\ \phi \approx 45°$$

The actual value of the current

$$i_C = \sqrt{(6.4)^2 + (6.74)^2}$$

$$= 9.3\,A$$

Voltage drop across branch C

$$= V_C = I_C Z_C$$
$$= (6.4 - 6.74j) \times (3 + 7j)$$
$$= 66.38 + 24.58j$$

or $\qquad |V_C| = \sqrt{66.38^2 + 24.58^2} = 70.8\,V$

Voltage drop across AB,

$$V_{AB} = 100 - V_C$$
$$= 100 - 70.8 = 29.2\,V.$$

From the figure

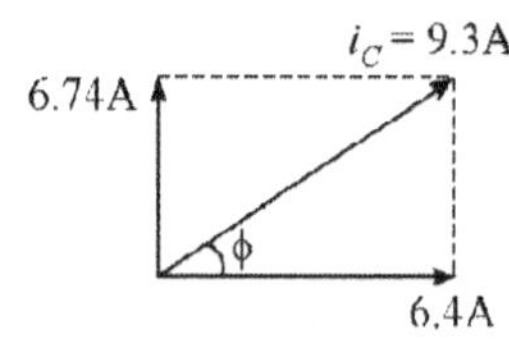

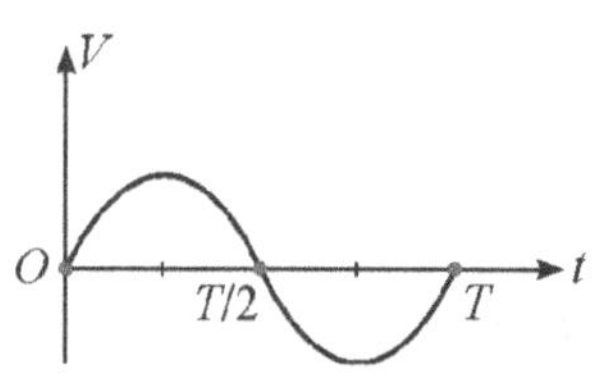

Fig. 9.40

$$\cos\phi = \frac{6.4}{9.3} = 0.69$$

Thus power

$$= V_0\, i_0\, \cos\phi$$
$$= 100 \times 9.3 \times 0.69$$
$$= 641.7\,W \qquad \textbf{\textit{Ans.}}$$

 **Note:**

1. When a value is given for alternating current or voltage, it is ordinarily the rms value.

2. The power rating of an element used in ac circuits refers to its average value not rms.

3. Though in a phasor diagram, voltage and current are represented by vectors, but these quantities are not really vectors themselves. They are scalar quanties.

4. Only resistor is the dissipative element and so no power losses associated with pure inductances or capacitances.

5. A transformer (step-up) changes a low-voltage into a high voltage. The current is reduced by the same proportion. This does not violate the law of conservation of energy.

Ex. 16 In LR series circuit, a sinusoidal $V = V_0\sin\omega t$ is applied.

It is given that $L = 35\ mH$, $R = 11\ \Omega$, $V_{rms} = 220\ V$, $\dfrac{\omega}{2\pi} = 50$Hz and

$\pi = \dfrac{22}{7}$. Find the amplitude of current is steady state and obtain

the phase difference between the current and the voltage. Also plot the variation of current for one cycle on the given graph.

Fig. 9.41

Sol.   The impedance of the circuit is given by

$$Z = \sqrt{R^2 + X_L^2}$$

where $\qquad X_L = \omega L = 2\pi \times 50 \times 35 \times 10^{-3}$
$$= 11\Omega$$

$$\therefore \qquad Z = \sqrt{11^2 + 11^2} = 11\sqrt{2}\ \Omega$$

Voltage amplitude $\quad V_0 = \sqrt{2}\,V_{rms}$

$$= \sqrt{2} \times 220\,V.$$

Current amplitude $\quad i_0 = \dfrac{V_0}{Z} = \dfrac{\sqrt{2} \times 220}{11\sqrt{2}}$

$$= 20\,A$$

If ϕ is the phase between V and i, then

$$\tan\phi = \frac{\omega L}{R} = \frac{11}{11} = 1$$

$$\therefore \qquad \phi = \frac{\pi}{4}\,rad.$$

Thus we can write

$$V = 220\sqrt{2}\,\sin\omega t$$

and $\qquad i = 20\sin\left(\omega t - \dfrac{\pi}{4}\right)$

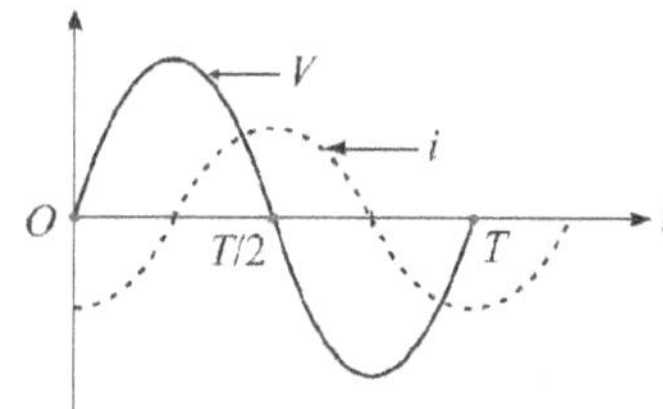

Fig. 9.42 Variation of V and i with time

9.10 ELECTROMAGNETIC WAVES

The idea of electromagnetic waves was proposed by Maxwell in 1864. The wave equation for light propagating in x-direction in vacuum may be written as

$$E = E_0\sin(kx - \omega t)$$

where E is the sinusoidally varying electric field.

The electric field E is in the yz- plane, that is perpendicular to direction of propagation of wave.

There is also a sinusoidally varying magnetic field associated with the electric field when light propagates. This magnetic field is perpendicular to both electric field and direction of propagation of wave. The magnetic field

$$B = B_0\sin(kx - \omega t)$$

Such a combination of mutually perpendicular electric and magnetic fields can represent an electromagnetic wave in vacuum.

More about displacement current

According to Kirchhoff's junction rule, for a conducting circuit, in the steady state, the total current into any given portion must be equal to the current out of that portion. But this rule is not obeyed for a capacitor that is being charged. In *fig. 9.43* there is a conduction current into the left plate but there is no conduction current out of this plate; similarly, there is conduction current out of the right plate, but not into it.

According to Maxwell, as the capacitor charges, the conduction current increases the charge on each plate, and this in turn increases the electric field between the plate. Because of the changing electric field there is a current between the plates, is called displacement current (i_d): A current without movement of electrons. For any charge density σ, electric field between the plates of capacitor

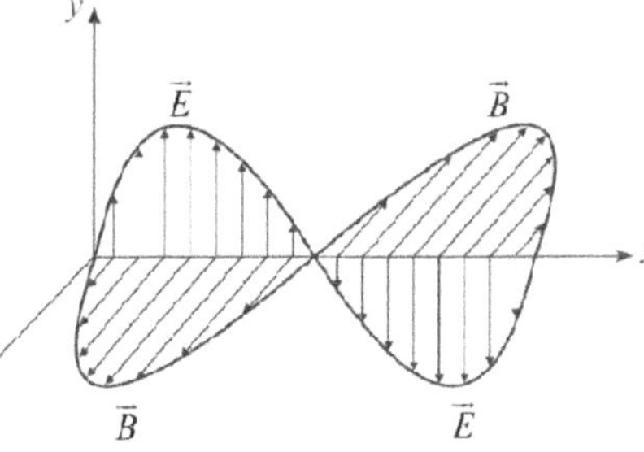

Fig. 9.43

$$E = \frac{\sigma}{\epsilon_0} = \frac{q}{A\,\epsilon_0}$$

$$\text{or}\quad q = \epsilon_0\, EA$$

$$= \epsilon_0\, \phi_E$$

And displacement current

$$i_d = \frac{dq}{dt} = \frac{d(\epsilon_0\, \phi_E)}{dt}$$

$$\text{or}\quad i_d = \epsilon_0\, \frac{d\phi_E}{dt}$$

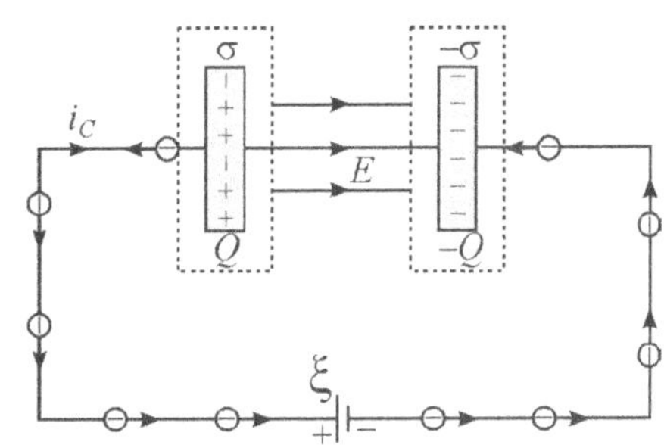

Fig. 9.44

Note: The current due to the flow of charges is often called conduction current.

Generalised Ampere's law :

It was James Clerk Maxwell who generalised Ampere's law. According to him, if there exists an electric current as well as a changing electric field, then Ampere's law can be written as:

$$\oint \vec{B}\cdot d\vec{\ell} = \mu_0\left(i_c + i_d\right)$$

$$\text{or}\quad \oint \vec{B}\cdot d\vec{\ell} = \mu_0\left(i_c + \epsilon_0\,\frac{d\phi_E}{dt}\right)$$

$$= \mu_0 i_c + \mu_0\,\epsilon_0\left[\frac{d\phi_E}{dt}\right]$$

In vacuum, $i_c = 0$ therefore

$$\oint \vec{B}\cdot d\vec{\ell} = \mu_0\,\epsilon_0\left[\frac{d\phi_E}{dt}\right]$$

Maxwell's equations :

Maxwell discovered that all the basic principles of electromagnetism can be formulated in terms of four fundamental equations called Maxwell's equations. They are

(1)   Gauss's law for electricity

$$\oint \vec{E}\cdot d\vec{A} = \frac{q_{in}}{\epsilon_0} \qquad \text{...(1)}$$

(2)   Gauss's law for magnetism

$$\oint \vec{B}\cdot d\vec{A} = 0 \qquad \text{...(2)}$$

(3)   Faraday's law of induction

$$\oint \vec{E}\cdot d\vec{\ell} \;=\; -\frac{d\phi_B}{dt} \qquad\qquad ...(3)$$

(4)   Ampere's law $\oint \vec{B}\cdot d\vec{\ell} \;=\; \mu_0\left(i_c + \epsilon_0\,\dfrac{d\phi_E}{dt} \right) \qquad ...(4)$

Faraday's law

$$\oint \vec{E}\cdot d\vec{\ell} \;=\; -\frac{d\phi_B}{dt}.$$

Consider a rectangular path *abcd* in the *xy*- plane as shown in *fig. 9.44*. The electric field is parallel to *y*-axis and magnetic field is parallel to *z*-axis. The circulation of $\vec{E}$ over the close path abcd,

$$\oint \vec{E}\cdot d\vec{\ell} \;=\; (E+dE)h - Eh$$
$$= hdE \qquad\qquad ...(i)$$

And the magnetic flux through rectangle,
$$\phi_B \;=\; B\,(hdx)$$

Differentiating, we get $\dfrac{d\phi_B}{dt} \;=\; hdx\,\dfrac{dB}{dt} \qquad\qquad ...(ii)$

Now from equations (1), (i) and (ii), we have

$$hdE \;=\; -hdx\,\frac{dB}{dt}$$

or $$\frac{dE}{dx} \;=\; -\frac{dB}{dt}$$

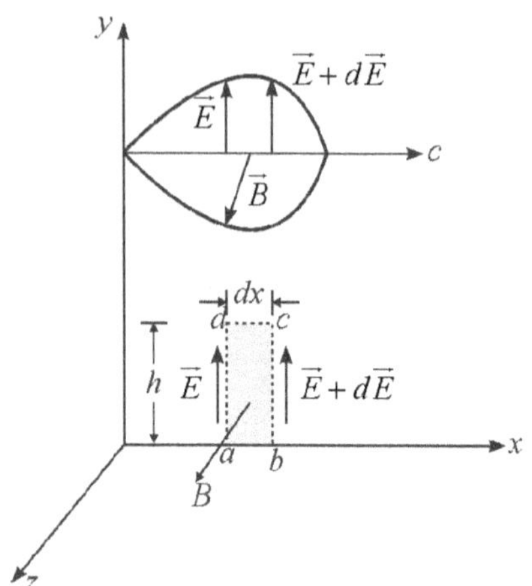

Fig. 9.45

or $$\frac{d\left[E_0 \sin\left(kx - \omega t \right) \right]}{dx} \;=\; -\frac{d}{dt}\left[B_0 \sin\left(kx - \omega t \right) \right]$$

$$E_0 k \cos\left(kx - \omega t \right) \;=\; B_0 \omega \cos\left(kx - \omega t \right)$$

or $$E_0 \;=\; \left(\frac{\omega}{k}\right) B_0$$

or $$E_0 \;=\; cB_0. \qquad\qquad ...(5)$$

where $\dfrac{\omega}{k} = c$, speed of the light wave.

Ampere's law $\oint \vec{B}\cdot d\vec{\ell} \;=\; \epsilon_0\,\mu_0\,\dfrac{d\phi_E}{dt} \qquad ...(2)$

Consider the rectangular path *efgh* in the *xz*- plane as shown in *fig. 9.45*. The circulation of $\vec{B}$ is

$$\oint \vec{B}\cdot d\vec{\ell} \;=\; Bh - (B+dB)$$
$$= -h\,dB \qquad\qquad ...(i)$$

The magnetic flux through the rectangle is
$$\phi_E \;=\; E\,(h\,dx)$$

On differentation gives

$$\frac{d\phi_E}{dt} \;=\; h\,dx\,\frac{dE}{dt} \qquad\qquad ...(ii)$$

Now from equations (2), (i) and (ii), we have

$$-h\,dB \;=\; \epsilon_0\,\mu_0\,h\,dx\,\frac{dE}{dt}$$

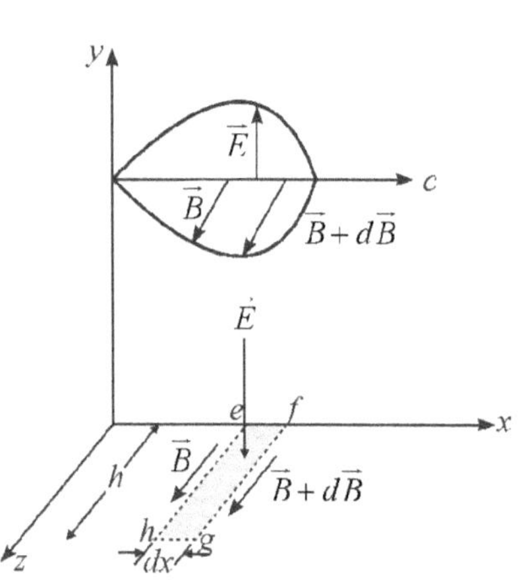

Fig. 9.46

or
$$-\frac{dB}{dx} = \epsilon_0 \mu_0 \frac{dE}{dt}$$

or
$$-\frac{d}{dx}\left[B_0 \sin\left(kx - \omega t\right)\right] = \epsilon_0 \mu_0 \frac{d}{dt}\left[E_0 \sin\left(kx - \omega t\right)\right]$$

or
$$-kB_0 \cos\left(kx - \omega t\right) = \epsilon_0 \mu_0 E_0 \left(-\omega\right)\cos\left(kx - \omega t\right)$$

or
$$B_0 = \left(\frac{\omega}{k}\right)\epsilon_0 \mu_0 E_0$$

or
$$\frac{E_0}{B_0} \times \frac{\omega}{k} = \frac{1}{\epsilon_0 \mu_0}$$

or
$$c \times c = \frac{1}{\epsilon_0 \mu_0}$$

or
$$c = \sqrt{\frac{1}{\epsilon_0 \mu_0}} . \qquad \ldots(6)$$

9.11 Poynting vector

The rate of energy transport per unit area in such a wave is described by a vector $\vec{S}$, called the Poynting vector after John Henry Poynting, who first discussed its properties. $\vec{S}$ is defined as

$$\vec{S} = \frac{1}{\mu_0}\left[\vec{E} \times \vec{B}\right] = \vec{E} \times \vec{H} . \qquad \ldots(7)$$

Its SI unit is W/m^2.

Energy transport

Figure shows a travelling wave, along with a thin box of thickness dx and area A. At any instant the energy stored in the box is

$$\begin{aligned}
dU &= du_E + du_B \\
&= (u_E + u_B)(A\,dx) \\
&= (u_E + u_B)\,dV
\end{aligned}$$

or
$$\frac{dU}{dV} = u_E + u_B$$

$$= \frac{1}{2}\epsilon_0 E^2 + \frac{B^2}{2\mu_0}$$

$$= \frac{1}{2}\epsilon_0 \left[E_0 \sin\left(kx - \omega t\right)\right]^2 + \frac{1}{2\mu_0}\left[B_0 \sin\left(kx - \omega t\right)\right]^2$$

$$= \frac{1}{2}\epsilon_0 E_0^{\,2} \sin^2\left(kx - \omega t\right) + \frac{B_0^{\,2}}{2\mu_0}\sin^2\left(kx - \omega t\right)$$

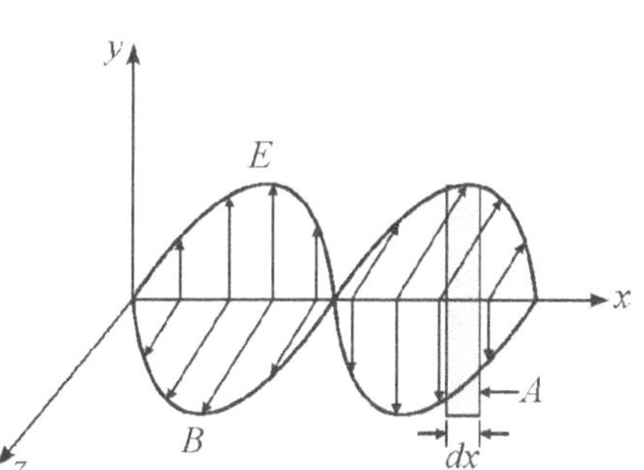

Fig. 9.47

The average of $\sin^2\left(kx - \omega t\right)$ over one complete cycle is $\frac{1}{2}$.

Therefore
$$u_{av} = \frac{dU}{dV} = \frac{1}{4}\epsilon_0 E_0^{\,2} + \frac{B_0^{\,2}}{4\mu_0} \qquad \ldots(8)$$

$$E_0 = cB_0 \text{ and } c = \sqrt{\frac{1}{\mu_0 \, \epsilon_0}}$$

$$\therefore \quad u_{av} = \frac{1}{2} \epsilon_0 E_0^2 = \frac{B_0^2}{2\mu_0}. \qquad ....(9)$$

Intensity of wave

The energy crossing per unit area per unit time perpendicular to the direction of propagation is called the intensity of wave. From above figure we have

$$dx = cdt$$

Energy contained
$$U = u_{av}(dV) = u_{av}(A\,dx)$$
$$= u_{av}\,Acdt$$

$\therefore$ The intensity
$$I = \frac{U}{Adt} = u_{av}c$$

or
$$I = \frac{1}{2} \epsilon_0 E_0^2 c. \qquad ....(10)$$

Momentum :

The electromagnetic wave also carries momentum with it. The momentum carried by the portion of wave having energy U is gives by

$$P = \frac{U}{c}.$$

9.12 ELECTROMAGNETIC SPECTRUM

Maxwell predicted the existence of electromagnetic waves. The only familiar electromagnetic waves were visible light waves. By the end of nineteenth century, X-rays and gamma rays had also been discovered. We know now were electromagnetic waves include infrared waves, visible light waves, X-rays, gamma-rays, radio waves, microwaves, and ultraviolet waves. Their classification according to frequency is called the electromagnetic spectrum.

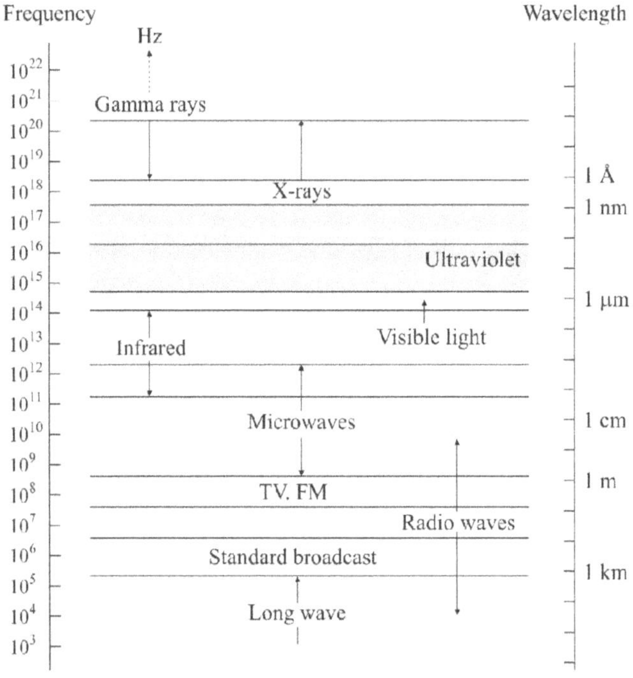

Fig.9.48 The electromagnetic spectrum. Note the overlap between one type of wave and the next. There is no sharp division between the different regions of em spectrum.

Ex. 17 A plane electromagnetic wave of frequency 25 MHz travels in free space along the *x*-direction. At a particular point in the space and time, $\vec{E} = 6.3\mathbf{j}$ V/m. What is $\vec{B}$ at this point ?

Sol. The magnitude of the magnetic field is given by

$$B = \frac{E}{c} = \frac{6.3}{3 \times 10^8} = 2.1 \times 10^{-8}\ T.$$

The vector $\vec{E} \times \vec{B}$ should be along *x*-direction, and so

$$\hat{j} \times (\hat{A}) = \hat{i}, \text{ indicates that } \hat{A} = \hat{k}.$$

Thus $\qquad \vec{B} = 2.1 \times 10^{-8}\ \hat{k}\ T.$ $\qquad$ ***Ans.***

Ex. 18 A light beam travelling in the *x*-direction is described by the electric field $E_y = (300\ \text{V/m}) \sin\omega\left(t - \dfrac{x}{C}\right)$. An electron is constrained to move along the *y*-direction with a speed of 2.0×10^7 m/s. Find the maximum electric force and the maximum magnetic force on the electron.

Sol.
The maximum value of electric field is 300 V/m. Therefore the maximum electric force

$$\begin{aligned}
F_e &= qE_0 = 1.6 \times 10^{-19} \times 300 \\
&= 4.8 \times 10^{-17}\ \text{N}
\end{aligned}$$

The maximum magnetic field

$$B_0 = \frac{E_0}{c} = \frac{300}{3 \times 10^8} = 10^{-8}\ T$$

The maximum magnetic force on electron

$$\begin{aligned}
F_m &= qvB_0 \\
&= \left(1.6 \times 10^{-19}\right) \times \left(2.0 \times 10^7\right) \times 10^{-8} \\
&= 3.2 \times 10^{-18}\ N.
\end{aligned}$$

Ex. 19 Calculate the electric and magnetic fields produced by the radiation coming from a 100 watt bulb at a distance of 3 m. Assume that the efficiency of the bulb is 2.5% and it is a point source.

Sol. Bulb radiates energy uniformly in all direction. At a distance of 3 m from the bulb, the surface area of the envelop

$$A = 4\pi(3)^2 = 113\ m^2.$$

The intensity of radiation at this distance is

$$\begin{aligned}
I &= \frac{\text{Power}}{\text{area}} = \frac{2.5}{100} \times \frac{100}{113} \\
&= 0.022\ \text{W/m}^2.
\end{aligned}$$

As half of the intensity is provided by the electric field and half by the magnetic field, so

$$\frac{I}{2} = 0.011.$$

Thus $\qquad \dfrac{1}{2}\,\epsilon_0\,E_{rms}{}^2 c = 0.011$

or $\qquad E_{\text{rms}} = \sqrt{\dfrac{0.011 \times 2}{\epsilon_0\,c}}$

$$= \sqrt{\frac{0.11 \times 2}{8.85 \times 10^{-12} \times 3 \times 10^8}}$$

$$= 2.9\ \text{V/m}$$

The peak value of electric field

$$\begin{aligned}
E_0 &= \sqrt{2}\,E_{\text{rms}} = \sqrt{2} \times 2.9 \\
&= 4.1\ \text{V/m} \qquad \textbf{\textit{Ans.}}
\end{aligned}$$

Now $\qquad B_{\text{rms}} = \dfrac{E_{\text{rms}}}{c} = \dfrac{2.9}{3 \times 10^8}$

$$= 9.6 \times 10^{-9}\ T,$$

and $\qquad B_0 = \sqrt{2}\,B_{\text{rms}} = 1.4 \times 10^{-8}\ \text{T.} \qquad \textbf{\textit{Ans.}}$

Review of formulae & Important Points

1. **Alternating current (AC) :** Alternating current is one whose direction changes periodically; $i = i_0 \sin\omega t$ is the sinusoidal alternating current.

2. **RMS value of AC :** For sinusoidal AC, $i = i_0 \sin\omega t$, the RMS value

$$i_{rms} = \frac{i_0}{\sqrt{2}} = 0.707\, i_0.$$

Similarly $\qquad V_{rms} = \dfrac{V_0}{\sqrt{2}} = 0.707\, V_0.$

For square wave AC, $i_{rms} = i_0$.

3. **Three simple circuits :**
   (i) Circuit having resistor only : The alternating potential difference across a resistor has amplitude $V_R = iR$; the current is in phase with the potential difference.

   (ii) Circuit having capacitor only : $V_c = iX_c$ in which $X_c = \dfrac{1}{\omega C}$ is the capacitive reactance : the current here leads the potential by 90°.

   (iii) Circuit having inductor only : $V_L = iX_L$, in which $X_L = \omega L$ is the inductive reactance; the current here lags the potential by 90°.

4. **Impedance and admittance :** The total resistance of AC circuit is called impedance Z, and reciprocal of impedance is called admittance A. Thus $A = \dfrac{1}{Z}$.

5. **In India domestic supply is 220 V, 50 Hz.** Thus

$$V_0 = 220\sqrt{2}\ V, \text{and}$$
$$V = 220\sqrt{2}\ \sin 100\pi t.$$

6. **Series RL C circuit :** For a series RLC circuit,

$$Z = \sqrt{R^2 + \left(\omega L - \frac{1}{\omega C}\right)^2},$$

and $\qquad \tan\phi = \dfrac{\left(\omega L - \dfrac{1}{\omega C}\right)}{R}$

current $\qquad i = \dfrac{V_0}{\sqrt{R^2 + \left(\omega L - \dfrac{1}{\omega C}\right)^2}}$

7. **Resonance :** The current amplitude i_0 in a series LRC circuit driven by a sinusoidal external emf is a maximum $\left(i = \dfrac{V_0}{R}\right)$ when the driving angular frequency ω equals the natural angular frequency ω_0 (resonance frequency) of the circuit. Then $X_C = X_L$, $\phi = 0$, and the current is in phase with the potential.

$$\omega_0 = \sqrt{\frac{1}{LC}}.$$

8. **Power in AC circuits :** In a series RLC circuit, the average power P_{av} equal to the production rate of thermal energy in the resistor :
$$P_{av} = V_{rms}\, i_{rms}\, \cos\phi.$$

Here $\cos\phi$ is called power factor and is equal to $\dfrac{R}{Z}$. Its value

$\cos\phi \le 1$. For purely inductive or capacitive circuit $\cos\theta = 0$ and so $P_{av} = 0$.

9. **EM-waves :** An EM-wave consists of oscillating electric and magnetic fields. An EM-wave travelling along an x-axis has an electric field $\vec{E}$ and a magnetic field $\vec{B}$ with magnitudes which depend on x and t :

$$E = E_0 \sin(kx - \omega t)$$
and $\qquad B = B_0 \sin(kx - \omega t).$

Electric field induces the magnetic field and vice-versa. The speed of EM-waves is c, which can be written as

$$c = \frac{E}{B} = \frac{1}{\sqrt{\mu_0\, \epsilon_0}}$$

10. **Maxwell's equations :** Maxwell discovered that all the basic principles of electromagnetism can be formulated in terms of four fundamental equations, called Maxwell's equations. These are :
   (i) Gauss's law for electricity
   $$\oint \vec{E}\cdot d\vec{A} = \frac{q}{\epsilon_0}.$$

   (ii) Gauss's law for magnetism
   $$\oint \vec{B}\cdot d\vec{A} = 0$$

   (iii) Faraday's law of induction
   $$\oint \vec{E}\cdot d\vec{\ell} = \frac{-d\phi_B}{dt}$$

   (iv) Ampere's law
   $$\oint \vec{B}\cdot d\vec{\ell} = \mu_0\left(i_C + \epsilon_0 \frac{d\phi_E}{dt}\right)$$

11. **Energy flow :** The rate per unit area at which energy is transported via an electromagnetic wave is given by the Pointing vector
$$\vec{S} = \frac{\vec{E}\times\vec{B}}{\mu_0}$$

12. **Intensity of EM-wave :** The time averaged rate per unit area at which energy is transported, is called the intensity of wave :
$$I = \frac{1}{2}\,\epsilon_0\, E_0^{\,2} c.$$

The intensity of the waves at distance r from a point source of power P is
$$I = \frac{P}{4\pi r^2}$$

13. **Radiation pressure :** When a surface intercepts electromagnetic radiation, a force is exerted on the surface. If the radiation is totally absorbed by the surface, the force is
$$F = \frac{IA}{c}$$

where A is the area of the surface perpendicular to the path of the radiation. If the radiation is totally reflected back along its original path, the force is
$$F = \frac{2IA}{c}$$

★ ★ ★

Magnetism | MCQ Type 1 | *Exercise 9.1*

LEVEL - 1

Only one option correct

1. A capacitor in an LC oscillator has a maximum potential difference of 17 V and a maximum energy of 160 μJ. When the capacitor has a potential difference of 5V and an energy of 10μJ, what is the energy stored in the magnetic field ?

(a) 10 μJ (b) 150 μJ
(c) 160 μJ (d) 170 μJ

2. If we increase the driving frequency in a circuit with a purely resistive load, then amplitude V_R

(a) remains the same (b) increase
(c) decrease (d) none

3. The figure shows a sine curve $S(t) = \sin\omega t$ and three other sinusoidal curves $A(t)$, $B(t)$ and $C(t)$, each of the form $\sin(\omega t - \phi)$. Which curve is according to the most negative value of ϕ

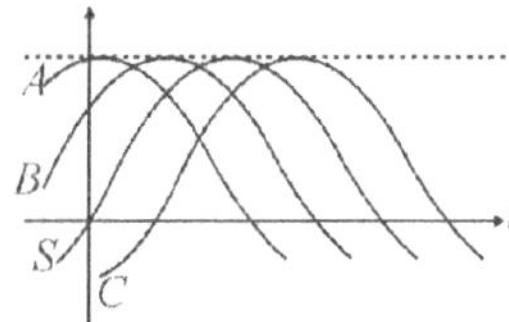

(a) A (b) B
(c) C (d) B and C

4. Figure shows three oscillating LC circuit with identical inductors and capacitors. If t_1, t_2, t_3 are the time taken by the circuits I, II, III for fully discharge, then

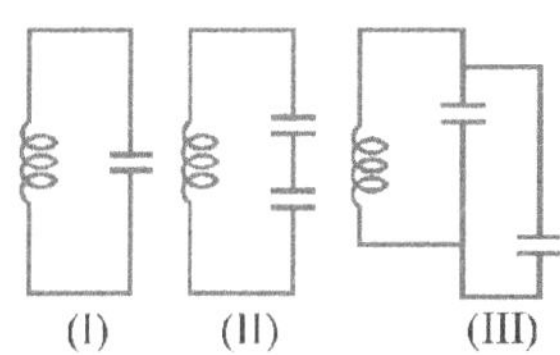

(I) (II) (III)

(a) $t_1 > t_2 > t_3$ (b) $t_1 < t_2 < t_3$
(c) $t_2 < t_1 < t_3$ (d) $t_3 = \sqrt{t_1 t_2}$

5. In an oscillating LC circuit with $L = 50$ mH and $C = 4.0$ μF, the current is initially a maximum. How long will it take before the capacitor is fully discharged for the first time :
(a) 7×10^{-4} s (b) 14×10^{-4} s
(c) 28×10^{-4} s (d) none

6. A charged capacitor and an inductor are connected in series at time $t = 0$. Read the statements : (T is the time period of oscillations)

(1) the charge on the capacitor is zero after a time $\dfrac{T}{2}$.

(2) The charge on the capacitor is zero after time $\dfrac{T}{4}$

(3) the energy stored in the capacitor maximum at $\dfrac{T}{2}$

(4) the energy stored in the inductor is maximum at $\dfrac{T}{4}$

Out of these statements; correct statement(s) is/are
(a) 2 (b) 3
(c) 1, 2 (d) 2, 3, 4

7. If we increase the driving frequency in a circuit with a purely capacitive load. Read the following statements :
(1) amplitude V_C increases (2) amplitude V_C decrease
(3) amplitude i_C increase (4) amplitude i_C decreases
Out of these, the correct statement(s) is/are
(a) 1 (b) 1, 2
(c) 3 (d) 2, 3, 4

8. If we increase the deriving frequency in a circuit with a purely inductive load. Read the following statements :
(1) amplitude V_L remain constant
(2) amplitude V_L increases
(3) amplitude i_L increases
(4) amplitude i_L decreases
Out of these, the correct statement (s) is / are
(a) 1 (b) 2
(c) 1, 2, 3 (d) 1, 4

9. Here are the capacitive reactance and inductive reactance, respectively, for three sinusoidally driven RLC circuits : (1) $50\,\Omega, 100\,\Omega$ (2) $100\,\Omega, 50\,\Omega$ (3) $100\,\Omega, 100\,\Omega$. Which is in resonance ?
(a) 1 (b) 2
(c) 3 (d) 1, 2

10. An alternating current emf device has a smaller resistance than that of the resistive load, to increase the transfer of energy from the device to the load, a transformer will be connected between two. Then
(a) N_S should be greater than N_P
(b) N_S should be less than $N/_P$
(c) $N_S = N_P$
(d) none

Answer Key	1	(b)	2	(a)	3	(a)	4	(c)	5	(a)
Sol. from page 613	6	(d)	7	(c)	8	(d)	9	(c)	10	(a)

11. An AC source is rated 220 V, 50 Hz. The average voltage is calculated in a time interval of 0.01s. It

(a) may be zero   (b) must be zero

(c) is never zero   (d) is $\dfrac{220}{\sqrt{2}}V$

12. An electromagnetic wave going through vacuum is described by $E = E_0 \sin(kx-\omega t)$; $B = B_0 \sin(kx-\omega t)$. Then

(a) $E_0 k = B_0 \omega$ (b) $E_0 B_0 = \omega k$

(c) $E_0 \omega = B_0 k$ (d) none of these.

13. Alternating current can not be measured by *dc* ammeter because

(a) ac cannot pass through *dc* ammeter

(b) average value of complete cycle is zero

(c) ac is virtual

(d) ac changes its direction

14. If a current I given by $I_0 \sin\left(\omega t - \dfrac{\pi}{2}\right)$ flows in an ac circuit across

which an ac potential of $V = V_0 \sin \omega t$ has been applied, then the power consumption P in the circuit will be

(a) $P = \dfrac{V_0 I_0}{\sqrt{2}}$ (b) $P = \sqrt{2}V_0 I_0$

(c) $P = \dfrac{V_0 I_0}{2}$ (d) $P = 0$

15. An alternating voltage $V = 200\sqrt{2}\sin(100t)$ is connected to a 1 microfarad capacitor through an ac ammeter. The reading of the ammeter shall be

(a) 10 mA   (b) 20 mA

(c) 40 mA   (d) 80 mA

16. A 220 V, 50 Hz ac source is connected to an inductance of 0.2 H and a resistance of 20 ohm in series. What is the current in the circuit

(a) 10 A   (b) 5 A

(c) 33.3 A   (d) 3.33 A

17. In the circuit shown below, the ac source has voltage $V = 20 \cos(\omega t)$ volt with $\omega = 2000$ rad/s. The amplitude of the current will be nearest to

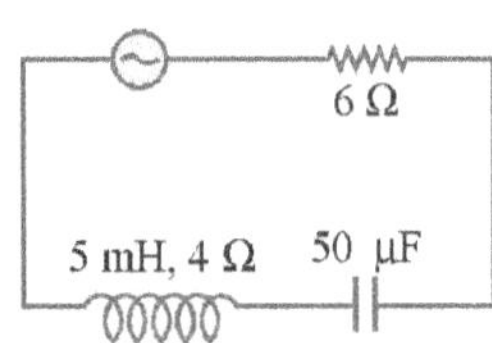

(a) 2A   (b) 3.3A

(c) $2/\sqrt{5}A$ (d) $\sqrt{5}A$

18. The power factor of an ac circuit having resistance (R) and inductance (L) connected in series and an angular velocity ω is

(a) $R / \omega L$ (b) $R/\left(R^2 + \omega^2 L^2\right)^{1/2}$

(c) $\omega L / R$ (d) $R/\left(R^2 - \omega^2 L^2\right)^{1/2}$

19. An inductor of inductance L and resistor of resistance R are joined in series and connected by a source of frequency ω. Power dissipated in the circuit is

(a) $\dfrac{\left(R^2 + \omega^2 L^2\right)}{V}$ (b) $\dfrac{V^2 R}{\left(R^2 + \omega^2 L^2\right)}$

(c) $\dfrac{V}{\left(R^2 + \omega^2 L^2\right)}$ (d) $\dfrac{\sqrt{R^2 + \omega^2 L^2}}{V^2}$

20. In an LCR series ac circuit, the voltage across each of the components, L, C and R is 50 V. The voltage across the LC combination will be

(a) 50 V   (b) $50\sqrt{2}V$

(c) 100V   (d) 0 V (zero)

21. A bulb and a capacitor are connected in series to a source of alternating current. If its frequency is increased, while keeping the voltage of the source constant, then

(a) bulb will give more intense light

(b) bulb will give less intense light

(c) bulb will give light of same intensity as before

(d) bulb will stop radiating light

22. An alternating e.m.f. of angular frequency ω is applied across an inductance. The instantaneous power developed in the circuit has an angular frequency

(a) $\dfrac{\omega}{4}$ (b) $\dfrac{\omega}{2}$

(c) ω (d) 2ω

23. The diagram shows a capacitor C and a resistor R connected in series to an ac source. V_1 and V_2 are voltmeters and A is an ammeter.

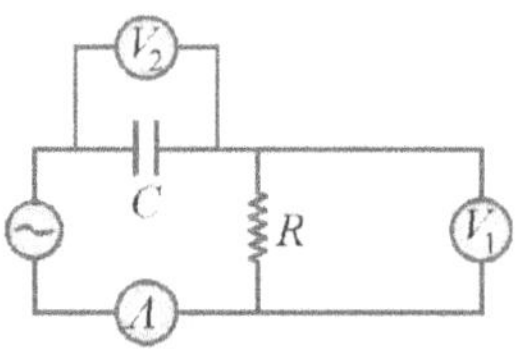

Consider now the following statements

I. Readings in A and V_2 are always in phase

II. Reading in V_1 is ahead in phase with reading in V_2.

III. Readings in A and V_1 are always in phase. Which of these statements are/is correct

(a) I only   (b) II only

(c) I and II only   (d) II and III only

Answer Key	**11**	(a)	**12**	(a)	**13**	(b)	**14**	(d)	**15**	(b)	**16**	(d)	**17**	(a)
Sol. from page 613	**18**	(b)	**19**	(b)	**20**	(d)	**21**	(a)	**22**	(d)	**23**	(d)		

24. At $t < 0$, the capacitor is charged and the switch is opened. At $t = 0$ the switch is closed. The shortest time T at which the charge on the capacitor will be zero is given by :

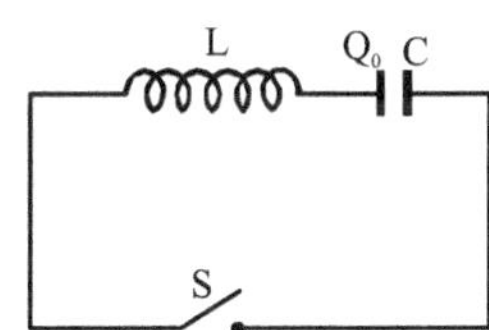

(a) $\pi\sqrt{LC}$

(b) $\dfrac{3}{2}\pi\sqrt{LC}$

(c) $\dfrac{\pi}{2}\sqrt{LC}$

(d) $2\pi\sqrt{LC}$

25. In an oscillation of L-C circuit, the maximum charge on the capacitor is Q. The charge on the capacitor, when the energy is stored equally between the electric and magnetic field is

(a) $\dfrac{Q}{2}$

(b) $\dfrac{Q}{\sqrt{2}}$

(c) $\dfrac{Q}{\sqrt{3}}$

(d) $\dfrac{Q}{3}$

26. Alternating current can not be measured by *dc* ammeter because

(a) *ac* cannot pass through *dc* ammeter

(b) average value of complete cycle is zero

(c) *ac* is virtual

(d) *ac* changes its direction

27. An alternating current is given by the equation

$i = i_1 \cos\omega t + i_2 \sin\omega t$. The r.m.s current is given by

(a) $\dfrac{1}{\sqrt{2}}(i_1 + i_2)$

(b) $\dfrac{1}{\sqrt{2}}(i_1 + i_2)^2$

(c) $\dfrac{1}{\sqrt{2}}(i_1^2 + i_2^2)^{1/2}$

(d) $\dfrac{1}{2}(i_1^2 + i_2^2)^{1/2}$

28. A choke coil has

(a) high inductance and low resistance

(b) low inductance and high resistance

(c) high inductance and high resistance

(d) low inductance and low resistance

29. An alternating voltage is connected in series with a resistance R and an inductance L. If the potential drop across the resistance is 200 V and across the inductance is 150 V, then the applied voltage is

(a) 350 V

(b) 250 V

(c) 500 V

(d) 300 V

30. The value of alternating emf E in the given circuit will be

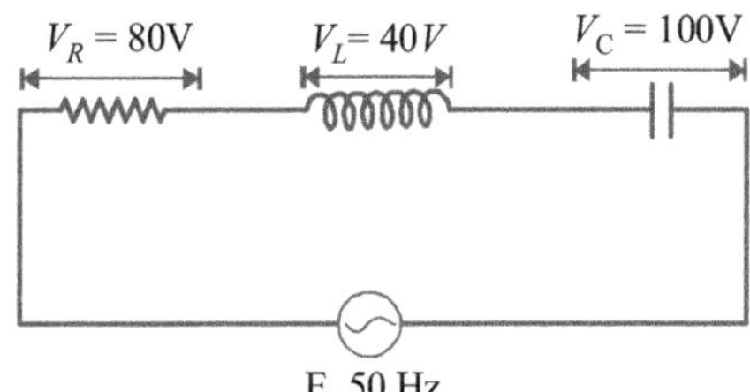

(a) 100 V

(b) 20 V

(c) 220 V

(d) 140 V

31. The power factor of LCR circuit at resonance is

(a) 0.707

(b) 1

(c) zero

(d) 0.5

32. The frequency for which a $5\mu F$ capacitor has a reactance of $\dfrac{1}{1000}$ ohm is given by

(a) $\dfrac{100}{\pi}$ MHz

(b) $\dfrac{1000}{\pi}$ Hz

(c) $\dfrac{1}{1000}$ Hz

(d) 1000 Hz

33. Two identical incandescent light bulbs are connected as shown in figure. When the circuit is an *AC* voltage source of frequency f, which of the following observations will be correct?

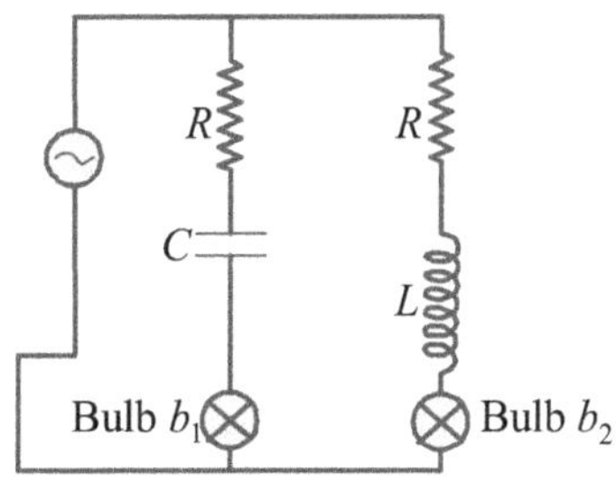

(a) Both bulbs will glow alternatively

(b) Both bulbs will glow with same brightness provided

$f = \dfrac{1}{2\pi}\sqrt{(1/LC)}$

(c) Bulb b_1 will light up initially and goes off, bulb b_2 will be ON constantly

(d) Bulb b_1 will blink and bulb b_2 will be ON constantly

34. For high frequency, a capacitor offers

(a) more reactance

(b) less reactance

(c) zero reactance

(d) infinite reactance

Answer Key	24	(c)	25	(b)	26	(b)	27	(c)	28	(a)	29	(b)
Sol. from page 613	30	(a)	31	(b)	32	(a)	33	(a)	34	(b)		

35. In a LCR circuit capacitance is changed from C to $2C$. For the resonant frequency to remain unchanged, the inductance should be change from L to

(a) $4L$ (b) $2L$

(c) $L/2$ (d) $L/4$

36. The current i in an inductance coil varies with time t according to following graph.

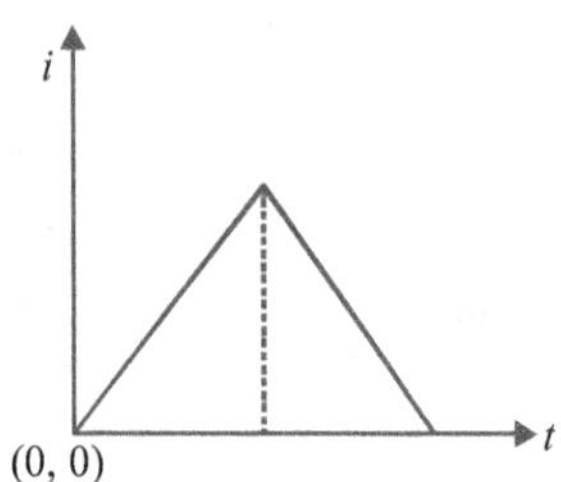

Which of the following plots shows the variation of voltage in the coil

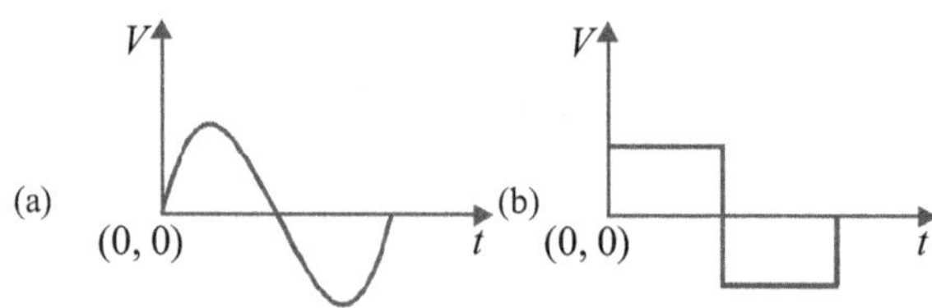

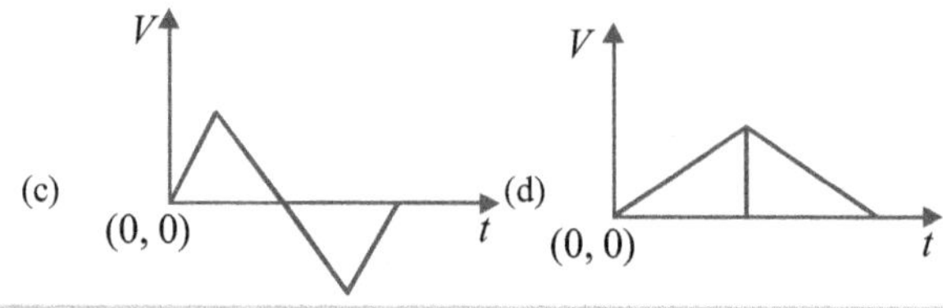

Answer Key	**35**	(c)	**36**	(b)
Sol. from page 613				

LEVEL -2

Only one option correct

1. A parallel-plate capacitor with rectangular plates is being discharged. A rectangular loop, centered on the plates and between them, measures L by $2L$: the plates measure $2L$ by $4L$. The fraction of the displacement current is encircled by the loop if that current is uniform

(a) 1 (b) $\dfrac{1}{2}$

(c) $\dfrac{1}{4}$ (d) $\dfrac{1}{8}$

2. Charges on the capacitors in four oscillating LC circuits vary as follows : (1) $q = 2\cos 4t$, (2) $q = 4\cos t$, (3) $q = 3\cos 4t$, (4) $q = 4\cos 2t$, with q in coulomb and t in second. In which circuit(s) current amplitude is greatest :

(a) (1) (b) (2)

(c) (3) (d) (4)

3. The figure here gives the electric field of an electromagnetic wave at a certain point and a certain instant. The wave is transporting energy in the negative z-direction. The direction of the magnetic field of the wave at that point and instant is :

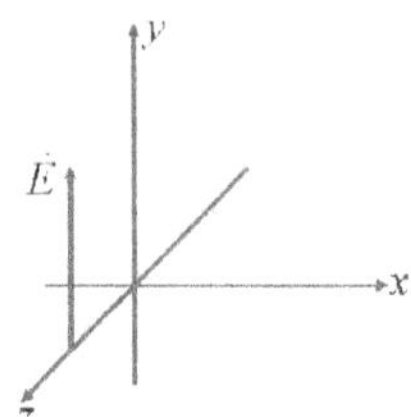

(a) $+$ ve x-direction (b) $-$ve x-direction

(c) $+$ve z-direction (d) $-$ve y-direction

4. Which of the following plots may represent the reactance of a series LC combination ?

(a) I

(b) II

(c) III

(d) IV

5. The voltage of an ac supply varies with time (t) as $V = 120\sin 100$ $\pi\,t\cos 100\,\pi t$. The maximum voltage and frequency respectively are

(a) 120 volts, 100 Hz (b) $\dfrac{120}{\sqrt{2}}$ volts, 100 Hz

(c) 60 volts, 200 Hz (d) 60 volts, 100 Hz

6. Match the following :

	Currents		r.m.s. values
(1)	$x_0\sin\omega t$	(i)	x_0
(2)	$x_0\sin\omega t\cos\omega t$	(ii)	$\dfrac{x_0}{\sqrt{2}}$
(3)	$x_0\sin\omega t + x_0\cos\omega t$	(iii)	$\dfrac{x_0}{\left(2\sqrt{2}\right)}$

(a) 1. (i), 2. (ii), 3. (iii) (b) 1. (ii), 2. (iii), 3. (i)

(c) 1. (i), 2. (iii), 3. (ii) (d) None of these

Answer Key	**1**	(c)	**2**	(c)	**3**	(a)	**4**	(d)
Sol. from page 614	**5**	(d)	**6**	(b)				

7. An ac source of angular frequency ω is fed across a resistor r and a capacitor C in series. The current registered is I. If now the frequency of source is changed to $\omega/3$ (but maintaining the same voltage), the current in the circuit is found to be halved. Calculate the ratio of reactance to resistance at the original frequency ω

(a) $\sqrt{\dfrac{3}{5}}$ (b) $\sqrt{\dfrac{2}{5}}$

(c) $\sqrt{\dfrac{1}{5}}$ (d) $\sqrt{\dfrac{4}{5}}$

8. The output current versus time curve of a rectifier is shown in the figure. The average value of output current in this case is

(a) 0

(b) $\dfrac{I_0}{2}$

(c) $\dfrac{2I_0}{\pi}$

(d) I_0

9. When an ac source of e.m.f. $e = V_0 \sin(100\,t)$ is connected across a circuit, the phase difference between the e.m.f. e and the current i in the circuit is observed to be $\pi/4$, as shown in the diagram. If the circuit consists possibly only of RC or LC in series, find the relationship between the two elements

(a) $R = 1k\Omega, C = 10\mu F$

(b) $R = 1k\Omega, C = 1\mu F$

(c) $R = 1k\Omega, L = 10H$

(d) $R = 1k\Omega, L = 1H$

10. The figure shows three circuits with identical batteries, inductors, and resistors. Rank the circuits, in the decreasing order, according to the current through the battery (i) just after the switch is closed and (ii) a long time later

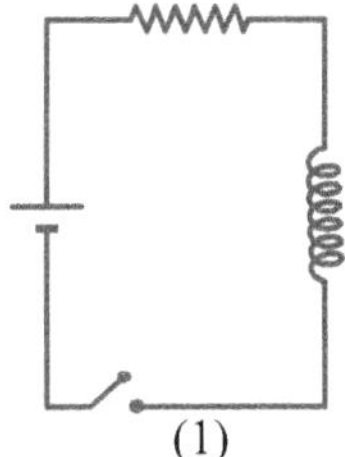 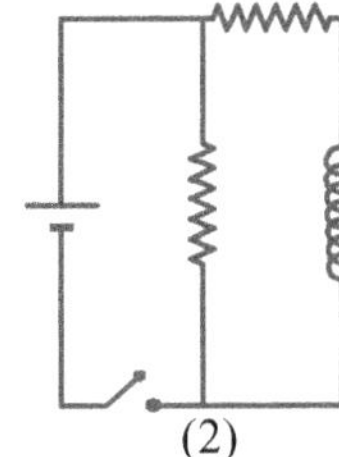 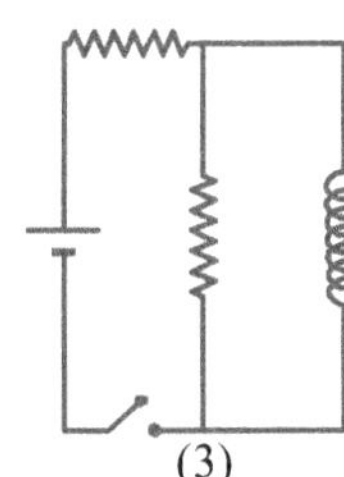

(1)   (2)   (3)

(a) (i) $i_2 > i_3 > i_1$ ($i_1 = 0$) (ii) $i_2 > i_3 = i_1$

(b) (i) $i_2 < i_3 < i_1$ ($i_1 \neq 0$) (ii) $i_2 > i_3 > i_1$

(c) (i) $i_2 = i_3 = i_1$ ($i_1 = 0$) (ii) $i_2 < i_3 < i_1$

(d) (i) $i_2 = i_3 > i_1$ ($i_1 \neq 0$) (ii) $i_2 > i_3 > i_1$

11. When 100 volts dc is supplied across a solenoid, a current of 1.0 amperes flows in it. When 100 volts ac is applied across the same coil, the current drops to 0.5 ampere. If the frequency of ac source is 50 Hz, then the impedance and inductance of the solenoid are

(a) $200\ \Omega$ and 0.55 henry (b) $100\ \Omega$ and 0.86 henry

(c) $200\ \Omega$ and 1.0 henry (d) $100\ \Omega$ and 0.93 henry

12. If the total charge stored in the LC circuit is Q_0, then for $t \geq 0$

(a) The charge on the capacitor is $Q = Q_0 \cos\left(\dfrac{\pi}{2} + \dfrac{t}{\sqrt{LC}}\right)$

(b) The charge on the capacitor is $Q = Q_0 \cos\left(\dfrac{\pi}{2} - \dfrac{t}{\sqrt{LC}}\right)$

(c) The charge on the capacitor is $Q = -LC\dfrac{d^2 Q}{dt^2}$

(d) The charge on the capacitor is $Q = \dfrac{1}{\sqrt{LC}}\dfrac{d^2 Q}{dt^2}$

13. In the circuit shown in the figure, the ac source gives a voltage V $= 20\cos 200\,t$. Neglecting source resistance, the voltmeter and ammeter reading will be

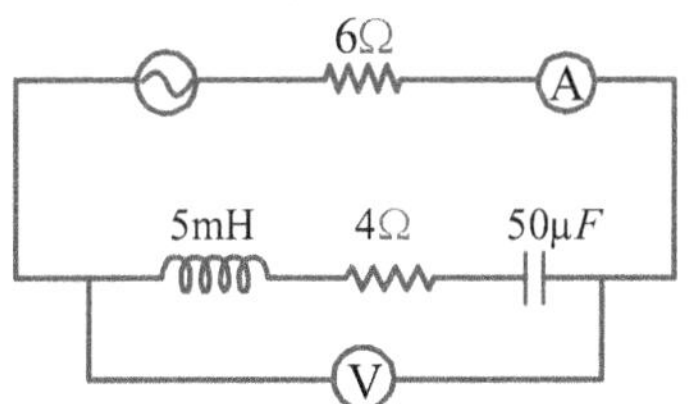
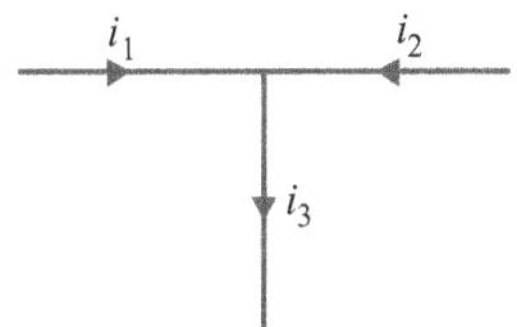

(a) $0V, 0.97\,A$ (b) $1.68\ V, 0.47\ A$

(c) $0V, 1.4\ A$ (d) $5.64\ V, 1.4\ A$

14. If $i_1 = 3\sin\omega t$ and $i_2 = 4\cos\omega t$, then i_3 is

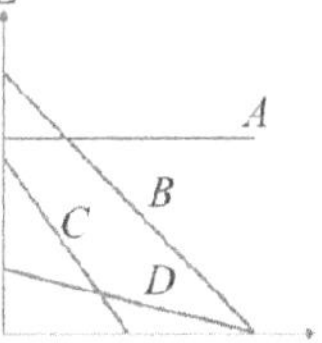

(a) $5\sin(\omega t + 53°)$ (b) $5\sin(\omega t + 37°)$

(c) $5\sin(\omega t + 45°)$ (d) $5\cos(\omega t + 53°)$

15. The figure shows graphs of the electric field magnitude E versus time t for four uniform electric fields, all contained within identical circular regions. Which of them is according to the magnitudes of the magnetic field greatest :

(a) A

(b) B

(c) C

(d) D

Answer Key	7	(a)	8	(c)	9	(a)	10	(a)	11	(a)
Sol. from page 614	12	(a)	13	(d)	14	(a)	15	(c)		

Magnetism   MCQ Type 2   Exercise 9.2

Multiple correct options

1. Figure shows a parallel plate capacitor and the current in the connecting wires that is discharging the capacitor.

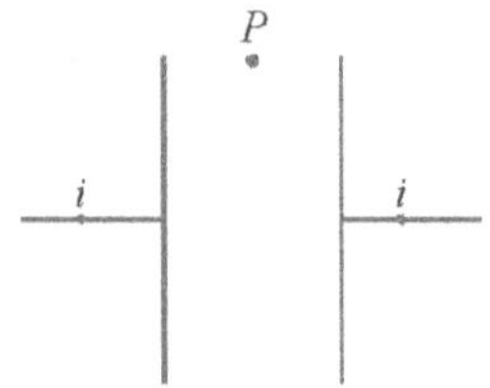

(a) The displacement current is leftward.

(b) The displacement current is rightward

(c) The electric field $\vec{E}$ is rightward

(d) The magnetic field at point P is into the page.

2. If the inductance L in an oscillating LC circuit having a given maximum charge Q is increased, then

(a) the current magnitude increases

(b) the maximum magnetic energy increases

(c) the maximum magnetic energy decreases

(d) current magnitude and maximum magnetic energy remain constant.

3. The reactance of a circuit is zero. It is possible that the circuit contains

(a) an inductor only

(b) a capacitor only

(c) an inductor and a capacitor

(d) a resistor only.

4. In an AC series circuit, the instantaneous current is zero when the instantaneous voltage is maximum. Connected to the source may be

(a) pure inductor

(b) pure capacitor

(c) pure resistor

(d) combination of an inductor and a capacitor

5. The magnetic field can be produced by

(a) a moving charge

(b) a changing electric field

(c) a non uniform field

(d) none of them

6. An alternating e.m.f. of frequency $f\left(=\dfrac{1}{2\pi\sqrt{LC}}\right)$ is applied to a series LCR circuit. For this frequency of the applied e.m.f.

(a) The circuit is at resonance and its impedance is made up only of a reactive part

(b) The current in the circuit is in phase with the applied e.m.f. and the voltage across R equals this applied emf

(c) The sum of the p.d.'s across the inductance and capacitance equals the applied e.m.f. which is 180° ahead of phase of the current in the circuit

(d) The quality factor of the circuit is $\omega L / R$ or $1 / \omega CR$ and this is a measure of the voltage magnification (produced by the circuit at resonance) as well as the sharpness of resonance of the circuit

Answer Key	1	(a, d)	2	(a, b)	3	(c, d)	4	(a, b, d)
Sol. from page 615	5	(a, b)	6	(b, d)				

Magnetism — **Statement Questions** — *Exercise 9.3*

Read the two statements carefully to mark the correct option out of the options given below:
(a) If both the statements are true and the *statement - 2* is the correct explanation of *statement - 1*.
(b) If both the statements are true but *statement - 2* is not the correct explanation of the *statement - 1*.
(c) If *statement - 1* true but *statement - 2* is false.
(d) If *statement - 1* is false but *statement - 2* is true.

1. *Statement - 1*
An alternating current is given by $i = 3\sin\omega t + 4\cos\omega t$. The. rms current of it is $\dfrac{7}{\sqrt{2}}A$.

Statement - 2
The rms current is $\dfrac{5}{\sqrt{2}}A$.

2. *Statement - 1*
A capacitor is connected to a direct current source. Its reactance is infinite.

Statement - 2
Reactance of a capacitor is given by $X_c = \dfrac{1}{\omega C}$.

3. *Statement - 1*
In a circuit containing a capacitor and an AC source the current is zero at the instant the source voltage is maximum. It is not consistent with Ohm's law.

Statement - 2
According to Ohm's law, $V = iR$.

4. *Statement - 1*
When the frequency of the AC source in an LCR circuit equals the resonant frequency, the reactance of the circuit is zero, and so there is no current through the inductor or the capacitor.

Statement - 2
The net current in the inductor and capacitor is zero.

5. *Statement - 1*
The alternating current legs behind the emf by a phase angle of $\dfrac{\pi}{2}$, when AC flows through an inductor.

Statement - 2
The inductive reactance increases as the frequency of AC source increases.

6. *Statement - 1*
The voltage and current in a series AC circuit are given by $V = V_0 \sin\omega t$ and $i = i_0\cos\omega t$. The power dissipated in the circuit is zero.

Statement - 2
Power in AC circuit is given by $P = \dfrac{V_0 i_0}{2}\cos\phi$.

7. *Statement - 1*
The power is produced when a transformer steps up the voltage.

Statement - 2
In an ideal transformer VI = constant.

8. *Statement - 1*
Hot-wire ammeter can be used to measure DC.

Statement - 2
DC produces heating effect.

9. *Statement - 1*
Choke coil is preferred over a resistor to control the current in an AC circuit.

Statement - 2
Power factor of an ideal inductor is zero.

10. *Statement - 1*
A bulb connected in series with a solenoid is connected to AC source. If a soft iron core is introduced in the solenoid, the bulb will glow brighter.

Statement - 2
On introducing soft iron in the solenoid, the electrical inertia increases.

11. *Statement - 1*
The figure is a view of one plate of a parallel-plate capacitor from within the capacitor. The dashed line show two integration paths (path-1 follows the edge of the plate). The value of $\oint \vec{B} \cdot d\vec{\ell}$ for the path-1 is smaller.

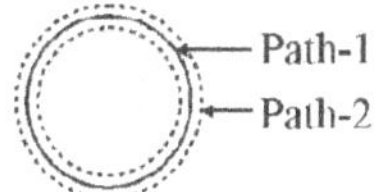

Statement - 2
The value of magnetic field for the path-2 is smaller.

12. *Statement - 1*
The displacement current in a parallel-plate capacitor of capacitance C can be written as $i_d = C\left(\dfrac{dV}{dt}\right)$, where V is the potential difference between the plates.

Statement - 2
The displacement current in free space is given by $i_d = \epsilon_0 \dfrac{d\phi_e}{dt}$.

Answer Key	1	(d)	2	(a)	3	(a)	4	(d)	5	(b)	6	(a)
Sol. from page 615	7	(d)	8	(a)	9	(a)	10	(d)	11	(d)	12	(a)

PASSAGES

Passage for Q.1 to Q.3

Two coils are connected in series. With 2A dc through the circuit, the p.ds. across the coils are 20 V and 30 V respectively. With 2 A ac at 40 Hz, the p.ds. across the coils are 140 V and 100 V respectively. The two coils are connected in series with a 230 V, 50 Hz supply.

1. The current in the coils is :
   - (a) 1 A
   - (b) 1.45 A
   - (c) 1.55 A
   - (d) 2.15 A
2. The power factor of the circuit is :
   - (a) 0.17
   - (b) 0.5
   - (c) 1
   - (d) none
3. The power dissipated in the circuit :
   - (a) 40 W
   - (b) 60 W
   - (c) 80 W
   - (d) 100 W

Passage for Q. 4 to Q. 6

A voltage $V = 100 \sin 314\,t$ is applied to a circuit consisting of a $25\,\Omega$ resistor and 80 µF capacitor in series.

4. The instantaneous current is given by :
   - (a) $i = 100 \sin (314\,t)$
   - (b) $i = 2.13 \sin (314\,t)$
   - (c) $i = 2.13 \sin (314\,t + \phi)$
   - (d) zero
5. The power consumed
   - (a) 35.5 W
   - (b) 50 W
   - (c) 56.7 W
   - (d) 90 W

6. The p.d. across the capacitor at the instant when the current is one-half of its maximum value :
   - (a) 60.7 V
   - (b) 73.5 V
   - (c) 95.0 V
   - (d) 100 V

Passage for Q.7 to Q.9

A parallel-plate capacitor has square plate 1.0 m on a side as shown in figure. A current of 2.0 A charges the capacitor, producing a uniform electric field $\vec{E}$ between the plates, with $\vec{E}$ perpendicular to the plates.

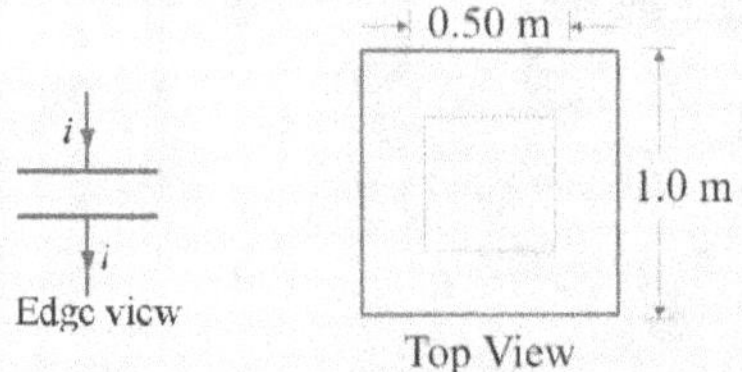

7. The displacement current through the region between the plates
   - (a) zero
   - (b) 1.0 A
   - (c) 2.0 A
   - (d) 2.5 A
8. The value of dE/dt in the region
   - (a) $1.1 \times 10^{11}\ V/m$
   - (b) $2.1 \times 10^{11}\ V/m$
   - (c) $2.3 \times 10^{11}\ V/m$
   - (d) $3.4 \times 10^{11}\ V/m$

9. The value of $\oint \vec{B}.d\vec{\ell}$ around the square dashed path
   - (a) zero
   - (b) 0.63 µT-m
   - (c) 0.75 µT-m
   - (d) none of these

MATRIX MATCHING

10. Consider the circuit shown in the figure. Currents in various branches of the circuit have been marked. Match the entries in Column I to the entries in Column II.

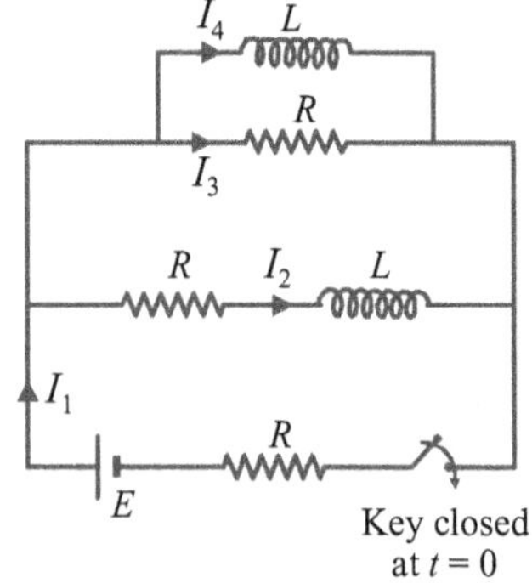

Column I	Column II
A. I_1 at $t = 0$	(p) 0
B. I_2 at $t = \infty$	(q) $\dfrac{E}{R}$
C. I_3 at $t = 0$	(r) $\dfrac{E}{2R}$
D. I_4 at $t = \infty$	(s) I_1 at $t = \infty$
	(t) I_2 at $t = 0$

Answer Key	1	(c)	2	(a)	3	(b)	4	(c)	5	(c)	6	(b)
Sol. from page 616	7	(c)	8	(c)	9	(b)	10	A-r ; B-p, t ; C-r ; D-q, s			

11. In an LCR sereis circuit connected to an ac source, the supply voltage is $V = V_0 \sin\left(100\pi t + \dfrac{\pi}{6}\right)$. $V_L = 40\ V$, $V_R = 40V$, $Z = 5\Omega$ and $R = 4\Omega$.

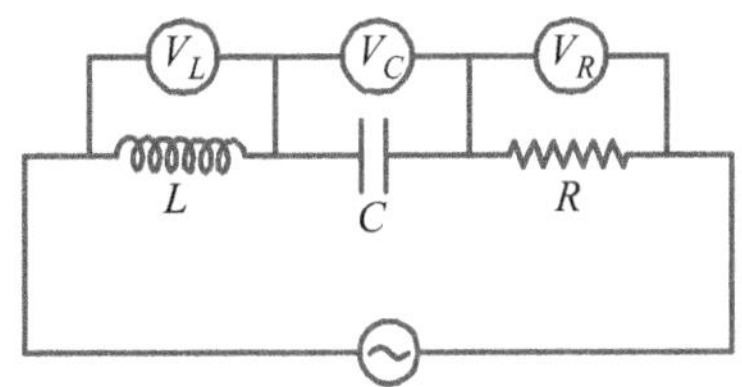

Column I		Column II	
A.	Peak current (in A)	(p)	$10\sqrt{2}$
B.	V_0 (in volts)	(q)	$50\sqrt{2}$
C.	Effective value of applied voltage (in volts)	(r)	50
D.	X_C (in Ω)	(s)	1

12. In a series LCR circuit, the e.m.f. leads current. Now the driving frequency is decreased slightly.

Column I		Column II	
A.	Current amplitude	(p)	Increases
B.	Phase constant	(q)	Decreases
C.	Power developed in resistor	(r)	Remains same
D.	Impedance	(s)	May increase or decrease
		(t)	Becomes maximum if resonace is achieved

Answer Key	11	A-p ; B-q, ; C-r ; D-s	12	A-p, t ; B-q ; C-p, t ; D-q
Sol. from page 616				

Magnetism   # Subjective Integer Type   *Exercise 8.5*

Solution from page 617

1. A 25.0 µF, a 0.10 H inductor and 25.0 Ω resistor are connected in series with an ac source whose emf is given by $e = 310 \sin 314\ t$.
(i) What is the frequency of emf ?
(ii) What is rms value of emf ?
(iii) What is reactance of circuit ?
(iv) What is impedance of the circuit ?
(v) What is the current in the circuit ?
(vi) What are the effective values of voltage across capacitor, inductor and resistor

Ans : (i) 50 Hz (ii) 219 V (iii) 96 Ω (iv) 99.2 Ω (v) 2.20 A
(vi) $V_R = 55$ V, $V_C = 280$ V, $V_L = 69$ V.

2. An inductor of inductance 100 mH is connected in series with a resistance, a variable capacitance and an AC source of frequency 2.0 kHz. What should be the value of the capacitance so that maximum current may be drawn into the circuit ?

Ans : 63 nF.

3. A 60 Hz AC voltage of 160 V impressed across an LR-circuit results in a current of 2 A. If the power dissipation is 200 W, calculate the maximum value of the back emf arising in the inductance. *Ans :* 125 V.

4. A LC circuit (inductance 0.01 H and capacitance 1µF) is connected to an AC source of variable frequency. If the frequency is varied from 1 kHz to 2 kHz, then show the consequent variation of current by a rough sketch.

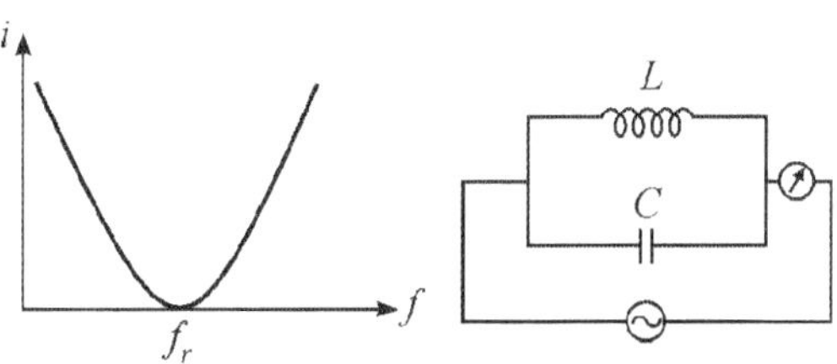

Ans : $f_r = 1592$ Hz

5. A 100 V AC source of frequency 500 Hz is connected to LCR circuit with $L = 8.1$ mH, $C = 12.5$ µF and $R = 10\ \Omega$, all connected in series. Find the potential across the resistance.

Ans : 100 V

6. An LCR series circuit with 100 Ω resistance is connected to an AC source of 200 V and angular frequency 300 rad/s. When only the capacitance is removed, the current legs behind the voltage by 60°. When only the inductance is removed, the current leads the voltage by 60°. Calculate the current and the power dissipated in the LCR circuit.

Ans : 2A, 400 W.

Solution from page 618

1. The electric current in a circuit is given by $i = i_0\left(\dfrac{t}{\tau}\right)$ for some time. Calculate the rms current for the period $t = 0$ to $t = \tau$.

Ans : $\dfrac{i_0}{\sqrt{3}}$

2. A current is made up of two components : a 5 *A DC* component and a 60 cycle AC sinusoidal component of peak value 4 A. Write an expression for resultant current and calculate the average current over a complete cycle and the effective value of current.

Ans : $i = 5+4 \sin 377t$; 5A; 5.75 A.

3. A current of 4 A flows in a coil when connected to a 12 V *DC* source. If the same coil is connected to a 12 V, 50 rad/s AC source. a current of 2.4 A flows in the circuit. Determine the inductance of the coil. Also find the power developed in the circuit if a 2500 µF capacitor is connected in series with the coil.

Ans : 0.08 H, 17.28 W.

4. A capacitor of capacitance 12.0 µF is joined to an AC source of frequency 200 Hz. The rms current in the circuit is 2.00 A. (a) Find the rms voltage across the capacitor (b) Find the average energy stored in the electric field between the plates of the capacitor.

Ans : (a) 133 V, (b) 0.106 J.

5. A coil has a resistance of $10\,\Omega$ and an inductance of 0.4 henry. It is connected to an AC source of 6.5 V, $\dfrac{30}{\pi}Hz$. Find the average power consumed in the circuit.

Ans : $\dfrac{5}{8}W.$

6. The energy in an oscillating LC circuit containing a 1.25 H inductor is 5.70 µJ. The maximum charge on the capacitor is 175 µC. Find (a) the mass, (b) the spring constant, (c) the maximum displacement, and (d) the maximum speed for a mechanical system with the same period.

Ans : (a) 1.25 kg (b) 372 N/m (c) 1.75×10^{-4} m (d) 3.02 mm/s

7. A LCR circuit has $L = 10$ mH, $R = 3\,\Omega$, and $C = 1$, µF connected in series to a source of $15 \cos\omega t$ volt. Calculate the current amplitude and the average power dissipated per cycle at a frequency that is 10% lower than the resonant frequency.

Ans : 0.704 A, 0.744 W.

8. An AC source is connected to two circuits as shown. Obtain the current through the resistance R at resonance in both the circuits.

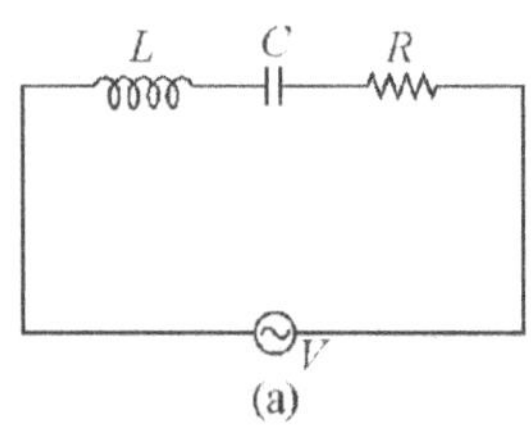

(a)

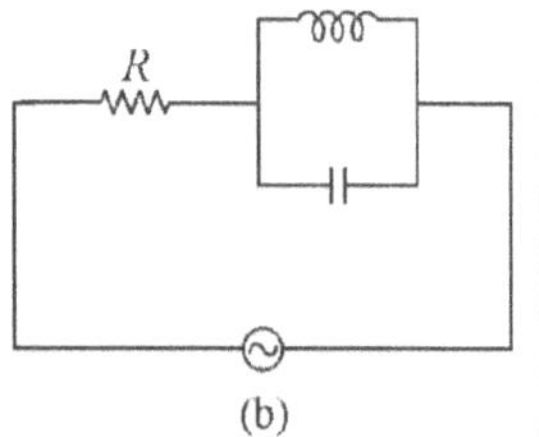

(b)

Ans : (a) V/R (b) 0.

9. A box contains L, C and R. When 250 *DC* is applied to the terminals of the box, a current of 1.0 A flows in the circuit. When an AC source of 250 V rms at 2250 rad/s is connected, a current of 1.25 A rms flows. It is observed that the current rises with

frequency and becomes maximum at 4500 rad/s. Find the values of L, C and R. Draw the circuit diagram.

Ans : $L = \dfrac{4}{81}, H, C = 1\mu F, R = 250\,\Omega$,

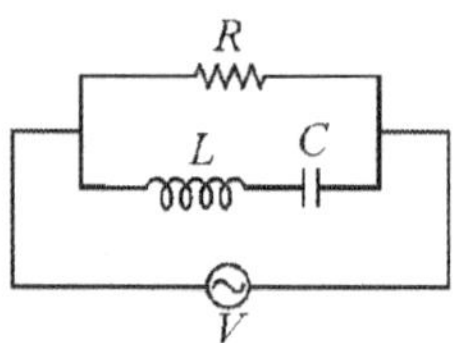

10. In the circuit shown in figure the switch is kept in position for a long time. It is then thrown to position *b*. (a) calculate the frequency of the resulting oscillating current. (b) What is the amplitude of the current oscillations ?

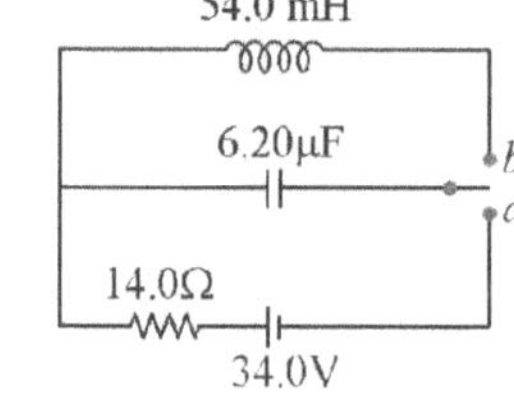

Ans : (a) 275 Hz (b) 364 mA.

11. In figure, $R = 15.0\,\Omega$, $C = 4.70$ µF, and $L = 25.0$ mH. The generator provides a sinusoidal voltage of 75.0 V (rms) and frequency $f = 550$ Hz. (a) Calculate the rms current (b) Find the rms voltages V_{ab}, V_{bc}, V_{ca}, V_{bd}, V_{ad}. (c) At what average rate is energy dissipated by each of the three circuit elements ?

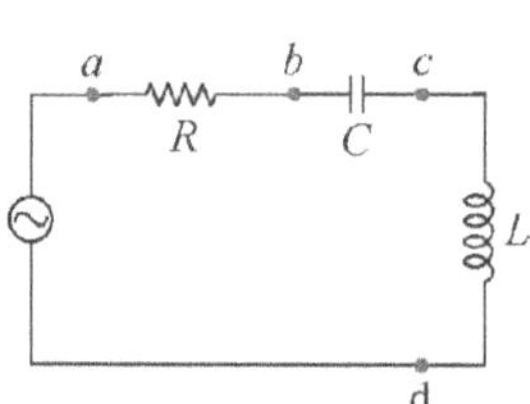

Ans : (a) 2.59 A; (b) 38.8 V, 159 V, 224 V, 64.2 V, 75.0 V; (c) 100 W for R, 0 for L and C.

12. In an oscillating series *RLC* circuit, show that the fraction of the energy lost per cycle of oscillation $\dfrac{\Delta U}{U}$, is given to a close approximation by $\dfrac{2\pi R}{\omega L}$. The quantity $\dfrac{\omega L}{R}$ is often called the *Q* of the circuit. A high-*Q* circuit has low resistance and a low fractional energy loss $\left(=\dfrac{2\pi}{Q}\right)$ per cycle.

13. A light beam travelling in the x-direction is described by the electric field $E_y = 300 \sin\omega\left(t - \dfrac{x}{c}\right)$. An electron is constrained to move along the y-direction with a speed of 2.0×10^7 m/s. Find the maximum electric force and the maximum magnetic force on the electron.

Ans : $F_e = 4.8\times10^{-17}$ N, $F_b = 3.2\times10^{-18}$ N.

14. A laser beam has intensity $2.5 \times 10^{14}\,\dfrac{W}{m^2}$. Find the amptitude of electric and magnetic fields in the beam.

Ans : $4.3 \times 10^8\,\dfrac{V}{m}, 1.44\,T.$

★ ★ ★

Hints & Solutions

1. **(b)** $U_e + U_m = 160$
$\therefore U_m = 160 - U_e$
$= 160 - 10 = 150\ \mu J.$

2. **(a)** V_R does not depend on the frequency of *ac*.

3. **(a)**

4. **(c)** Time period, $T_1 = 2\pi\sqrt{LC}$, $T_2 = 2\pi\sqrt{\dfrac{LC}{2}}$, $T_3 = 2\pi\sqrt{2LC}$.

Clearly $t_2 < t_1 < t_3$.

5. **(a)** Time period, $T = 2\pi\sqrt{LC} = 2\pi\sqrt{(50\times10^{-3})\times4\times10^{-6}}$
$= 28\times10^{-4}\ s$
Time taken by capacitor to charge fulley,

$$t = \frac{T}{4} = 7\times10^{-4} s .$$

6. **(d)**

7. **(c)** As $X_C = \dfrac{1}{\omega C}$, so with the increase in frequency, X_C decreases and so i_C increases.

8. **(d)** As $X_L = \omega L$, so with the increase in frequency, X_L increases and so current i_L will decrease.

9. **(c)** For resonance, $X_C = X_L$.

10. **(a)** To increase transfer of energy, V_s and hence N_s should be greater than N_p .

11. **(a)** The average of AC may be zero, when it is calculated between $+i_0$ to $-i_0$.

12. **(a)** We know that, in EM-waves $E_0 = C\,B$.
Also, $C = \dfrac{\omega}{k}$, and so $E_0 k = B_0\omega$.

13. **(b)**

14. **(d)** Power, $P = V\,I\cos\pi/2 = 0$

15. **(b)** $X_C = \dfrac{1}{\omega C} = \dfrac{1}{100\times10^{-6}} = 10^4\Omega$

Thus $i_{rms} = \dfrac{V_{rms}}{X_C} = \dfrac{200}{10^4} = 20\times10^{-3}\,A.$

16. **(d)** $X_L = \omega L = (2\pi\times50)\times0.2 = 62.8\Omega$

$Z = \sqrt{R^2 + X_L^2} = \sqrt{20^2 + 62.8^2} = 65.91\Omega$

$\therefore i = \dfrac{V}{Z} = \dfrac{220}{65.91} = 3.33\,A.$

17. **(a)** $Z = \sqrt{R^2 + \left(\omega L - \dfrac{1}{\omega C}\right)^2}$

$= \sqrt{10^2 + \left(2000\times5\times10^{-3} - \dfrac{1}{2000\times50\times10^{-6}}\right)^2}$

$= 10\ \Omega$

$i = \dfrac{V_0}{Z} = \dfrac{20}{10} = 2A$.

18. **(b)** $Z = \sqrt{R^2 + X_L^2} = \sqrt{R^2 + (\omega L)^2}$

Power factor, $\cos\phi = \dfrac{R}{Z} = \dfrac{R}{\sqrt{R^2 + \omega^2 L^2}}$.

19. **(b)** $P = \dfrac{V^2}{Z}\cos\phi = \dfrac{V^2}{Z}\times\dfrac{R}{Z^2} = \dfrac{V^2 R}{(R^2 + \omega^2 L^2)}$.

20. **(d)** $V = 50 - 50 = 0$

As $X_C = \dfrac{1}{\omega C}$, so with increase in frequency of *ac*, X_C decreases and so current in the bulb wil increase.

21. **(a)**
22. **(d)**
23. **(d)** Current in resistor and p.d. across it are in same phase. Also p.d. across resistor is $\pi/2$ ahead of p.d. across capacitor.

24. **(c)** The time period of LC oscillations, $T = 2\pi\sqrt{LC}$.

The time at which charge on the capacitor will be zero is $\dfrac{T}{4}$.

So $t = \dfrac{\pi}{2}\sqrt{LC}$.

25. **(b)** If q is the required charge, then

$$\frac{q^2}{2C} = \frac{1}{2}\frac{Q^2}{2C}$$

$$\therefore\ q = \frac{Q}{\sqrt{2}} .$$

26. **(b)**

27. **(c)** $i^2 = (i_1\cos\omega t + i_2\sin\omega t)^2$

$= i_1^2\cos^2\omega t + i_2^2\sin^2\omega t + 2i_1 i_2\cos\omega t\sin\omega t$

$\overline{i^2} = i_1^2\times\dfrac{1}{2} + i_2^2\times\dfrac{1}{2} + 0$

or $i_{rms} = \sqrt{\overline{i^2}} = \sqrt{(i_1^2 + i_2^2)/2}$

28. **(a)** $\cos\phi = \dfrac{R}{Z} = \dfrac{R}{\sqrt{R^2 + \omega^2 L^2}}$. For low value of $\cos\phi$, R should be small and L should be large.

29. **(b)** $V = \sqrt{V_R^2 + V_L^2} = \sqrt{200^2 + 150^2} = 250V$.

30. **(a)** $V = \sqrt{V_R^2 + (V_L - V_C)^2} = \sqrt{80^2 + (40-100)^2} = 100V$

31. **(b)** At resonance LCR, $Z = R$,

and so $\cos\phi = \dfrac{R}{Z} = 1$.

32. **(a)** We have

$$X_C = \frac{1}{\omega C}$$

$$\therefore\ \omega = \frac{1}{X_C C}$$

or $\quad f = \dfrac{1}{2\pi \times \dfrac{1}{100} \times 5 \times 10^{-6}} = \dfrac{100}{\pi} MHz$

33. (a)

34. (b) As $X_C = \dfrac{1}{\omega C}$, so at high value of ω, X_C will be small.

35. (c) Resonance frequency,

$$\omega_0 = \dfrac{1}{\sqrt{LC}} = \dfrac{1}{\sqrt{L'(2C)}} \qquad \therefore \ L' = \dfrac{L}{2}.$$

36. (b) $V = L\dfrac{di}{dt}$. For constant value of $\dfrac{di}{dt}$, V is also constant

So, in first half V is positive and next half it is negative.

Solutions EXERCISE 9.1 LEVEL -2

1. (c) As $i_d = \in_0 A\dfrac{dE}{dt}$

$\therefore \dfrac{i_1}{i_2} = \dfrac{A_1}{A_2}$ or $i_2 = \dfrac{A_2}{A_1}i_1 = \left(\dfrac{L \times 2L}{2L \times 4L}\right)i_1 = \dfrac{i_1}{4}$

2. (c) $i_1 = \dfrac{dq}{dt} = \dfrac{d}{dt}(2\cos 4t) = -8\sin 4t$,

$i_2 = \dfrac{dq}{dt} = \dfrac{d}{dt}(4\cos t) = -4\sin t$,

$i_3 = \dfrac{dq}{dt} = \dfrac{d}{dt}(3\cos 4t) = -12\sin 4t$,

$i_4 = \dfrac{dq}{dt} = \dfrac{d(4\cos 2t)}{dt} = -8\sin 2t$.

Clearly, amplitude of i_3 is greatest.

3. (a) Direction of energy progration of EM-waves is given by

$\vec{D} = K(\vec{E} \times \vec{B}) \qquad$ or $\qquad -\hat{k} = K(E\,\hat{j} \times \vec{B})$

Clearly direction of magnetic field is along positive x-axis.

4. (d)

5. (d) Given, $V = 120\sin(100\pi t)\cos(100\pi t)$.

$= 60[2\sin(100\pi t).\cos(100\pi t)]$

$= 60 \sin 200\,\pi\,t$.

Thus, $V_0 = 60$ V, $\omega = 200\pi$ or $f = \dfrac{200\pi}{2\pi} = 100 Hz$.

6. (b) (1) $i = x_0\sin\omega t$; $i_{rms} = \dfrac{x_0}{\sqrt{2}}$.

(2) $i = x_0\sin\omega t\cos\omega t = \dfrac{x_0}{2}\sin 2\omega t$; $i_{rms} = \dfrac{x_0}{2\sqrt{2}}$.

(3) $i = x_0\sin\omega t + x_0\cos\omega t$; $i_{rms} = \sqrt{\dfrac{x_0^2 + x_0^2}{2}} = x_0$

7. (a) $i = \dfrac{V}{\sqrt{R^2 + \left(\dfrac{1}{\omega C}\right)^2}}$

or $\quad I = \dfrac{V}{\sqrt{R^2 + \dfrac{1}{\omega^2 C^2}}} \qquad \dots \text{(i)}$

and $\dfrac{I}{2} = \dfrac{V}{\sqrt{R^2 + \dfrac{\omega^2 C^2}{9}}} \qquad \dots \text{(ii)}$

On simplifying above equations, we get

$\dfrac{X_L}{R} = \dfrac{\omega L}{R} = \sqrt{\dfrac{3}{5}}$.

8. (c) See theory of the chapter.

9. (a) $\tan\theta = \dfrac{X_C}{R} \qquad$ or $\qquad \tan\dfrac{\pi}{4} = \dfrac{X_C}{R}$

or $\ 1 = \dfrac{X_C}{R} \qquad \therefore \ X_C = R$.

Also e lags i, so (a) is correct.

10. (a) Just after closing of switch,

$i = i_0(1 - e^{-t/\tau}) = \dfrac{\varepsilon}{R}(1 - e^{-t/\tau})$

At, $t = 0$, $i_1 = 0$, $i_2 = \dfrac{\varepsilon}{R}$, $i_3 = \dfrac{\varepsilon}{2R}$

After a long time, $t = \infty$,

$i_1 = \dfrac{\varepsilon}{R}$, $i_2 = \dfrac{\varepsilon}{R/2}$, $i_3 = \dfrac{\varepsilon}{R}$

11. (a) $R = \dfrac{V}{i} = \dfrac{100}{1} = 100\,\Omega$

and $Z = \dfrac{V}{i} = \dfrac{100}{0.5} = 200\,\Omega$

Now $Z = \sqrt{R^2 + X_L^2}$

or $\ 200^2 = \sqrt{100^2 + (\omega L)^2}$

$\therefore \qquad L = 0.55$ H

12. (c) If Q is the instantaneous charge on the capacitor, then

$\dfrac{Q^2}{2C} + \dfrac{1}{2}Li^2 = \dfrac{Q_0^2}{2C} \qquad$ or $\qquad \dfrac{d}{dt}\left[\dfrac{Q^2}{2C} + \dfrac{1}{2}Li^2\right] = 0$

or $\dfrac{2Q}{2C}\dfrac{dQ}{dt} + \dfrac{L}{2} \times 2i \times \dfrac{di}{dt} = 0$ $\therefore \ Q = -LC\dfrac{d^2Q}{dt^2}$.

13. (d) $Z = \sqrt{R^2 + (X_L - X_C)^2}$; $R = 10$ Ω,

$X_L = \omega L = 2000 \times 5 \times 10^{-3} = 10\,\Omega$

$X_C = \dfrac{1}{\omega C} = \dfrac{1}{2000 \times 50 \times 10^{-6}} = 10\,\Omega$.

Thus, $Z = 10\,\Omega$

$i_0 = \dfrac{V_0}{Z} = \dfrac{20}{10} = 2A$; $i_{rms} = \dfrac{2}{\sqrt{2}} = 1.4A$

$V_{rms} = 4 \times i_{rms} = 5.6A\,V$.

14. (a) $i_3 = i_1 + i_2 = 3\sin\omega t + 4\cos\omega t$

$= 5\sin(\omega t + \phi)$, where $\tan\phi = \dfrac{3}{4}$ or $\phi = 53°$.

15. (c) $\oint \vec{B}.d\vec{\ell} = \mu_0 \in_0 \dfrac{d\phi}{dt}$

or $B \times 2\pi r = \mu_0 \in_0 A\left(\dfrac{dE}{dt}\right) \qquad \therefore \ B \propto \left(\dfrac{dE}{dt}\right)$

Solutions EXERCISE 9.2

1. (a, d) According to conservation of charge, the displacement current must be leftward.

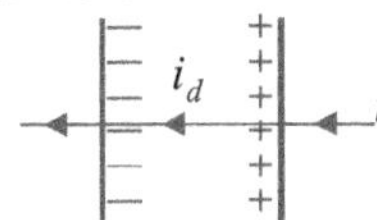

2. (a, b) As $U = \dfrac{Q^2}{2C}$, so with the increase in Q, current will increase and U also increases.

3. (c, d) **4.** (a, b, d) **5.** (a, b)

6. (b, d) For $f = \dfrac{1}{2\pi\sqrt{LC}}$, $\omega = 2\pi f = \dfrac{1}{\sqrt{LC}} = \omega_0$.

This is the condition of resonance of LCR circuit.

At resonance, $Z = R$, and so $V = iZ = iR$.

Solutions EXERCISE 9.3

1. (d) $i_{rms} = \sqrt{\dfrac{i_1^2 + i_2^2}{2}} = \sqrt{\dfrac{3^2 + 4^2}{2}} = \dfrac{5}{\sqrt{2}} A$

2. (a) As $X_C = \dfrac{1}{\omega C}$, so for $\omega = 0$, $X_C \to \infty$.

3. (a)

4. (d) The currents in capacitor and in inductor are opposite and so net current is zero.

5. (b) In case of inductive circuit emf leads current by $\pi/2$ rad

6. (a) $V = V_0 \sin \omega t \quad i = i_0 \cos \omega t = i_0 \sin(\omega t + \pi/2)$

$\therefore \phi = \dfrac{\pi}{2}$, and $\cos\phi = 0$.

7. (a) Transformer cannot produce power, but it transfer from primary to secondary.

8. (d) Hot wire ammeter is based on heating effect; dc produces heat.

9. (a)

10. (d) When soft iron rod is inserted in solenoid, its electrical inertia increases, but ultimate intensity of bulb remains same.

11. (d) $\oint \vec{B}.d\vec{\ell} = \mu_0 i_{in}$; i_{in} is same for both the paths and so $\oint \vec{B}.d\vec{\ell}$ is same for both the paths.

Also $\oint \vec{B}.d\vec{\ell} = \mu_0 i_{in}$

or $B \times 2\pi r = \mu_0 i_{in}$

$\therefore B \propto \dfrac{1}{r}$

As r is greater for second path and so B is smaller for second path.

12. (a)

Solutions EXERCISE 9.4

Passage Q.1 to Q.3

$R_1 = \dfrac{V}{i} = \dfrac{20}{2} = 10\Omega$ and $R_2 = \dfrac{30}{2} = 15\Omega$

$Z_1 = \dfrac{V}{i} = \dfrac{140}{2} = 70\Omega$ and $Z_2 = \dfrac{100}{2} = 50\Omega$

For first coil;

$Z_p = \sqrt{R_1^2 + \omega^2 L_1^2}$

or $70 = \sqrt{10^2 + (2\pi \times 40)^2 \times L_1^2}$

$\therefore L_1 = 0.2764$ H

For second coil ;

$Z_2 = \sqrt{R_2^2 + \omega^2 L_2^2}$

or $50 = \sqrt{15^2 + (2\pi \times 40)^2 L_2^2}$

$\therefore L_2 = 0.19$ H

At $f = 50 Hz$, $Z_1 = \sqrt{10^2 + (2\pi \times 50 \times 0.276)^2} = 87\Omega$

$Z_2 = \sqrt{15^2 + (2\pi \times 50 \times 0.19)^2} = 61.5\Omega$

1. (a) Now $Z = Z_1 + Z_2 = 148.52 \ \Omega$, $R = R_1 + R_2 = 25 \ \Omega$

$i = \dfrac{V}{Z} = \dfrac{230}{148.52} = 1.55 A$

2. (a) Power factor, $\cos\phi = \dfrac{R}{Z} = \dfrac{25}{148.52} = 0.17$

3. (b) Power dissipated, $P = V_{rms} i_{rms} \cos\phi$
$= 230 \times 1.55 \times 0.17 = 60$ W

Passage Q.4 to Q.6

$X_C = \dfrac{1}{\omega C} = \dfrac{1}{314 \times 80 \times 10^{-6}} = 40\Omega$

$Z = \sqrt{R^2 + X_C^2} = \sqrt{25^2 + 40^2} = 47.17\Omega$.

4. (c) $i_0 = \dfrac{V_0}{Z} = \dfrac{100}{47.17} = 2.13 A$

5. (c) $\cos\phi = \dfrac{R}{Z} = \dfrac{25}{47.17} = 0.53$

$P = V_{rms} i_{rms} \cos\phi$

$= \dfrac{100}{\sqrt{2}} \times \dfrac{2.13}{\sqrt{2}} \times 0.53$

$= 56.7 \ W$

6. (b)

Passage Q.7 to Q.9

7. (c) The displacement current, $i_1 = i = 2A$.

8. (c) We know that, $i_d = \epsilon_0 A \left(\dfrac{dE}{dt}\right)$

$\therefore \left(\dfrac{dE}{dt}\right) = \dfrac{i_d}{\epsilon_0 A} = \dfrac{2}{8.86 \times 10^{-12} \times 1^2}$

$\simeq 2.3 \times 10^3$ V/m.

9. (b) $\oint \vec{B}.d\vec{\ell} = \mu_0 i_{in}$

$= 4\pi \times 10^{-7} \times (2 \times 0.5^2)$

$= 0.63 \times 10^{-6}$ T-m

10.   A-r : At $t = 0$, inductor offers infinite resistance, and so circuit is completed through I_1 and I_3 .

Thus $i_1 = i_3 = \dfrac{E}{2R}$.

B-p, t : At $t = \infty$, inductor will offer zero resistance, and so

$$I_2 = I_3 = 0 , \; I_1 = I_4 = \dfrac{E}{R}$$

C-r : $i_3 = \dfrac{E}{2R}$.

D - q, s : $i_4 = \dfrac{E}{R}$

11.   A - p : $i_{rms} = \dfrac{V_R}{R} = \dfrac{40}{4} = 10A$; $i_0 = \sqrt{2}\,i_{rms} = 2\sqrt{2}\ A$

B-q ; $\therefore\ V_{rms} = iZ = 10 \times 5 = 50V$; $V_0 = \sqrt{2}\,V_{rms} = 50\sqrt{2}\,V$

C-p :

D-s : Now $V^2 = V_R^2 + (V_L - V_C)^2$

or $\; 50^2 = 40^2 + (40 - V_C)^2$

$\therefore\ V_C = 10V$,

and $X_C = \dfrac{V_C}{i} = \dfrac{10}{10} = 1\Omega$

12.   See theory of the chapter.

Solutions **EXERCISE-9.5**

1.   Given, $C = 25 \times 10^{-6} F$, $L = 0.10 H$, $R = 25\Omega$ and $e = 310 \sin 314t$

On comparing with , $e = e_0 \sin \omega t$, we have

$$\omega = 314 ,$$

(i) $\therefore$ $f = \dfrac{\omega}{2\pi} = \dfrac{314}{2\pi} = 50\,\text{Hz}$

(ii) $e_{rms} = \dfrac{e_0}{\sqrt{2}} = \dfrac{310}{\sqrt{2}} = 219\ V$

(iii) $X_L = \omega L = 314 \times 0.10 = 31.40\ \Omega$

and $X_C = \dfrac{1}{\omega C} = \dfrac{1}{314 \times (25 \times 10^{-6})} = 127.38\Omega$

The reactance, $X = X_L \sim X_C = 96\ \Omega$

(iv)   Impedance, $Z = \sqrt{25^2 + 96^2} = 99.2\Omega$

(v)   Current, $i = \dfrac{e_{rms}}{Z} = \dfrac{219}{99.2} = 2.2\ A$

(vi) $V_R = iR = 2.2 \times 25 = 55\Omega$

$V_C = iX_C = 2.2 \times 127.38 = 280\ \Omega$

$V_L = iX_L = 2.2 \times 31.40 = 69\ \Omega$ **Ans**

2.   For the maximum current,

$$X_C = X_L$$

or $\quad \dfrac{1}{\omega C} = \omega L$

$\therefore \quad C = \dfrac{1}{\omega^2 L} = \dfrac{1}{(2\pi f)^2 L}$

$$= \dfrac{1}{(2\pi \times 2 \times 10^3)^2 \times 100 \times 10^{-3}}$$

$$= 63 \times 10^{-9} F \qquad \textbf{Ans}$$

3.   The impedance, $Z = \dfrac{V_{rms}}{i} = \dfrac{160}{2} = 80\Omega$

We know that, Power,

$$P = \dfrac{V_{rms}^2 R}{Z^2}$$

or $\quad 200 = \dfrac{160^2 \times R}{80^2}$

$\therefore \qquad R = 50\ \Omega$

We know that, $Z = \sqrt{R^2 + X_L^2}$

or $\qquad 80 = \sqrt{50^2 + X_L^2}$

$\therefore \qquad X_L = 62.5\ \Omega$

The back emf, $V_L = iX_L = 2 \times 62.5$

$\qquad\qquad = 125\ V.$ *Ans.*

4.   Resonance frequency,

$$f_r = \dfrac{1}{2\pi} \sqrt{\dfrac{1}{LC}}$$

$$= \dfrac{1}{2\pi} \sqrt{\dfrac{1}{0.01 \times 1 \times 10^{-6}}}$$

$$= 1592\ \text{Hz} \qquad \textbf{\textit{Ans.}}$$

5. $X_L = \omega L = (2\pi \times 500) \times 8.1 = 25.4\,\Omega$

and $X_C = \dfrac{1}{\omega C} = \dfrac{1}{(2\pi \times 500) \times (12.5 \times 10^{-6})} = 25.4\ \Omega$

As $X_L = X_C$, so resonance will occur and $V_R = 100V$.

         Ans.

6.   If first case, $\tan 60^\circ = \dfrac{X_L}{R} = \dfrac{\omega L}{R}$

or $\qquad \sqrt{3} = \dfrac{300 L}{100}$

$\therefore \qquad L = 0.58\ H$

In second case, $\tan 60^\circ = \dfrac{X_C}{R} = \dfrac{1}{\omega C R}$

or $\qquad \sqrt{3} = \dfrac{1}{300 C \times 100}$

$\therefore \qquad C = 19.2\ \mu F$

The impedance of the circuit is

$$Z = \sqrt{R^2 + \left(\omega L - \dfrac{1}{\omega C} \right)^2}$$

$$= \sqrt{100^2 + \left(300 \times 0.58 - \dfrac{1}{300 \times 19.2 \times 10^{-6}} \right)^2}$$

$$= 100\ \Omega$$

Current, $\quad i = \dfrac{V}{Z} = \dfrac{200}{100} = 2A$.

Power dissipated $= V_{rms} i_{rms} \cos\phi$

$\qquad\qquad\qquad = 200 \times 2 \times 1 = 400\ W$ *Ans.*

1. Given,
$$i = i_0 \frac{t}{\tau}$$

$$\therefore \quad i^2 = i^2 \cdot \frac{t^2}{\tau^2}$$

$$\overline{i^2} = \frac{\int_0^\tau i^2 \, dt}{\tau} = \frac{i_0^2}{\tau^3} \int_0^\tau t^2 \, dt$$

$$= \frac{i_0^2}{\tau^3} \left| \frac{t^3}{3} \right|_0^\tau = \frac{i_0^2}{3}$$

and
$$i_{rms} = \sqrt{\overline{i^2}} = \frac{i_0}{\sqrt{3}} \qquad \textbf{Ans.}$$

2. Given,
$$i = 5 + 4\sin\omega t$$
$$= 5 + 4\sin(2\pi \times 60)t$$
$$= 5 + 4\sin 377t$$

The average value of current
$$i_{av} = \frac{\int_0^T i \, dt}{T} = \frac{\int_0^T (5 + 4\sin 377t) \, dt}{T}$$
$$= 5 \text{ A.}$$

For rms value, $\quad i^2 = (5 + 4\sin\omega t)^2 = 25 + 16\sin^2\omega t + 40\sin^2\omega t$

and
$$\overline{i^2} = 25 + \frac{16}{2} + 0 = 33$$

$$\therefore \quad i_{rms} = \sqrt{\overline{i^2}} = \sqrt{33} = 5.75 \text{ A}$$

3. The resistance of the coil,
$$R = \frac{V}{i} = \frac{12}{4} = 3\Omega$$

Impedance, $\quad Z = \frac{12}{2.4} = 5\Omega$

As
$$Z = \sqrt{R^2 + X_L^2}$$

$$\therefore \quad X_L = 4\Omega$$

and
$$L = \frac{X_L}{\omega} = \frac{4}{50} = 0.08 \text{ H}$$

The reactance, $\quad X_C = \frac{1}{\omega C} = \frac{1}{50 \times 2500 \times 10^{-6}} = 8\Omega$

The total impendance,
$$Z = \sqrt{R^2 + (X_L - X_C)^2} = \sqrt{3^2 + (4-8)^2}$$
$$= 5\Omega$$

Power
$$= \frac{V_{rms}^2 R}{Z^2} = \frac{12^2 \times 3}{5^2} = 17.28 \text{ W} \qquad \textbf{Ans.}$$

4. **(a)** The capacitive reactance
$$X_C = \frac{1}{\omega C} = \frac{1}{(2\pi \times 200) \times 12 \times 10^{-6}}$$
$$= 66.35 \ \Omega$$

$$V_C = i_{rms} X_C = 2 \times 66.35$$
$$= 133 \text{ V} \qquad \textbf{Ans.}$$

(b) Energy stored,
$$U = \frac{1}{2} C V_C^2 = \frac{1}{2} \times 12 \times 10^{-6} \times (133)^2$$
$$= 0.106 \text{ J} \qquad \textbf{Ans.}$$

5. Average power consumed is given by
$$P = \frac{V_{rms}^2 R}{Z^2},$$

where
$$Z = \sqrt{R^2 + (\omega L)^2} = \sqrt{10^2 + \left(2\pi \times \frac{30}{\pi} \times 0.4\right)^2}$$
$$= 26\Omega$$

$$\therefore \quad P = \frac{6.5^2 \times 10}{26^2} = 0.625 \text{ W} \qquad \textbf{Ans.}$$

6. We know that, $\quad U = \frac{Q^2}{2C}$

or
$$5.70 \times 10^{-6} = \frac{(175 \times 10^{-6})^2}{2C}$$

$$\therefore \quad C = 2.69 \times 10^{-3} \text{ F}$$

(a) The mass m is corresponding to the inductance so,
$$m = 1.25 \text{ kg}$$

(b) Force constant $k = \dfrac{1}{C} = \dfrac{1}{2.69 \times 10^{-3}}$
$$= 372 \text{ N/m.}$$

(c) The maximum displacement is corresponding to the maximum charge, and so
$$x_{max} = 175 \times 10^{-6} \text{ m.}$$

(d) The maximum speed v_{max} corresponds to the maximum current. Thus
$$v_{max} = i_{max} = \frac{Q}{\sqrt{LC}} = \frac{175 \times 10^{-6}}{\sqrt{1.25 \times 2.69 \times 10^{-3}}}$$
$$= 3.02 \times 10^{-3} \text{ m/s} \qquad \textbf{Ans.}$$

7. The resonance frequency,
$$\omega_r = \sqrt{\frac{1}{LC}} = \sqrt{\frac{1}{10 \times 10^{-3} \times 1 \times 10^{-6}}}$$
$$= 10^4 \text{ rad/s}$$

Thus
$$\omega = 0.90 \, \omega_r = 9 \times 10^3 \, rad/s$$
$$X_L = \omega L = 9 \times 10^3 \times (10 \times 10^{-3})$$
$$= 90 \ \Omega$$

and
$$X_C = \frac{1}{\omega C} = \frac{1}{9 \times 10^3 \times 10^{-6}}$$
$$= 111.11 \ \Omega$$

The impedance, $\quad Z = \sqrt{R^2 + (X_L \sim X_C)^2}$
$$= \sqrt{3^2 + (111.11 - 90)^2}$$
$$= 21.32 \ \Omega$$

The current amplitude,
$$i_0 = \frac{V_0}{Z} = \frac{15}{21.32} = 0.704 \text{ A}$$

Average power, $\quad P_{av} = \frac{V_0^2 R}{2Z^2} = \frac{15^2 \times 3}{2 \times 21.32^2}$
$$= 0.74 \text{ W} \qquad \textbf{Ans.}$$

8. In series circuit at resonance

$$\text{impedance} \quad z = R, \qquad \therefore \ i = \frac{V}{R}$$

In parallel circuit at resonance

$$\text{impedance}, \quad z = \infty \qquad \therefore i = 0,$$

9. When DC is applied, the resistor is effective

$$\therefore \qquad R = \frac{V}{i_1} = \frac{250}{1} = 250\,\Omega$$

The impedance of LC-branch,

$$z = X_L - X_C = \left(\omega L - \frac{1}{\omega C}\right)$$

Current in LC- branch,

$$i_2 = \frac{V}{Z} = \frac{250}{\left(\omega L - \dfrac{1}{\omega C}\right)} \qquad \dots (i)$$

The net current, $\quad i = \sqrt{i_1^2 + i_2^2}$

$$\therefore \qquad i_2 = \sqrt{i^2 - i_1^2}$$

$$= \sqrt{1.25^2 - 1^2} = 0.75\ \text{A}$$

From equation (i), we have

$$0.75 = \frac{250}{\left|\omega L - \dfrac{1}{\omega C}\right|}$$

$$\therefore \qquad \left|\omega L - \frac{1}{\omega C}\right| = \frac{1000}{3} \qquad \dots (ii)$$

Also, $\qquad \omega_0 = \dfrac{1}{\sqrt{LC}}$

or $\qquad 4500 = \dfrac{1}{\sqrt{LC}} \qquad \dots (iii)$

After substituting $\omega = 2250$ rad/s and simplifying equations (ii) and (iii), we get

$$L = \frac{4}{81}\,\text{H}, \ C = 1\mu\text{F} \qquad\qquad \textbf{\textit{Ans.}}$$

10. (a) The frequency of oscillations

$$f = \frac{1}{2\pi}\sqrt{\frac{1}{LC}}$$

$$= \frac{1}{2\pi}\sqrt{\frac{1}{(54\times10^{-3})\times(6.20\times10^{-6})}}$$

$$= 275\ \text{Hz} \qquad\qquad \textbf{\textit{Ans.}}$$

(b) The maximum charge stored on the capacitor

$$Q = CV = 6.20\times10^{-6}\times34$$
$$= 210.8\times10^{-6}\ \text{C}$$

If i_0 be the amplitude of current, then

$$\frac{1}{2}Li_0^2 = Q^2/2C$$

or $\qquad i_0 = \sqrt{\dfrac{Q^2}{LC}} = \sqrt{\dfrac{(210.8\times10^{-6})^2}{54\times10^{-3}\times6.20\times10^{-6}}}$

$$= 0.364\text{A} \qquad\qquad \textbf{\textit{Ans.}}$$

11. (a) Impedance of the circuit

$$z = \sqrt{R^2 + \left(\omega L - \frac{1}{\omega C}\right)^2}$$

$$= \sqrt{15^2 + \left[(2\pi\times550)\times25\times10^{-3} - \frac{1}{2\pi\times550\times4.70\times10^{-6}}\right]^2}$$

$$= 28.5\ \Omega$$

$$\therefore \qquad i_{rms} = \frac{V_{rms}}{Z} = \frac{75}{28.5} \simeq 2.6\text{A}$$

(b) $\qquad V_{ab} = i_{rms}R = 2.6\times15 = 38.8\,\text{V}$

$$V_{bc} = i_{rms}X_C = 2.6\times\left[\frac{1}{2\pi\times550\times4.70\times10^{-6}}\right]$$
$$= 159\ \text{V}$$

$$V_{cd} = i_{rms}X_L = 2.6\times[2\pi\times550\times25\times10^{-3}]$$
$$= 224\ \text{V}$$

$$V_{bd} = V_{cd} - V_{bc} = 224 - 159 = 65\ \text{V}$$

$$V_{ad} = \sqrt{V_{ab}^2 + V_{bd}^2} = 75\,\text{V} \qquad \textbf{\textit{Ans.}}$$

(c) Power dissipated by resistor,

$$P = V_{rms}i_{rms}\cos\phi$$

$$= 75\times2.6\times\left(\frac{15}{28.5}\right)$$

$$\simeq 100\ \text{W}$$

The power dissipated by inductor and capacitor will be zero.

12. If U_0 be the initial energy stored in the capacitor, then energy at any time t

$$U(t) = U_0 e^{-Rt/L}$$

and $\quad U(t+T) = U_0 e^{-R(t+T)/L}$

The fractional loss in energy is

$$\frac{\Delta U}{U} = \frac{U(t) - U(t+T)}{U(t)} = \frac{e^{-Rt/L} - e^{-R(t+T)/L}}{e^{-Rt/L}}$$

$$= (1 - e^{-RT/L})$$

Assume that $\dfrac{RT}{L}$ is small compared to 1, (as resistance is small).

Also $\qquad e^{-RT/L} \simeq 1 - \dfrac{RT}{L}$

$$\therefore \qquad \frac{\Delta U}{U} = 1 - \left(1 - \frac{RT}{L}\right) = \frac{RT}{L}$$

$$= \frac{2\pi R}{\omega L} \qquad\qquad \textbf{\textit{Ans.}}$$

13. $E_0 = 300\,\text{V/m}$, $\ \therefore B_0 = \dfrac{E_0}{C} = \dfrac{300}{3\times10^8} = 1\times10^{-6}\ \text{N/A-m}$

The maximum electric force,

$$F_0 = E_0 q = 300\times1.6\times10^{-19}$$
$$= 4.8\times10^{-7}\ \text{N.}$$

The maximum magnetic force,

$$F_b = qvB = (1.6\times10^{-19})\times(2\times10^7)\times(1\times10^{-6})$$
$$= 3.2\times10^{-18}\ \text{N.} \qquad \textbf{\textit{Ans.}}$$

14. The intensity is given by

$$I = \frac{1}{2}\epsilon_0 E^2 C$$

or $\qquad 2.5\times10^{14} = \dfrac{1}{2}\times(8.86\times10^{-12})\times E_0^2\times(3\times10^8)$

$$\therefore \qquad E_0 = 4.3\times10^8\ \text{V/m}$$

and $\qquad B_0 = \dfrac{E_0}{C} = 1.44\,\text{T} \qquad\qquad \textbf{\textit{Ans.}}$

★ ★ ★